Tiger!

To Noni

Eternal Butterfly

Tiger!
The de Havilland DH.82 Tiger Moth

Stuart McKay

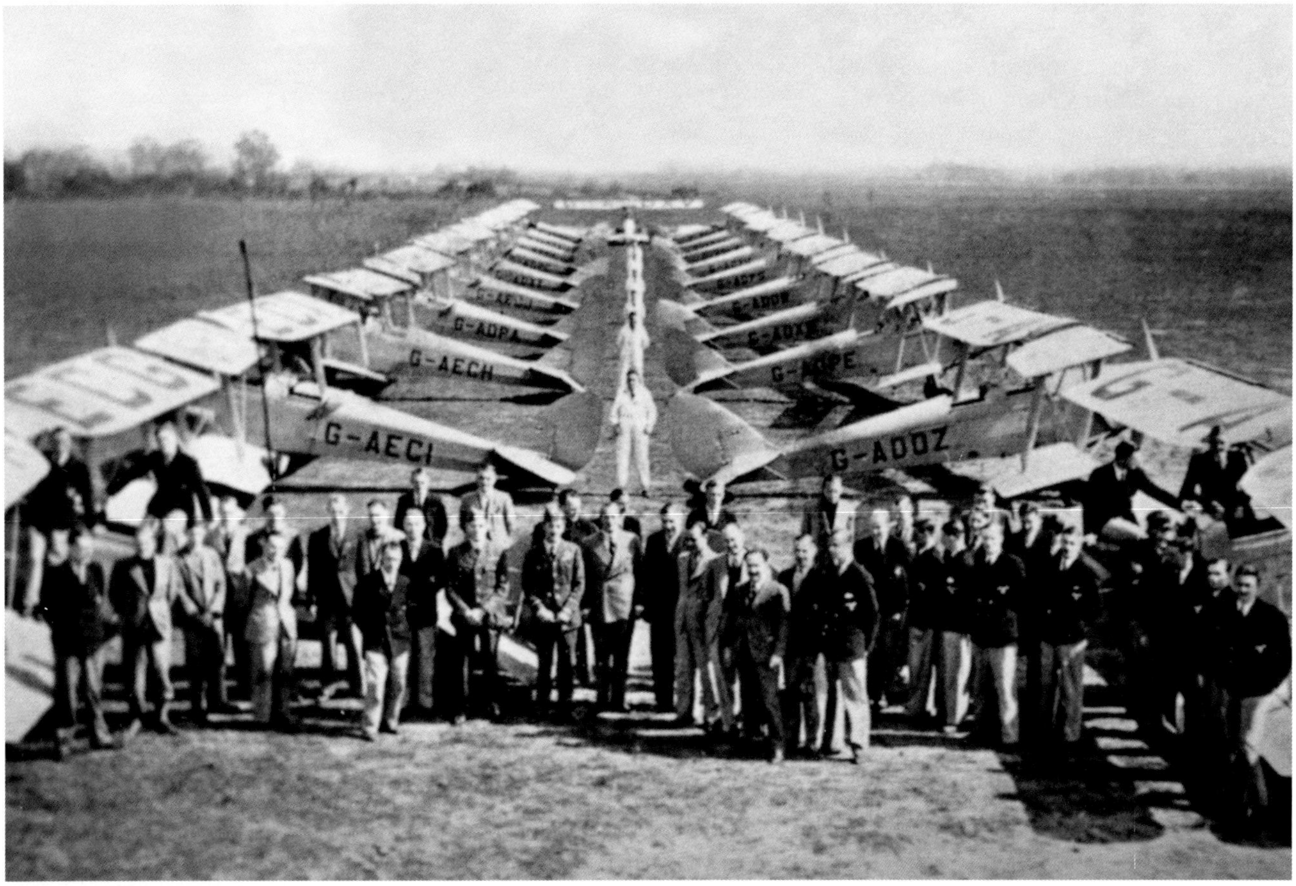

Crécy Publishing Ltd

First published in 1999 by Midland Publishing Ltd
Fully revised and updated in 2014
by Crécy Publishing Ltd

Copyright © Stuart McKay MBE 1999 and 2014

All rights reserved. No part of this book may be reproduced or transmitted in any form or by any means electronic or mechanical, including photocopying, recording or by any information storage without permission from the Publisher in writing. All enquiries should be directed to the Publisher.

A CIP record for this book is available from the British Library

ISBN 9780859 791823

Printed in Slovenia by GPS Group

Crécy Publishing Limited
1a Ringway Trading Estate, Shadowmoss Road, Manchester M22 5LH

www.crecy.co.uk

Front cover: DH.82A Tiger Moth G-ANFM at Baxterley, Warwickshire in 2008. Built by Morris Motors in 1941, G-ANFM is something of a film star having appeared in *Thunderbirds* (1968), *The Little Prince* (1974), *Agatha* (1979) and *The King's Speech* (2010). © Derek Pedley/Air Team Images

Rear cover background: DH.82A Tiger Moth K4288 cavorting above the clouds when on strength with 18 ERFTS Fairoaks in 1938. *deHMC Archive*

Rear cover bottom: The rear instrument panel of a Tiger Moth operated by Brooklands Aviation. Where the pre-war ERFTS was managed by a civilian organisation also offering Club flying in parallel, Reserve aircraft were usually set aside for exclusive use although instrumentation and equipment carried does appear to have been at the discretion of the operator rather than an Air Ministry specification. *via Ted Lawrence*

Rear cover top: During the Invasion scare in 1940 instructors were allowed to indulge in some authorised low level activity after normal working hours. *deHMC Archive*

Front flap top: Gawpers on the flying bridge of HMS *Eagle* in June 1964 had the perfect opportunity to compare the arrival techniques of each visiting Tiger Moth. *Royal Navy*

Front flap bottom: Location of the propeller and a check on the starboard slat completes the task in assembling NL913 at the Cowley works in November 1943. Manoeuvred clear of the pillars and into natural daylight, engine checks were next on the list. *Morris Motors*

Half title page: Whether she is in her element or a fleeting shadow on the sand, there is nothing more distinctive than the outline shape of a Tiger Moth, an inspiration for generations of pilots, engineers and enthusiasts, past, present and future.

Title page: An impressive line-up at 7 ERFTS Desford during an inspection by AOC Training Command, September 1938. The instructors in blazers and slacks are at right. *via John Collier*

Table of Contents

Acknowledgements 6
Chapter 1 A New Specification 7
Chapter 2 Developing Market Share 25
Chapter 3 Chasing the Export Trade 41
Chapter 4 A Time for Decisions 55
Chapter 5 An Acceleration of Effort 65
Chapter 6 A Matter of Desperation 79
Chapter 7 Getting Into a Spin 90
Chapter 8 A Job To Be Done 109
Chapter 9 Beyond the Call 128
Chapter 10 Perpetual Phoenix 141
Chapter 11 European Variations on a Proven Theme 157
Chapter 12 Adventure in Canada 169
Chapter 13 Industry for the Antipodes 179
Chapter 14 Honeymoon in New Zealand 191
Chapter 15 Going for a Song 203
Chapter 16 Resisting the Change 232
Chapter 17 The Great Commonwealth Rundown 247
Chapter 18 Back to the Drawing Board 266
Chapter 19 The Grand Tourists 288
Chapter 20 The Agriculturalists 305
Chapter 21 All in a Day's Work 315
Chapter 22 Front Page News 336
Chapter 23 Out and About 348
Chapter 24 The DH.82 Queen Bee 358
Chapter 25 The DH.82A(Mod) Thruxton Jackaroo 372
Chapter 26 The Circus Comes to Town 380
Appendix 1 Variant Specifications 392

Bibliography 393

Index 394

Acknowledgments

During the preparation of this manuscript, much assistance and encouragement was provided, often against short order requests, but always willingly and generously by those who responded. In some cases the answers were in handy reference files, but in others it was necessary to tease out long forgotten memories from still active minds. In having the privilege of stringing some of the facts together, I hope I have done adequate justice to this remarkable aeroplane, the Tiger Moth, and the men and women who designed and built her and to those who flew her, and continue to do so.

My special thanks are due to the following: Therese Angelo, Royal New Zealand Air Force Museum; Nigel Arthur, British Aerobatic Association; Captain David Becker, South African Air Force Museum; Lewis Benjamin, the Tiger Club; Philip Birtles; Garry Bisshopp; Bruce Bosher; Bill Bowker; Philip Bremridge; Charles Caliendi; John Collier; Charles Cornish; Darryl Cott; Sheila Courts; Frank Cox; John Cunningham; David Cyster; Mel Davies; Bert Davis; Roy Day; Roger de Mercado; Iain Dick; Colin Dodds; Gary Dolski, Bombardier Aerospace; Neville Duke; David Edwards, British Motor Industry Heritage Centre, Gaydon; Jonathan Elwes; Peter Elliott, Royal Air Force Museum Hendon; Joan Ellis; Ken Ellis; Gordon Evans; Pat Fillingham; Malcolm Fillmore; John Fisher; David Freeman; Ben French; Ken Fulton; Ron Gammons; Michael Geoghegan; Pamela Guess, Barry Guess and Mike Fielding, British Aerospace Heritage Collection, Farnborough; Peter Gould; Ian Grace; Paul and Liz Gliddon; Tony Haigh; Bernie Halliday; Patricia Hammond; Charles Hastings-Winch; Terry Heffernan; Peter Henley; Bertil Henrikson for translation services; Bill Hitchcock, the Tiger Club of Australia; Kenneth Holliday; Terry Holloway; Michael Hooks; Carol Horton; Fred Hotson; Stuart Howe; Geoff Hulett; Michael Inskip; John O Isaacs; Cliff Jenks, Aviation Historical Society of New Zealand; John King, the Tiger Moth Club of New Zealand; Colonel Knut Kinne, Kjeller Flyhistoriske Forening, Norway; Henry Labouchere; Ted Lawrence; Ted Leonard, de Havilland Moth Club of Canada; Neil Lewis; Wolf Letsch, for translation services; Tony Lloyd, British Aerobatic Association; George Mackie; Barry Markham; Melissa McKay; Dr Ivan McLannahan; Jack Meaden; Mark Miller, de Havilland Support, Duxford; Morten Myhr; Michael Oakey; Bob Ogden; Anita Paalanen, Bombardier Aerospace; Norman Parry; Tom Payne; Murray Peden; Desmond Penrose; Bo Vincent Petersen, for translation services; Eva Peverett for translation services; Staff of the National Archives at Kew, formerly the Public Records Office; Melvin K Rees, The British Patent Office; Richard Riding; Bill Sarjantson; Gerry Schwam, US Moth Club; Commander Philip Shaw, RN; Colin Smith; Mitch Stirling; Rusty Tack; Luis Tavares; Bill Taylor, de Havilland Support, Duxford; Bill Teague; Captain Fred Terry; David Tipper; Guy Tucker; Chris Tucker; United States Air Force Museum, Wright-Patterson AFB, Ohio; Michael Vaisey; Pim Van Dam; Steve van Dulken, The British Library; Captain David Vernon; Jan Voeten; Monica Walsh, Royal Australian Air Force Museum; Roy and Courtney Watson; David Welch; Tim Williams; Bruce Winley; Christine Woodland, University of Warwickshire.

In addition, thanks to all who have contributed with letters, memories and photographs gathered together since the formation of the de Havilland Moth Club in 1975, much of which archive has provided valuable source material, and to those who today enjoy the unique opportunities offered by an association with the Tiger Moth, for they continue to extend an already noble history.

Stuart McKay
Berkhamsted
Hertfordshire

June 2014

Right: One of the early birds: DH.60T Tiger Moth G-ABPH in playful mood over Stag Lane Aerodrome in the late summer of 1931. The aircraft was sold to de Havilland's Portuguese Agent in time for Christmas.

Below: Two 'solo' members of the de Havilland Moth Club's 'Tiger 9' formation team proving that in the right hands the Tiger Moth, designed for military training, can be much enjoyed when flying for fun.

CHAPTER ONE

A New Specification

The Royal Air Force had been a supportive customer for de Havilland's DH.60 Moth series, which first flew in 1925, from wooden airframes with 60hp Cirrus engines to others specially adapted to take the Armstrong Siddeley Genet and used for display purposes. However, the vast majority of orders placed in 1929/1930 had been for the DH.60M Metal Moth with a 100hp Gipsy I engine.

The RAF took delivery of 135 DH.60M Moths between October 1929 and March 1931 under the terms of four separate contracts. While nearly all the British civil aero clubs used Moths for training, only the first eleven of the Air Ministry order were scheduled for school work. The remainder were scattered across Great Britain attached to fighting units, various trade schools, communications squadrons, practice and station flights, an anti-aircraft co-operation unit and the RAF Colleges at Andover and Cranwell. One aircraft was used to test an experimental seaplane hull at Felixstowe, others went as vehicles of communication to Aden, Iraq and Malta. Six aircraft joined the Central Flying School (CFS) in 1930 and flew as a five man team at that year's RAF Pageant followed by a team of new aircraft the following year. In spite of the aircraft's non-intensive training role, her exposure within a practising, high mobility Air Force was wide, and senior rank officers had sampled her delights as both pilot and passenger, raising a catalogue of opinion both for and against.

The de Havilland Company took note and developed the DH.60M into a multi-role aircraft aimed specifically at the military under the designation DH.60T Moth Trainer:

> "Throughout the design the importance of interchangeability, together with ease and simplicity of repair and replacement has been kept uppermost. All points which need periodical inspection are readily accessible and, if damage is done, repairs can generally be localised and new sections can be fitted without disturbing the main structure."

Provision was made for dual control but more particularly for items such as camera guns, mapping, reconnaissance and wireless equipment, and practice bombs slung from an underfloor rack. The aircraft was heavier and stronger than the DH.60M with power provided by the uprated Gipsy II delivering 120hp. An improved escape path for the occupant of the front seat was engineered by routing the exhaust system vertically down immediately behind the propeller, thus allowing deep doors to be provided on both sides of the cockpit. As crew abandonment had previously been impeded by the convergence of the rear flying wires at the root end of the bottom

Everybody loves a Tiger Moth, even to the exclusion of heartier beasts. Empire Air Day at Hendon, 1935, and a hands-on experience for many a starry eyed schoolboy little realising, perhaps, that within a few years they would be more closely associated on a professional level. *Keystone*

Arthur Hagg, who became Chief Designer of the de Havilland Aircraft Company, and Frank Halford, designer of the Gipsy range of engines that proved to be fundamental to the success of the company's efforts.

DH.60T Moth Trainer G-ABKM clearly illustrating how the occupant of the front seat could be enmeshed in rigging wires during an attempted escape by parachute. Partial resolution of the port side clutter was achieved by routing the exhaust pipe vertically downwards just behind the propeller. This aircraft was sold to the Swedish Air Force in June 1931. *deHMC Archive*

wing's rear spar, the geometry was altered to permit grouping of the cluster at the front spar root, ahead of the cockpit and away from the passage of anxious feet propelling a parachute encumbered body.

Following flight trials at Stag Lane in April 1931 orders were secured for ten DH.60T Moth Trainers for the Royal Swedish Air Force (re-designated Sk.9 in their inventory), forty for the Brazilian Government to be divided by the ratio of 3:5 in favour of the Navy, and one for China, two for Iraq and six for Egypt.

Engineering practice and a degree of common sense ruled that the cylinders and heads of an aero engine should be positioned above the crankcase, protected from the internal deluge of oil that would otherwise surely engulf them. But if the engine could be arranged to run efficiently when 'inverted' not only would the top cowling line provide a better forward view for the pilot, but the thrust line would be raised providing a greater ground clearance for the propeller tips or, alternatively, an opportunity for blades of a greater diameter. Major Frank Halford and his engine design team had been considering the prospects for the last several years and after relatively straightforward modifications were applied to a Gipsy II, the engine was persuaded to run 'upside-down' by Eric Mitchell in the Experimental Department at Stag Lane in 1929. The team had created the Gipsy III for an increase in weight of 7lb, but no additional horsepower, and the engine was tested in a DH.80 Moth Three (later renamed Puss Moth), a new high-wing, cabin monoplane for which type in early production it became the standard power unit. The same engine was fitted to a sporting development of the wooden DH.60, the DH.60GIII Moth, and earmarked for the DH.60T Moth Trainer.

Early in 1931 the Air Ministry called for design submissions for a completely new basic training aircraft for the RAF. Particular emphasis was to be applied to the ease with which the instructor might escape from his front office. Armed with an ideal engine and Service experience of the basic airframe, the Stag Lane team was well placed to meet the challenge.

The venerable Avro 504N, whose core dated back to 1912, had been replaced in 1929 by the Air Ministry's pre-conceived ideal, the Hawker Tomtit. The fabric covered tubular steel fuselage frame, fitted with a 150hp Armstrong Siddeley Mongoose five cylinder radial engine, had been chosen partly on account of the dwindling number of RAF tradesmen capable of maintaining a more complicated structure. The Tomtit was built to Air Ministry specification 5/29 with an emphasis on simplicity and safety: slats

Avro 621 Tutor K1797, powered by a Lynx engine, was a one-off order delivered to the RAF in October 1930 and seen here as a visitor to Stag Lane. *Richard Thompson*

Lynx powered Avro 621 Tutor K1237 was one of ten aircraft delivered to the RAF between May and June 1930. During a visit to Stag Lane that summer she was subjected to close scrutiny by de Havilland staff. *Richard Thompson*

were fitted to the top wings which were arranged with forward stagger to improve ease of evacuation; there were no mainwheel brakes, an adjustable rear seat was standard and there was provision for a blind flying hood. Only 25 Tomtits were built, serving with 3 FTS at Grantham and the Central Flying School at Wittering.

Ordered a year later against specification 3/30 was the Avro 621, which, when re-engined with the 240hp development of the Armstrong Siddeley Lynx, became the Tutor, well equipped with mainwheel brakes, a tailwheel, adjustable seats and rudder pedals, variable incidence tailplane, leading edge slats, ailerons fitted to both top and bottom wings and whose front cockpit was free of obstruction. Almost 400 Tutors were eventually in widespread and active circulation throughout the home based training establishments but at a time of financial constraint it was regarded as a relatively expensive aeroplane to operate.

Flying Officer Peter Heath, soon to become acquainted with the fruits of de Havilland's thinking on a new trainer, flew several hundred hours instructing on Tutors and described it as a 'bad trainer'. "It was far too forgiving and suffered fools too gladly. The result was that when the fools went on to more advanced types and tried things with which they had got away on Tutors, they were surprised when they killed themselves."

de Havilland's DH.60T proposal fitted with a Gipsy III engine and revised cockpits and rigging was considered a prime contender for the new basic trainer for which the Air Ministry had issued specification 15/31, especially so in view of the Ministry's heavy investment in the DH.60M. The commonality of engine and airframe spares and servicing requirements were all viewed with favour, but there was still one glaring problem which had to be addressed: the biplane geometry of the DH.60T still left the occupant of the front seat surrounded with cabane struts and a fuel tank situated immediately overhead. There were no solutions more obvious than to move the tank or the cabane structure or to delete the top wings altogether but time and the need to utilise as much of the existing structure as possible in the bare interests of economy were paramount if the tender was to be realistic in meeting the terms of delivery and price.

A popular myth suggests that this essential new training aeroplane was not so much designed by anyone in particular rather than that it evolved from ideas promoted by a group of fiercely interested individuals. In his privately circulated book of de Havilland reminiscences Richard Clarkson perpetuates the story that "Messers Nixon and St. Barbe, directors of finance and sales, acutely aware of the significance of such an Air Ministry contract, got together and sketched on the back of an envelope what needed to be done to the Moth's centre section and upper planes and presented it to the designers. Hence the story that the Sales and Finance Directors designed the Tiger Moth!"

Enlisting the skills of the shop floor specialists and their supervisors, they gathered round what has been described as a skeletal metal airframe in a quiet corner of the Stag Lane factory, adjacent to the Puss Moth assembly area. There is some suspicion that the airframe might have been that of a DH.60T Moth Trainer, G-ABKS

de Havilland Tiger Moth and arch rival for the 1931 RAF trainer contract, the all-metal, side-by-side seating Blackburn B2. In the event only Blackburn's Reserve School at Brough was equipped with a fleet of B2 aircraft, later superseded by the Tiger Moth. DH.82A G-ANCS and sole surviving airworthy Blackburn B2 G-AEBJ were photographed at Brough. *via Roger Reeves*

Stag Lane Aerodrome in March 1933, a hive of activity with DH.60 Moth, DH.82 Tiger Moth, DH.80 Puss Moth and DH.84 Dragon all clearly visible. Features, viewing from left (north) clockwise are private owner lock-ups, Service Department and London Aeroplane Club, Engine Division, Aircraft Company, Flight Test and Technical School. Stag Lane can be seen running eastwards from behind the buildings of the Engine Division to join the Edgware Road immediately opposite the white fronted structure with a three apex roof: this was de Havilland's 'local', the Bald Faced Stag. *de Havilland Aircraft Co*

Captain Geoffrey de Havilland, founder of the company that bore his name and Chief Designer in 1930 when the specification for a new RAF training type was being evolved. *deHMC Archive*

(1705), which had been registered to the company in April 1931, the last of a batch of six. Whilst the other five (1700-1704), had all been sold to the Royal Swedish Air Force in June 1931, G-ABKS was retained as a test and demonstration aircraft but never aspired to a full Certificate of Airworthiness (C of A), and the registration was finally cancelled against de Havilland's own description of it having been 'reduced to redundant stock'.

Chief Designer Arthur Hagg and General Manager Frank Hearle were on hand to assist company stalwarts Fred Plumb and Douglas Hunter to progress the situation. Fred Plumb had joined the company soon after its establishment at Stag Lane in 1920 with all the qualifications of a skilled aircraft woodworker and was personally responsible for much of the earliest manufacturing development of the DH.60 Moth. As Superintendent of the Experimental Shop he was closely associated with all subsequent prototype building, completing a high percentage of the work by hand, and was inextricably involved with the later DH.88 Comet and DH.98 Mosquito programmes. It was the need to adapt the Mosquito to limited production facilities that took him to Canada during the Second World War.

Assigned as project engineer, Douglas Hunter had joined the Stag Lane Drawing Office in 1925 where he had been closely involved with development of every project since. Like Fred Plumb his expertise was eventually required in support of the Canadian Mosquito programme and, as Director of Engineering to de Havilland Aircraft of Canada, his responsibility in 1946 was to oversee the company's efforts in producing a successful replacement for the Tiger Moth, the DHC.1 Chipmunk.

At Stag Lane the team's first agreed task was to move the fuel tank forward, away from the Moth's front cockpit, and under Douglas Hunter's direction to rearrange the geometry of that specimen airframe, reversing the cabane 'V' strut effectively to provide the basis of a forward platform onto which the fuel tank could be re-positioned. The move proved to be 18in measured at the wing root and the trial installation was shown to Captain de Havilland and test pilot Hubert Broad who tried the cockpit but was not totally convinced. After lunch, Hubert Broad is believed to have revisited the site to amplify his concern with the result that, according to Fred Plumb, the centre section was moved forward again by a further 4in. Based on a DH.60T fuselage side frame there would have been no braced pickup joint at this new position which was only satisfied by on-the-spot local engineering.

The change in geometry successfully solved the problem of cockpit accessibility, but the aircraft was now seriously out of balance, and some simple method of re-establishing an equitable centre of gravity (CG) had to be determined. The only real option was to sweep back the wings, an exercise accomplished by shortening the spindled rear spars of each wing, and adjusting the fittings to suit. By calculation it was agreed that a sweep of 9in measured from the original position of the interplane struts should be sufficient to restore the CG to lie within a practical and workable range, but it proved not to be. The remedy, and most expeditious course, was simply to add extra sweep to the top wings only, and again using the interplane struts as a datum, a further 2in of sweepback was added at which the CG conditions were considered to be satisfied. *Flight's* correspondent commented that the solution was 'not altogether beneficial in the matter of looks, but having probably no other disadvantages'.

Having established the basic geometry of the airframe recording of the detail differences could now begin prior to issue of manufacturing drawings. Following Stag Lane practice of structural testing, prototype wings were built, attached to stanchions in one of the workshops and loaded with sandbags against a defined schedule. The new geometry precluded the ability to fold back the wings, a practical way to save on storage space and expenses and a major selling feature of all other Moth aeroplanes, but the market for this

This very rare photograph of the DH.60 Training Moth T1 (E.4) fitted with a Gipsy II engine, clearly illustrates the sweep and stagger of the mainplanes after the centre section had been moved forward in an effort to comply with the Air Ministry specification. The top wings are fitted with leading edge slats. *Richard Thompson*

machine was perceived as being an almost exclusively military one where hangarage and storage facilities would be amply provided.

On 10 July 1931 an aircraft identified by the company as a 'DH Training Moth T1', fitted with a Gipsy II engine, was weighed at Stag Lane. In most respects she was noted as being identical with the final specification of another aircraft which had been recently flight tested using identity E.3, DH.60T G-ABNY (1724), one of six destined for China. The exception was that the weighing report identified that DH Training Moth T1 was fitted with swept mainplanes, the top set staggered forward of the lower wings. Her centre of gravity in this configuration was closely compared with aircraft 1724 and found to be further forward, the difference recorded as being due to an increased tare weight and *'the forward shift of petrol'*.

The increase in weight was accounted for by the addition of 'a controlled slot locking device' and 'a drop door (four) fuselage'. The petrol tap was described as being 'cockpit controlled' rather than positioned on the cabane where it could not have been reached from the rear cockpit. The Training Moth T1 had been configured by moving the whole of the cabane structure forward of the front cockpit, removing the petrol tank from immediately above the occupant's head. This move would satisfy the views of the Canadian authorities who had declared they would buy no more aircraft without an easy escape path for the instructor, a resolution which had already caused as much concern at Stag Lane as at de Havilland's Canadian factory at Downsview, Toronto, in addition to fulfilling the requirements of the Air Ministry's trainer specification 15/31 which embodied the same philosophy. If the Training Moth T1 was in fact the resurrected G-ABKS, she carried the test marks E.4 when flown by Jack Tyler on 21 July 1931 and by Hubert Broad in August. E.4 never qualified for a C of A before she was declared redundant and dismantled having proved the concept.

A small batch of aeroplanes built to this new formula but fitted with the 'inverted' Gipsy III engine was approved by the company board and, in view of the competition for RAF orders, the aircraft was to be called DH.60T 'Tiger Moth', 'T' not only denoting 'Trainer', but acting in compliance with the Air Ministry's contemporary naming policy (Tomtit/Tutor).

Not all found favour with the new name. A correspondent who reported on his experience of flying the machine for *The Aeroplane* wrote:

> "Personally we are inclined to be sorry that this name should be used again as a machine so utterly different from the tiny and fiery monoplane on which Mr H S Broad made, and still holds, the World's speed record for light aeroplanes in the Third Category. From the fanciful standpoint also, the name suggests something far less tractable than the new trainer."

A demonstration by a parachute-clad instructor of the obvious advantage of moving the centre section forward to allow much easier egress in the event of an emergency escape. *deHMC archive*

The first DH.60T Tiger Moth (1727), was delivered by Hubert Broad to the A&AEE at Martlesham Heath on 18 August 1931 identified by the manufacturer's Class II serial 'E.5', an alpha-numeric system allocated to aircraft companies by the Air Ministry strictly for experimental flying. Civil registration G-ABNJ had been issued to the aircraft in June but was not carried.

The general impression when investigative flying and assessment began four days later was favourable except that, in the opinion of the Establishment's test pilots, landing in a crosswind put the into-wind wing tip perilously close to the ground, and that when taxiing across uneven territory, any down aileron was liable to make contact and trail across the surface.

Hubert Broad, Chief Test Pilot to the de Havilland Aircraft Company, seated in a single seat DH.60 Moth and carrying a trophy after another success for the combination. *deHMC Archive*

Students of the de Havilland Aeronautical Technical School showing a marked interest in DH.60T Tiger Moth E.5 in the early summer of 1931. The aircraft was delivered to Martlesham Heath by Hubert Broad in August and although issued with registration G-ABNJ the letters were never carried. *Phil Hagger*

An apocryphal story which circulated in and probably emanated from the bars of the Stag Lane factory's 'local' on the Edgware Road, the Bald Faced Stag, suggested that part of an Air Ministry 'competition' was judgement of the time taken to remove all four wings. A de Havilland engineer had picked up a snatch of conversation in an Ipswich pub and, in association with his colleagues on detachment, serviced the aircraft in the Martlesham hangar the night before the assessment, during which they removed all the appropriate split pins, substantially reducing the clocked time and earning the aircraft top marks for maintenance accessibility!

At Stag Lane, a second DH.60T Tiger Moth, G-ABPH (1732), was re-rigged to accept 4° 30' of dihedral on the lower wings only, an increase of 1° 45' over the setting of the top wings, and the aircraft was delivered to Martlesham Heath by Hubert Broad on 3 September. In this configuration the type was cleared in an A&AEE report dated 7 September: "Cross-wind landings and take-offs were carried out and with the increased dihedral there was found to be no extra risk of touching the wing-tip. Taxiing cross-wind was also found to be easy." The change in rigging made no difference in handling when compared with recorded flight trials conducted on aircraft E.5 the previous month. In this new configuration the design received A&AEE clearance as a military trainer acceptable to the Air Ministry.

Due to the introduction of sweep and revised bottom wing dihedral, the distance between locating pin centres at the top and bottom of the front and rear interplane struts was now unequal by one sixteenth of an inch, the rear strut being the longer. Although it was minimal the difference did have an effect on rigging and was to prove the bane of many an engineer's life in the future if front and rear struts were mis-identified, even though their cross sections were also slightly dissimilar.

Adding sweep to a wing of constant chord and section changed the relationship between the angle of the ribs and the airflow, resulting in a less efficient section. de Havilland viewed the prospect of modifying their jigs to accommodate wings built with realigned ribs with some alarm. What would be the advantages if such an investment were made? The aircraft was designed as a trainer, not a high efficiency, long distance tourer or a racing vehicle, or a commercial aircraft reliant on good economics for survival. The RAF 15 (modified) wing profile, described by the Aerodynamics Department as 'a flat bottomed section', had been carefully chosen: when stalling, the lift fell off gradually and smoothly, not abruptly, and the spin was normal with immediate recovery. The company decided to make no immediate change to the layout of the wing. During subsequent commercial production of probably in excess of 40,000 Tiger Moth wings, nobody ever did.

Three aircraft had been built to the DH.60T Tiger Moth specification in the summer of 1931, each fitted with the Gipsy III engine: G-ABNI (1726), G-ABNJ (1727) and G-ABPH (1732). G-ABNI was despatched to Canada in August where she was registered CF-APL (known locally as 'The Apple') and operated as a demonstrator for barely a year, ending her days as an instructional airframe with Toronto Central Technical School during the Second World War. G-ABPH (1732), was officially sold to Carlos Bleck, de Havilland's Portuguese agent, in December 1931 and was registered CS-AAF to the Aero Clube de Portugal before suffering an accident the following year after which she was 'dismantled'.

Also in December, in the depths of the Swedish winter, DH test pilot Hubert Broad drew the short straw and was delegated to fly G-ABNJ to the military airfield at Barkarby, north of Stockholm and mid-way to Uppsala, where in conditions of extreme cold and deep snow he demonstrated the open cockpit biplane over several days to government officials and Air Force officers. It was something of a change from the summer trials flown by this same aeroplane under designation 'E.5' at Martlesham Heath the previous August but Hubert Broad's considerable talent as a sales representative, in addition to his flying skills, assisted in selling the aeroplane, quite literally. G-ABNJ remained in Sweden, acquired by the Air Force, where she operated alongside a fleet of DH.60T Moth Trainers under the new designation Sk.11, serial Fv562, until July 1934. It was an important sale which led to an order for twelve type DH.82 Tiger Moths and licensed manufacture of both the DH.82 and later the DH.82A in pre-war Sweden.

Above: This unmarked DH.60T Tiger Moth is believed to be No 1732, G-ABPH which qualified for her C of A in September 1931 and was tested at Martlesham Heath the same month. The aircraft was later sold to Portugal. *Richard Thompson*

Right: DH.60T Tiger Moth G-ABPH was constructed with the typical stringer turtle deck, deep front door and prominent air scoop for a rear mounted carburettor fitted to the Gipsy III engine. This aircraft was the first to be tested with increased dihedral on the lower wings and is seen here indulging in a session of sustained inverted flight over Stag Lane. Note the angle of the elevators. *deHMC Archive*

DH.82 Tiger Moth K2570 at Stag Lane illustrating the dissimilarity between the dihedral angles of top and bottom mainplanes. *deHMC Archive*

(The Barkarby exercise was still considered remarkable in 2007 when, under very different conditions, Swedish Tiger Moth owners flew into Barkarby Aerodrome on 17 December to commemorate the 75th anniversary of Hubert Broad's phenomenal resilience.)

At Stag Lane it was decided that a sufficient number of major alterations had been absorbed for the DH.60T Type Number to be amended. This was not a hasty decision for all design and stress calculations, modification summaries and flight test reports collectively formed the aircraft Type Record held by the Design Authority, the de Havilland Aircraft Company Ltd. The Type Record for a 'modified' aircraft, no matter how major the modification, was considered progressive development of the same series and in 1931 all de Havilland biplane Moth documentation was predicated on the standard of the DH.60X. In theory, the change of Type Number signalled an entirely new design of aeroplane in which case the regulatory authority, in the shape of the Air Ministry, could have argued and insisted that a whole new Type Record be established from scratch, a time consuming and expensive exercise, to be avoided if possible.

In the event the option of a new Type Number was chosen: DH.82, one number on from the soon to be abandoned DH.81 Swallow Moth, a victim of financial stringency as much as anything, but the Type Record for the DH.82 continued to be referenced to the DH.60X, under whose protection it has remained ever since. The Air Ministry awarded the company a contract for a single prototype DH.82 to be built, fitted with a Gipsy III engine. Originally scheduled to be a DH.60T Tiger Moth, work's number 1733, painted silver

While production of the DH.80A Puss Moth was in full swing construction of the first DH.82 Tiger Moth, G-ABRC, made quiet progress in the same facility. The interruption of the top longeron to facilitate a deep front door is clearly visible. *Richard Thompson*

overall and carrying test serial 'E.6', was flown from Stag Lane on 26 October 1931 by Hubert Broad, who positioned her to Martlesham Heath for the standard acceptance trials on 11 November.

And how did Hubert Broad record what is now seen as the historic first flight of the re-designated DH.82 Tiger Moth in his logbook? There is no entry! de Havilland's Chief Test Pilot was so committed to testing and demonstrating Moths and a miscellany of other aircraft that the events of 26 October 1931 were of no greater significance than those of any other day. Admittedly, he did rely on the watch office for much of the detail he was obliged to record, and there is evidence that on some occasions his logbooks were completed by third parties acting on his behalf.

K2570, one of the first batch of DH.82 Tiger Moths for the RAF, photographed at Stag Lane in October 1931. She was delivered to Grantham by an RAF Ferry Pilot at the beginning of November. *Flight*

DH.82 Tiger Moth prototype G-ABRC, first flown by Hubert Broad on 26 October 1931, survived until 1956 when, not recognised for her historic value, she was broken up and burned at Croydon. *Charles Holland*

An analysis of Hubert Broad's recorded work pattern for dates either side of 26 October illustrates the significant level of company activity at the time. Between 12 October and 6 November he test flew the DH.81 Swallow Moth on three occasions, made sixteen test or demonstration flights in DH.80 Puss Moths, production tested two new DH.60 Moths and a reconditioned one, and flew five of the RAF's new DH.82 Tiger Moths, although three of these are listed as DH.60s. On 3 and 6 November respectively, K2570 and K2573 were flown under the heading 'DH.82', the first such mention. The twenty minute test of DH.82 prototype 'E.6' on 4 November is listed as that of a DH.60.

Later registered G-ABRC, 'E.6' was fitted with the new Gipsy Major engine early in 1932 and during the 1933 season was attached to Alan Cobham's National Aviation Day Displays before joining the de Havilland School of Flying at Hatfield where she was part of the fleet operated on behalf of No 1 Reserve Flying School (RFS). Geoffrey Bartlett was sent solo on the aeroplane by instructor Vic Moon, a member of the 1932 Tiger Moth equipped CFS Aerobatic Team, at 1535 local time on 15 July 1936, a date, time and place never to be forgotten by any first soloist. Geoffrey Bartlett also remembered that, as a pilot trainee it was absolutely forbidden for him to enter the hangar-workshops, a practice that was continued later at the wartime Elementary Schools. "Trainee pilots were not welcomed inside the maintenance hangars except to help sweep the floors on Saturday mornings, and then only under close supervision!"

The historic aircraft remained firmly in the grip of the military, taking on impressment serial BB723 in October 1940, continuing to operate at Hatfield with No 1 Elementary Flying Training School (EFTS). Transferred to the Royal Navy in 1943 one of her many different bases was Heathrow where she stayed for six months from November 1944. Sold out of the service in 1951 as just another Tiger Moth, BB723 was not recognised for the treasure she surely was and is believed to have been one of nine Tiger Moth airframes burned at a Bonfire Night party at the Five Ways Night Club at Hamsey Green near Croydon in November 1956.

In his Foreword to the DH.82 Tiger Moth Maintenance Manual, Albert Brant of the de Havilland Service Department wrote:

"Guided by the accumulated experience of years, especially that since 1925, during which over 2,000 Moths have been built, mainly for training purposes, and kept in continuous service in every part of the world, the de Havilland Aircraft Company Limited is now producing the Tiger Moth, specially designed, arranged and equipped as a General Training and Practice type.

There is one right and many wrong ways of doing most things and the operation and maintenance of an aeroplane is no exception. The object of these Notes is to point out the right way of doing the few small jobs necessary to ensure completely satisfactory and trouble-free operation. Due to its straightforward design and robust construction, the Tiger Moth needs a minimum of attention, but this very simplicity of maintenance must not be allowed to engender carelessness."

DH.82 Tiger Moth G-ABRC undergoing inspection at Hatfield in 1936. The twenty one year old Don Lawrence seems to be reminding trainee pilot Geoffrey Bartlett of the divide between pilots and engineers. *Geoffrey Bartlett*

Prototype DH.82 Tiger Moth G-ABRC during her working life with the de Havilland School of Flying at Hatfield. The aircraft has been subject to a number of upgrades (see the cutaway rear doors) whilst retaining the fabric covered rear turtle deck. *Geoffrey Bartlett*

What manner of machine was it that had been created at Stag Lane which was now called 'the DH.82 Tiger Moth'? By definition it was a simple biplane, built up on enhanced principles whose roots could be traced back to the First World War. There can be little improvement on the description penned by the manufacturer in 1931:

Main Planes:

The single bay biplane structure has a pronounced stagger and sweepback achieving the visibility and ease of egress from both cockpits aimed at. Each plane consists of two heavy 'I' section spruce spars with leading and trailing edge and ribs of normal wood structure. The tip bends are of light alloy tubing. The drag struts are of steel tube, the lugs for the swaged rod and light tensile steel wire bracing being integral with the tube, completing a structure which is not affected by any slight shrinkage which might take place in the wooden spar. The interplane struts are of spruce with steel end sockets and the drag bracings are duplicated.

Fuselage:

The sizes of tubing to specification DTD.89.A used for round tubes in the construction of the fuselage, and DTD.113 for square tubes, are shown on Drawing M.1698. In addition to the above, there are the lower cross members terminating with attachment fittings for root ends of the lower planes, which are especially constructed parts. The various stiffening plates at the welded joints are mild steel plate to specification S.3.

The front fuselage, the sides of which are parallel in plan view, is constructed of two flat sides, the junction joints of the structure and diagonal members to the longerons being welded in a jig. All joints are reinforced with side plates welded on. All holes in these side units are also jig drilled, and the side forms a replaceable unit should the need arise. The side units are assembled with no welding by the bolted cross members, which complete the front fuselage framework.

The rear fuselage from the rear of the pilot's seat to the stern post, is a completely rigid welded-up unit, jig built, and is a replaceable unit. The four longerons are of square tube and struts, diagonals and cross members of round tubing. All joints are reinforced by side plates welded on. A small quantity of quarter inch diameter by 22G commercial quality steel tubing is also used as stays for the rear fuselage fairing formers.

The engine bay structure consists of two side frames, each constructed of three square tubes in triangular form, welded flat in a jig at the joints. The joints are reinforced with steel plates welded on. The side units are assembled to the front fuselage section by bolted fishplates, and being jig made and drilled, form replaceable units. A stay tube from the right-hand rear engine foot to the bottom left-hand joint of the fuselage braces the structure against side loads.

It will be appreciated from the foregoing description that in the event of major damage the replaceable section can be obtained and fitted with little or no constructional experience.

Empennage:

The empennage follows the normal de Havilland practice and is constructed of wood and fabric covered. The control surfaces have trailing bends of light alloy tubing.

The tailplane is not adjustable in flight, but longitudinal trim is attained by adjustable spring loading on elevators, which has proved so satisfactory on other Gipsy Moth types.

Undercarriage:

The undercarriage is of the divided axle type. Spring legs embodying rubber-in-compression springing are used. The top end is attached to the fuselage lower longeron and the other end to the wheel end of the

The anatomy of a Tiger Moth revealed during a trial rig of PH-TYG by the Royal Netherlands Air Force Historic Flight during major overhaul of the aircraft at Gilze Rijen. *RNAFHF*

cranked half axle, which terminates at a tripod fitting under the fuselage. The structure is completed by a forwardly inclined stay tube from the lower end of the leg casing to the fuselage.

Controls:

All machine control operating gear is housed in a control box running centrally along the cockpit floor, forming a unit which can be easily removed for periodical inspection. The controls in the front cockpit are quickly detachable, the control columns by withdrawing a safety locking pin, and the rudder by removing the connecting rod.

The two control columns connect with a shaft carrying a lever which transmits side movement to the ailerons by cables, and fore and aft movement by link tubes to a cross shaft behind the pilot's seat, from which cables run direct to the elevator levers. Rudder cables run direct from attachment on the outer end of the rear rudder bar to the levers on the rudder."

Unable to raise patents against the DH.82 Tiger Moth design, de Havilland were content to label each aircraft with a reminder that it carried three patented features:

> GB 184,317. Improvements in or relating to aileron controlmechanism (aileron differential), registered in the name of Chief Designer Arthur Hagg and dated 1922.
> GB 277,914. Improvements in or relating to air speedindicators for aircraft (strut mounted ASI) registered in the name of Geoffrey de Havilland and dated 1927.
> GB 297,541. Improvements in or relating to harness for airmen (three point seat restraint) registered in the name of Hubert Broad and dated 1928.

In her final configuration the dimensions of the DH.82 Tiger Moth were remarkably similar to those of the DH.60M: span at 29ft 4in was six inches less than the DH.60M and wing area was 239sq.ft. compared with 243sq.ft, but length at 23ft. 11in and a height of 8ft 9½ in were identical. Tare weight of a basic DH.82 Tiger Moth had risen from 962lb to 1,075lb.

Reporting for *The Aeroplane*, Francis Bradbrooke wrote:

> "In the new Tiger Moth the de Havilland Company has succeeded in producing a machine which has all the flying qualities of the Moth either unimpaired or improved, and at the same time incorporates a number of special features for Air Force training requirements which make it substantially a different aeroplane.

The wings and bracing have been so stiffened up that the most violent aerobatics can be performed in these machines when they are in constant service and carrying parachutes, complete dual sets of instruments and controls, and various extras such as camera or machine gun equipment.

The standard Moth cellule is simplicity itself compared with the new staggered and swept back arrangement, from the designer's point of view, but the complicated problems involved have been solved with remarkable rapidity by the drawing office, inspection departments and shops in turn."

Following Martlesham Heath's approval, the Air Ministry placed an order with de Havilland (contract No 120255/31) for the supply of thirty five aircraft to be built to specification 23/31, essentially the same as the build standard of DH.60T Tiger Moth G-ABPH (1732). The first batch of fifteen aircraft was to be air delivered to 3 FTS at Grantham where they would be used as primary trainers, replacing the popular Hawker Tomtit. Each of the remaining twenty was required 'less engine' to be delivered by surface, as directed.

The first six, K2567-K2572, (1739-1744), were scheduled for delivery to Grantham on 9 November 1931, but the weather, very cold and accompanied by poor visibility, ensured the flight was postponed until the following day. The delivery pilots, drawn from 24 (Communications) Squadron based only a few miles west of Stag Lane at Northolt, were entertained by de Havilland staff and invited to thaw out after local flight testing by sampling freshly brewed coffee liberally laced with rum. While waiting, F/O Peter Heath was moved to assess the crazy flying qualities of the DH.82 in comparison to the DH.60 with which he was already familiar, and believed his twenty minute low level routine proved that the new aeroplane was considerably more versatile. Peter Heath later recalled that nobody in the de Havilland organisation objected to his exhibition, but his own Commanding Officer was far from amused.

A sunny day at RAF Grantham on 10 November 1931 when the RAF's first DH.82 Tiger Moths were delivered from Stag Lane by pilots of 24 (Communications) Squadron. Partly masked by the fin and rudder of K2572 just inside the hangar is a Hawker Tomtit, a type replaced at No 3 FTS by the new arrival. *Peter Heath*

This 'ticking off' of an RAF Tiger Moth pilot occurred even before the aircraft had been delivered into service, but no official action was taken to impede Peter Heath's long career in the Royal Air Force from which he retired with the rank of Group Captain.

Conditions had improved sufficiently the following day for the task to be completed: nothing was considered remarkable, the squadron pilots were merely delivering another batch of aeroplanes. Leaving Stag Lane at 0945 hrs the flight to Lincolnshire took exactly sixty five minutes. Having handed over his own machine, K2572, and received the necessary signature, Peter Heath accepted Avro Tutor K1579 in exchange and flew her back to Northolt. It was all in a day's work.

At the time of the Tiger Moth's entry into RAF service, pilots were being trained under a number of different schemes as described in this contemporary appraisal:

"If a man joins the Reserve of Air Force Officers, he is taught to fly at one of the civilian training schools approved for the purpose by the Air Ministry, where the training methods are kept closely to the lines adopted in the RAF itself. If he joins the Auxiliary Air Force he is taught to fly in the squadron which he joins, under the care of the Adjutant, who is always a regular officer and a qualified instructor. Officers of the Special Reserve are taught at one of the civilian schools, while regular officers with short-service commissions are taught at one of the RAF Flying Training Schools. The permanent officers who have learnt elementary flying at Cranwell, Oxford or Cambridge, are also sent to a Flying Training School for further instruction before being posted to a squadron.

"There are four approved civilian training schools: the de Havilland school for London, the Bristol school for the West, the Blackburn school at Brough in Yorkshire, and Flying Training Services at Hamble near Southampton. The Flying Training Schools of the RAF are at Digby in Lincolnshire, Grantham, also in Lincolnshire, Sealand near Chester, and Abu Sueir in Egypt. At the Flying Training Schools officers who can fly receive instruction in aerial gunnery, photography and other necessary duties. They leave these schools fully trained pilot officers.

"Considerations of economy have often turned attention to the possibility of using a smaller and cheaper machine than the Avro for elementary training, for minor mishaps to undercarriages and propellers are bound to be not infrequent. A great deal of good training work has been carried out on the de Havilland Moth, and the Tiger Moth is now also used. The Hawker Tomtit is another type which has done good service. The exponents of the Avro type for training now admit that after so many years of redoubtable service it is time that the 504 type should go on the half pay list."

The student pilots of 'A' Flight, No 3 FTS Grantham (also known as Spitalgate or Spittlegate), were all approaching solo standard on their Hawker Tomtits when the Tiger Moths arrived, bearing an order from the Air Ministry that type conversion was to begin without delay. In spite of protests, additional pre-solo hours had now to be flown by students and instructors, none of whom were seduced by the new aeroplane which they compared unfavourably with the Tomtit except in the arenas of price, economy of operation, reliability and baggage space, the latter proving a bonus for weekends away.

Of the residual nine aircraft from the first batch, a further six, K2573-K2578 (1744-1750), were flown to Grantham on 16 November; K2579 and K2580 (1751-1752) joined them on 2 December and K2581 (1753), twelve days later. All twenty aircraft ordered for delivery 'less engines', K2582-K2601 (1754-1773), were transported to the Home Aircraft Depot (HAD) at Henlow between 16 December 1931 and 4 February 1932, arriving singly or in pairs in fifteen separate consignments.

On 2 February 1932 Mr Charles Power of Renfrew, Pennsylvania, USA, wrote to the Sales Office of the de Havilland Aircraft Company Ltd. at Stag Lane Aerodrome, Edgware, North London, and requested details of the firm's DH.82 Tiger Moth.

The letter arrived on the desk of Business Director Francis St Barbe only eight days later and, as it was just another routine enquiry, one of the office staff replied politely to advise that they were enclosing a reprint of an article first published in *The Aeroplane* giving full particulars of the company's Tiger Moth Military Training Machine, receipt of which it was hoped would be to Mr Power's satisfaction.

Above: Mike Russell used an amalgam of Tiger Moth parts to assemble a DH.82 style airframe registered G-MOTH and painted to represent K2567, the first of the marque delivered to the RAF in November 1931. *deHMC Archive*

Right: Francis St Barbe, Business Director of the de Havilland Aircraft Company, whose grip on publicity, sales contracts and finance ensured stability and measured growth during difficult times. The Tiger Moth continued in production largely due to his faith in the continuation of sales around the world. *via BAE Systems*

There was no suggestion that the correspondent from Pennsylvania should visit the company in London although that offer was undoubtedly made to Dr H J van der Maas from the Rotterdamse Aeroclub in the Netherlands. The Club's board of directors had suggested that an evaluation of the Tiger Moth would be required in advance of any prospective order, and Dr van der Maas was duly entertained by one of the de Havilland sales and demonstration pilots, Hugh 'Jimmy' Buckingham, on 28 June 1932.

While the de Havilland company was in a position to extract £5 per flying hour from the Air Ministry for Moth aeroplanes operated by their flying school on behalf of the Royal Air Force Reserve, St Barbe's instructions to his salesmen were almost certainly centred around minimum flight time or the least that could be considered polite. In the event, and after a check flight, Dr van der Maas was permitted to fly solo and the de Havilland reward was the sale of one Tiger Moth which was delivered, as requested, almost exactly a year later.

The Sales Office at Stag Lane was, perhaps, taken by surprise at the rapidity of the changes which had resulted in the new type designation, else instructed to exercise economy by the Business Director, for in an uncharacteristic practice sales leaflets were distributed, originally produced under the heading "de Havilland 'Moth' (Military Training Type DH.60T)", badly amended by typewriter with the name 'Tiger' inserted before 'Moth' and the DH.60T nomination merely struck through. The change of engine specification had been accomplished by the simple expedient of adding a further 'I' to the two existing Roman numerals. There was just sufficient space at the bottom of the page, tucked in between notification of colour options and the de Havilland trademark symbol, to advise interested parties that the price of the new aircraft was '£1,045. Landplane ex-Works, ready for Flight or Packing'.

Under a sub-heading, the aircraft was again described as a 'Tiger' Training Type Moth, and there followed a list of what a would-be purchaser might expect: standard instruments in both cockpits, mounted on a board, and supplied in what were described as 'English' or metric units, and faces printed in any desired language. Items featured as 'Equipment' might well have been subject to query by anybody seeking a contractual definition of the aeroplane for they included fundamentals such as seats and three-piece unsplinterable glass windscreens, controls and ignition switches, aerobatic harness and special wide doors for emergency exit. Particular reference was made to the Dunlop air wheels and low pressure tyres which were described very specifically as being 'fitted on ball bearings'.

Altogether it was a very uninspired document, liberally spiced with the considerable mis-use of capital letters, and ending with a statement clarifying the ex-factory colour schemes, advising that all covered surfaces would be, to quote, 'Alluminium', while 'Fuselage Strut and Undercarriage' colours were optional, excepting white or gold. But promotional material was scheduled to change and heavy emphasis on the potential of the Tiger Moth, 'As Supplied to the British Royal Air Force', was soon reviewed in a three page brochure which proclaimed the aircraft as: 'One machine adaptable for every branch of training'. Short descriptive paragraphs under the headings of Flying, Fighting, Bombing, Photography and Wireless were followed by a statement that interested parties would be sent 'fully illustrated literature upon request'.

Six DH.82 Tiger Moths were removed from store at the Home Aircraft Depot at RAF Henlow in April 1932 and delivered to Stag Lane where they were extensively modified to become the display team of the Central Flying School, primarily to take part in the RAF Pageant at Hendon in June. *Phil Hagger*

In support of the Royal Air Force Pageant at Hendon in 1927, the Central Flying School had raised a formation display team with an establishment of six DH.60 Moths. They were powered by the Armstrong Siddeley Genet I engine, chosen for its ability to cope with sustained inverted flight. Gipsy-powered DH.60M Moths with full inverted systems were provided for the 1930 and 1931 Pageants. In 1932 six Tiger Moths were removed from store at Henlow, K2582-K2587 (1754-1759), and transferred back to Stag Lane in pairs on 4, 6 and 8 April. The fleet was modified to permit sustained inverted flight and a prominent red and white chequerboard colour scheme was applied to the top surfaces of all mainplanes, tailplanes and elevators: those surfaces, due to the inverted nature of much of the display, most on view to spectators on the ground. Operating in a single seat configuration with the inverted fuel system hidden inside the front cockpit, the team was to display in a formation of five, leaving one aircraft in reserve.

To enable familiarisation, K2582 was delivered to CFS on 26 April 1932 and the remaining five aircraft joined the school at Wittering in May where the routines were perfected under the team leadership of Flt Lt P M Watt. At Hendon on 26 June four of the five aircraft team (Flt Lt L K Stokes, F/Os D D Christie and V R Moon, and Sgt Pilot S J Mansell), engaged one another in a slow speed race, during which they were not permitted to lose height.

A contemporary report was headed 'The Tortoise Race':

"First the four Tiger Moths flew past at normal speed in line astern, then they flew over the aerodrome across wind in line abreast, each pilot checking his speed by a series of stalls. At first the third machine rapidly 'underhauled' his rivals, but lost altitude in his effort. Finally, No 3 machine fell behind in fine style with only a comparatively small loss in altitude. It was quite an interesting event, which certainly tortoised a lot regarding the advance made in present-day flying with the help of automatic slots etc."

In 1932 the Royal Air Force Central Flying School display team painted the tops of the flying surfaces of their Tiger Moths in a red and white chequerboard to improve the crowd's appreciation of which aircraft were inverted at any one time. In 1995, John Pothecary's restored G-BJAP made her first appearance at the Woburn Abbey Moth Rally in an identical scheme. *Mansfield Spong*

The 1932 RAF Central Flying School Display Team, in the form of K2583, K2584, K2585, K2586 and K2587, at altitude in perfect formation, inverted. The top surfaces of the mainplanes and horizontal tail were painted in a large red and white chequerboard pattern for maximum visual effect when playing to the crowd. *via Darryl Cott*

The CFS aerobatic team was part of an impressive show of RAF support at the opening of Portsmouth Airport in July 1932. The photograph gives the impression that the dihedral on the Tiger Moth's top wings may have been reduced to zero, possibly in a quest to improve the quality of sustained inverted flight. *via Mike Jerram*

The team aircraft were returned to Stag Lane in mid-August for conversion to standard configuration, after which they were flown into storage at 2 Aircraft Servicing Unit (ASU) Cardington. Perhaps this was a questionable decision, for the Air Ministry moved all six back to de Havilland in March and April 1933 where the inverted systems were refitted and the team reformed at Wittering on 9 May. But it was to be their second and last season: the aircraft were all delivered to Henlow on 24 July, standardised, and finally allocated to other less arduous duties.

Having ordered the type into service as a new trainer, the history of the Tiger Moth with 3 FTS might be described as brief. By August 1933, K2569 had been struck off charge at Grantham; three aircraft had been transferred to communications duties with 24 Squadron at Hendon, followed by a further five in 1934; four aircraft were transferred to the Home Aircraft Depot (HAD) at Henlow in August 1933 and had been broken up within a year, and another had been allocated to an Air Armament School where it was scrapped in August 1934. The previous May, K2570 (1742), was featured in a magazine article, photographed with the hood erected, 'for instruction in the art of blind flying', said the caption, whilst confirming that 'the particular machine illustrated' belonged not to a flying training establishment, but to No 24 (Communications) Squadron. K2586 (1758), was transferred to 24 Squadron at Hendon late in 1934 for a four year posting, during which time the aircraft was used to conduct civilian 'B' (commercial) cross country tests of about two hours average duration. Intended to become an instructional airframe in October 1938, K2586 was instead broken up for spares.

DH.82 Tiger Moth K2573 wearing the chevrons and titling of No 24 (Communications) Squadron, RAF, after a short posting to Grantham. The distinctive DH trademark symbols applied to the interplane struts of all civil and military biplanes supplied pre-war, have been painted over or removed. *Frank Bentley*

Remarkably, the first of the Grantham batch lived longest: K2567 spent several weeks at RAE Farnborough early in 1932, engaged on 'experimental work of a secret nature, instrument testing and as a communications aircraft'. In fact, K2567 was employed in early trials in support of a programme which resulted in the introduction of the de Havilland DH.82 Queen Bee, a remotely controlled, pilotless gunnery target aircraft, her specific function to demonstrate the ability of the Gipsy Major engine to be advanced from idle in a glide to the instant application of full power. Following time in the care of 12 Maintenance Unit (MU) Kirkbride, in June 1940 she was 'converted' into an instructional airframe (2049M), by 4 MU at Cowley, probably as an educational aid in support of Tiger Moth production which was just gaining momentum at the Morris Motors' works.

In reply to criticism of the first aircraft completed at Cowley in April 1940, the Works' Superintendent had replied that the job had been copied from 'a de Havilland fuselage held at these works'. In July 1940, indicating that she had remained entirely passive, 2049M was surprisingly and unusually returned to flying duties at Fairoaks where she remained with 18 Elementary Flying Training School (EFTS) until December 1941. After a service life of just ten years, the RAF's first Tiger Moth was cut up for scrap.

Two major criticisms continued to be expressed by pilots: the lack of an adjustable seat and the degree of the forced draught which was channelled into the rear cockpit from around the front windscreen. The seat was a matter of continuing experimentation whilst some attempt was made to counter the draught by extending laterally the plywood framework in which the front seat was located. Under the hopeful title 'draught excluder', the spare parts inventory was increased to include delicately tailored strips of plywood which were glued and pinned in their strategic locations.

Permitted to solo one of the RAF's new Tiger Moths from Stag Lane prior to delivery, and in some soupy winter weather, journalist Francis Bradbrooke touched on points with which later generations of Tiger Moth pilots might beg to disagree:

"When flying the machine has most of the standard Moth characteristics with all its sensitiveness on the elevators and lightness on ailerons. Like the other Moths it can be turned by the use of aileron alone without need for ruddering, but unlike the great majority of light aeroplanes it will fly a perfectly straight course with both hands and feet off the controls at cruising speed. When throttled down a slight swing to the left sets in.
When the rudder bar is left alone the machine can be turned to the right quite readily by means of aileron and elevator but the left hand turn only begins after some side slipping, presumably because the slipstream swirl imparts a right handed tendency which is overcome when the rudder is held solidly as part of the fin, but not so well when the rudder floats free.
The slot locking device made possible a comparative experiment which we have never previously been able to make on a Moth, or any other machine with ailerons on the bottom wings only.
The Tiger Moth can just be kept straight at 40 indicated mph with the slots locked shut. At less than this speed, with the rudder straight, a brisk right handed spin develops. An equally brisk left hand spin can be induced by the rudder.
With slots free there is no difficulty in keeping straight at 35mph but the nose cannot be kept up to that speed except in successive pull ups, unless the engine is used to provide a little slipstream for the elevators. With extreme use of all controls a spin in either direction can be started, even with slots open, but we did not stay in to see what happened because too much right hand spinning makes us come all over queer abdominally.
The windshields are quite as effective as usual but we should have preferred a sinkable seat so that when the excellent visibility is not vital, as on cross country flights, we could retire into seclusion out of the fresh air. We are becoming cabin conscious. When we mentioned this point to Mr Broad he said that this feature of up and down seats, adjustable while flying, was being incorporated."

Writing a series of reminiscences fifty years after Francis Bradbrooke's contribution had appeared in *The Aeroplane*, John Fricker wrote of the Tiger Moth:

"Like all de Havilland aeroplanes of the 1930s, the Tiger Moth is somewhat short of vertical fin area and directional stability. Application of the non-Frise and wide-chord ailerons on the lower mainplanes also results in generous amounts of adverse yaw, despite their differential action, calling for further and carefully co-ordinated use of the sensitive rudder."

For pupils and instructors with differing leg lengths there was provision by simple adjustment for presentation of the rudder pedals in both cockpits. The idea of an adjustable seat in the rear cockpit was first addressed as early as 1 October 1931 when experimental modification drawings M1678, M1679 and M1680 were raised to cover the arrangement and assembly of such a seat and associated changes to the controls and structure necessary to accommodate it.

When allocated to the de Havilland School of Flying in March 1933, second production DH.82A Tiger Moth G-ACDB (3176), was fitted with an adjustable rear seat for which the weight increase was noted at 4lb. This may have been an experimental version used for evaluation ahead of the next series of design studies which were not signed off until January 1934. The two aircraft for the Bristol Aeroplane Company's Reserve School at Filton, the orange and black G-ACVK (3224), and G-ACVL (3225), were both delivered with adjustable rear seats in August 1934 following which, and until November 1938, a mere handful of modified aircraft was sold.

The de Havilland Drawing Office maintained a grip on the development of seats until what appears to be their final draft of 'experimental' drawing M1679 at Issue 8, dated 11 September 1935. In spite of what some actual or potential customers considered a deficiency, the lack of an adjustable seat seems not to have been a

This scene was shot at Old Rhinebeck Aerodrome, New York State, in the summer of 2005 after locally based Tiger Moth N3529 was repainted in the colours of the de Havilland School of Flying. The same aircraft had previously carried registration G-ACDA but owner Bill King made a change after the real G-ACDA was restored in England. *Clive Abbott*

Complete with flowing white silk scarf Bill King taking off in a crosswind at Old Rhinebeck Aerodrome, New York in his Tiger Moth N3529 painted to represent G-ACDB of the de Havilland School of Flying. *via Bill King*

de Havilland demonstrator G-ABYJ was fitted with a Gipsy Major engine and listed as a DH.82A in the company register in July 1932. The aircraft was flown with distinction by Christopher Clarkson in Portugal and France and was photographed between sessions on a wet 12 October 1932 at Stag Lane. *Christopher Clarkson*

major deterrent to continued sales of the Tiger Moth. The fact that no such installation was specified by the British Air Ministry may have been a deciding factor in termination of further research.

K2579 (1751), was withdrawn from Grantham in May 1932 and contributed to a programme of performance measurement at Martlesham Heath during which she was dived at speeds up to 225mph IAS. In December, K2578 (1750), arrived to begin flutter trials with the result that having dived the aircraft to 215mph IAS, mass balance weights were recommended for attachment to the ailerons. K2570 (1742), joined the programme in February 1933, spending additional time investigating the inverted envelope from 120mph to the inverted stall which was recorded at 60mph.

K2583 (1755), one of the 1932 CFS Team, began trials on 13 November 1933 which resulted in a report published the following January recommending mass balancing of the rudder, a feature not universally accepted, and never fitted to Tiger Moths later manufactured in Australia. At Martlesham Heath, Tiger Moth K2583 had been temporarily loaned the mass balanced rudder of DH.60M K1864 (1604), an aircraft posted-in during September from communications duties on behalf of the Air Ministry's 'Air Defence of Great Britain' organisation, and herself scheduled for further flight investigation of DH.60 aileron control. The rudder was returned in good order to permit K1864 to take up a new post with 24 Squadron early in 1934.

The de Havilland Aircraft Company was particularly keen to sell into overseas markets, and their network of local agents and associated companies always had a demonstration aircraft on hand with which to entertain potential customers. The company policy directed from the Sales Office at Stag Lane and later at Hatfield required that agents bought their own demonstrators and payment was required prior to delivery, a policy not always appreciated but one which safeguarded the business structure and added an imperative to the local sales efforts.

Few would have denied that the most famous display of flying in Europe was the annual RAF Pageant at Hendon. Following the 13th Pageant on the last Monday of June in 1932, the Air Ministry encouraged members of the Society of British Aircraft Constructors (SBAC) to set up shop and to exhibit their latest airframes and engines to an exclusive list of guests specially invited from around the world. The de Havilland Company flew three aircraft into Hendon from Stag Lane, just a few miles over the hedge: Gipsy III versions of the DH.80 Puss Moth, DH.83 Fox Moth and DH.82 Tiger Moth. *Flight* magazine thought it a capital idea allowing visitors to make the acquaintance of these new machines in the flesh, but in contrast to their effusive descriptions of the Puss Moth's 'comfort' and Fox Moth's 'obvious economy' leaving a marked impression on the visitors, no such supportive comments were reserved for the new Tiger Moth.

In October 1932 at thirty years of age, Christopher Clarkson was already into his third year of retirement as a veteran instructor from the RAF Central Flying School. For this gifted pilot, retirement actually meant establishing the Aviation Department of Selfridges' London departmental store, operating from the Heston base of old school chum and business partner Brian Lewis, later Lord Essendon.

Brian Lewis & Co. Ltd. had been appointed British agents for de Havilland aeroplanes in an interesting arrangement announced in March 1932, and which divided England into three business regions, although the agents' offices were all within a radius of 25 miles of one another: Brian Lewis at Heston, Brooklands Aviation at Weybridge and Phillips and Powis at Woodley. Stag Lane/Hatfield controlled sales in Northern Ireland, Scotland and Wales.

When the manufacturer was called upon to demonstrate the latest model of DH.82 Tiger Moth in Lisbon, competing for a trainer aircraft contract for the Portuguese military, Christopher Clarkson was recruited as pilot nominee.

The contemporary demonstration aircraft was G-ABYJ (3137), registered to the de Havilland Aircraft Co. Ltd. on 14 July, 1932 and issued with a Certificate of Airworthiness (C of A) eight days later. Apart from a long range fuel tank installed in the front cockpit, G-ABYJ had been fitted with the new Gipsy Major, production number 5003, and was listed in the de Havilland inventory as a DH.82A. She carried the legend *'Tiger Moth'* inelegantly stencilled in large capital letters along the fuselage sides. At least showing some consistency, all reference to the aeroplane in surviving de Havilland documents identify her as 'G-ABYT' due to nothing more sinister than bad hand-writing or third copy typed memos.

G-ABYJ was flown to Lisbon early in September, transiting via Paris, Tours, Biarritz and Burgos. On previous occasions a routing via Madrid had resulted in Christopher Clarkson having to use his hat as a petrol filter due to the primitive state of the refuelling facilities, but apart from that disincentive the city was not on the direct routing, and he had not been asked to make a diplomatic landing there.

On arrival in Lisbon three other aircraft were found to be competing for the same business: a Bluebird from Blackburn Aircraft flown by an old friend, Patrick Johnson, a Fleet Trainer and an Italian Caproni Ca.100, built with DH.60 parts supplied by de Havilland. The Caproni was soon eliminated in spite and because of its confused pedigree, a situation richly exploited by the de Havilland team; relations between the two companies were anything but cordial. The Bluebird went next because the military did not like the side-by-side seating arrangement, an ideal which, to save trouble and expense, could have been transmitted to Blackburn before arrival. Johnson threw in his lot with the Tiger Moth, exhibiting a broad band of patriotism in an effort to unsettle the obvious pretensions of the American Fleet.

During exercises held over the next few days, Johnson climbed out onto the wing of the Tiger Moth in flight in an effort to prove the strength of the airframe after the pilot of the Fleet had been seen on the ground, jumping on and off his tailplane in an effort to demonstrate a similar point. A few days before an aerobatic competition which had been arranged at the local aero club the Fleet went to Madrid for a presentation to the Spanish Air Force, but forced landed due to the loss of a cylinder during the return flight to Lisbon, and effectively was ruled out. But Fleet supporters managed to delay the contest by a week in view of the forecast weather conditions which, in spite of the dire prognosis, turned out bright and clear.

With the aid of the local agent, Carlos Bleck, authority was secured for the two British aircraft to fly a mild aerobatic display over an exhibition site situated on a hillside, followed by a loop and a roll over the local football stadium where the host country was to play Spain.

What happened after that is best expressed by Christopher Clarkson himself:

> "All our long years of RAF training and discipline found their reward that sunny day in Lisbon. Never before and never again could such a thing happen. We worked out a beautiful programme. Johnson on the Bluebird and I on the Tiger Moth. Fix the exhibition first, we thought, then maybe stop the soccer match.
>
> The field was good and big and lent itself to some low flying. After that? Well, why not fly upside down in formation above the main street from the top of the hill to the harbour? It had a gentle slope which just about took care of the sinking speed of an inverted Moth or Bluebird. And so it was. If it was enjoyed by the participants, it certainly was by the populace. All the populace, that is, except the protagonists of the Fleet who realised too late that we had got away with a publicity stunt of far, far greater value than the local aero club meeting. And for the participants, it was nice to think that they had at least been able to fly upside down along the main avenue of a European capital and not be clapped in jail. What we did not know, however, was that there were wires of some sort strung across our path. But we missed them."

The promised aerobatic competition was held at the local aero club as planned, but the Fleet did not manage to get back to Lisbon in time, and the Tiger Moth in the hands of Christopher Clarkson took all the honours, securing the contract for de Havilland. Soon after, and at another venue, the engine of the Fleet Trainer failed again during a low level aerobatic display and the aircraft crashed, killing the pilot.

Tiger Moth G-ABYJ returned to a demonstration career with her makers at Stag Lane where she was modified in December to accept a revised exhaust system, a long tail pipe which curved gracefully back underneath the fuselage, terminating at the trailing edge of the lower wings. It was in this configuration that Christopher Clarkson was invited to display her at the Saint Germain Aviation Meeting on 22 May 1933, an event held annually at the picturesque aerodrome situated a few miles south west of the centre of Paris, on the edge of the Bois de Boulogne, and within sight of the Eiffel Tower.

Following the flight of a 'chicken-coop' Farman which carried Miss Paris 1933 around the circuit, an 'International Stunting Exhibition' was opened by Gerhard Fieseler piloting his new biplane, the Tiger II, powered by a 420hp Walter engine which, should there have been any confusion over names, certainly distinguished it from the 130hp de Havilland's Tiger Moth. Clarkson was introduced as 'the well known English aerobatic pilot' whose display was reported as "... a novel exhibition of crazy flying. Side-slipping around the field, letting one wheel touch on the ground, then rising a short height, as if bouncing up, and again letting a wheel touch on the ground, Clarkson encircled the aerodrome, having his 'plane under perfect control all the time. All of his evolutions in the air, barrel rolls, loopings, nose dives etc., were all done in that smooth continuous manner that has so often been admired in the Royal Air Force displays."

Like all other demonstrators, G-ABYJ soon was passed on, making way for another factory fresh example. She joined de Havilland's fleet at White Waltham where she was operated on behalf of 13 ERFTS, by which time she had been fitted with a new Gipsy Major engine, No 5519. On 13 July 1936, a pilot with eight hours solo time was authorised to conduct forced landing practice at the Relief Landing Ground (RLG) at Winkfield. During one approach, excess height was lost by attempting gliding turns to left and right, but the aircraft stalled at low level and crashed causing damage from which the airframe failed to recover. G-ABYJ was replaced on the establishment by G-AEMF (3514), delivered to White Waltham following issue of her Certificate of Airworthiness on 19 September, and fitted with Gipsy Major engine No 5519 salvaged from G-ABYJ.

At Stag Lane the Sales Department had redesigned their brochures and a standard Price List appeared in November 1931 under designation 'Form 253' which initially was re-published in a modified state every two months, not because the price was increasing at an alarming rate, but rather as the requirement to include extras and options for which verified prices to supply and fit could be quoted. Although Price List No 2 dated January 1932 had been subjected to a mild attack of updating by typewriter prior to publication of List No 3 in March, the changes reflected the rapid progression of modification, development and customer requirements.

The heading 'Equipment' as specified in the early and amended DH.60T leaflet had been revised to read 'Normal Standard Fixed Equipment' but still carried details of seats, harness and controls. The option for special wide doors had been deleted but replaced with a note that cushions could be supplied as standard but only if specified during the sales negotiations. The information on colour remained as before, except the subject was referred to as the 'Normal Standard' colour scheme, and the spelling of 'aluminium' had been corrected. Whereas the price for supply and fitting of certain lighting electrics and instruments had been reduced, the cost of installing remote control gear for the Hythe Mk IIIA camera gun had almost doubled to fifteen guineas, reflecting the difficulties introduced by incorporation of the mechanism.

Hughes IIIA compasses were mounted on top of the control boxes in both cockpits, forward of the stick position, excepting when Marconi AD22 wireless (or as specified) was fitted in the front cockpit. In this configuration it was necessary to move the compass to a port side shelf where it effectively blanked off the low speed scale of the engine revolution indicator, but left the right side of the cockpit clear for installation of the wireless trailing aerial reel and winch.

Handley Page automatic slots had always been a feature of de Havilland aeroplanes scheduled for club or training duties and were a safety device recommended by the manufacturer, at extra cost. During Captain de Havilland's famously public accident during the demonstration of an experimentally slotted DH.60 Moth at Stag Lane in March 1928, the wooden fuselage was broken in two but the pilot walked away practically unscathed and the press was there by invitation to report the event in graphic detail but not quite from the angle they had expected. Accident inspectors thereafter nearly always recorded whether the subject aircraft had been fitted with slots or not.

All Tiger Moths ordered by the Air Ministry were fitted with slots on delivery as part of the standard specification. Only the six aircraft operated by the CFS formation team during the summer of 1932 flew with the slots removed, and then only on a temporary basis.

The de Havilland Aircraft Company was being honest with its customers when it quoted the cost of supplying and fitting slots to a

Tiger Moth early in 1932 as £18.0s.0d with a further ten guineas required for a cockpit locking device, but advised that an additional sum of £38.11s.6d was to be paid to Handley Page Ltd. as a royalty on each set fitted. There is every reason to suppose that this financial burden was the main reason why the de Havilland company did not fit the devices to its own demonstrator aircraft until they were sold or re-deployed, when the costs could be recovered from the client.

Subsidiary items specified for an early export order to Persia, and which filtered into the first few issues of the price lists as an incentive to prospective customers, included a drinking water tank and a ration box in each cockpit, neither of which could have been treated as anything short of emergency equipment, although as a subject of its own that particular title was never used in any published schedule of spare parts.

The Persian order, booked against the name of the Imperial Persian Army Flying Corps, was for twenty aeroplanes serialled 101-120 and which were allocated production slots 17-36, very early positions from which any customer could reasonably be expected to dictate specification and terms. But the manufacturer was not unhappy: the order for twenty identical aircraft had been won after mutually beneficial negotiations between Francis St Barbe assisted by the General Production Manager, Harry Povey, in Berne. The Persian delegation of Colonel Issa Khan and Major Arfa were accompanied by Swedish Captain Alis Nordquist who had been appointed to modernise the Air Force and select a new military training aircraft in Europe. They were impressed with the de Havilland approach to business which required cash payments in advance and the balance before delivery. St Barbe knew that other manufacturers had offered better terms including a promise to accept local produce as part-payment, a potentially disastrous spiral into which he refused to be drawn. Avro had demonstrated an Avro 626 Trainer in Tehran but the type had been rejected.

A modification to satisfy the Flying Corps' requirement for the aerobatic weight to be increased by 100lb to 1,750lb was achieved by strengthening the front spars of the top mainplanes by adding ash 'packing pieces' (cappings) and doubling up on some rib lattice slats. When introduced to the Tiger Moth in October 1931, *Flight's* correspondent had assumed that the next logical step in development would be an all-metal wing, and this was perhaps the opportunity to provide one, but at no time in any of the subsequent discussions regarding an upgrade of the aeroplane was a metal wing put forward as a subject for further investigation. However, the Persian Army clearly specified that Fairey-Reed fixed pitch metal propellers were to be fitted to their Gipsy III engines.

Further development of the Gipsy III, which in the DH.82 Tiger Moth was inclined to overheat when the climb speed was too low, included an increase in bore from 114mm to 118mm, raising the capacity from 5.71 to 6.12 litres, and the maximum output by 10hp to 130hp, a figure achieved at 2,350rpm. The improved engine was initially designated Gipsy IIIA, but the military connection was considered vital, and the name Gipsy Major was adopted on full production in 1932. Unprecedented for aero engines of the period, the Gipsy Major I was introduced into service with an overhaul life of 450 hours, a 50% increase over the Gipsy I of 1927. By July 1933, the figure had risen to 750 hours, and by August 1937 the value had been extended to the accompaniment of universal acclaim, to the magic one thousand. And even that was not the end of the story.

Until production of the Gipsy III was halted potential customers were offered DH.82 Tiger Moths with a choice of engine, although the Gipsy Major powered aircraft attracted a premium of slightly less than 5%, increasing the ex-factory price to £1,095. And what could be expected for the money? At the same maximum permitted all up weight of 1,825lb, the performance variation offered by the extra power of the Gipsy Major was neither startling nor surprising. Maximum speeds at all levels up to 10,000ft were about 4mph greater than the Gipsy III model, 109mph quoted at sea level reducing to 99mph at 10,000ft, and the cruising speed of 93mph maintained the average difference. Petrol consumption had risen by four pints to six gallons per hour reducing the miles per gallon by slightly more than half a mile. Operating with a fuel capacity quoted as eighteen gallons (later increased to nineteen gallons), ultimate range was reduced slightly by little more than 4% to 279 miles. In all other respects, the new engine improved basic performance as anticipated with a reduction by some 17 yards to achieve a take-off run of 156 yards measured from a standing start to lift off.

In 1933, performance was calculated against criteria defined by the Paris based International Commission of Air Navigation (ICAN), a necessary regulation which permitted easier acceptance of performance values obtained world-wide which could be judged against the same benchmark.

One curiosity of the system was in timing the take-off run. A Gipsy Major powered Tiger Moth at maximum authorised weight was clocked at twelve seconds for 'take-off' compared with just over thirteen for the Gipsy III variant and sixteen or eighteen seconds for a similarly loaded seaplane. A parameter deleted from the system of performance analysis universally adopted in 1939 included aircraft

Some of the first batch of twenty DH.82 Tiger Moths ordered on behalf of the Imperial Persian Army Flying Corps in 1932 under construction at Stag Lane. Build numbers chalked onto trestles identify the four aircraft on the right of the group as 110, 109, 107 and 108. *The Aeroplane*

The Stag Lane engine factory working to its limited capacity in 1929. Massive orders for the Gipsy Major engine ensured a major expansion until by 1934 and on closure of the aerodrome the Engine Division was in control of the whole Stag Lane factory site. *deHMC Archive*

height after take-off, measured 500 metres 'from rest'. Figures quoted as 119ft and 143ft respectively served to confirm the better rate of climb on 130hp: 673 feet per minute at sea level, an improvement of 15% over the Gipsy III.

For an aircraft designed primarily for circuit training, the thought of a service ceiling of 13,600ft operating at maximum weight behind the Gipsy Major might have seemed fairly academic, (12,100ft for the Gipsy III), or an absolute value of 18,100ft at normal weight (1,650lb) compared with 16,800ft. But de Havilland's main thrust early in 1933, and for some time to follow, was to promote acceptance of the Tiger Moth as a multi-role military training aircraft under which heading bomb aiming and photographic reconnaissance from such altitudes would have been normal operational practice. The company published a sixteen page booklet promoting just these ideas which included performance figures not found in any other publicity material.

During the summer vacation of 1932, two young students, Messrs Naish and Page, using generally available data, constructed a formula from which the relative efficiency of a range of fully laden civil aircraft could be generated and the resultant 'unit values' compared. Although their endeavours were not intended to be anything more than for personal interest, the results were published in the aviation press. Several de Havilland aircraft were included although DH.82 analysis was limited to the Gipsy III powerplant:

DH.83 Fox Moth (Gipsy Major)	56.2
DH.83 Fox Moth (Gipsy III)	52.0
DH.60G Moth Major (Gipsy Major)	50.4
DH.82 Tiger Moth (Gipsy III)	46.2
DH.60G Gipsy Moth (Gipsy II)	45.3

Seriously intentioned or not, de Havilland might have been alarmed to see that in the complete list, the most efficient aircraft judged against the common formula at 59.7, was a Percival Gull powered by a Cirrus Hermes IV engine.

Upgrading of the basic DH.82 Tiger Moth into the Gipsy Major powered 'A' model was the result of natural development, allied to the considerable experience gained from operation of the 103 Gipsy III powered DH.82s listed in the de Havilland order of manufacture. The transition from DH.60T Tiger Moth (Gipsy III) to DH.82 Tiger Moth (Gipsy III) with DH.60T Moth Trainers (Gipsy I and Gipsy II)

and DH.60M Metal Moths (Gipsy I and Gipsy II) on the factory floor at the same time, appears to have been handled by the progress clerks with some equanimity, but a greater clarity of order was introduced when the DH.82 Tiger Moth was issued with its own unique series of works' identification numbers commencing from No 3100, an unregistered aircraft shipped early in 1932 to Arnhold & Co, de Havilland's successful agent in Shanghai.

Although the first 'A' designated Tiger Moth is listed as G-ABUL (3107), the original airframe was merely re-engined with a Gipsy Major for use by Sir Alan Cobham and his National Aviation Day Display during the 1933 season.

The company demonstrator G-ABYJ and an aircraft ordered for the Deutscher Reichverkenes Ministerium in Berlin, D-2357 (3142), to which a British Certificate of Airworthiness was issued in October 1932, were similarly, production DH.82 airframes fitted with the new engine. In contrast, the Bristol Aeroplane Company accepted delivery of a pair of basic DH.82 aircraft, complete with Gipsy III engines, G-ACZY (3315), and G-ACZZ (3316), as late as December 1934. These were the last of the Gipsy III powered Tiger Moths and followed two others, G-ACVK (3224), and G-ACVL (3225), which had been delivered the previous July, no doubt to maintain standardisation of the Filton-based fleet.

DH.82 Tiger Moth D-2357, fitted with a Gipsy Major engine, was registered to the German Government in October 1932 and operated by the German Airline Pilots Flying School at Munich. Civil letters D-EVYN were allocated in 1934. No repeat orders followed. The aircraft was still listed in September 1939. *BAE Systems*

The facilities established by Brooklands Aviation at Sywell Aerodrome, Northamptonshire, for operation of 6 ERFTS. Nearly all the buildings have survived, have been improved and extended, and are in current daily use. *Richard Riding*

CHAPTER TWO

Developing Market Share

With the installation of the first Gipsy Major I engines in the summer of 1932 the opportunity was also taken to tidy up, standardise and refine the Tiger Moth airframe. The fabric covered hoop and stringer arrangement which formed the rear fuselage top decking, although common to other types, was seen as vulnerable to ground handling damage and was replaced with a single wooden construction which encapsulated the production subtleties of bending a ply skin around three bulkheads incorporating variable radii and differences in depth and width, while maintaining an unkinked curved surface which tapered and sloped over a length of eight and a half feet! Adding further complication was a cut-out for the luggage locker door situated just behind the rear cockpit on the starboard side. However, de Havilland was a company rich with experience in designing and building wooden aeroplanes and the new rear decking which, in unity with the wooden structures forward of each cockpit were known officially and confusingly in the company parlance as 'cowls', used less resource and a tiny fraction of that knowledge which soon would be focused on a unique racing aeroplane, a four engined transatlantic mail carrying airliner, and a military twin of sensational performance and adaptability.

The rear cowl was part of a series of improvements already on the drawing board in the spring of 1932 and which were leached progressively into the approval system. In the light of experience and for the sake of expediency further changes were made to the top wings to introduce a standard maximum aerobatic weight of 1,750lb. Simple modifications to the front spar root end fittings reduced bending moments in the wing bays and eliminated the requirement for the ash cappings first fitted to the Persian aircraft. An extra gallon was engineered into the centre section fuel tank by rounding out the leading edge and the oil tank was reshaped too, increasing capacity from 1.25 gallons to 2.1 gallons.

A year after her unveiling the DH.82's port and starboard front fuselage side frames were redesigned to delete the complications surrounding the deep door at the front cockpit position, now considered unnecessary in view of the greater ease of egress. The requirement had necessitated a serious interruption in the natural line of the top longeron, and the tidied assembly effectively created a straight edge running from the front cups on the engine bearers to the top of the sternpost. Front and rear cockpit doors were thus standardised, for a short while at least, and certainly until instrument flying 'under the hood' became more urgently needed as part of the training syllabus.

An interesting line of enquiry pursued into the origins of the DH.82A fuselage believe it to have been developed not merely as a series of modifications applied to the DH.82 but rather from the proposed metal fuselage of the unbuilt DH.60M III Moth Major. This aircraft would have been the logical progression from the wooden DH.60G III Moth Major as was the DH.60T from the DH.60G and M, and a series of fuselage drawings and those for hundreds of fittings dated around the middle of 1932 refer their eligibility both to the DH.60M III and the DH.82A. In New Zealand in 2013 Stan Smith closely examined the fuselage structure of a DH.82A and compared his findings with early drawings to establish a theory that fuselages for the DH.60M III were probably in production at Stag Lane. The straight winged design would probably have been aimed at the slim market into which the Avro Cadet had made some progress and the lively DH.60G III had proved a relative disappointment. The need for an improved military trainer overcame that for a sporting type in a world still recovering from a Depression and the fuselages were usurped in order to boost the earliest availability of the DH.82 Tiger Moth model 'A'.

First aircraft to take advantage of the Gipsy Major engine, revised weights and rear cowl construction was work's No 3148, supplied with the serial 33-1 to the Aeronautical Department of the Ministry of War in Madrid at the end of 1932.

The evident military connection between the civilian contractors and their Reserve School aircraft was well illustrated by an order from the Air Ministry in 1932 for seven DH.82 Tiger Moths for No 2 Elementary and Reserve Flying Training School (ERFTS) operated by the Bristol Aeroplane Company. The first of these, G-ACBA (3152), was delivered in February 1933 with a cockpit equipped for blind flying and provision for a camera gun, Aldis sight and a P.7 camera installation. There is no reason to believe the equipment was not still on board when G-ACBA collided with a Hawker Hart over Filton in May 1939 and was destroyed in the subsequent crash.

The request by Brooklands Aviation that provision for a floor mounted P14 camera, and installation of a camera gun and sight should be made in each of the eleven new aircraft scheduled for delivery to No 6 ERFTS at Sywell during the early summer of 1935 was answered by clearance of the equipment in the first of the batch, G-ADGS (3337), on 29 May. This was less than three weeks after authorisation of a further nominal increase in the maximum permitted aerobatic weight, rising by a mere 20lb to 1,770lb. The improvement was necessary to accommodate the gently creeping increase in tare weight and, without physical modification was applied retrospectively and equally to all civil and service aircraft which currently enjoyed a 1,750lb aerobatic maximum.

G-ADGS provided faithful service at Sywell from June 1935 until 1944 when as BB705, an impressment serial adopted from September 1940, she was transferred to the Royal Navy. Surviving the war and the rigours of demobilisation in 1951, she was used as a source of spares by Rollason Aircraft at Croydon until with no more to offer, she was ignominiously burned during a Bonfire Night party at the Fiveways Night Club, Hamsey Green, near Croydon, in 1956.

Final customers for the basic DH82 model, although fitted with the Gipsy Major engine, were the Portuguese Ministry of War in Lisbon who took eleven (3159-3169), all delivered without military serial numbers, and Haerens Flyvertropper, the Danish Army Air Corps. Their five DH.82 Tiger Moths (3170-3174), acquired at a total cost of £5,910.10s.10d, and identified on the Air Corps inventory as Type 1S (School aircraft, Trainer type), were shipped on board the SS *Margrethe* in March 1933. On arrival at the Flying School at Lundtofte, the aircraft were issued with serial numbers S-358 to S-362, changed a year later to S1-S5, coincident with a change of base to Vaerlose.

The first Tiger Moth built at Stag Lane which incorporated all the cleared design improvements in addition to installation of the Gipsy Major I, was No 3175, registered G-ACDA to the de Havilland Aircraft Co. Ltd. at Hatfield on 6 February 1933. This machine is acknowledged as the first definitive DH.82A and was one of a batch of ten scheduled for service with No 1 RFS. The new Tiger Moths were to replace thirsty Armstrong Siddeley Jaguar powered DH.9Js which had been operated specifically for advanced training alongside a dedicated 'Reserve Only' fleet of civil DH.60 Moths.

Prototype DH.82A G-ACDA in the colours of the de Havilland School of Flying picketed in company with an unidentified sister aircraft, Waco U1C G-ACGJ and other types at an away event, probably in 1934. *Richard Riding*

Some of the hardy ground crew servicing civilian registered Tiger Moths of No 6 ERFTS in the snow at Sywell Aerodrome in about 1937. In the centre wearing Wellington boots is Frank Golding who was still attending to the needs of Tiger Moths at Sywell until his death in 2013. *via Chris Parker*

de Havilland DH.82A Tiger Moth, G-ADGX, No 6 ERFTS, Brooklands Aviation Ltd, Sywell, 1938. 'Shadow compensation scheme' of Dark Earth/Dark Green on upper surfaces with Light Earth and Light Green on top of lower wings. Trainer Yellow undersides, vertical tail surfaces, elevators and outer top half of wings. Night registration, repeated below wings, Night registration above top wing over the yellow section, white over the camouflaged area. The aircraft was impressed as BB698 in 1940. Sold to the Wiltshire School of Flying in 1951 the aircraft crashed on landing at Thruxton in 1953. *Artwork ©Richard Caruana, 1:72 scale*

The de Havilland Aircraft Company progressively transferred its manufacturing and operating businesses to its new headquarters at Hatfield Aerodrome between late 1930 and July 1934 when Stag Lane Aerodrome was sold for domestic housing, leaving the plant and workshops in the good hands of the Engine Division. Before delivery to Hatfield, and immediately after qualification for her civil Certificate of Airworthiness on 10 March 1933, G-ACDA flew a series of trials at the A&AEE, Martlesham Heath, not only as a matter of routine expected of all civil prototypes, especially in view of the number of changes incorporated since the type's last visit, but also with a view to the military future. Later that same year G-ACDA and her sister aircraft G-ACDB (3176), were used to test experimental wooden propellers of relatively fine pitch but principally of revised construction. As an exercise, the Airscrew Company of Weybridge had built one propeller to de Havilland design 5220/H entirely from birch and another with an inner core of traditional mahogany but outer laminations of birch. The material had been selected from a small sample of boards tested at RAE Farnborough in connection with a programme of airscrew research on behalf of the Air Ministry. The two Tiger Moths were chosen as test vehicles because of their expected high utilisation during Reserve School operations, such that a steady plot of condition could be maintained following regular twenty five hourly inspections from October until the end of 1933.

The restored G-ACDA taxying out for a test flight from Kemble in June 1979. The engine stopped during a mild aerobatic routine and the aircraft was impaled on an electricity pylon where she caught fire and was severely damaged. *Richard Biddle*

Coil springs replacing rubber-in-compression was one of the detail changes designed into the undercarriage of the DH.82A. The new legs designed by Dowty were incorporated by students of the de Havilland Aeronautical Technical School into their own DH.60G Moth G-ABTS (1900), when the aeroplane was rebuilt in June 1933 after it had landed on the roof of a house in Edgware the previous year. The new system was considered to be worthy of comprehensive handling trials conducted by Hubert Broad at Stag Lane the following month.

While the first Tiger Moths delivered to Grantham were being posted away and replaced on a temporary basis by the assuredly more expensive Avro Tutor, the Air Ministry was professing acute awareness of the constant need for economy in the Service and in March 1934 announced an order for fifty DH.82A Tiger Moths, to be known as Tiger Moth Mk II. Unlike their predecessors all were to be delivered by surface, less engines, to RAF Kenley between November 1934 and the following February. Manufactured to specification T.26/33 under contract No.307395/34, the aircraft were to carry serial numbers K4242 to K4291 (3238-3287), and eventual allocation was to be throughout the Royal Air Force mostly not as trainer aircraft, but to serve with squadrons and Station Flights, communications units, Practice Flights, and an Army co-operation unit.

The de Havilland Company issued a 'Bulletin' in 1934 which analysed the costs of training groups of pilots on the Tiger Moth. Assuming fifty pilots each flying 40 hours, the Bulletin suggested that 2,000 hours could be flown in one year by four machines averaging 500 hours each.

> 2,000 hours flying at 5.5 gallons per hour. 11,000 gallons at one shilling and six pence per gallon: £825.0s.0d.
> 2,000 hours flying with an oil consumption of 1.5 pints per hour. 375 gallons at 7s 8d per gallon: £143.15s.0d.
> Cost of materials at 1s.0d per hour (airframe) and 1s.0d per hour engine: £200.
> Cost of materials used at annual overhaul (airframe), four machines at £30 each annually: £120.
> Cost of material for engine overhaul every 750 hours at £37.10s.0d per engine, 2.66 overhauls: £100.
> Total £1,388.15s.0d.

For a group of 100 pilots flying seven machines averaging 572 hours each the grand total was £2,747.10s.0d.

DH.82A Tiger Moth K4288 cavorting above the clouds when on strength with 18 ERFTS Fairoaks in 1938. Note the code number '3' painted unusually on the top decking behind the rear cockpit. *deHMC Archive*

de Havilland DH.82A Tiger Moth, G-ACDA, de Havilland School of Flying, Hatfield, 1933. Maroon fuselage, spinner, undercarriage and interplane struts. Silver wings and tail. All lettering in white. The aircraft was sold to a civilian owner in 1943 and was restored to airworthiness in 1979 but suffered an accident on a test flight. Rebuilt, the aircraft is currently based on a private strip in Hampshire. *Artwork ©Richard Caruana, 1:72 scale*

In 1935 under a British Government initiative created through the Air Estimates of March the previous year, the Air Training Plan expanded the four civilian operated Reserve Schools at Bristol, Brough, Hamble and Hatfield to offer primary training in a pseudo-military environment to large numbers of cadet pilots who either were streamed straight into a Royal Air Force career or remained in their civilian occupations but joined the RAF Volunteer Reserve (RAFVR). From August 1935 the scheme required civilian pupils to complete their courses at an Elementary and Reserve Flying Training School (ERFTS) in eight weeks as opposed to twelve months at an RAF Service Flying Training School (SFTS). In addition to fifty hours flying, a mixture of dual and solo, each course included a comprehensive range of classroom studies. Nine more Reserve Schools were established in 1936 and a further twenty the following year.

The Tiger Moth Mk II military specification called for a number of detail changes and minor modifications in and around the cockpits which were drawn up between April and October 1934 as the result of substantial operational experience at de Havilland's Reserve School. K4242 (3238), was nominated for performance trials at Martlesham Heath in September and November 1934 and, prior to delivery in December 1934, K4288 (3244), was selected as a representative aircraft for further tests: the blind flying hood attachment was modified to permit a greater tension in the elastic cords which held it in the erected position; the auto slot pulley brackets were revised and alterations to the safety harnesses were called up to conform to changing Service requirements. The accumulator was repositioned to the front cockpit floor where it was clamped between the rudder bar supports on a plywood surface specially prepared against damage from anticipated acid spillage. It was the only practical position for the accumulator owing to centre of gravity limitations and special protection was necessary when an auxiliary fuel tank was installed inside the wooden cowl just above it. It was not a totally satisfactory arrangement and de Havilland could only argue that they had made the accumulator lid and leads 'as petrol tight as possible'.

Additional changes were incorporated against Drawing Office Instructions (DOIs), by which method the industry could assess their suitability, or not, as the result of in-service use prior to committing to approved drawings and the laborious procedure of subsequent amendment. Enduring changes made after October 1934 included spacer plates for the external routing of the duplicated rudder cables, a board to mount fuse boxes and terminal blocks, deletion of the master switch and provision of an intricate thin brass frame screwed to the inside walls of the cockpit cowls, whose sole purpose was to house a compass correction card or performance data plate. In subsequent revisions, K4242-K4265 were all modified to accept navigation lights on the tips of both upper mainplanes and the trailing edge of the rudder, while all fifty aircraft of the March contract were subject of petrol drain pipe modifications following engine installation by the RAF.

At a later date two small modifications were introduced without which a Tiger Moth airframe could almost be labelled an impostor. Square cut doors could not easily be opened by the occupant of the rear cockpit when an instrument hood assembly was fitted, but by the simple expedient of cutting off the bottom rear corners and replacing them with amazingly complex and handed, curved triangular fabrications in plywood and spruce, glued, pinned and screwed to the rear decking superstructure, and officially listed as 'fillings', the pilot regained his freedom. British built aircraft acquired the Mk VIIA pitot/static head with its characteristic bend, (Mod No 19), a feature intended to protect the system from the ingress of rain water.

Distribution of the new aeroplanes from Kenley was extraordinarily protracted and especially so in view of the stated aims for economy: as a basic training machine, only three aircraft were posted to No 1 Flying Training School (FTS) Leuchars between September 1935 and October the following year; one went to 14 ERFTS at Castle Bromwich on formation of the establishment at the beginning of July 1937, and six others to 16 ERFTS at Shoreham at the same time. Four aircraft were posted overseas: K4252 and K4255 to RAF Hinaidi, Iraq in January and March 1936 respectively, as replacements for a pair of DH.60M Moths on charge with the Iraq Communications Flight, and K4253 to Singapore, but the aircraft appears to have been diverted to Aden where she was on charge with 8 Squadron in June 1937, joining Vickers Vincents and Hawker Demons at Khormaksar.

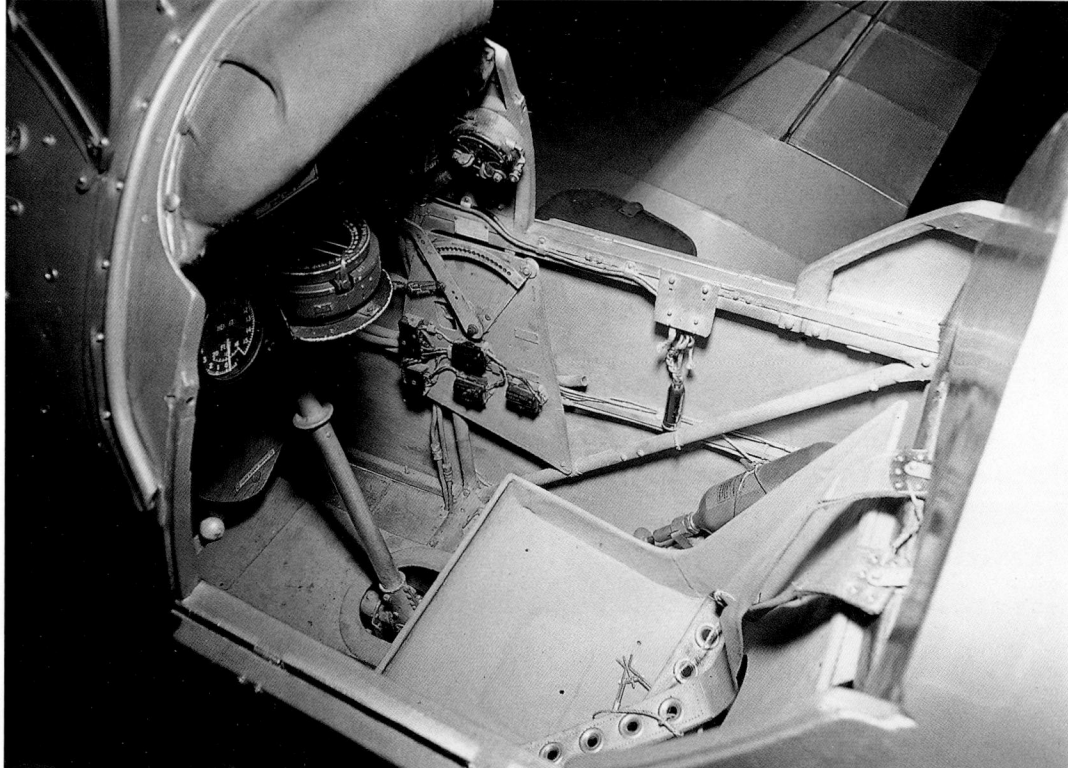

A general view of the rear cockpit of a post-war RAF DH.82A Tiger Moth showing the electrical fuse panel below the Morse tapper, junction box for the electric intercom with an RAF type socket, fire extinguisher, parachute seat pan and Sutton harness. *via British Aerospace*

Tiger Moth K4259 (3255), spent some time with No 24 (Communications) Squadron at Hendon before a period of storage at Waddington, but in June 1937 the aircraft was loaned to the British Air Attaché in Paris for a month before returning to serve with 19 ERFTS at Gatwick. It was there during a sunny day in March 1939 that K4259 managed to taxy into Hawker Audax K7461 which was hidden in a shadow. The aeroplane completed a war service training career with a number of Elementary Schools and was one of the last operational Tiger Moths on the RAF inventory, honourably retiring from the Grading Unit at Kirton in Lindsey in 1953. As a civil aircraft registered G-ANMO, but painted in RAF camouflage, the aircraft was involved in a spectacular mid-air collision with Stampe SV-4 G-AYGR during an air display at Weston-super-Mare on 30 July 1972.

K4284 (3280), was allocated to the use of the British Air Attaché in Berlin in December 1937 and the sensitivity of the posting required that the aircraft be operated in civilian guise. Registration G-AERM was allocated under the ownership of The Air Council for the ten month posting which ended with the aircraft's restoration to military markings with 24 Squadron at Hendon where, ironically, she was destroyed during a German air raid on 8 October 1940.

K4268 (3264), on the other hand, appears to have been shuffled between Maintenance Units from delivery in February 1935 until she was sold for scrap from storage at Hullavington in 1950 with no recorded history of a day's active service in between.

Further feedback from the civilian marked fleet based with de Havilland at Hatfield, an arrangement which provided excellent on-site contractor liaison possibilities, suggested that a slight alteration to the recommended rigging of the control stick coupled with a two degree change to the aileron sprocket differential would result in better handling during aerobatics and was particularly relevant to inverted flying. This observation may have referred to inverted time spent during the course of normal aerobatics for, with the exception of the six aircraft used by the Central Flying School team which were modified for sustained but short duration inverted flight in 1932, and the National Aviation Day aircraft, inverted flying systems were not fitted to standard school machines.

Survivor of the pre-war de Havilland School of Flying at Hatfield, G-ACDJ was a participant in the de Havilland Moth Club's Vintage Air Tour which arrived at Kemble in May 2002. *Clive Abbott*

Approved for experimental purposes was an adjustable trimmer set into the trailing edge of each elevator. Known as an 'elevator flap' the installation was in its third revision by the time it was flight tested on mass balanced elevators fitted to G-ACDJ (3183), in March 1935. For all its worth the system was complicated and infinitely more expensive than the simple spring loading of the control stick which was retained in preference. Drawings for the deletion of the trimmer and associated controls were issued the following October. Only when the Tiger Moth was designed for Canadian conditions as the DH.82C, and built in Toronto from April 1940, was a cockpit adjustable elevator trimmer incorporated as standard, although the experimental DH.82B Tiger Moth E.11 had enjoyed a brief flirtation with a similar system at Hatfield in the summer of 1939.

G-ACDJ is another survivor of the pre-war fleet operated by the de Havilland School of Flying at Hatfield. In 1994 she took part in the de Havilland Moth Club's annual Charity Flying Day which moved to Old Warden following the closure of Hatfield Aerodrome. *deHMC Archive*

de Havilland had developed the Tiger Moth as a military trainer and the majority of their effort in selling the type was directed towards that cause. A major promotion surrounded the ability of the aircraft to offer practical through-training from school to squadron, and the company presented a carefully reasoned argument in support of their case which was summed up as follows under the heading: 'The One Type Trainer':

The essential attributes of a 'one type trainer' are:
a. Versatility, or adaptability to the varying uses to which first-line service aircraft are put.
b. Performance, or the capability of reproducing, on a small scale, the handling characteristics and performance of the different types of first-line aircraft.
c. Economy, in first cost, maintenance cost and running cost.
d. Strength, which involves reliability.
e. Safety.

"Examination of the trainer aircraft now in existence shows that the de Havilland Tiger Moth embodies in balanced form all these essential features. It is a scaled-down edition of the full-size, high powered, high-performance military aircraft, and reproduces with remarkable fidelity the characteristics of the larger machine.
Moreover, the pupil who has never been in the air before can, on this one type alone, be thoroughly trained in every branch of aerial manoeuvre and pass direct from the Tiger Moth to any of the various high-performance types which he may be ordered to fly on service.
The Tiger Moth has been specifically designed as a one-type trainer. It is the outcome of the experience gained by the de Havilland Aircraft Company with over 2,000 Moths of other types in actual service, both civil and military, all over the world in extremes of temperature and humidity and under the most difficult operational conditions."

The full presentation was an over-worded and fairly thin argument, and just how successful the 'One Type' campaign was might be judged from the following figures. Of the 400 Tiger Moths, DH.82 and DH.82A, built at Stag Lane and Hatfield between January 1932 and May 1936, distribution was to air arms, ministries of war or government departments in varying proportions: Austria 2, Brazil 17, China 4, Denmark 9, Germany 1, India 4, Iraq 7, Palestine 1, Japan 1, Persia/Iran 69, Poland 1, Portugal 21, Spain 5, Sweden 16 and Uruguay 6.

The motives behind the acquisition of a single aircraft, 3116, by the Mosawa Company of Japan in July 1932 can only be surmised. Supplied in an airworthy condition and with a British Certificate of Airworthiness, the aircraft's subsequent history is completely unknown. More than half the 400 were sold to the British Air Ministry: 51 directly into RAF service and 158 to the civilian operated schools at Brooklands, Desford, Filton, Hatfield, Prestwick, Perth and Reading.

A lead customer for the Tiger Moth, the Imperial Persian Army Flying Corps was as pleased to have their new aircraft equipped to the latest standards as was de Havilland to supply, and the spin-off in terms of publicity and prestige was as valuable as the knowledge gained in designing, manufacturing and fitting out the aircraft. In September 1932, Persian Tiger Moth 113 (3129), was the development aircraft at Stag Lane for a new blind flying hood, B.S.2C bomb sight, arrangement of bomb gear, navigation lights, Holt flares and Very pistol, together with the mounting for a ten gallon auxiliary fuel tank. The following month, aircraft 104 (3120), was fitted with a nine gallon auxiliary tank of new design which replaced the approved ten gallon tank in this aircraft, almost certainly to create space for additional equipment. By November, 113 had been further modified to accept a second bomb rack with the associated bomb release gear, an Eagle III camera with electrical control equipment, and arrangements for mounting either Williamson Mk I or Mk III cameras.

E.6, the de Havilland 'Class 2' markings used for test flying purposes, applied to a single seat fighter version of the DH.82A Tiger Moth developed for the Persian Government. A machine gun straddles the faired-in front cockpit, firing through the arc of the propeller. *de Havilland Aircraft Co*

Machine gun and magazine installed in the front cockpit of a Persian Government Tiger Moth. Note the streamlined windscreen fitted for the pilot. The curved ply fairing below the screen was a simple device to prevent rain water running back along the decking and dripping into the cockpit. *de Havilland Aircraft Co*

A line-up of DH.82A Tiger Moths of the de Havilland School of Flying outside the hangars and classrooms built at Hatfield Aerodrome to accommodate aeroplanes, engineers, pupils and instructors operating on behalf of No 1 ERFTS. *deHMC Archive*

As the result of experience operating from rough desert airstrips, by February 1936 when an order for ten DH.82A Tiger Moths for the 'Imperial Iranian Ministry of War' was progressing through the Hatfield shops, 160 (3464), and 169 (3473), were supplied with special tailplanes incorporating plywood skins on the under surfaces as a guard against damage from stones thrown up by the wheels. The Persian aircraft were the only ones ever to specify this modification which may not have found general favour on the grounds of extra weight and its influence on the already critical aft CG position. At least for aircraft 160 and 169, the additional weight at the tail neutralised the nose heaviness induced by the mass of the Fairey-Reed metal propeller, and tare CG was restored to a more comfortable situation.

The most radical of all modifications resulted in the Tiger Moth Fighter, 122 (3201), which was unveiled in October 1932. As far as the engineering approvals were concerned, Hatfield's Resident Technical Officer (RTO) reported on 11 October that regarding safety considerations the installation of a machine gun mounting, cockpit control for the interrupter gear, and ammunition container had all been completed in conformity with the drawing schedule.

Shortly afterwards the de Havilland sales office was moved to provide more information:

The view from the rear cockpit of a Persian Air Force Tiger Moth fitted with a machine gun in the front seat position. The gun was synchronised to fire through the arc of the metal propeller. The instrument faces carry Arabic script. *Flight*

"We are now able to offer the Tiger Moth as a single seater fighter with a machine gun firing forward through the propeller, and also capable of carrying eight bombs of 20lb each. Fuel can be carried for a range of over 500 miles, with gun, gun sight and four bombs of 20lb each, but if eight bombs are carried, range would be reduced to approximately 250 miles, the range being limited by the all up weight of the aircraft.

The gun and mounting are easily removable, so that the machine can be readily converted to a training type aircraft and for any other of the duties for which the Tiger Moth was primarily designed."

The Gun: The machine gun is air-cooled, weighs only 9.5kg, and is manufactured by the Czechoslovakian Arms Factory of Prague. The muzzle velocity is 839ms, and the maximum rate of fire 900 +/− 100 rounds per minute. The bore is 7.92 mm. A Pratt and Whitney synchronising gear is fitted, which is very light and efficient, the drive being taken from the top half of the rear cover of the engine, where provision for hand starting gear is normally allowed for.

Location and mounting: The gun is mounted in the front cockpit, and shoots directly over the top engine cowling. It is fixed to the machine mounting by two bolts only, the rear bolt incorporating a vernier adjustment for direction and elevation. The ammunition box, holding 200 rounds, and the cartridge chute, are fixed to the mounting itself, and the only connections between the gun, gun mounting and fuselage, are four holding down bolts. The mounting rests at four points on the two top longerons with one bolt at each of these points. No extra holes are drilled in the longerons.

It takes one man fifteen minutes to install, or to remove the gun. With the latter operation the machine becomes a normal two seater. The whole installation is extremely simple and very effective, as only eight bolts have to be removed to take off the complete gun and sight. The cocking handle is connected only by a cotter pin to the lever which acts on the gun. In order to protect the workings of the gun it has been cowled in, which cowling is held by four butterfly nuts.

The trigger is located on the control column, and its action is conveyed to the gun by means of a Bowden cable. It is actuated very easily by closing the hand round the trigger and the handle of the control column.

Sights: The Aldis telescopic gun sight is provided for long distance firing. The ordinary ring and bead sight for dog fighting can be fitted as an alternative, or together with the Aldis sight.

Ammunition box and chute: The ammunition box can be taken out, refilled and put back, without disturbing the rest of the mounting or gun. The top chute is for the spent belt and the larger one below for the spent cartridges.

Tests: The results of the official ground and air acceptance tests were as follows:

1. Pulling over the propeller by hand, the first round penetrated the disc nineteen and a half degrees after top dead centre.
2. Dispersion throughout the entire speed range occurred between the angles of 45 and 86 deg., that is to say through an arc of 41 deg.
3. Propeller speeds varied from 800rpm to 2,400rpm.
These results are absolutely satisfactory.

In none of the contemporary publicity material did de Havilland ever once mention the identity of their customer, and it was left to the aviation press to speculate, as predictably they did: "The machine looks a very nice little job and should be very useful for ground strafing, for which purpose it was probably designed, more than for actual aerial fighting. A detachment of this machine has been ordered by a foreign government and has already been packed up for despatch." Some years later, a connection was assumed between the fighter and the training on Tiger Moths at Panshanger and Wolverhampton of many Iranian flying instructors. Yet another link was seen in the adaptation of the Pratt and Whitney E-4 Gun Synchroniser which was believed to have been specified to standardise on such equipment already in use by the Air Corps and after Sydney Camm had rejected a proposal to fit a Pratt and Whitney Hornet engine to his elegant Fury.

The Tiger Moth fighter was probably intended only as a training vehicle but whether aircraft additional to the example fitted up at Stag Lane were equipped with guns has not been confirmed. Equally, Persian authorities had made suggestions in some quarters that the Tiger Moth fighters had been secured for the defence of the oil installations at Abadan. After the end of the Second World War an informed source revealed that a secret 'Q Site' had been established on Abadan Island in 1942 where a dummy oil refinery had been constructed, protected by a flight of three Tiger Moths.

A DH.82A Tiger Moth was the first aircraft purchased by the official Jewish institutions in Palestine in 1934 when attempts were made to establish a joint Jewish-British-Arab Flying Club, 'The Flying Camel'. Although this attempt failed a follow-up club, the Palestine Flying Club, was set up as a wholly Jewish organisation. In the autumn of 1934 a group of Palestine officials who dealt with immigration matters in Poland, met with David Ben-Gurion, Head of the Jewish Agency, and obtained the necessary funds to acquire the Tiger Moth which was delivered in October. Registered G-ACYN (3314), the aircraft operated with the Aviron Flying School, a front for Hagana, a military organisation set up before the establishment of Israel. In addition to training duties the aircraft was also used for military spotting purposes and missions in support of national defence such as the protection of groups of workers engaged in building roads and other construction projects. She was also used for dropping essential supplies of food and ammunition to settlers, especially those in newly developed areas, when the winter was at its height. By the end of 1938 operations were judged to have been so successful that it was decided to list the Tiger Moth in the Palestine Civil Register as VQ-PAN.

Isaac Hennenson, later a senior captain with the airline El Al, began his flying training in G-ACYN and on 15 April 1939 was flying with his instructor, Mr Tzoorberger, whose habit it was to test fly the Tiger Moth every morning before instruction commenced. With ten hours in his logbook Isaac Hennenson was in the rear cockpit with Tzoorberger flying from the front seat. Operating from the airstrip at Kibutz Afikim in the Jordan Valley the aircraft commenced a tight turn at very low level but a wingtip scraped the ground and the aircraft crashed, demolishing all but the front fuselage section where only the instructor was slightly hurt.

Two of a batch of twelve Tiger Moths registered to the Bristol Aeroplane Company in October 1935, G-ADNW (3417), and G-ADNY (3419), were involved in a mid-air collision over Westerleigh Common near Avebury, Wiltshire, on 3 December 1938 while operating from Yate, a site often used as a satellite for Yatesbury and Filton. G-ADNW, abandoned by her crew, crashed in a cornfield at Nibley while the two pilots descended by parachute, one of them landing in a disused quarry full of water where he managed to prevent himself from drowning by clinging to a wooden raft which, by some miracle, was floating on the surface. G-ADNY was successfully put down at Yate and survived her ordeal for she was one of the entire Bristol fleet that was packed into crates and seconded to Indian 'military' service in 1940. Although she retained civil markings (VT-AOB) until February 1941 she was absorbed into the military training machine and ultimate obscurity.

One early civil Tiger Moth had been sold directly to the Netherlands, and another, G-ADSI (3423), to the Egyptian branch of the RAF Flying Club, although the aircraft was delivered to their Hatfield base in October 1935 and was written off in a crash at Nithsdale, Dumfries in 1938, almost certainly having never seen the waters of the Nile.

de Havilland also supplied their associated companies and agents: one aircraft was crated to Australia, a pair to South Africa and five to Canada. OA-CCH (3289), went to Peru in June 1934, OE-DAX (3494), to Nikolaus von Eltz, de Havilland's agent in Austria and LY-LAT (3493), to the Lietuvos Aero Club in Lithuania, both in April 1936.

The Marquess of Douglas and Clydesdale received G-ADUC (3425), at Prestwick in November 1935. Together with David McIntyre and Stewart Kennedy, they had set up Scottish Aviation Ltd. the previous August. This company was to manage the first civilian flying school in Scotland to become part of the Air Ministry's expanding ERFTS scheme and G-ADUC was operated by No 12 ERFTS and No 12 EFTS until after the end of the war when she joined the Royal Navy. The de Havilland Aircraft Company supplied sixteen Tiger Moths to Scottish Aviation at a price of £750 each, but astutely opted for a shareholding in the new business rather than taking a cash payment, an interest that lasted almost until the end of the war when Stewart Kennedy joined de Havilland at Hatfield as part of a redeployment of top management following the retirement of Frank Hearle. Stewart Kennedy learned to fly at his own Scottish school but on his first solo the rudder bar contrived to jump off its bearing, leaving him with only one-way movement, committing him, as he put it, "to skidding round the sky somewhat slowly."

Yatesbury Aerodrome, August 1937, and Tiger Moths of 10 ERFTS, operated by the Bristol Aeroplane Company, are paid a visit by an unidentified DH.90 Dragonfly. The rudder of G-ADNY appears to be at variance with the remainder of the fleet whose house colours were thought to be purple fuselage and custard yellow wings, a combination still seeking verification by historians almost eighty years later. *Richard Riding*

Tiger Moth G-AOXG was one of a number purchased in the civil market by the Royal Navy in 1956 for operation by Britannia Flight from Plymouth. Allocated new serial XL717 the aircraft was later retired to the Fleet Air Arm Museum at Yeovilton where, with assistance from Cobham plc, she was painted and configured as G-ABUL to represent her service with Alan Cobham's pre-war National Aviation Day display. *Paul Kirby*

Only eleven Tiger Moths were released into the UK civilian market between March 1932 and April 1936: prototype G-ABRC (1733), G-ABUL (3107), G-ACEZ (3186) and G-ACFA (3187), all operated with National Aviation Day Display Ltd., the flying circus based at Ford in Sussex. Each aircraft survived trial by bunt, loop and falling leaf to have a long career in aviation; hard daily use was a sure way of ironing out the bugs and the best possible form of publicity for the aeroplane. de Havilland were quick to recognise and promote this exposure and those vital appearances of the RAF teams at Hendon and encapsulated the detail in their subsequent advertising material:

"A training aircraft must of necessity be of exceptionally strong construction as it has not only to withstand the stresses of normal flying and landings, but also to the abnormal strains imposed by the performance of violent aerobatics.
The exhibition of formation aerobatics at the Royal Air Force Display by the Instructors of the Central Flying School demonstrated beyond doubt that the Tiger Moth will stand up to any aerobatic manoeuvre which it may be called upon to perform.
A further remarkable testimony is contained in a letter received by the de Havilland Aircraft Company from Sir Alan Cobham, who used a standard Tiger Moth for the demonstration of aerobatics in his 1932 propaganda tour of Great Britain. For six months this machine gave eight displays of aerobatics daily, including such violent manoeuvres as upward rolls and inverted loops. It performed a total of 2,520 landings, 345 half outside loops, 300 upward rolls, 1,440 loops, 1,080 rolls and upwards of 90 hours inverted flying in that period; it was never under cover, never failed to give its display and, when returned to the factory for overhaul, was found to be in perfect condition. Sir Alan expressed the opinion that this machine has put up a greater number of aerobatic displays than any other aeroplane in history."

Not such a happy story surrounded G-ACDY (3189), which was delivered to the Scottish Motor Traction Co at Renfrew in April 1933. The brief was to perform public aerobatic displays as a means of promoting the company's internal Scottish airline services shortly to be flown with DH.83 Fox Moths, but G-ACDY crashed into the River Don at Aberdeen less than five months later. G-ABTB (3101), was registered to The Standard Telephone & Cable Co. Ltd. in January 1932 and handed over in March at a ceremony at Stag Lane attended by all the directors. The aircraft was used in experimental work connected with development of airborne wireless transmission equipment on behalf of the Air Ministry but her demonstration at an air display in Belgium in May was curtailed due to interference generated by the large steel hangars! G-ADWG (3492), spent the 1936 season with C W A Scott's Flying Display Ltd before moving into Club use at Lympne and the remaining four civil aircraft were all operated by the London Aeroplane Club at Hatfield: G-ACSK

One of the rare pre-war British civil Tiger Moths was DH.82 G-ABTB, registered to the Standard Telephone and Cable Co Ltd in January 1932, and used for air to ground wireless communication experiments. Aerials can be seen on the top of the port upper mainplane and just behind the rear cockpit, while the front cockpit has a non-standard rounded screen. Unusually for a display aircraft G-ACEZ was not fitted with slats. *deHMC Archive*

Right: During her time with Alan Cobham's National Aviation Day display Tiger Moth G-ACEZ was frequently flown by Geoffrey Tyson who on hundreds of occasions collected a handkerchief from the grass with a wire prong fixed to the wingtip. *Flight*

Below: Tiger Moth G-ACEZ was operated by Alan Cobham's National Aviation Day for several seasons during the 1930s which served to highlight any design faults or deficiencies, details of which could be fed back to the manufacturer. *deHMC Archive*

The fuselage of Tiger Moth G-ADWG was painted in a red and white chequer scheme when operated by C W A Scott's Flying Displays Ltd for the 1936 season. The following year she was sold to the Cinque Ports Flying Club and in 1940 was despatched to the Madras Flying Club where she was written off in 1941. *Eddie Riding*

(3223); G-ACWB (3226); G-ADLU (3357) and G-ADUK (3426).

In 1930, the de Havilland Aircraft Company had bought the London Aeroplane Club on the closure of Stag Lane and relocated it to their new aerodrome at Hatfield where it became one of London's centres for society and civil flying. Later still, the once fashionable Club was adopted as the vehicle through which employees of the company could learn to fly at a rate which barely covered the cost of the petrol. In 1940, the Club's entire Tiger Moth fleet was packed into crates and shipped south, sold to the Royal New Zealand Air Force.

With the immediate requirements of the military appearing to have been met, the destinations of the 250 Tiger Moths built at Hatfield between April 1936 and August 1938 indicated that de Havilland had broadened their sales base, and their efforts in now promoting the type as the natural successor to the DH.60 as a civil training aircraft were bearing fruit. The RAF took only thirty five of these aircraft, mostly at the end of this audit, although they were but a prelude; the advance party of what shortly was to develop into a veritable avalanche of orders. The supply of aircraft to the established ERFTS contractors accounted for forty three of the sales, thirteen of which in ones and twos, possibly ordered as replacements, were unsystematically scattered though the period.

No 1 ERFTS established at Hatfield flew 6,000 hours in 1935 and, partly due to seven days a week operations, increased that to 9,000 hours in 1936 and 11,400 hours in 1937. Their sister organisation, 13 ERFTS at White Waltham, flew 7,500 hours in its first year, 1935/1936, then beat the parent school with 12,300 hours in 1937. By the end of 1937 the establishment at British ERFTSs was estimated to be 175 Tiger Moths. By comparison, in 1941 the Hatfield school alone flew a total of 43,693 hours.

During such utilisation there was bound to be wastage and a constant need for additional or replacement aircraft. A block of thirty aircraft laid down against civilian specification in June 1937 was purchased off the line by an Air Ministry acting with a sudden degree of urgency. Carrying military serials, these hybrids were distributed amongst selected schools: four to Brooklands, seven to the new Airwork organisation at Castle Bromwich, three to Desford, four to the Bristol Aeroplane Company at Filton, and seven to Scottish Aviation at Prestwick. Five aircraft were delivered to the de Havilland school at White Waltham, while one of the batch, L6923 (3558), remained with the home team at Hatfield where she was exposed to intense air-to-air photographic coverage, much of which later appeared in promotional articles and advertisements.

All aircraft in the batch were gradually converted to military standard and L6923 subsequently led a varied life: she became part of Hatfield's No 1 EFTS on the outbreak of war (when all ERFTS were renamed EFTS, discarding the 'R' for Reserve) but crashed in September 1940 and was rebuilt by the de Havilland Civil Repair Unit (CRU) at Witney, a job which began in early October but was not completed until Christmas, the aircraft transferring to No 19 Maintenance Unit (MU) at St Athan on New Year's Day 1941. Allocated to 'A' Flight of 1 Anti Aircraft Co-operation Unit (AACU) in June 1941, L6923 crashed again in November and was repaired at the Taylorcraft CRU, Thurmaston, before transfer to 5 MU at Kemble on the last day of 1941. A month later, the aircraft was delivered to No 6 EFTS Sywell where she remained for the rest of the war until allocated to storage with 38 MU at Llandow for over four years, only to be cut up for scrap in 1950.

The instructors of No 13 ERFTS White Waltham in 1937. All flying staff wore a civilian 'de Havilland' uniform until the outbreak of war when the school became an EFTS, the uniforms changed to standard RAF dress and civil administration was overtaken by King's Regulations.

Above: A rare pre-war colour image of a Brooklands Flying Club Tiger Moth parked on the tarmac early in 1937 alongside the familiar control tower at Brooklands Aerodrome, set within the confines of the race track at Weybridge. The tower has survived and is a listed building; the Tiger Moth was wrecked in September 1937 only six months after delivery. *deHMC Archive*

Left: The rear instrument panel of a Tiger Moth operated by Brooklands Aviation. Where the pre-war ERFTS was managed by a civilian organisation also offering Club flying in parallel, Reserve aircraft were usually set aside for exclusive use although instrumentation and equipment carried does appear to have been at the discretion of the operator rather than an Air Ministry specification. *via Ted Lawrence*

Below: Brooklands Flying Club Tiger Moth G-AESD during a local sortie near Weybridge. The aircraft was delivered in April 1937, impressed in August 1940 and served as an instructional airframe until 1945 when she was scrapped. *deHMC Archive*

Pre-war, Brooklands Aviation operated not only a Reserve School at Sywell but a civil flying club from their Surrey headquarters, the famous motor racing circuit near Weybridge. For many years the Brooklands Flying Club had been a major user of DH.60 Moths and through their parent company acted as sales agents and a major force in the training of aeronautical engineers. Early in 1937 some of the DH.60 Moths were replaced by the purchase of six Tiger Moths and, after a year's activity, the first of the new aircraft, G-AESA (3544), was taken in for overhaul when it was revealed the aircraft had accumulated 850 flying hours and 7,000 landings. de Havilland promoted the fact that the cost of materials used during overhaul amounted to just £21, the most expensive single item being the provision of one new mainwheel tyre.

Doing his best to keep up the hours on the Tiger Moth fleet at £2 per hour, was Charles Nepean Bishop who, together with two fellow Club members, organised a unique 'weekend' formation team of four and later six Tiger Moths. The team was only disbanded when several of the members qualified for their commercial licences and went off to earn instead of spend. Started almost by accident in 1937 when a trio of aircraft would travel around the south of England 'in close proximity' attending the standard club Breakfast Patrols, matters changed in 1938:

"In April came our first really organised flight of this description, this being a special luncheon flight to Hanworth Aerodrome at the invitation of the London Air Park Flying Club. Four Tiger Moths and a Gipsy Moth took off from Brooklands, and as the distance to Hanworth was only seven miles we made a slight (?) detour by way of Reading at which aerodrome we landed in formation, much to the consternation of certain military instructors at the resident FTS.

Having calmed them down and refuelled ourselves we took off, again in formation, and headed for Hanworth. The Gipsy Moth pilot having found that he could not keep up when on the outside of a turn came along separately, so the four Tiger Moths were flown in diamond formation, this being the first occasion on which this particular formation had been tried out. At Hanworth the advent of our four machines caused quite a sensation, and by a modern miracle we all touched down at the same moment on landing. This made our stock quite high, and when we left, after an excellent lunch, we were asked to fly past for the benefit of the local photographer, which we did. All went well until the landing at Brooklands, when our leader glided in at no feet and very little speed with us behind him stalling visibly. In the end we landed quite safely, but after the flight the order came forth that in future we must not land in formation unless there was an instructor in at least one of the machines."

An aircraft which spent her entire war-time life with Brooklands Aviation at Sywell was Tiger Moth R5042 (82943), delivered from Hatfield to 6 MU Brize Norton in March 1943 and arriving at Sywell six months later. During forced landing practice in February 1944 the

Above: This replica Tiger Moth marked 2-1-2 was built by Darci Assis for the Brazilian Navy and is used as a backdrop on ceremonial occasions at the Museum of Naval Aviation. One original aircraft, 2-1-10, at the Museu Aeroespacial at Campo dos Afonsus, is being returned to flying condition. *E Viroli*

Below: Replica Tiger Moth marked 2-1-2 has been based at the Brazilian Museum of Naval Aviation since the mid 1990s and represents an aircraft delivered from Stag Lane when hopes for large pre-war export orders for South America were anticipated with great optimism. *deHMC Archive*

Tiger Moth L6923 was one of thirty aircraft built to civilian specification but bought straight off the line by an Air Ministry seriously worried about its lack of Reserve training aircraft. The thirty were widely dispersed amongst the schools but L6923 was retained at Hatfield for publicity purposes before release to the home based 1 EFTS. *de Havilland Aircraft Co*

Tiger Moth G-ANEM owned and flown by Peter Benest with Lady Carnarvon as passenger, flying close to the scene of Geoffrey de Havilland's first aerial experiments at Seven Barrows, part of the Highclere Castle estate. The picture was taken by Lord Carnarvon flying with Steve Bohill-Smith in Tiger Moth G-AOBX.

aircraft collided with the airfield boundary hedge but most damage was restricted to the rear fuselage. She was repaired on site, probably at a time when Tiger Moth L6923 was also on jacks, for when long after civilianisation as G-ANEM she was stripped down for overhaul in 1992, irrefutable proof was discovered that her rear fuselage was that of the much photographed, civil specification, L6923.

Between 1932 and 1934, thirty nine DH.60T Moth Trainers had been sold in South America, followed by orders for twelve DH.82A Tiger Moths for delivery to Brazil and five for Uruguay. The de Havilland agents in South America, Walter and Company in Brazil, Regusci and Voulminot in Uruguay and Morrison and Company in Chile, were directed by the company's 'Special Representative in South America', W T W Ballantyne, whose responsibility for the entire continent was effected from the portals of the English Club in Buenos Aires.

Ballantyne was well qualified for what the company considered an important post, having joined the de Havilland School at Stag Lane as an officer in the Reserve, he qualified for his 'B' commercial pilots' licence before he could drive a car. Following a spell in the de Havilland Drawing Office at Stag Lane and on detachment with Arthur Hagg working in isolation on the DH.61 Giant Moth in 1927, the increase in business activity found him promoted to the Sales Department in June 1929, where he became Technical Assistant to Francis St Barbe, and revelled in the opportunities offered to ferry and demonstrate the company's products.

The decision to set up a permanent office in South America, and staff it from London, was something of a financial gamble but Ballantyne agreed to take up the post as full time representative, visiting England as the situation demanded. On one occasion he returned to duties in South America by flying a DH.84 Dragon across the South Atlantic to Brazil for delivery to VASP.

In March 1933 the British Air Ministry offered scholarships for two Uruguayan officers from the Military Aviation School (E.M.Aer.) based at Captain Boiso Lanza Aerodrome at Paso de Mendoza, to train at an RAF school in England. When the two successful candidates returned home in December, one an instructor, both had completed ninety flying hours in Tiger Moths. The following May the Director of the E.M.Aer. received Presidential approval to sign a contract for the purchase of five DH.82A Tiger Moths at a total price of £7,527, to be paid in three instalments. The aircraft (3288 and 3310 to 3313), painted with green fuselages and silver wings were allocated serials 1 to 5, and were carried on board the SS *Avila Star*, arriving in Montevideo in January 1935.

The customer's specification did not include leading edge slats but their options were for navigation lights, a landing light positioned under the port lower wing, bomb cradles under the fuselage, a camera gun, a hood and instrumentation necessary for blind flying, equipment for towing gliders and target drogues, a survey camera and a tank fitted in the luggage locker for a smoke system. By 1942 target towing was undertaken by Tiger Moths operating in pairs while the training role was undertaken by fleets of Curtiss SNC-1, PT-19, Canadian manufactured PT-26 and North American AT-6.

Uruguayan Military Tiger Moth marked E-4 operating in a single seat configuration with a camera gun fixed to the starboard lower fuselage side. *FAU Archive via George Boubeta*

Uruguayan Military Tiger Moth BI-605 airborne from Aerial Base No 1 in September 1945 by which time, apart from the national insignia, the colour scheme had been changed to all-over green. *FAU Archive via George Boubeta*

Following erection the test flights were carried out by de Havilland's 'Special Representative' himself, Nos 2 and 3 on 25 January and the remaining three on 28 January. It was timely for on that day an armed uprising broke out in the north east region of the country and President Gabriel Terra 'took all necessary measures' to quell it, including the immediate despatch of four of the new Tiger Moths with their photographic reconnaissance kit but also armed with bombs. They were in action from 30 January until 14 February completing a total of fifty missions. A military spokesman later explained that bloodshed was not the object of the exercise. The bombs, he insisted, were dropped near the rebels' horses in an attempt to frighten them!

DH.82A Tiger Moths Nos 1 and 4 were delivered to Montevideo for the Uruguayan military in January 1935 and although the basic colour scheme of green fuselage and silver wings was retained for ten years, the allocation of serial numbers changed several times during the same period. *via George Boubeta*

Uruguayan Military Tiger Moth No 5 was delivered to Montevideo in January 1935 and was test flown by de Havilland's Special Representative in South America on 28th January. In February she took part in an action against a revolt led by Basilio Munoz. *Gualberto Trelles*

The accident to Uruguayan Military Tiger Moth E-600 occurred at Mazangano, Cerro Largo on 18 December 1947 when the aircraft was fitted with a pesticide tank in the rear cockpit. *FAU Archive via George Boubeta*

At the end of the year the system of allocating serial numbers was changed when a prefix was added to the numeral on the fuselage (but not that displayed on the rudder) indicating to which unit the aircraft belonged: E, B1, B2 and S were established for the E.M.Aer., aeronautical bases and Service divisions. This was further changed to a three number group in 1941. From April 1945 the colour scheme was altered from green fuselage and silver wings and empennage to green overall but the process was slow and it is unlikely that all the aircraft were repainted before they were withdrawn from service.

Ballantyne firmly believed that his company was ideally placed to exploit the market for trainer aircraft in South America and was greatly anticipating the brand new design from Hatfield proposed for 1936, and which at the suggested price of £1,850 for the basic machine was competition for the Waco and Curtiss SNC-1. Pitched at its current level of specification the Tiger Moth had proved generally unpopular throughout the region and at home the Air Ministry was perceived as being positively unhelpful by prevaricating over a decision on whether or not to adopt the aircraft as an 'official training type' for the RAF.

The promised new trainer from Hatfield never came and in spite of his best endeavours and optimism that there was a prospect of twenty five sales to Argentina, Brazil and Chile, only thirteen additional Tiger Moths were sold in the whole of South America pre-war: two repeat orders for the Uruguayan Ministry of War. The aircraft, serials 6-9 (3499 and 3503-3505), were delivered on board the SS *Andalucia Star* in August 1936 and 10-18 (3612-3620), in two shipments in October and November the following year after an initial and temporary difficulty in effecting payment had been overcome, and with the capable Ballantyne taking passage with them. The aircraft were different from standard in that reverse action throttle controls were specified and approval for the unusual configuration was signed off after flight testing at Hatfield in June 1936.

On 20 November 1937, Uruguay's 21st Anniversary of Military Aviation, all eighteen Tiger Moths assembled at Pando Aerodrome, twelve miles from the capital, for the Montevideo Fiesta de Aviacion and to mark the official opening of Pando (General Artigas Military Aerodrome) as the new training headquarters for 'Military Aviation, the fifth branch of the army.' Ballantyne was on hand as de Havilland

What the well dressed Uruguayan military pilot was wearing in 1940: Junior Lieutenant Luis Alfaro at the Captain Boiso Military Aerodrome. Note that Tiger Moth No 16 is fitted with bomb racks under the fuselage floor. To have been absolutely correct he aircraft should have displayed serial B2-16 at this time. *FAU Archive via George Boubeta*

On a cold and blustery April day in 1940 the senior flying and engineering staff assigned to the formation of a French civilian flying school to be based in Indo China were hosted at Hatfield. By agreement of the Allied powers, the school was to operate Tiger Moths fitted with the latest RAF equipment. However, the agreement was cancelled and the aircraft, already fitted with reverse action throttles and flight tested, were re-directed. *Flight*

Representative and was able to report that: "the flying display did great credit to Major Gestido, organiser of the military school, and besides clean formation and aerobatic flying by the Tiger Moth trainers and the reconnaissance and day bombing types, (Potez and Breda), they demonstrated the Dragon Rapide ambulance which the military operate for the Ministry of Health."

The next and probably the only other customer for 'reverse' throttle action was the French Government which ordered a trio of Tiger Moths for delivery to a new civil flying school established in Indo-China. The aircraft were identified simply as '8', '9' and '10' and allocated Hatfield build positions 83364-83366. Four officials from the school visited Hatfield in April 1940, including two engineers, Chief Pilot Maurice Thoroval and the Commandant, Louis Costex. The Allied governments had agreed to the sale on the grounds that pupils were civilians, but the technical specification called for a deal of standard RAF equipment including blind flying instruments and navigation lighting.

Pat Fillingham flew 83365 on tests of ten and fifteen minutes on 29 May 1940 and a civil Certificate of Airworthiness was issued on 4 June. But the delivery was frustrated by the changing pace of world events and eventually the aircraft were transferred to the RAF as T5883-T5885, when the reverse action mechanism was dismantled. All three served with the training schools, T5884 (83365), ending her career in Southern Rhodesia in 1950 as the result of an indiscretion when overshooting at No 4 Flying Training School at Heany.

In contrast to the slow rate of orders for South America, the de Havilland company in South Africa had taken forty four aircraft, with a further sixteen shipped to New Zealand and seventeen to Australia. Closer to home, the British based private owners and clubs, having no affinity with military training contracts, took twenty six aircraft but precious few additional civil machines were to be completed. Escalating Air Ministry orders filled nearly all the delivery positions, a degree of exclusivity which effectively closed the Hatfield line to outsiders from mid-1939. They were lucky it was still in operation.

CHAPTER THREE
Chasing the Export Trade

The de Havilland Aircraft Company had always enjoyed a harmonious relationship with that particular section of the aviation fraternity who, by force of circumstance or out of preference, operated from water or any other precipitation covered surface. At one time or another almost the entire range of Cirrus and Gipsy powered designs had been persuaded onto floats or skis for experimental or commercial purposes. It was no surprise that from the earliest publication of brochures the company had alluded to the Seaplane version of the DH.82 Tiger Moth and, although they were specific with details of charges for packing and delivery from Stag Lane to the London Docks, '£59 for a single Tiger Moth Seaplane or £93 for a pair, packed into three high specification wooden cases', the cost of a complete machine was never quoted. Prospective customers were advised that prices were available on application, and that the quotation provided for collection ex-works, ready for packing, or 'ex-Seaplane Station, ready for flight' at extra cost.

A friendly and fruitful business relationship had always been maintained with Short Bros and it was their 'metal floats' that were specified for Moths built in England. Although de Havilland were unwilling to make a public revelation of prices the company did have sufficient experience to quote with confidence against a whole range of essentials for an aircraft operating in a marine environment. Special anti-corrosion treatment for engine and airframe was offered at just over £130, attachment fittings for the float chassis (but less chassis and floats) was £25 and the charge for supplying and fitting water rudder controls was an equal sum. The difficulties of hand swinging a propeller at a mooring were recognised by the offer to modify the engine and airframe to accept an Eclipse starter at a little over £85 extra, a geared mechanism wound with a detachable handle from the port side of the engine by an engineer, or more frequently in remote areas the pilot, precariously standing on a float. When the landplane fighter was developed for the Persian Air Force the Pratt and Whitney E-4 Gun Synchroniser occupied the same position.

Additional Seaplane accessories were all available to assist the marine aviator: float bilge pumps, boat hooks, mooring cables, anchors and paddles, not to mention a beaching trolley. Floats and the float undercarriage were also referenced under 'accessories' and a note emphasised that water rudders, a highly desirable device to assist taxiing, were 'extra', but declined to quote by how much.

The Air Ministry dutifully ordered a pair of Tiger Moth Seaplanes in 1931 under contract No 113208/31, and built to specification T.6/33. The two Gipsy III powered aircraft, S1675 and S1676 (1774/1775), were erected for trial purposes at Stag Lane in March 1932 and later were delivered to the Short Bros. factory at Rochester for water trials on the river Medway. S1675 subsequently flew with the Marine Aircraft Experimental Establishment (MAEE) at Felixstowe before a short posting to the Seaplane Training Flight

DH.82 Tiger Moth S1675 fitted with Short floats, underwent manufacturer's trials from the river Medway in Kent in 1932. Service pilots later found against the suitability of the type as a vehicle for seaplane training although as a result of sifting through subsequent information it is likely that training may not have been what the Air Ministry had in mind. *Short Bros*

The second of two DH.82 Tiger Moth Seaplanes, S1676, during a trial erection on Short floats at Stag Lane in March 1932. After trials at Felixstowe she was last reported to be in Hong Kong in December 1933. *Flight*

(STF) at Calshot in May 1932. The following year the aircraft was in Singapore, sharing space with the Hawker Horsleys operated by 36 Squadron from Seletar, but during a flight near Pasir Ris in Johore Strait on 14 August she forced landed due to engine failure. S1676 also passed through the MAEE at Felixstowe and was last reported at Kai Tak, Hong Kong in December 1933.

Hubert Broad conducted further Tiger Moth Seaplane trials on the river Medway on 9 October 1933 when he flew two different aircraft under Class 2 markings 'E.2' and 'E.3'. Four days later further trials were flown in which the aircraft were listed as 3203/3204, identifying them as P125 and P126, two of the second batch of aircraft ordered by the Imperial Iranian Ministry of War. Although there was never any suggestion that the Iranian Tiger Moths would be operated on anything but wheeled chassis, three sets of floats and two sets of skis were prepared and delivered but are thought never to have been used.

Apart from the obvious differences of alighting gear, the Tiger Moth Seaplane was little changed from the Landplane, although the fundamental requirement to hoist the aircraft in and out of the water dictated modifications to allow attachment of slinging cables to the centre section. An auxiliary ten gallon tank was fitted as standard inside the front cockpit top decking, a measure considered necessary to combat higher consumption, a result of the extra drag of the float configuration rather than the anticipation of long duration standing patrols. Additional instruments conducive to low level operations over water were also specified and a Turn Indicator and Fore and Aft Level were fitted to redesigned instrument panels; the occasion seen too as an opportunity to make provisions for a blind flying hood. Specification T.6/33 also called for complete engine and airframe protective treatment and an element of stress analysis to ensure that the centre section attachment was adequate to support the entire weight of the structure when suspended by cables from the jib of a dockyard crane.

The Air Ministry ordered that five of the standard Tiger Moths delivered into store at Henlow in January 1932 should be converted to Specification T.6/33. Aircraft serialled K2588-K2592 (1760-1764) were all allocated to de Havilland at Stag Lane on 20 June 1933 and by 29 March 1934 the five machines had each been signed off as a 'conversion of Landplane to Seaplane' at their new maximum weight of 1,825lb.

The quintet subsequently lead what on paper appears to have been an unimpressive life: K2588 undertook trials at MAEE Felixstowe before delivery to Sealand in May 1934, where she was processed for shipment to Singapore the following month. It is not clear how long she served the colony as a Seaplane, but suspicions are that she had been converted back onto a wheeled undercarriage long before she was taken on charge by Tengah Station Flight late in 1939. K2589 also routed via Sealand in May and June, but her ultimate destination was Kai Tak, Hong Kong, where she survived to be broken up for spare parts in August 1937. This fatalistic decision might have been taken in support of K2592 which had accompanied her during the voyage to Asia. This aircraft was posted on from Hong Kong to Singapore, converted to a Landplane, and operated by 4 Anti Aircraft Co-operation Unit (AACU) before joining K2588 at Tengah Station Flight.

K2591 was another candidate for Singapore, shipped in June 1934 and almost immediately after arrival re-converted to a Landplane for service with 4 AACU. The machine was written off after suffering a take-off accident at Seletar the following November and was replaced by sister aircraft K2590 which, following conversion at Stag Lane, had been placed into temporary store as a Seaplane at RAF Kenley. Shipped to Singapore in January 1935 she too was re-converted to a Landplane on arrival. None of the aircraft survived the war.

The Norwegian Navy had rejected the Tiger Moth as a suitable candidate for a float mounted training aircraft in February 1934 so to some observers there may have been surprise at the Air Ministry's decision to sign contract 419031/35 in 1935 for the supply of two further Tiger Moth Seaplanes, K8336 (3500) and K8337 (3501), which were to be delivered less engines, and approved for operations at a further increase in maximum permissible weight of 1,875lb. At a tare weight of 1,350lb and assuming a combined crew weight with parachutes of 400lb and the essential oil capacity of sixteen pints, no more than thirteen and a half gallons of fuel could be uplifted. But perhaps it was never intended that a crew of two should ever be carried!

There is every possibility, given the timing, type of conversion, postings and duties that all, or at least some, of the Tiger Moth Seaplanes were not being assessed for their potential as waterborne trainers at all, rather than as part of the development programme for the DH.82 Queen Bee whose specification had been laid down in 1933. The aircraft and her function were only publicly revealed in the summer of 1935 until which time details of the project, her role and particularly her remote control and guidance system, had been a closely guarded secret. The Queen Bee programme flirted with the Tiger Moth almost until the remotely controlled target aircraft was declared obsolete at the end of the Second World War.

Both K8336 and K8337 were taken on charge at No 2 Aircraft Servicing Unit (ASU) Cardington in October 1936 and on the last day of that year the Air Ministry's Resident Technical Officer at Hatfield, W T Sandford, signed the approval for their increased operational weights. Unless the aircraft were used for unreported trials during which they might have incurred structural distress, their next documented move seems to have been to 6 MU at Brize Norton on 30 January 1939 where, with the Air Ministry's requirement for training aircraft seemingly insatiable, they were re-categorised as Instructional Airframes (1506M and 1505M respectively), the former moving to Brighton Technical College and the latter to Stepney Mens' Institute, both transfers occurring in June. The two airframes were soon re-united: 1505M was relocated to No 3 School of Technical Training at Blackpool in November 1939 followed by 1506M the following month.

By April 1933, only eighteen months after launch of the DH.82, and six weeks since introduction of the improved 'A' version, de Havilland were disappointed to receive strong criticism of the aeroplane channelled back from agents and field representatives. The new three seater Avro 640 Cadet was being discussed in the corridors as a 'formidable competitor' powered by a Cirrus Hermes IV, and arrangements were put in hand for Captain de Havilland to fly and assess one, probably with Scottish Motor Traction at Renfrew, although there is no evidence that he did. In the event, only six Avro 640 Cadets were built in 1933, with another trio three years later, and although collectively the Cadet series did undoubtedly deprive de Havilland of orders, like the limited success of the Avian before it, ultimately the de Havilland team was able to shrug off the 'formidable competitor' almost as an irrelevance.

At their monthly meeting in June 1933, the company directors had actively debated their belief that an entirely new aircraft to replace the Tiger Moth might be required, but as an interim measure. Before any design work could be authorised St Barbe's Sales Department was called upon to explore an amelioration of the criticism not by structural modification but by offering agents a price reduction or the incentive of special rates of commission.

At the same time de Havilland's Belgian agent, Jean Stampe, partner in the Stampe and Vertongen company, was suggesting that they might be allowed to market a machine similar to the Moth, a request that raised no objection on the grounds that locally manufactured aircraft would usually be given preference if customers were allowed a choice, and ought to provide additional opportunities for the sale of Gipsy engines, an argument exemplified at that time by the encouragement offered by the Dutch National Aviation School to design submissions made by the Koolhoven Company.

The year 1933 ended with a flurry of proposals and considerations which in hindsight had little or no obvious effect on the long-term future of the Tiger Moth except that in making no firm decisions the company maintained the status quo and permitted slow but steady and uninterrupted production, the stability of which was vital for the slam acceleration that was demanded, and achieved, almost five years later.

Communicating with the managers of all the Associated Companies in November 1933, Francis St Barbe confirmed that the Gipsy Major powered Tiger Moth was 'of course' to be continued, and sold at the advertised price of £1,095. Although the aircraft was selling in a manner which he considered to be satisfactory, and a small price reduction was feasible, a view confirmed by analysis of expenses at the request of the management meeting in June, St Barbe was obdurate in his opinion that business negotiation, especially with foreign governments, was a costly exercise, often necessitating "expensive demonstration exhibitions, certain terms of payment hazards, and other considerations which justify as comfortable a price as possible."

By coincidence, and at a time when St Barbe's November letter was still in transit, de Havilland were advised by 'a reliable source' that the Air Ministry was not entirely satisfied with performance of the Avro Tutor as a training type and in all probability would be seeking to replace it within two years. It was another blow to Avro and the de Havilland board must have been delighted at the prospects. But the Tiger Moth was far from being the perfect replacement: it was certainly a more economical aircraft but had already been criticised by the military for having insufficient cockpit space, hardly enough performance and no facility for the training of observers or for air-to-air gunnery. Many of these points had been specifically tackled in the 1933 brochure which promoted the aircraft under such headings as 'The Foundations of an Air Force', and 'The One Type Trainer', apart from laying heavy emphasis on versatility, economy and performance.

Tiger Moth K2593 (1765), one of the group delivered into store at Henlow in January 1932, was returned to Stag Lane in 1933 for experiments into the feasibility of heating front and rear open cockpits. A system had been designed in July to tap hot air from a muffler fitted to a long exhaust pipe running underneath the floor on the starboard side of the front fuselage. Heated air was drawn through a 3in pipe running vertically upwards inside the cockpit and connecting with another of half the diameter, about 4ft long, and secured horizontally to the fuselage side frame. The forward end was turned down to discharge warm air 12in above the front rudder pedals, a particularly cold area for the feet of a passive instructor, or more probably, in view of the aircraft's limited contemporary use for training and preferential employment for communications, a lightly clad staff officer or minor official. In the rear cockpit the pipe was bent horizontally to form a 4in stub, discharging behind the rear instrument panel some 10in below the level of the top longeron.

The system was approved in April 1934 for Service trials at Martlesham Heath where there was criticism that the final installation did not fully comply with the original Design Memorandum in that through-ventilation of the heater muffler was not provided in the event that both front and rear cockpit control valves were closed. A circulated note was emphatic that the installation was not to be considered for any aircraft carrying an auxiliary fuel tank in the front cockpit. Trials at A&AEE were flown in the late spring and early summer of 1934, which may or may not have been the best time of year to conduct such experiments, and the results were disappointing. The aircraft was returned to Stag Lane where modifications were made to the system during the winter, including a redesign of the exhaust pipe muffler and a seventh re-arrangement of the hot air feed into the cockpit. K2593 was flown again in May 1935 after which all future developments in England were abandoned. By November 1936 the aircraft had passed into the care of No 2 ASU Cardington before transfer the following February to 24 Squadron, for communication duties from Hendon.

Probably hoping for an instantly successful heater system were the seven pilots of the Danish Army Air Corps (Haerens Flyvertropper) who arrived at Hatfield in mid-March 1934, each to collect a new DH.82A Tiger Moth. The Danish Army Air Corps had decided that operating a mixed Army Aviation School fleet of DH.60s and DH.82s was not efficient, in spite of the aircraft sharing a pedigree, and negotiations with de Havilland resulted in the company taking five DH.60 Moths in part exchange for the seven new DH.82A Tiger Moths and two DH.84 'Dragon Moths', plus a cash balance of £12,480. The DH.60 Moths were immediately resold in Denmark to civilian operators by de Havilland's local agent, Christian Thielst of Aero Material.

Senior Officer of the Danish party, Capt C C Larsen, was to lead the flight from the comfort of his newly acquired DH.84 Dragon, a machine intended for troop transport, observation and general liaison duties. A photographic session held at Hatfield in the pouring rain was the perfect occasion upon which the engineers could display the

Swinging a propeller from behind is considered to be the safest method but it helps if the swinger is tall and with a long arm. These Danish military pilots demonstrate the technique with hands on throttle and switches and a flying boot acting as precautionary chock. *BAE Systems*

Tiger Moth's tailored cockpit and propeller covers to good effect. The seven aircraft (3196-3199 and 3209-3211), which joined up with the Dragon after take-off for an immaculate formation flypast were a follow-on order from the five DH.82s which had been delivered from Stag Lane by surface a year previously. The new batch arrived at Kastrup Aerodrome, Copenhagen, on 24 March 1934 and was allocated military serial numbers S-6 to S-12.

During a training flight from Vaerlose on 11 August 1934, S-3 (3172) was abandoned by her crew who took to their parachutes, the aircraft crashing near Smorum. A replacement was purchased, at a cost of £1,029 5s 0d, and delivered from Hatfield to Copenhagen by Capt Larsen on 20 February 1935, where serial S-13 was applied. In August the same year, during an instrument flying exercise, the crew of S-1 (3170), experienced a control lock in flight and abandoned the aircraft over Amager. The student pilot, LMS Jacobsen, had parachuted from S-3 exactly twelve months previously.

Tiger Moth S-14 (3336), was purchased by the Haerens Flyvertropper in February 1936 at a price of £1,196.8s.10d, and delivered to Copenhagen by Premierlieutenant Michael Hansen. For her routing across Germany, the aircraft carried the spurious civil registration OY-DOK, although these letters were never officially allocated for the purpose, and were more legitimately worn by a DH.87B Hornet Moth (8065), delivered shortly afterwards to de Havilland's Danish agent Christian Thielst. A month after the arrival of S-14, the first of the DH.82A Tiger Moths was lost when S-6 crashed at Stenlille, and was in turn replaced by the last of the pre-war Danish orders when S-15 (3611), was delivered by E B Meincke at exactly one o'clock on the afternoon of 16 October 1937.

Led by Captain C C Larsen of the Danish Army who was to fly the DH.84 Dragon, this party of pilots gathered at Hatfield in the rain in March 1934 prior to taking delivery of seven additional Tiger Moths. The fleet arrived at Kastrup Aerodrome, Copenhagen in good order on 24 March. *Flight*

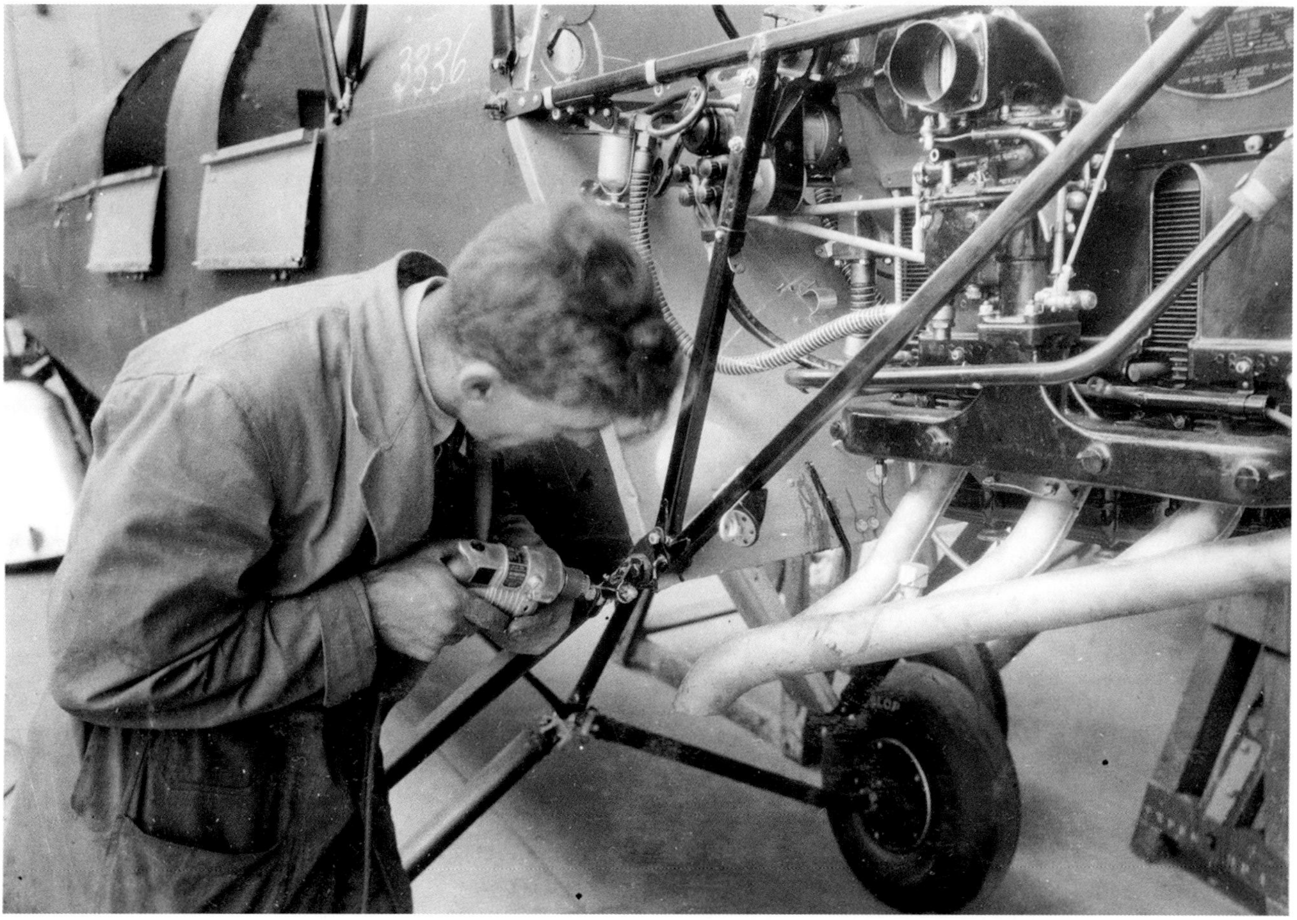

Above: A Hatfield engineer drills a bolt for split pinning on aircraft No 3336, a one-off order on behalf of the Danish Army. The aircraft carried the spurious civil registration OY-DOK for the delivery flight but was allocated military serial S-14 in 1936. *de Havilland Aircraft Co*

Top: Five of the seven Tiger Moths delivered from Hatfield to Copenhagen on 24 March 1934 are paraded at Kastrup Aerodrome for the benefit of the military photographers. *Haerens Flyvertropper*

Right: Danish Army Tiger Moth S-15 was loaned to an expedition to north east Greenland in July 1938 when she was operated on floats by Michael Hansen, a competitor in the Mildenhall to Melbourne Air Race four years previously. When under tow the aircraft's upwind lower wing was stabilised by a ballast weight. *deHMC Archive*

de Havilland DH.82A Tiger Moth, 30-107. Spanish Air Force, post civil war. Silver overall with Azure Blue underside of wings and tailplane. White wingtips and rudder. All markings in black, with three black bands above top and below lower wingtip.
Artwork ©Richard Caruana, 1:72 scale

A matter of days before an expedition was due to leave Copenhagen on board the MV *Gamma* in July 1938, bound for north east Greenland, funds became available for the hire of a spotter aircraft. The Danish Government agreed to loan Tiger Moth S-15 and after a set of suitable floats had been located in and collected from Stockholm, and fitted to the aircraft at the KZ factory, Michael Hansen flew a series of trials from Copenhagen Harbour in the only Air Corps aeroplane ever to operate on floats.

The expedition proved a great success thanks to the efforts of the wireless equipped Tiger Moth and her pilot who was able to survey a passage free from ice and report directly to the ship's captain. S-15 operated mostly at a height of 3,000ft and carried life belts, parachutes, flares, emergency rations for two days and fuel for two hours. On one occasion when the ship was difficult to locate due to its black hull, the Tiger Moth flew just above the surface from which position the *Gamma's* superstructure was spotted on the horizon.

Following the German invasion on 9 April 1941, eleven of the twelve surviving Air Corps' Tiger Moths were flown into storage at Avedore and the remaining one to Klovermarken. The whole fleet was confiscated by the Germans in August 1943 and offered for sale. With only 270 hours recorded, S-15 was sold to a Swedish company, Bjorkvallsflyg, early in 1944 for 6,300 Reichmarks and registered SE-ADK on 29 February for operation by the Halmstad Aero Club. During take-off on 8 September 1946 with a glider on tow the aircraft crashed and was written off.

Plans were drawn up in December 1942 for the loan of four Tiger Moths to Det Danske Luftfartsselskab in anticipation of the isolation of several small islands due to severe winter conditions, and registrations OY-DBA, OY-DBE, OY-DBI and OY-DBO were earmarked, but the scheme did not materialise.

Following the disbandment of the Danish Army in August 1943 and until June 1944, correspondence was exchanged between the Berlin office of the German Ministry of Aviation (Business Group, Overseas Department) and an address in Dessau, concerning the sale of ten Tiger Moths then based in Denmark. On 10 June 1944 the Luftwaffe High Command in occupation in Denmark was advised by Dr Pesch, on behalf of the German Government, that the aircraft had been withdrawn from sale pending their allocation to other duties. Pesch made no mention of what these duties might have been or where, and although there is some suspicion that the customer might have been the Governments of Portugal or Spain, the ultimate fate of the Danish Tiger Moth fleet remains a mystery.

During the spring of 1934, the Students of the de Havilland Aeronautical Technical School were working on the scheme to install a Gipsy III engine in their successful T.K.1 biplane in addition to finalising the layout for T.K.2, a low wing monoplane racer with an enclosed cockpit. In the workshops, and registered G-ACPS against one of de Havilland's 'special' build numbers, 1993, stood a Tiger Moth, built from scratch by the students and scheduled for service with the London Aeroplane Club at Hatfield. The aircraft qualified for a Certificate of Airworthiness in April 1934. In order to maintain momentum, a second Tiger Moth was laid down, registered G-ADGO (2262), to the London Aeroplane Club in May. A year later the aircraft spun into the ground during exuberant but poorly executed aerobatics at low level near Dunstable, but was repaired to live on. Perhaps it was the unexpected effort required in repairing G-ADGO that resulted in the School's third Tiger Moth production, G-AEVB (2264), not appearing until April 1937. This aircraft was registered in the name of the de Havilland Aircraft Company, and was immediately employed as part of the Reserve School establishment at Hatfield.

With the third Tiger Moth safely delivered, G-ACPS was sold to the Aero Club de France in Paris and registered F-AQDP in October 1937, but appears not to have survived the war. The Certificate of Airworthiness of G-ADGO lapsed in May 1940 before she could be impressed and it is believed she may have been written off as the result of a crash in March and reduced to spares. G-AEVB took up military markings as BB739 in October 1940 but was burned out after a take-off accident at Hatfield the following September.

In June 1934 the first World Cup competition for aerobatics was organised at Vincennes in France, a two day affair attended by 150,000 spectators. Six nations were represented by their finest aerobatic pilots and aircraft capable of performing all the manoeuvres necessary for the free and compulsory sequences.

Christopher Clarkson was the sole British entrant, nominated by the Royal Aero Club and flying a borrowed Armstrong Whitworth AW16. Just before the competition was due to start Christopher Clarkson was advised the AW16 was not available and at very short notice his friends at de Havilland offered a DH.82A Tiger Moth, G-ACJA (3191), in which Clem Pike had just completed a demonstration tour of the Balkans. The aircraft was made available for collection from Le Bourget.

"Although this was very sporting and generous of them it was not much of an aeroplane – a tired workhorse, weighted down

Above: The de Havilland Company progressively shifted all airframe production from Stag Lane to Hatfield between 1930 and 1934. Manufacture of Tiger Moth and Leopard Moth fuselages continued in parallel at an unhurried pace. *deHMC Archive*

Right: The much travelled demonstration Tiger Moth G-ACJA preparing for a solo flight during an aviation gathering in Europe, probably in Germany, sometime after her presentation at the Geneva Aero Show in April 1934. *deHMC Archive*

by a large extra tank in the front. If that was not enough it had no inverted flying engine modification."

The competition was fierce and on the second day a French pilot and a Portuguese competitor were killed with an hour of one another. The winner was Gerhard Fieseler from Germany flying his specially prepared F2 Tiger with a very disgruntled Frenchman, Michel Détroyet, second in a Morane Saulnier 225. And what of Christopher Clarkson? A report in a French newspaper read:

> "The Englishman Clarkson, although a brilliant pilot was desperately handicapped by the meagre power-weight ratio of the Tiger Moth and its inability to perform negative manoeuvres severely limited his repertoire of figures in the competition. But, having entered, he was sporting enough to see it through. Though not by any means disgracing himself, he predictably came in last."

Within the space of six months late in 1934, the de Havilland Company had rejected the idea of a substantial redesign of the Tiger Moth in favour of a review of prices for the existing model, but now found themselves being shepherded, however unwillingly, into a major policy change in the wake of a substantial re-equipment programme being pursued by the Royal Air Force. The most obvious requirement for an improved training type was likely to be a more powerful engine, and the six cylinder Gipsy Six was the natural candidate with which to replace the Gipsy Major. Good take-off and climb performance was necessary while speed was of little consequence. To be even more ambitious there were thoughts that in addition to spacious cockpits the aircraft should be provided with facilities for a manoeuvrable observer's gun to the rear and a synchronised forward firing machine gun.

Immediate thoughts were that the new design should have a fabric covered metal frame fuselage and wings, and would sell at between £1,600 and £1,800. Furthermore, if the type was termed 'experimental', a company funded prototype could be constructed relatively quickly, leading to the prospect of an Air Ministry development contract. The board agreed just before their 1934 Christmas holiday that significant opportunities were to be offered by the provision of a new Service trainer aircraft.

Early in January 1935, shortly before delivery of the 1,000th Gipsy Major engine, the directors declared themselves to be divided in their opinion on whether a bigger, all-purpose development was after all preferable to a modified version of the standard Tiger Moth in which the front fuselage could be suitably adapted to provide more spacious cockpits and other refinements, whilst retaining the Gipsy Major powerplant. Whatever the final decision, capacity was not available for any further progress to be made until after May 1935, but even that was conditional on the decision whether or not to proceed with a four seat cabin type replacement for the DH.83 Fox Moth, or the 'very cheap' light aeroplane which was considered even more essential. The production of Gipsy Major engines was scheduled to remain at thirteen per week, although the output of Gipsy Sixes was to be increased by one to a total of eight.

The matter had still not been resolved by April when Frank Hearle proposed that in order to reduce the necessity for the company to hold up to 18,000 part numbers in support of the current product range, (he quoted that in the USA, Waco held less than 4,000), the DH.83 Fox Moth (selling at £995) should be phased out after current orders had been fulfilled, and that the DH.60G Moth Major at £695, should be dropped when the new DH.87 Hornet Moth was in production. A 'General Purpose Advance Trainer' designed as a Tiger Moth replacement was still under consideration, and although the military Tiger Moth selling price had been reduced by £50, the estimated cost of the proposed new project had risen to between £1,850 and £2,000 per production aircraft.

The opinion of the company's Special Representative in South America that training aircraft were vital, but the Tiger Moth was probably not the machine for the local market, was confirmed during the summer of 1934 when the Brazilian Government passed over de Havilland's proposals for forty five Tiger Moths in favour of fifteen Curtiss Wright Primary Trainers and Waco F.3s. By the mid-1930s, Brazil had discovered with others, that pilots of high performance military aircraft required a stepped level of training. If de Havilland were to remain competitive, a new aircraft was required sooner rather than later, and with an emphasis on speed and capacity for armament training rather than manoeuvrability. An improved Tiger Moth with a Gipsy Six engine and variable pitch (VP) propeller was a prospect else a completely new design complementing the standard DH.82A which would continue in the role of primary trainer. The company believed the Air Ministry was bound to announce soon an interest in an advanced training type and that their own promotion of the Tiger Moth as the 'one-type' trainer could no longer be vindicated.

Undeterred, Hatfield continued to exercise development effort on behalf of the DH.82A and in October 1935 an experimental exhaust manifold was authorised for flight trials. The following month G-ADUC (3425), an aircraft purchased by the Marquess of Douglas and Clydesdale in support of his initiative to form a local airline based at Prestwick, was fitted with a full set of Demec navigation lights to a similar standard of installation as that employed two years previously on Lindsay Everard's DH.60GIII G-ACBX, a machine used for all-weather operations from his private airfield at Ratcliffe.

Before delivery, G-ADUC received a 6in Harley landing light: the unit was housed in the floor of the front cockpit, situated between the runners of the rudder bar support. Bowden cables operated by a small winch adjacent to the throttle controls in the rear cockpit permitted the lamp to be lowered or retracted into a position flush with the underside. The beam was directed 15° off-centre rather than straight ahead and under the nose, eliminating the nuisance of flickering propeller interference and providing the pilot with a better chance of seeing it in contact with the ground.

In addition to managing the Reserve Flying Schools at Desford, Stapleford and Meir, the Reid and Sigrist Company manufactured aircraft instruments, the most famous and perhaps widely appreciated being the ubiquitous 'Turn and Slip' indicator which took centre place in many instrument panels. In 1935 the company designed a new instrument, the Gyorizon, described as a combination of a rate of turn indicator with a visible horizon created using coloured fluid. By the simple expedient of allowing a pair of wings to sprout at the pivot point of the turn indicator needle, the lateral relation of the aircraft could be represented against an imaginary horizon. Since this horizon was itself affected both by gravity and by centrifugal force, the pilot was given an easily understood diagrammatical picture of the angular motion as well as the attitude of the aeroplane.

Early in 1936 the Gyorizon was installed and flight tested in a Desford Reserve School Tiger Moth, G-ADPD (3394), and at the end of February it was arranged that a practical demonstration of the safety potential of the device should be given to the press. This would be in the form of an aerobatic routine by a solo pilot flying from the rear cockpit and under the blind flying hood; probably the first time in the world that the aircraft had been flown in such a configuration. A contemporary report of the proceedings at Desford duly appeared in *Flight:*

> "After only half an hour or so of practice under the hood with George Lowdell, Chief Instructor, in the front seat, Flight Lieutenant H A Howes took off by himself, lowered the hood and proceeded to carry out a series of very presentable slow rolls interspersed with odd half minutes of inverted flying. The sensations cannot have been too pleasant when another machine was known to be formating close by. Flight Lieutenant Howes suffered a bad ten seconds or so when his engine blew back with such force that he felt convinced that the photographic machine had touched his. He admitted that his only real difficulty consisted in stopping the roll in a squarely inverted position so that the machine would not fall out at once in one direction or another."

As if to confirm the attitude prevailing in South America, in November, 'Jimmy' Buckingham reported back from the Initial Training School (5th Air Corps) of the Royal Swedish Air Force at Ljungbyhed where he had been demonstrating a DH.89 Dragon Rapide, that the Tiger Moth had fallen into disfavour. Instructors believed the aircraft was too small and too easy to fly, and that the cramped cockpits were not compatible with a pilot encased in a winter flying suit. Neither the aircraft nor the natural environment had changed since the first sales in 1931 and Sweden continued to build Tiger Moths under licence until June 1937.

Swedish debate on the likely specification of an improved aircraft was in tune with de Havilland's own thoughts, but of more immediate concern to Hatfield was that a Focke-Wulf Stieglitz with a 150hp Siemens engine had already been delivered to Ljungbyhed for assessment and Swedish authorities confirmed that another British aircraft was also being considered, almost certainly a trainer from Avro. Both types could offer *ab initio* and a degree of advanced training. Should either be recruited, de Havilland stood to lose the advantage for follow-on commercial aircraft orders which had proved to be so beneficial. The company's fears were realised in December when the Swedish Air Force announced an order for twelve Stieglitz and the prospect of more to follow.

One of a pair of unidentified Tiger Moths in this picture caught in severe European weather before or during the Second World War. Traces of a civil registration under the wing, a long exhaust pipe and glider towing hook point towards a one time Austrian civil aircraft. *de Havilland Aircraft Company*

Tiger Moth A-78 was a direct export to de Havilland's Austrian agent, Nikolaus von Eltz in 1934. She was registered OE-DAM to the Austrian Aero Club in 1935 but joined the Austrian Army that same year. *Hugh Evans*

Within nine months, Nikolaus von Eltz, de Havilland's agent in Vienna, communicated criticism of the Tiger Moth as addressed to him by the Austrian Air Force. Von Eltz had suggested that a crashed aircraft, probably A-81 (3191), a previous de Havilland demonstration aircraft sold second hand in 1934, might be replaced by a new Tiger Moth but he was advised that the DH.82 was an old design; in 1936 nobody had control cables running outside the fuselage and stretched across a non-adjustable tailplane. The aircraft had no mainwheel brakes, nor a tailwheel, and was, according to the Air Force, not very good at aerobatics.

Apart from the reliability of the Gipsy Major engine, reported the Austrian agent, his customers perceived the Tiger Moth and her sisters the Leopard Moth and Hornet Moth, as old fashioned and uncompetitive. If the developing policy of buying from a near neighbour due to ease and reliability of delivery and subsequent support was to be challenged, then it could only be as the result of a higher quality product offered at an appropriate price. The Austrian Air Force had declared itself in favour of the new Bücker machine which, at about the same cost as the Tiger Moth, was more economical on fuel and a greatly improved aerobatic platform. The message from Nikolaus von Eltz was clear enough: if the Tiger Moth was not modernised, nobody would buy it.

The gauntlet flung down in Vienna was picked up by the de Havilland team at Hatfield. The company was only too aware that it had a serious problem on its hands. A massive effort spent on designing, building, delivering on time and selling (at a huge predicted loss) the trio of DH.88 Comets which distinguished themselves in the 1934 MacRobertson Races; the major effort with the DH.91 Albatross, including new twelve cylinder engines, and modernisation of the DH.89 Dragon Rapide into the elegant but already dated DH.92 Dolphin, had caused the company to neglect the trainer programme and the private owners and clubs upon whose support the very foundation of the company had been laid. "Drifting away from the Training markets," is how St Barbe described it, with other companies offering new designs (notably Miles Hawks and Percival Gulls) and some even considering alternative powerplants. Phillips and Powis, de Havilland's West Country agents based at Woodley were openly courting the prospect of manufacturing the American Menasco engine in support of its Miles aircraft production, not only to relieve its dependence on de Havilland, but to cream off a greater share of the revenues.

In April 1936 St Barbe admitted that had it not been for those other recent preoccupations the Tiger Moth would have been replaced some time previously, but on Captain de Havilland's initiative, some consideration was now being given to setting up a semi-independent unit to address the whole issue of trainer aircraft. An alternative was to buy a controlling interest in a competitor offering an appropriate design. St. Barbe considered the Tiger Moth to be "on its last legs" and at the current price of £1,100, unlikely to attract any more orders. His decision was to cut the price to £850, a figure at which the aeroplane could be produced at 'no loss', maintaining his salesman's belief that the move would revive interest in the type, "leading possibly to the construction of two or three hundred more."

By the end of 1936, the company was considering a three year plan during which design capacity was to be allocated to a Tiger Moth replacement, probably from April 1937, but only after the development of a military trainer of a different kind had been well established. Built to Air Ministry specification T.6/36, and excessively, continuously and disastrously modified by interfering official dictate, the DH.93 Don, powered by a 525hp V-12 Gipsy King engine, finally emerged as a total inadequate, soaking up massive effort before and after the first flight of the prototype on 18 June 1937. Contracted production was still incomplete when the entire project was cancelled and unflown airframes and engines were scrapped.

A de Havilland publicity shot of Hatfield-based Tiger Moths and others awaiting delivery taken in the late summer of 1935. In November, G-ADJB went to Phillips and Powis, civilian operators of 8 ERFTS at Woodley, but was written off the following March. *via Richard Riding*

In December 1936, the same month that brought confirmation of the Swedish Air Force order for the Stieglitz, forty Tiger Moths were ordered by the Air Ministry for distribution amongst the still expanding Reserve. The contract called for delivery by 1 April 1937, a situation demanding re-organisation of the production programme. Capacity had already been sold until mid-March and only sixteen machines were scheduled from then until the end of April, after which production of four Tiger Moths per week was planned until the middle of July.

In January 1937, the prospective Argentinean order was reported lost to the American Fleet in a deal which included six spare Kinner engines, and at a price said to be greater than the de Havilland proposal. Just over a year later, the Inspector General of Aviation in Peru called for a tender against training aircraft to be based in Lima, but to be fitted with Wright engines, a number of which were held as surplus on his spares inventory. As the Tiger Moth was not a suitable candidate, Ballantyne passed the enquiry on to Avro, anticipating the normal introductory commission.

Money as much as anything was a factor behind the Austrian Air Force's eventual order for the Stieglitz. In a transparent display of political economics, the Austrian Finance Minister was reported as having instructed the Air Force to buy German aircraft not only as a good propaganda exercise but due to unmatchable terms for long term credit.

An enquiry from Portugal suggested a further eight Tiger Moths might be required, but there were grounds to believe that the Portuguese were also interested in acquiring licensed manufacturing rights. Arrangements were made for the Portuguese agent, Carlos Bleck, to accompany a government delegation to Hatfield, arriving in early June. There was little further news until October when a contract for eight aircraft (3645-3652), was signed on behalf of Oficinas Gerais de Material Aeronáutico, in an arrangement which included purchase of a manufacturing licence. The eight aircraft were amongst thirteen delivered from Hatfield in December.

At the beginning of 1937 the company was still soul searching, believing that in spite of a slight acceleration in interest, probably assisted by St Barbe's price reductions, the Tiger Moth was near to its end and accepting that a replacement was long overdue. The image of a wooden winged biplane was no longer compliant with a once universally perceived view of excellence and imagination in the company's designs, they admitted. But enquiries continued to arrive at Hatfield and in January and February were received from Turkey and Egypt whilst deliveries were made to South Africa, Ceylon, Iraq and Malaya. Orders were also confirmed for thirteen Tiger Moths for the Reserve Schools at Bristol, Sywell and Desford, including one for the Airwork syndicate's school at Castle Bromwich.

In April a Reserve aircraft scheduled for delivery to the Newcastle upon Tyne Aero Club, G-AEWG (3589), was tested with a Rotax K625 signal navigation light installed under the floor, part of a continuing development strategy. In spite of having now sold practically all of its sanctioned Tiger Moth build positions the company sensed that the Reserve requirements were still not completely satisfied and laid down a further 'small' batch, all in the face of increasing Air Ministry orders for Miles Hawk Trainers from Phillips and Powis, to whom the Stag Lane factory continued to supply Gipsy Major engines.

With the continuing trickle of orders, an analysis of the production cost was called up in May 1937, and concluded that per pound of empty weight (1,125lb quoted) the price of aircraft materials amounted to three shillings and a halfpenny and the labour content to two shillings and a halfpenny. Against these economics it was considered prudent to make an upwards adjustment in the currently advertised price from £875 to £925, still more than 11% below the 1931 listing, although by September the figure had been amended again to read £1,095, an amazingly brash move which took it to within £5 of the highest ever quoted price.

Above: Tiger Moths of the Egyptian Air Force with tails towards what appear to be substantial brick-built facilities in the desert. *Hugh Buckingham*

Left: Peter de Havilland (left) and Hugh Buckingham with Tiger Moth G-ACJA during one of their ranging sales and demonstration tours on behalf of the de Havilland Company. *Hugh Buckingham*

Tiger Moths of the Egyptian Air Force being inspected by a party of officers who appear to have arrived at their desert airfield in the unidentified aircraft to the right of the corrugated iron hangars. *Hugh Buckingham*

Since the introduction of the DH.82 Tiger Moth examples of all models had been purchased by the Persian authorities following their approval of the de Havilland business ethic. It was the Persians who had initiated many of the earliest military modifications, culminating in the fully fledged Tiger Moth 'Fighter' in 1932. Their support of the order book was satisfyingly constant, but each contract would appear to have been negotiated under a different bureaucracy:

1932: Imperial Persian Army Flying Corps, 3117-3136 (20), serials 101-120
1933: Imperial Iranian Ministry of War, 3200-3208 (9), serials 121-129
1934: Le Ministere de la Guerre, Imperial de Perse, 3228-3237 (10), serials 130-139
1935: Imperial Persian War Ministry, 3290-3309 (20), serials 140-159.
1935: Imperial Iranian War Ministry, 3464-3473 (10), serials 160-169
1938: Imperial Iranian Army, 3930-3934 (5 as supplied ex Hatfield), but serials quoted are for six aircraft, 170-175; 82005-82009, serials 176-180; 82047-82051, serials 181-185; 82092-82096, serials 186-190, (20)
1940: 83352 (191), 83353 (192) and 83355 (193), 83357-83363 serials 194-200 (10) supplied less engines.
1940: 83774-83783, serials 201-210 (10)

The first 105 aircraft were manufactured at Hatfield and the last ten by Morris Motors at Cowley which were delivered for assembly at the Shahbaz State Aircraft Factory at Dushan Tappeh.

Early in December 1932 crates holding the first aircraft were unloaded at the port of Khoramshahr and the following month de Havilland demonstration pilot Hugh Buckingham accompanied by engineer Brett Johnson arrived to start training the Tiger Moth force. Hugh Buckingham had travelled out by DH.83 Fox Moth G-ABZN, which he delivered to a customer in Cairo on the way home. Following assembly at Khoramahahr the aircraft were flown in three groups between 12 December and 23 January 1933 to Tehran via Ahvaz, an airfield five miles north of Abadan at the head of the Persian Gulf. One aircraft crashed during the delivery phase and was written off. Apart from fifty one aircraft assigned to the Advanced Pilot Training School established at Mehrabad in 1933, where instrument training was conducted under a locally designed and manufactured hood, others were stationed with Army regiments at Tehran, Tabriz, Mashhad and Ahvaz.

Observers were trained to fire rifles and throw grenades from the back seats and thirty eight Tiger Moths were fitted with bomb racks. To expedite training using European methods a number of Swedish instructors arrived in 1934 followed in the same year by ten Belgians and although training was greatly improved almost forty Tiger Moths were lost in accidents, several due to the harsh environment in which they operated. Before the Second World War Iranian pilots trained on Tiger Moths at home regularly travelled to the RAF base at Habbaniyah in Iraq to fly front line fighters. Continuation of this agreement may have resulted in the regular throughput of Iranian pilots who were being coached in the art of flying instruction by the de Havilland School at Hatfield and later Panshanger until at least 1944.

The last Shah of Iran, HRH Mohammad-Reza-Shah Pahlavi, made a solo flight in a Tiger Moth marked 166 in 1946 but there is doubt as to whether this was the 'original' 166 (3470), delivered in 1935. The type is understood to have been 'much enjoyed' and remained in military service until 1953 when the majority was replaced by the North American T-6 Texan. Three redundant aircraft were stored at Dushan Tappeh where they were still in evidence ten years later. The Islamic Revolution of 1979 resulted in closure of the Air Force Museum and attempts to re-establish it at Ghale Morghi in the 1990s were thwarted when the Chief of the Iranian Air Force was killed in the crash of a Lockheed Jetstar near Isfahan.

In January 2011 a dilapidated Tiger Moth marked '166' was moved from the historic hangars at Ghale Morghi which were threatened with demolition and moved to Dushan Tappeh. This aircraft was fitted with spin strakes, almost compelling evidence to suggest this was not the genuine 166 (3470), but another aircraft from an unknown source and possibly that flown solo in 1946 by the Shah which was the singular reason for its survival.

Bomb racks were fitted to a number of aircraft exported to military air arms, one of the first was the 1932 delivery to Persia. The whole arrangement was revisited at Hatfield early in 1940.
de Havilland Aircraft Company

Left: A Tiger Moth marked '166' was scheduled for the Iranian Air Force Museum at Ghale Morghi before the project was shelved. Semi-abandoned the aircraft is fitted with spin strakes which means it is unlikely to be the original bearer of that serial. *Babak Taghvaee*

Below: Dilapidated Tiger Moth '166' was dismantled at Ghale Morghi Aerodrome on 19 January 2011 and taken by lorry to Dushan Tappeh where a new museum is in prospect. *Babak Taghvaee*

The Hatfield Sales Department had made a surprise announcement in June 1937 that seven Gipsy Major engines had been sold to Iran (Persia) and were to be fitted to Tiger Moths built under licence in that country. There is no evidence to support the claim that up to twenty aircraft were manufactured at the Shahbaz factory between 1938 and 1940 rather than being assembled there from imported British kits nor that the engines, together with five more which were ordered in 1939, were purchased as anything other than replacements or spares.

In August 1937 the company returned to its earlier sales philosophy and released another brochure extolling the multi-role virtues of the Tiger Moth, 'The One Type Trainer' with the sheer reliability of the Gipsy Major engine:

> "Possessing adequately high performance to permit instruction without loss of time in securing height, reproducing perfectly the handling characteristics of first-line aircraft and having ample accommodation for the installation of all forms of military equipment, the Tiger Moth is equally recommended for *ab initio*, intermediate and advanced flying training as well as for instruction in specialised military duties.
> The adoption of Tiger Moths spells absolute standardisation in training aircraft, eliminates completely the need for a variety of different types for individual phases of military instruction and ensures the most economical training of efficient Air Force personnel."

It was a fairly lightweight document compared with the solidity of the 1932 booklet although the message was substantially the same and the promotion very much in line with St Barbe's business instinct that irrespective of criticism, a renewed interest and requirement was beginning to emerge. The brochure was a reminder to all that the aircraft's capabilities were already well recognised in air arms and civil organisations around the world.

The recent substantial increases in price had little or no connection with any rise in production costs; there was no follow-on aircraft, no updated Tiger Moth to sell or to buy, and the Business Office had little to lose in exercising its talents to achieve those 'two or three hundred' predicted sales of the aircraft which they had already declared to be 'on its last legs'.

The price list which followed in September 1937 was greatly expanded and included details of all the 'subsidiary equipment' which previously had been supplied to individual customer specification, not unnaturally with a heavy bias towards military installations. No firm commitment to price was offered on items such as machine guns, bombing sights or wireless, all of which depended on the operator's choice of supplier, although de Havilland revealed that they could offer two alternative types of inverted flying conversion kits: £58 would buy the three minute system, but an extended period of ten minutes was available at £73.15s.0d per aircraft, supplied and fitted.

In a report to the board, the Business Department was able to record that 108 Tiger Moths had been sold during the twelve month period until 30 September 1937, but at an average price allowing for variations in equipment and commissions of only £780 each, and that an allowance for fifty sales might be made for 1938. There was no projection beyond that in anticipation of a new, low priced practical two seater that might be expected to fulfil the roles of both the Tiger Moth and the generally unpopular Hornet Moth. In prospect was a new advanced light trainer for 1941, doubling in an alternative model as a high speed civil tourer.

The publicity drive caused no immediate impact on sales. During the last quarter of 1937, only eighteen Tiger Moths were ordered: three for the associated company in South Africa, one each for India and New Zealand, and the anticipated eight aircraft order from Portugal. Five were ordered by French agent Costa de Beauregard, operating from his offices in the Champs Elysées, followed by a further five early in 1938. This second order had been accepted against a spring delivery in the confident expectation that the French authorities would present no difficulties, but by the end of February when eight aircraft had been completed, import licences for only three had been granted and the group sat somewhat disconsolately in the Hatfield factory, just recovering from the effects of a fortnight's strike. A third batch of six aircraft was ordered for delivery in June and one other aircraft for July.

Initially all the aircraft were registered in the names of individuals, the first, F-AQJU (3655), to Dr René Arbeltier of Coulommiers, a member of the French Parliament and Vice Président of his local flying club, the Cercle Aéronautique de Coulommiers et de la Brie. Once delivered to France and without operating at Coulommiers, registered ownership was immediately changed to the Société Française de Transports Aériens, a front organisation which channelled the aircraft to the Aeroclub de Catalunya and thence to the Spanish Republican training bases at Murcia of Los Alcázares and La Ribera in Spain. Dr Arbeltier organised training of Republican pilots in the dim recesses of the Brie and later a 'reseau' for smuggling aircraft to them.

F-AQOS (3677), issued with a C of A in May 1938 for Roger Levy at Neuilly, was cancelled from the register in London in August and the eventual fate of the aircraft is unknown. F-AQOX (3688), was registered to two different individual names in Coulommiers in July 1938 before transfer to the Société Française de Transports Aériens the same month. It is thought she may not have been smuggled to Spain as she was registered to owners in Gaillac and Vannes in April and June 1939 before returning to England for maintenance by Airwork at Heston where she was stranded at the outbreak of the Second World War. Events then took a strange twist; the aircraft was delivered by train to Glasgow and, registered G-AGAP, she was issued with a British C of A on 6 March 1940 at Renfrew before acquisition by broker W S Shackleton two days later, the same date upon which the registration was cancelled as sold to Australia. Delivered to the Newcastle Aero Club in June 1940 she was impressed into military service as A17-681 the following month, sold to the Australian Associated Aero Clubs in 1947 and probably broken up for spares.

St Barbe must have been heartened to receive from the Chinese Government an invitation to tender for sixty Tiger Moths, but equally frustrated that he could not offer a reasonable delivery schedule. Advised that Chinese contacts had re-focused their attention on the American Fleet, Hatfield immediately revised their schedule but it was too late and nothing further was heard.

Eastern Europe had proved to be a profitable trading area for de Havilland since the company chairman, Alan Butler, toured the area extensively in his personal DH.37, G-EBDO, in 1924 seeking government contracts and licensing agreements. When in October 1937 the Government of Bulgaria asked de Havilland to tender for twenty Tiger Moths the company was dismayed to be advised that their usual terms of business were not acceptable. The proposal was for 50% of the total value to be paid only after all the aircraft had been delivered to Sofia, where they would be regarded as in 'temporary reception' for six months, after which the remaining 50% would be negotiated for 'definite reception'. In common with competing British and American manufacturers, de Havilland refused the terms which they were later advised by 'informed sources' were part of a ploy to ensure that the order went to Germany. The intelligence was not without foundation for, in May 1938 it was announced that the Bulgarian order had indeed been placed as anticipated.

Although St Barbe would rarely view a lost order with anything but disappointment, contemporary systems of international control and transfer of currency could create uncertainty and possibly danger for the unwary business dabbler. de Havilland's Business Director was both worldly and wise and had only recently rejected the opportunity to tender for a Turkish order purely on the grounds of what he perceived to be a bad long-term currency situation. At the first opportunity following advice that Bulgaria was in a position to place Sterling in London, he appointed an agent in Sofia. It was a shrewd move. In August 1938 only months after the loss of the government order to Germany, and against all predictions, there arose the slightest prospect for an order for Tiger Moths. de Havilland were anxious enough to send General Manager Lee Murray to Sofia to enter into discussions, and Major Ivan Nojaroff led a Trade Mission to Hatfield in January 1939, during which visit he said that much as he liked the Tiger Moth, he preferred a low wing monoplane made from wood, suitable for manufacture under licence in Bulgaria. The Tiger Moth order did not materialise.

The Romanian agent, Mr A Mano, called from Bucharest in January 1938 to seek confirmation of prices and terms for between ten and twenty Tiger Moths. The Romanian Government had recently purchased twenty five Nardi trainers from Italy, powered by Gipsy engines built under licence by Alfa Romeo. Hatfield knew from past experience involving the sale of DH.89 Dragon Rapides to the country that negotiations were liable to continue for many months. The enquiry itself almost certainly resulted from Clem Pike's demonstration of Tiger Moth G-ACJA (3191), in Bucharest three and a half years previously but in spite of his warm welcome then, and an enduring relationship between the two countries and their aviation interests, no order was received.

Under the big sky in Africa, Tiger Moth VP-YBW of the touring Southern Rhodesia Flying Training School. Operations were confined to early mornings and late afternoons due to heat and turbulence. *The Aeroplane*

In July 1938, funded by a donation from the Abe Bailey Aviation Coronation Gift, and a small subsidy from the Government of Southern Rhodesia, Tiger Moth VP-YBW (3701), was test flown at Hatfield and shipped to the de Havilland associated company in South Africa where it was prepared for delivery to the 'Travelling Flying School' recently established in Southern Rhodesia. Representatives of the Southern Rhodesian Government and of the de Havilland Aircraft Company, which was already operating flying schools at Salisbury and Bulawayo using DH.60 Moths and DH.82A Tiger Moths, had visited several towns to discuss with local flying clubs how to overcome the financial problems of maintaining facilities for what would always be a limited number of members. As a result, the Southern Rhodesia Flying Training School was inaugurated at Que Que on 25 October 1938, consisting of: "Tiger Moth VP-YBW, complete with slots and a fixed pitch metal propeller, an instructor, Mr D D Longmore, accompanied by an A and C licensed ground engineer, Mr T H Gundry, a tent, a box of tools and spares, and half a dozen sets of helmets, earphones and goggles."

Que Que was the first town visited where seven members of the flying club were helped to obtain their 'A' licences. The next move was to Gatooma where on 7 January 1939 nine members of the club started their flying training in climatic conditions that seriously limited the number of hours available for useful instruction. It was usual to start flying as early as 5.30am but finishing by 8.30am and then starting again after 4.00pm when the heat of the day had diminished and with it the turbulent conditions that *ab initio* pupils found impossible to cope with. In company with other civil aircraft in the region, VP-YBW was impressed into the Southern Rhodesia Air Service just eight months later.

The subject of de Havilland's new *ab initio* trainer had been raised again during a review of the company's design programme conducted by Frank Hearle and Lee Murray in October 1937. The new 'cheap aeroplane', the DH.94, was first flown by Captain Geoffrey de Havilland at Hatfield on 23 June 1937, his last 'first' flight, but deliveries were not expected before October 1938 and, more realistically, six months later than that due to difficulties in development of its new engine, provisionally named the Gipsy Junior. The trainer project was now being referred to as the DH.96 but due to pressure on the overall programme a further postponement was suggested, unless the responsibility could be switched to the new department specially created to work on the DH.94. On their own initiative they were already attempting to fit a Gipsy Major engine into the DH.94 airframe and would need high level direction to delay that project indefinitely in favour of the DH.96.

The review concluded that money and effort expended on the current level of design and development in both Engine Division and Aircraft Division was too high. Priorities would need to be identified and adhered to, and the new trainer was high on the list. Should there have been doubt word came from Belgium that the Military Flying School had rejected the Tiger Moth on the grounds that both construction and performance were below the current level of their specification which, for the same reason, had eliminated both the Bücker Jungmann and the Gipsy Major powered Stampe SV-4B, a type submitted by de Havilland's Belgian agents. The company hoped that as no firm decision had been made the competition would remain open until after the DH.96 had been launched. Preliminary drawings revealed the proposed aircraft to be an open cockpit, tandem two seat low-wing monoplane, looking for all the world like a Miles Magister.

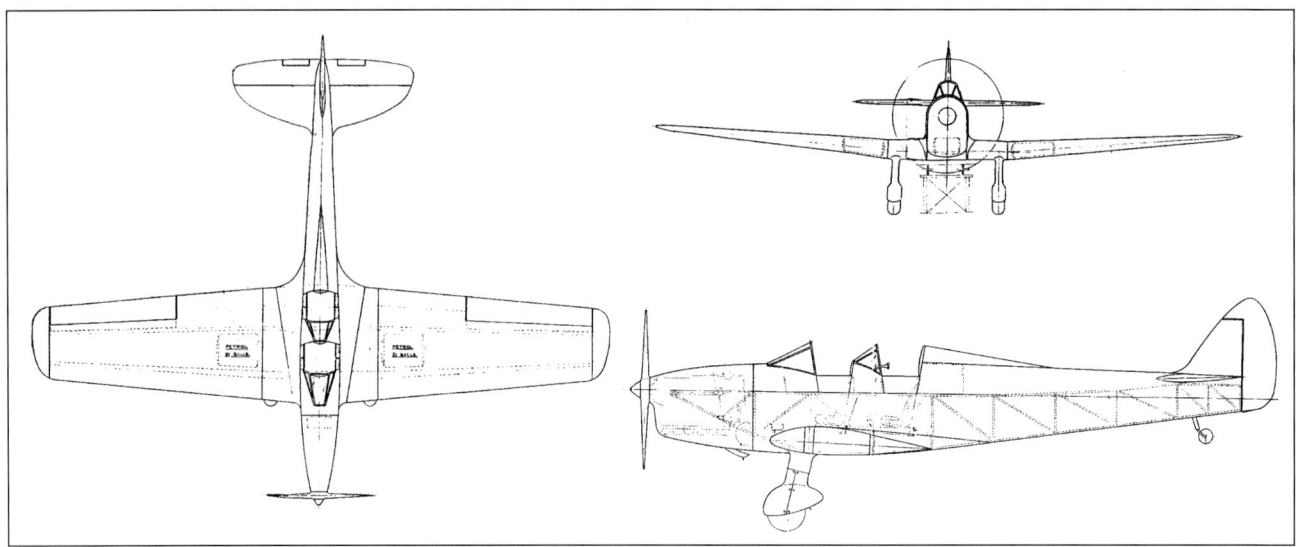

The unnamed DH.96 might have replaced the Tiger Moth after de Havilland finally acknowledged that change was necessary, but world events moved too rapidly and the project progressed no further than the drawing boards at Hatfield. *de Havilland Aircraft Company*

CHAPTER FOUR

A Time for Decisions

In view of his most recent sales promotions Francis St Barbe must have been surprised to take a telephone call in February 1938 from the Directorate of Aeronautical Production (DAP) at the Air Ministry, asking whether the company was still in a position to supply Tiger Moths! On hearing that they were, the caller confirmed that a further order was being considered. Possibly, it had been brought to his attention that the Gipsy Major engine had just been approved for a 1,000 hour overhaul life, a figure without precedent. In March, officials from the DAP visited the Stag Lane engine factory on two occasions to enquire after the company's position if large numbers of engines should be required at short notice in the event of a national emergency. The Air Ministry was already critical of the de Havilland company's Engine Division for not maintaining the Gipsy Major delivery schedule contracted for Miles Magisters, forcing some airframes to be accepted into pre-flight storage, but General Manager Frank Hearle was confident that all current obligations would be honoured by October 1938. For the time being the Air Ministry was also reasonably content to accept delivery, without engines, of Tiger Moth airframes intended for storage as part of the Strategic Reserve.

At their current rate of production the factory was able to provide twenty Gipsy Major engines per month although the company would have preferred to have been in a position offer twenty five. To increase production significantly it would be necessary to invest heavily in a new range of tools and jigs which, for the level of civil orders being received, could not be justified. It was a problem that only government money together with de Havilland effort could hope to resolve and the urgency of the situation resulted in an almost immediate authority for the Engine Division to proceed with a major re-development of the production shops at Stag Lane, following which it was expected that an additional 120 engines per month could be supplied.

Although the Munich Agreement signed in September 1938 provided a year's grace before Great Britain actually declared war on Germany there was an increasing pace of rearmament with the commissioning of new aircraft, equipment and ships including sixteen battleships. The Royal Air Force structured a Reserve Command with the responsibility of refreshing active reservists; a school was formed at Gatwick with an establishment of nine instructors and sixteen Tiger

The Stag Lane factory site in 1935, marooned within a sea of actual and pending housing development. Engine production was housed in the block nearest the camera. Most of the buildings survived until demolition and clearance of the historic site in 1997 to be replaced with more houses.
de Havilland Aircraft Company

Above: A corner of the greatly expanded de Havilland Engine Division shops at Stag Lane, an area specialising in connecting rods and pistons and, at the time of the photographic session, busy with throughput for the twelve cylinder Gipsy King. *via British Aerospace*

Left: Tiger Moths ready for a day's work at an ERFTS managed by the Airwork company in Great Britain. Airwork was by far the largest civilian contractor with schools in operation at Perth, Castle Bromwich, Manchester (Barton), Gatwick, Gloucester and Cheltenham (Staverton), Grangemouth and Birmingham (Elmdon). *deHMC Archive*

Below: Bathed in pale winter sunshine Tiger Moths of No 1 ERFTS at Hatfield lined up in preparation for another duty day in 1937. Some of the aircraft are already painted in an early camouflage scheme. *Ben French*

Note quite in alphabetical order, three new Tiger Moths for the Midland Aero Club await delivery to their base at Castle Bromwich on 4 February 1939. That site would soon be more famous as a massive factory under the Nuffield Organisation, building Supermarine Spitfires and Avro Lancasters.
de Havilland Aircraft Company

Moths to train personnel from the Royal Navy Air Branch. Secret meetings held by the Air Council Committee on Supply were to agree that Hatfield had a major role to play with its current products, and that more Tiger Moths built to the standard specification, out of date, uncomfortable, under powered, lacking performance, and on its last legs, were needed as quickly as possible.

The Air Ministry became embroiled in a round of correspondence in April 1938 when Air Service Training (AST), ordered a trio of Tiger Moths for operation either at Hamble where they managed No 3 ERFTS or Ansty on behalf of 9 ERFTS. The Ministry advised de Havilland that in their tender to operate a Reserve School, AST had stipulated the use of Miles Magisters and asked Hatfield not to supply Tiger Moths against the threat of a refusal to recognise the order. AST countered that their submission had been against 'aircraft of an approved type'. The Tiger Moths were not delivered. The loss of a potential order for three aeroplanes might have caused greater concern had not Frank Hearle reported to his fellow directors on 27 May 1938 that the company was to be in imminent receipt of a contract to supply 400 Tiger Moths to the Air Ministry, the last of which was to be delivered by 30 September 1939. Notice of confirmation of no additional requirement beyond 400 was to be posted not later than 31 March.

In July 1938, de Havilland Aircraft of Canada placed an order with Stag Lane for fifty Gipsy Major engines to be delivered as sub-assemblies and suggested that a further fifty were in prospect. Deliveries were promised from September starting at two engine sets per week but soon rising to four. Slightly later than forecast, the first fifteen kits for Canada were despatched in October with fifteen more the following month. In August 1938 the Air Ministry's concurrent order for Miles Magisters resulted in the Engine Division receiving a revised contract for the supply of Gipsy Majors increasing the requirement from 810 to 1,020.

Tiger Moth fuselages under construction in the Downsview plant of de Havilland Aircraft of Canada. The shape of the middle decking on fuselages furthest from the camera identify them as DH.82C, following on from the orders already completed and exported to the parent company at Hatfield.
de Havilland Aircraft of Canada

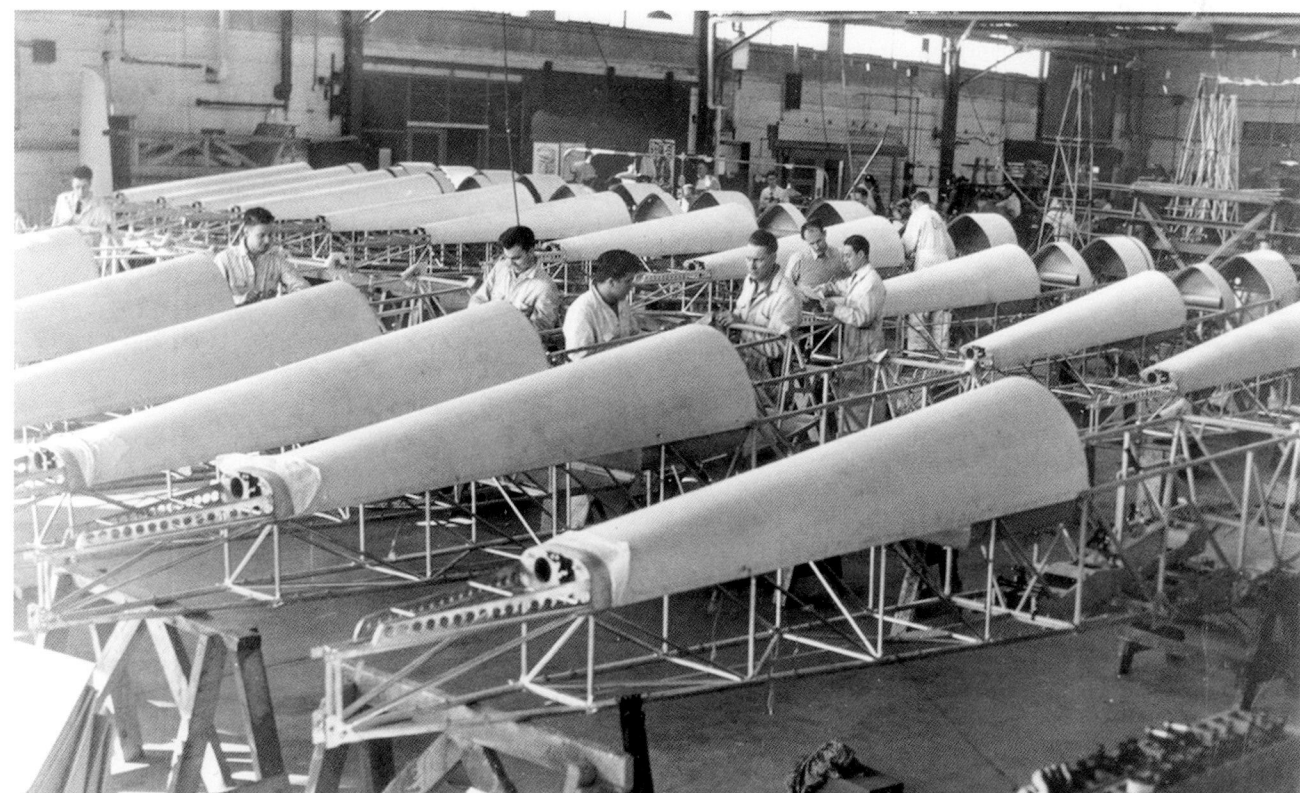

de Havilland DH.82A Tiger Moth, G-AELB, Merseyside Aero and Sports Co Ltd trading as Liverpool and District Aero Club, 1936-39. Yellow overall with silver undersides of wings, tailplane and fin/rudder. Yellow/green trim on vertical tail surfaces. Green registration on fuselage sides, black under lower wings. The aircraft was impressed as AX781 in August 1940 but was broken up for spares in September 1941. *Artwork ©Richard Caruana, 1:72 scale*

At a required average production rate of twenty five aircraft per month it was impossible for Hatfield to fulfil the Tiger Moth contract without assistance and the Air Ministry agreed to allow de Havilland's Associated Company in Canada to provide metal parts from its factory at Downsview, Toronto, assuming the need not to increase the workforce there. Hatfield was to source a major woodworking company who, under de Havilland control and supervision, could produce high quality sub contract work, graduating towards manufacture of complete aircraft.

As an interim measure the Air Ministry placed an order with de Havilland in May 1938 for the supply of fifty Tiger Moths to be built against contract 778402/38, and extended this the following month by a firm order for the 400 machines alluded to by Frank Hearle against a schedule which required delivery of twenty in December 1938, thirty in January 1939, thirty six in February and each month thereafter until completion, and assumed Canadian participation.

Frank Hearle advised the Ministry that the aircraft with Canadian components would be 30% to 40% more expensive than a pure Hatfield product on the grounds of freight charges alone: an estimated increase in cost of between £600 and £800 per airframe. This revelation brought only another question: "can you make fifty Tiger Moths a month?" The Air Ministry was now looking towards an anticipated requirement for 896 training aircraft in addition to those already contracted, and were beginning to believe that these numbers would provide such an ample margin over Hatfield's capacity to supply as to be of real interest to an outside contractor.

The company was pleased to have the immediate order for fifty Tiger Moths as it plugged a gap in the current schedule of work and prevented a prospective loss of labour which even on a temporary basis at a time of growing crisis was barely imaginable. An order for 200 Airspeed Oxfords to be built at Hatfield was also secured in May 1938 for delivery by March 1940, much to the displeasure of the Airspeed Company who adopted an uncooperative attitude. Hatfield was permitted to increase floor space by the addition of a new shed of 80,000sq.ft. and abandoned plans to develop the wooden DH.91 Albatross as a high speed bomber, although not the concept. The additional Tiger Moth orders also appeared to put an end to speculation that the Air Ministry was considering purchase of the North American NA-16. The government's own advisors had already suggested that at such a time the British aircraft industry would hardly welcome any further interest in that direction.

Such momentous activity made the Coventry Aeroplane Club's order for a single Tiger Moth, G-AFHI (3682), delivered to Whitley in May, look rather insignificant but the Air Ministry eventually had that too, impressed into military service just over two years later. G-AFHT (3695), was another refugee from the immediate pre-war flying club movement which was just managing to drag itself out of recessionary times to re-equip. Delivered to the Merseyside Aero and Sports Company Ltd. in July 1938 for operation by Liverpool Aero Club from Hooton Park, and painted in the traditional colours of yellow fuselage with silver wings, the aircraft was impressed exactly two years later, survived the war, including eight years with the Royal Navy, and was sold to New Zealand in 1952 where she crashed ten months after arrival.

Encouraged by the Air Ministry's massive order against a strict timetable, the company put up its own proposal for a follow-on run of 500 additional Tiger Moths and also solicited further enquiries from any quarter. Although the political situation in the world at large was deteriorating there was always hope that diplomatic efforts would reverse the trend and it was essential that civil and commercial lines of business were maintained. The London Aeroplane Club and Liverpool Aero Club both enquired after additional Tiger Moths in July, and from Syria a request to tender against the provision of twenty touring aircraft was met by the offer of civil specification Tiger Moths, and refused. Hatfield admitted that even with the current level of commitment to the Air Ministry, it could still squeeze in one 'independent' order each week.

Tiger Moth G-ADLZ (3362), fresh from the factory and with a C of A dated 16 August 1935, left Hatfield in the early hours seven days later bound for Lympne. The famous grass aerodrome on the south coast of England had, in course of its rich history, despatched and received many record breaking flights and provided a safe haven for ever optimistic or totally exhausted light aeroplane pilots. G-ADLZ was using Lympne as a stepping off point before crossing the English Channel bound for Brussels, Cologne and Frankfurt where pilot Hugh Buckingham was scheduled to spend the night. The following day the aircraft flew via Linz, Vienna and Budapest to Belgrade, and on the third day, 25 August, travelling via Skopje and Salonica she touched down at her destination, Athens, after a total flight time of twenty one hours. During the course of the next six weeks, 'Jimmy' Buckingham lived in the Air Force Mess where he was introduced to some extraordinary drinking games, but still managed to accumulate more than twenty eight hours of test and demonstration flying. The end result was nothing; the authorities decided to buy the Avro Cadet instead, a decision they were later to regret.

Having travelled deep into the Balkans, G-ADLZ was required to fly on to Turkey, demonstrating at Ankara on 10 October and flying more than ten hours at Eskisehir during a week's stay. No sales resulted. The aircraft was delivered back to Heston rather than Hatfield, arriving on 31 October, operating from Frankfurt via Brussels in two sectors of more than three hours each. In spite of the pilot acting as his own operations staff and engineer it was an expensive trip, logging 100 flying hours alone.

G-ADLZ joined the de Havilland fleet at White Waltham operating in support of 13 ERFTS until she was impressed as BB752 in October 1940. In June 1941 the aircraft was transferred to 21 EFTS Booker, and on 28 January 1942 suffered engine failure during take off from the Relief Landing Ground (RLG) at Garston, stalling into the ground from 30ft and sustaining damage which was not considered economical to repair.

Hugh Buckingham's demonstration in Athens did leave one good impression. Amongst the Tiger Moths ordered in July 1938 was one listed under 'Private Club Greece'. The aircraft, SX-AAK (3721), had been sold to Sqn Ldr Stephan T Zotos of Athens, a retired Greek Air Force officer, and although the British airworthiness certificate was dated 27 September 1938, there are no records to confirm that the aircraft was ever delivered although she was reported to have been seen in Paris in August 1939 and in a dismantled condition at Hatfield the following October. In April 1940, the registered ownership was changed to Technical and Aeronautical Exploitations Ltd. (TAE), a company owned by Stephan Zotos, and through which he was trying to persuade the Greek Government to establish a fully fledged Air Force Reserve based on the operating principles established by the British. Zotos knew the Greek Air Force was keen to be rid of its expensive-to-run Avro Cadets, an aircraft not liked by instructors, and which could easily be replaced by more economical Tiger Moths.

de Havilland backed the plan as an important entree. Zotos was a most valued ally, having bought his own demonstration aircraft, and there was no coincidence in the fact that he and the company's Greek agent, Mr Coutroubie, were at Hatfield together when the Tiger Moth order had been placed. They returned to Greece in Sqn Ldr Zotos' new Hornet Moth, SX-AAI, also destined for ownership by TAE before her impressment into local and emergency service with the Royal Air Force in 1941. Any record of SX-AAK held on file in Athens was lost after the Italian invasion in 1940. The Greek Air Force did receive Tiger Moths, eventually, although they had to wait until after the war was over.

Stephan Zotos would still have been on his protracted four week journey back to Athens, meandering across Europe in his Hornet Moth during the summer of 1938, when the British Air Ministry announced that 300 more Tiger Moths were to be added to the 450 of the current contract. At Hatfield, the de Havilland sales team was also receiving orders for the DH.94, now named Moth Minor, and inviting clubs and other bodies participating in the Civil Air Guard scheme to come and fly the new aeroplane although, due to its uncertificated status, this would have to be within the boundary of the airfield.

Although it was August the Hatfield works was hardly on summer holiday but only two Tiger Moths were delivered that month, one to New Zealand and the other to the Aero Club de Suisse, HB-OKU (3702), which was written off in a crash at Saleve within a few weeks of arrival and was not replaced. Much attention was being paid to the new DH.94 Moth Minor and 111 delivery positions were reserved during September, all but five from the home country and mostly in support of the Civil Air Guard initiative. Two Tiger Moths reserved for India were subsequently cancelled due to problems with payment; the customers had no money. Meanwhile in France, Costa de Beauregard, not in the least diverted by his contracted re-direction of Tiger Moths, nearly all of which had flown on to the conflict in Spain, was negotiating with the French Naval Air Service for the provision of thirty more, but the quoted delivery dates may not have been acceptable and no firm order was placed.

News that the British and Canadian Governments had been holding talks on the prospect of the Dominion providing facilities for a substantial military training programme soon reached the redoubtable Phil Garratt, General Manager of de Havilland Aircraft of Canada. Phil Garratt had received a copy of an RCAF specification for a proposed new training aircraft which, because of limited design capacity at Downsview, he had forwarded to Hatfield suggesting that it was very close to the company's own proposals in the shape of the DH.96. Phil Garratt was informed that in view of the workload then being experienced in England the DH.96 project had been dropped. The General Manager believed this was a serious mistake and confirmed that Fleet Aircraft were working on a trainer designed around the RCAF specification and which would, if successful, undoubtedly satisfy the Canadian market at least. He complained that the British company had invested too heavily in the DH.91 Albatross and DH.93 Don leaving him nothing to offer except the prospect of a few Moth Minors, and that for many reasons the DH.96 was urgently required. But his pleas were to no avail; at Hatfield the decision had been made and all work on the new trainer had been brought to a halt. As it transpired none of the aircraft designed and built in Great Britain to the same general specification as the proposed DH.96 was accepted by the Air Ministry. Following flight trials of those that were built all were rejected as unsuitable and the specification was allowed to lapse.

During the late summer of 1938 the Canadian company had asked Hatfield to investigate prospects for an uprated engine for Tiger Moth operations in Canada. The basic Gipsy Major I had already been developed into the 1C version specifically for Canada ('C' for Canada): domed pistons raised the compression ratio from 5.25 to 6:1, and aluminium alloy heads were fitted, a revived form of the old Gipsy I and Gipsy II heads but with an improved technique for inserting the valve seats. The engine was in most other respects identical to the Gipsy Major I, except that it could burn leaded fuel without fear of damage to the valve seats, and maximum power output was raised from 130bhp to 142bhp at little increase in turning speed and with a reduction in weight.

On 18 November 1938 approval was received for Hatfield to begin flight trials of a Tiger Moth fitted with a Gipsy Major Series II engine and Fairey Reed fixed pitch metal propeller. A review of airframe stressing suggested no changes were necessary except that the mounting had to be moved forward by two inches to provide clearance between the engine back cover and the fireproof bulkhead. Compared with a basic Gipsy Major I, the Series II engine had grown in weight by about 14lb and the metal airscrew was 18lb heavier than its wooden counterpart but, perversely, the increases were beneficial to the position of the centre of gravity (CG) which, other than in a fully loaded Tiger Moth, was near to the permitted aft limit.

As the result of research and laboratory analysis of vibration, many of the components in the Series II had been redesigned, and a stiffer crankshaft had been specified with a splined nose which could accept in addition to a fixed pitch propeller, a two pitch or constant speed unit. High compression pistons and new aluminium heads with increased fin area were fitted to permit a higher cruising output, and the crankcase was cast from Elektron magnesium alloy rather than aluminium in an effort to save weight. The timing gear cover on the back of the engine had been redesigned to accommodate a vacuum pump, double scavenge pump, a constant speed unit (governor) and a small generator. The forward shift of the mounting necessitated fitting a V bracing in the engine bay to cope with side and torsional loads which replaced the single diagonal brace acceptable on the Gipsy Major I. Other minor modifications were made to the oil system and exhaust manifold and the whole new installation was approved on 16 January 1939.

Conducting a vibration check on a running Gipsy Major engine at Hatfield. The aircraft is painted in the accepted pre-war style of semi-camouflage with large areas of 'sunshine' yellow dope to signify 'trainer'. *de Havilland Aircraft Company*

Downsview's orders for Gipsy Major 1C engines placed in July 1938 were in anticipation of a contract for 100 Tiger Moths expected to be placed shortly by the Canadian Government. At the beginning of August with no order confirmed Phil Garratt was in discussion with Hatfield concerning the prospects of his currently under-utilised factory capacity assisting with large orders for Tiger Moths then being contemplated in England. It was agreed that the best practical assistance from Downsview would be to supply 200 fuselages built to the British specification. A Canadian order, should it come, could not be satisfied concurrently within existing facilities and on 19 August Phil Garratt cabled Hatfield to request a substantial cash loan in order to undertake immediate plant extensions, the loan to be serviced by the shipment of Tiger Moth fuselages to England.

Hatfield was already showing concern over the financial state of the Canadian company and were interested to learn whether they were intending to make a profit on the prospective government order and if so, how much? When the order was completed would they find themselves with a surplus of personnel and other commitments? Lee Murray and Hatfield Chief Designer R E Bishop visited Canada to see for themselves and returned home feeling assured. The agreement for 200 fuselages and additional metal parts was confirmed, plus the approval for considerable modification and expansion of the Downsview plant into a facility which was described as having the capacity to produce 300-400 aircraft per annum. The building extension work was begun in September 1938 and completed in time for a Christmas dinner party and dance in one of the new shops on 23 December. After what must have been anxious times the anticipated order for Tiger Moths was placed by the government, but not until February 1940.

Downsview allocated build numbers E1-E200 to the fuselages scheduled for delivery to Hatfield beginning in the autumn of 1938, 'E' representing 'export' or 'England', perhaps? A photograph which appeared in the *de Havilland Gazette* for November 1938 was accompanied by a caption which indicated that the aeroplane-sized wooden crate being prised open in the rain by an extraordinarily tall man (for the benefit of the photographer no doubt), was the "first of many packages received from Canada containing Tiger Moth metal components."

Hatfield had shipped a DH.82A Tiger Moth to Downsview in 1935. Registered CF-AVG (3348), the aircraft was used for demonstrations and trials and in 1937, following some time with the RCAF, was dismantled. The Canadian fuselages despatched to Hatfield were manufactured against British drawings when pattern parts donated by CF-AVG were not available and were identified by the serial number, an inspection stamp and date all embossed on a small plate of about 1½ in by ½ in, most often tack welded onto the outer face of a front fuselage side frame and visible through a window sewn into the fabric covering. Inspection of the first units on arrival in England brought forth howls of anguish and pages of snag sheets which were expeditiously communicated to Downsview. Not unnaturally Canada was far from amused but Chief Designer Don Long was summoned to Hatfield in December to defend his company and explain the situation. Six months later similar problems arose when Morris Motors suffered slings and arrows after building fuselages to drawings supplied from Hatfield.

Posed for the benefit of the PR photographer and enlisting the tallest man working on the Hatfield site, attention is paid to one of a stream of boxes delivered from Toronto each containing at least one and probably two complete Tiger Moth fuselages and other parts. *de Havilland Aircraft Company*

G-AJOA was one of the first British based Tiger Moths to be fitted with a tailwheel and parking brake after the new owner of Fairoaks Aerodrome decided he did not approve of skids tearing up his grass. During a major overhaul in 1990 evidence was found that suggested the rear fuselage had once been exchanged with that from another aircraft, a frame manufactured in Canada. *Peter March*

In his logbook entries for 1939, amongst seventy nine individual Tiger Moth production test flights, de Havilland test pilot Lionel 'Wilf' Clark noted 'DH.82C' against just three: N9266 (82367), N9305 (82386), and N9452 (82506). Had the Flight Test foreman tipped him off about Canadian components or was the 'C' just the slip of a busy pen?

Hatfield absorbed the fuselages into their production schedules for 400 aircraft built between November 1938 and June 1939 (commencing 3773); 300 aircraft between July 1939 and January 1940 (commencing 82227), and another 400 aircraft between December 1939 and May 1940 (commencing 82551). Hatfield build positions 82599 to 82692 inclusive were never allocated any identity (on paper) giving some authority to a belief that they were reserved for Canadian imports and the order for all 200 fuselages was never fulfilled. This is almost certainly not the case. However, there is an anomaly in the 1939/1940 sequence. Aircraft 82554 was issued with serial R4751 and taken on RAF charge on 11 January 1940; 82693, the first aircraft identified after the blank spaces on the production lists, was issued with consecutive RAF serial R4752 and taken on charge on 13 February 1940 as part of the continuation of Air Ministry contract 20916/39. The twenty positions from 82555 were engineless fuselages for Australia followed by 82575 to 82598 which were all built to civilian specification for owners in Great Britain, India and Southern Rhodesia, a total of twenty four aircraft. All of these twenty four were issued with Certificates of Airworthiness between April and August 1939, that is several months before completion of the military aircraft that bracketed them. One of the possibilities for the apparent anomaly is that positions 82599 to 82692 were reserved for pre-war civilian orders that were not forthcoming and the military sequence was resumed from 82693, continuing until June 1940, punctuated by small batches allocated to France, India, Iraq, New Zealand and South Africa.

During subsequent major overhaul or repair of Hatfield built Tiger Moths close scrutiny has revealed a number of Canadian inspection plates attached to fuselages from a build sequence which would indicate that the 200 fuselage contract was fully serviced. RAF Tiger Moth N6478 (3815), taken on charge in December 1938, carried a plate to identify her as E17; in November 1990 a major overhaul of G-AJOA (83167), revealed a docket lodged in the rear fuselage which proved the assembly to be of Canadian manufacture and originally allocated to N6588 (3889), a Hatfield assembled aircraft of February 1939. During the mid-1980s a bare fuselage was exported from Australia to Canada which carried a plate identifying it as 'E75', possibly one of the 100 aircraft consignment shipped from the RAF's Strategic Reserve in 1940. Hatfield supplied an engineless fuselage, 82562, as part of the order for kits to enable the line at Mascot to get started in 1939. The completed aircraft was taken onto RAAF charge as A17-8 in July 1939. On her civil registration as VH-RAW in 1957 her build number was notified as 'DHC-78' which was accepted as a corruption of her RAAF serial but it is much more likely that her fuselage was actually E78, a fact that must have been recorded somewhere.

G-AFSU (82588), carried the identification E104 and a date, 27 January 1939; the aircraft had qualified for a C of A in the following July. RAF T6365 (84739), a Morris Motors' product of 1941, was found to be carrying a plate embossed with E122 and dated February 1939, a clear case of identity exchange at some time in her career and E143 was allocated to N6948 (82196), taken on charge on 13 July 1939. The highest referenced example which adds to the argument that the contract was fulfilled is E190. The frame dated 4 May 1939 was built into N9372 (82442), taken on charge on 27 October 1939. All of these identified serials fall before the block of Hatfield's unallocated build numbers.

The year 1938 ended with a flurry of activity: during the last quarter thirty four Tiger Moths were ordered including twenty kits of 'fuselages and metal parts' listed against build numbers 82555-82574 scheduled for completion by de Havilland in Australia where they were to be fitted with Gipsy Major Series II engines, and 102 aircraft were delivered of which eighty were for the Air Ministry. British based flying clubs continued to show interest as did those in New Zealand and India where a scheme of government subsidies was being proposed. The Iranian Army said it wanted another twenty aircraft and placed a firm order in January; the Port of Spain Aero Club booked two for operation in the Caribbean. The Midland Aero Club at Castle Bromwich asked for a reservation on six on the grounds that they were unable to wait for delivery of Moth Minors, but a month later when confirming the Tiger Moth order, they declared their intention to take five Moth Minors too.

With the continued growth of the de Havilland Aircraft Company, John Parkes was promoted to the position of General Manager of the Engine Division at Stag Lane (it would become a separate company in 1944) and Lee Murray to a parallel situation within the aircraft factory at Hatfield, succeeding Frank Hearle who was appointed Managing Director of the Company with effect from the beginning of 1939. Critical timing allowed him to inherit guidance of the DH.95 Flamingo programme, the prototype of which had flown on 22 December 1938 and was the subject of intense promotional activity.

In January 1939 New Year discussions revolved around the company's anticipated programme for 1940. Following enormous increases in unrecoverable development costs incurred by the Aircraft Division for the past several years, a situation likely to be balanced only by the substantial Air Ministry contracts currently going through the shops, it was planned to launch a major civil aircraft sales campaign which, if successful, would absorb 70% of available production capacity and to fill the remaining 30% with Air Ministry orders against a limited but guaranteed profit. Sights were set on the sale of fifty DH.95 Flamingos, twelve DH.91 Albatross, forty DH.89 Dragon Rapides and at least 250 DH.94 Moth Minors. Continuance of the current production contract for Oxfords would be sought although the type was on the prohibited export list which restricted any extension of sales other than to the Air Ministry. The Tiger Moth remained in the mind of the company very much as a 'military contract' aeroplane, and was useful to balance the loss of Oxford export opportunities. "From that point of view it is very desirable that we should maintain a good production of Tiger Moths or its successor," wrote Lee Murray. It was essential that an early decision be made regarding the 1940 programme, he urged the Directors, both from a production point of view and in formulation of design policy.

Encouraged by the Directorate of Civil Research and Production, by mid-February the company was actively considering involvement in another new project, a small twin to accommodate perhaps eight or ten passengers, and the study had already been allocated an identity, DH.97. Much as he was in favour, and concerned that a rival manufacturer might take up the specification and compete in the markets currently and adequately satisfied by the Dragon Rapide, St Barbe still believed that for business reasons, amongst others, a new training aircraft was more urgently required.

The New Year order book was primed and expectant when news was received that five Tiger Moths were required in Java (Netherlands East Indies) for the earliest possible delivery in 1939, and the de Havilland agents in Bandoeng, Rous and Meeuwenoord, were cabled from Hatfield offering one delivery position in March, April and May and two in June. In return, Hatfield was advised that Bücker in Germany were offering delivery three weeks following receipt of order and their quotation was 30% below de Havilland's published list price. Nothing more was heard until March when Hatfield was advised that the order would definitely be placed with Bücker on the grounds of better delivery, price and payment terms. The Bücker offer had resulted in an affordable order which for the same cash sum would now provide six machines.

But the East Indies were to have Tiger Moths; five aircraft were delivered to the Northern Aviation School and Club at Barton in August 1939, two weeks before war was declared: G-AFTI (82233), G-AFXZ (82234), G-AFYB (82593), G-AFYC (82594), and G-AFZD (82595). All escaped immediate impressment but were sold to aircraft brokers W S Shackleton Ltd., operating from their London office in Piccadilly. G-AFZD was flown to the de Havilland Civil Repair Unit (CRU) at Witney on 6 July 1940 where she was converted to South African Air Force specification and crated for despatch in September. The remaining four aircraft from Barton were shipped to the Netherlands East Indies, arriving in August 1940, two months later than planned due to problems with the issue of export licences. Assistance in this matter was volunteered by Jonkheer Krayerhoff, one time chairman of the Soerabaja Flying Club, and conveniently positioned in London working with Royal Dutch Shell. The aircraft were scheduled for operation by flying clubs scattered through the islands and had been paid for by the Netherlands Indies Aviation Fund. Three aircraft had been sought but the Fund was adequately solvent and provided finance for four. More than fifty additional Tiger Moths were ordered from Australia in 1941, and subsequently led dramatic lives.

The DH.91 Albatross was caught in the spotlight as the result of an undercarriage failure in public at Croydon and subsequent temporary grounding of the fleet. Maintaining composure the Hatfield Public Relations Office reported that it had supplied photographs 'of a Tiger Moth (with girl)' at the request of a printing house to illustrate a calendar which, hopefully, was scheduled for 1940 publication. The Sales Department bagged a pair of Tiger Moths, one each for India and New Zealand, in addition to the orders for the Midland Club and Iran (twenty eight for the month) and was delighted to take deposits on another sixty seven Moth Minors.

Planning stability was vital to Lee Murray's perception of the company's future programme and he teased out some of the views of the Aeronautical Inspection Directorate (AID) at a meeting in March 1939. Although discussions were wide ranging, considerable time was spent on the subject of the Tiger Moth, development or replacement? Colonel Harold Outram, Director of AID, commented that prospects for the continuance of the Tiger Moth programme would be greatly enhanced if the company could offer a version with a bigger cockpit and an improvement in the efficiency of its production. The possibility of a larger engine was also discussed, a six cylinder in preference to the Gipsy Major, or perhaps the Series II which was then engaged in flight trials.

G-AFGZ was registered to the de Havilland Company in May 1938 for operation by No 13 ERFTS at White Waltham. She was militarised in 1940 and after White Waltham had been allocated to the ATA as headquarters and the school closed down, the aircraft joined the Royal Navy until the end of the war. *Barry Dowsett*

No trace seems to have survived of records surrounding experiments with a rocket propelled Tiger Moth which were conducted in Scotland by a group of model aircraft engineers some time after 1934, most probably in 1938 or 1939. Their interest had been kindled by reports that a schoolboy living in Glasgow had, in 1920, flown a 4ft span model aircraft a distance of three miles in one minute: an average speed of 180mph. The powerplant was a crude rocket motor mounted on a cardboard tube fuselage and the implications of the feat had been largely ignored until the group of five engineers, one of whom had been working on a military rocket programme, combined their talents and were able to use sparsely inhabited areas of Sutherland and Cumberland, testing devices on bicycles and operating from the surface of Loch Lomond with rowing boats and float equipped models. They even laid a concrete track with a diameter of 60ft for captive trials on which speeds of up to 200mph were claimed to have been achieved.

The group turned its attentions to full size aircraft when they proved to their own satisfaction that skilfully designed and made 'ejectors' were more efficient than airscrews, and that it was perfectly possible to scale up their experiments, either to consider aircraft operating at very high speed (over 1,000mph) when rocket propulsion was at its most efficient but sadly outside their level of resource, or to harness thrust to provide what they described as 'really useful acceleration'.

Against this latter principle, a re-usable rocket motor and ejector were designed for trials to accelerate a Tiger Moth into the air. The device was 11ft long and 22in in diameter, and weighed 34lb including a 1lb charge of explosive fuel. Measured thrust was 150lb up to a speed of 50mph, falling to 100lb at 100mph. Cost per launch was estimated at about 1s.8d. There is no evidence to assume that the motor detached after its fuel was exhausted.

Regrettably, no performance figures have been found nor other details of any modifications to the basic Tiger Moth airframe which allowed it to absorb the slam accelerations which it obviously endured. Who sanctioned the rocket assisted take-off tests, where were they undertaken and whose aeroplane was used? The questions remain unanswered, but the experimenters are reported to have said that when faced with the test results in 1939 the Air Ministry classified them as being of 'low value'.

The views of the AID were evidently taken to heart for during 1939 the company prepared a scheme for a DH.82B Tiger Moth which incorporated answers to all the major criticisms of the DH.82 and DH.82A. The fuselage was widened by about 4in to offer more shoulder room for the crew and a larger fin and horn balanced rudder were designed to provide inherent stability. Elevator trim tabs and horn balances were installed to improve aerodynamic fore and aft trim, replacing the crude but cheap and effective method of spring tensioning applied to the control column. The most important airframe upgrade was perhaps the design of a Hornet Moth style undercarriage, offering a track wider by about 8in and with the wheels set further forward to permit functional cable operated brakes, augmented by a tailwheel, a configuration long sought by the overseas agents. Power was provided by a Gipsy Major IIA engine.

At a time of considerable development within the Engine Division, and continuing investigation of the Gipsy Major Series II, another experimental powerplant was the Gipsy Major IIA, forerunner of the Gipsy Major III scheduled for the Queen Bee, which produced 160bhp at 2,500rpm, and was different in having both magnetos mounted on top of the Elektron crankcase. Had the project reached maturity, the Gipsy Major III, a four cylinder engine and itself a predecessor of the supercharged military specification Gipsy Major 10 developed for use in the Saunders-Roe Skeeter helicopter, might have been chosen for the proposed new trainer airframe against the trend which popularly assumed a six cylinder powerplant. The moderate increase in power of the Gipsy Major II or III series engines was considered sufficient for the immediate needs.

The Gipsy Major IIA was described in a secret document dated 15 September 1942, and written by Hatfield's Public Relations Manager, Martin Sharp, as "a lash-up to obtain the power output of the proposed Gipsy Major III but using modified Gipsy Major II components." The Gipsy Major IIA engine had been civil type approved to permit Phillips and Powis to fly it in Miles M.18 and M.28 trainer prototypes, and a third engine had been installed for trials in Captain de Havilland's DH.85 Leopard Moth G-ACKP. Apart from those few and the engine fitted to the sole DH.82B, it is believed only one other unit was built.

The installation required mounting the engine 8in further forward when compared with the standard Gipsy Major I, not only in an effort to restore or improve fore and aft balance but to accommodate the redesigned timing gear cover. Production aircraft were planned to carry a larger capacity fuel tank to maintain endurance otherwise reduced by the increased consumption of the new engine.

Very little is known about the DH.82B Tiger Moth, a designation often and erroneously applied to the DH.82 Queen Bee, apart from the fact that the aircraft was first weighed on 30 September 1939 and subsequently flown by several Hatfield test pilots. The one prototype

Unpainted Tiger Moths and Queen Bees covering the assembly floor at Hatfield, summer 1939. Note DH.89 Dragon Rapides against the far wall, and Airspeed Oxfords to the right. The three aircraft nearest the camera have airframe and engine numbers chalked on the rudders: 82115/82517; 82116/82511 and 82117/82515, just to prove how confusing the similarity in block serials could be. *British Aerospace*

aircraft was allocated a construction number, 1989, and flight tested at Hatfield using the Class II markings E.11. Carrying this identity the aircraft was flown by de Havilland test pilot Lionel 'Wilf' Clark on 1 October 1939 who clearly labelled the aeroplane as a DH.82B in his log book, and added the note 'Production test. Elevator'.

As a young man from the Aerodynamics Department, David Newman remembers watching the DH.82B as it landed after its first flight. One of the elevators had broken up due to what was assumed to have been flutter, possibly associated with the introduction of a trimmer built into the trailing edge, and the aircraft touched down with the elevator reduced to a spar and some stumps of the rib caps. Chief Aerodynamicist Richard Clarkson subsequently worked on a layout for a revised Tiger Moth empennage although he recoiled from the suggestion that he had 'designed' it.

In other respects, trials are believed to have been considered successful. A new weighing report was compiled on 11 January 1940 and Geoffrey de Havilland Jnr flew the aeroplane again on 16 and 18 January, on at least two occasions in March and once in May. There is only one further entry for the type in Wilf Clark's logbook, that for 8 May 1940 when the note reads 'Experimental. To 12,000ft'. Twelve days later she was flown by Geoffrey Pike for flow tests assisted by Pat Fillingham.

Improvements over the standard Tiger Moth were certainly considered worthwhile, but the more pressing need for immediate, high volume production of a primary trainer overtook the need for refinement. The eventual sub-contract to Morris Motors coupled with acceleration of the Mosquito programme brought the DH.82B project to a premature end in 1940 and the aircraft was scrapped.

In hindsight it would appear that Lee Murray was never entirely convinced of the need for an improved trainer, Tiger Moth or otherwise, especially when the factory was already working at almost full capacity, for he queried the real need for wheel brakes, tailwheel, coupe top and cabin heater. The Air Ministry had not said they would stop buying the currently configured aircraft unless and until it was improved, neither had they confirmed additional orders if it were. Should the refinements be considered necessary, he proposed a Canadian example be imported for test purposes. No evidence suggests that this was ever done. As if to emphasise the point of the argument to leave well alone, a record number of sixty five Tiger Moths was delivered during March 1939, fifty one of which were for the Air Ministry, and eleven new orders were received, all for overseas customers.

In April 1939 the Air Council decided that following a general review of the state of the aircraft industry, the de Havilland Aircraft Company required more orders to be placed for Tiger Moths or Oxfords, using as its gauge for commitment a date some nine months prior to the estimated completion of current contracts. The orders would be part of an immediate £30M production plan authorised by the Treasury in a bid to provide 1,000 aircraft prior to the prospect of war breaking out in 1940. The Treasury had agreed in 1938 that as far as budget sanctions were concerned, a Tiger Moth and other trainers should count only as half of one aircraft unit. By July 1939 the 1,000 aircraft production plan had been increased to 2,400, of which 650 were anticipated to be trainer types. Two days before war was declared, the Air Council was advised that Tiger Moth production capacity under current circumstances could not be greater than ninety aircraft per month. Three weeks later the same body was reviewing the requirements of trainer aircraft by types for inclusion in a total production programme of 2,000 aircraft per month supplemented by 250 aircraft per month supplied by the Dominions. On 23 September 1939 the committee decided that an immediate order should be placed with de Havilland for the supply of a further 1,000 Gipsy Major engines.

Over a period of some years under a scheme initiated by Sir Ernest Lemon, a man who previously had worked near miracles by massive re-organisation of supply and production within the British railway industry, the Air Ministry had championed the cause for heavy sub contracting of all aircraft component parts, ensuring that manufacturers received supplies from at least one alternative source. Ernest Lemon's investigations had revealed that aircraft manufacturers tended to want to make every component part themselves on their own main factory sites and each individual machine was essentially hand-made under regimes and practices that were simply not geared for mass production. As early as 1933 the de Havilland Company had found it necessary to approve an alternative supplier for Tiger Moth undercarriage compression legs (shock absorber struts) and new internally sprung units were eventually sourced from Aircraft Components Ltd., a Dowty-owned company based in Cheltenham. The new multi-spring legs replaced the original design of rubber blocks in compression, a feature revived when purity and simplicity was being sought in support of the DH.98 Mosquito design programme.

To clear their own decks for receipt of Air Ministry contracts, de Havilland nominated Morris Motors as a company capable of accepting the mantle of sub-contractor to the British Tiger Moth programme, not merely to make components but to take responsibility for manufacture and assembly of whole aircraft. Why should not the principles of mass motor production, or at least some of them, be applied to the quantity and quality construction of a basic aeroplane too?

With war declared the camouflage scheme applied to Tiger Moths ex-factory deleted the all yellow tail surfaces and wing tips. Three aircraft await collection from Hatfield on a frosty morning, 10 January 1940. *de Havilland Aircraft Company*

CHAPTER FIVE

An Acceleration of Effort

The immense effort of Hatfield's DH.91 Albatross programme had resulted in a total of seven aeroplanes; DH.95 Flamingo production reached sixteen. Both aircraft types served their country well and the Flamingo would, without doubt, have been a commercial success had its arrival on the scene not coincided with a world in turmoil. The DH.93 Don was unsuited to most of its specified tasks and the anticipated order for 250 was reduced to fifty, and twenty of those were delivered as incomplete and engineless shells for technical training purposes. The Hatfield workforce was seriously concerned about a large scale layoff, and when thirty of the shop floor staff were given notice on the grounds that they were 'not required', representations were made in July 1939 directly to the Air Minister, Sir Kingsley Wood, citing any 'discharge of labour' as having very serious repercussions at a time of gathering uncertainty. Had none of these aircraft programmes been so demanding, would an improved Tiger Moth have been developed, or possibly an entirely new aircraft designed as a replacement, both options discussed so often at the Hatfield board meetings? Would either or both have been available or suitable for accelerated mass production when the need arose?

Above: The allocation of space for a task within any factory needs careful planning. By April 1939 the pace of production of Tiger Moths at Hatfield was accelerating but having to share resources with contracted manufacture of Airspeed Oxfords. Work on this ordered line of Tiger Moth fuselages progressed away from the camera. To ensure maximum use of available space each mainwheel is located on a spot painted on the floor. *BAE Systems*

Right: Interim camouflage colours had been applied to aircraft with No 1 ERFTS at Hatfield by January 1939 when this shot was taken of Tiger Moth G-ACDG, CFI Clem Pike and one of his instructors in their military style de Havilland uniforms. *de Havilland Aircraft Company*

When a state of war was declared between Great Britain and Germany on 3 September 1939 some 1,300 Tiger Moths had been built in eight years at Stag Lane and Hatfield, of which the Hertfordshire factory alone had delivered 660 in 1939. Until September the Air Ministry had administered 35 Elementary and Reserve Flying Training Schools (ERFTS) managed and operated under contracts let to civilian companies throughout the country and which, under a preconceived plan, were immediately re-organised into 20 Elementary Flying Training Schools (EFTS) where all matters were conducted in accordance with King's Regulations. Instructors took RAF rank and uniform and aeroplanes with civil registrations were 'impressed' into Crown service and allocated military serial numbers under Air Ministry Directive 364041/34/CH8 (d). Distinctive colours, proudly worn as emblems of their school parentage, gradually disappeared under coats of camouflage dope, often hastily applied by brush during scheduled maintenance checks.

When Tiger Moth G-AHVU was rebuilt at Farnborough in 1983 research on colours turned up this faded pre-war camouflage scheme. Spin strakes were not valid for the period but were still the subject of confusion within the airworthiness authorities and had to be carried. *deHMC Archive*

A year after painting in her faded camouflage scheme, and as the result of many enquiries asking whether the yellow rudder was a temporary replacement, it was decided to camouflage it too. In the original RAF scheme the tailplane and elevators would have been yellow also. *deHMC Archive*

To assist the Airspeed Company with production of wooden Oxford twin engine trainers, de Havilland had accepted an Air Ministry contract to build the aircraft at Hatfield and completed an initial batch of 150 in 1939. Towards the end of the year contracts for the supply of large numbers of Tiger Moths were being discussed, and de Havilland recommended that their sub-contracted Oxford production be transferred to a new shadow factory established at their Scottish aerodrome at Grangemouth, mid-way between Edinburgh and Glasgow. The Air Ministry rejected the offer and a further 1,290 Oxfords were constructed at Hatfield before their place was taken by a wooden twin of greater potency, the DH.98 Mosquito. From May 1940 Hatfield was in receipt of damaged Hawker Hurricanes and Rolls-Royce Merlin engines at an increasing rate, all seeking rapid and urgent repair and return to service. Moth Minor production had already been shut down and materials, tools, jigs, engines and incomplete aircraft packed off to the Australian company at Mascot near Sydney. Hundreds of orders were left unfulfilled although the majority, all connected with the Civil Air Guard, were negated by the declaration of war and the cancellation of the scheme.

In 1938 millionaire motor magnate Sir William Morris was elevated to the Peerage and, as Lord Nuffield, headed the 'Nuffield Organisation', a huge motor engineering conglomerate akin to de Havilland's own world-wide 'Enterprise'. One of Nuffield's companies, Wolseley Motors, had dabbled with aero engines but never quite managed to bracket power, size, weight and reliability with the rapid developments taking place in the airframe industry.

From the mid 1930s implementation of Ernest Lemon's government sponsored initiatives to disperse production by the creation of 'shadow factories' was gaining momentum. Lord Nuffield's 'Organisation' was approached to supervise the erection of a new plant at Castle Bromwich, near Birmingham, there to organise the mass production of Spitfires. Nuffield was reluctant to co-operate having developed a poor relationship with the incumbent Air Minister, Lord Swinton, as a result of receiving no recognition and no orders following considerable work on the development of the Wolseley Aero Engine Company's Scorpio and Leo. The factory was eventually built following persuasion from his own top management team, but Lord Nuffield refused absolutely for the Castle Bromwich works ever to be referred to as a 'shadow' factory, and in all official communication it was never called anything less than the Castle Bromwich Aeroplane Factory.

Following Sir Kingsley Wood's appointment as Secretary of State for Air and creation of the Ministry of Aircraft Production (MAP) under Lord Beaverbrook, Lord Nuffield was offered and accepted on 6 October 1939, without remuneration, the post of Director General of Repairs and Maintenance for the Royal Air Force with offices in London. He soon tired of the bureaucratic life-style and removed himself to his own office at the Morris Motors plant at Cowley, Oxford. His responsibilities as Director General were for the organisation of repair of aircraft and ancillary equipment for the RAF, and as far as facilities were concerned his brief was 'to make the fullest and most efficient use of industrial undertakings not engaged on essential production'.

Administered from Magdalen College, Oxford, the first Civil Repair Unit (CRU) of the Civil Repair Organisation (CRO), together with its associated salvage facility, was established at Cowley in September 1939 specifically to cater for fighter and trainer aircraft, and a number of badly damaged airframes were shipped in at an early stage for educational purposes. The de Havilland Service Department

Following declaration of war in September 1939, all civil registered Tiger Moths found suitable after technical inspection were gradually 'impressed' into military service, including the aircraft previously operated by the Reserve schools. Painted in the contemporary camouflage scheme, civil registrations were later changed to military serial numbers allocated from the batches specially created for impressed machines. G-ADWM was on establishment with 12 EFTS Prestwick where camouflage of the buildings was treated just as seriously. *C Nepean Bishop*

G-ADGG of 6 EFTS Sywell and two flight cadets, now in full RAF uniform and with sergeant's stripes. The mustard-yellow 'gas patch', with an orange border, on the top decking above the unit code '2', was supposed to change colour if the aircraft's surroundings were ever subjected to gas attack. *Richard Saward*

was moved from Hatfield to establish itself in the spring of 1940 at the old Witney Aerodrome, a few miles to the west of Oxford, where initially their priority task became the overhaul and repair of Spitfires and Hurricanes. Not unnaturally the site was soon also required to offer specialist services for most de Havilland light aeroplanes which had been enrolled into the war effort, breaking down many damaged airframes for the recovery of spare parts after production had been curtailed on the outbreak of war.

With normal business in terminal decline and before war contracts could be let, Morris Motors' 5,000 workforce had already been reduced by 2,000 and for the survivors' major re-direction was as welcome as it was inevitable. With Lord Nuffield's personal interest in tanks, aeroplanes and aero engines, and the clearest brief on industrial efficiency and essential production, consideration of the Morris Motors' Cowley works as an appropriate site at which to provide facilities for Tiger Moth manufacture was obvious should there be an evident necessity.

The Air Council promised Lee Murray in October 1939 that the de Havilland Company was shortly to receive contracts for the supply of 2,000 new Tiger Moths, and reservedly agreed that 1,000 of these could be sub-contracted to Morris Motors, but reminded the company of their current obligations for Oxford aircraft and completion of the last contracted Flamingos. It was suggested too that de Havilland should not lose sight of the provisioning of spare parts for some aircraft types still in worldwide use.

Hatfield, confident of its productive capability and anxious to retain as much business for itself as was practical, requested that it retain the right to export any production in excess of that required by the Air Ministry's contracted delivery schedule. This was agreed by the Air Council subject to the surplus production being no greater than 10% of the planned output, and that no exports would be permitted until the Air Ministry's requirement had been fully satisfied. It seemed to be a polite way of saying 'home team first'. St Barbe took up the matter again in November when his request that the Morris allowance be reduced to 900 aircraft was agreed. As events rapidly unfolded and changed, new situations were experienced with increasing frequency. After 3 September 1939 and until Morris Motors took complete charge of manufacture from June 1940, the total Hatfield contribution was restricted to an output of only 795 machines.

Two weeks after the declaration of war, Alan Butler in his capacity as Chairman of the de Havilland Aircraft Company Ltd., was minded to bring to the attention of the Air Minister that Hatfield Aerodrome and works had been provided with no defensive armament. The reason quoted by official channels for this apparent oversight was that the factory was 'only making training aircraft'. Alan Butler stressed the opinion that Tiger Moths today could become fighters and bombers tomorrow should vital production facilities elsewhere be 'knocked out' and this was the greatest possible case for a strong defence. Sir Kingsley Wood replied that there was an acute shortage of guns, but that he was looking into the supply of some light automatic weapons.

In the event, Hatfield Aerodrome was attacked, but on only one occasion: 3 October 1940. An opportunist Junkers Ju88 bounced four bombs from low level into the workshops recently vacated by the Moth Minor, and then full of Mosquito parts. The '94 Shop' was destroyed and twenty one people killed, but the intruder paid the price and was shot down by local defences, crashing into a field three miles to the south. In passive resistance, and with the intention of drawing attention away from the real site, the Relief Landing Ground (RLG) at Holwell Hyde, later known as Panshanger Aerodrome, was converted into an 'aircraft factory' with the creative aid of the film industry who built an expansive decoy structure which, to aerial reconnaissance, was indistinguishable from a productive unit. To add an air of authenticity a number of dummy aircraft and requisitioned civilian DH.60 Moths were picketed out but did not survive the rigours of the English climate for more than one winter.

At Hatfield, while design office capacity was available and desperately in need of a project, shop floor space was severely limited. The company was advised that Oxford production was to be given priority and there were suggestions (some believed threats) that the company might be required to build Armstrong Whitworth Albemarles, later changed to an agreed monthly output of 300 Vickers Wellingtons. Subsequently, in order for Hatfield to concentrate wholly on Mosquito matters, for which de Havilland were awarded a contract for a prototype and forty nine production models in March 1940, the company agreed to a total transfer of all Tiger Moth production on a sub-contract basis to Morris Motors. The aircraft were to be built at the Morris car factory at Cowley, just south of the university city of Oxford, commencing immediately and eight aircraft were required to be completed by the end of April 1940.

When allocating works' airframe construction numbers, the new de Havilland Aircraft Company Ltd. had, upon commencing operations at Stag Lane in September 1920, not unnaturally started at No 1. Strangely, this was a Hendon (Airco) built DH.18, G-EARI, fitted with a Napier Lion engine for service with Air Transport & Travel Ltd. (AT&T), and first flown under the test markings E.52. As additional shop floor projects were commissioned the numerical listing continued, taking in a range of DH.9 variants and a miscellany of other DH types until No 168 which was allocated to the first DH.60 Moth in 1925. From then until No 400, DH.60 Moths took the lion's share of positions, occasionally making way for a substantial run of DH.9 work but including DH.56, DH.61, DH.65, DH.66, DH.71, DH.72, DH.75 and DH.80.

Apart from numbers 704-710, allocated to a DH.9J, five DH.75 Hawk Moths and the unique DH Autogyro based on a DH.80 Puss Moth fuselage, DH.60 Moth build numbers run consecutively and uninterrupted until 1739, the first nominated DH.82, and from 1740 to 1927, the last DH.60G. Numbers 1988-1999 were allocated separately to 'special' projects: DH.100 light twin; DH.82B experimental Tiger Moth; DH.81 Swallow Moth, a Jaguar engined DH.9J, a quartet of DH.88 Comets, DH.87 Hornet Moth prototype, and the Technical School's T.K.2 and a hand made Tiger Moth.

With a range of new types becoming established and DH.60 production coming to a natural conclusion, it was decided to split the numbering sequences into easily recognisable groups. The 2000 block was allocated to the DH.80 Puss Moth (DH.86 from 2300 and Airspeed Oxford from 2400); 3000 to DH.82 Tiger Moth; 4000 to DH.83 Fox Moth; 5000 to DH.60GIII, Moth Major and Queen Bee; 6000 to DH.84 Dragon (DH.89 from 6250); 7000 to DH.85 Leopard Moth (DH.90 Dragonfly from 7500); 8000 to DH.87 Hornet Moth; 9000 to DH.93 Don and, somewhat confusingly, 9400 and 94000 to the DH.94 Moth Minor.

When DH.82A Tiger Moth allocation reached build number 3999 the opportunity was taken to start a new series, and the inspired figure was 82000. Gipsy Major engines manufactured by the Engine Division began their numeric sequences at 5000-5999, and 8000-8999 before adding a digit and starting again at 80000. This latter means of identification was to cause unforeseen confusion, especially during later civil operations when ex-military aircraft were occasionally and erroneously registered against their engine numbers. Engine production being speedier than airframe the allocation quickly 'caught up' with the Tiger Moth build positions, and RAF aircraft N9498 (82525), for example, was fitted with Gipsy Major I, engine number 82524. Acting in the capacity of sub-contractors to de Havilland, Morris Motors were not obliged to continue the numerical progression although they did.

It was agreed that the first Cowley aeroplane would be constructed against drawings supplied by Hatfield aided by component parts delivered from de Havilland and other major sub-contracted sources. The prototype Morris Tiger Moth was to be 83176, serial T7011, available for inspection from the beginning of April, followed by seven others which were expected to be cleared that month. Cowley was to take sole responsibility for production from June 1940.

Some of Cowley's first efforts in the manifested form of T7013 (83179) were the subject of critical analysis at Hatfield after the aircraft had been delivered there by road at the beginning of April. The Cowley line had been established and initial manufacture supervised by Hatfield staff with additional assistance drafted in from nearby Witney, and the report from A H Povey at Hatfield and addressed to Mr S V Smith, Works' Superintendent at Cowley, indicated that every inch of T7013 had been examined in minute detail, resulting in sixty seven observations worthy of comment.

Harry Povey, de Havilland's General Production Manager, had joined the Stag Lane Drawing Office in 1926 where he was responsible for the design of teak production jigs for the DH.60 Moth, a move not supported by the then Works' Manager, Frank Hearle, until the scheme had proved spectacularly efficient and effective. In 1928 Harry Povey succeeded Arthur Morse as Chief Inspector, and it was his ideas that were developed into concrete moulds for the manufacture of Mosquito half fuselages. His value to the company was recognised by promotion to the board of the de Havilland Aircraft Company in 1951.

It was Harry Povey's lot to advise S V Smith, a man with an iron fist reputation within the motor industry, of the Hatfield team's assessment. Mr Smith received the report with reasonable humour and replied to each of the sixty seven points by letter on 24 April, quoting A F Houlberg, Chief Inspector from the Aeronautical Inspection Directorate (AID) as his mentor. This was evidently a prudent move as the Works' Superintendent had already caused some dismay among the de Havilland advance party in claiming that the assembly of an aircraft should be treated no differently from that of a motor vehicle. Perhaps the eventual output of 3,210 Tiger Moths from Cowley in the next four years vindicated this philosophy to some degree, and assisted in his promotion by 1946 to the post of General Manager.

By September 1940 Tiger Moth production was well established in the Morris Motors' factory at Cowley. Applying mass production philosophy fuselages were mounted on wheeled frames that could easily be shifted to the next phase. *Morris Motors*

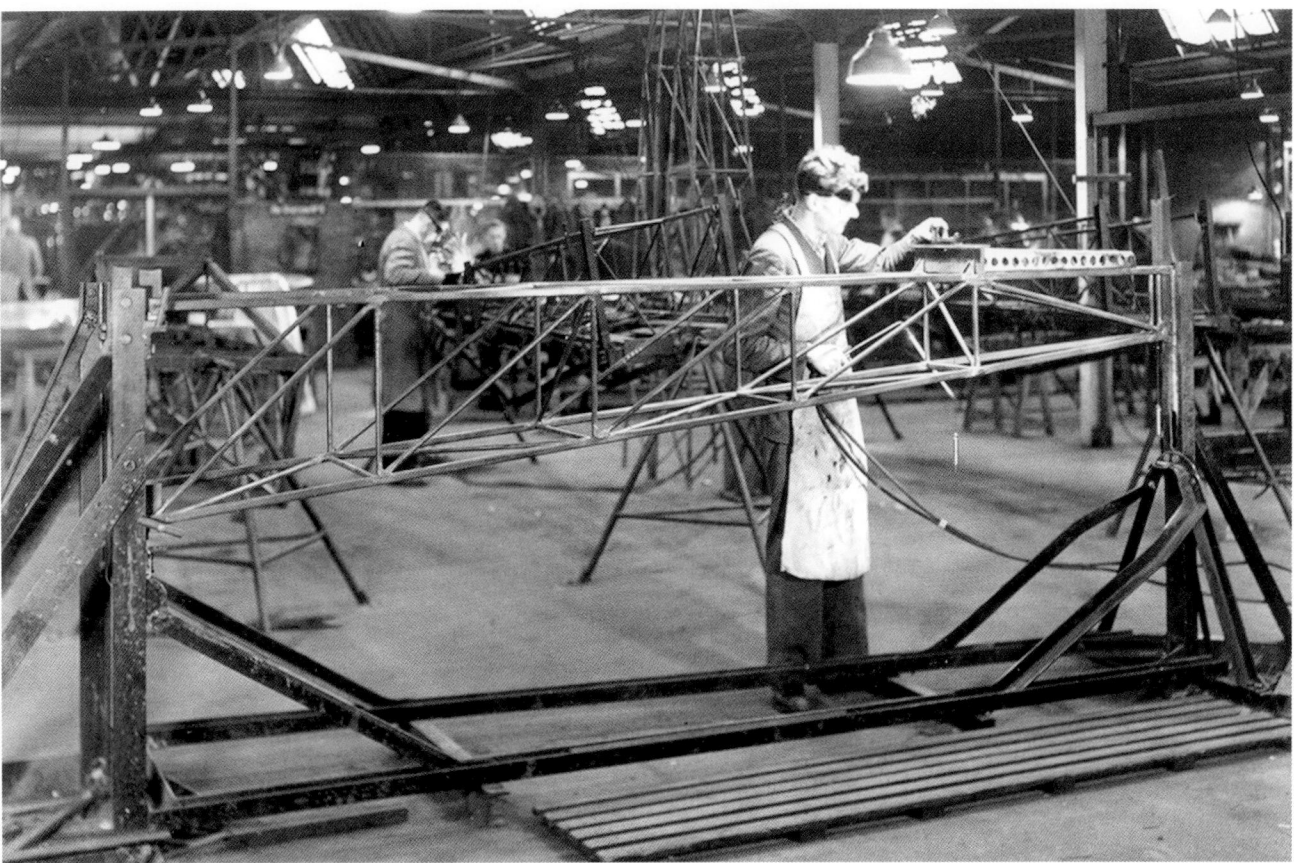

The Tiger Moth fuselage was designed as a series of separate components bolted together which could be quickly and easily removed and replaced for overhaul or repair. The rear fuselage pylon was constructed from round and square section Reynolds T45 steel tubing welded in a jig. *Morris Motors*

Front fuselage handed sideframes were jig drilled to provide pick up points for fittings and accessories. The correct positioning of each hole was critical in what was the most highly stressed area of the whole structure. *Morris Motors*

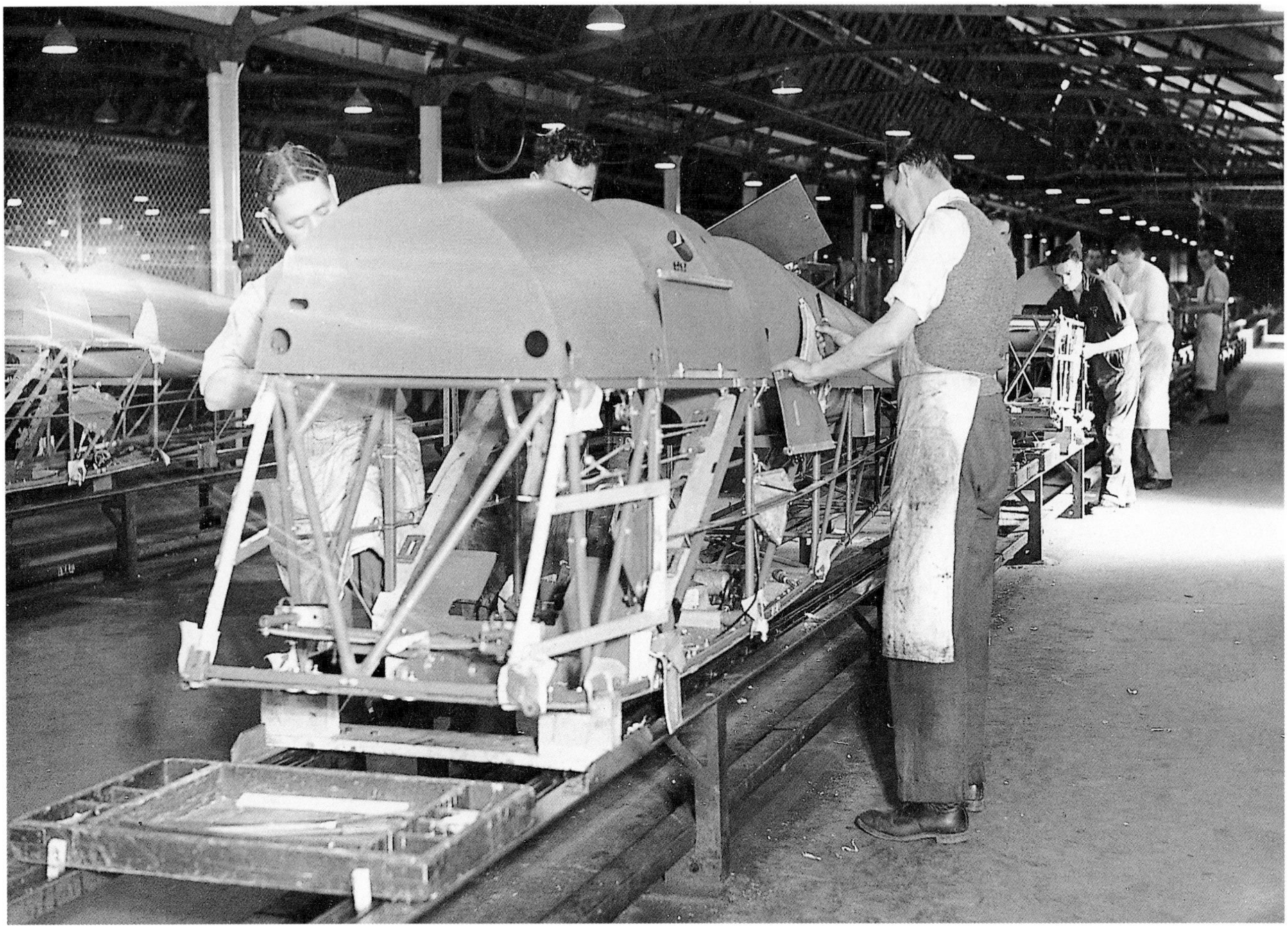

A basic Tiger Moth fuselage in the final stages of fitting out at Morris Motors, Cowley. The first Cowley aircraft were built in 'F Block', part of the North Side factory. *The Aeroplane*

At Cowley, completed fuselages were spray painted to a standard camouflage pattern and, in this posed shot, with an apparent minimum of masking. *Morris Motors*

External fittings were applied to the wings and control surfaces after covering and doping. A relatively small section of the Cowley workforce was allocated to Tiger Moth production of which a high proportion was women. *Morris Motors*

AID at Cowley agreed that in order to clear the first eight aircraft due for delivery in April, forty three of the points identified by Harry Povey's team would be addressed immediately. These mostly concerned the absence of clips and chafe protection for electrical wiring, missing washers and misaligned installation of moving parts which caused fouling, under-and over-tightened bolts, badly aligned greasers, etc. Cowley undertook responsibility to revise other points but only on account of expediency; they would ensure that the steel bolts holding the compass brackets were replaced with brass ones, but in mitigation revealed that both steel and brass nuts and bolts had received a cadmium finish making it difficult on sight for the operatives to distinguish between the two. The engine nose cowling, according to Hatfield, had been poorly finished and badly fitted, and incorrectly drilled holes had been filled with rivets. Cowley replied that while they did not disagree, the standard of the cowling as supplied left much to be desired.

In response to Hatfield's claim that the anti-vibration leather strap looped around the torque tube in the control box was too loose, Cowley responded with an accusation that straps fitted to a Hatfield built fuselage they had inspected were not to drawing, and that extra holes had been cut by erecting shop staff to facilitate their installation. "This would appear to be a point to be cleared up by de Havilland as well as here, if a standard is to be ensured," suggested AID.

Regarding other matters, Cowley believed that misalignment and distortion might have been caused during transportation of the aircraft by road to Hatfield. On a further twelve points AID confirmed that manufacture had proceeded strictly in accordance with the current issue of drawings, and the criticism levelled from Hatfield was because the drawings were either wrong or contained insufficient detail or guidance; their suggestion was that such matters should be corrected without delay. Perhaps it was the classic case of Hatfield being too close to the wood to see the trees: Canada had expressed similar views on drawings when contracted to build 200 fuselages in 1938. Errors and omissions were easily circumvented by the Hatfield workforce who had absorbed all the necessary production changes as a matter of daily routine, irrespective of the state of validity of the drawings.

Cowley was not in the least vexed by the criticism: where they had been in error they recognised and admitted to the fault and took immediate steps for correction. It was a remarkable achievement that they had been able to adapt to the delicate complications of building light, fabric covered structures involving many processes so different from motor manufacture, and to harness them so efficiently to almost instant mass production. They were not averse to offering advice either. On the matter of fuselage side frames they put forward an honest and practical opinion:

"We think that during manufacture we could eliminate a number of drilled holes which we understand were for both RAF and civilian requirements in the past, and as this machine is now to be used expressly by the Air Ministry, will you please confirm and modify the drawings accordingly."

To conclude his response, Mr Smith underlined AID's belief that Hatfield were building some parts of the aeroplane to a more practical or convenient standard by local agreement rather than to detail shown on the drawings, and Cowley was in receipt of unfair criticism for simply following the approved path. In respect of Hatfield's assertion that inspection tabs on control cables should be turned to enable the inspection stamps to be clearly seen, the Works' Superintendent and his AID Chief Inspector were agreed: "this is a matter of opinion and not a fault," they replied.

When a large batch of Tiger Moth spares was imported into England from India in 1980, it was found that the hinge pin holes drilled in the rudder posts were half an inch off centre. The inspecting engineer was beginning to form the impression that it was a manufacturing error when coincidentally he was asked to assist with the upgrade of a Morris Motors built Tiger Moth, in fairly original condition, which had been retrieved from France. Much to his surprise the rudder post was drilled in an exactly similar manner. Was it a production error, misinterpretation of the drawings, incorrect drawings or a local modification tied in with tugging target sleeves or gliders?

The first of the Cowley built aircraft to fly was T7011 (83136), transferred to nearby Witney by road and test flown from there by

Guy Tucker on 15 May 1940. The aircraft was eventually posted by coincidence to two reasonably local airfields: first 3 EFTS at Watchfield and later with the same school at Shellingford, spending her entire working life with the unit until sold into obscurity in 1951.

In early May T7013 was returned to Cowley from her brief expedition to Hatfield, and the catalogue of shared errors was corrected, following which she was moved to Witney and test flown from there. The aircraft was allocated to 24 Maintenance Unit (MU) at Ternhill on 25 April 1940 and delivered on 13 May. There she remained until allocation to 12 EFTS at Prestwick on 20 September. Prior to closure of that establishment in April 1941, T7013 was transferred on 14 March to 19 EFTS Sealand where she remained until transfer on paper to 24 EFTS which re-formed at the same airfield on 7 February 1942. Cowley's much inspected Tiger Moth crashed there on 10 June 1944 when a pilot on his second solo flight held off too high and stalled into the ground. The pupil's instructor received the blame for permitting him to fly a one hour session and become fatigued. The considerable damage caused when the undercarriage collapsed resulted in T7013 being officially written off nine days later.

Guy Tucker, inevitably known as 'Tommy' or 'Tiger', was a de Havilland test pilot temporarily detached from Hatfield who eventually took up full-time residence at Cowley test flying production Tiger Moths and later repaired Spitfires. A further eighteen aircraft experienced maiden flights from Witney while the airfield facilities at Cowley were being prepared, the last being T7028 (83309), which flew on 24 June. Three days later Guy Tucker flew T7029 (83310), from Cowley's own barely adequate little grass aerodrome.

In its initial stages production at Cowley was sited at the southern end of 'F Block, North Side Factory', a single storey red brick building typical of the inter-war period, under a blacked out northlight truss roof. The line was set up in what appeared to visitors to be a corridor running east-west, abutting a vast floor space devoted to the manufacture of Bren Gun Carriers. The wood mill and sub assembly area was at the eastern end of the block and fuselages were built up on wheeled dollies running in floor mounted guide rails which gradually were processed towards the west, shifted manually as required. These mobile jigs have given rise to a popular myth that Cowley's mass production motor methods included a continuously moving assembly line. This was never the case and at a steady and acceptable productive rate of about forty Tiger Moths per week, was never necessary.

Following completion accumulated groups of six red doped fuselages complete with empennage were pushed on their own wheels on a southerly heading out of F Block and to the end of a wide covered passageway between C Block to the right and GK vehicle paint and finishing lines to the left, now assembly areas for torpedoes and armoured cars. Headed due east as far as the end of L Block, it was necessary to turn sharp right to head south again, past the P Block trimshop and the wages office, through Gate 16, across the busy Garsington Road, and immediately right into R Block of the South Side Factory. Here the Gipsy Major engine was installed, the fuselage sprayed with camouflage paint and the wings and empennage fitted. Now complete, the aircraft was weighed before engine runs and final checks were signed off and she was handed over for test flying.

The tiny airfield which had been used on at least one occasion pre-war by a DH.51 visiting from Stag Lane, hosted thousands of maiden and post-repair flights, not only by Tiger Moths in the hands of resident test pilot Guy Tucker, but Geoffrey de Havilland Jnr, John de Havilland and Pat Fillingham who flew across from Hertfordshire in a company communications aeroplane, staying for three week assignments to assist with a seemingly endless backlog.

Flt Lt Richard Jones was occasionally loaned from similar duties with repaired Tiger Moths and Spitfires at Witney. Richard Jones had been posted to de Havilland in April 1941 for a 'rest' from operations with 19 Squadron and their Supermarine Spitfires operating during the summer of 1940 as part of the Duxford Wing commanded by Douglas Bader, and stayed at Witney as resident test pilot until 1945. He enjoyed flying Tiger Moths, remembering that his first solo in 1937 was in a Miles Magister which carried a label on the instrument panel on which was inscribed in bold red letters: "This aircraft will not, repeat will not, come out of a spin."

Pre-war record breaking pilot Alex Henshaw, based at Castle Bromwich, was a regular visitor to Cowley Aerodrome, squeezing in and out when helping to test Spitfires after attention by the resident CRU, and John Grierson, 'Cloudy Joe' to his chums, who flew long distances in a Fox Moth, exercised mended Hurricanes.

Pat Fillingham remembers the days at Cowley as very routine, but the social life was good. He and Geoffrey de Havilland Jnr would stay with Guy Tucker in his cottage at Old Marston and try to enjoy their time off duty as much as wartime shortages and an annual salary of £175 would permit. In such dark times maximum effort was required and the Cowley test pilots found space in their busy schedule to join the Oxford Local Defence Volunteers (LDV), the Home Guard, with whom they were engaged on night patrols by launch along the river Thames, armed with ancient rifles, seeking parachuted spies.

Between 3 July and 24 July 1940, Pat Fillingham made ninety seven test flights on Tiger Moths, including a batch of civil aircraft destined for the Indian Government. It was fair game when the wind was right, to fly between the two tall chimneys of the power house which still bore the traces of wartime camouflage paint before demolition over fifty years later, but happily no scars from wingtip scrapes.

Hooper & Co. (Coachbuilders) Ltd., the bespoke coach building company based alongside the Grand Union Canal at Park Royal on the northwest fringes of London, was founded in 1805 and amongst their regular customers for horse drawn carriages and later, motor car bodies, were many of the crowned heads of Europe. They were sub-contracted by Morris Motors from late 1940 to manufacture and supply to Cowley finished Tiger Moth fuselages complete with fabric covering. One of the young apprentices involved in their manufacture was Alan Harris:

> "They gave me the drawings of the Tiger Moth fuselage, a bunch of jigs and a hacksaw and told me to draw out from the stores lengths of Reynolds tubing, boil them in a large gas-heated bath of caustic soda to remove the grease and cut them into lengths ready for welding into the shape of Tiger Moth fuselage frames and engine bearers. The longerons had to be bent cold and the creases hammered flat afterwards. I got through a pack of high tensile hacksaw blades every day cutting the 17 gauge tubing. I would prepare the tubes in batches sufficient for one aircraft and then pass the lot on to the welders, some of whom were girls.
> Bare wings were delivered from an outside contractor and they and our fuselages were covered with Irish linen by girls working in a special climate-controlled room. When covered, taped and stitched, it was time for hand doping the fabric with a dark red gooey substance which would tighten the fabric prior to spraying on the colours and markings. The wings and also the fuselages were sprayed yellow overall and were certainly not camouflaged.
> A group of us would have to act as fire-watchers at night twice a week to guard the factory and attempt to put out any fires. We were hit by an incendiary bomb during an air raid one night and a couple of Tiger Moth fuselages were burned out but within two days we were back in full production.
> We never saw the finished product because the aircraft were sent by lorry to Morris Motors at Cowley for assembly. I cannot recall more than three or four completed fuselages

The facade of the Hooper factory at Park Royal, north-west London, a bespoke coach-building company where from late 1940 Tiger Moth fuselages were manufactured under sub contract to Morris Motors. *via Bernard King*

standing ready for transportation at any one time or any parts of the empennage, undercarriage, centre section or fuel tanks, and definitely no engines."

Alan Harris continued working on Tiger Moths at Park Royal until 1942 when he disentangled himself from his reserved occupation as a skilled fitter, volunteered for aircrew duties and was Graded as a pilot. Following training in the USA he returned to England and to 'keep his hand in' flew Tiger Moths at Shellingford before posting to a Dakota squadron in the Far East and later Sunderland flying boats. His evidence that the Hooper made fuselages were painted yellow overall may suggest that whilst the emphasis at Morris Motors was concentration on aircraft for the RAF, others known to have been supplied from Cowley to India and New Zealand may largely have been constructed by Hooper and other outside contractors. A clue would be to find an 'H&C' inspectors' stamp on the throttle levers, assembly of which was one of Alan Harris' specialities.

Location of the propeller and a check on the starboard slat completes the task in assembling NL913 at the Cowley works in November 1943. Manoeuvred clear of the pillars and into natural daylight, engine checks were next on the list. *Morris Motors*

NL911 was set up on the camouflaged concrete base adjacent to Cowley Aerodrome ready for swinging both bowl compasses. Two Supermarine Spitfires and the nose of what possibly is a Dragon Rapide can just be seen on the left edge of the picture. *Morris Motors*

Export orders satisfied by Cowley were crated and sent out via the factory's own railway branch line. Domestic collection and delivery was handled by civilian pilots of the Air Transport Auxiliary, an organisation with pilot 'Pools' established in different parts of the country. These lady pilots of the ATA were introduced to the press at Hatfield in January 1940. *de Havilland Aircraft Company*

Many Air Transport Auxiliary (ATA) pilots completed their first assignments by delivering Tiger Moths to RAF Maintenance Units from the holding area at Cowley, situated next to what had become one of the country's two biggest aircraft reclamation and salvage dumps, where they were held under the authority of Hatfield nominated Chief Inspector Terry Dunworth. Flying usually in gaggles of three or four or sometimes more, the numbers were probably reflected by the carrying capacity of the ATA's taxi Avro Ansons used for delivery and collection of crews. Pat Fillingham once took off on a routine production test flight during the late summer of 1940 as six new Tiger Moths were being taxied out by ATA pilots. His brief was standard: a routine test lasting between ten and twenty minutes during which he was scheduled to check engine performance, general handling, especially with respect to trim and setting of the aileron differential. Occasionally it was necessary to change a rogue propeller or an oil gauge if the indications looked bad. Climbing between 500ft and 1,000ft Pat Fillingham happened to glance back to see six Tiger Moths climbing after him. When he turned, they turned, and it soon became clear that they were trying to formate on him, wrongly suspecting him to be their group leader. Not wishing to prolong their agony, he took evasive action and hurriedly returned to land.

In order to join the ATA, pilots were required to fly an 'acceptance test' with the chief instructor, A R O MacMillan, flying Tiger Moth G-AFSX (82004), at Whitchurch Aerodrome, Bristol. In view of their experience and following interview, the flight test was almost a formality for most, and usually consisted of little more than a wide circuit and landing. The first tests were completed on 6 September 1939 as the result of which twenty six pilots acceptable to the ATA were invited to fly a North American Harvard at the RAF Central Flying School, Upavon, and so qualify to ferry all RAF single engine aircraft. Selection and training later moved to ATA Headquarters at White Waltham although an Initial Training Unit was eventually established using Tiger Moths and based at Barton le Clay, near Luton, Bedfordshire.

The first flight acceptance aircraft, G-AFSX, originally had been assigned to RAF care as N6731 but was re-directed to 'The Secretary of State for Air' and allocated to the Director General of Civil Aviation. She was delivered to No 3 Ferry Pilots Pool at White Waltham in February 1940 and took on the new military serial AX856 the following July, but evidence of her hard life style was revealed during a major inspection in August 1942 and she was scrapped.

With an increased operational need ATA pilots later were called upon to ferry Spitfires from Cowley too. One such was Diana Barnato Walker whose father had raced Bentley cars at Brooklands. It was almost inevitable that she should join the Brooklands Flying Club in 1936 where she learned to fly on Tiger Moths at a cost of £3 per hour. Her family was not amused and cut off her allowance which meant she was not in flying practise at the beginning of the war and took up duties as an ambulance driver. She joined the ATA in 1942 and her first delivery flight was on 25 March when she ferried Tiger Moth DE410 (85418), on a forty minute trip from Cowley to Hullavington. An ATA taxi Anson returned Diana Barnato Walker and her colleagues back to Cowley the same day to allow her to deliver DE569 (85536), to Kemble from where she was airlifted back for tea at White Waltham in the faithful Anson again.

Having been invalided out of the RAF Anthony Phelps returned to civilian life as a Fleet Street journalist but was persuaded to join the ATA. A few days after his flight test at Whitchurch he was welcomed to a snow covered White Waltham Aerodrome from where he was immediately invited to deliver a brand new Tiger Moth, a feat he described in his book '*I Couldn't Care Less*':

> "Apart from my short flight test I had not flown a Tiger Moth since before the war started, and, forgetting just how cold they could be, especially when the temperature at ground level is two degrees below, had neglected to attire myself suitably.
> For the first few minutes after taking off I could hardly breathe. It was just like diving into an icy cold pool. Then I became wildly exhilarated. To be flying again, on a real job, when I had given up all hope of flying until the war finished. The wind whipping my face was like champagne that had been on ice for a long time.
> Like champagne too it was not long before the exhilaration began to wear off, until finally I was conscious of nothing except that I was cold.
> I glanced at my compass. Yes, I was on the course. Then I looked at my map and was not so sure. I had another look and became equally sure that I was not.
> Now aerial navigation is one of those many things in which the theory at times seems somewhat far removed from the practice. Also, of course, there is a vast difference between navigating a light aircraft like a Moth and modern service types for which the drift is much less. Furthermore, the fighter pilot often has very little time for serious navigation and tends to rely more and more on wireless.
> Hence, although my theory was sound, my practice, (may I admit, never brilliant), was a little rusty. To add to my difficulties, the entire country was covered with snow, which renders many landmarks difficult of recognition.

I began to get a little worried, but stuck grimly to my course, I think I must have been frozen to it anyhow, until a certain town came into view, and I heaved a sigh of relief. I realised that the low ground speed of the Tiger Moth had fooled me and in consequence I had been navigating somewhat ahead of myself. Furthermore, I had been guilty of neglecting my watch, which would have told me that everything was in order. All this of course is very elementary, but it really is surprising how easy it is to get out of the habit of navigating, and I was terribly nervous of making a mess of my first job: even a simple one like a Tiger Moth. I know my luck.

For nearly two hours after that all I had to do was to sit like a piece of chilled mutton waiting for the refrigerator door to open. When I saw my destination I was too cold even to feel happy about it. Had the machine started to break up in mid-air I would not have cared. All I wanted was to get it over."

Although 154 ATA personnel died in the service, often the result of accidents caused by bad weather, only one pilot was killed when ferrying a Tiger Moth amongst the 171,934 single engine delivery flights completed between February 1940 and November 1945. As a grand total, the ATA pilots delivered 309,011 aircraft during which they achieved 414,984 flying hours.

Tiger Moth G-AEEA (3495), was part of the establishment of 11 ERFTS Perth at the beginning of the war and took on military markings BB691 in September 1940. During landing practice at Buttergask Relief Landing Ground (RLG) on 19 November 1941, BB691 had undershot and collided with a wall. Damage was severe and the aircraft was routed to the de Havilland CRU at Witney where, following repairs, she was test flown by Richard Jones on 27 December.

Second Officer J A Nathan had joined the ATA in April 1941 with a total of seventy two hours experience. On 8 February 1942 he was engaged on his sixty sixth single engined ferry during the course of which his total flight time had increased to 188 hours. Nathan's aircraft was BB691, assigned to Prestwick, and he took off from Witney in the early afternoon bound for RAF Ouston near Newcastle upon Tyne, where he was scheduled to stop for fuel. The aircraft arrived at 1530 hours and landed normally, but swung badly when taxying clear such that it re-entered the active runway and was rammed by a Spitfire which had landed immediately behind, wrecking the Tiger Moth and killing Second Officer Nathan.

The entire production facility at Cowley was set up around a shop foreman (Mr Coles) and charge hand (Percy Saunders) in a cell of about fifty employees. These included some Morris Motors' male permanent staff and others with woodworking skills recruited from the building industry and augmented by a number of local women and girls. The group worked long hours, 7.30am to 7.30pm, six days a week, and occasionally seven, (there was no night shift), or for as long as parts and supplies were to hand. In addition there was a compulsorily rostered fire watching duty on two nights per week for each male employee. The F Block men patrolled their own roof, operating from a small hut inside the Block where they could brew tea and sleep in rotation.

As a nineteen year old, Les Gurl (Snowball to his workmates), assisted Archie Penn in fitting control boxes, and at least once on a daily basis was required to lift a tail to push a fuselage on the half mile journey through the factory and across the public road to R Block. It was a tough physical exercise and the one way push took about fifteen minutes. The covered walkway had to be navigated with care as the factory had taken on emergency assembly of thousands of American Mack and White army lorries, diverted from France and delivered in kit form to England instead to fill every vacant corner of the site. Les Gurl left Cowley in the late summer of 1940, part of an emergency draft redirected to work at the Cunliffe Owen company at Eastleigh where his talents were employed in assisting to accelerate the production of Spitfire wings. From there he joined the Royal Navy, and was, therefore, not part of the Cowley team which moved out of F Block in 1942, and consolidated the whole of the production and assembly process more efficiently in R Block, leaving the vacated space for the assembly of Horsa gliders.

With the military training machine in top gear at home and overseas, the immediate requirement for a continuous supply of new Tiger Moths diminished from February 1944 and increasing numbers of complete but dismantled aircraft were delivered by road into hastily secured 'Purgatory Stores' in and around Oxford, all under the authority of 15 MU Wroughton. From June to October 1945, many were routed back to Cowley where they were updated, customised, erected, test flown and delivered to MUs at Aston Down, Colerne, Little Rissington and Llandow, prior to sale or gift-in-aid to the Air Forces of Belgium, France, the Netherlands and Yugoslavia. At Witney, every square inch of available hangar floor space had been utilised for the repair and overhaul of Spitfires and Tiger Moths. Additional storage was requisitioned in the adjacent Blarney Garage and Tower Hill Garage, and dismantled Tiger Moths were stored in the basement of the Haines' repair workshop at Staple Hall. Dent's glove factory at Charlbury was the site of major wood repairs and fabric work including the covering of the majority of reconditioned Tiger Moth wings.

While the Cowley factory manufactured Tiger Moths and repaired Spitfires, repair and overhaul of Tiger Moths was accomplished at designated RAF Maintenance Units or civilian contractors. They were never short of work. The Taylorcraft Company operated a Tiger Moth repair unit at Thurmaston in Leicestershire which employed a lot of local women.
via de Havilland Support Ltd

The de Havilland contribution was limited to the repair and overhaul of Tiger Moths (and Queen Bees) at Witney. What component parts Morris Motors themselves did not manufacture in-house they sub contracted to suppliers sometimes with the capability of repairing major damage to aircraft that were allocated to them following assessment at an RAF MU. Lundy and Atlantic Coast Airlines at Barnstaple was one such, operating behind a name selected to disguise the company's true activities. Others were William Mumford at Billacombe near Plymouth, Southern Aircraft at Gatwick and Taylorcraft Aeroplanes at locations in Leicestershire but principally at Thurmaston. Spare parts were supplied by, amongst many small companies, William Lawrence and Co. Ltd. of Colwick, Nottingham, Entwistle and Kenyon of Accrington and James H. Sutcliffe and Son Ltd. of Todmorden, both in Lancashire.

The last Tiger Moth to be wholly constructed at Cowley was PG746 (86632). Taken into care by 15 MU Wroughton on 24 July 1944, PG746 was routed to 38 MU Llandow, a major Tiger Moth refurbishment centre near Cardiff, on 8 July the following year and on 12 September 1946 she was transferred to 47 MU, a specialist packing unit based at Sealand. It seems astonishing that instead of air delivery to the Royal Netherlands Air Force, to whom the aircraft had been sold, PG746 along with several others, was dismantled, crated, transported to Dagenham Docks from Cheshire, and ferried across the North Sea on board the SS *Ponto* to take up duties with the Air Force at Woensdrecht, and later the Dutch Navy at Valkenburg. Withdrawn from use in December 1965 and sold in January 1966, the aircraft is thought to have been purchased as a source of spare parts by a naval gliding club in the Netherlands.

For Morris Motors, building Tiger Moths was just another mass production job to be completed against a high specification and to a strict timetable and price agreed under conditions of national emergency. The company was not involved in promoting any form of development or experimental flying. Miles Thomas, a senior executive with the Nuffield Organisation, makes not a single mention of the Tiger Moth in his otherwise meticulously detailed autobiography. Apart from a series of photographs taken on behalf of a news agency in F Block in January 1941, a further sequence covering detail work and assembly in R Block was not recorded by Morris Motors until October 1943 after which the negatives were misfiled for over thirty years. Five decades after the last Tiger Moth had flown away from Cowley, an exhibition held in Oxford and which included a major feature on the contribution made by the Cowley site in times of war and peace, failed to acknowledge any association with Tiger Moths.

After the war the British motor industry underwent massive changes both in company identity and organisation. In latter days Cowley was operational under the banner of the Rover Group, a company purchased by an irony of politics and economics by British Aerospace who ran down the works before closing the whole of the North and South Factories, to embark on a planned and systematic programme of demolition. F Block and R Block went down to the bulldozers in 1993, together with Lord Nuffield's offices. So too did all the post-war additions to the South Factory, releasing for a short period the outline of a dusty patch of a one time small grass airfield from which more than 3,000 Tiger Moths first took wing.

With dispersal of production and the establishment of new facilities across the country, some of the British aircraft manufacturers discovered that it was impossible to move key personnel, test pilots, drawings, spares or urgently needed supplies with any alacrity. The railway service throughout the British Isles was liable to disruption and long road journeys were tedious.

Westland Aircraft were the first to raise the subject of production companies using 'communications' aircraft when, early in 1941, they were faced with regular liaison between their Somerset factory and 263 Squadron operating Whirlwind 1s from Montrose in Scotland. Other companies were soon anxious to be included in any realistic scheme which could be devised and the Civil Service went into top gear establishing committees to study the appropriate rates for aircraft loan and flight time, depreciation, insurance, maintenance, and even the operational competence of the company personnel who would fly the government's property.

It was recognised at an early stage that aircraft 'hire' charges made by the Ministry of Aircraft Production (MAP) or on behalf of the Director General of Research and Development (DGRD) would only be included in company overheads and recovered by the manufacturers in due course, thus the basics of Third Party insurance, fuel, oil, servicing and repairs were agreed as the maximum contribution which could realistically be expected from the users.

Westland had asked for a multi-seat transport, a DH.89A Dragon Rapide for example, but currently these were all fully committed and supplies of the alternative Avro Anson were earmarked for export. Vickers, MAP decided, were to be given priority anyway, with dispersal factories and operational squadrons across the country busy with Wellingtons and Spitfires. In June 1941 the company was allocated a G.A.L. Monospar, Percival Vega Gull, Miles Falcon and a pair of DH.90 Dragonflies, AV992 (G-AEDJ) and AV993 (G-AFRF) which, after clearance of all the necessary paperwork by 41 Group at Andover, were to be collected from the Ferry Pool at White Waltham. Thereafter and until further notice, the fleet was to be the responsibility of Vickers. In its submission for the allocation of a communications aircraft the company had included the Morris Motors aerodrome at Cowley as a base of operations, hinged to the CRO Spitfire salvage and repair programmes.

In common with all British based motor engineering companies, the Rootes Group became heavily involved in military aircraft production and by June 1941 their association with the Bristol Blenheim occupied facilities at Shawbury, Stoke, Burtonwood and Speke. The company complained that test pilots were having to rely on the good offices of the RAF Overseer to be chauffeured around the network in his duty Miles Magister. Perhaps Rootes did not have the same political clout as Westland which resulted in allocation of a brand new Dominie (Dragon Rapide), for DGRD's committee thought that a Tiger Moth could be made available to Rootes after all the formalities

When restoring Tiger Moth G-AMTF for ex-Lightning pilot Mark Zipfell, the New Zealand based Croydon Aircraft Company in association with the owner paid special attention to the colour scheme in which T7842 had left the Cowley factory in 1941. *Steve Barnes*

had been approved. However, having received the green light, a Tiger Moth was allocated but not until June 1943 when T7842 (84207), was delivered to Standard Motors from 10 MU Hullavington and remained on charge with the company until January 1945. Following more than three years of training activity with 11 EFTS/11 RFS at Perth, T7842 was declared surplus and took up an agricultural appointment in New Zealand until she was grounded and dismantled in 1963. The aircraft was acquired by the Croydon Aircraft Company of Mandeville and rebuilt to her 1942 configuration for Mark Zipfell, an ex-RAF English Electric Lightning pilot, who returned her to the luxury of a private landing ground in Suffolk during the summer of 1995. She moved to a similar facility in Kent in 2006 where her new owner, Hamish Monro, named her 'The Inheritance'.

The availability of light aircraft, especially Tiger Moths, after the early pressures had been removed from the British based training programme were evidenced by their allocation to Airspeed, Short Bros, Power Jets, Westland, Vickers, Vosper and Bristol. Although de Havilland did operate Tiger Moths for company communications they much preferred the extra speed and comfort of the Leopard Moth, Hornet Moth and Dragon Rapide, all of which types were procured. Tiger Moth PG624 (86533), was delivered across the hedge from Cowley to de Havilland at Witney in March 1944, officially for 'modifications', and nominal ownership passed to the government's Controller of Research and Development in August 1945. Under de Havilland control she was extensively flown during the course of communications and weather observation duties until she was purchased outright by the company in April 1946, registered G-AHIZ and posted to the London Aeroplane Club at Panshanger, in whose yellow and silver colours she continues to operate training and recreational sorties with the Cambridge Flying Group.

Before the war and under civil contract, The Air Operating Company Ltd. flew missions over the British Isles on behalf of the Home Office to identify sites which would be best protected by camouflage in the event of a national emergency. On the outbreak of hostilities the Camouflage Flight was taken over by the RAF and operated by 24 Squadron from Hendon under an arrangement with RAF Fighter Command. Renamed No 1 Camouflage Unit, they were ordered to commence operations at Baginton, Coventry, from 9 October 1939.

Following complete refurbishment in New Zealand Tiger Moth G-AMTF was delivered to her owner in England painted in the scheme with which she left the Cowley factory in 1941. She made her first public appearance at the de Havilland Moth Club's International Rally at Woburn in 2002. *J D Gretton*

The Unit flew a variety of aircraft including at least two Leopard Moths, Dominies and requisitioned Dragon Rapides. The first of two Tiger Moths, T7604 (84001), was on strength for general duties from 31 July 1942 after the Unit's Commanding Officer had been delivered to High Ercall from Stapleford Tawney to collect her from 222 MU, a packing unit more associated with shipping Tiger Moths out of the country than to despatching them by air to a grassy British aerodrome. The second aircraft, T7723 (84100), had been on strength briefly with 55 Operational Training Unit (OTU) at Annan before allocation to the Unit, but was written off as the result of a landing accident at Stapleford Tawney on 13 April 1943. With 23 hours solo time on Tiger Moths the pilot had approached to land in a steep sideslip but had misjudged his recovery, probably due to failing evening light, touched down heavily, bounced and dived into the ground. "Careless and over confident," was the Station Commander's assessment!

After a stay of only five months T7604 was posted in January 1943 to 167 Squadron flying the Supermarine Spitfire Vc at Ludham, and was not replaced. Six weeks later the aircraft joined 164 Squadron when they moved into Middle Wallop with Hawker Hurricane IVs and

Tiger Moth G-AHIZ operated by the Cambridge Flying Group since 1956 is painted in the yellow and silver scheme once the house colours of a previous owner, the London Aeroplane Club. *Ian Oliver*

is believed to have remained with them during a re-equipment programme which saw the introduction of the Hawker Typhoon 1B and nineteen changes of airfield including forward bases on the Continent. Retired to 39 MU at Colerne in November 1944, T7604 aircraft was held in storage until declared surplus in 1950 and cut up for scrap.

The Ministry of Home Security established a wartime unit at Leamington Spa from where schemes were raised to disguise everything of strategic value, and the Camouflage Unit was tasked with the job of photographing and reporting. All aircraft factories and aerodromes were divided into categories and the Morris Motors works was classified as '2A', a site in which the Air Ministry, specifically, had no direct interest although a plethora of other government agencies did. In consequence, the Ministry of Home Security was responsible for the design, execution and maintenance of the whole camouflage scheme applied to the Cowley factory.

Painting a wall in brown and green drab was fairly basic and three dimensional devices were permitted but only as long as they were removable at twenty four hours notice, and consultations on their possible effect on the normal operation of the factory or aerodrome were to be held between the Ministry and the Superintending Engineer of the site. Having erected any such devices on facilities such as those in the Cowley category, however, their ultimate removal was regarded as the responsibility of the Air Ministry. As a result the Tiger Moth production facilities in Cowley's R Block sprouted dormer windows constructed from wire mesh and doors and windows painted on the external walls.

Manufacturers became uneasy when the airfields at some production sites were selected for training-related activities. They believed the inevitable high rate of utilisation would draw unwelcome attention. Phillips and Powis were still applying the finishing touches to a new shadow factory built at South Marston near Swindon in 1940 for the production of Miles Masters when news reached them that the airfield was to be added to the list of Relief Landing Grounds already established for the Elementary Schools which proliferated throughout the area.

During construction of the factory, and with nearly all the steelwork for the main assembly hall already erected, the Air Ministry themselves had decided that the site was too attractive a target and two thirds of it was dismantled and rebuilt into two additional and separate units elsewhere in the locality. Having insisted on such an expensive and disruptive measure, added to which the company had already planted trees for screening and made further efforts to disguise the taxyways leading from factory to aerodrome, plans for utilisation by the training schools were cancelled.

The inherent dangers of a high utilisation aerodrome at a production site were experienced by Luton Corporation's airfield at the top of the town, overlooking the hat factories and the Vauxhall motor plant, where the Percival Aircraft Company had been joined by the Miles Magisters of 29 ERFTS in August 1938, contracted to Birkett Air Services Ltd., an organisation with roots at Stag Lane. The ERFTS had been closed as a result of the September 1939 reorganisation, reforming at Clyffe Pypard two years later as a Tiger Moth equipped EFTS for training pilots for the Fleet Air Arm. On 22 July 1940, the void was filled when 24 EFTS was transferred to Luton from Belfast and the Percival Aircraft Company immediately expressed their feelings of nervousness. Percival had complained to the MAP that the intensive flight training operations at Luton were drawing attention to the airfield and consequently to the aircraft factory, quite apart from the other local activities in support of the war effort. The camouflage experts at Leamington Spa were drawn into the argument and presented a report in December 1941 which was critical of the RAF Station Commander and OC 24 EFTS, Wing Cmdr Chambers. Although the camouflage of the buildings was satisfactory an enormous muddy scar had been allowed to develop on the grass manoeuvring area, the result of intensive ploughing in a confined space by Tiger Moth tailskids, a situation exacerbated by the movement of support vehicles, refuelling bowsers etc.

The aerodrome manager, Mr Rushton, acting on behalf of Luton Corporation, had asked that the area be fenced off and re-seeded to allow the healing process to take its course. The camouflage agency had agreed that this was necessary and easily accomplished. The Station Commander had retaliated by reiterating that he was duty bound to produce target results in the form of hours and pupil accomplishment and had positively refused to co-operate. The report suggested the scar was associated with one of the "usual problems of an EFTS; lack of proper control over taxiing aircraft etc." There might have been more than just coincidence in the closure of the Luton based school and transfer to Sealand only two months later.

The whole business of flying training operations conducted from MAP airfields was considered very seriously and at the height of the Luton dispute the Ministry published a list of aerodromes at which they declared themselves 'very anxious' not to accommodate or offer facilities to training units. Included were Morris Motors at Cowley and de Havilland at Watford Aerodrome (Leavesden). There was no mention of Hatfield or Windsor (Smiths Lawn) where Vickers maintained a shadow installation and the polo fields were extensively used as a Relief Landing Ground by Tiger Moths operating beyond the circuits of White Waltham and Fairoaks.

Engine runs, adjustments and determination of fuel flow were completed in the shadow of some fancy camouflage design and construction on the outside of Cowley's R Block. Having built Tiger Moths all day, male workers were compelled to spend two nights every week patrolling the factory roof, on fire watching duties. *Morris Motors*

Bombs fitted to underfloor carriers on Tiger Moth T5610, 1940 style, photographed at RAE Farnborough with the aid of some strategically placed cardboard sheets. *RAE Farnborough*

CHAPTER SIX

A Matter of Desperation

Tiger Moth bombers were the secret ingredient of a clandestine anti-invasion plan devised by the Air Staff in the spring of 1940 as the result of representations by No 2 School of Army Co-operation. Training Command Operational Order No 1 issued on 23 May 1940 called for the Command in a time of declared national emergency, ie. invasion, to reinforce the efforts of Bomber Command. As originally devised the overall scheme was called 'ZZ' and known as 'The Julius Caesar Plan' by Army Co-operation, but was renamed 'Banquet' on 27 May. Between 179 and 247 miscellaneous bomber training aircraft were expected to be deployed at fourteen Bomber Command airfields. At the same time, the factor of light primary training aircraft was added to the equation. This extension to the Plan was coded 'Banquet Light' and dictated that improvised striking forces, a 'cooks and butchers air force' to quote one senior officer, raised from within the elementary training establishments, would be allocated to stations where Army Co-operation Westland Lysander squadrons were located. There, they were to come under the jurisdiction of the local RAF operational commander and were to attack targets allocated by the Army or Corps headquarters. As many of the airfield assembly sites were likely to be remote from prospective action aircraft were scheduled for re-deployment as necessary to advanced landing grounds where they would be fuelled and armed and maintained at full alert.

Additional Banquet plans included the use of civil transport aircraft, 'Banquet Civil', although the perceived requirement for extensive modification and subsequent training and maintenance, not to mention a greater usefulness in their transport role rather than deployment as light bombers, tipped the balance against the idea which was dropped. 'Banquet Comm' was intended to relieve Communications Flights of their Tiger Moths and Magisters, but the idea was also abandoned in the face of realisation that good and flexible communications in an emergency situation would be absolutely critical. 'Banquet CB' involved integration of some 251 obsolescent bombers of the Hawker Hart variety, of which 174 had already been earmarked at storage units for service overseas, which could be retained and integrated as part of the Flying Training Command contribution. 'Banquet Master' was intended to employ the Miles Master trainer as a fighter but the fitting of Browning machine guns had caused such disruption during manufacture that Lord Beaverbrook, Minister of Aircraft Production, had agreed to an abandonment of the concept.

At the end of May 1940 the Deputy Director of Home Operations asked for a quantification of the light aircraft immediately available and was advised that 663 RAF Tiger Moths could be mustered together with 410 light civil aircraft.

At the start of another day. Just part of the post-war establishment of 6 EFTS Sywell viewed from the roof of the flight cadet's mess. *Ken Ellis collection*

"In the last resort they might enable us to hit the enemy," he wrote. The civil aircraft were identified as Gipsy Moth 12; Moth Minor 11; DH.60 Moth 5; DH.60A Moth 1; DH.60G Moth 119; DH.60M Moth 23; DH.60N Moth 1; DH.60X Moth 23; DH.82 Tiger Moth 69. Containing a number of spurious entries the author of the accompanying note could hardly have realised the unintended irony:

"It is impossible to say how many of these are in serviceable condition or, in fact, really exist at all, until they have been inspected, as the records kept have been found to be very inaccurate."

On the basis that an Elementary Flying Training School (EFTS) may have two or three or four Flights (some had more), it was considered that the strength of the light bomber force should be drawn in proportion: a four Flight EFTS would provide thirty aircraft for example, while a two Flight school would allocate half as many. Fifteen of the twenty four Avro Cadets of 3 EFTS at Hamble were to be included as no reason could be seen for excluding them, providing bomb racks could be fitted, and five more schools were to allocate a total of 120 Miles Magisters. The remaining thirteen schools, all equipped with Tiger Moths, were scheduled to release a total of 350 aircraft. At this time the active training fleet was assessed at 756 aircraft, but a drawback was in pilot strength; for the 485 operational light bombers, only 378 instructor pilots could be mustered.

One solution to the shortage of pilots was to consider withdrawing students who had recently joined Service Flying Training Schools (SFTS) and who could be regarded as competent on recently vacated light training types; another was the redirection of more senior pilots over the age of thirty, and then forty, who were involved in administrative duties.

The de Havilland Aircraft Company was urgently required to assess the practical implications of converting innocuous Tiger Moth training aeroplanes into front line light bombers. It was a case of back to the wall offensive defence for which every option had to be considered. A scheme to carry a single 250lb bomb was proposed, and Major Hereward de Havilland, Captain de Havilland's younger brother who had been a fighter pilot during the First World War, flew a trial installation at Hatfield, but the dummy bomb fell off prematurely and embedded itself in open ground near the main factory buildings, fortunately without damage or injury. Geoffrey de Havilland Jnr was co-opted into the trials and dropped a 250lb bomb over the airfield which test pilot 'Baron' Cross and systems engineer Charles Caliendi from the Aerodynamics Department, and a future Chief Engineer of the Company, were detailed off to recover. In spite of their intensive searches no trace of it was ever found.

An installation to accept eight Cooper or 'F' type bombs of 20lb each was approved on 12 June 1940. Hereward de Havilland conducted release trials near the northern perimeter of Hatfield Aerodrome following which 1,500 sets of racks ('carrier, bomb, light series, type B, de Havilland'), were ordered. The first 100 sets were delivered to 25 Maintenance Unit (MU) Hartlebury at the beginning of July and the remainder followed at the rate of 200 sets per week to join 240 sets of 'old type carrier' originally intended for DH.9s and which were already in stock.

The scheme was not exactly original. As part of their sales campaign dating from early 1932 de Havilland had presented the Tiger Moth as a machine with great military versatility, and, amongst much besides, aircraft were configured to carry eight 20lb bombs capable of release from either seat, implying no perceived problem with operational weight or centre of gravity (CG) limitations. In January 1932, a 'Light Series Bomb Rack and Release Control (less Bowden Cable)' was being advertised in lists of subsidiary equipment available to customers: racks could be supplied at a cost of £24.0s.0d plus a fitting charge of £9.15s.0d each. Alternatively, the aircraft could be prepared for later installation for just ten shillings less.

Geoffrey de Havilland's younger brother Hereward, a fighter pilot during the First World War, conducted bomb dropping trials from a Tiger Moth over Hatfield Aerodrome. *BAE Systems*

While the Royal Air Force as lead customer chose to ignore most of the options, allocating its first Tiger Moths to basic flying training, a formation display team and a communications squadron, the offer of an aggressive Tiger Moth was far from shelved but rather refined. In October 1933 the company had unveiled their Tiger Moth Fighter which in addition to carrying a machine gun mounted over the front seat position, was scheduled to carry eight 20lb Cooper bombs slung from racks under the rear cockpit floor. The bomb carrying option taken up first by Persia was followed by others including Uruguay.

Drawing on this experience in 1940 de Havilland were able to provide early detail for manufacture of kits of the thirty eight individual component parts required for the bomb racks and their installation, including the plumbing of release gear up into the front cockpit. The kits were distributed from Hartlebury together with detailed instructions on how to undertake the conversion. Unlike some instruction leaflets AP.1449B/C.2-W could only have been compiled by a secretary noting every action during a trial installation at Hatfield: "If necessary, bend the pitot tubes to clear the aileron cables," mechanics were urged, no doubt as a result of such a requirement being discovered during the 'on the job' modification.

A total of fifteen man hours was required to complete the conversion of each aircraft in the field but was applicable only to Tiger Moth IIs held at certain Home Units which effectively meant all the Elementary Schools. Some of the modifications necessary to accept the installations were embodied on production aircraft at Cowley from October 1940 where T7266 (83764), was the first. The production standard saved ten hours of in-service engineering time and although updated instructions on how to complete the job were still being published as late as December 1941 the greater urgency had passed.

To maintain the CG when bombs were carried, and equally after they had been dropped, under the 1940 de Havilland scheme it was necessary for the pilot to operate solo, and from the front seat. Included in the thirty eight piece kit was a placard: 'When bombs are carried, rear cockpit must be empty'. Fixing the label was the very last action on the conversion instructions which instructed that it should be positioned to the top left-hand corner of the instrument panel and screwed in place with two ⅜ inch No 4 roundhead nickel-plated woodscrews. Nobody could have been left in any doubt.

It was anticipated that instructors would be operating the aircraft during their raids who were more used to the front seat position and which many preferred anyway, believing it to be less draughty than the rear cockpit.

Bomb release was activated by a pair of Bowden cables routed up through the floor on the starboard side and then outboard of the fuselage side frame to run between that and the fabric covering. Both

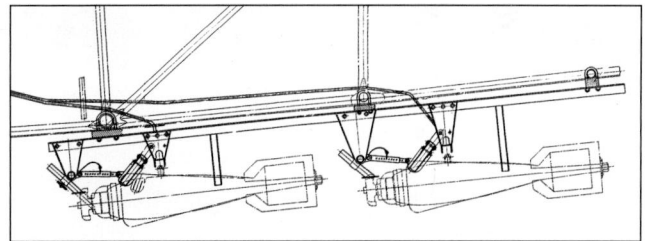

Bombs and racks located with respect to the lower longerons of a Tiger Moth fuselage. Bombs were rarely carried; racks and rails were often retained during training sorties. *de Havilland Aircraft Company*

cable outer sleeves were secured to the frame's mid-depth wooden stringer before looping up and back to link onto a pair of long throttle-type levers assembled in a quadrant and clamped to the structure near the slat cable pulley. A single plain split pin acted as safety guard and prevented inadvertent operation of the levers which were pulled backwards for release: the longer, outer lever for the rear salvo and the semi-arched inner lever for the forward four. There was no provision for dropping the small bombs singly, not that any prospective bomber pilot would have wanted a choice other than to drop the whole load on one pass and get on his way.

The two levers were grouped for ease in releasing both salvos together, controlled by the pilot's right hand, and assuming the throttle to have been pre-set for maximum power with the stick in his left, an unnatural situation for any instructor or long term habitué of the front cockpit of a Tiger Moth.

The bomb 'rack' was a box which could easily and quickly be fitted to a pair of fixed parallel rails situated under the floor of the rear cockpit and, unlike the inflexible installation on the Magister, were designed to accommodate either eight 20lb or 25lb bombs arranged transversely in two rows of four.

At the time the Tiger Moth Coastal Patrol Flights (CPF) were being re-equipped with Lysanders and Avro Ansons, the Assistant Chief of the Air Staff, aware that "DCAS has laid on a scheme for arming a number of Moths with light bomb racks," advised his colleagues that they should bear in mind "the Coastal Command Moths of which there are Flights of six at ...." But those particular birds had already flown.

In April it had been discovered that the Magister was capable of carrying only an old style 20lb Cooper bomb and by June it was admitted that modifications necessary to convert the aircraft into a light bomber were seriously interfering with production and that after the twenty eighth job the programme had been stopped. While the converted aircraft would be available for use, a much greater reliance would now be placed on the Tiger Moth. An urgent request from the Air Ministry was received by the Deputy Director of Operational Requirements: "Please signal number of Moths fitted with bomb racks as at 1200 hours June 25 1940, rate of fitting, and number still to be fitted," it asked.

Tiger Moths on the establishment of No 12 ERFTS Prestwick on a calm day in February 1936. Four years later the Air Ministry was asking how many of the aircraft were serviceable. *Flight*

Instructors were allowed to indulge in some authorised low level activity after normal working hours. *deHMC Archive*

Instructors from the schools were allocated 'after hours' flying sessions in which they were to practise low level flying at maximum speed. It was regarded by many as a welcome relief from their normal day in which six hours of instructional flying divided into forty five minute sessions was routine. Although each station had its own prescribed low-flying area the instructors made the most of their opportunity to indulge in authorised and legitimate hedge height inspection of the English countryside during transit.

At 22 EFTS Cambridge instructors were briefed to fly their Banquet Tiger Moths just above ground level until the enemy was identified and then climb to 800ft before diving down to 500ft to release their bombs. There were no dummy bombs available and practice attacks were carried out with the aircraft flown from the front cockpit by an instructor while, on his command, house bricks were thrown out of the rear cockpit by a senior student. The exercise was stopped after it was realised that a house brick fell faster than a diving Tiger Moth which risked catastrophic damage to the airframe or propeller.

Exercises with army units were encouraged and pilots from 3 EFTS Watchfield were invited to hurl make-believe bombs at troops positioned with camera guns around their detachment headquarters in the manor house at Coleshill. More seriously, during the early summer 15lb smoke bombs were dropped onto targets set up on the Salisbury Plain ranges. Pilots were gathered together at Old Sarum and taken by bus to assess form as Army Co-operation Lysanders attempted to lob practice bombs into the target circle. Returned to Old Sarum by road the Tiger Moth crews were given their heads and a stream of biplanes was let loose at 90mph, operating below the tree line, with the object of achieving a maximum score at the end of a shallow diving approach. It was all good fun and a break from the responsibilities of formal training but, of course, the only aggressive opposition was offered by army referees armed with nothing more lethal than their cameras, clipboards and Very pistols.

Part of the administrative task of civilian clerks employed in the watch offices at the school aerodromes was the regular update of flying logbooks and aircraft technical records, but instructors found that details of their practice sessions were not being recorded as a matter of official policy, a dictate resulting from the near tangible levels of secrecy and security being imposed on Plan Banquet at the time.

The imposition of the high level of alert was reflected in the fact that some senior personnel remained on station for long periods during the Battle of Britain in the summer of 1940. Flt Lt Monty Cox, Chief Flying Instructor (CFI) of 13 EFTS White Waltham, set up domestic and sleeping arrangements in his new office immediately after taking over from Sqn Ldr Bob Reeve in August 1940. The new CFI would have viewed the prospect of action with a greater clarity than most, having bombed and strafed the enemy from a Sopwith Camel during the latter days of conflict on the Western Front in 1918, operations which, combined with other duties, resulted in the award of a Military Cross.

At 1 EFTS Hatfield, volunteer engineers were called for to position with a pre-allocated pilot to their prescribed assembly point, and to be ready to service the aircraft and bomb-up whenever the call should come. Ben French ran his finger down the list of names which had been presented to him and selected Flt Lt V R Moon whom he regarded as a 'steady type'. Reggie Moon knew a thing or two about Tiger Moths. In 1932 as a Flying Officer he had been one of the five pilots from CFS who had flown formation aerobatics at the RAF Pageant at Hendon, a display which included sustained inverted demonstrations in close order.

In June 1934 Flying Officers Moon was one of a pair of instructors from the de Havilland School of Flying who had taken part in the display organised by the Royal Air Force Flying Club at Hatfield. Before an audience which included HRH Prince George, the future King George VI, Marshal of the Royal Air Force Lord Trenchard, and the Director of Civil Aviation, Lt Col Francis Shelmerdine, F/Os G S King and V R Moon were credited with "a lurid and very hair raising exhibition termed on the programme 'Eccentric Aerobatics'. They were! Their Tiger Moths were put into every conceivable position which, had we not known who they were, would have condemned them as the world's worst and most dangerous pilots."

A pleasing study of Tiger Moth R4922 in flight with the instrument hood erected. The Holt flareholder can be clearly seen trailing beneath the starboard lower mainplane, and was often confused with under-wing, as opposed to under-fuselage, bomb racks. Note the negative angle of the elevator in level flight. *deHMC Archive*

On Empire Air Day 1938, George King, 'Whizzy' to his friends, put on a show for the public who were invited into Hatfield Aerodrome to inspect the School facilities. Whizzy gave a display of crazy flying operating from the rear cockpit with the blind flying hood erected. The public was not aware that small wooden blocks prevented the hood from fully closing, allowing the pilot some slight visual reference. The finale of his display was to fly across the aerodrome skipping from one mainwheel to the other. Unfortunately, one touchdown was too heavy which caused the port side front fuselage frame to buckle, although he taxied in cheerfully enough to the accompaniment of loud applause from the crowd. Eager to see action, George King joined a Bristol Blenheim squadron in 1939 and was shot down and killed in one of the first raids of the war.

The blind flying hood, often referred to as the 'pram hood' due to its similarity in structure and operation to that supplied with a child's perambulator, was in use as a serious teaching tool by flying schools around the world until the Tiger Moth was replaced. In addition to taking off and flying aerobatics 'under the hood' students were also 'talked down' to a blind landing by their instructors, all in an effort to get them to understand and interpret exactly what their instruments were and were not indicating. Otherwise, the exercise was of no practical value.

From 1941, Reggie Moon instructed on Night Fighter Blenheims at Church Fenton where he was awarded a Bar to his Air Force Cross earned at Hatfield. Promoted to command 219 Squadron, he returned with the rank of Wing Commander to the appointment as CFI with 1 EFTS which had long since moved to the Hatfield satellite aerodrome at Holwell Hyde, (Panshanger). It was from there that he acted as instructor to Don Stoneham in Tiger Moth DE836 (85734), in the first sortie flown post-war by the renamed No 1 Reserve Flying School (RFS) on 13 June 1947.

All volunteer 'Banquet' engineers were issued with a standard service flying kit: Sidcot suit, parachute and leather helmet, in addition to the obligatory tin hat, gas mask and cape, all of which were stored in steel lockers inside the school hangar. Each volunteer was advised to prepare an overnight bag and rations for two days and was read the Official Secrets Act. Nobody outside of their immediate circle of fellow travellers was to be allowed the slightest hint of the plans.

The establishment of every EFTS included a civilian armourer and in the summer of 1940 the post at 1 EFTS was filled by Len Gaskin, later to remuster in the handsome Hatfield tower as an air traffic controller. The technician was called upon to provide essential instruction in loading the bomb racks while maintaining the highest standards of safety. This aspect was high in the minds of the pilots and engineers as dummy drops were made onto a carpet spread on the hangar floor. Rumours had filtered down from the Experimental Department that the prototype trials had been made with a live round included amongst the clutch.

While Hereward de Havilland progressed the release and delivery trials near the carefully tended woodland on the north eastern perimeter of Hatfield Aerodrome, the scene of seasonal shooting parties organised by the de Havilland directors in happier days, the school instructors were emulating their colleagues elsewhere and flying along the hedges in their designated low level zone at Wheathampstead. Touch-and-go forced landings at No Man's Common were practised with a new relish.

Ben French was on permanent standby to contact all personnel who were not on site 'should the balloon go up'. He was authorised to fill the petrol tank of his motorcycle and call on the names and

The Home Command markings and serial batch of this Tiger Moth are evidence of a deception. The aircraft is EM836, the place Hatfield Aerodrome, and the date, 2 June 1944. Attaching the bombs is believed to be Hereward de Havilland. The scene was set up by Merton Park Film Studios and incorporated into the classic de Havilland film biography of the Mosquito.
de Havilland Aircraft Company

addresses provided against a secure list. His sole message was to be 'Banquet Light'; all other communication was forbidden. If the intended recipient was not at home, a message was to be left asking that they should telephone the chief engineer as soon as possible.

Regarded as an emergency and hopefully temporary measure, proper testing of the Tiger Moth with her military ordnance still had to be completed to an agreed schedule and performance measured and recorded. How would this trainer aircraft behave with up to 250lb of small bombs slung underneath the rear seat, and just as relevant, how would she handle with empty cradles? The Aeroplane and Armament Experimental Establishment (A&AEE) at Boscombe Down was tasked with the job of finding out.

Two Tiger Moths, N9454 (82508), and T5610 (83303), were delivered to A&AEE in the summer of 1940 to become the responsibility of 'A' Squadron, Performance Testing Squadron. N9454 had been built in November 1939 and although allocated to storage at 20 MU Aston Down, may have been retained by de Havilland as a trials aircraft. T5610, a brand new machine from the June production batch, was fitted with bomb racks and after a prolonged one hour flight test by de Havilland test pilot Pat Fillingham on 28 July, during which he encountered no peculiarities in handling, was despatched to Boscombe Down. The initial briefing was to investigate 'Handling and Diving', but at the request of Flying Training Command the remit was widened to include spinning.

A series of flight tests at varying weights and CG positions, with the pilot operating in either front or rear cockpits, showed the aircraft to behave much as expected but in level flight at an extended aft CG position it was noted that there was insufficient trim to allow hands-off flight at full throttle. This may have been considered a serious deficiency in view of the revised control layout of the bomber cockpit conversion.

The diving tests were conducted at one third throttle setting or less in order to limit the engine to its maximum permitted rotational speed of 2,350rpm which was reached very rapidly. At engine speeds of 1,500rpm to 2,000rpm, and dive angles of 50° to 55°, indicated airspeeds of 160mph to 170mph were recorded operating from 5,000ft, speeds which it was considered would be difficult to better within a reasonable loss of height due to the extra drag effected by the racks and bombs.

'A' Squadron reported that they were satisfied with the aircraft's diving performance and control and proceeded with bomb release tests conducted when in level flight, a prolonged dive, and from a dive following a half roll. Spinning trials were flown only with bombs removed and with solo pilots operating first from the front and then the rear seat. At each loading situation spins of eight turns were made both to the right and to the left, during which it was noted that the control column tended to move in the direction of the spins which were described as being steady and of a normal attitude. The aeroplane responded to the standard method of spin recovery which resulted in spins stopping within half a turn. Height lost during the eight turn sequence amounted to about 2,000ft. Boscombe Down's secret report concluded that in their opinion, the behaviour of the military Tiger Moth II in general handling, diving and spinning, was satisfactory.

There was some debate at Chief of Staff level on whether, once fitted, bomb carriers should remain fitted to the aircraft. One line of thought was that carriers should be removed and stored until the Plan Banquet force was called to readiness. It was decided, however, that it would be better to leave them permanently in place "provided they did not seriously affect the performance of the aircraft in its role as a trainer." One senior staff officer was moved to point out that it would be uneconomical to leave bomb carriers attached as they would be written off every time an aircraft was crashed!

Flying Training Command expressed concerns over spinning with the racks in position and on 16 August 1940 Albert Brant, Hatfield-based Service Manager of the de Havilland Aircraft Company, wrote to all Elementary Schools to advise them that to improve flying characteristics during training the entire bomb rack, or at least the rear crutch boards fitted in accordance with modifications 'Moth 11/73 and 11/77', should be removed. The Air Ministry confirmed the detail of the letter by signal to all units on 25 September and the instruction was re-emphasised in an Air Ministry circular although this was not published until the following April.

It was inevitable that some schools flew the aircraft with the carriers permanently attached while others removed them for training during the working day, refitting the selected aircraft to coincide with the instructors' practice sessions after normal hours. While it was simple enough to schedule modification of the sixty nine Tiger Moths confirmed by the RAF to be in Reserve Storage on 1 June, conversion of the working aircraft had to be integrated into the school programme. For minimum disruption slave aircraft were rotated through the system, enabling establishment Tiger Moths to be temporarily withdrawn and modified on site.

The two trials' aeroplanes went their separate ways. In November, N9454 flew from Boscombe Down into a period of eighteen months storage at 10 MU Hullavington before allocation in June 1942 to a detachment of 2 Squadron operating their North American Mustang 1s from Gatwick. Within a month the aircraft had been broken and was routed through the locally based Southern Aircraft CRU for repair. After a few weeks with 1424 Flight, N9454 crashed on 1 December 1942 and, having been repaired by Taylorcraft at Thurmaston, passed through Hullavington again en-route to the packing unit at High Ercall, from where she was despatched for service in South Africa. During passage in convoy LS33, her freighter, the SS *Djambe*, was attacked and sunk.

T5610 fared better. The aircraft was returned to de Havilland at Hatfield by the end of 1942 where she was used extensively during the next two years in development of improved 'suction' systems, especially with regard to night flying instrumentation, and occasionally for the airborne inspection of the factory camouflage scheme, both exercises often flown by Pat Fillingham accompanied by Resident Technical Officer (RTO), Ray Fitch. The aircraft was eventually posted to Scotland and spent a few weeks with Station Flight at RAF Kirkbride early in 1945 before heading south again and disposal into the civil market from 5 MU Kemble in July 1947.

Meanwhile, in 1940 all was still not well in the training units who, not reassured, were advised to mark bomb racks with the serial numbers of the aircraft from which they had been separated. In addition, the tireless engineering staff was encouraged to ensure there would be no delay in the event of a national emergency by periodically practicing refitting the crutches in position on the racks.

In addition to what might be considered the conventionality of bomb racks, Tiger Moths were involved in two other bizarre anti-invasion schemes in 1940. Although its origins have been dimmed, the aircraft was fleetingly involved in a plan to spray invading forces with a poisonous bright green insecticide called Paris Green. In powder form this was to be carried in a tank installed in the front cockpit and dispensed through nozzles situated under the floor. No details of the installation or of its sponsors or trials appear to have survived.

The 'Paraslasher' was, on the other hand, tried and tested but not taken up in spite of impeccable credentials. The idea was originated by George Reid of the Reid and Sigrist Company who, apart from being the contracted civil operators of 7 EFTS and its Tiger Moths at Desford, were designers and builders of aircraft instruments, parts and equipment. A garden scythe attached to an 8ft pole was stowed underneath a Tiger Moth fuselage, pivoting about the knuckle joint of the split undercarriage. In the extended position it was intended to trail the scythe through massed ranks of descending parachutists, ripping canopies and causing mayhem. Jack Bentley, Chief Engineer at MRC Ltd. (Teleflex Controls), was ordered to Desford with great urgency in March 1940, there to liaise with Reid and Sigrist's Chief Designer Chas Bower, a talented engineer previously involved with the Hawker Hart and later responsible for the twin engined Desford. The urgency, he discovered to his surprise, centred on how the paraslasher pole could be shifted through a 90° arc, controlled by Teleflex cables.

George Reid obtained permission for the conversion of one aircraft, G-ADPG (3397), and the system was demonstrated at Braunstone Aerodrome, Leicester, on 12 June 1940 by the CO of 7 EFTS, Squadron Leader George Lowdell, a pre-war air display pilot. Through his contacts at the Air Ministry at which institution he had variously been a member of the Air Inventions Committee and Training Departments, George Reid arranged for a further trial to be conducted for officials on 7 July, following which his offer to attack weighted parachutes descending over Henlow was rejected. In spite of his submission that the device was cheap, effective, non-intrusive to training duties, and required no back-up service or maintenance, the scheme was dropped because, according to official belief, pilots less competent than George Lowdell would be unable to wring out maximum benefit. Perhaps to ease his frustration, on occasions the scythe had been observed menacingly trailed across the ground at high speed. Another reason for the rejection of the idea might have been that the time between troop transports appearing overhead and parachutists touching down was probably a lot less than the warm-up time on the ground for a recently activated Gipsy Major engine.

During the course of normal school activities, when being flown by a pilot with three hours solo time engaged in landing practice at Desford on 27 September 1940, G-ADPG levelled out too high, stalled from 10ft and was written off as a result of the damage sustained.

No documentation can be traced which details the authorised installation or use of bomb racks fitted under the wings of Tiger Moths based in Great Britain, but the number of sightings and reports would indicate that such a provision may have been made as the result of local initiatives when necessity once again proved to be the mother of invention. The habit of Boscombe Down and Farnborough test pilot Allen Wheeler in referring to 'wing' racks in all written communication on the subject, has done nothing to lift the veil of confusion.

At least one Tiger Moth with a pair of 25lb Cooper bombs fitted to racks carried under each lower wing was observed by the Spitfire pilots of 603 Squadron to be operational for a few days in January 1940 at Dyce Aerodrome, Aberdeen. This was an aircraft from 1 Coastal Patrol Flight (CPF), a unit which had been established as unarmed reconnaissance patrollers in December 1939. The on-site modifications may have pre-empted what was already being considered elsewhere and are unlikely to have received approval from anywhere but within the unit. Much to the consternation of the Spitfire air and ground crews, not to mention the CPF pilots, the bombs were inclined to fall off the racks when manoeuvring on the ground, particularly during touchdown, and apart from familiarisation only two operational sorties are believed to have been flown before the experiment was halted and the racks removed.

Possibly the idea for wing mounted bomb racks migrated with ex-CPF aircraft to 11 EFTS at Perth during the late summer of 1940. A pupil pilot recorded, long after retirement as a Consolidated Catalina captain and Station Commander based in India, that during his initial training at Perth in August and September of that year, some of the establishment's Tiger Moths were fitted with what he clearly described as bomb racks fitted 'outboard of each landing wheel' and that each rack was capable of carrying four bombs. In the evenings the instructors were seen carrying out practice dive bombing attacks on a target set up in the corner of the airfield.

While wandering around the dispersals at 13 EFTS at White Waltham in August 1940, pupil pilot Neville Duke noticed that the aircraft of one Flight were fitted with what appeared to be racks under each lower wing capable of carrying four bombs. The school's recently appointed CFI, Flt Lt George 'Monty' Cox MC, advised his instructional staff that when armed, these aircraft should only be flown solo. A misinterpretation of this order seems to have been that 'with a full bomb load and two up, it is not possible to carry full fuel'.

No 13 EFTS was operated under contract by the de Havilland Aircraft Company and, although administered as a completely autonomous body, ultimately reported back to the Enterprise at Hatfield. The de Havilland technical archive makes no mention of any modification which involved fitting bomb racks anywhere except underneath the fuselage, and although it may appear improbable that an operational establishment so closely tied to its manufacturing parent would effect such a radical modification at a local level, August and September 1940 were desperate times calling for dramatic initiatives.

As recently as 3 July 1940 a Dornier Do217 had attacked the airfield at White Waltham, laying two sticks of small fragmentation bombs

For the benefit of new groundcrew recruits at No 9 EFTS Ansty, a civilian instructor at the rear cockpit demonstrates the operation of the Holt flare system. This underwing device has often been confused for a wing mounted bomb rack. *Flight*

across the dispersal, destroying six Tiger Moths and damaging twenty five more. A year later, 13 EFTS was closed down and the premises vacated for use as Headquarters by the Air Transport Auxiliary, a move which greatly displeased de Havilland who in pre-war days had planned and built the site for maximum efficiency and long term use. Although they would have much preferred a move to nearby Benson the company was tasked with organising ninety Tiger Moths for 17 EFTS based at Peterborough until the unit there was disbanded in May 1942.

What chance that underwing racks may have been confused with single point Holt flare carriers bolted through the lower pickup bracket for the forward interplane strut? The carrier arms were designed to fold backwards when not in use, an additional safety feature intended to prevent them hooking onto obstructions during landing. The flare carriers were not easy to see on casual inspection when standing near a Tiger Moth but their location at 8ft from the root end was not in conformity with the opinion of most observers which put the racks close to the fuselage sides, and definitely within the first bay.

In the intervening years, restorers opening up wings for structural inspection prior to application of new fabric have occasionally reported the presence of apparently redundant fittings. The lack of part numbers stamped on some of them would indicate local modification, the absence of identification certainly hampering any serious investigation of what might be just another red herring.

At 22 EFTS Cambridge in November 1940, pupil pilot Idris Griffith was sent solo in a Tiger Moth which he described as having been subject to 'considerable usage'. The pre-flight inspection was inadequate, the pilot paying greater attention to his cockpit drill and the prospects of what lay immediately ahead. After what appeared to be a normal take-off, the aircraft refused to fly straight and level and it was with great difficulty that the first soloist managed to land back only to be met by an exasperated instructor, not with a congratulatory smile but a demand to know what had happened to standard technique. A closer look at the aircraft revealed that the 'bomb rack' underneath the starboard lower wing had been removed but perhaps the arrival of the NAAFI wagon had interrupted the mechanic's schedule, and the aircraft had been presented to the flight line with the port side unit still firmly attached.

No 116 Squadron was disbanded in 1918 and its Handley Page 0/400 bombers struck off charge. From the nucleus of 1 Anti-Aircraft Co-operation Unit the squadron was re-formed at Hatfield in February 1941, operating Westland Lysander IIIs, but moved to Hendon in April of that year where Hawker Hurricane Is were inherited. The squadron was headquartered at a number of different airfields all located around London until disbandment in May 1945, by which time DH Hornet Moth, Airspeed Oxford II and Avro Anson I and XII had all been part of the establishment. The nature of the squadron's business, partly the provision of flying services for anti-aircraft gun and radar alignment in various areas of the country, necessitated the regular deployment of small detachments. In July 1942 Detachment D5 equipped with Lysander IIIs was stationed at Church Fenton, Yorkshire.

Mindful of the continuing and crucial need to economise on fuel the Air Ministry believed that D5's non-fighting role could equally well be achieved by substituting Gipsy Major powered Tiger Moths for the Mercury engined Lysanders, consuming about a quarter of the precious liquid for the same end result. Tiger Moth DE680 (85621), was one of a total of thirty four brand new aircraft allocated to 116 Squadron on 1 July 1942 and was delivered a few days later by a pilot of the ATA positioning from 38 MU Llandow. On arrival the Detachment crews were astonished to discover what to their minds were tiny bomb racks fitted to the undersides of both lower wings, and the fighting potential of the aircraft was the matter of much discussion and playful demonstration.

The Commanding Officer of D5, P/O Jenkins, freely discussed the options: in case of an invasion, still a possibility in July 1942, he and his fellow pilots W/O Morgan and Sgt Evans, would fight with the Lysanders, leaving the Detachment's two Wireless Operator/Air Gunners Kydd and Hawkesworth to fly the Tiger Moth. Jenkins repeated his philosophy so often that Sgts Kydd and Hawkesworth realised he was not joking at their expense, especially when the tactics to be employed at hedge top height were debated and briefed.

Sgt Hawkesworth's first 'training' flight took place on 16 July 1942 and he logged a total of almost eighteen hours with the squadron pilots on 'familiarisation' work plus additional unrecorded sorties. The invasion did not come, the crisis was eased, and DE680 was transferred in May 1943 to 486 Squadron, a New Zealand unit operating Hawker Typhoons from Tangmere.

NEW ZEALAND

With the Japanese on the rampage throughout the Pacific even New Zealand was vulnerable to their unwelcome attentions and the Tiger Moth was immediately considered part of a greater effort to develop the best line of defence: offence! Grp Capt Michael Keogh, Director of Repair and Maintenance, Royal New Zealand Air Force, had been trained as a pilot before joining the Engineering Branch and had been awarded the Albert Medal for rescuing a pilot trapped in a crashed and burning aircraft. Taking a leaf from the Japanese book on tactics it is alleged that 'Micky' Keogh proposed to the Air Staff that Tiger Moths carrying bombs, and flown by the more elderly officers and men who had previously received some form of pilot training, such as himself, should be deliberately crashed into ships carrying the invading hordes.

That may have been the version which filtered down through the ranks but the Air Staff did take the matter seriously enough to draw up plans in December 1941 for every available training aircraft to be converted to a fighter or a bomber, including a force of eighty Tiger Moths. 'Light Series Mechanically Actuated Bomb Carriers' were fitted under the fuselages, initially with a capacity for four 20lb bombs, later increased to eight. Due to weight and balance limitations, the aircraft could only be flown solo and from the front seat. Not for the Tiger Moth was the prospect of a machine gun equipped rear cockpit to emulate the Hawker Hinds, Vickers Vincents, Fairey Gordons and Vickers Vildebeeste, or a forward firing gun which converted North American Harvards and Airspeed Oxfords into potent fighter bombers.

Hugh Buckingham, General Manager of the de Havilland Aircraft Company of New Zealand's factory at Rongotai, Wellington, was asked to design in great secrecy a bomb rack system which could be fitted to the underside of each of the country's civilian owned DH.89 Dragon Rapides and his basic but practical suggestions were conveyed to Hatfield for approval. In the event the Dragon Rapides were not armed and in accord with British belief were considered to be of greater value in a transport configuration.

The Tiger Moth fleet was accorded the lowest priority in provisioning of offensive equipment, not least in view of their primary and continuing role of training new pilots. Courses of fifty five pupils continued to join the Elementary Schools every four weeks.

The New Zealand Defence Plan as approved by Air Commodore R V Goddard, Chief of the Air Staff, was issued under the 'secret' classification from Air Force Headquarters in Wellington on 17 January 1942. Known as the FAFAI Scheme (Forces Available For Anti Invasion), the Tiger Moth element was clearly defined. Four operational light bomber squadrons of 'Moths' were to be formed (41, 42, 43 and 44 Auxiliary Squadrons), provided from the resources of 1, 2, 3 and 4 EFTS, together with 51 Auxiliary Squadron created from the Central Flying School. Each squadron was to have an initial establishment of eighteen aircraft and instructor pilots, later increased to twenty four. Administered as 'paper' squadrons within their host organisations, each school was required to nominate a Squadron Commander and conventional chain of authority for flying, maintenance and administrative duties. Officers with recent operational experience were appointed by Air Force Headquarters to advise school commanders on the best tactics to be taught during squadron training. From July 1942 the eighth week in each course was dedicated to concentrated operational training for the instructors, either on a local basis or as dictated by exercises organised from HQ, during which the local hedges were subject to constant low level review.

Each of the new Moth auxiliary squadrons was initially divided into two Flights of nine aircraft each, with a Pool Reserve composed of all remaining aircraft on the establishment strength and fitted with whatever left-over equipment could be made available. The Chief Flying Instructor was usually appointed Squadron Commander, and it was the Station Commander's prerogative to nominate Flight Commanders and other officers with a similar authority within the Pool Reserve.

Due to a shortage of practice bombs the CFI/Squadron Commander was advised to arrange training on the most appropriate ranges with aircraft operating in sections of three or by Flights, when imaginary bombs would be dropped against a pre-arranged signal to simulate the attack window. Methods of ordnance delivery were the subject of discussion between squadrons and for their declared role of beach reconnaissance and troop harassment a low level shallow diving technique, using the cross-over of the centre section bracing wires as a reference, was considered to be the most productive, endorsing what had been discovered in England during the tense days of 1940.

After the danger was past a trainee pilot at 2 EFTS New Plymouth explained that previously, on all solo flights except when aerobatics were expected, pilots flew with a clutch of four anti-personnel bombs attached to the aircraft which were to be dropped on invading troops, after which instructions were quite clear: "We were to fly inland, land somewhere, take off our uniforms, camouflage the aircraft, and get the hell out of it."

Bomber squadrons of Tiger Moths temporarily repainted in camouflage colours were allocated to pre-planned airfield and satellite locations dotted around the major cities which were considered the most obvious enemy targets and stocks of bombs, spares and fuel sufficient for twenty flying hours per aircraft were scheduled to be laid down. In the event, neither of the code words required to spring the trap were ever broadcast. 'FAFAI' would have brought units to a four hour state of readiness with all flying training stopped in favour of essential test flying only and the immediate equipping and provisioning of aircraft. 'LAFRAF' was the signal to bomb-up and for armouries to issue the available supply of revolvers and tin hats. 'Fly-off to rendezvous' instructions were then tensely awaited from Air Force Headquarters.

Although the FAFAI scheme was never tested in anger the plan was conceived with the best of motives, was well organised and the aircrew thoroughly briefed and trained. Their period of legal low level activity was considered a welcome break from the exigencies of circuit discipline.

No 44 Auxiliary Squadron was disbanded along with 4 EFTS on 9 March 1942 when the aerodrome at Whenuapai was handed over to operational squadrons. The aircraft and trained staff were absorbed by the three remaining units, all of which were located by design in South Island and whose establishments were subsequently increased to at least fifty five Tiger Moths each. CFS renounced its anti-invasion status in July 1942 when 51 Auxiliary Squadron was stood down, and 41, 42 and 43 Squadrons were formally disbanded on 5 April 1943.

Possibly there were few in New Zealand who realised that machine guns had been fitted to Tiger Moths in Persia and Norway else they may have saved much effort. In 1942 a RNZAF Tiger Moth was positioned to Rongotai where three de Havilland engineers were tasked with fitting a 0.303 Lewis gun on the centre section above the fuel tank in the style of a First World War scout. After a few days of complete frustration the job was abandoned.

With the disbandment of the FAFAI units and feeling still vulnerable the personnel with No 20 Squadron based at the northernmost station at Onerahi decided to investigate the possibility of fitting two 0.303 Bren Guns above the leading edges of the top wings of their resident Tiger Moth NZ1441 (DHNZ121), firing outside the arc of the propeller and fed by modified belts originating from ammunition boxes located in the front cockpit. The idea was never put into practice and shortly after its demise Tiger Moth NZ1441 was itself wrecked in an accident in the main street of Whangarei.

AUSTRALIA

In 1942 Australia also was concerned about the prospects of a Japanese invasion and for what protection could be provided had moved the majority of her slender defence resources to the areas of most immediate danger in the north. Supposing the Japanese invasion fleet merely bypassed the obvious landing sites and their defences and hit hard straight at Sydney and the extensive beaches on the eastern seaboard? What was left in the country's armoury?

The answer was a few armed Commonwealth Aircraft Corporation Wirraway trainers and Lockheed Hudsons which could operate from only a small number of adequately large airfields, and about 700 Tiger Moths with nearly 1,000 experienced pilots, mostly instructors, stationed at the Elementary Schools. One such instructor, a Flight Commander at 4 EFTS Mascot, was John Kingsford-Smith, a nephew of Sir Charles Kingsford-Smith, the legendary 'Smithy'.

John Kingsford-Smith devised a plan to fit stocks of redundant under-wing bomb racks to Tiger Moths at the schools scattered throughout Victoria and New South Wales. He had discovered nearly 100 bomb rack sets originally designed for Westland Wapitis in store at Richmond, together with others from DH.9s and Hawker Demons. Additional racks were later discovered at Laverton.

The proposal for the emergency arming of Tiger Moths was submitted to the Commanding Officer of Eastern Command Headquarters at Port Piper, Air Commodore Lachal, who was impressed sufficiently to stand down Kingsford-Smith from his instructional duties, probably coincident with the closure of 4 EFTS in April 1942 anyway, and to appoint him to head a small team to develop the scheme.

The installation was designed by two friends of Kingsford-Smith, both of whom worked for de Havilland at Mascot: Johnny Larkin and Norman Lennon. In their design the pilot's bomb release controls were divided between the port and starboard side of the rear cockpit: the 'safety' device was cable operated, using as a locator the top rail of a Tiger Moth door and bolted with a slight nose down bias just below the slat operating quadrant on the starboard fuselage sideframe.

Bomb release was effected by cables connected to a pair of T handles operating in a nearly vertical orientation on the port side, forward of the trimmer quadrant and below the combined throttle/mixture levers. The starboard bombs were released by the handle in a lower and more rearward position when compared to the port control, a configuration which permitted a firm grip on both handles at the same time to encourage a simultaneous drop. If the pilot forgot which release was appropriate to which rack, a diagrammatic scheme was stencilled onto an adjacent facia. Unlike their British counterparts, however, and those across the Tasman Sea, the aggressive Australian Tiger Moth was not intended to double as a trainer after conversion. The aircraft was designed to be flown solo from the rear cockpit with the front instrument panel and windscreen removed and a fairing secured over the void. In this configuration and with her bright yellow training colours hidden under

The only Tiger Moth known to have carried under wing bomb racks, and for which incontrovertible photographic evidence exists, is A17-330 of the Royal Australian Air Force, converted to the specification called up by John Kingsford-Smith in 1942. *RAAF Museum*

Left: A clear view of the underwing bomb rack positions on A17-330. The de Havilland factory at Mascot and other interesting hardware can be seen in the background. *via Bruce Winley*

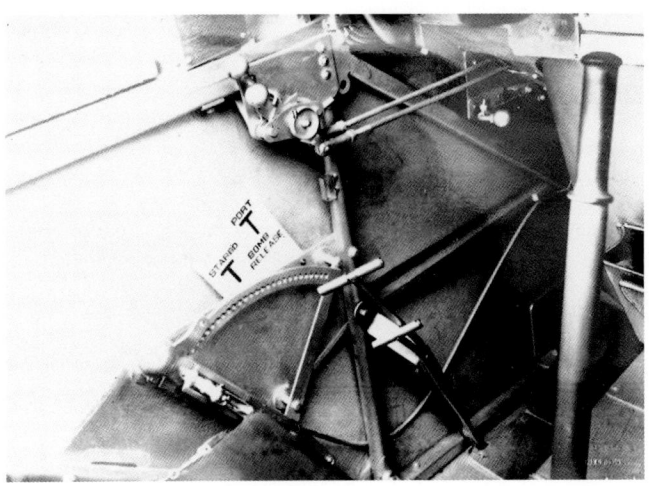 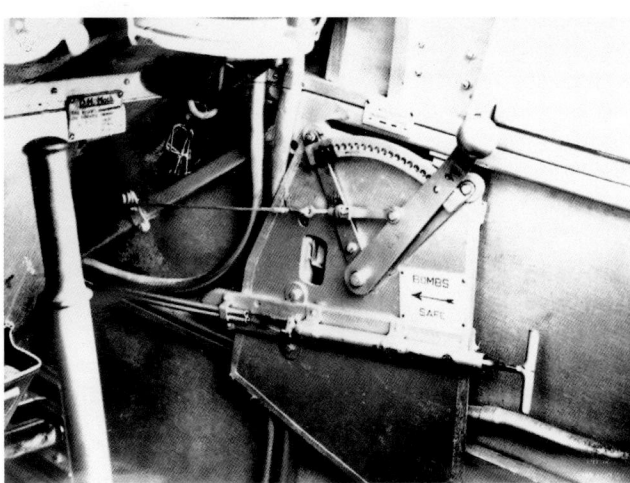

Bomb release T handles on the port side of the rear cockpit of A17-330, together with an illustrated placard indicating what does what. *via Bruce Winley*

The Australian underwing bombs could be armed or made safe in the air via an arrangement on the starboard side of the rear cockpit, utilising the top rail of a Tiger Moth cockpit door. *via Bruce Winley*

a faded camouflage scheme, Tiger Moth bombers were to be deployed to their operational sites and scheduled to remain there for as long as was considered necessary.

The de Havilland Aircraft Company at Mascot was formally involved with the trials and conversion of Tiger Moth A17-330 (DHA349), a judicious decision considering the clamour for conversion kits which might be expected if the prospect of invasion loomed large. A17-330 had been based with 4 EFTS on home ground at Mascot before transfer to 2 Communications Flight, also at Mascot, remaining with that unit until May 1942 when the Flight moved to Wagga Wagga. However, the aircraft was re-allocated to 3 Communications Flight which formed at Mascot just as soon as their predecessors had shifted their kit and was retained for what was officially described as 'photographic duties'. This was a euphemism driven by security for 'bomber conversion trials'. The aircraft was featured in a number of official photographs released after the war in which a 40lb bomb is displayed in each under-wing cradle adjacent to a placard warning that the maximum design load for the configuration under normal conditions was never intended to be greater than a 30lb bomb in any one position.

Having established the credibility of the mechanism it was necessary to test the concept and release trials were conducted at Richmond where it was established that remarkable accuracy could be achieved when operating at high speed and at low level. Kingsford-Smith had already given considerable thought to the theoretical disposition of this new offensive defence force and ideal sites were considered to be the fifty two golf courses situated within a fifteen mile coastal band between Newcastle and Wollongong. Assisted by two other RAAF pilots operating standard aircraft, Kingsford-Smith and his team surveyed each site and rejected only four as unsuitable for operational use.

Flight trials were conducted from all the selected fairways much to the consternation of some club officials. The secretary of the Royal Sydney Club at Rose Bay suffered a fit of apoplexy when he saw the damage being inflicted by the Tiger Moth's tailskid and a popular rumour has it that he was doubly outraged to discover that the responsible pilot was not a club member. But it was just a rumour. Having threatened police action and complaints directed at the highest seats in government, the secretary was told to expect ten aircraft to arrive for trials the following day on the authority of the same government.

From the trial fitting of the first rack to completion of the fifty second site survey, only four weeks had elapsed. The plan had proved feasible and de Havilland were immediately commissioned to produce 800 sets of standard conversion kits which would include the sets of old bomb racks previously discovered in store.

Plans were in hand to issue location maps and to provision each fairway with a 44 gallon barrel of petrol and a supply of anti-personnel bombs when the cavalry arrived in the form of two squadrons of American Curtiss P-40 Kittyhawks, posted into the area. Tested and ready for action, the Tiger Moth bomber project was shelved.

A17-330 was delivered into store at Canberra the following year, perhaps as an insurance, but having been stripped back to her standard configuration she joined an Air Ambulance Unit in Queensland in June 1943. Following spells with 8 and 9 EFTS and another period in storage, the aircraft was sold for £305 in April 1946 to the Royal Aero Club of Western Australia in Perth where she was broken down for spare parts.

CHAPTER SEVEN

Getting Into a Spin

Possibly the first recorded Tiger Moth spinning accident, one which involved a civilian aircraft, occurred on 15 December 1933 near to Hatfield Aerodrome when G-ACJA (3191), failed to recover from a spin initiated at about 1,500ft, and fell into trees just outside the airfield boundary. The pilot was a recently qualified student of the de Havilland Aeronautical Technical School who was working towards his 'B' commercial pilot's licence. G-ACJA was a demonstration model on loan to the London Aeroplane Club and with only 115 flying hours logged since the previous August, most of which were accumulated during a demonstration tour to the Middle East. After taking off from Hatfield the previous afternoon the pilot had flown to Stag Lane and engaged in the exuberant low level antics of a man with ninety seven hours experience, a display for the benefit of his ex colleagues which earned him what was politely termed 'a caution' from a senior member of the de Havilland staff.

The following morning G-ACJA returned to Hatfield and indulged in a further series of indifferent aerobatics. The left hand spin was intentional but in the opinion of the accident inspector it was

DH.85 Leopard Moth CH-368, DH.60GIII Moth Major, probably CH-369, a DH.60M Moth and DH.82A Tiger Moth G-ACJA together with some splendid carpets and 'office' furniture, represented the de Havilland Aircraft Company at the Geneva Aero Show in April 1934. *P Geiselhard*

a dangerous error of judgement to spin from such a low altitude during which manoeuvre the pilot failed to make proper use of the controls to effect a rapid recovery. The report included a note to the effect that G-ACJA was not fitted with Handley Page automatic slots, an optional extra rarely fitted to de Havilland's demonstration aircraft due to the substantial royalty levied on each installation.

At the time of the accident the aircraft was painted in a style most unlike any de Havilland demonstration aircraft with the fuselage displaying a broad two-tone spiral which required the letters of the registration to be painted in alternative colours. Following repairs G-ACJA was displayed in an overall silver scheme, looking pristine and with a blind flying hood in the raised position, at the Geneva Aero Show in May 1934 when she shared stand space at the indoor exhibition with DH.85 Leopard Moth CH-368 (7045,) and a DH.60GIII. Soon after the aircraft was photographed at an unknown location fitted with a metal propeller and painted in the maroon and silver colours of the de Havilland School of Flying. In September 1934 G-ACJA was sold to Austria, joining the Luftschutzkommando as A-81, but only three months later she was lost in unrecorded circumstances and the entry was cancelled.

Operating from Hatfield in 1936 the London Aeroplane Club's G-ADGO (2262), a Tiger Moth built as a practical exercise by members of the de Havilland Aeronautical Technical School, and not

Above: G-ADXB spun into the ground near Hatfield in 1933. The relatively undamaged fuselage was repaired and having been mated to new wings was returned to service. She was impressed into military markings in 1940 and collided with a Bristol Blenheim over Halton. *Phil Hagger*

Right: Painted in very un-de Havilland style for a company demonstrator, G-ACJA on a scrubby airfield far from home in 1933. *Hugh Buckingham*

Below: Nine days before Christmas 1933, Tiger Moth G-ACJA spun into trees just outside the boundary of Hatfield Aerodrome, assisted by the pilot, according to the accident inspector's report. Four months later G-ACJA was an exhibit at the Geneva Aero Show. *deHMC Archive*

fitted with slots, was seen to dive towards the Dunstable clubhouse of the London Gliding Club before climbing away to perform two loops. At the end of the second manoeuvre the aircraft commenced a spin from less than 1,000ft but recovery was very late and during the pull-out the aircraft flew into the ground. An embarrassed pilot afterwards admitted that the second 'loop' was a failed attempt at a stall turn to the left from which the aircraft had spun off. In this case the accident inspector expressed no opinion other than that the aeroplane appeared to have suffered no pre-crash defects or failures. Given just another 10ft perhaps, G-ADGO might have survived.

Before the critical need for offensive equipment had even been contemplated, an instructor from 1 ERFTS Hatfield experienced a fright when spinning a Tiger Moth with a pupil early in 1938. Until now he had regarded the type with great respect, and was confident enough in the structural integrity to have tried a bunt, a half outside loop. After four turns of a spin with recovery due to be effected following the appearance of St Albans Abbey for the seventh time, the aircraft seemed to lose momentum before quite suddenly rearing up into a climbing attitude to enter what was described as a fast, unbanked turn with the wings parallel with the horizon. The instructor, John Nesbit-Dufort, 'Whippy' to close friends, reported no skidding sensation; he considered that he was sitting above the vertical axis of rotation and that the aircraft had no forward speed whatsoever, a fact verified by the needle of the Air Speed Indicator (ASI) flickering around the lowest graduations on the dial.

Realising the aircraft was in a flat spin the instructor took control and at first attempted normal recovery action, but the controls appeared to be stuck fast and he was suspicious that the pupil pilot was still clinging on. Following a burst of high volume communication via the Gosport tubes the pupil exposed both gloved hands simultaneously but the stick remained obstinate, forced back against the stop as the elevators were deflected upwards with the rapid descent of the aircraft. On the point of ordering abandonment at 1,000ft, 'Whippy' Dufort remembered he had not enlisted the aid of the gently ticking engine and in a last chance effort slammed on full throttle. With some elevator power restored the Tiger Moth almost instantly flipped into a normal spin from which a standard recovery was made at 150ft. He later wrote that his post-flight report was treated with some disbelief. Soon after he was posted to Central Flying School (CFS) to attend a re-categorisation course after which, and with two and a half hours of night flying experience, he was judged sufficiently qualified to teach others.

On 13 September 1940 Tiger Moth N6948 (82198), an aircraft reported as being fitted with 'bomb racks' and operating with 7 EFTS from Desford, was conducting spinning tests with a pupil but in spite of all efforts was unable to recover into stable flight. The instructor, Flt Lt F W Moxham, ordered his pupil to abandon the aircraft immediately after which control was regained and the Tiger Moth safely landed flown solo and from the front seat.

Bill Oliver, a DH.60 Moth pilot from Stag Lane days, and inventor of a banned flick manoeuvre which quickly became known as 'the Oliver Twist', was 'B' Flight Commander at 31 EFTS Elmdon during the summer of 1940. He initiated a deliberate spin in a Tiger Moth equipped with bomb rack rails close to the airfield boundary at 3,000ft and was surprised that in spite of applying all known methods of recovery absolutely nothing happened. Continuous pumping of the throttle resulted in sudden and unexpected recovery at a height to quote Bill Oliver, "down amongst the bird's nests." Having mentioned the incident to fellow instructors, Bill Oliver was astonished at the incredulity and derision which resulted and allowed the matter to pass. Soon after he was posted overseas and unable to pursue his concerns, only learning of the possible causes more than forty years later.

As a trainee, Geoffrey Alden flew seventeen different Tiger Moths at 10 EFTS Weston-super-Mare between 3 August and 28 September 1941 and remembers that bomb rack rails were still fitted to some of the unit's aircraft. One of them, R5129 (83011), was considered to be a rogue. A ban on Tiger Moth spinning had been imposed by Flying Training Command as the result of a series of accidents early in 1941, but was later lifted. Almost immediately R5129 was involved in a delayed recovery and had been grounded. Meanwhile the spinning ban had been re-imposed.

At Weston-super-Mare trainees were advised that in the event of an invasion selected senior pupils would be expected to fly Tiger Moth bomber conversions into battle. This was a story leaked by instructors (who were already allocated to the task) perhaps in the hope of improving standards. It was not unusual for a pupil to be advised that he would have nothing to worry about: "When the invading hordes saw the way this pilot flew, distressed enemy troops would drop their weapons and run back into the sea."

In spite of Albert Brant's letter from Hatfield dated August 1940, where a proportion of 1 EFTS aircraft always operated with complete racks attached, by mid-summer 1941 Flying Training Command was continuing to receive complaints about the randomly poor

Instructors of 1 ERFTS Hatfield in 1936. L-R back row: John Nesbit-Dufort, Michael Daunt, Lieutenant Commander Morgan, George Weighill, Bill Wilson. Front row: Reggie Moon, Eddy Fulford, Clem Pike (CFI), George King and Gordon Carey. A formidable pool of talent. *via Ben French*

performance of a few Tiger Moths during spinning demonstrations. Specific aircraft appeared to behave more erratically than others and spin recovery had proved difficult for both seasoned instructors and solo pupils. In some cases failure to recover from spins had resulted in abandonment or a crash with fatal results.

An engineering check was carried out on Tiger Moth N9437 (82491), of No 4 Service Flying Instructors School at Cambridge in April 1941 after the aircraft had entered a flat spin at 4,000ft and recovered at 800ft. The rigging was considered to be satisfactory, but the port elevator was found to be warped and both port and starboard surfaces were changed. An air test, which included spinning to left and right, reported no difficulty in recovery from up to one and a half turns, but after three turns "there was a little tendency for the spin to flatten." The control column flicked over in the direction of the spin and required sheer brute force to centralise. Spins resulting from different methods of entry all led to the same result but it was found that if instead of moving the control column to the centre and then forward, it was moved forward and then to the centre, as the aircraft came out of the spin the pressure on the control column was quite gentle. N9437 was restricted to non-spin training until after her next scheduled maintenance during which a new set of wings was fitted and the tailplane stripped and reassembled. A check on the alignment of the fuselage proved it not to be twisted and following reintroduction to service no further difficulties were experienced.

In July 1941, officials of the Ministry of Aircraft Production (MAP) based at Hatfield wrote to Flying Training Command authorising return to the factory of Tiger Moth components, especially wings, which it was thought might have a bearing on the bad spinning habits. Mainplanes salvaged from T5692 (83407), arrived at Hatfield on 9 July from 2 EFTS Staverton where the aircraft had crashed on 24 June. It had been a classic case: at 5,500ft with instructor and pupil on board, the aircraft had been eased into a right hand spin and after about seven turns full left rudder was applied with no result. Opening the throttle had only increased the speed of the spin which also flattened, at which point the crew had baled out.

More wings were in prospect from N9464 (82518), which had experienced difficulties in recovering from a spin at 10 EFTS Weston-super-Mare on 11 July. After landing the instructor had demanded an engineering inspection during which it was discovered that the trailing edge and the extremities of all the ribs of the starboard upper mainplane were warped, the effect being that the rib ends were curled upwards by approximately 20°, carrying with them the trailing edge section. In addition the aileron cables were slack and the rudder cable 'very slightly' slack. The defective wing was removed and replaced with a serviceable unit but before a comparative flight test could be arranged Flying Training Command had imposed a ban on all Tiger Moth spinning exercises and the opportunity was lost.

In his signal reporting the incident to the MAP Overseer at Hatfield the Commanding Officer of 10 EFTS confirmed what would eventually be discovered during the investigations at Farnborough. "The trouble is always rectified when the control column is moved right forward."

On 21 July Albert Brant visited 2 EFTS at Staverton and was introduced not only to a pilot who had already baled out of Tiger Moth N9464 (82518), but to another recalcitrant machine, T8240 (84513). This aeroplane had flown barely fifteen hours since manufacture at Cowley and the only defects which the Hatfield Work's Manager could determine was a warped rudder due to very tight fabric which had twisted the trailing edge by about half an inch along its length, and a stern post which was on the top limit of permissibility for being out of plumb. It was also noted that the setting of the tailplane was about half a degree above the authorised maximum.

In chasing every possible cause for the spinning problems Albert Brant was also moved to report back to Hatfield that he had discovered that the slot locking device had been wired up to make it inoperative, "meaning that aerobatics have been indulged in with the slots free. It has also been observed that the machine collected from Ansty for tests at Hatfield has the slot locking device made inoperative, meaning that they too are indulging in aerobatics without the slots being locked."

A second series of spinning investigations was programmed for Boscombe Down where test pilot Wing Commander Allen Wheeler considered that instructors and pupils alike might unwittingly have developed a culture of not allowing normal recovery action to take effect before trying a different control configuration. Also, a developed spin is likely to rotate faster and at a steeper angle just before recovery, a situation that may have been misinterpreted.

Conducted again by 'A' Squadron on behalf of the Director General of Research and Development, the brief was to establish a reason for the normally docile Tiger Moth becoming, on occasions, an aggressive old dog, and biting. Although dangerous spins may have occurred before, only after bomb rack rails were fitted did the volume of complaints increase and the new appendages were easily the most natural target for further investigation. It was recognised that both centre of gravity and moments of inertia had been changed, but only slightly, leaving disturbed airflow over the rear fuselage and tail unit as probable causes.

Why were only some Tiger Moths subject to dangerous spin characteristics? Rigging errors had been investigated and discounted. The CG position was not a primary issue either. Had the blind flying hood and bomb rack rails together caused a new reaction? Each report received was carefully analysed and, in addition to the fuel and baggage loads, crew composition and nature of the exercise, one column of information was reserved for the identity of the aeroplane's manufacturer. Flying Training Command nominated three aircraft reported to have particularly bad spin characteristics: N5468 (3736), and N6621 (3922), both from 9 EFTS Ansty, and R4760 (82701), from 10 EFTS Weston-super-Mare.

A serious degree of briefing being exercised at 10 EFTS Yatesbury early in 1940 while the Gipsy Major engine ticks merrily away in an unattended aircraft not hindered by chocks. *Richard Riding*

N5468 had refused to recover from what developed into a flat spin on 16 June, and according to the Ministry of Aircraft Production's Directorate of Technical Development, had been abandoned by the crew after the controls became unresponsive following two turns of an intentional spin commenced at 4,500ft. The MAP Overseer at Hatfield requested that de Havilland receive and inspect the aircraft "which was finally landed with only slight damage and is being repaired by the EFTS at Ansty." The full story was that having given orders to abandon the aircraft the instructor baled out, but partly because of a loose helmet the pupil, who was a qualified pilot undertaking a refresher prior to attending an Instructor's Course at the Central Flying School, could not hear what was said. He was astonished to see the instructor jump over the side at which point the Tiger Moth recovered from the spin. Still not sure about the nature of the problem, but with the engine and controls still apparently functioning normally, N5468 was immediately landed in a suitable field, a safe arrival marred slightly by the experience of breaking the port front interplane strut on a wire obstruction and denting the engine cowling undertray. Subsequent inspection concluded that all controls were functional, the rudder was not warped, bomb racks were not fitted, the petrol tank was half full and there was no significant weight in the rear locker. N5468 was eventually flown to Hatfield and arrived on 18 July where the tailplane was re-fabriced after several broken ribs had been repaired.

Operating from Lulsgate Bottom on 6 February 1941 R4760 had entered a conventional spin at 3,800 ft which had quickly flattened and the aircraft had been extracted at 600ft only after extensive use of the throttle. An engineering check showed that the rigging was almost symmetrical and within limits, but the rudder hinges were very slightly out of alignment as was the rudder trailing edge. Bomb racks, it was noted, were not fitted.

The incident which booked N6621 a place in the trials was very similar to that of N5468: a conventional spin commenced at 4,000ft had gone flat after fewer than two turns, and the instructor could get no response from the controls which he later described as 'sluggish'. At 2,000ft the instructor ordered the pupil to bale out but, before he could, and while the instructor also was preparing to abandon the aircraft, the spin stopped and the pupil regained control at about 1,000ft.

Both N6621 and R4760 were delivered to A&AEE in July 1941, neither with racks nor rails fitted, where 'A' Squadron concentrated their initial attentions on operations with the blind flying hood stowed or removed and with one or both of the leading edge slats locked. Each aircraft was spun on thirty three separate occasions.

While these intensive trials were in progress, on 9 August another aircraft from 10 EFTS, R5129 (83011), an aircraft built at Hatfield in March 1940, was added to the programme when she was delivered to A&AEE by the CFI. Instructors agreed that R5129 was not a good aircraft for spinning training as almost five turns were necessary to effect recovery.

The aircraft had arrived at Boscombe Down with what was described as 'bomb racks' fitted, although they were almost certainly just the rack rails attached to the lower longerons under the cockpit floor. The first three in a series of seven programmed spins were conducted by the 'A' Squadron Commander with the rails remaining in place, after which they were removed. The blind flying hood had been eliminated as a potential source of significant disturbance and was not fitted at any time during the programme. The test pilots discovered that recovery from a right hand spin was quite normal (a half turn), but exit from left hand rotation was delayed, even when standard methods of entry and recovery were used, with an average of about four turns required. Removal of the port navigation light made no apparent difference and two subsequent left hand spins had still resulted in four and five turns before full recovery.

It was quickly realised that spinning characteristics were very sensitive to aileron setting and flatter spins resulted from the input of small amounts of out of spin aileron, varying in degree between individual aeroplanes. R5129 was found to require only one inch of sideways control stick deflection to change the spin incidence by between 40° and 50°.

In such tests, accurate counting of fractions of turns was essential, and with a need to record a number of additional parameters the test pilots relied not on visual reference beyond the nose, but on the angle of the sun shining into the cockpit, where the instruments were illuminated long enough for a full scan and afforded the opportunity to note the altimeter readings.

Boscombe Down's report forwarded to the Ministry of Aircraft Production, dated 22 August 1941 was distilled from analysis of the flight tests and said in part:

"The tests made by us on three aeroplanes show that a different number of turns were required to recover, varying from three quarters to four and threequarter turns. Because of this discrepancy on three aeroplanes tested, one might reason that recovery from spins on some Tiger Moths might be impossible and in consequence that spinning should be banned until some remedial action has been applied to make recovery more consistent and in general, quicker. Though we accept this reasoning, some considerable time may elapse before the present investigation being conducted by the Royal Aircraft Establishment (RAE) at Farnborough is completed and a further period will be required before remedial steps can be taken to make recovery quicker on all Tiger Moths in Flying Training Command.

In the interim, therefore, much valuable spinning instruction will be lost if spinning on the type is banned. With this in view, we consider that spinning should still be allowed on the type and in order to reduce accidents to a minimum we now propose that the minimum height at which recovery is initiated be increased from 3,000ft, previously recommended, to 4,000ft. Also, in order to provide sufficient height for spinning instruction to be given, the minimum height at which spinning should be started should be increased from 5,000ft, previously recommended, to 6,000ft. In addition, we propose that the number of turns during spins should not exceed three.

We feel confident that most, if not all, of the accidents will be eliminated if the above procedure is followed until such time as a more permanent solution to the problem is found."

The A&AEE report published for internal circulation on 15 September 1941 and classified 'secret', concluded that one test aircraft did not behave in a manner properly associated with Tiger Moths in which it was usual for recovery from spins to be effected immediately rudder was taken off, and that the reason for this misbehaviour was unknown. In the case of N6621 and R4760 delayed recoveries had only been induced by artificial means and when using the standard method of entry and recovery both aircraft had reacted normally with a maximum delay of not more than two and a quarter turns.

R5129 was considered not to be a satisfactory aircraft for training purposes and was to be retained for further investigations. N6621 and R4760 were both thought certain to recover from spins no matter how unconventional the entry configuration and subsequent use or misuse of the controls, provided the standard method of recovery was eventually applied.

N6621 rejoined 9 EFTS on 28 August where she remained in harness for most of the next three years. R4760 was routed through the Civil Repair Unit operated by Lundy and Atlantic Coast Airlines at Barnstaple in August 1941, probably for routine maintenance, and was posted to training duties with 4 EFTS Brough on 10 September.

Allen Wheeler recalled that his Squadron Commander at A&AEE was very excited after analysis of the first results showed there to be a positive link between the bomb rack rails and a change in the aeroplane's behaviour. He subsequently became almost totally committed to the programme experiencing about 120 rotations, but the job was still not finished.

Four Tiger Moth Mk.IIs drawn from RAF sources were co-opted into the continuing test programme and all had been assessed by Aero Flight at RAE Farnborough by the end of 1941:

N5468 (3736), from 9 EFTS Ansty which had been posted into the care of the de Havilland Company at Hatfield on 18 July was fitted with an anti-spin safety parachute on the tail and test flown by Pat Fillingham on 6/7 August and 18 September, and also by Geoffrey de Havilland Jnr before referral to the RAE.

During the trials at Hatfield spins were completed at varying positions of Centre of Gravity, and operating at the aft-most limit N5468 was entered into a fourteen turn spin to the right from which recovery was described as being 'excellent'. In a report to Richard Clarkson in the Aerodynamics Department, Geoffrey de Havilland Jnr wrote: "During this sequence of tests the machine did not show the slightest tendency to flat spin or to become uncontrollable in any way."

The aircraft was never again used for flying training: following nine months in store with 33 MU at Lyneham N5468 was operated by 1483 Flight before she was moved to RAF Halton and converted to a ground instructional airframe, 4439M, in December 1943. By March 1945 the aircraft had been relocated to RAF Locking where she was scrapped in May 1947.

R5180 (83042), from 10 EFTS Stoke Orchard had been considerably spun during her twelve month training assignment and had shown no dangerous tendencies when recovering. It is not clear whether she returned to Stoke Orchard, but from July 1942 she was posted to 16 EFTS Burnaston where she remained for three years. In July 1945 she was placed in store with 8 MU Little Rissington and remained there until March 1950 when she was sold for scrap.

T6035 (84214), from 26 EFTS Theale was a brand new aeroplane which was with her home unit for exactly a month before delivery fifteen miles across the open fields to Farnborough on 3 September. Following the trials T6035 spent seven months in store with 33 MU at Lyneham before transport to 222 MU High Ercall where she was packed for despatch to South Africa in September 1942.

T6615 (84929), another brand new aeroplane, was allocated directly to Farnborough. No 26 EFTS had formed at Theale on 20 August 1941 and after the trials T6615 was posted to that unit, arriving ten days after the commencement of operations and remaining until the school closed in July 1945. Relocated to Woodley she continued in service with 8 EFTS and the post-war Reserve Flying School (RFS) until May 1948 when she crashed on landing and was written off the following month.

In addition, BB727 (3178), described as a 'reconstructed civil type Tiger Moth' but fitted with wings incorporating some Mk.II features, was made available to join the investigation at a late stage and was to provide direct comparisons with the performance of pedigree Mk.II specification airframes. In civilian life BB727 had been registered G-ACDE to the de Havilland School of Flying at Hatfield where she was operated as part of the establishment of 1 ERFTS and 1 EFTS from the outbreak of war. The aircraft received a coat of camouflage to obliterate her maroon and silver house colours and with her impressed military serial allocated from 30 October 1940 continued with her daily tasks much as always. The aircraft arrived at Farnborough on 13 September 1941 and remained until the end of October.

As a result of the aileron mass balance trials with K2583 at Martlesham Heath in 1933 all Tiger Moth aircraft were specified to carry them. The RAE had targeted the balances as a possible cause of trouble: a lead weight attached to a long lever arm and weighing just under 4lb each. The spinning characteristics of a slightly staggered biplane deteriorate with an increase in the rolling moment of inertia, and the removal of the mass balance served to reduce or improve the longitudinal moment (A) by 5% and the vertical (normal) moment (C) by 3%.

To create a Tiger Moth II and permit unrestricted aerobatic operations at an improved maximum weight of 1,770lb, an increase of 120lb, a number of modifications to the Mk I wing had been approved from January 1937. These were designed to allow all aircraft to be brought to a common (higher) standard and whilst factory-new wings were manufactured with the modifications incorporated, aircraft in the field were subject to longer term retrofit action. The 1937 upgrade was extensive, affecting both top and bottom mainplanes, and called for new spars; aileron gearbox structure and mounting; strengthened ribs at the control box, root end and walkway; special aileron hinge bolts to accommodate the aileron mass balance (and increased from three to four in accordance with the post trial requirements), new wing tip bows, trailing edge and associated wiring plates, modified fittings, stiffening struts and support tubes.

These were additional to other airframe changes which filtered through to constitute the current in-service specification of the aircraft: rudder mass balance, slot locking gear, strengthened undercarriage, navigation and identification lights, flare holders, an electrics panel, first aid box and amended instrument fit and layout, improved treatments for protection of the wing panels, revisions to aileron differentials, a blind flying hood and camouflage dope scheme.

All had contributed to a not insubstantial increase in tare weight (over 113lb), and to moments of inertia, 'A' by 10% and 'C' by 7%. Bomb rack rails and associated release cables, guides and levers accounted for an additional 30lb.

The reasoned removal of the aileron balance weights would go some way toward restoration of the known situation. de Havilland calculated that when compared with a standard civil flying school Tiger Moth, the RAF 'Contract Tiger Moth' showed an increase in weight of 223lb.

The opportunity of test flying the nearest equivalent civil Tiger Moth BB727/G-ACDE was a bonus. The results indicated that even with some Mk II features in her wings, spinning properties were very similar to the best of the standard RAF aircraft. The civil aircraft's wings were subsequently loaded with lead weights to simulate a full Mk II version and bomb rack rails were fitted to the lower longerons, after which a further flight test resulted in a spin of eight turns before recovery, a situation comparable with the worst of the military machines.

Immediately after the trials had been completed Hatfield was anxious to reclaim the anti-spin parachute which had been fitted to R5129 as a precaution as some of the component parts had been borrowed from other firms. This had been deployed once to good effect when, during a trial with rails and mass balances in position, the aircraft failed to respond to any pilot induced recovery action and control was regained only after thirteen full turns had been completed.

Further trials with the aileron mass balance weights removed (but with bomb rails in position) indicated a marked improvement in recovery no matter what mis-positioning of the ailerons, averaging about four turns. With ailerons held in the neutral position recovery was effected after two and a half turns.

R5129 was then subjected to a series of tests with, as far as was practical, many of the Mk II modifications deleted. Normal recovery was again achieved after about four turns. However, little further improvement was registered when neither aileron mass balances nor bomb rack rails were present on the same test. Equally, the effects of removing the 2lb 4oz of fabricated lead which formed the rudder mass balance were small, as were the effects of changing aileron differential ratios and sprocket angles.

During the course of the trials, Service Tiger Moths were still earning their daily crusts and on 19 August 1941, N5455 (3718), entered a left spin at 5,000ft near Booker where she was part of the establishment of 21 EFTS. After the application of normal corrective action, the instructor, whose favourite aeroplane this was, found there was no resistance to application of the rudder and in spite of 'rocking' the control column without resorting to bursts of full throttle, the spin merely increased in speed and the aircraft tended to go over the vertical. Without warning the Tiger Moth snapped out of the spin with a jerk having lost 3,000ft. A post flight engineering check confirmed that the rigging was within limits and apart from warping at the top of the rudder and the tip of the starboard aileron, the aircraft was serviceable. Bomb racks were not carried and the luggage locker was completely empty.

Having identified what was believed to be the root cause of the spinning difficulties, and believing that references to 'flat' spins in accident reports were misleading, A&AEE recommended that the current ban on spin training should be lifted. More attention was now to be paid to the prospects of correcting the situation. At a meeting convened at Hatfield on 22 September 1941, one of a series which had been held throughout the summer, Richard Clarkson and Percy Bryan of the de Havilland Company, accompanied by the Aeronautical Inspection Directorate's (AID) Resident Technical Officer (RTO) R W Fitch, were joined by Messrs Stevens (Air Ministry), Lyons and Finn (RAE). Their brief was to agree a programme of alternative modifications in order to improve Tiger Moth spinning performance.

As the aircraft currently displaying the worst spinning characteristics, R5129 was to be routed back to Hatfield as soon as possible for de Havilland to incorporate two specific modifications: horizontal strakes, aluminium pressings, fitted to the top of the rear fuselage immediately forward of the tailplane leading edge and an increase in the depth of the rear fuselage immediately below the tailplane effected by installation of a detachable fairing.

Farnborough was tasked to design a method of increasing the rudder area by filling the gap between the rudder and the hinge line at the bottom of the finpost. Airframe modifications were to be completed at the RAE if required. It was also agreed that Farnborough would design and manufacture a rudder of revised outline which effectively shrouded the tailskid cut-out and increased the surface area. In addition a revised dorsal-like fin fairing would be sought, but no installation or any trials were to be authorised without presentation first to Hatfield, affording the company the opportunity to check the integrity and strength of the proposals.

A basic drawing of one proposal for a new empennage for the Tiger Moth, possibly the Mk.III, which has been attributed to Richard Clarkson. The dashed line represents the outline of the standard fin and rudder fitted to the Tiger Moth. *deHMC Archive*

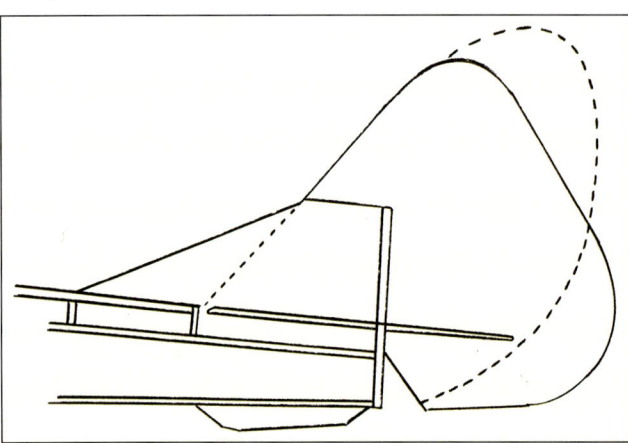

Perhaps this was the most crucial of all the meetings between de Havilland and government scientists that summer. As a result of the post trial report written by D J Lyons with R H Francis, spin strakes were adapted throughout the RAF's Tiger Moth fleet. Percy Bryan had advised the Hatfield gathering that strakes were by far the easiest of the proposed modifications to fit retrospectively and that there should be very careful consideration before fitting any of the other suggested devices. The incorporation of strakes was considered a worthwhile insurance against any future non-training demands that might be under consideration for the aircraft. Strakes had been used previously to improve the spinning characteristics of other types and they were thought likely to be especially effective with the fuselage cross section employed on the Tiger Moth. In her modified form de Havilland had promised that Tiger Moth R5129 would be ready for further testing from 1 October.

Richard Clarkson revealed to the meeting that the company had previously studied prospects for a Tiger Moth Mk III, the elusive DH.82B, and a rudder similar to that now proposed by the RAE had been built and flight tested. He would endeavour to find the rudder somewhere in the Experimental Department, he promised, or at least have copies of the drawings forwarded to Farnborough.

Based on the knowledge that spin characteristics of some other aircraft types had been varied by changing the arc within which the rudder could operate, flight tests were conducted with a conventional empennage but with a 10° reduction in pro-spin rudder and 4° increase in anti-spin rudder during which both entry and recovery were found to be substantially unaltered. Only slight improvement resulted from the increase in rudder area effected by the modification to fill the gap at the bottom of the finpost.

The conclusions drawn from the Farnborough report were that all the Tiger Moths sent to the RAE as part of this investigation had spun correctly and recovered quickly when the controls were applied as prescribed. A mishandled Tiger Moth Mk II could spin dangerously and if the control column was not held centrally flat spins could be effected. The greatest difficulty in recovery was obtained with full opposite aileron. With full pro-spin aileron the spin was again flat.

Agreeing that a considerable number of modifications had been incorporated into the aircraft since the type had last been tested by the A&AEE or RAE there remained little doubt that the spin would become safer if aileron mass balance weights and bomb rack rails were removed.

There was no evidence to suggest that the six Tiger Moth Mk I and eighty seven civil Tiger Moth Mk II then operating with the military and not fitted with aileron mass balances had ever experienced difficulty, but in association with the removal of the balances on RAF aircraft a reduction in the maximum diving speed from 210mph to 170mph was recommended which, together with the maintenance of regular inspections of the rigging and control circuit, were considered a sufficient guard against flutter. The Air Staff was to be approached over the matter of the bomb racks; de Havilland were to prepare modification drawings for the removal of the mass balances, a job which they estimated would take about an hour, and the advisability for proper centralisation of the control column during recovery was to be made clear to all users through Flying Training Command. In the revised configuration, it was also recommended that the restriction regarding the commencement of spins at a height of not less than 5,000ft be removed.

Results of the British flight tests had been transmitted to de Havilland Aircraft of Canada where, in the late summer of 1941, an exhaustive series of normal and what the company referred to as 'crossed aileron' spinning tests was completed on a DH.82C model Tiger Moth. Towards the end of October, the report landed on the desk of Managing Director Phil Garratt:

"Tests were carried out on the aircraft with and without navigation lights being fitted. No appreciable difference was noted during the spins or at the time of recovery although some slight rudder flutter was noted on machines fitted with navigation lights.

All spins were maintained for a minimum of seven turns before recovery was commenced and several tests were undertaken which included a maximum of twelve turns.

Using the normally accepted method for spinning to the left or right, recoveries were immediate in every case. Specifically, *immediate* should be read to indicate a maximum of three quarters of a turn. Some increase in the speed of normal spinning can be obtained by applying full inside aileron. The spin continues normally although somewhat steeper and faster. This procedure has no effect upon normal recovery.

When a spin is made to the left or right with crossed ailerons the spin becomes quite flat, the nose rises quite appreciably and a very definite whipping occurs once in each revolution. The spin is unpleasant and would tend to alarm an inexperienced pilot. Recovery can be effected in the normal way, that is to say, the usual procedure as laid down in the Air Force Manual of Training is sufficient to produce a normal dive. However, it should be noted that the time for recovery is much longer and takes a minimum of one and a half turns and a maximum of two and a half turns. Furthermore, it will be found that when applying opposite rudder to recover from the spin it is necessary to exert quite a considerable pressure on the rudder bar over and above that usually necessary to recover from a normal spin. Pilots should be informed that an earlier recovery from the 'crossed aileron' spin can be effected by applying inside aileron or, in other words, uncrossing the ailerons towards the direction of the spin.

There is an average altitude loss of 150ft per turn on the 'crossed aileron' spin and 250ft per turn on the normal spin. Exhaustive tests have shown that spins to the right require a little longer to recover than spins to the left."

Copies of the de Havilland Canada report were sent to the RCAF Director of Training, Air Vice-Marshal E W Stedman, and to Lee Murray at Hatfield. In its conclusion it was fairly specific on how the matter of spinning should be treated during pilot training:

"Allowed sufficient height there is no more difficulty in recovering from the 'crossed aileron' spin than from the normal spin but in the case of the 'crossed aileron' spin, additional altitude should be allowed. In other words, Elementary Flying Training Schools should be instructed that 'crossed aileron' spins should not be made on Tiger Moths under an altitude of 2,000ft. Also, it might be as well for instructors to inform their pupils that there is no cause for alarm arising out of the peculiar attitude or behaviour of the aircraft during the 'crossed aileron' spin, since it is apparent that crossing of the ailerons changes the nose position and at the same time brings on an unpleasant whipping motion which can be dampened out immediately."

As far as the DH.82C Tiger Moth was concerned there appeared to be no unforeseen spinning problems but Lee Murray was moved to remind his colleagues that the Canadian Tiger Moth did have "a large fitted canopy, undercarriage moved forward for brakes and a tailwheel." And much else besides.

R5129 was subjected to a further programme of intensive spinning checks at A&AEE in November 1941. A series of twenty seven spins was completed without aileron mass balance weights but with bomb rack rails fitted under the fuselage and strakes forward of the tailplane. The blind flying hood was discounted but the tail parachute was again carried as a precaution. With centralised ailerons the spin stabilised at 20° incidence and flattened only marginally with application of opposite aileron, in which configuration spins were arrested in less than two and a half turns. Standard recovery was effected in less than one turn. Apart from the various modifications agreed the previous August, the aircraft was to current RAF standard Tiger Moth Mk II configuration.

The biggest single improvement in spin recovery resulted from the fitting of the strakes: light alloy extensions of the tailplane running forward onto the rear fuselage top cowl, and picking up on captive nuts that were attached to the inside. The addition of strakes had moved the CG rearwards by six tenths of an inch and tests were conducted both at the normal load case and at the 1% Mean Aerodynamic Chord (MAC) extension to the new aft limit. A sequence of normal aerobatic manoeuvres was flown during which both slats were either locked or left free. The tests confirmed a vast improvement in the spin recovery performance of R5129 while maintaining the general handling characteristics of the type, although it was reported that aileron snatch could occur at about 80mph, accentuated by turbulent air conditions, and also during inverted flight.

The Establishment's earlier recommendation that R5129 was unsuitable as a training vehicle was heeded even after her absolution. The aircraft was posted from Boscombe Down to 15 MU Wroughton and issued to 654 (AOP) Squadron for barely three weeks towards the end of August 1942, immediately before the unit's new Taylorcraft Auster Is were delivered. She spent the next several years shuffling between Maintenance Units until September 1946 when she was sold to a civilian owner for operations with the Nottingham Flying Club at Tollerton. Re-sold to India in 1949 the aircraft was destroyed by fire at Safdarjung, New Delhi, after an Indian Air Force DH.100 Vampire collided with her hangar.

Inevitably, every production run using identical jigging could spawn a rogue aeroplane: the sum of all the minor differences in degrees of straightness, thickness, weight distribution and alignment. Bad rigging had never been a perceived problem, but A&AEE and RAE test pilot Allen Wheeler had nagging doubts throughout his involvement with the trials that the bomb racks and their fittings were the sole cause of the Tiger Moth, a docile old friend, turning into a vicious animal. Why were all Tiger Moths not affected, and why did the bad ones appear to degenerate gradually?

Having taken ten turns to recover from an intentional spin initiated at 8,000ft, an instructor at 10 EFTS, Weston-super-Mare, had ordered Tiger Moth T7047 (83417), to be removed to a hangar where his suspicions of mis-rigging or bad load distribution were not substantiated. The aircraft was returned to service with a cautionary note attached blaming the climate for a temporary distortion of the structure. The CFI later flew the aircraft and carried out an extensive spinning exercise without any recovery problems, followed by the original instructor, again with no difficulties.

Rapidly expanding flying schools in Great Britain did not always have facilities at main base, not to mention satellite fields, to shelter these open cockpit, fabric covered airframes. The aircraft establishment at 6 EFTS Sywell was 140 Tiger Moths by the end of 1940, most of which were forced to endure the English climate picketed at dispersal. No matter how securely covered, it was almost inevitable that rainwater and the effects of condensation were likely to accumulate especially in the rear fuselage, adding invisible weight at the rate of 10lb per gallon, and causing gross distortion of any calculated CG position. A modification which removed corrugated aluminium clips, originally designed to segregate fabric bagging from the fuselage bottom longerons, was found necessary after the clips were proved to provide a series of perfect reservoirs for the retention of moisture. Checks on the level of corrosion suffered by the rear fuselage lower longerons subsequently became a matter of major concern when aircraft were recovered or rebuilt in later years.

Drain eyelets were occasionally found not to have been opened up after fabric re-work or new painting and were especially critical in the tailplane and elevator where they might equally have become blocked with mud or grass during extraordinary manoeuvrings on the ground. At altitude, trapped moisture could freeze, spraying out in the relative warmth of the lower levels as the result of centrifugal force, permitting eventual but worryingly delayed recovery from spins and leaving no obvious trace for subsequent investigation. Pre-war colour schemes had been hastily covered with camouflage dope, often by mechanics wielding brushes, and coupled with patched repairs weighty layers of paint estimated in some quarters to be as heavy as 60lb per aircraft had been gradually propagated.

In May 1940, *Flight* published an article on flying training with the Royal Air Force, which carried a specific passage dedicated to spinning:

"A lot has been said about spinning during the past year, particularly by the non- flying public who can hardly know what it is all about. One of the early lessons in flying is in how to recover from a spin, having purposely got into it. From the safety point of view, which is most important in a trainer, the Tiger Moth, representative of biplane trainers, is ideal in this respect. A Tiger Moth will, in fact, recover from a spin unaided. Certainly, it is sufficient on all occasions to centralise controls. This method is not, however, suitable for getting the majority of monoplanes out of a spin. It is essential, if the practice is to be valuable, at least to hold on sharply full opposite rudder and then ease the control column well forward to dive the aeroplane to full flying speed. This practice seems rather to trouble pupils, and only with the greatest difficulty can they be persuaded to put on more rudder than is required for recovery on the Tiger Moth. Spinning is considered important enough to be a compulsory practice each week, and is the only manoeuvre outside straightforward flying which is taught previous to a first solo. Later at a Service FTS, pupils are taught other or extra movements to facilitate recovery from spins. These include the use of throttle."

By December of the same year, the same correspondent was writing an amended story:

"The control technique for getting out of a spin has now been slightly altered. Previously it was to put on opposite rudder and then, about two seconds later, to bring the stick forward. Not too far forward, as this leaves the aeroplane in a steep dive after the spin has been stopped, a decided disadvantage if near the ground. Now it is to put on opposite rudder and stick forward simultaneously, and with no apologies, as the instructor said. It is permissible to put the stick right forward, although this is not necessary on a Tiger Moth. The reason for the change seems to be that the procedure is necessary with some of the advanced trainer types, the North American Harvard, for example, and so it is taught right from the start. A Tiger Moth loses about 300ft per turn in a spin, but a Harvard between two and three times that height. A safe height for a spin in a Harvard is to start at 9,000ft."

Allen Wheeler suspected not only the spin recovery techniques employed by some pilots, but also the position of the centre of gravity which would be different for every individual aircraft. In 1954, Air Registration Board (ARB) surveyor Michael Inskip was checking the weight schedule for a civil Tiger Moth and was amazed to find that the basic centre of gravity (CG) was so far aft that it would be impossible to load the aircraft and stay within the prescribed limits. He then checked through ninety other weight schedules and found that only ten were satisfactory for flight where no spin strakes were fitted, seventy three needed strakes to stay within limits and the remaining seven were well outside the envelope. Mike Inskip wrote a paper on the subject which was circulated within the ARB on 24 March 1954, AW/151, all traces of which have disappeared from official files.

The major points of issue could well have read back to 1940:

1. It is imperative to rig the stagger of the centre section to the foremost limit, on the dot, and square with the fuselage.
2. Accurate weighing is essential and must be completed with the tail up 4° rather than in a horizontal position which would be more usual. A 1° difference will result in significant inaccuracies in the measurement of lever arms.
3. A build up of additional weight in the tailskid shoe will move the CG aft.
4. Too many coats of paint on the rear fuselage structure allied with too many coats of dope on the covered rear fuselage and tail unit. Two full coats of dope in these areas will move the CG aft.
5. Be aware of the night flying lamp on the rudder, not fitted to all Tiger Moths, and the lead mass balance weight in the rudder horn.
6. Monitor the load carried in the baggage locker. A 20lb load will move the CG aft 0.78in when the aircraft is flown dual and 0.92in when flown solo.

An additional factor to be considered in relation to wartime production was a possible variation in the radius or gauge of the steel tubes supplied batch upon batch, for building into rear fuselage structures. Was there no difference at all between the fuselages supplied from Canada and those built at Hatfield in 1938 and subsequently, and those manufactured at Cowley?

At the time of Michael Inskip's survey there were additional considerations, all of which tended to shift the CG to the aft position: a glider tow hook at 3lb moved the CG 1.16in; aluminium cylinder heads fitted to a Gipsy Major engine moved the CG 0.31in; replacement of a Schwartz covered wooden propeller with a modern lightweight example, radio kit and wiring situated in the rear fuselage, and removal of slats and mechanism from the upper mainplanes, all resulted in an increased 'positive' moment.

Bad spinning characteristics were sometimes blamed on poor rigging or a Centre of Gravity out of limits. One secret in the black art of rigging is to ensure absolute integrity of the centre section. The C of G can only be calculated with any accuracy when a Tiger Moth is weighed and measured with the tail above the horizontal as described in the Care and Maintenance manual. *Terry Dann*

A view of the port upper mainplane showing the fairing and lens of the navigation light, leading edge slat in the extended (open) position, and the shroud at each of the three slat hinge points. *Darryl Cott*

The official capacity of the rear luggage locker has varied across the range of manuals published since 1931, and actual contents of the lockers of RAF aircraft involved in spinning incidents and accidents in 1940 were carefully analysed. In Australia the initial limit of 60lb, later amended to 40lb, was further reduced to 30lb when operating with two crew. Air Publication (AP) 1449B, the standard RAF work of reference for dimensions, weights and tolerances, makes no mention at all of locker limitations.

de Havilland admitted post-war that the Tiger Moth had imposed practically no work-load on design staff during the conflict: straightforward production was contracted out. However, the operational behaviour of the aeroplane was always accepted as a prime de Havilland Aircraft Company responsibility and they ensured a close liaison was maintained with all owners, users and servicing units in addition to the production centres in Australia, Canada and New Zealand.

Almost inevitably the Drawing Office had, of course, devoted some time to the aeroplane during which they pursued a number of interesting lines of research. In December 1939 the DH.82B project was still live and attention was being paid to a redesign of the elevator ribs and static tests to establish satisfactory load factors whilst the New Year found attention being paid to a revised tailskid for the DH.82A assuming a maximum loaded weight for an aeroplane to be 1,825lb. In February 1941 mahogany brown vulcanised fibre was tested for suitability as material for the luggage locker tray as a substitute for grey can fibre then in use and during the same month Hatfield's Plastics Department provided two different examples of slats of different weights manufactured in Bakelite to be considered as a substitute for the standard metal slats made from L.16 sheet.

A significant amount of research and testing to destruction of Tiger Moth control columns manufactured from different materials occurred in September 1940 including duralumin, non-magnetic steel, laminated wood and Bakelite. Extending into March 1941 were experiments with a control column made from Texolex which was described as a fibre-resin material used in the manufacture of helmets worn by Welsh coal miners. It was proposed to fit a Texolex A.C.35 (Mod) control column to Tiger Moth G-ACDB (3176), then in daily operation with No 1 EFTS and based only a few hundred yards from the Design Office, for what was termed "pilots' criticism", but the same aircraft was officially 'impressed' the following month which may have cancelled the trial and as no results appear to have survived it is unknown whether the trials were even begun. Whatever the outcome Morris Motors continued to turn out aircraft fitted with standard steel control columns until the end of their contract in 1944.

Prior to the transfer of Tiger Moth production to Cowley and in an effort to conserve stocks of Grade A spruce, Hatfield began a series of investigations into the prospects of manufacturing laminated main wing spars utilising spruce of Grades A, B and C. To a world leader in wood technology the task was fairly straightforward but it was necessary to treat each mainspar, upper and lower, front and rear, as separate studies. The top front spar was tackled first and a specimen manufactured using twenty two laminations. A top rear spar consisting of nineteen laminations was glued up on 6 October and tested to destruction alongside a conventional spar on 16 November 1942, one of the main purposes being to observe the behaviour of the glue joints between flanges and web. In comparing the results the subsequent report concluded that where the standard spar was considerably above minimum quality the laminated spar was of minimum quality but satisfactory as regards strength. In the event Grade A spruce supplies were maintained at an acceptable level throughout the war and laminated spars were used sparingly, mostly during repairs.

Two similar investigations in October and November 1943 centred on the manufacture of front interplane struts from three laminations of Sitka Spruce or the substitution of Western Hemlock for spruce in both front and rear interplane struts. In all cases test results proved the schemes to be satisfactory.

Well after their production had ceased, Cowley reported in January 1945 that a supplier of material used to manufacture the rear centre-section cross spar had declared their belief that a consignment of their tubes was well below the specification for T.45. The problem was immediately passed to Hatfield where it was assessed that the number of man hours required to replace the spars, all fitted to aircraft which had flown, was considerable and it would be prudent to apply static tests to a batch of suspect material. The results were entirely as expected which proved the tubes to be up to strength, a finding corroborated in February when the supplier confirmed that on further investigation it was revealed that the alleged faulty batch had not been used at all.

Valuable Drawing Office time was devoted to Mod.103, the 'mandatory' removal of Tiger Moth aileron mass balance weights which also imposed a restriction on the 'never exceed' speed (Vne) of 170mph, a reduction of 40mph, as a precaution against aileron flutter.

Drawing M7685 was the vehicle which conveyed detailed instructions for the application of 'Modification 112', published on 17 October 1942: light alloy pressings, Part Nos 62976 and 62977 (left and right hand), which formed the core of the strake modification

The fabric and stringer turtledeck of a DH.82 Tiger Moth would have caused serious problems for the designers had it been necessary to fit spin strakes to the structure. Part of the reason for change to a ply decking was reported to be the high level of damage caused to the fabric covering by poor ground handling. *Mark Miller*

Spin strakes fitted comfortably to the ply rear decking of the DH.82A Tiger Moth, blending in to the leading edge of the tailplane. Critics of the scheme were vocal in their belief that the strakes were not the answer to alleged spinning problems and may even have assisted in getting an aircraft into the situation. *Mark Miller*

and which had been conceived and fitted to R5129 a full year previously. Including pins, screws and washers, 304 individual parts were called up to complete each field modification kit. From unlacing the fuselage belly fabric for access to the inside of the rear cowl, to the final licks of green and dark earth paint, the job was estimated at eight man hours per aircraft. Classified as *'desirable'*, Mod 112 was applied to all RAF Tiger Moths in service and aircraft on the Cowley line were fitted with strakes on production from September 1942, nine months after a trial batch of conversions on aircraft serving with 1 EFTS at Hatfield, including R5082 (82977). This aircraft had been repaired at Witney in April 1941 following an accident at Church Fenton and the strakes could have been fitted then but the 'system' was not yet in gear. Displaying her new appendages, R5082 was subjected to an official photographic session in the pouring rain at Hatfield on 27 December 1941.

A story circulating at 6 EFTS Sywell late in 1941, where there was knowledge of strakes, suggested that they had been invented as a morale booster in the light of the reported spinning accidents and the idea had been pinched from the Miles Magister. It is doubtful whether the Air Ministry had communicated any part of the 'secret' reports being compiled at Boscombe Down and Farnborough at that time and the tales remained a matter of pure conjecture. A more malicious rumour suggested that only the Morris Motors built aircraft were affected, a fact that was blatantly untrue. Following a degree of initial criticism of the quality of the Morris product, de Havilland test pilot Guy Tucker, responsible for testing the vast majority of Cowley built Tiger Moths, repudiated absolutely any suggestion that quality was inferior in any way to products of the parent company.

One Cowley built Tiger Moth did come under scrutiny in the late summer of 1941 when operating with 17 EFTS Peterborough. In the rear seat the pupil pilot heard a loud crack as the fuselage tie-rods snapped and watched bemused as the starboard lower wing detached from its root end pickup. The instructor only realised his pupil had baled out when he saw the descending parachute at which point the aircraft broke up and he too abandoned what had become a spinning fuselage. Devoid of all wings the structure landed on a house in Peterborough alongside the engine which had already buried itself in the garden. The salvage recovery team reported that when they reached the site they found the fuselage covered in jam, the product of an industrious British housewife and not in any way connected with the theme of an enduring First World War song describing the last moments of a bold aviator.

Flying at 17 EFTS was suspended for two days while the tie rods of the entire fleet were examined in detail, partly by engineers wielding magnets. There was some suspicion that during assembly or later maintenance, tie rods manufactured from dural instead of high tensile steel had been installed or substituted, and the whiff of sabotage as much as carelessness in quality control was prevalent, although the engineering staff was never advised of the outcome.

Philip Bremridge, an instructor at Yatesbury with 10 ERFTS from October 1938 and a Flight Commander with 3 EFTS at Watchfield and later Shellingford between 1940-1942, clearly remembered strakes being fitted to the school's Tiger Moths, but with equal clarity he recalled never having been advised of the reason. Following a six month posting as Deputy Chief Flying Instructor (CFI) with 21 EFTS Booker he was appointed CFI at 22 EFTS Cambridge until he was promoted Wing Commander and posted away to undertake experimental work on training methods in May 1943. During five intensive years of instruction Philip Bremridge could recall no spinning incidents of any malevolence involving Tiger Moths, and only discovered in 1997 that strakes had resulted from the investigations called for by his own Command.

Inevitably, and for some considerable time, all schools flew Tiger Moths both with and without strakes and no obvious attempts appear to have been made to segregate non-straked aircraft from spinning exercises which continued relentlessly, an essential part of the daily training syllabus.

Modification 112 was never incorporated into DH.82A Tiger Moths built in Australia or New Zealand, nor into the DH.82C models rolling off the line in Canada and aircraft in the field were never retro-fitted as was the case in Great Britain. Tiger Moths used extensively for training in Rhodesia, an amalgam of British and Australian factory output, were regularly spun from only 3,500ft. When operating from the high elevations of the base airfields instructors decided it just took too long to climb any higher. Spin recovery was never considered a problem although it was noted that Tiger Moths flying here solely in support of *ab initio* training did not require heavy wingtip navigation lights, neither did they have occasion to carry bomb racks.

de Havilland DH.82A Tiger Moth, G-ADZN/30, No 10 Elementary Flying Training School, RAF, Yatesbury, April 1940. 'Shadow compensation scheme' of Dark Earth/Dark Green on upper surfaces with Light Earth and Light Green on top of lower wings. Trainer Yellow undersides, vertical tail surfaces and elevators. Night registration, repeated below wings. Blue/red roundels above top wings. *Artwork ©Richard Caruana, 1:72 scale*

For Tiger Moth G-AKXO (83548), 13 March 1964 was not a good day. She spun off a climbing turn at 500ft after taking off from Shoreham Airport in the late afternoon and the rotation was checked only as the result of colliding with the roof of a house in Buckingham Road. The accident inspector concluded that the fatal spin had followed a stall and there was evidence to indicate that the amount of alcohol found in the pilot's blood could have resulted in a diminution of attention and a reduction in both judgement and efficiency. Clearly, whether the aircraft was or was not fitted with strakes was of no consequence on this occasion but, after the war, the whole question of Tiger Moths operating with or without spin strakes was raised again, notably by the Dutch Government who requested assistance from the British Air Registration Board (ARB) following a series of accidents which had occurred with newly imported ex-RAF Tiger Moths during the summer of 1946.

The ARB called upon one of its expert consultants, none other than Air Commodore Allen Wheeler, test pilot during the Tiger Moth's wartime trials at Boscombe Down and later Commanding Officer of A&AEE's Performance Testing Squadron and RAE's Experimental Flying Department. Accepting Allen Wheeler's first hand experience and advice the Board's considered reply was fairly unequivocal:

"The horizontal stabiliser modification was incorporated at the instigation of Flying Training Command but whether it was really necessary is doubtful.

The reason for the modification was to decrease the time taken for spin recovery but it has been suggested that although they fulfil this function, they also may slightly increase the tendency to spin when near the stall.

Although this modification was classed as 'essential' by RAF Flying Training Command it was not considered so by the Air Registration Board and is not included in the list of essential modifications which must be incorporated for the issue of a civil certificate of airworthiness."

In 1982, the British Civil Aviation Authority (CAA), successor to the ARB, issued a Certificate of Airworthiness to a British civil registered Tiger Moth which, in the small print, declared that aerobatics were prohibited unless spin strakes were fitted. The aircraft had been imported from South Africa where, by coincidence at much the same time, an unstraked Tiger Moth, ZS-DFM (84478), an RAF import from 1941, was regularly recovering from twenty eight turn spin demonstrations at air displays flown by her owner, Dr H J 'Manie' Coetzee, a pilot with only one leg. When challenged to explain their decision, imposed without consultation, the CAA referred back to the wartime test reports and quoted the RAE's recommendation that strakes were a *'desirable'* modification, a grading which they would not challenge, but clearly using an interpretation different from that of the hands-on test pilot turned consultant, the now retired Air Commodore Wheeler. The CAA's reply continued:

Alan Wesson's Tiger Moth ZS-DFM in her July 2013 scheme reflecting an image of a First World War fighter. In a previous life and without spin strakes the same aircraft had demonstrated twenty eight turn spins at air displays flown by a pilot with an artificial leg. *Alan Wesson*

"Our conclusions are that as anti-spin strakes are a desirable modification, backed by a considerable body of evidence, then they should be fitted to Tiger Moths certificated for spinning. As we also argue that aeroplanes intended for aerobatics must be cleared for spinning – this rule is applied rigorously to British aeroplanes – then if a Tiger Moth is to be aerobatic, it should have anti-spin strakes.

Just because one Tiger Moth can be spun for twenty five to thirty years without strakes, it does not follow that all Tiger Moths will behave in the same way on all occasions with all pilots. That is the reason now, with hindsight, for restricting spinning and aerobatics without spin strakes."

The term 'anti-spin' strake used by the CAA was, perhaps, misleading. In all contemporary discussions between de Havilland, RAE, A&AEE and RAF, the part in question was never referred to as anything but a 'strake', and Tiger Moth part numbers 62976/62977 refer to 'strake, fairing, port (or starboard), Mod 112' and are listed under the 'aerofoils, arrangement of tail unit' section of the Schedule of Spare Parts, rather than 'fuselage' which is where most maintainers might tend to look first.

Allen Wheeler's personal views on the matter were expressed not only with the first hand knowledge of his own military test flying but also as the owner of a number of Tiger Moths at different times, one of which, G-ADGV (3340), was an aircraft he had regularly flown and aerobatted since restoration in 1978. Operated in the 1935 colours of the aircraft's first owners, Brooklands Aviation, G-ADGV would not have been authentic with spin strakes and so none was fitted.

Allen Wheeler considered that whether or not strakes were fitted the matter was entirely by choice of the owner whom he assumed would not be carrying bomb racks and would take care with any weight distribution. His own enquiries of the CAA were answered by a reply which put the emphasis on flight safety in the modern age and with which there was no argument. "...we accept that particular pilots may have considerable experience and skills ... (but it is advisable) ... to increase the level of safety for the average pilot ..."

Air Commodore Allen Wheeler refused to fit spin strakes to his personal Tiger Moth G-ADGV and flew virtuosic aerobatic sessions which included spins and exceptional demonstrations of the falling leaf. *deHMC Archive*

Unfortunately, these views were expressed almost simultaneously with publication in 1973 of an article by an anonymous hand in the General Aviation Safety Council's *Flight Safety Bulletin*, under the title 'Beware Tiger' which implied that all Tiger Moths Mk II had never been safe until strakes were fitted. The article was severely criticised by another anonymous hand described as being in an official position enabling judgement of the statements to be made realistically:

"From the evidence it can be seen that the presentation is far from accurate in many respects. Some of this is due to a lack of knowledge of Ministry procedures and some to misinterpretation of the evidence."

Pressure from the Tiger Moth owning fraternity resulted in the CAA granting dispensation which permitted aerobatics to be flown by non-straked aircraft following application on an individual basis but in 1983 the system was changed again. An Airworthiness Directive (AD) was issued listing the fitment of strakes under 'Mandatory Modifications' with an Information Leaflet available for those who required amplification. Under the new rules, applications for aerobatic Certificates of Airworthiness for private aircraft not fitted with strakes would only be considered after flight testing of Tiger Moths on an individual basis by a CAA test pilot and at the owner's expense.

This concession was further amended in June 1992 when the CAA issued a revised version of their Information and Procedures Leaflet which prohibited aircraft operating in the Transport and Aerial Work category from spinning and aerobatics unless strakes were fitted and, in order to qualify for a Transport Category certificate at all the individual aircraft was to be subject to a spin recovery check performed by a CAA test pilot. Owners and operators were left wondering what difference a piece of paper with an official stamp on it, and left in the filing cabinet, could possibly make to the airborne capabilities of a Tiger Moth and conditional upon whether or not the pilot was being paid to fly her.

Prompted by the British AD of 1983 the Airworthiness Division of Transport Canada was stirred into action. Shocked owners of Tiger Moths bearing Canadian registrations were advised that under the Directive effective from 9 September 1985, no DH.82C Tiger Moth would be permitted to fly aerobatics or to spin unless strakes were fitted and that cockpits were to be placarded to this effect. Companies engaged in commercial operations with the DH.82C model were to fit strakes as a mandatory modification. British built DH.82A Tiger Moths registered in Canada were already subject to the conditions laid down by the British CAA and enforced by the Canadian authorities.

The reason for implicating the DH.82C model, reported Transport Canada, was because neither British Aerospace, inheritors of the de Havilland technical archive, nor the de Havilland Aircraft of Canada could shed light on any aerodynamic differences which could lead to a variation of spinning characteristics between the 'A' and 'C' models. The DH.82C was an innocent, and the thousands of hours which had been flown without complication when training pilots in Canada for over forty years, seemed to have been forgotten, as was the report which had dropped onto Phil Garratt's desk during the summer of 1941. But the views of the owners supported by the Moth Clubs of Canada, USA and Great Britain were soon well voiced in the corridors of power following study of which Transport Canada were roundly applauded for their early and complete acceptance of the fact that they had made a mistake. In their own words:

"Subsequent to the initial issue of this Directive, sufficient new information has been received which leads Transport Canada to believe that the configuration differences and Canadian service experience are such as to conclude that the unacceptable spin recovery characteristics of the DH.82A do not warrant airworthiness action on the DH.82C."

"Unacceptable spin recovery characteristics of the DH.82A" was an unwarranted comment, but if it helped to establish the DH.82C as an independent force and free of the strictures of the misguided AD, it was acceptable.

Test pilot Bob Cole joined the British CAA after a distinguished RAF career during which he had graduated from the Empire Test Pilots' School (ETPS) and later had been involved with a number of new civil light aeroplane projects. He inherited all the simmering discontent displayed by owners of British registered Tiger Moths and made it known that he was very willing to fly and spin unstraked aircraft in a coordinated attempt to build a dossier on the subject. Bob

Cole subsequently wrung out many aircraft, mostly with their owners on board, and the result was publication of an Airworthiness Information Leaflet dated February 2001 which said, in part:

> "The addition of strakes to civil Tiger Moth aircraft has never been made mandatory. The experience of the CAA of Tiger Moth aircraft without strakes has been increased with successful flight tests on twenty nine aircraft so that the differentiation between C of A category is no longer deemed to be necessary.
> Part (j) of the Certificate of Airworthiness will be amended as follows:
> > Aerobatics and spinning are permitted on this aircraft subject to the following conditions.
> > In the event of any change that could affect spinning characteristics (eg. modifications affecting aerodynamic features, replacement of major parts such as a main aerofoil or control surface, changes affecting weight and balance) no aerobatics or spinning shall be permitted until such time as the aircraft has been re-evaluated by further test flights by the CAA, and declared to be satisfactory."

Was Transport Canada aware that in 1947 two DH.82C Tiger Moths, CF-CJA (DHC1747), and CF-CTB (DHC1653), were operational with the Aviron Company, later the Palestine Flying Club, in Tel Aviv? Both aircraft operated for a time in their original configurations, complete with yellow colour schemes and Canadian registrations but, in the summer heat, flying with the canopy closed was found to be barely tolerable. The situation resulted in one aircraft, CF-CTB, having its canopy removed on a trial basis coincident with local registry as VQ-PAU, leaving a wide fixed windscreen and long bath-like open cockpit behind it.

A Club pilot accompanied by an engineer flew the aircraft in this configuration and from a good altitude tempted her into a spin. It proved to be a frightening experience for all concerned, not least the bathers on the sun drenched beaches below, but after three full turns the aircraft recovered having taught another lesson which was not to be repeated and the canopy was replaced.

During the production life of the Tiger Moth in New Zealand, fifteen local modifications of consequence were introduced between April 1940 and May 1944 which were identified separately from those called up by the Royal Air Force or the parent company in England. Although Mod NZ104 dated 28 October 1941 called for removal of the aileron mass balance weights there was no suggestion that spin strakes should be fitted and none of the aircraft imported from England for local assembly, nor any of those manufactured at Rongotai, was ever modified. After the war the New Zealand airworthiness authorities insisted that strakes be fitted to all Tiger Moths in use by aero clubs but the mandatory requirement was lifted after substantial input of pilot opinion suggested the strakes made no appreciable difference to the spin characteristics.

A programme of performance testing for agricultural Tiger Moths to judge the effects of 'excrescences in the form of hopper tanks' was conducted between 9 April and 9 May 1952 when ZK-ALK (3795), was hired from the Wellington Aero Club and flown in various configurations, including with and without strakes, to measure amongst the usual parameters, longitudinal stability, stalling and spinning. The results were later reported in the *Journal of the Aviation Historical Society of New Zealand*:

> "The spinning tests involved four turns in each configuration, one in which three turns were made before beginning recovery, and one for eight turns, each of these being carried out both to the left and to the right. The aircraft was at 1,675lb, and with the centre of gravity fully aft.
> The results were interesting. For all spins to the right, the excrescences had no effect, but to the left they improved recovery characteristics for three turn spins, and were the same or slightly worse for eight turn spins.
> What were more interesting were the spins performed with the aircraft in a clean (unmodified) configuration and with no spin strakes. For eight turn spins to the right, removing the strakes had no effect, but to the left the number of turns to recover and the height lost were greater than with strakes. For three spin turns, however, removal of the strakes had improved recovery characteristics for spins in either direction."

The protectionist powers of the Tiger Moth might be judged from an incident that occurred in the United States in 1980. A flying instructor who claimed experience in Moth aircraft from the 1930s and 1940s persuaded the owner of a recently imported DH.82A Tiger Moth to allow him to fly it. With the owner in the front seat and no method of communicating with the rear cockpit the aircraft took off to fly a standard circuit, but the first landing was a disaster: the Tiger Moth was dropped in from 10ft and witnesses on the ground said they could see the wings flex. Without stopping to inspect the aircraft the instructor immediately took off again. At a point where the aircraft would normally expect to be 600ft-700ft it was at 200ft and continued to climb. Having reached 400ft the aircraft was banked into a left turn but immediately entered a spin which was only arrested when the Tiger Moth hit the ground. The owner suffered a back injury as the result of failure of the shoulder harness but was fit again within a month; the instructor sustained a minor cut on his arm. The FAA Investigator commented that the chances of anyone surviving a similar impact in a modern light aircraft would have been slim indeed. As it was, the

DH.82C Tiger Moth CF-CTB was one of a pair operated by the Aviron Company, later the Palestine Flying Club at Remleh in 1947. This aircraft caused concern when deliberately spun with the canopy removed. *George Nelson*

Tiger Moth protected her charges and was herself rebuilt to fly again.

During the period from immediately after the war until the early 1950s the RAF sold off the majority of its still considerable stockholding of now obsolete Tiger Moths, by which time all had been fitted with Modification 112. Aircraft sold or gifted as aid by the British Government to overseas air arms were already fitted with strakes and these were normally retained. In most cases the Tiger Moths were used to supplement or even modernise emerging Air Force training schemes. Glider tugging was an important task in post-war France where 200 Tiger Moths were employed at one time, some serving the sport well for almost thirty years.

In the Netherlands the bad spinning habits reportedly developed by the wartime Tiger Moth were noted by the authorities. Ex-RAF machines delivered to the Government Aviation School (RLS) and National Aviation School (NLS) were found to have an increased angle of rudder deflection when compared with the trio of Dutch civil registered examples from pre-war days: N V Avon's PH-AJO (3101); PH-AJD (3188), owned privately by J Montauban van Swijndregt from May 1933, and PH-AJG (3190), the aircraft originally used as a test vehicle for Dutch certification.

In the late 1920s the Rotterdamse Aeroclub had been selected to train Dutch civil airline pilots, effectively becoming the first National Aviation School, and by December 1930 had a growing requirement for improved equipment, favouring a local manufacturer if one could be found. Of three prospective candidates, Fokker would only undertake to build a minimum of twelve aircraft while Pander and Koolhoven were essentially prototype constructors. Koolhoven was willing to design to the school's requirements but was slow in delivering promises and completing what eventually became the FK-46, a tandem seat, open cockpit biplane.

During this time of uncertainty the school sent Dr H J van der Maas to de Havilland at Stag Lane where he flew a DH.82 Tiger Moth accompanied by Hugh Buckingham at first, and then solo with 40lb of ballast lashed down in the rear locker. In his report to the school board Dr van der Maas made specific reference to the controls being heavier than he was used to and that "spinning is positive and quick and easy to recover from: nose slightly down; rudder in centre for a quick response. The aircraft can be regarded as very promising."

Other virtues openly discussed included low initial cost due to series production; the immediate availability and low cost of spare parts; incorporation of improvements resulting from an ordered test flight programme and the fact that deliveries could be fulfilled almost immediately. He recommended that the school should buy two Tiger Moths without delay. Bowing to opposition from officials who still preferred to buy locally only one aircraft was ordered and PH-AJG was delivered to Waalhaven on 1 July 1933 where it was subjected to intensive flight trials in an effort to alleviate a major concern still being expressed over the use of the rudder and entry to the spin.

Koolhoven flew their promised FK-46 on 18 August 1933 and, after she was fitted with a Gipsy I engine in January 1934, the aircraft proved to have a very impressive performance. A Gipsy Major was installed early in 1935 which transformed the aircraft and the NLS board honoured their intention to buy locally by ordering five aircraft with no further orders in prospect for de Havilland except the supply of engines and spares. Tiger Moth PH-AJG was hangared at Schiphol on 10 May 1940 where she was destroyed in an air raid. The Koolhoven works at Waalhaven were destroyed at about the same time.

Although the two other Dutch registered Tiger Moths had returned to Great Britain pre-war, PH-AJD to the Cinque Ports Flying Club as G-ACGE in March 1936 and PH-AJO to Brooklands Flying Club as G-ABTB the following June, the Dutch authorities had created an extensive technical file on the type which they dusted off in 1946 in order to make comparisons with the new intake.

The RLS commenced flying training at Gilze-Rijen airfield in March 1946 but four major crashes were experienced that summer and the loss of PH-UAK (86303), in a landing accident on 26 August, in which the 19 year old pilot was killed, was believed to have been caused by spinning off an unbanked turn at slow speed during the approach to land. This accident triggered the investigative research which resulted in major modifications to the areas always viewed with deep suspicion: the fin and classical de Havilland rudder.

An increase in the degree of rudder movement compared with that afforded PH-AJG in 1933 was considered by the Dutch authorities to be a contributory factor in post-war spin related accidents. In addition, all the Gilze-Rijen aircraft which had crashed had been fitted with spin strakes and these also were allocated a share of the blame. Assistance requested from Great Britain resulted in Allen Wheeler's opinion, delivered via the Air Registration Board, that strakes were not really necessary and may have increased the tendency to spin when near the stall.

The Tiger Moth was subjected to yet another series of official tests, this time under the authority of the Dutch Department of Civil Aviation (RLD) and which were conducted by Captain H J van Overvest of the National Flying Laboratory (NLL) on 5 and 9 September 1946. The subject aircraft, PH-UAM (86536), was one of several brand new Tiger Moths which had been upgraded by the de Havilland company early in 1946 and, with civil letters painted over their RAF camouflage, delivered with British export Certificates of Airworthiness. PH-UAM was registered to the RLD on 9 May 1946 and prior to the trials was modified to restrict the range of available rudder movement. The structure of the fin and rudder was subject to a number of alterations designed by the Fokker Aircraft

A fully camouflaged Tiger Moth of the Royal Netherlands Air Force shortly after delivery with national insignia applied to wings and fuselage but still carrying RAF serial T5820. The aircraft later became 'A-11' at Woensdrecht. *via Herman Dekker*

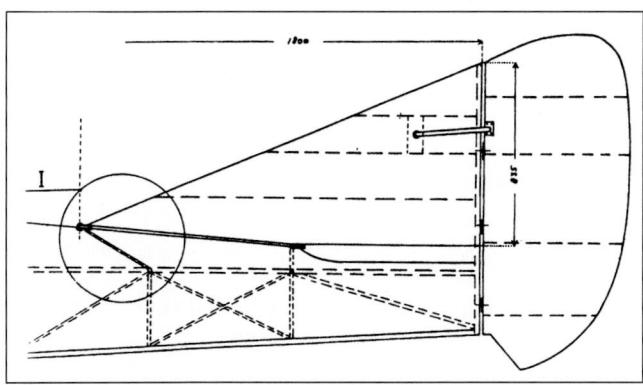
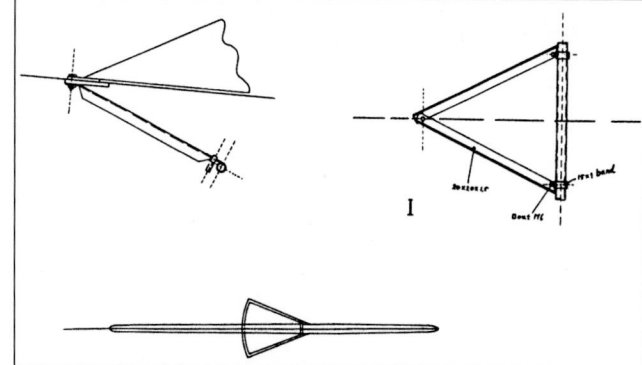

A drawing for the Tiger Moth's Fokker designed tail as approved by the Dutch RLD in September 1947. The modification increased the area of the fixed fin at the expense of the rudder and introduced a limiter for rudder deflection.

Post war all Tiger Moths operating on the civil register in the Netherlands were obliged to carry the Fokker fin and rudder; Dutch military Tiger Moths operating in the same airspace were not. *Ton Noors*

Company: the area of rudder forward of the hinge line was deleted and substituted with an exactly similar area added as an upper extension to the fixed fin. The aircraft was found to perform normally in a straight and level attitude but showed her wrath by developing bad stall characteristics, especially during turns.

The NLL report (V.1388) was finally published on 9 December 1946 and said in summary: "In its present form the aircraft is considered less suitable to be used as an initial trainer" and concluded, "the aircraft could be improved and made safe by further aerodynamic under-balancing of the rudder and enlargement of the fin."

A further series of test flights by Captain J K Hoekstra resulted in another report (V.1406) which in turn was responsible for major surgery on de Havilland's trademark empennage. Three stages of development were tested by Captain Hoekstra using PH-UAM. On 21 March 1947 the aircraft was flown with a dorsal fin added to the existing modified fin, superimposed along almost the entire length of the strakes which remained in position. On 9 April the same tests were flown with the strakes removed. Finally, a new dorsal fin was fitted which enlarged the fin area by almost half a square metre. In this configuration PH-UAM was flown on 22 April.

The greatest improvement in spin control was achieved using the configuration which embodied the larger of the dorsal fins and no strakes, a situation which tended to confirm opinions expressed on the validity of the strakes. The publication of report V.1407 confirmed that spinning was entered 'calmly' and a more vertical position was held while height was lost at almost 295ft per rotation: a rate of one turn in about two seconds. Two bonus situations arose as might have been expected: the CG aft limit was extended rearwards by almost 2%, and landings on hard runways or grass were achieved without problems in cross wind speeds of up to 19mph, somewhat different from the manufacturer's suggested limit of zero. In addition to the recommendation that the revised fin and rudder be adopted, providing its lightweight structure could be made strong enough to permit aerobatic manoeuvres, and that the revised rearward CG was acceptable, Mr T van Oosterom, investigator from the NLL, proposed deletion of the Tiger Moth rudder balance area and its static balance weight and that spin strakes should be removed too.

The Royal Netherlands Air Force was not obliged to conform to this civil aviation report and even after their camouflaged aircraft had been dismantled and re-painted yellow overall, the fin and

A post-war formation of three yellow painted Tiger Moths of the Royal Netherlands Air Force. Supplied from RAF surplus stocks in Great Britain with Mod 112 incorporated, no attempt was made to remove strakes from Dutch military aircraft and replace them with Fokker tails. *via Herman Dekker*

rudder shape remained pure de Havilland. None of the military aircraft had their strakes removed. All civil registered Tiger Moths operated by both the RLS and NLS were modified with the ugly fins and rudders which were known most politely as 'Fokker Tails' else 'Bedboards'. All Tiger Moths civil registered in the Netherlands and aspiring to an unrestricted Transport Category C of A during the next forty years were required to carry this modification. It was the most compelling reason for imports and restorations during the period to be registered at convenient addresses in Great Britain, Belgium and the USA which aircraft, without undue difficulty, continued uninterrupted operations through Dutch airspace. Persuaded that the rules now applied only to a handful of privately owned Tiger Moths, and no longer the great fleet of aircraft maintained to provide a new generation of pilots for the national airline, the Dutch authorities were encouraged to fly a further series of trials in 1985 as the result of which they removed the mandatory requirement for a 'Fokker Tail' for locally registered aircraft.

An enquiry made of RLD in 1998 to explain why the authorities had changed their views was answered only with copies of correspondence dating from 1946 explaining why the Fokker modification was to be mandatory and accompanied by a metaphorical shrug of the official shoulders. It is believed the 1985 tests had shown there to be very little difference between the new results and those recorded fifty years previously.

Thought to have been the last aircraft in the world operating with the Fokker tail was PH-CSL (86609). The aircraft had been delivered to the Lucht Strijd Krachten, predecessor to the Royal Netherlands Air Force, as PG712 in 1946 taking up serial '2' then 'A-2' in 1948. Between December 1956 and January 1961 she operated as a glider tug at Gilze Rijen until she was sold to Belgium in 1962 for similar duties as civil aircraft OO-DJU. Acquired by Henri Smeitink in 1968 she was returned to the Netherlands in 1974 where fitting of her Fokker tail became mandatory. As part of the celebrations of the 60th anniversary of Schiphol Airport on May 16 1980, Henri Smeitink was invited to land with PH-CSL carrying wartime Tiger Moth pilot Prince Bernhard as passenger. Sold to a syndicate at Seppe in 1999 the aircraft made her final flight with the Fokker tail in October 2002 and was returned to her original RNethAF specification and colours by Aard Schenk at Rotterdam where the task consumed 3,500 man hours over three and a half years.

PH-CSL was the last of the airworthy Dutch registered Tiger Moths to be operated with a Fokker fin and rudder. Now painted in her original RAF camouflage colours she flies in standard de Havilland configuration. *deHMC Archive*

Miklos Schermer Voest owned Tiger Moth ZS-DLK in South Africa. By the time he had returned to the Netherlands with his aeroplane and taken up Dutch registry the rules had changed and there was no need for major modification apart from the paint scheme. *Terry Burke*

In honour of the occasion and emerging in dramatic fashion from clouds of stage smoke, PH-CSL was 'rolled in' to the RAS/IAS hangar at Rotterdam Airport on 1 June 2006, there to be greeted by 200 guests at a special reception exactly sixty years after the aeroplane had first been delivered across the North Sea.

In Australia strakes were not fitted to aircraft of local manufacture and the 100 Tiger Moths imported from Great Britain between February and September 1940 for service with the RAAF, all of which retained their RAF serial numbers, were not retrospectively converted. Strakes were never carried by the 345 Tiger Moths built by de Havilland in New Zealand, and the modification was never called up during the FAFAI Scheme early in 1942.

For the greater understanding and benefit of all those involved with the growing phenomenon of ownership and operation of Tiger Moths in Australia, it was decided by a few friends in 1992 that a civil aircraft should be subject to a thorough flight test under peacetime conditions and the results freely published. The candidate aircraft was VH-SSK (DHA885), a standard Tiger Moth built at Mascot in 1942, owned by Ken Broomhead, marked in RAAF Training Yellow as A17-468, and resident as a flying exhibit in the RAAF Museum at Point Cook.

The trials were to be the responsibility of Flt Lt Antony Morris, an RAAF pilot assigned to fast jet duties at the Aircraft Research and Development Unit, and a graduate of the Empire Test Pilots' School. Tony Morris had experience on more than forty different types of aircraft and volunteered to conduct the trials as a civilian, purely out of private interest, and the results would have no official standing in the eyes of authority. The assessment was conducted at Point Cook between 1-8 January 1993 against the following brief:

"... to produce a document outlining the recommended operating techniques and describing the aircraft's handling characteristics both on the ground and in the air. The existing Pilot's Notes for the aircraft (based on RAAF Training Notes dated 1948) are brief and do not describe major flight characteristics such as stalling and spinning, nor is any guidance given for recommended operating techniques for ground handling, take-off, aerobatics or landing. This report seeks to rectify that deficiency by providing guidance to pilots converting to the Tiger Moth who have little or no biplane or tailwheel experience ..."

Tony Morris asked readers to consider his report as a complete document rather than a series of isolated parts, but his investigation into the spinning characteristics of the Tiger Moth are of specific interest here:

"After the completion of the first turn the aircraft was defined as being in a steady state spin. The steady state spin was characterised by a 60° nose-low attitude, with no detectable

Although Tiger Moth G-AJHS has been based in the Netherlands with the Flying Wires syndicate since 1991 it proved more convenient to maintain her British registration. PH-VMS was Dutch registered using her owner's initials due to a farcical situation concocted by bureaucracy when registered in Belgium. *via Jan Voeten*

oscillations or hesitations in roll or yaw rates. The time per turn was quick (approximately 2-3 seconds), however the motion was quite smooth and no disorientation was experienced. Altitude loss was between 200ft and 300ft per turn. The forces required to hold the pro-spin controls were light to moderate (with outspin force required to keep the aileron neutral), and no stick or rudder buffeting was observed. During the spin the pilot remained firmly restrained and determining spin direction from outside reference was easy. The engine rpm remained stable throughout the spin and no rough running was noticed. Airspeed during the spin was observed at 48kts indicated (KIAS) and 36 KIAS for left and right spins respectively. No other significant differences were observed between left and right spins. The aircraft remained in the steady state spin while the pro-spin controls were applied and no tendency to transition to a spiral dive was noted. Only small differences between the slots locked and unlocked case were observed, although the slots deployed symmetrically during the spin when unlocked.

Recovery from the baseline spin was made from both the incipient and steady-state cases. Incipient recovery (which merely required centralising the controls) was rapid, with yaw and roll ceasing within a half a turn after recovery control application. Full power was then applied and the wings levelled. Height loss from the application of recovery controls to wings level, climbing flight at 58 KIAS was approximately 250ft. Once the spin had progressed to the steady state phase, recovery was effected by applying full deflection rudder opposite to the direction of spin, and simultaneously moving the control column forward to the elevator neutral position, maintaining neutral aileron. Following the application of recovery controls, the rotation ceased abruptly (within one turn), providing the pilot with a good cue to centralise the rudder. Full power was applied after the rotation had ceased, and the wings levelled. Height loss from the application of recovery controls to wings level, climbing flight at 58 KIAS was 300ft. The recovery technique was straightforward to fly and only required moderate control forces. Once the rotation had ceased, prompt centralisation of the rudder was required to prevent departure in the opposite direction.

To establish the recovery technique providing the minimum altitude loss, four additional recovery variations were examined. The baseline spin entry technique was used in each case:

Controls central recovery: The effect of centralising the rudder and control column (longitudinally and laterally) was examined during one left and one right spin. From a left spin, this technique resulted in a recovery 2.5 turns after the centralisation of the controls, consuming significantly more altitude than the baseline recovery. Similar results were observed during the right spin.

Controls free recovery: The effect of abandoning the controls during the spin was examined during one left and one right spin. For each direction of spin, releasing the controls did not effect a recovery after a further four turns, and a standard recovery was then made.

"Pro-rudder recovery: The effect of maintaining full rudder deflection in the direction of spin, while applying forward control column was assessed during one spin in each direction. In both cases the aircraft failed to recover and standard recovery action was required.

Aft stick recovery: The effect of applying full rudder deflection opposite to the direction of spin, while maintaining full aft control column was examined during one spin in each direction. In the case of the left spin, after applying the opposite rudder the spin rotation ceased after less than one turn. For the right spin, the recovery was slightly slower, requiring 2.5 turns.

Minimum altitude recovery: In all cases, minimum altitude loss for the spin recovery was achieved by applying full rudder opposite to the direction of spin and moving the control column forward. This is the recommended spin recovery technique.

The effect of introducing aileron during the spin was evaluated for both the in-spin and out-spin cases during the left and right spins. Lateral control column displacement in both directions generally increased the rate of rotation, but did not inhibit recovery if inadvertently applied while moving the stick forward. Lateral control displacement was not required to maintain a stable spin.

Military flying training post-war was dedicated towards creation of an 'all weather air force' which was so vital an ingredient in the safe and efficient operation of the new generation of aeroplanes, especially low endurance jets. Pilots of the RAF Volunteer Reserve who maintained their flying skills on Tiger Moths into the early 1950s were expected to cope with instructor induced 'unusual attitudes' under the blind flying hood. John Fricker, reminiscing in 1982, wrote:

"Unusual attitude training included spin recovery (under the hood) on primary instruments, which is a pressing invitation to vertigo and air sickness if you are that way inclined. A spin is fairly easy to identify on instruments since the needles stay in line, although way off centre, and the ASI remains steady at a bit above the normal stalling speed. The bottom needle is centred, unusually, by rudder in the direction of its displacement, and the wings are then held level by maintaining the turn needle in the middle. All controls are neutralised before easing out of the ensuing dive, remembering to relax back pressure on the stick momentarily if excessive 'g' causes the bottom needle to precess into a sudden maximum rate turn indication."

So, was the Tiger Moth an inherently dangerous beast, ready to ensnare pupil and seasoned instructor alike, or were her unpredictable moods of savagery a direct result of creeping military overload and lack of appreciation? Were the remedial measures of 1940 and later adequate or even necessary? The arguments are guaranteed to continue whenever the nose is high with the ASI showing barely 35kts.

CHAPTER EIGHT

A Job To Be Done

The state of the pilot's feet was the subject of a lesson in flying taught by a pre-war instructor with 12 ERFTS at Prestwick. The pupil had been practising forced landings under instruction on Ayr Racecourse and due to the wintry conditions had elected to wear his heavy flying boots. These had reduced his dexterity on the rudder bars and his instructor was becoming frustrated at the lack of co-ordination. Finally putting the aircraft down on the snow covered grass the instructor told his pupil to take off his boots and stow them in the locker and then to get back into his seat. Although his feet were frozen the following session was considered productive and worthwhile due to the extra sensitivity transmitted through the pupil's soles.

Thirty years later a similar tale told in New Zealand could have had fatal consequences. Dr Bernie Gunn remembers a pilot who used to fly a Tiger Moth from Tauranga to visit friends at Kawerau and on one occasion had suffered the embarrassment of getting a new flying boot jammed between the end of the rudder bar and the fuselage side frame. The experience had caused the pilot to investigate control with unshod feet and on one sunny and unusually mild winter's day he took off without footwear and clad in just a shirt and shorts. Soon feeling very cold a brief session of aerobatics did nothing to relieve the creeping numbness and the situation was not improved when he found Kawerau shrouded in fog and almost landed in a field off the aerodrome by mistake.

Flight Lieutenant Richard Jones RAFVR, took a break from flying Supermarine Spitfires with the Bader Wing at Duxford, to become resident test pilot with the de Havilland CRU at Witney, flight testing Spitfires and Tiger Moths. 'Nichi' the bulldog belonged to Witney's much respected General Manager, Philip Gordon-Marshall. *deHMC Archive*

Some time after a safe touchdown club members found the pilot still sitting in the aircraft with the engine running, unable to taxy or to speak. They switched off the ignition and managed to lift him out of the cockpit, but it was only after half an hour in front of a gentle heater that he recovered the powers of speech. More drastic action to relieve a classic case of hypothermia, said Dr Gunn, could have resulted in death.

At an estimated cost of £5 per flying hour for RAF Tiger Moth pilot training in 1940 the high rejection rate of would-be pilots at the flying schools was not only bad economics, but the unsuccessful candidates were slowing the passage of waiting recruits and consequently the flow of trained pilots to operational squadrons. The problem was exacerbated with the establishment of the Air Training Scheme when pupil pilots were transported to overseas schools and only then found not to be suitable, by which time they had already been subject to high levels of expenditure and logistical support.

A correspondent of the day was partially right in his assessment of the situation:

"We are practically mass producing pilots for the first time in our history. In the First World War, a man became a pilot by grit and a good modicum of luck which gave him time to complete his flying training while on actual service. This time a pilot who has passed through elementary, intermediate and advanced schools, and has sampled squadron work, can call himself experienced. It is unlikely that anyone who is unsuitable for active service will get past the elementary stage."

In order to reach the elementary stage in the first instance pilot recruits passed through an indoctrination process at an Initial Training Wing and were required to undertake both written and mechanical

During the early part of the Second World War Tiger Moth circuit training in Great Britain was almost continuous, often in marginal weather, by day and by night. The introduction of the Grading System and opening of schools in the Commonwealth, considerably eased the home situation. Note the two styles of camouflage still in use. *via Richard Riding*

There is no obvious reason why this exercise with a plum-bob should be taking place on what appears to be a very cold day, especially when the aircraft's mainwheels are not chocked. The instructor will have his reasons. *Flight*

It turned out to be a very wet day at No 10 ERFTS at Yatesbury when the press were invited to meet instructors and trainees in April 1939. Nearly all the aircraft are painted in the pre-war camouflage scheme whilst retaining civil registrations. *Flight*

aptitude tests, in addition to a stringent medical, before even getting close to a Tiger Moth weeks later. In Great Britain, aircrew cadets were mustered as Aircraftmen 2nd Class (AC2) with pay at the rate of two shillings per day during training. Those going on to become pilots were promoted to Leading Aircraftmen with pay raised to five shillings per day with an additional two shillings on account of 'flying instructional pay'. It was important to score good marks at the end of the EFTS course as these dictated possible reclassification and promotion. A sergeant pilot could expect a rate of twelve shillings and sixpence a day.

The length of time spent at a British EFTS, eight to twelve weeks, might depend on the season of the year although course duration varied as the war progressed, on global location and the urgency or otherwise for speeding up or slowing down the throughput. Working to a standard syllabus the trainees flying Tiger Moths could expect to fly for fifty hours of which five hours would be under the blind flying hood coping with instruments, five hours navigation work including a first solo cross country exercise, and at least twenty five hours dual.

Precious to the memory of every trainee was the number of the 'Exercise' and the order in which they progressed:

01	Air Experience
01A	Familiarity with cockpit layout
02	Effect of controls
03	Taxiing
04	Straight and level flight
05	Climbing, gliding and stalling
06	Medium turns
07	Taking off into wind
08	Powered approach and landing
09	Gliding approach and landing
10	Spinning
11	First solo
12	Side slipping
13	Precautionary landings
14	Low flying (with instructor only)
15	Steep turns
16	Climbing turns
17	Forced landings
18	Action in the event of fire
18A	Abandoning the aircraft
19	Instrument flying
20	Taking off and landing out of wind
21	Restarting the engine in flight
22	Aerobatics

As part of their training every aircrew cadet was instructed in the art of propeller swinging. The RAF method was to stand in front of the propeller ensuring chocks were in place. When starting an engine use of the correct litany was emphasised in addition to the fact that the person outside the aircraft was in command of the operation. *Flight*

de Havilland DH.82A Tiger Moth Mk II, EM-973/YO, No 401 Squadron, 1943. Dark Earth and Dark Green upper surfaces with Trainer Yellow undersides. Codes in Medium Sea Grey, serials in Night. Black/white/red 'sharkmouth' motif on engine cowling. Squadron hack, carrying the YO codes applied on the squadron's Spitfires at the time. *Artwork ©Richard Caruana, 1:72 scale*

SOUTHERN RHODESIA RATG

About 430 Tiger Moths were shipped from RAF stocks in Great Britain to Southern Rhodesia after the Empire Air Training Scheme (EATS) established Elementary Flying Training Schools (EFTS) there. No 25 EFTS was opened at Belvedere near Salisbury in May 1940; No 26 at Guinea Fowl (Gwelo) in August; No 27 at Induna (Bulawayo) in November and, following expansion, No 28 at Mount Hampden, an airfield twelve miles outside Salisbury, in April 1941. The aircraft were sent by sea to Cape Town then via the rail link to Bulawayo and on to Induna where they were repainted yellow overall, erected, and distributed as necessary around the stations of what became the Rhodesian Air Training Group (RATG). Administratively controlled by the Rhodesian Minister of Air with Air Vice-Marshal C W Meredith, pre-war Director of Civil Aviation, as Commanding Officer, the ultimate direction was vested in the Air Ministry operating from London.

Belvedere opened on 25 May 1940, the first EFTS in the Training Scheme, beating Canada by just a few days. Under the terms of the Agreement, Southern Rhodesia was to provide buildings and facilities at a cost of about £950,000. The aircraft and staff and four fifths of the running costs were all the responsibility of the British Government.

Cranbourne Air Station had been designated an EFTS in December 1939, utilising eight Tiger Moths and some instructors

Trainee pilot Stanley Hoddinott with an all-yellow Tiger Moth at Induna, Southern Rhodesia in 1942 where open neck shirts and shorts were the order of the day. *Stanley Hoddinott*

from the Bulawayo and Salisbury Flying Clubs. Under these arrangements, sixty two pupils qualified for advanced training with No 4 Service Flying Training School (SFTS) at Habbaniya in Iraq until the new system became operational when Cranbourne itself took on the role of an SFTS.

RATG flying instructor Charles Nepean Bishop remembered that affiliated to RATG was the training unit of the Royal Hellenic Air Force which flew as part of No 28 EFTS at Mount Hampden:

"To start with they had a special flight of their own under Flt Lt Jack Collins but were later divided amongst the other four Flights at that station. They were under their own administration, had their own senior officers at Group HQ, and carried out no station duties whatsoever. They also broke aeroplanes with the same gay abandon as others amongst our gallant allies, but they were good fellows and we liked them. Recruits arriving at the Hillside Initial Training Wing (ITW) in 1941, formerly Bulawayo's agricultural showground, found a Tiger Moth on display adjacent to the parade square, placed no doubt in an effort to raise spirits, but on closer inspection new arrivals would have discovered it was merely a loose assemblage of parts mostly salvaged from those rearranged during training by their predecessors.

Bernie Halliday met T8113 (84425), at 26 EFTS Guinea Fowl on 22 July 1943, "a lovely bright yellow Tiger Moth. I had dreamed of this moment for years," and was soon enveloped into the ordered routine of an RAF flying training syllabus. Apart from the patient entreaties of his flying instructor pupil pilot Halliday remembers his early flying hours for other reasons:

> The Rhodesian bush offers an uninteresting vista, but not from a Tiger Moth at 2,000ft, (6,840ft above mean sea level), for the first time. I looked around the horizon: the blue sky met a sunlit ground. Breathtaking! Only those privileged to have flown in an open cockpit aircraft on such a day would fully appreciate my feelings. The war was a long way away. My instructor asked me where we were in relation to the airfield. I had not a clue! But it was one of the first lessons to be learnt, and from early on too."

Guinea Fowl was the second Rhodesian EFTS to open. The whole station had been constructed in twelve weeks and was declared operational on the day 500 trainees arrived at the end of a three day train journey from Cape Town. The weather was not always so ideal and, due to a peculiar gathering of dust devils on the aerodrome one morning, Bernie Halliday's course picked up the dubious distinction of establishing the record for the most prangs before breakfast: nine! Tiger Moth T8113, delivered to Rhodesia in May 1941, was one of forty three flown south to the SAAF on 31 May 1944, and from whose charge she was sold as surplus in October 1946.

T7513 (83924), had been shipped on 30 November 1940, one of three paid for by Mr and Mrs G R Milne. The Tiger Moth was named *Mary Ann* after their third daughter, and in January 1942 was adopted as his personal aircraft by the 'A' Flight Commander at 28 EFTS Mt. Hampden, Flt Lt C A Nepean Bishop, he of the pre-war civilian formation team which had operated informally from Brooklands. The legendary 'Bish' was to maintain an active association with Tiger Moths for another twenty years as post-war Chief Flying Instructor (CFI) of the Tiger Club at Croydon and later Redhill. On 13 January 1944, T7513 accrued her 2,000th flying hour and, in accordance with standing orders, was withdrawn from use and broken down for spare parts, to be replaced in RATG by one of an increasing fleet of unsuitable Fairchild Cornells.

A productive use for at least one of the time-expired RATG Tiger Moths was reported to have been conceived by instructors in 1942 on behalf of the many Air Training Corps (ATC) cadets who flew with the units on a regular basis, and was featured in contemporary British magazines. A training device known as the 'Hoppity' allowed cadets the opportunity to gain valuable taxy and handling time on the ground in company with a unit instructor. A Tiger Moth fuselage with the centre section removed was fitted with a shortened undercarriage, a precaution to displace the centre of gravity and dissuade the machine from standing on her nose. Operation of the rudder on the ground, the only method of steering the craft, was made easier by the installation of a double kingpost. Fed from a one gallon fuel tank hidden underneath the front decking, the standard Gipsy Major engine was governed to reduce maximum speed to 1,400rpm, turning a cropped wooden propeller. With the exception of the oil pressure gauges, all the other instruments were painted onto flat dashboards, otherwise the cockpit controls and seats were pure Tiger Moth.

Lower mainplanes were cropped at the root end to permit standard interplane struts, attached at their normal wiring plate positions, to pick up on the fuselage top longerons and act as bracing. In this configuration, somewhat reminiscent of the 'penguins' used during the First World War to teach embryonic pilots the art of running 'straights' at speed across the aerodrome without fear of getting prematurely airborne, ATC cadets acquired useful and practical manoeuvring skills. Cadets with experience of the 'Hoppity' were actively encouraged by the RATG instructors to taxy their real Tiger Moths from and to dispersal, before and after flight.

'Hoppity' was constructed from scrap Tiger Moth components at Induna in Southern Rhodesia in 1942, and wrecked after the craft was persuaded off the ground for a moment of glory. Note the wingless Fairchild Cornell behind the tail unit. *via Richard Riding*

Hatfield built Tiger Moth R4916 was shipped to the Southern Rhodesia Air Force early in 1940 and served at 25 EFTS Belvedere until scrapped in 1945. To relieve the duties of the RAF Regiment, aircraft and airfield equipment was placed under the protection of an Air Askari Corps raised for the purpose from several Central African countries. *deHMC Archive*

Flt Lt Nepean Bishop championed the idea of turning irreparable or redundant Tiger Moths into more Hoppities for the benefit of ATC Squadrons in Great Britain and possibly elsewhere, although New Zealand provided their ATC units with a Flight of real Tiger Moths operating on a touring basis. It was hoped that Hoppities would come to represent a realistic complement to the basic gliders then in widespread use, but the idea was never taken up.

Almost fifty years later, a slightly different story emerged which cast some doubt on the optimism shown in 'Bish's' original report, and also highlighted technical differences which might have indicated that two different standards of machine were involved. This Hoppity, built from scratch using Tiger Moth parts salvaged by engineers at 27 EFTS Induna, was offered to the Bulawayo Grammar School. Len Bracey, one of the instigators of the scheme, described how it all went together:

"A Tiger Moth fuselage was constructed complete except for the centre section and fuel tank, then fitted with a normal cockpit including controls, instruments etc. A standard tailplane, rudder and skid were fitted and a fuel tank was manufactured by the station tinsmith to fit under the fuselage decking behind the engine bulkhead. The 'powers that be' decided that, in order to make propeller swinging easier, the undercarriage was to be shortened. This was achieved by removing the main spring from the oleo leg which, when this latter part was bolted to the fuselage proper, gave the desired result.

The bottom mainplanes only were attached in the normal way, supported by four struts from the fuselage centre section lugs to the main spar. Fittings were manufactured and the spars drilled at the required location. By doubling the length of the tailplane support struts by welding pairs together, four very suitable wing struts were manufactured. Wood and fabric fairings completed the job and the whole assembly, when completed, took on the looks of a very racy little trainer.

A normal Gipsy Major engine was installed, minus four plugs and one magneto and fitted with a propeller reduced in diameter by twelve inches. Once the engine had been finally cowled, a ground test was declared. Several instructors tried their hand and pronounced it to be a very successful design. The engine, on four plugs, required some careful adjustment with the slow running which an engine fitter and I carried out. This necessitated a ground run and we saw no harm in removing the chocks and trying things out for ourselves. I found she was good fun to taxy around and we were really enjoying ourselves when an officer saw us and threatened to throw the book at us, courts martial etc. We reasoned that the Hoppity was not really an aircraft and managed to escape by the skin of our teeth.

For some time the EFTS pilots used the trainer but the Grammar School never took up the scheme so Hoppity became the station 'fun machine' until one day a pilot tried to get her off the ground, and succeeded, gaining an altitude of about four feet before the bracing struts failed at the welds and the wings folded up."

In England during the 1950s the Wiltshire School of Flying at Thruxton, having established themselves with a Tiger Moth four seat conversion to create the Jackaroo, commissioned a low wing monoplane from their associate, Jackaroo Aircraft Ltd. Called the Paragon the layout was not dissimilar to the Hoppity but on the engineering mock up wings were standard Tiger Moth lower mainplanes, slightly swept, and braced by external 'V' struts mounted between the fuselage top longeron and the main spars.

Flt Lt Micklethwaite, CFI at Guinea Fowl, laid claim to a personal Tiger Moth which he graciously shared with the Station Commander: T5475 (83200), painted silver overall and named *Inez* after his wife, was another aircraft which had been presented privately to the RAF. The machine was rigged perfectly and sensitive controls lulled one pupil into applying less rudder than was necessary to get cleanly out of a test spin, earning him a private lecture. The candidate's own instructor subsequently took him to 4,000ft and demonstrated the not very gentle art of extraction from inverted spins. *Inez* later served with 4 Flying Training School (FTS) at Heany and 5 FTS at Thornhill before sale to the Government of Kenya in 1952. Registered VP-KKA in June that year and operated by the Aero Club of East Africa from Nairobi West, she was written off on 28 August 1953. The pilot, a man of 1,800 hours experience, was cleared to fly with a false right hand and on the day of the accident was engaged on a local sightseeing trip with a high time RAF pilot as passenger. The aircraft had no form of intercom between cockpits, and after the crash from which both men escaped relatively unscathed, the pilot made the following statement:

"It was arranged with my passenger that when I was ready to hand the aircraft over I would raise my hands above my head. The aircraft was then started up and I taxied out after normal checks and took the aircraft off on the duty runway. I climbed straight ahead to about 1,000ft, carried out a climbing turn to the left and when at approximately 1,200ft to 1,500ft, my passenger took over the controls without any pre-warning and banged the stick abruptly over to the right, whereupon I held my hands above my head to indicate that he had control.

de Havilland DH.82A Tiger Moth Mk II, 680/12, No 28 EFTS, Rhodesian Air Training Group, Mount Hampden (Southern Rhodesia), May 1942. Trainer Yellow overall. Serial in black, code on engine cowling in white. Red/white checks around rear fuselage. Roundels in six positions. *Artwork ©Richard Caruana, 1:72 scale*

He then attempted to carry out a roll. This manoeuvre did not appear to be successful and the aircraft came out of the manoeuvre in a diving turn to the left. I did not attempt to interfere with the control of the aircraft at this point, believing that my passenger was demonstrating his ability prior to carrying out some further manoeuvre, and it was not until we were dangerously near the ground, that I realised that some corrective action must be taken. I made a very coarse corrective movement in an attempt to rectify the attitude of the aeroplane, but this was too late and the aircraft struck the ground."

In the official report which was published within four weeks of the accident, highlighting a number of offences and breaches which had been committed, the Inspector suggested that it was possible that the aircraft had not been under the control of either occupant for some portion of the flight which had taken place after a heavy drinking session at lunchtime, during which the pilot admitted to having consumed at least six single gins.

Canadian-built Fairchild Cornells were supplied to RATG as Tiger Moth replacements from late 1943 when all Tiger Moths with more than 2,000 airframe hours were withdrawn and scrapped. It was intended that 200 Cornells would be provided to the Joint Air Training Scheme (JATS) in South Africa, but trials with a pair of Cornells from February 1944 convinced the South African Air Force that the aircraft was quite unsuitable for their needs. While Cornells were taken on charge in Rhodesia, eighty one Tiger Moths were released from RATG, ferried south and integrated into the JATS programme, taking up SAAF serial numbers in the process.

One instructor was not over-impressed with the condition of some of the aircraft, a view thoroughly endorsed by SAAF engineers who scrapped several on arrival:

"With the number of aircraft on the station after the arrival of the Cornells, there was certainly no room for Tiger Moths in the hangars with the result that they had to stand outside with disastrous results to their general condition, especially as regards rigging. As the decision to send them to South Africa was not made at once they were out some weeks, so when the time came to get them ready for the flight to Induna, it needed considerable work to get them flying straight and level once again, especially level. During the first two weeks of February 1944, I made over sixty test flights to get twenty nine aircraft flying really to my liking. After they had been ferried down to Induna they joined many others which were waiting in the open to be taken on the next stage to the Union, and from all reports they were still there some weeks later, so one shudders to think about the state in which they eventually arrived."

A contingent of surplus Tiger Moths from 26 EFTS Guinea Fowl were flown by instructors and pupils directly to the SAAF Base at Zwartkop near Pretoria on 21 May 1944. The total flight time was over eight hours and the aircraft arrived in the twilight and very low on fuel.

A Tiger Moth supplied from Hatfield to the South African branch of the company in 1937 (3606), was delivered to the Aero Club de Moçambique in Lourenço Marques (Maputo) as CR-AAG, but was flown into a hillside in 1943 and effectively demolished. By whatever reasoning, the remains of the aircraft were delivered to the engineering section of 28 EFTS Mount Hampden, where they arrived in a number of sacks. Under the supervision of F/O Pennant-Rea, a former de Havilland employee based in Southern Rhodesia, CR-AAG was carefully reconstructed using mostly new spares drawn from stores and the rear fuselage of DX544, an Australian built aircraft, (DHA 605), which had been struck off charge under unknown circumstances in September 1942.

The 'new' CR-AAG was found to be faster than all other locally based Tiger Moths, even the most recently delivered, by an astonishing 20mph, and was duly returned to Mozambique only to crash into the Zambesi River in May 1948 when operated by the Aero Club at Beira.

The remains of Tiger Moth CR-AAG were delivered to RAF Mount Hampden, Southern Rhodesia, in a number of sacks. Nobody questioned the authority under which this 1937 civil aircraft was rebuilt and could only speculate on the reasons why she subsequently became the station's fastest Tiger Moth by a margin of 20mph. *C Nepean Bishop*

Student pilot Cyril Saward and much patched Tiger Moth N6983 of 6 EFTS Sywell about October 1939. All three Tiger Moths which appear in the photograph are at different stages in the camouflage change-over programme. *Richard Saward*

TRAINING

Neville Duke, a naturally talented pilot, had flown his first RAF familiarisation trip at 13 EFTS White Waltham in Tiger Moth N6790 (82060), on 20 August 1940. On 6 September at the height of the Battle of Britain, he flew solo after eight and a half hours dual and, two days later such was the urgency, he flew seven sorties between dawn and dusk of which four were solo. He described the whole experience of solo flight as 'exhilarating'. Following a successful career as an RAF fighter pilot, Sqn Ldr N F Duke DSO, OBE, DFC and 2 Bars, AFC, flying a Hawker Hunter, became the holder of the world air speed record in 1953.

Early in April 1941 when working on Tiger Moths grounded at dispersal at 17 EFTS North Luffenham due to poor weather, one of the two duty engine fitters suddenly appeared from their crew hut wearing a flying suit and carrying a helmet, parachute and maps and announced his intention of flying. He persuaded his reluctant colleague to start the engine, taxied out and took off. It was suspected that the man already had some flying experience and the fact that he owned an Alvis open tourer put him in a different league from most of the other airmen.

After lunch the Tiger Moth landed back at North Luffenham and was met by an officer and two military policemen. The officer was heard to say "good show" before inviting the two MPs to make their arrest. The pilot was charged with taking an aircraft, the property of His Majesty the King, without permission, stealing petrol and endangering life. He was court martialled, found guilty and sentenced to three months confined to barracks which he served at RAF Wittering, mostly in the Sergeants' Mess where he was treated like a hero before returning to duties at North Luffenham.

On the day of the adventure he had landed at Bristol where he was presented with a chit commending his good landing. Then it was to Hendon where, due to the worsening weather, the Duty Officer was reluctant to let him take off until he was persuaded that the pilot had flown for Imperial Airways before the war and was used to the conditions. The flight had been a protest against the system for rejecting his application for aircrew on account of poor eyesight.

Derek Piggott made remarkable progress during his Grading course and his instructor was willing to allow him to go solo after only four hours dual. He relished the experience, noting especially the improved performance of the Tiger Moth without the mass in the front seat. Derek Piggott later learned that the Flight Commander had mistakenly believed he was already an accomplished glider pilot, (he did become a world class glider pilot and instructor after the war), and had encouraged his progress, but the overheard discussions had actually

"A bit murky and rather cool, but the wind is down the runway, the forecast is better and the aeroplane is serviceable. Shall we go, gentlemen?" Flight Lieutenant Godfrey Bremridge, a member of the pre-war Brooklands Aviation sales team based at Weybridge, joined the instructional staff at 6 EFTS Sywell where he was later killed when his Tiger Moth collided with an Airspeed Oxford during a weather check overhead the airfield. *Richard Sayward*

The crude but reliable and effective 'Gosport' dynamic tube communications system which remained the only contact between student and instructor until electric intercom was installed post-war. If ever a student chose to shower retribution on an unfriendly instructor he could choose to be sick into the mouthpiece, and blow!

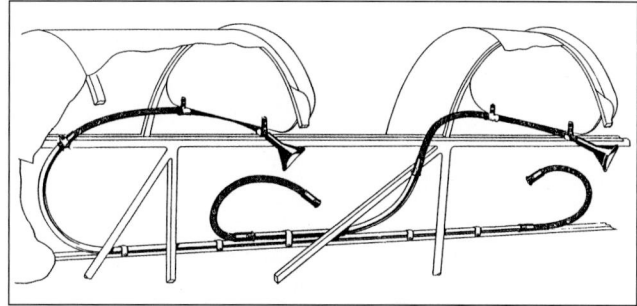

Instructors and trainee pilots confirm their pre-flight briefing at No 1 EFTS at Hatfield whilst the School engineers ready the aircraft in the background. *Flight*

concerned flying model gliders. Nevertheless, with a natural ability and 'above average' assessment, within the twelve hour allowance he managed the obligatory spinning exercises and several hours solo.

The Glider Pilot Regiment was regarded as simply another unit of the British Army and volunteers were lured into the ranks by the enticement of additional allowances. Serving with the Black Watch in Scotland in 1942 Bill Sarjantson was offered an extra two shillings a day to join the Parachute Regiment, but three shillings and six pence if he became a glider pilot. He opted for the additional pay, was taught to fly Tiger Moths with 3 EFTS at Shellingford in October 1942, but transferred to 21 EFTS at Booker for refresher training early in 1943.

The occupant of the front cockpit appears to be taking command during this engine starting exercise, unaware perhaps that the engineer has forgotten to place the chocks in front of the wheels. *deHMC Archive*

Army glider flights were, inevitably, one way trips, and Bill Sarjentson's Tiger Moth training led him to a final landing at Arnhem in 1944 where a non-fatal shot in the head put paid to his flying career.

British Army glider pilots had trained with the RAF at Booker from June 1941 and, due to the matured size of the establishment it was necessary to base E and F Flights at Denham as a means of relief. Although related there was a marked degree of rivalry between the two airfields and aerobatic competitions were regularly organised for the instructors of all the Flights.

A peculiarity of circuit flying at Denham was that against accepted practice it was usual to operate right hand, taking aircraft around the substantial facility that was the local film studios and where one of the Denham based instructors, David Tomlinson, spent some of his off duty hours in front of the cameras. On 6 April 1985, David Tomlinson was the compère at a concert in support of the Bomber Command Museum at Hendon and between renderings of the Spitfire Prelude and the Dam Busters March, the former instructor alluded to his previous associations with Tiger Moths at which some of the audience sniggered. Whether in anger or jest or frustration, David Tomlinson retorted: "Well I don't know what's funny about that!"

In action it was always believed that British trained pilots would naturally break left if attacked from behind and one successful German fighter pilot said that his deflection shooting always assumed that would be the case. It was the built-in instinct of Denham trained pilots to break right and against convention, which unexpected reaction might have saved their lives.

A legendary instructor at 21 EFTS Booker had recorded 500 flying hours in his first logbook which was dated 1915, and was still adding hours in his tenth when the total had passed 17,000. One morning he looked casually at the names chalked on the flying rota together with achieved hours and called out a student listed for some dual. After two circuits the instructor climbed out of the front cockpit, tidied up the straps, offered a word of encouragement to the prospective soloist and shambled back to the hut. Enter the Flight Commander, scheduled to fly with the same student, only to be told that he had just been sent off solo. Now somewhat concerned the instructor looked again at the chalked hours to read 1 hour and 15 minutes and not 11 hours 50 minutes as he had believed. The student managed to land the Tiger Moth safely and in one piece, on his sixth attempt.

While prospective glider pilots were learning to fly in Tiger Moths the Airborne Forces Establishment (AFE) at Ringway kept a number of the type on charge for light tugging duties alongside Hawker Hectors and heavy duty machines. The Tiger Moths were used to develop new or experimental towing techniques, climbing with their charges to thousands of feet before casting off. One was fitted with a Chance sector light to enable a following glider to maintain station in darkness.

At No 1 Glider Training School (GTS) Thame in 1941 trainee army glider pilot instructors were themselves instructed whilst flying Kirby Kites towed in formation by Tiger Moths and Hawker Hectors, during which the aerial convoys were subjected to mock attack by Hawker Hurricanes. Drawn from all regiments, the situation at Thame was described by Lawrence Wright in his book *The Wooden Sword:*

An instructor at No 18 ERFTS Fairoaks briefs his pupil in advance of his first solo flight. It was standard practice to tie together the harness straps in the front cockpit and to remove the control column to avoid any chance of conflict. *Flight*

The instructor's work is done, for the time being, and he expresses no obvious emotion as his pupil taxies away for his first flight as pilot in command. *Flight*

"The informal air of the camp was matched by its inmates, the instructors to be, and a rum lot they were, as the devil said when he first saw the Ten Commandments. Their clothing was the opposite of uniform. All of them glider pilots, hurriedly secured by posting, by attachment, by seconding or by shadier means."

In November 1941, the Hatfield factory, ever mindful of the importance of communication, introduced a pocket sized newsletter for fortnightly circulation within the local workforce. It was inexpensively produced on cheap utility paper and the first edition of eight sides carried three photographs, none of which showed the image of an aeroplane, a cartoon and a short report under the heading 'Our stinger on show':

'Some hundreds of people who are very close friends of ours came to the aircraft factory on Saturday and saw something they are all helping to make.'

The 'close friends' were all sub-contract suppliers and the 'stinger' they had come to see fly was the DH.98 Mosquito, which it did, capably demonstrated by Geoffrey de Havilland Jnr, although the report was restrained from saying so. Entitled *Our Job*, issue 1 of the new publication carried the title-page sub-heading: "which deals informally with matters of interest to everyone in the de Havilland organisation," and on the reverse side, a warning: "Published for private circulation only. The contents are not to be communicated to anyone not in the employ of the de Havilland Aircraft Co Ltd."

Due to very strict censorship, perhaps, it was probably something of a relief for the Editor to be able to include real aeroplane facts in issue 34 dated 11 February 1943, for hidden amongst the continuous text which allowed not a blank line for fear of infringing the paper regulations, and which included news of fund raising for Merchant Navy Week, the Aircraft Division Sports Club, the need to save fuel in the factory heating system and distribution of prime cuts from the Pig Club, not to mention the call for editorial contributions of the right material, was a choice piece entitled 'The Ubiquitous Tiger'.

The editorial spoke of four Tiger Moths which were in service at an Elementary Flying Training School in the West Country, which between them had amassed a total of nearly 13,000 flying hours, and were still going strong. Curiously, for a publication of limited circulation which had been concerned enough about security in its first issue not even to mention the name of its own company product, the reporter quoted the serial numbers of all four aircraft. To have achieved an average of over 3,000 hours even by mid-1942, each Tiger Moth would surely have required substantial investment in pre-war activity to have boosted her totals, and so it proved to be.

BB694 (3340), had operated as G-ADGV before military impressment with 6 ERFTS, contracted to Brooklands Aviation at Sywell since May 1935. BB791 (3382), was another Sywell aircraft, having joined 6 ERFTS in August 1935 as G-ADJF. BB742 (3182), was the ninth production DH.82A and the veteran of the piece, having been delivered to the de Havilland administered 13 ERFTS at White Waltham in February 1933 as G-ACDI.

The youngest of the quartet was BB860 (3436), delivered to Reid and Sigrist on behalf of 7 ERFTS Desford as G-ADXT in December 1935; she was probably also the most fortunate of the group to have survived for inclusion in the *Our Job* list. On 22 September 1939, her pupil pilot choked the engine during an attempted overshoot, stalled and crashed, causing substantial airframe damage. On 4 January 1940, without assistance from the pilot, the engine failed just after take off and during the inevitable straight-ahead landing, BB860 ran into a concealed ditch which wrecked the undercarriage and caused a re-arrangement of the engine bay. As if that was not a sufficient indignity, during circuit activity on 17 June 1941, Tiger Moth R4776 (82720), managed to land on top of her. BB860 was conveyed to the de Havilland Civil Repair Unit (CRU) at Witney where she was eventually wheeled out to be test flown on 5 September by resident RAF test pilot, Flt Lt Richard Jones.

In addition to the four old stagers, the *Our Job* Editor highlighted a further four Tiger Moths in his thirty fourth issue, each of which was involved in an unpublished story every bit as interesting as the morale raising facts appearing in print.

BB675 (3402), was declared to be a 'redoubtable veteran' with 2,600 hours since her registration as G-ADOI on 11 October 1935, and posting to Perth for duty with 11 ERFTS. By the time news of her status was published in *Our Job* early in 1943, she had been repaired in Devon twice, firstly after a major landing accident at Perth and then following a mishap at Yeovilton while serving with Station Flight at RAF Hawkinge. At the moment of publication BB675 was with 16 EFTS Burnaston and remained there apart from terminal leave at 9 MU Cosford until sold, coincidentally to the de Havilland Aircraft Company, who refurbished her at Witney prior to sale in Ethiopia.

DE241 (85287), was hailed as the first Tiger Moth to be fitted experimentally with a full blind flying instrument panel, "and the experiment has proved a success." The aircraft was delivered to 22 EFTS Cambridge in January 1942 where a pupil made three attempts to land during his first night solo and on his final approach dragged the aeroplane in low and slow but collided with a blister hangar near the perimeter track. Following repairs at Llandow the aircraft returned to operate at Cambridge until 1950.

G-ACDI was delivered new to No 1 ERFTS at Hatfield in February 1933 and later served with the second de Havilland managed ERFTS, No 13, based at White Waltham. In 1954 the aircraft crashed on take-off when operating with Christchurch Aero Club but her remains were stored and following a long-term rebuild by John Pothecary she flew again in 2008. *Geoff Collins*

Right: One of the aircraft featured in the de Havilland Aircraft Company's wartime in-house publication 'Our Job' was G-ADXT, delivered to Desford in December 1935. The aircraft is currently used for trial lessons at Compton Abbas. *Barry Dowsett*

Below: This picture was released on behalf of the Admiralty in March 1940, accompanied by the following statement: "The Fleet Air Arm, the speedy infant of the Royal Navy, plays an important part in modern warfare. At the Elementary Flying Training School where this picture was taken, the Rating pilots undergo ten weeks intensive training in all branches of aeronautics."

Above: No 29 EFTS at Clyffe Pypard was operated by the Marshall Company of Cambridge and was contracted to train pilots for the Fleet Air Arm. As RAF aircrew cadets wore a white flash in their caps so naval cadets wore a most distinguishable white band around theirs, otherwise in Sidcot suits and against a background of Tiger Moths, who could tell the difference? *Marshall Aerospace*

Below: An unidentified Tiger Moth in the R-4000 serial range, probably painted all over silver and with a gas patch at the rear of the fuselage top decking, on charge with the Royal Navy at HMS *Phoenix*, Egypt, in November 1942. There appears to be an inverted tin can over the fuel tank sight glass and non standard head rests for the occupants of both seats. *Howard Levy*

T6683 (84983), collided with another aircraft when landing at Clyffe Pypard, a fact willingly acknowledged in the *Our Job* report, but it was very much a case of the other fellow coming off second best. While T6683 suffered a broken top wing and damaged fuel tank, repairs to which kept her off the circuit for only two days, the second aeroplane was said to have been cut in half. On 6 May 1943, T6683 is reported to have 'crashed' and was sent to Taylorcraft at Thurmaston for repairs. Damage must have been severe for her incapacitation lasted for an almost unprecedented eight weeks before she was positioned to 5 MU Kemble. Nine weeks later she was allocated to the Pilotless Aircraft Unit (PAU) at Manorbier, five miles south east of the flying boat activity at Pembroke Dock in West Wales, where on 22 November 1943 she was selected for conversion to a Queen Bee.

Why was what is assumed to have been a perfectly serviceable Tiger Moth removed from the training programme, when production of new aircraft was scheduled to continue at Cowley for another eight months, and be slated for conversion after lengthy repairs? However, T6683 was spared. A fortnight later she was posted to the Glider Pilot Exercise Unit (GPEU) at Shrewton, Wiltshire, and a week after that to the Operational and Refresher Training Unit (ORTU), but only on account of the fact that the establishment had changed its name!

Was there something odd about Tiger Moth T6683, something that had been discovered during that extended repair schedule at Taylorcraft? Had she developed a personality disorder after her accidents at Clyffe Pypard when the de Havilland publicity machine had described her as being 'sturdy'? After spending more than five years in storage with 10 MU Hullavington from January 1945, the aircraft was sold for scrap.

The final aircraft of the batch chosen for publicity was R4962 (82771), another Tiger Moth based with 22 EFTS at Cambridge. "A cadet pilot making his first night solo trip was suddenly confronted by a Nazi swooping from the cloud. Although the enemy attacked fiercely and the British pilot was wounded, he succeeded in evading his formidable opponent and brought his unarmed machine safe home," read the report. In truth the action was much more serious. R4962 was operating from Caxton Gibbet, one of three satellite airfields for Cambridge's main aerodrome at Teversham, and where night flying facilities were available. At 0230 hours on 16 July 1941, the Tiger Moth was attacked in the circuit by a German prowler, thought to have been a Messerschmit Me 110, lurking with just such an intent. Against a blacked-out background the appearance of a lighted flarepath was an obvious draw and training aircraft showing navigation lights as they flew sedate circuits made easy and attractive targets. R4962 received two bursts of machine gun fire which badly damaged the tail but the pilot, LAC Hassall, was praised for the confidence he displayed when forced to crash-land the aircraft in the darkness. His personal injuries amounted to a cut on his neck which received one stitch. 'Safe home' it might have been but R4962 was classified as having been shot down as the result of enemy action and written off. Not for publication in 1941 was the fact that the enemy aircraft also dropped 10 delayed action bombs across the landing ground. An area of some 250 yards radius around each was cordoned off but training continued unabated by day and by night for the next four days by which time the Bomb Disposal Squad had removed them from the site. Neither was it revealed that two other Tiger Moths were shot down over Caxton Gibbett in 1941 with the loss of instructors and pupils. The marauding Ju88c Night Fighter actually believed he was operating over RAF Wyton and claimed a Bristol Blenheim.

Caxton Gibbet was the source of another interesting story which circulated amongst the stations of Flying Training Command. Pupils from one resident Cambridge Flight, intent on demonstrating their abilities to fly in formation, but denied the opportunity by the CFI, are said to have locked their instructors into the crew room one day and enjoyed a brief and unauthorised interlude in close harmony.

The 'Grading System' introduced into the RAF in November 1941 and based on a points score for ability and aptitude awarded at each of ten phases, functioned as an integral part of the Elementary School programme within which selected pilot candidates were

The RAF's top scoring fighter pilot of the Second World War, 'Johnnie' Johnston, was trained to fly on Tiger Moths at 22 EFTS Cambridge, a school managed by the Marshall Company. When the new AirSpace Centre was opened at Duxford in 2006, Sir Arthur Marshall commissioned a non-flying composite of Johnnie Johnston's first solo aircraft, N6635, which now hangs from the ceiling of the museum. *Bill Taylor*

The Grading System was introduced by Flying Training Command in an effort to prevent waste and speed up the selection process but some unlikely candidates still managed to impress their instructors. The shadowy pressmen still managed to immortalise themselves. *deHMC Archive*

allowed up to twelve hours of instructional flying. At six hours and twelve hours, their suitability, or not, to go forward for further training was assessed following a check flight, usually conducted by the CFI and with reference to the accumulated points total. Within the twelve hour allowance pupils were not expected to achieve solo standard although many did and were sent off for their never-to-be-forgotten ten minute circuit. Some instructors held back pupils just on the edge of solo standard to prevent the prospect of a bad solo flight 'score' spoiling an otherwise exemplary course result.

Achieving a high standard during the grading process did not automatically guarantee further advancement. Successful candidates were matched to the availability of berths on sailings to Canada or southern Africa, or to a sudden increased demand due to heavier than expected casualties, or the total opposite. Such circumstances dictated how many aspiring trainees could be accommodated, and the percentage of the total was never constant, varying from as little as 5% to 40% or more.

The Grading System had an unforeseen secondary effect. By providing a stream of higher quality trainees the wastage rate at any EFTS was significantly lower, resulting in qualified pupils queuing for vacancies at Service Flying Training Schools (SFTS). To counter this situation there was a corresponding reduction in the intake of EFTS pupils and, towards the end of the war when the training machine was running down, a total cancellation of options against modest compensation.

Grading was scheduled to be swiftly and efficiently completed within fourteen days but a candidate could be a victim of circumstances. Don Roskilly flew solo on Tiger Moth T7472 (83901), during grading at 15 EFTS Carlisle on 28 February 1944, having received eleven hours and fifteen minutes dual instruction during eighteen sorties, in ten aircraft with eight instructors spread over seven weeks. Prior to the issue of proper log books to those scheduled for further instruction, preciously accumulated flight times were recorded on log sheets (Form 4148). Fortunately, dates of birth were not recorded for, in spite of the delays, Don Roskilly soloed at 17 years of age having persuaded the recruiting officer that he was a year older.

Soon after the Grading System was introduced, 22 EFTS Cambridge was asked to conduct an experiment to train six pupil pilots of average ability to fly a Tiger Moth, to and beyond solo standard, entirely at night. The six candidates were to be divided into two groups: one to be trained solely with the aid of visual references, feel and the basic instrumentation of a Tiger Moth, and the second to work with instruments as the primary guide aided by visual indications. Three instructors were selected, each taking one pupil from both groups. Four Tiger Moths were fitted with artificial horizons in front and rear cockpits and were scheduled to operate at the main base at Teversham Aerodrome and Caxton Gibbet Relief Landing Ground (RLG) where an electrically lit flare path was available. As the flying experiment progressed, and in order to achieve maximum practical value, the aircraft were converted to accept full blind flying panels in both cockpits, and a twin flare path was introduced.

To coincide with maximum darkness and also, by definition, the coldest weather conditions, flying training started in January 1942. Oliver Wells, a 19 year old flying instructor at 22 EFTS was an interested observer but could never be clear about the reasons for the experiment, except perhaps as a scheme to accelerate the supply and quality of night fighter pilots:

"The flying started with the instrument cadets being given experience of the feel of the controls and instrument reactions to their use. The visual cadets were given experience of the effect of the controls, straight and level climbing, gliding, stalling and medium turns. Reference was made to stars and landmark beacons and sometimes a faintly visible horizon or bank of clouds allied with reference to the artificial horizon. Recovery from a spin could not be taught due to the unsuitability of the Tiger Moth battery fittings for such a manoeuvre, apart from any other considerations, so emphasis was placed on familiarity with the stall and recovery, both with and without the engine, and the attitude and feel of this manoeuvre. There was a tendency for cadets to be unconcerned by unusual flying attitudes or speeds since darkness cloaked the fact that the ground was in the wrong place or rushing up to meet them, but they were firmly taught to avoid steep turns or violent manoeuvres."

All six cadets went on to complete their first solo flights at night after an average 16 hours 30 minutes dual instruction, having never flown in daylight. They enjoyed certain advantages in that the flare path was always laid into wind and being mostly alone in the circuit not troubled with the need to avoid up to an average of thirty other active aircraft. On one occasion local resident and aviation historian Michael Bower counted sixty six aircraft in the Teversham circuit. After twenty five hours dual and six hours solo, all at night, the six cadets were introduced to daylight flying and soloed after an hour of dual instruction and detailed briefings on what to expect in the real world. Their experiment had proved that it was possible to teach a pilot to fly safely by night using instruments and visual references, and although wheel landings were taught everybody agreed that a tricycle undercarriage would have saved time and reduced the risk of accidents.

It was later revealed that the experiment had been suggested by Arthur Marshall in 1941 in an effort to speed up the training of bomber pilots, not night fighters as Oliver Wells had considered, on the grounds that they may never fly in daylight at all.

An Insurance Schedule correct to March 1942, listed 152 active Tiger Moths on charge with 22 EFTS against an agreed value of £1,200 each, plus fifteen Miles Magisters which were considered to be worth more at £1,600.

Tiger Moth T5467 (83192), had been posted to 4 EFTS Brough in March 1941 and was to remain in service there until August 1947.

She had been adopted by a test pilot with the resident Blackburn Aircraft Company, who assisted the resident instructors with grading by flying with trainee pilots recommended to undertake their solo flight tests. Mr Richardson was a big man at around eighteen stone and found the narrow width of a Tiger Moth front cockpit was limiting his movement. The doors were removed and the aircraft was fitted with side flaps which provided extra shoulder space. As he removed himself from the cockpit and tidied the straps in preparation for Tom Payne to taxy away for his first solo, he reminded his trainee to expect a much better rate of climb now that his great weight had been removed from the front seat.

George Mackie had learned to fly on Magisters at Meir, a station situated amongst the Staffordshire Potteries, and where he said the horizon was never properly visible due to the smoke haze that was encouraged as a means of camouflage. Via Oxfords at Cranfield and Wellingtons he had graduated to Short Stirlings and by August 1942 was an instructor at 1651 Heavy Conversion Unit based at Waterbeach near Cambridge. During the afternoon of 28 August the CO, Wing Commander Menaul, tired of flying ATC cadets in the Station Tiger Moth N9326 (82413), had motioned W/O Mackie to take over without asking the vital question. George Mackie had flown a Tiger Moth before, once, and for a reason he could not remember, but had never been officially converted and signed off.

After three or four circular trips he was coping well enough and ventured off the circuit to fly along the river Cam at 50ft where he was spotted by two WAAFs who waved from the bank. On his next flight he returned to the spot and indulged himself in some tight turns at low level during which the aircraft stalled and was recovered just before she settled into the water. The crew escaped unhurt and whilst the pilot rescued Cadet Harris, whose chief concern was the state of his best uniform which he had planned to wear at a dance the following evening, the two WAAFs ran off to raise the alarm.

At his subsequent interview with the Wing Commander details of the accident were received with equanimity and George Mackie never received any reprimand or punishment for his self confessed mishandling. According to the Station Operations Book the dunking of N9326 occurred at 1835 hours local time and the reason for the accident was attributed to 'aileron failure'. "The aircraft (identified as a Puss Moth) fell into the river Cam," it says. Following a survey N9326 was struck off charge on 17 September.

The wartime press was always anxious for whatever good news could be willingly released by the authorities and posed pictures were bread and butter. An RAF flying instructor explains the theory of level flight to a group of Turkish pilots under training in England.
deHMC Archive

Ron Hitchcock joined the RAF in 1940 as an instrument fitter and was posted to Singapore to join 36 Squadron. In May 1941 he signed up for aircrew training and in December, during a trek up country with a salvage squad to retrieve instruments from a crashed aircraft, the Japanese landed at Kota Bahru and began to move south. On 13 February 1942 he arrived back in Singapore where he was advised his aircrew application had been agreed and as he was posted back to England he should go to the harbour immediately and find his own passage. Two days later Singapore fell to the Japanese and about 70,000 British and Commonwealth troops were led into captivity.

Ron Hitchcock secured a passage to Calcutta and by various means travelled to Southern Rhodesia where he trained as a pilot on Tiger Moths and qualified for his wings in January 1943. He was posted back to England as a flying instructor having been assessed during training as having the necessary aptitude to be a good teacher. In May 1943 at No 10 Flying Instructors School at Woodley, two trainee instructors, P/O Hitchcock and Sgt Elsnorth, took-off in a Tiger Moth to practise their newly-learned patter and found themselves stooging around the Berkshire countryside at about 2,000ft. They circled over a large country house with surrounding fields which had been put down to vegetables where Ron Hitchcock noticed a Land Girl with a hoe who looked up and waved. Now he turned his attention to his co-pilot who had obviously decided that a brief stop near the house (and prospect of tea on the terrace) would be a welcome change from practising patter.

The Tiger Moth straightened up and gently descended to make a perfect wheeler landing on the unkempt lawn but seemed reluctant to stop although a collision with an oak tree was avoided when the wheels ran into a shallow ditch at the edge of the lawn, tipping the Tiger Moth forward and breaking the propeller. Both pilots jumped out with accusing thoughts only to realise nobody had been in command and to dissolve into laughter. Soon they were enjoying their afternoon tea on the terrace waiting for a squad to arrive from Woodley to remove the aeroplane. What did they hear later about their accident? Nothing at all! Ron Hitchcock went on to complete 500 hours in his role as an instructor before progressing to Hurricane IIs and Spitfire XIVs in a tactical photo reconnaissance unit based in post-war Germany.

Flying Training Command's reaction to the worrying intruder incidents had been to launch a thorough investigation of night flying techniques which could be adapted to safer daylight conditions and these resulted in the simple and effective Day/Night Flight (DNF) systems of Two Stage Blue, Two Stage Amber and Two Stage Brown. Invented by the brothers Wood, professional photographers from Bradford, and developed by Wg Cdr Philip Bremridge and his teams of the Day/Night Flight and Flying Training Research Flight, part of the Empire Central Flying School (ECFS) at Hullavington, the two-stage system became the standard method of converting pilots into night owls during the hours of daylight.

To permit DNF training in a Tiger Moth a new version of the instrument flying hood was designed which incorporated a transparent blue panel sewn into the fabric, also acting as a windscreen. Known as the Brown Two-stage DNF Hood, the tent-like device was of much lighter construction than the heavy canvas-covered 'pram hood' then in daily use. Following flight trials conducted with Tiger Moth T7809 (84187), at Boscombe Down on 18/19 June 1943, it was recommended that for aerobatic flight, and to prevent damage, the hood should first be removed on account of what was described as "its relatively flimsy construction".

At the end of the day when the hangar is as full as the Clubhouse bar, a pair of old blind flying hoods make handy cockpit covers. *deHMC Archive*

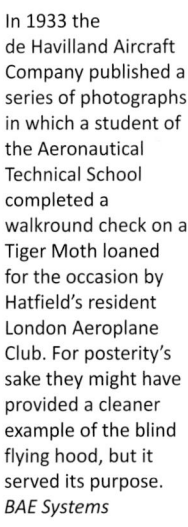

In 1933 the de Havilland Aircraft Company published a series of photographs in which a student of the Aeronautical Technical School completed a walkround check on a Tiger Moth loaned for the occasion by Hatfield's resident London Aeroplane Club. For posterity's sake they might have provided a cleaner example of the blind flying hood, but it served its purpose. *BAE Systems*

The lightweight Brown Two Stage DNF Hood, developed by Flying Training Command at RAF Hullavington and flight tested at A&AEE Boscombe Down in 1943. *Crown Copyright*

At Boscombe Down T7809 was flown with two crew and tested with the hood erected when it was found difficult to engage the locking catch, else folded down, transiting between the two positions in the air without difficulty. In the folded down position the crew noted that the hood lifted about 12in from the rear decking in a dive at 140mph but remained in that position in diving speeds up to 155mph. Unlike the standard blind flying hood the lightweight construction of the Brown DNF Hood caused it to buffet when erected, transmitting an intermittent shudder through the airframe. In all other respects the hood caused no significant difference to the handling characteristics of the aeroplane which was stalled, aerobatted and spun without difficulty. In view of their previous association with Tiger Moth spinning trials the Boscombe Down test pilots were pleased to report that with the hood either up or down, behaviour in three turn spins, left or right, was perfectly normal, recovery being effected after half a turn.

At the time of the trials T7809 was operational with the Empire Central Flying School at Hullavington, conveniently placed within thirty minutes flight time of Boscombe Down, and remained on strength there until September 1948 when she was posted to 10 MU, just across the airfield, and listed for sale. In February 1949 the aircraft was acquired by W A Rollason Ltd. at Croydon and civilianised as G-AMEG before she was sold into the employ of the Royal Thai Navy.

Pilots posted from the rigours of operational flying where they would say somebody on the 'other side' was trying to kill them, often were remustered for 'rest' as flying instructors at the elementary schools where they would say that somebody from their own side was trying to kill them. Frustration was vented in all manner of different ways, especially through flying low and as fast as a Tiger Moth would permit, or even slowly when the occasion demanded. On his first familiarisation flight one pupil was conducted on a low level tour of the area surrounding the Solway Firth during which his instructor pointed out all the spots where parts of a body had been discovered during a murder inquiry.

Early in 1944 at low level and high speed, a Tiger Moth was seen to fly through a blister hangar at Alton Barnes RLG near Devizes. The eye witness report stated, perhaps unnecessarily, that the aircraft achieved this feat without touching the sides of the hangar and that the heavy tarpaulin curtains were open. The pilot, who was a resident instructor, had just received his notice of posting.

A practice was introduced in 1944 of posting instructors to Bomber Command stations for a period of up to a month in order that they could observe how trainees had become an integral part of mature crews. There they were also invited to fly on operations to act as second pilots and to be generally useful particularly by lending a hand with the distribution of 'window'. Charles Cornish was sent to join the Halifax equipped No 76 Squadron at Holme-on-Spalding Moor in August 1944 with whom he flew four missions which led him to conclude that it was an 'easy' war he was having. The following October he began a two year tour with a Spitfire equipped meteorological reconnaissance unit and in January 1947 returned to instructing on Tiger Moths with No 24 RFS at Rochester.

A famous Air Ministry form was the 'A25', designed to record details of all military flying accidents. Those aspiring to become Fleet Air Arm (FAA) pilots were graded in a manner identical to their counterparts for the RAF, except that all FAA pilot training was completed in Great Britain. One of their number composed a song about the Form A25, one verse of which went:

> "They taught me to fly in an old Tiger Moth,
> A fantastic contraption of wood, string and cloth,
> The take off is great and the climb is fantastic,
> A bloody good show for some string and elastic.
>
> Chorus:
> Cracking Show, I'm alive,
> But I still have to render my A25."

A figure of perfection. Not a scratch on her; everything new and serviceable. Chocked on a dispersal area at Hatfield in 1940, Tiger Moth T6297 survived all tutorials to become a civilian in 1951. *de Havilland Aircraft Company*

On 29 June 2013 the second and third Tiger Moths to be returned to their original delivery specification by Kevin Crumplin, G-ADWJ and G-ANEW, began operations at Tiger Moth Training Ltd at Henstridge Airfield in Dorset. The aircraft, joined by a third in May 2014, are fully equipped to serve the initial training needs of any Twenty First century aspiring pilot.
Neil Wilson

Although the reference is to 'an old Tiger Moth' how many of those nautical gentlemen singing the ditty realised that most of the aircraft in use were of fairly recent manufacture?

In austerity-hit Great Britain immediately post-war the operational Tiger Moths were expected to continue to cope with equally miserable weather conditions. R5219 (83094), had been allocated to 3 EFTS Watchfield in July 1942, moving to the grass field at nearby Shellingford when the Beam Approach facilities at Watchfield became more intensively occupied by bigger and more competitive training traffic.

Charles Hastings-Winch was posted to Shellingford in December 1945 as a preliminary to undertaking a Flying Instructors' Course, (No 44), flying Tiger Moths at 10 Flying Instructor School (FIS) at nearby Woodley. The course was scheduled to run between February and April the following year. During the previous three years he had flown a variety of aircraft in and around North Africa, India and Burma as a ferry pilot. Between November 1943 and May 1945, he had delivered 45 Republic P-47 Thunderbolts, 63 Supermarine Spitfires, 197 Hawker Hurricanes, 15 Vultee Vengeances and 15 North American Harvards, in addition to an assortment of Austers and Fairchild Argus, and four Tiger Moths. These flights involved 543 sorties and landings at 168 different airfield sites.

Some of the Tiger Moths, EM893 (86087), EM951 (86134), NL735 (86218), and NL817 (86276), had been operated on 'communications' duties from the famous Red Road Airfield situated in the middle of Calcutta, and from where regular operations were conducted with Hurricanes and on one notable occasion, a Bristol Blenheim. Charles Hastings-Winch was no stranger to Tiger Moths having trained on the type at No 5 Air School, Witbank, South Africa, in 1942 where, under training and operational conditions, a major effort had been made in trying to keep cool. Now, in the heart of a British winter, as he inspected R5219 prior to departure it began to snow. But the flying programme was arranged and the detail was completed as expected.

The shock to the trainee instructor's system was contained. At Shellingford he flew in thirteen different Tiger Moths in December and January, followed by a further seventeen during his course at Woodley. The Air Ministry's posting system ensured that as a Tiger Moth trained instructor they would extract maximum value from him and during his thirteen month posting to 28 EFTS Wolverhampton, May 1946-April 1947, he flew thirty nine different Tiger Moths. He met the type again on posting to Cranwell (April 1947-January 1950) where forty three aircraft were flown and at Barton (February-August 1950), where the establishment of Manchester University Air Squadron was ten. Only the final removal of the Tiger Moth from RAF training schedules broke the link, although when posted to Debden as a Flight Commander (September 1950-August 1953) additional hours were flown in seven Tiger Moths on behalf of various Establishment, Command and Group Communications Flights.

The aeroplane which welcomed Charles Hastings-Winch back to the English winter of 1945, R5219, had like so many taken up a civil career when sold out of the Royal Air Force in June 1949. Registered G-ALUC she served in a training role at Coventry until 1961 when she overturned on landing and sustained damage which was then considered uneconomical to repair. The airframe was discovered near the south coast of Hampshire in 1974 and partially rebuilt as a single seat S.E.5A lookalike, although she finally emerged as a standard two seat aircraft but with a psudo First World War colour scheme. She was maintained as such on a private aerodrome at Laddingford in Kent from July 1986 until February 2012 when she was sold to become a joyriding aircraft in Yorkshire.

The Services have always paid particular attention to sport and offered encouragement to participants in all the popular team games through the legendary Wednesday afternoon sessions set aside for endeavour on the station playing fields. Inter-service rivalry could only be matched by inter-Command or station or unit competition, therefore, the briefing that was held behind closed doors at 7 EFTS Desford on 25 March 1946 would have been serious and secretive. The School's rugby team was scheduled to play a needle match with their rivals from 16 EFTS Burnaston two days later and the briefing at Desford was more than a discussion on tactics. The Chief Flying Instructor, Sqn Ldr Wardell, was detailing his pilots to their positions in a formation of thirty six Tiger Moths that was to arrive overhead Derby precisely on time and in sharp order; a reminder of the talent that was routinely available at Desford. The rugby match was another problem altogether. Was there significance in the fact that during the day following the match 7 EFTS was inspected by the AOC?

By mid-1947 the Tiger Moths at 15 EFTS Carlisle had been fitted with battery operated electric intercom, replacing the original Gosport systems which remained in the aircraft. Iain Dick recalled that when flying south of Carlisle over the hills towards Shap Fell, it was possible to pick up the BBC Overseas Service in the headphones which created a pleasant interlude. The down side was that the intercom required the pilot to wear a face mask from which the oxygen tube had been removed. During the course of flights in winter condensation would drip out of the mask and promptly freeze on the compass. All crews found it handy to carry some small sharp tool to chip away the ice.

From September 1947 Pete Thorn, son of Avro test pilot Bill Thorn, was a pupil with the Fleet Air Arm intake at 3 EFTS Shellingford where his instructor was 'Dusty' Miller. The school operated on Saturday mornings to make up for time lost by the compulsory Wednesday afternoon games and the absence of injured pupils and instructors on Thursday. On Saturdays Dusty Miller encouraged his pupils to fly low while he potted rabbits with his shotgun aimed carefully through the rigging from the front cockpit. One by-product of his low flying routine was to smarten up tight turns. Any pupil found wanting discovered soon enough that the Tiger Moth was amongst the weeds and the pupil was being invited to execute 45° banked turns without losing height.

The Grading System remained an essential part of the military selection process after the war and a fleet of RAF Tiger Moths was maintained for the purpose at Digby and Kirton in Lindsey until the type was finally withdrawn from service in 1953. Situated in Lincolnshire they were cold stations in winter from which would-be RAF pilots were asked to display a high degree of aptitude and dedication when coping with an open cockpit biplane.

Long after his short association with Digby, one pupil revealed that when taxiing out in the morning the instructors would often sit on the leading edge of the Tiger Moth's lower mainplanes spotting for mushrooms. On one occasion a pupil taxied his Tiger Moth into the tail of the preceding aircraft, causing considerable damage, but both machines were spirited away for repair and nothing further was heard of the incident. The trainee believes he was removed from the prospect of a pilot's course and remustered as a navigator, not because of the mushroom hunting accident, but due to getting lost on his first solo and putting the Tiger Moth down again on a different aerodrome.

Mick Rogers, whose three week 'grading' occurred between 26 January and 18 February 1953, recalled that in spite of all the warm clothing the RAF provided he could long remember how frozen he would feel after a 40-50 minute sortie. On the heavily frosted morning of 5 February 1953 the engine of DE694 (85635), was being warmed when the chocks slipped on the grass and the aircraft moved away. An alert instructor grasped a wing tip but only succeeded in turning the aircraft sufficiently for her to collide with T6903 parked alongside. The following month both aircraft were flown away to MUs and retirement.

The eventual withdrawal of the Tiger Moth from her primary role in the Royal Air Force in 1952 was the occasion for many to vent their opinions for and against what had become an institution, this clutter of technology with roots in the era of the First World War. The following thoughts were expressed by an RAF pilot who, with thousands of others, had trained on Tiger Moths:

> "The Tiger Moth will be missed chiefly, of course, by the old air dogs, those tough, nerveless instructors who were so much a part of their aircraft that they positively preferred to impart their instructional patter while hanging upside down in the straps. One could not but admire their ability, developed through long years of practice, to roll the Tiger Moth about a very small dot on the horizon; but for the novice, the slow roll was the grimmest trial of the lot. Mental preparation was useless, for by reading up beforehand the mechanics of the roll, outlined in half a page of close print detailing the succession of stick, rudder and throttle movement, the pupil was apt to be conditioned in a mood of despair before even attempting the manoeuvre. The time for doing aerobatics was usually chosen by the instructor to be in that part of the day when the morale and metabolic rate of the pupil was at its

Above: Cadets from E2 Flight, No 1 Grading Unit, RAF Digby, November 1952. The picture could have been taken more than ten years previously. Nobody would have known. Nothing had changed. *via Bill George*

Left: The Tiger Moth joined the establishment of the Royal Air Force in 1931 and twenty one years later was still the best tool in the bag for grading young men who sought to fly front line jet fighters. George Jones was one of the last aspirants to pass through No 1 Grading Unit at RAF Digby in November 1952. Sixty years later he still regretted his failure to go solo following which he elected to become an MT fitter instead. *via Bill George*

lowest; that is to say, immediately after breakfast, or after a long day's flying. It must be admitted that the condition of the pupil after five hours of bumpy flying was such as to excite compassion. His nerves, jarred by the incessant vibration, had gone completely numb. His brain was dulled by the scream of the wind about his head; and in his ears there was the high singing note left by the roaring of the engine. He was now entitled to a little quiet and relaxation. At this point the kindly instructor, who possessed a cast iron stomach, would gently insinuate himself into the consciousness of the pupil, and quietly suggest an hour's aerobatics before tea. He would ask his pupil what he was looking so glum about: Do you not like aerobatics? The pupil would choke back an oath, and restrain himself from yelling at his tormentor that the mere thought of them filled him with such a fierce loathing that to give proper expression to his feelings would entail resort to the use of language rivalling the most vitriolic excesses of an eighteenth century pamphleteer. Instead, he would merely crawl out to the Tiger Moth again. The system had him in thrall."

Nostalgia being a marketable commodity, perhaps it was surprising that it took until 1984 for enterprise to surface at Staverton Aerodrome, Cheltenham. The glossy brochure advertised a Nostalgia Holiday in the form of: "Full board for the week in a purpose built Sergeant's billet (£145) or for an extra £100 per week languish in luxury in Officers' quarters. A full week's course of flying instruction on a Tiger Moth starts at £195. Sample the same sizzle of bacon and eggs before flying briefing, and the same tankards of fiery local brew after the sun has set and the Tiger Moths are silent." The business did have takers, but not enough to go into a second season.

Although designed, sold, bought and operated as a pilot training aeroplane, during the Second World War the Tiger Moth was enrolled into a wide diversity of essential military activities, all of which were, seemingly, accomplished with a minimum of effort. Such dexterity added immeasurably to the type's universal appeal, popularity and lasting affection: the very stuff of legend.

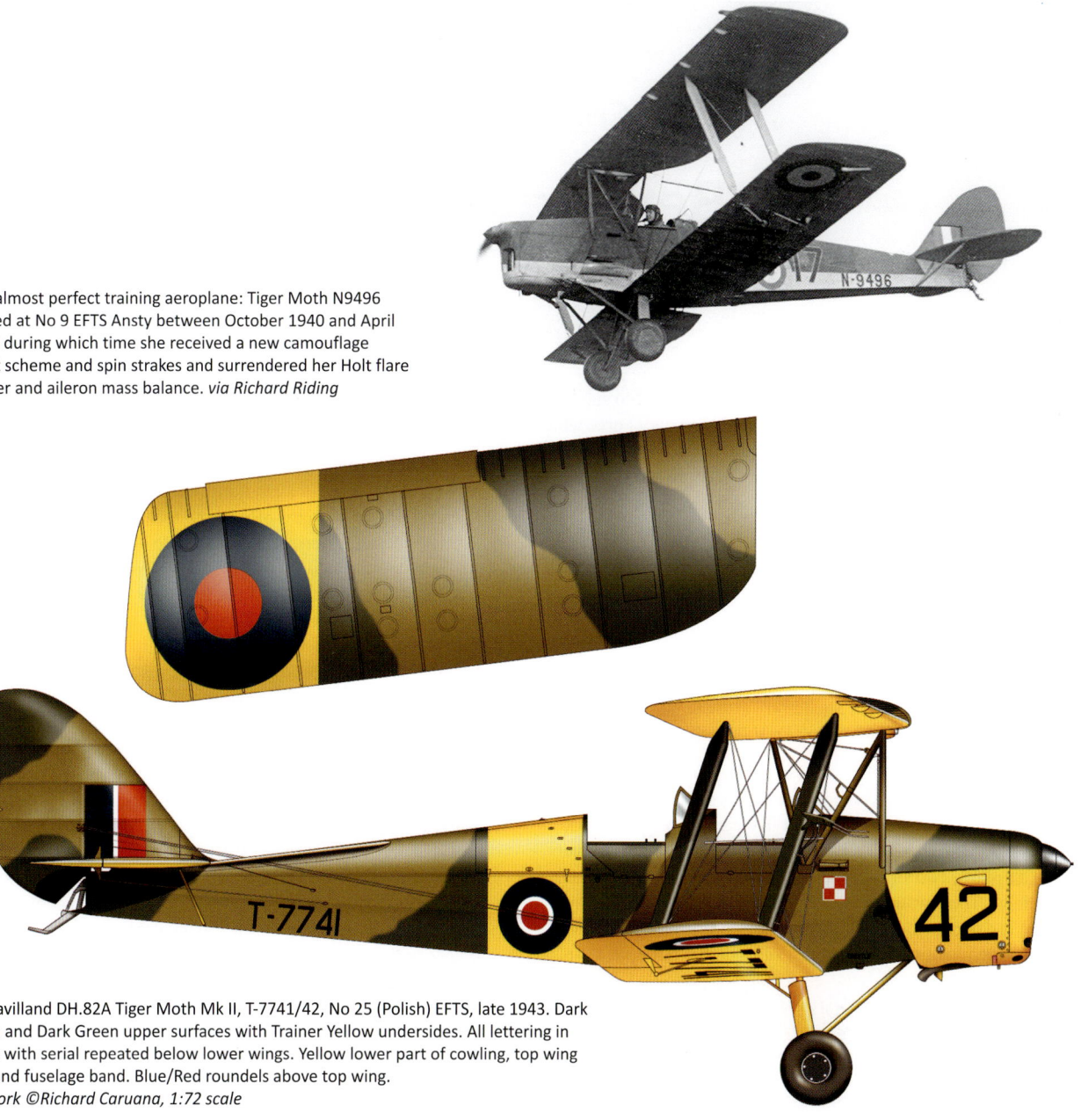

The almost perfect training aeroplane: Tiger Moth N9496 served at No 9 EFTS Ansty between October 1940 and April 1944 during which time she received a new camouflage paint scheme and spin strakes and surrendered her Holt flare holder and aileron mass balance. *via Richard Riding*

de Havilland DH.82A Tiger Moth Mk II, T-7741/42, No 25 (Polish) EFTS, late 1943. Dark Earth and Dark Green upper surfaces with Trainer Yellow undersides. All lettering in black with serial repeated below lower wings. Yellow lower part of cowling, top wing tips and fuselage band. Blue/Red roundels above top wing.
Artwork ©Richard Caruana, 1:72 scale

CHAPTER NINE

Beyond the Call

The British Expeditionary Force

Woefully short of equipment the RAF was required to subscribe an 'Air Component' to the British Expeditionary Force which set off for France in September 1939. In anticipation an 'Avro Tutor Communications Squadron' was established on paper, utilising aircraft drawn from the University Air Squadrons, falling back on an organisation when Tutors had been operated by No 24 Squadron for communications duties from Northolt between November 1931 and October 1932. When inspected, however, only four aircraft were considered to be in any fit condition to go to war and they were replaced at very short notice in August and September by brand new Tiger Moths delivered to Andover from RAF Maintenance Units. From 28 August 1939 the assemblage formed the Air Component 'Tiger Moth Communication Squadron'.

The Squadron's medical officer, Dr V P Geoghegan, recorded the following memories:

> "I found a mixed lot of commissioned pilots posted from various squadrons and not very pleased at finding themselves in what they naturally regarded as a second class outfit, and four or five NCO pilots, two of them qualified instructors, with similar feelings. There was a veteran Flying Officer from the Reserve who had done some of his early training on Bristol Fighters and had joined his first squadron in 1927, but had not been in an aircraft for five years. He arrived shortly before the Air Party was due to leave for France and when told he was to fly a Tiger Moth over there in a couple of days he mildly suggested that a few circuits and bumps might be a wise preliminary. One of the instructors took him up for an hour and he coped perfectly well, becoming a tower of strength from then on.

During the first two weeks of September the plans for our move to France began to emerge. There were to be three parties: the Air Party divided into 'A' and 'B' Flights would fly to France in true RFC tradition with a fitter in each front seat; the Road Party would be shipped with all the vehicles from Southampton and the Main Party would also cross from Southampton. Security was tight: nobody knew where we were going or how long it would take, and it was forty three years later that I discovered we were a small part of 'Operation Violet'.

There were about a dozen 3-ton Crossley 6-wheelers and as many 4-wheeled trailers all pre-packed with the necessary spare parts, engines etc. for, yes, Avro Tutors. The Engineer Warrant Officer lost a lot of hair in the ten days or so before embarkation, trying to persuade Equipment Officers in Maintenance Units up and down the country to swap Lynx engines for Gipsy Majors and Avro Tutor airframe spares for Tiger Moth. He was largely successful, but we still arrived in France with some of the wrong bits.

The CO, Sqn Ldr George Ashton, would not agree to 'A' Flight flying in formation: he decided the aircraft would fly in line astern with F/O Bevis as Tail End Charlie, Flt Sgt Carver leading with the CO tucked in behind him. Bevis was advised to watch out for any machine that went down into the

Aircraft allocated to the Coastal Patrol Flights in 1939 were standard Tiger Moths drawn from stock. Operating with no wireless communication, and armed with only a Very pistol, the pilots flew regular 'Scarecrow Patrols' over the sea searching for enemy submarine activity during one of the worst winters on record during which they exhibited extremes of endurance and courage.

drink, and if it did, to mark the spot and fly around until help arrived. In reply to his question: "And what if I go down?" he was told; "That's your bad luck!"

The CO had very little idea of navigation, or on what course the aircraft should all be flying. Carver, the most experienced pilot, flew in front and was to be seen signalling his CO to go left or right when he veered off course. The Flight refuelled at Shoreham and crossed the Channel to Le Tréport before heading for Poix. Getting close to their destination the CO made no attempt to lose height or make an approach. Carver waved at him and pointed downwards emphatically, whereupon the CO went into a steep dive and landed straight off the bottom. When the aircraft stopped, well out in the field, he was seen throwing off his Sutton harness and parachute, leaping out and having a long pee by the tailplane. Meanwhile two of the junior officers dutifully followed their Squadron Commander and landed down wind while Carver led the remainder round the circuit to land into wind, a performance which resulted in Tiger Moths landing in all directions, but nobody hit anybody else and the aerodrome authorities did not turn a hair."

'A' Flight moved on to Montjoie by the end of September where they were joined by 'B' Flight on 6 October, detaching elements to Arras, Abbeville, Poix and Metz. On 21 November 1939 the Tiger Moth Communications Squadron was formally listed as No 81 Squadron RAF with Headquarters at Montjoie, a few miles north east of Amiens, although the unit recalls that it was not advised of its new name until 1 December which is the date it records as that of its formation.

The squadron had previously disbanded in January 1920 when operating S.E.5As at Shoreham and under the reformation acceded as the only RAF squadron ever to be solely equipped with Tiger Moths. For a brief period in December 1939 the Tiger Moths were uniquely joined by a Cierva C.40 Autogyro, 'the whirling spray', a device which was said to have frightened the life out of some high ranking Staff Officers.

Dr Geoghegan recalls some of the Squadron's unique operations in France:

"During the Phoney War which lasted until 10 May 1940, 81 Squadron sat at Montjoie, survived the cold spell when the temperature fell as low as 0°F, and provided a minicab cum postal service for the Air Component and GHQ. There was a daily milk run to Arras, navigated by following the HT wires from Amiens, and it was whispered that staff officers were occasionally flown to Le Touquet on golfing weekends. Machines were detached to various aerodromes: 57 and 59 Squadrons, both with Bristol Blenheim IV, were at Poix or Crecy, and others were at Rosieres where we used to fly for Sunday lunch, returning in the afternoon, more or less in formation.

At Montjoie the circumstances were ideal for learning to fly: Tiger Moths with dual control and a number of qualified instructors. On one occasion under instruction, the aircraft was taken off smoothly and climbed gently as I kept my hands and feet well clear of the controls. My instructor who was sitting in the back seat then asked quietly at about 500ft whether I might flatten out and pay attention to the speed. We discovered that the aircraft had climbed away quite happily without human interference.

When a new pilot was posted in he was introduced to the daily routine by taking the front seat on the morning mail run to Arras. On return to base the pilot in command confessed that the man could not fly although he had claimed to be just out of current practice. After some persuasion he was forced to admit that he had joined the RAF in 1918 and after a few hours instruction the war had ended and he was sent home. In 1939 he had re-enlisted and managed to convince the chain of authority that he was a qualified pilot, but all his records had been destroyed. When the CO was confronted with the story he decided that the best method of escaping the inevitable deluge of forms and trouble was to teach the man to fly at Montjoie, which is what happened. When the Squadron returned to disband in England it is believed the pilot was transferred to another squadron flying Hurricanes.

When the shooting war started some of the pilots encountered the enemy and quickly found that by flying low and as slowly as possible, they were moderately safe. Johnny Sayer described how he saw coloured balls coming from astern and passing between the upper and lower mainplanes. He managed to shake off his attacker by making a tight turn at low level. Another pilot was advised that the Squadron had moved from Montjoie and relocated to Abbeville, but when he landed there he found the airfield had been captured and he and his Tiger Moth were taken prisoner. One Tiger Moth landed near a farmhouse where the pilot, F/O Gautier, was asking for directions as a German motorcycle combination complete with machine gun arrived in the field. Fortunately, the Gipsy Major had been left ticking over and the aircraft quickly took off on a direct heading for England but ran out of fuel in mid-Channel. Gautier managed to parachute into the sea near a passing French Navy destroyer and was picked up safely."

A signal delivered by motor cycle was received at Montjoie instructing the Squadron to reassemble at Boulogne 'with all dispatch'. The serviceable aircraft left for home and two unairworthy Tiger Moths were disabled and abandoned together with some of the transport. After several noisy and nervous days in and around the port the personnel of 81 Squadron returned to Dover Harbour on board the SS *King George V*, a MacBrayne steamer from Oban whose inbound cargo of ammunition they had helped to unload at full speed. Although some of the aircraft eventually returned to Andover, 81 Squadron regrouped at Hendon to be officially disbanded there on 15 June, only to reform on 29 July 1941 equipped with Hawker Hurricane IIBs in preparation for a posting to Russia.

The evacuation of the unique Tiger Moth Squadron from France had been agreed by Air Vice-Marshal Charles Blount, AOC of the Air Component, after his Command had all but ceased to exist. The Air Marshal was persuaded to fly himself home in a Tiger Moth found abandoned amongst a collection of Bristol Blenheims and Westland Lysanders after the basic controls of the aircraft, a type he had never flown, had been explained to him and an army greatcoat squabbed into the seat pan to replace the missing parachute. His overall emotions on landing safely at Hawkinge can only be imagined.

The story behind the incident is unknown but a Tiger Moth in RAF markings appears to be in enemy hands and an attempt to fly her has ended with the engine becoming detached. Could this have been a case of the withdrawing 81 Squadron sabotaging aircraft that had to be abandoned in France?
via Mike Dalton

On formation eighteen new Tiger Moths had been posted to 81 Squadron, all of which are thought to have served in France. A further ten aircraft were allocated during March and May 1940 which permitted five of the first batch, N9154-N9158 (82273-82277), to fly back to England for servicing at 6 MU Brize Norton.

One of the replacement aircraft, N9433 (82487), collided with a tree on arrival in France on 11 March and was written off before handover. Eleven other aircraft were lost during the Expedition including two that were written off as the result of operational accidents, two that were deliberately burned at Arras, and one that went missing during operations on 20 May 1940 and probably was the aircraft captured at Abbeville.

Three of the squadron's aircraft survived their battle training and subsequent exposure to wartime conditions in England: N6847 (82102), was refurbished at 39 MU Colerne in July 1940 and took on standard duties with Flying Training Command until declared surplus in 1953. In 1958 and registered G-APAL, the aircraft was converted into the sixteenth Jackaroo at Thruxton but was converted back into a Tiger Moth at Gransden in 1984. N6946 (82196), was operated by 24 Squadron at Hendon from October 1940 and served with various units until sale in 1955. Registered G-AOEI the aircraft has been offering *ab initio* training in company with G-AHIZ (86533), with the Cambridge Flying Group, established in 1953 and based at the previous home of 22 EFTS, Teversham Aerodrome, now Cambridge Airport.

Above: An 81 Squadron Tiger Moth which escaped from France was N6847. She survived the home-based wartime training programme until 1953 and registered G-APAL was converted into a Jackaroo in 1958 but reverted to Tiger Moth configuration in 1984 and later took up a new career as a joyrider. *Darryl Cott*

N6965 (82203), also served with 24 Squadron at Hendon immediately after she was relinquished by 81 Squadron and then completed the rounds: Northolt Station Flight, 418 Squadron with their Douglas Boston III at Bradwell Bay, and 488 Squadron with de Havilland Mosquitos at West Malling. N6965 maintained her Mosquito connection when she was posted to 13 Operational Training Unit (OTU) at Middleton St George in December 1945. In conditions of drizzle and poor visibility on 11 March 1946 the aeroplane was being flown by the unit's Senior Air Staff Officer (SASO), Group Captain Christopher Paul:

"The Tiger Moth became my early morning jaunt: it was my custom, after my morning half hour, to land the aeroplane on the small patch of usable grass outside the hangar in which she was kept. When the SW wind was right this could be done neatly, so that a slight swerve at the end of the minuscule landing run, and by cutting the engine just before finish, resulted in our arrival neatly, with engine stopped, just inside the hangar doors. It was of course sheer showing off, but the crew enjoyed it, and I was not above the belief that a little showmanship of the right kind can sometimes help in a Service which likes to see its commanding officers flying and enjoying it.

This arrival at the hangar doors required a nicely judged approach over the roof of the hut in which the radar operators did their ground training. This produced no problems until one day they had erected a co-axial cable suspended between two low masts along the whole length of the building; as I afterwards found it ran about three feet above the top pitch of the roof. I found it by hitting the cable in such a way that it slid over the top of the Tiger Moth landing wheels and acted as a splendidly efficient arrester cable; the only trouble was that it brought the Tiger Moth to a standstill about 20ft up, from which height it descended nose first.

The immediate results were dramatic. The crash alarm went, the ambulance, fire crews and rescue teams sprang into lightning action, and the senior air traffic controller in the tower immediately rang my wife in our married quarter, and gave her a running commentary on proceedings. I myself, having descended with a bump had only one thought which was to get

Below: G-AOEI joined the Cambridge Flying Group at Cambridge Airport in 1958 with whom she continues to operate. At one time CFG was the only flying training organisation in Great Britain offering ab initio training through to licence qualification using Tiger Moths. *Reg Bonner*

As N6965 with Station Flight at RAF Middleton St George in 1946 the aircraft picked up a newly rigged co-axial cable during an approach to land and crashed in front of her hangar. She survived several incidents in her later civilian life but was rebuilt at Tibenham in 2014 and offered for sale at a local auction.
Richard Flagg

out of the cockpit fast in case anything went on fire; in fact I was able to watch from a comfortable distance the very efficient operation of all the fire and rescue services which we took great pains to keep at concert pitch for a Mosquito, for example, could go up, if things went wrong, very quickly.

But the most serious immediate effect was that, by some means which only an electronic genius could explain, the radar people's co-axial cable had become tied up with the perimeter telephone circuit which went all round the airfield, and was in some way linked up to the station Tannoy system. We were all to become aware of this when the Tannoy began to recount to us, all over Middleton, in clear girlish voices, the conversation of two young women describing in uncensored detail their previous night out in Darlington. This incident happened when the AOC was away on leave; as Station Commander it was my duty to write on the accident report my opinion as to the reason, and responsibility. On this one, having got all the detail filled in, I wrote my own comments: 'The pilot was showing off and is entirely to blame'."

N6965 was sold by the RAF in 1947 and, registered G-AJTW, was operated by Short Bros from their factory at Rochester. The aircraft subsequently passed through a number of different hands until allowed to go derelict. Rebuilt to qualify for a new C of A in 1988, G-AJTW's former history was recognised when the aircraft was painted in the wartime colours of 81 Squadron.

Andover Aerodrome became used to the sight and sound of itinerant Tiger Moths. Station Flight was host to at least two examples including T7359 (83669), which later went on to a Pilots' Advanced Flying Unit (PAFU). She was sold onto the civil market as G-AHRX in 1946, ending her days with the Oxford Aeroplane Club in 1953 when she lost the argument with a fence during take off from Kidlington. R5135 (83017), arrived to join Station Flight on 23 May 1941 and N9386 (82456), touched down four days later. Together with the resident Miles Magisters the Station Flight aircraft were required to operate regular patrols within an eight mile radius of the airfield seeking out 'action of an obvious nature by enemy agents'. Trying to locate the proverbial needle in the haystack might have been easier but no doubt the occasions provided some relief to the crews. R5135 moved on to 15 PAFU in company with T7359 on 21 June 1943 where she was damaged beyond what was then considered to be economical repair on 20 September 1944. N9386 served with No 7 Anti-Aircraft Co-operation Unit and 289 Squadron from the end of 1943 supporting Miles Martinets from Catterick until the Squadron re-equipped with the Vultee Vengeance in May 1945 and moved to Acklington. N9386 was sold from 12 MU Kirkbride in 1951 and was almost certainly used as a source of spares by a civilian operator based in Blackpool.

Coastal Patrol Flights

One of the most bizarre tasks Tiger Moths were called upon to perform occurred between December 1939 and May 1940. In spite of the massive programme of re-armament embarked upon in 1938 the shadow factories and tens of thousands of new aircraft contracted by the multifarious government committees under the co-ordination of the Ministry of Aircraft Production (MAP), RAF Coastal Command had little in the locker with which to effect anti-submarine patrols within the vicinity of some of the country's biggest, busiest, most vital and vulnerable ports. It was known that Germany had pre-positioned its submarine fleet and the sinking of the liner SS *Athenia* on the day war was declared was a sobering reminder of the prospects for the future.

In an act of near desperation a theory was devised which it was hoped would keep prowling submarines below periscope depth where they would be blind and relatively harmless. Working on the belief that any submarine commander would submerge at the sight or sound of an approaching aircraft, Coastal Command proposed to establish a number of units strategically stationed around the British coastline which would operate as non-aggressive, unarmed spotters and nuisances. It was appropriate that somebody coined the name 'Scarecrow' to cover the proposed operations. There was precious little equipment to choose from, but given the nature of the task and the immediate availability of suitable aircrew from the Auxiliary Air Force and Volunteer Reserve, it was confirmed that there existed a stored adequacy of one type: the Tiger Moth.

The prime object of the units was the detection of submarines; their additional brief was to record the fullest details of all shipping and coastal movements. At first it was believed that resident Coastal Command squadrons would absorb the intake of new aircraft and assume the role. The planned locations reflected that view: Aberdeen, Dyce Aerodrome, 612 Squadron (Avro Anson 1); Belfast, Aldergrove Aerodrome, 224 Squadron (Lockheed Hudson); Liverpool/Birkenhead, Hooton Park Aerodrome, 206 Squadron (Avro Anson I), posted in from Bircham Newton to supplement 502 Squadron, already on site sharing facilities with the Supermarine Spitfire Is of 610 Squadron. 217 Squadron (South West England and South Wales) was based at St Eval in Cornwall with a detachment of Avro Anson 1s at Carew Cheriton, was 217 Squadron (South West England and South Wales). Their brief was to cover the southern coast of the Gower Peninsula and much of the Cornish Peninsula within a 100 mile radius of Newquay. While the northern units would be watchful of the sea lanes leading to and from their own major port facilities, those situated in the south west would be on the alert for submarines taking advantage of the shelter afforded by the myriad of coves and bays, conveniently situated adjacent to the North Atlantic shipping lanes.

Although the subsequent allocation of Tiger Moths was initiated against the disposition of Squadrons in September 1939 plans quickly changed and, instead of detachments, new self-contained units were formed to be known as Coastal Patrol Flights (CPF). With the exception of the addition of Glasgow, their operating bases remained as forecast:

No 1 CPF – Aberdeen (Dyce)
No 2 CPF – Glasgow (Abbotsinch)
No 3 CPF – Hooton Park
No 4 CPF – Belfast (Aldergrove)
No 5 CPF – Carew Cheriton
No 6 CPF – St Eval

Each Flight was to operate with an establishment of nine Tiger Moths, all new and drawn from Reserve storage. The only exception was No 6 CPF which was allocated ten impressed Hornet Moths, capable of exploratory flights of longer duration around the rugged coastline and in considerably more comfort. There was no wireless, no offensive equipment with the exception of a Very pistol which, together with a standard downward facing signalling light, were the only method of communication. As additional emergency equipment the Tiger Moths were to carry semi-inflated rubber rings in their lockers and two carrier pigeons in a basket strapped to the front seat. In the event of a ditching the pilot was expected to record his position, place a scroll in a thimble tied to a bird's leg, and release one or the pair before the aircraft sank, leaving the pilot to wallow in his Mae West and rubber ring.

With little time available, and much to achieve, an element of confusion and awakening of the system had to be expected. Five officer pilots and five airmen were posted to Abbotsinch from St Athan on 9 October 1939 with little knowledge of their purpose and no idea of the name of their unit. Nine days later, the Station Adjutant gave verbal instructions for the formation of No 2 Coastal Patrol Flight, although the Flight still had no aircraft. By 22 October seven more airmen had arrived and the following day written instructions were received outlining their duties which were amplified by further instructions two days later.

In order to establish some degree of formality and set up a Headquarters the Flight requested paperwork and publications, but station authorities at Abbotsinch refused to recognise their lodgers, believing them to come under the administrative authority of Leuchars. That station subsequently returned all requisitions, not recognising the Flight either, and suggesting it direct its enquiries elsewhere.

On 3 November three pilots travelled to 6 MU Brize Norton to collect a trio of Tiger Moths which were delivered on 6 November having spent the previous night at Hooton Park. Three more Tiger Moths were delivered from Brize Norton on 9 November and the final three, collected from 10 MU Hullavington on 19 November, arrived at Abbotsinch the following day having operated via West Freugh.

Meanwhile, a meeting with the Senior Naval Officer, Clyde, had identified duties and established the most appropriate areas in which No 2 CPF should operate: anti-submarine patrols in the Clyde Approaches and act as escort to the passage of armed merchant cruisers through the same waters.

The Flight's Commanding Officer, P/O Tillett, had his nine aeroplane establishment but no operational equipment and sent urgent signals on 23 November which resulted in the arrival and practical test of a consignment of Very pistols and cartridges three weeks later. With the end of the month looming and the Flight still non-operational it was decided that, in view of their wide area of responsibility, accurate fuel consumption figures would be essential for individual aircraft and each was subsequently flown for precisely one hour at 75mph and again at 90mph. With little else to do Tillett advised all concerned that "as there is time during the week to get in all the practice flying needed, the Flight is closed on Sundays."

Two additional pilots arrived before the end of the year, directed straight from the Reserve system. Sgt Perkins had flown 1,400 hours in Moths as a civilian instructor and had attended an RAF elementary instructors' course, and Sgt Carter could claim 200 hours. Neither had been awarded an RAF pilots' flying brevet, and both required instruction in formation flying and the daily routines expected of a Sergeant pilot posted to an operational unit.

In working up towards their first serious operation on 17 December, location of a convoy (which they failed to find), when detached to Prestwick, the No 2 CPF pilots were all encouraged to fly locally and familiarise themselves. Knowledge of landmarks could make all the difference between returning safely home and perhaps landing out. Abbotsinch was greatly affected by industrial haze and smoke generated by the nearby city of Glasgow, and November and December had already demonstrated how prone the area was to lingering shrouds of mist and fog.

Each CPF worked to the same basic plan under the operational title of 'AS' (Anti-submarine patrol). How this was achieved efficiently and economically was left to the initiative of the local commander, bearing in mind the limitations of the Tiger Moth as a patrol aircraft, and the scandalous lack of equipment. While all Flights operated each patrol with two aircraft, one to remain overhead the contact but making attempts to interest any conveniently positioned naval vessel by firing off recognised flare patterns, and the other to scurry back to base or the nearest facility in order to report, No 2 CPF put up three aircraft on each sweep. With an establishment of only six pilots the scheme was impossible to maintain but the theory was right: two aircraft were to remain on patrol for two hours whilst the third returned after an hour and a half. The returning pilot then briefed the second patrol as to the expected position in which to establish contact with the two aircraft still airborne and waiting to be relieved. It was the only practical solution to having no wireless communication.

Unlike the pilots at Abbotsinch, amongst whom the Flight aircraft were rotated as required, the Aberdeen based pilots of No 1 CPF maintained close contact with individual aircraft and always hunted in pairs. Their operations began on 14 December when Tiger Moths N6664 (3968), and N6800 (82070), took off at 1350 hours local time and landed one hour and twenty eight minutes later, having jointly consumed thirty gallons of petrol to reach and return from a point some twenty five miles south of Aberdeen. Absolutely everything seen then and on all subsequent patrols was noted in meticulous detail: every vessel of whatever size, patches of oil, floating debris. Two or even three patrols were undertaken every day: the early afternoon sweep was expected to be fairly routine, but it was during the dawn and dusk patrols that submarines were more likely to be found on the surface.

Only nine days after their initial operation the Flight's Commanding Officer, P/O Child, together with P/O Hoyle, had been on early morning patrol for twenty minutes when from a point about one mile off shore, Hoyle noticed what appeared to be a flashing light. He turned the Tiger Moth towards the source and as he approached the light disappeared to be replaced by a much brighter light nearby which was exposed and extinguished several times, and appeared to be transmitting 'S' in Morse Code. Hoyle took N6841, carrying unit code 'TA', down to 25ft and, having established the source as a house, flew round it several times noting its position, layout and identifying features such as the shape of the roof and chimney stacks, all of which detail was passed on to the local police after landing.

It was P/O Hoyle who answered the challenge of a patrolling Avro Anson at 0800 hours on Christmas Day by firing off the colours of the day, but on 25 January 1940 he used his Very pistol in anger for the first time. Having sighted what seemed to be a drifting line of oil on the water Hoyle established that it appeared to be bubbling up from below the surface. By firing off green flares and repeatedly diving on the spot, he managed to attract the attention of a destroyer, HMS *Jackal*, 'F22', which, captained by Cmdr Charles Firth, RN, arrived overhead the source twenty minutes later and dropped a pattern of depth charges. The explosions resulted in the appearance of considerably more oil accompanied by large air bubbles and shortly afterwards the destroyer signalled 'AAA', (proceedings now at an end), at which point the circling aircraft returned to Dyce. However, post-war records indicate that no submarine was lost in that position on that day and the discharge of oil and air became well known as a submariner's ploy in an attempt to create a false impression of a successful kill and dissuade further attacks.

Tiger Moths 'TA' and 'TJ' (N6845), were back on early patrol the next morning. Some of the Flights worked a roster which required the late patrollers to sleep at dispersal and fly the dawn patrol too, after which the crews had a whole day to themselves, to be disturbed only in the case of extreme emergency. Tiredness and monotony are believed to have lulled two pilots airborne from Abbotsinch into momentary sleep. One of them hit the sea with both mainwheels causing waterspouts which were observed by the coastguard on the shore and a belief that the aircraft was dropping bombs. On another occasion an aircraft returned to base with ribbons of seaweed wrapped around the tailskid. Neither pilot could remember anything about either incident.

The first northern winter of the Second World War was one of the worst on record and even the hardened Tiger Moth pilots of the CPFs were grounded for days on end. No patrols could be flown from Dyce between 27 January and 7 February. The nights were so cold that engines could not be started, and on one morning at Hooton Park the engineers started swinging at 0830 hrs and finally succeeded in running up at 1100 hrs. Abbotsinch decided to leave arc lights near the aircraft all night to provide security and a source of directable heat.

No 3 CPF at Hooton Park and No 4 at Aldergrove had evolved into operational units along much the same paths as those experienced in Scotland. No 3 CPF flew its first patrols from Hooton Park at 0800 hrs and 1350 hrs on 1t December, and apart from authorised shipping had nothing to report. Bad weather caused strings of cancellations: fog and snow and intense cold all took their toll. Engines could not be started and aircraft standing in the open at dawn were susceptible to complete coating in rime ice. There was no flying at all during the first week of February when the aerodrome disappeared under deep snow drifts. The engineers busied themselves with a programme of engine runs and also tried to alleviate the problem of sea spray freezing on the aircraft by applying a proprietary Kilfrost paste to all leading edges. Although this had some benefit if it was renewed on a routine basis, the chemical reaction damaged alloy parts and on 26 February, N6779 (82043), had to be fitted with a new oil tank and N6780 (82044), with a replacement pair of slats.

Six Tiger Moths had been delivered to Aldergrove from Little Rissington on 13 November for use by No 4 CPF but two weeks later they were still operationally ineffective due to the lack of equipment, quite apart from the state of the aerodrome surface which rendered it completely unserviceable. A change of policy resulted in the entire Flight moving to Hooton Park in December where they maintained their identity but operated in parallel with No 3 CPF very much on the basis of a squadron. The six new Tiger Moths which had never flown an operation were ferried to Silloth on 4 December but due to poor visibility, low cloud and heavy rain, they put down for a convivial night in Blackpool.

During peacetime the decision on whether to fly or not rests with the owner. Some choose to take the opportunity during the calm that often follows a period of winter snow as did Danny Linkous on Christmas Day 2010 when he flew his Tiger Moth N28681 from Miller Field, Mooresville, North Carolina. *Danny Linkous*

Not quite the same as the harsh conditions endured by the pilots of the Scarecrow Patrols in 1939 although the crew of Tiger Moth G-ANFV operating from Shempston Farm near Elgin, Scotland early in 2011 reported the temperature on the ground to be 'minus lots'. *John Farquhar*

Open cockpit flying during the winter in Indianapolis calls for an iron constitution and more than ordinary levels of kit. Alan Reber wears full facial protection but with the ability to speak into his boom microphone. The Scarecrow pilots had no wireless to concern them and piled on the layers. *Alan Reber*

Still nominally non-operational, No 4 CPF loaned pilots on a short term basis to Aberdeen whose manifest gratitude was exemplified by the loan of equipment to get two aircraft into an operational condition on 18 December, on which day No 4 CPF's last three establishment Tiger Moths were delivered, all arriving from Little Rissington.

The New Year started badly when the first patrol of 1940 took off into poor visibility which suddenly deteriorated even further. The pilot of N6722 (3995), lost sight of the aerodrome and attempted to land in a ploughed field whose surface was heavily disguised by snow. The Tiger Moth turned over, breaking all four wings, the rudder, centre section and propeller. It was considered expeditious to effect repairs on site, although the necessary spares did not arrive until 18 January.

All CPF pilots complained about the insidiously creeping cold and the constant draught experienced in their open cockpits. The front windscreens were removed as an experimental measure and although this did reduce the turbulence around the rear cockpit it also steered an icy blast more piercingly into that same position. Circulating draughts also picked up the loose contents of the carrier pigeon baskets and channelled them into the pilot's face causing cases of sickness due to sore eyes and throats. Just after take-off from Dyce on 21 May, P/O Cole received the full impact of wood shavings and pigeon droppings, some of which managed to evade the protection of his goggles and affect his eyes, forcing him into an immediate return to land. The pigeon passengers were the cause of the denial of a request to allow the front cockpit to be faired over, a simple enough exercise which would have improved conditions immensely.

The great diversity of flying experience amongst the hastily assembled pilots was demonstrated by an incident on 27 February when two crews from No 3 CPF were returning to Hooton Park after their uneventful evening patrol. P/O Hodgkinson and Sgt Galt encountered conditions of practically zero visibility, and Hodgkinson immediately put down in a small field on the coast. Galt made six attempts to land in the same field but a lack of experience in the necessary forced landing technique prevented a safe touchdown. Hodgkinson recognised the problem and took off again, shepherding the other aircraft back to Hooton Park in near blind conditions and a safe landing just after dark.

The sun was just setting at Aberdeen on 14 April as P/O Child landed back in his N6664 'TB' after a patrol of two hours and twenty minutes, but with nothing to report. The action had started with P/O Hoyle taking off on his afternoon patrol at 1350 hrs in N6841 'TA' and observing a periscope. Having fired off his green Very lights he sighted a second periscope, and both remained tantalisingly above the surface while he continued to circle completely impotent for fifteen frustrating minutes. Having been alerted, P/O Burgess in N6800 'TH' took off to join 'TA' for about forty minutes before Hoyle returned to base. Burgess was in turn joined and relieved by P/O Boyes flying N6711 'TD' before Child arrived to round off the day. Hoyle, Boyes and Child each uplifted fifteen gallons of petrol on return to Aberdeen but the refuellers were able to deliver the maximum capacity of nineteen gallons to the tank on 'TH', somewhat to the concern of her pilot.

The exercise proved a number of points. The endurance without long range tanks was insufficient, although whether or not the crew could have coped with longer patrols, especially in poor conditions, was open to debate. The need to fly Tiger Moths in pairs to maintain some degree of flexible communication and security whenever possible was valid. Had the enemy now been advised that they were in no danger from Tiger Moths operating without teeth? CPF pilots had always been aware of the impossibility of sighting a submarine once it had slipped below the surface of the waters surrounding the British coastline and, on this occasion, in spite of a positive double sighting and intensive effort, nothing further was ever heard.

Having suffered some of the most atrocious weather conditions ever experienced on the north west coast of England the CPF pilots based at Hooton Park received an issue of electrically heated Sidcot suits on 10 March 1940. Their standard mode of protective dress was described as a Sidcot, a monkey suit, three pairs of gloves, a balaclava under the leather helmet and a Mae West and parachute harness. In 1942, David Masters wrote quoting the Commanding Officer of No 1 CPF:

> "It was exceptionally hard to turn one's head let alone get at the signal pistol and flares, but all this difficulty was well worth while because the uninterrupted view from the back seat of a Tiger Moth could not be beaten, and the aircraft could be flown slowly."

The arrival of heated clothing was somewhat ironic in view of a decision taken to supplement Nos 3 and 4 CPFs with impressed civilian DH.87B Hornet Moths which began to trickle through from 22 January, much to the astonishment of P/O E H Fuller of No 4 CPF who received G-ADKH on 14 February. Following impressment serialisation as W5747, application of camouflage and installation of a First Aid satchel, Fuller flew the first Scarecrow Patrol by a Hooton Park Hornet Moth on 16 March. In civilian life, Edward Fuller had owned the same aircraft at Heston.

Hornet Moths in greater profusion were taken on charge with Nos 3 and 4 CPFs at Hooton Park and twenty two of the type eventually worked alongside the establishment of eighteen Tiger Moths until both units were disbanded in May 1940. The weather in late March had seen a procession of deep Atlantic depressions sweeping across the country bringing low cloud, heavy squalls, poor visibility and gale force winds. The Hornet Moths were thought better able to survive in such conditions. Tiger Moths were banned from operating whenever a gale warning was in force but a famous party trick exploited by barnstorming circus pilots and hard bitten instructors alike was the ability to hover a biplane when headed into a strong, steady wind. While learning to fly at Carlisle, Iain Dick well remembers the performances which took place during the early morning weather check. Almost immediately after an apparently normal take off the Tiger Moth seemed to stop and maintaining its climbing attitude was lifted vertically upwards. At about 500ft the pilot levelled out and the aircraft flew backwards, headed against the wind, its airspeed being less than the wind speed, until it reached the down-wind boundary when it dipped down and landed on the spot alongside a group of airman who had been pre-positioned to catch the wingtips.

Jim Robson, an instructor at 15 EFTS Carlisle in 1942, had once soared a Tiger Moth with engine throttled back from 2,000ft to 5,000ft in the lee side of the Pennines when the Helm wind was blowing. He also once achieved a vertical roll in a Magister whilst in the climb but on the numerous occasions he tried the same in a Tiger Moth met with no success.

Carew Cheriton had received its establishment of nine Tiger Moths for No 5 CPF by 21 December 1939, although N9337 (82424), had been lost on 15 November when the aircraft was ditched into the sea off the South Wales coast at Tenby during her delivery flight and was almost immediately replaced by N9441 (82495), which arrived on 2 December. The Tiger Moth strength was eventually increased to eleven and these were joined by six Hornet Moths in mid-January and another trio in March, all of which attempted to operate in pairs for standing patrols timed at 0530 hrs, 1000 hrs and 1930 hrs every day. They meshed with the activities of No 6 CPF based at St Eval across the Bristol Channel, and nine new Tiger Moths were allocated only three weeks before the unit disbanded on 27 May. No 6 CPF flew ten impressed Hornet Moths around the coastline on five pre-determined routes from early February 1940.

No 1 CPF made a final patrol on 28 May 1940 after which duties were assumed by armed Westland Lysanders and an increased fleet of Avro Ansons of Coastal Command, aircraft with longer range and provision of some degree of comfort for the crew. No 2 CPF stood down at Abbotsinch at the end of the month, like her sister unit at Aberdeen having operated Tiger Moths through the worst of the weather until the spring when eight DH.87B Hornet Moths had been allocated to them. Although more comfortable than a Tiger Moth and with a considerably extended range, the Hornet Moths were not best suited to the Scarecrow role due to the blanketing effect of the lower wings on downward vision from the cabin and the semi-opaque nature of scratched windscreens and side windows.

During the six months of Scarecrow operation, although there had been some engine problems, not surprisingly in view of the environmental conditions in which the aircraft were dispersed and expected to fly, and in spite of the very high percentage of flight time spent cruising at relatively low level, no Tiger Moth or Hornet Moth was lost at sea. But two of the Scottish based aircraft were lost, over land, on consecutive days and within a relatively few hours of the Flights' disbandment.

On 26 May No 2 CPF Tiger Moth N9202 (82319), left Abbotsinch in darkness just after 0400 hrs in order to be on station at dawn. Heading out over Ladyland Moor the pilot took late evading action to avoid entering a low lying cloudbank and the aircraft's wingtip hit the ground. The pilot was injured but the aircraft was wrecked. The Commanding Officer thought that the pilot, a relatively senior officer who had trained at Cranwell should, with his experience, have decided to fly round the cloud somewhat earlier. The following day, Tiger Moth N6785 (82055), up from Dyce, was engaged in an afternoon's exercise of forced landing practice near Fintroy when she stalled off a steep gliding turn and flew into the ground, killing the pilot. Another CPF Tiger Moth flew over the scene shortly after the accident and her crew reported very severe downdraughts which were thought to have contributed towards the accident.

David Masters summed up the Coastal Patrol Flights in his 1942 book *'So Few'*:

> "There was nothing spectacular about the Scarecrow Patrols, nothing to win high honours. Of the six pilots who formed the first flight, three alas are no more. But the amateur pilots who joyfully risked their lives without question for day after day flying far out to sea, sitting in open cockpits exposed to all the rigours of a terrible winter, until fully-armed aircraft were manufactured to take up the task, won, by their quiet confidence and their physical endurance, a worthy place in British history."

Having relinquished them to the distribution system, the subsequent rate of attrition amongst ex-CPF aircraft was no worse than for any other group and they suffered their share of accidents during the next decade. N6719 (3992), previously with No 4 CPF at Hooton Park was posted to No 1 Anti-Aircraft Co-operation Unit and with great irony was lost when she hit the sea in January 1942 when low flying for the local battery off the Norfolk coast at Weybourne, adjacent to the Queen Bee launch site. Another Tiger Moth from No 4 CPF N6722 (3995), was actually converted into a Queen Bee and crashed on landing at her home base at Manorbier in June 1944. Two Tiger Moths from No 3 CPF were abandoned in flight: N6724 (3997), during an aerobatic sortie when operating with 29 EFTS at Clyffe Pypard in January 1943 and N6726 (3999), when she suffered jammed controls in April 1945, also on the establishment of 29 EFTS at the time.

One time Carew Cheriton Tiger Moth N6798 (82068), dived into the ground at Croy, Invernesshire, in December 1942 when serving with No 2 Air Gunners School, and another machine not to reach an EFTS, and which may not have been delivered to St Eval prior to the closure of the CPF, Tiger Moth N9196 (82313), was abandoned overhead that same airfield in January 1941 as the result of bad weather when operating with No 1 Photographic Reconnaissance Unit.

What of the remaining Tiger Moths which had spent the first six months of their active lives gallantly defending the British coastline? Twenty were relocated to 11 EFTS Perth after overhaul at 45 MU Kinloss and six more found their way to 4 EFTS Brough. The remaining twenty five were scattered around the system: fourteen went to British based flying schools and the others joined a miscellany of Flights, Squadrons and Units. A total of twenty one ex-CPF Tiger Moths survived their military service to be sold 'as standing' in conformity with the prevailing disposals policy, and nine of those subsequently endured almost half a century of civil ownership.

N6720 (3993), No 4 CPF Hooton Park, served with 11 EFTS Perth and a number of University Air Squadrons before recategorisation as an instructional airframe (7014M) in 1953, and served with Air Training Corps squadrons for almost forty years. A rebuilding programme to airworthy condition was begun by Bryn Hughes in 1993 in Bedfordshire and civil registration G-BYTN was allocated in November 1999. The aircraft was restored with meticulous care to her 1939 military specification and flew again in August 2004 carrying her former No 4 CPF code 'VX'. She joined Blue Eye Aviation in Yorkshire in January 2014 to become a joyriding aircraft specialising in following the routes once flown by 617 Squadron during preparations for their famous Dams raid in May 1943.

Following her wartime service with No 4 CPF at Hooton Park and later with various training establishments Tiger Moth N6720 spent almost 40 years as an instructional airframe. An eleven year restoration programme was completed in 2004 and in 2014 she became a professional joyrider in Yorkshire. *Geoff Collins*

Tiger Moth SE-FNA served with No 3 CPF at Hooton Park and remained in RAF service until 1952 when she was retired from Grading duties at Kirton in Lindsey. She joined a Swedish museum as a non-flying exhibit in 1986 but was returned to airworthiness twenty years later. *Bjorn Svedfelt*

N6730 (82003), No 3 CPF Hooton Park, served with a number of training units until 1951 and was one of the last active Tiger Moths in RAF service, retiring from No 2 Grading Unit at Kirton in Lindsey in June 1952. Converted for the German civil market in 1961, the aircraft was resold to Sweden in 1976, registered SE-FNA, and was displayed as a non-flying exhibit at the Svedinos Bil Och Flygmuseum at Ugglarp, Halmsted, from 1986. She was returned to airworthy condition for owner Bjorn Svedfelt in 2006.

N6779 (82043), No 4 CPF Hooton Park, suffered a number of accidents during service at 11 EFTS Perth but ended her RAF career with two years at Station Flight, West Raynham. She was acquired by the Wiltshire School of Flying at Thruxton in July 1954 and was one of fifteen Tiger Moths sold at £80 each to Father Peter Schulte and his flying training organisation in West Germany. Registered D-EDON she was used by the Flugsport-vereinigung Speyer at Birkenheide until 1967. Following sale to Denmark, the prospect of a new life in Canada and time spent in England, she was eventually returned to Germany in 1986 and rebuilt to static condition. Painted in camouflage colours and carrying false RAF serial DE623, she has been on display at the Auto Techniks Museum at Sinsheim since 1988.

On the establishment of No 4 CPF at Hooton Park in 1939, N6779 was one of a batch of fifteen Tiger Moths delivered from the Wiltshire School of Flying at Thruxton to West Germany at a price of £80 each. Since 1988 and marked as DE623, the aircraft has been on display at the Auto Techniks Museum at Sinsheim. *Paul Kirby*

N6837 (82086), No 5 CPF Carew Cheriton, was operated by 11 EFTS and later 11 RFS at Perth until 1951 when she was posted to No 2 Aircrew Grading School at Digby, later renamed Airwork Grading Unit then No 1 Grading Unit. She was withdrawn to 33 MU Lyneham in February 1953 but between June and October was loaned to No 215 Advanced Flying School (AFS) at Finningley until returned to Lyneham from where she was sold to Universal Flying Services in March 1954. Registered G-ANOM the aircraft led a hectic existence at Fairoaks for almost ten years but in 1965 started the first of many protracted rebuilding programmes with different owners which resulted in her completion in 2013 when she flew again from a private strip in Northamptonshire.

N6849 (82104), No 1 CPF Dyce, spent the remainder of her RAF career at 11 EFTS Perth, and was one of the first Tiger Moths in April 1946 to be sold into the civil market following a campaign led by the Royal Aero Club. Registered G-AHRV and operated by a number of owners until 1967, the aircraft was sold to Denmark as OY-DNR in December 1968. The engine failed on take-off during a filming session for a Swedish television channel in November 1974 and the damaged aircraft, which was not repaired, was put into store at Greve Strand until sold late in 1998 to Captain Aharon Sagi, a senior El Al pilot based in Israel. With the aid of additional airframes sourced from the same store at Greve Strand and delivered to Israel in February 1999, the aircraft was rebuilt, registered 4X-AAA and reflown in February 2008.

N9128 (82247), No 5 CPF Carew Cheriton, was sold as part of the 1946 disposal programme having spent over four years with 11 EFTS Perth and a few months at Cranwell. Registered G-AHLT and operated by the Thanet Aero Club at Lympne, she crashed into trees near Hythe in June 1957 and was not repaired. Acquired by Roger Bailey in 1974,

A former member of No 1 CPF at Dyce, N6849 was damaged in Denmark in 1974 and following a period in store was rebuilt in Israel by Captain Aharon Sagi. Her first landing after restoration was on the concrete runway at Megiddo Aerodrome on 7 February 2008. *via Aharon Sagi*

Tiger Moth N9128 was posted to No 11 EFTS at Perth following service with No 5 CPF at Carew Cheriton. Between major accidents in civil life the aircraft has been flown on long touring missions in Europe. *Damien Burke*

a complete restoration was completed for the aircraft to fly again in 1997. Sold the following year the aircraft spent some time based in the Netherlands before returning to Lee on Solent in 2003. During an attempt to land in a short field near Wrexham in August 2012 G-AHLT collided with a tree during a go-around and demolished almost her entire starboard side. She was returned to Lee on Solent for major repairs.

N9191 was operational with No 6 CPF at St Eval and spent six years in store at Aston Down from 1941. Due to the Royal Navy titling carried when as G-ALND she was an entrant in the 1979 Famous Grouse Rally she inadvertently attracted more attention from the BBC film crew carried on board a Royal Navy Lynx helicopter than the Tiger Moth entered by the FAA Historic Flight at Yeovilton. *David Welch*

N9191 (82308), No 6 CPF St Eval, spent the winter of 1940/1941 at Duxford and later with 19 EFTS at Sealand before joining Technical Training Command at Locking for two years from October 1941. After six years in storage with 20 MU Aston Down, she was sold in March 1949 and registered G-ALND to lead a varied life as a professional school trainer, group owned aircraft and circus performer. Severely damaged in an accident on take-off from Panshanger in March 1981, the aircraft was sold as a long term restoration project in 1990 and having passed through several hands eventually settled at Pontypool in 2009 where further progress was delayed due to the owner's ill health.

N9240 (82335), No 5 CPF Carew Cheriton, was overhauled at 19 MU St Athan and spent time with 10 EFTS Weston-super-Mare, 3 EFTS Shellingford and 14 EFTS Elmdon until withdrawn to 9 MU Cosford in January 1946. She was operated by London University Air Squadron and 24 RFS Rochester during the summers of 1951 and 1952 before receipt at 10 MU Hullavington from where she was sold in 1953. The aircraft was allocated registration G-ANDM but was actually painted as G-ANDI when she was civilianised at White Waltham in 1958. She was sold to the USA in 1970 but after several misadventures was returned to England in 1982, rebuilt by April 1988 and sold to Germany where she was registered D-ENDI and is currently owned and operated by Dr Martin Knebel.

Following service with No 2 CPF at Abbotsinch Tiger Moth N9241 was attached to the station's Torpedo Training Unit before transfer to Flying Training Command. In civilian life she was converted as a cropsprayer and film prop for *The Blue Max*. *Barry Dowsett*

N9241 (82336), No 2 CPF Abbotsinch, joined the Torpedo Training Unit at Abbotsinch before transferring to basic duties with 10 FIS and 8 EFTS at Woodley and eventual sale in August 1946 to the West London Aero Club at White Waltham, an organisation founded very largely by ex members of the ATA, to whom she was registered G-AIRK. Converted for use as a cropsprayer in 1961 and a film prop for *The Blue Max* in 1965, she was sold to a co-ownership group in Suffolk in 1966 under whose guiding hand she remained fully operational until 2005 when she was acquired by new owners at Lavenham and dismantled pending a complete overhaul.

Unlike the pilots of the British Coastal Patrol Flights in 1940 amongst whose enemies were extreme cold and frustration, obstacles of a different nature confronted the patrolling Tiger Moths of No 5 Coastal Defence Flight (CDF), Royal Indian Air Force Volunteer Reserve, in October 1942. Based at Cochin on Willingdon Island, South India, the Flight's establishment of two DH.86s and a pair of Westland Wapities was allocated to shipping and anti submarine sweeps while two Tiger Moths flew regular beach patrols searching for signs of Fifth Column infiltration. Many other coastal areas were shadowed by CDFs operating Tiger Moths and a veritable mix of additional types.

Patrols ranged equidistantly about 125 miles north to Cannanore and south to Trivandrum. A task on 1 October 1942 was to fly a naval officer to Trivandrum to interview the captain of the SS *Camilla*. The ship had been discovered drifting and ablaze by another aircraft from the Flight a few days before and together with lifeboats had fetched up on the beach where an aerial survey conducted by a low flying Tiger Moth had confirmed her to be a total loss. The ship's crew was later to explain how they had been attacked by gunfire from a surfaced submarine.

The Tiger Moths of No 5 CDF were ideally suited to their task and on many occasions were able to put safely down on the sandy beaches when faced with ferocious storm activity which brewed sullenly over the Arabian Sea. The coastal storms were, on occasions, so severe that the aircraft were forced to take shelter on the nearest beach for hours at a time to allow torrential rain to move away. Forced landings following attempts to resume patrols interrupted by weather and unserviceability due to water in the carburettor were common occurrences. A brief diversion on 21 November 1942 was the carriage of spare parts almost 200 miles inland to Salem where a Wapiti had

Dr Martin Knebel has owned Tiger Moth D-ENDI since 1988 during which time he has crossed the English Channel on numerous occasions but probably has spent less time over water than when the former N9240 was part of the establishment of No 5 CPF at Carew Cheriton. *Dr Martin Knebel*

forced landed. It was a passing interlude for only five days later the CDF Tiger Moths were flown over 1,200 miles to join a Communications Flight in Calcutta while Cochin was formalised as an RAF Station and the coastal defence duties were taken over by detachments of 353 Squadron flying Lockheed Hudson IIIAs.

AMBULANCE

The evacuation of wounded troops from positions close to the front line has always demanded priority and the prospects of operating light aircraft into forward strips with a view to airlifting out serious cases demanded attention as the Allied armies moved forward during the latter stages of the war in Asia. Two schemes to employ Tiger Moths in this role were developed after 1944, almost certainly independently of one another, but following exactly similar methods.

While Tiger Moths in standard configuration could cope with wounded soldiers capable of sitting normally in a cockpit, it was those who were completely incapacitated that had to be moved quickly and aeroplane types chosen for the task usually required conversion or modification to the total satisfaction of that need. With careful remodelling of the Tiger Moth decking aft of the rear instrument panel, and deletion of the rear cockpit, it was possible to create a platform on the tapering rear fuselage frame capable of accepting a stretcher, using the top longerons for anchorage. Protection of the patient was then possible by design of a new superstructure which hinged, or unbolted completely, for ease and care of loading.

The Australian Army required an aerial evacuation system towards the end of 1944 when they returned to the offensive in New Britain and New Guinea where Tiger Moths could be operated at low level into small airstrips hastily hacked out of the jungle and frequently within sight of the enemy.

The first full conversion of a Tiger Moth to the ambulance role undertaken on behalf of the RAAF was relatively simple. A17-57 (DHA 54), was modified by removing the forward 6ft of rear decking, including the luggage locker, and building a lightweight tapered frame with cross webbing, a Norcom Stretcher, which filled the entire created space including that of the redundant rear cockpit. A modified decking built to the original profile was then latched down onto the top longerons. The patient's head was left exposed at a cutout where the rear instrument panel would have been, and he was restrained by a wide webbing belt laterally across his thighs and a four strap Sutton harness placed conventionally across shoulders and stomach. The system was crude but effective although A17-57 appears to have been used only for Australian based trials during a nominal allocation to storage at Temora.

The better known ambulance conversion was A17-450 (DHA655), which had passed through Laverton in April 1945. Following the installation of long range tanks at Breddan the aircraft had been dismantled and shipped to Nadzab in New Guinea for service with No 8 Communications Unit (CU) based at Madang, an organisation formed from what was previously No 1 Rescue and Communications Squadron (RCS). The Unit operated eleven different Tiger Moths in its time and A17-450 was one of the last four, sold locally for £200 in April 1946.

RAAF Tiger Moth A17-450 was converted into a flying ambulance in 1945 and served in New Guinea where she was sold for £200 in April 1946. *RAAF Museum*

This ambitious conversion to ambulance role included provision of a new fixed windscreen and enclosed cockpit for the pilot. *RAAF Museum*

Below: RAAF Tiger Moth ambulance A17-543 was commissioned in June 1942 and remained in that configuration following civil acquisition by Connellan Airways in 1951, operating an essential community service centred on Alice Springs. *Neville Parnell*

One of a number of different casualty evacuation conversions applied to Tiger Moths, in which fuselage space under the rear decking, sometimes including the rear cockpit, was re-engineered to accept a stretcher. This RAAF conversion dates from September 1945. *RAAF Museum*

Former RAAF ambulance conversion A17-543 was sold as surplus in 1946 and after a spell with the Hamilton Downs Pastoral Company as VH-BIW was operated from Alice Springs by Connellan Airways from 1951. She was sold to Doggett Aviation in Perth in 1958 and converted for agricultural use. *via Bill Teague*

Following their surrender in 1945 RAAF Tiger Moth A17-489 was enrolled to ferry the Commander of Japanese forces in New Guinea from Cape Wom to Kiarivu. Alan Reber's Tiger Moth of unconfirmed identity and registered N17489 is painted to represent the original aircraft. *via Alan Reber*

Whilst the original A17-489 would have sweltered in the heat of New Guinea, Alan Reber's lonely look-alike aircraft faces the bleak and snowy outlook at Eagle Creek Airpark, Indianapolis. *Alan Reber*

No 9 Communications Unit at Port Moresby in New Guinea, and later Lae, flew a total of eight Tiger Moths from November 1943 until November 1944 when their last aircraft, Mascot's much publicised A17-565, the 1,000th Tiger Moth to be assembled by the de Havilland Company in Australia, was returned home to storage.

A17-180 (DHA181), was converted into an air ambulance at Laverton in June 1945, the final touch being to spray her 'foliage green' overall, but following installation of a long range fuel tank at Breddan in August the aircraft was placed into storage without allocation and sold for £100 in September 1946. Acquired by Connellan Airways at Alice Springs and registered VH-BAA, she was operated as a civilian air ambulance in company with a similarly converted Tiger Moth, VH-BIW (DHA978). This second aircraft, formally A17-543, used the same basic principles of a stretcher mounted on the top longerons, and a detachable rear decking, but a more spacious hinged hood with windows which completely enclosed the patient and front seat pilot, mating with a tall wrap-around fixed windscreen. The aircraft had preceded A17-180 from conversion at Laverton to Breddan, also for long range tank installation, but was delayed there, placed into storage, and sold for £100 in September 1946.

Ten other Tiger Moths which had received long range tankage at Breddan, but probably little else by way of ambulance conversion, had been shepherded as a group by an Avro Anson 2,500 miles north to Jaquinot Bay in New Britain. At the last minute they had been re-routed further north to Tadjj due to the uncertainty of whose troops held the landing strip at Jaquinot Bay. It was a grand adventure, the aircraft left Breddan on 3 April 1945 and nine of them arrived near their destination forty nine days later. The tenth aircraft, A17-506 (DHA929), had been abandoned at Atkinson Strip, near Milne Bay in New Guinea after turning over there during transit for refuelling and was later dismantled for spares at Port Moresby. The aircraft had probably been intended to reinforce Nos 8 and 9 CU, although No 33 Squadron RAAF also operated a total of eighteen Tiger Moths at various locations in New Guinea between December 1942 and January 1945.

A17-489 (DHA912), operated by 12 Local Air Supply Unit (LASU) based at Aitape, New Guinea from April 1945, and coded TA-L, was commissioned to fly the Japanese Commander, Lieutenant General Hatazo Adachi, from Cape Wom to Kiarivu on 14 September 1945, following the surrender of Japanese forces in the region.

Elsewhere, as the South East Asia campaign moved into Burma, the need for casualty evacuation from the front line was equally well recognised by the RAF and a similar arrangement to that employed

by the Australians in the conversion of A17-57, but pre-dating it, was applied to an unknown number of Tiger Moths in India late in 1943. The whole of the rear decking was reconstructed to shield a patient strapped onto a plywood baseboard occupying space from the stripped out rear cockpit towards the tail. The aircraft was flown from the front seat which maintained its open cockpit configuration.

The conversion and trials were completed at the RAF's Research and Development Unit at Cawnpore and the Tiger Moths were operated by 224 Group Communications Squadron, notionally based at Chittagong, and in some reports referred to as the Air Ambulance Detachment of the 3rd Tactical Air Force Communications Squadron. Exactly which aircraft were converted is not recorded, but DG456 (83571), was photographed at Cawnpore during trials, a one-time Indian civil aircraft, VT-AMI, requisitioned in 1941 and struck off charge without explanation in December 1944. Her sister aircraft, DG455 (83572), the requisitioned VT-AMJ, had remained with 1 EFTS at Begumpet since impressment and was not selected for ambulance duties but during an aerobatic sortie on 22 May 1945, the engine fell out. The pilot managed to regain some measure of control before the aircraft crashed at Shaikpet and was written off. DG493 (83704), another conversion from an impressed civil aircraft, VT-ANG, overshot a forward landing ground at Bongya on 11 November 1944, damaging the undercarriage and causing the aircraft to be abandoned on site.

Flying a training sortie as part of a SAAF Reserve scheme out of Wonderboom, north of Pretoria in the early 1950s, one blade of the propeller detached itself and before the instructor could close the throttle the Gipsy Major engine vibrated itself out of the bearers. Due to the nature of the flight both crew members were wearing parachutes and the pupil was ordered to bale out. In the front cockpit the instructor found that he had a degree of control and managed to glide down to land in a field.

Two DH.82A Tiger Moths and a pair of DH.60GIII Moth Majors of the Karachi Aero Club in 1943. VT-AKS was a pre-war Indian import, impressed as MA947 in 1943. VT-AOG was registered to the Government of India in 1941, part of the Bristol Reserve School fleet exported from Yatesbury. *de Havilland Aircraft Company*

A film clip which was included in a 2013 BBC Television documentary covering the wartime activities of ENSA (Entertainments National Service Association) briefly showed a Tiger Moth ambulance being loaded in Burma. The aircraft was NL732 (86215), sporting an extraordinarily battered engine top cowl, which had been delivered to Bombay from 222 MU on board the SS *Ocean Vestel* on 27 September 1943 after which, like many others, she had simply been absorbed into the system.

Philip Gordon was trained 'to inflict defeat' but before progressing in that task found himself flying casualty evacuation Tiger Moths in what he described as "the wild mountains of the Arakan Yoma, just inland from the impassable wilderness of the mangrove swamps of Burma's coast." His RAF Detachment flew Tiger Moths and Stinson Sentinels, "both as expendable as food, petrol, ammunition and men's lives."

"We had five Tiger Moths and smashed all five within a few weeks for most of our landing strips were short and rough, embedded deep in the valley bottoms between steep and jungle-covered mountains. The aircraft had been modified to take a single stretcher-case in a long coffin-like compartment behind the forward cockpit, where the rear cockpit had been and aft behind that, with an adjusted centre of gravity. The coffin-lid was hinged along its length to fold back sideways to admit the casualty on his stretcher, which was strapped down on a little deck built to accommodate them. There was a small circular Perspex-covered window on either side to enable the man to see outside and for medical staff to look inward to see if he had gone grey or green or was still breathing.

This claustrophobic arrangement was unpopular with the clients, for too many of them arrived dead although most of these were already dying anyway. The tougher and less seriously wounded normally survived, some semi-catatonic with terror because these were West African troops and for many of them this was their first flight. An added factor was that their Regimental Sergeant Major (RSM) was also their witch doctor and he had put a ju-ju curse on our Tiger Moths. As each one was reduced to mangled matchwood in turn so his reputation grew. One of our last Tiger Moth passengers actually threw-up as he was loaded aboard for the flight back to our base strip beside the tented hospital on Ramree Island, just off the coast, such was his fear. Ginger Moxon flew back again to get the last casualty of the day and upon arrival earned two beautiful black eyes when he spectacularly smashed his Tiger Moth into scrap wreckage strewn down the length of the short jungle-strip. The RSM probably said something like "told you so," when his ju-ju curse was vindicated. Ginger had a very disturbed night as ferocious battle was rejoined soon after dark, with screaming charges and counter charges. We flew him out next morning, a bit frayed at the edges but still cheerful.

Another West African soldier was collected from the battlefield, wounded, booted and clothed, and loaded into the casualty compartment of the Tiger Moth. When he was off-loaded after a flight of about ninety minutes his boots were neatly parked beside his hip. How, we asked, can anyone take their own boots off when encased inside a coffin? He was clearly akin to Houdini."

A year after the action around those remote reaches of the river Kaladan in Arakan, a report published in Great Britain coincided with the award of the Distinguished Flying Medal to Flt Sgt J K Davies of Yorkshire, and the Distinguished Flying Cross to W/O M L Cecil of Western Australia:

"The story behind the work of these pilots began early in 1944 when the West Africans made their advance along the Kaladan and evacuation of the wounded became a problem. The answer lay in employing Tiger Moths and Fox Moths, modified to take stretcher cases. As the West Africans advanced, they built small landing strips in paddy fields or on dry river beds. These strips were never more than a few hundred yards from Japanese positions, and were almost continually under mortar or machine-gun fire. During engagements with the enemy a call would be sent back, and the ambulance pilots at once set out to pick up the casualties. Their journey, a little over fifty miles there and back, was mostly over enemy territory and entailed a double crossing of a 3,000ft high range of hills. Sgt Davies and W/O Cecil flew an average of ten hours a day to evacuate wounded. Sergeant Davies flew over 100 sorties.

At one position where casualties were being evacuated the enemy made an attack and the West Africans withdrew to another point. Wounded still remained to be evacuated, and the pilots flew in to pick them up until they were forced to stop. Even on that occasion, W/O Cecil insisted on his last run and taking in a pilot to fly out a damaged Tiger Moth, he collected the last casualties from the deserted strip under mortar fire, a few minutes before the Japanese arrived.

Between 16 February and 8 May 1944, over 2,000 casualties were brought out to forward bases, where they were put into hospital or transferred to Dakotas and flown to the rear."

CHAPTER TEN

Perpetual Phoenix

With thousands of Tiger Moths in use all over the world, operating in a variety of climatic conditions and under the guiding hands of every calibre of air and ground crew from polished professional to the newest recruits in the wartime 'cooks and butchers air force', so described by a senior RAF Staff Officer, it should be no surprise that incidents and accidents occurred on a daily basis until the very end of the Tiger Moth's Service life and continued under civilian colours. There were many reasons: first solo and low time pilots bouncing their landings, ballooning and stalling into the ground with or without an undercarriage; pupils straying off the centreline of the flarepath during night training and colliding with other aircraft in the air or waiting to take-off, even vehicles and buildings shrouded by the darkness; aircraft being blown over after landing or during unaided taxiing in strong winds or behind other larger aircraft with turning engines.

Forced landings as the result of bad weather, getting lost, running out of fuel, engine misbehaviour or simply unauthorised practice, frequently resulted in Tiger Moths turning over after touching down on soft or otherwise unsuitable surfaces. Low flying, approved and not, letting off steam or relieving boredom, accounted for the disappearance of miles of telephone wires and electricity cables and the tops of trees and hedges all over the Empire.

Pilots more used to higher performance aircraft were sometimes prone to take the Tiger Moth very much for granted and as something of a toy, attempting to take-off with most of the available runway still behind them, for example, or with extraordinarily heavy loads on board and, realising too late that the approaching hedge could not be cleared, could do little but shut off the engine, metaphorically apply the brakes, and rely on the decelerating powers of the enveloping foliage. In post-war days the cockpits of aeroplanes employed by the Tiger Club carried an additional placard instigated by Norman Jones: 'All aeroplanes bite fools'.

Ground crews were occasionally taken to task for bad handling when assisting with parking or taxiing and the enduring problem of turning a propeller with the switches inadvertently left on, and sometimes off, only to receive a crack over the hand, or worse, as the engine fired and the blade came powering round. Although they did their best in times of forecast gales and filthy weather, the ground staff often could do little but watch as aircraft were tossed into the air, picket lines flailing, as huge gusts, cyclones, 'willy willies' and revolving storms hit the dispersals, the damage compounded, especially in Australia and southern Africa, by torrents of destructive hail. In many cases whole replacement aircraft were easier to obtain than spare parts with which to apply the magic fix.

In Australia two RAAF Tiger Moths were officially posted as 'missing'. Julian Forsyth noted in his book *'The Tiger Moth in Australia'* that A17-476 (DHA893), of Station Headquarters, Townsville, disappeared on a flight between Townsville and Cairns on 20 July 1942 and A17-589 (DHA1024), on her way to join 33 Squadron at Port Moresby, did not arrive at Daru after leaving Horn Island at night on 24 September 1944. Adding to the catalogue, in their book *'New Zealand Tiger Moths'*, Cliff Jenks and David Phillips cite the case of five post-war civilian Tiger Moths that simply disappeared: "In three cases the aircraft were very likely lost at sea. A fourth was possibly lost at sea and the fifth is likely still rotting in some central North Island forest. Tiger

Just one more shot! After the official poses at Yatesbury early in 1940, there was time for another pass by the photographic Tiger Moth which took in the whole panoply of the station and the urgency of frail, frozen humans to seek the comforts of the NAAFI wagon. *Flight*

A not entirely unexpected occurrence at any time during the working day of a Reserve School: Tiger Moth G-ACDC over and out at Hatfield in 1938, sustaining standard damage in the process: undercarriage, rudder, propeller, cowlings and fuel tank. *Ben French*

Moth ZK-ATL (DHNZ92), took off on 28 September 1958 with a full spray load for a job less than twenty miles from Napier. The pilot and aircraft were never seen again."

Jack Franklin learned to fly with the de Havilland Reserve School at Hatfield:

"The time came for my first solo cross-country to Abingdon. Carefully trying to hang on to my correct course, I soon lost the pencil line across the map, and when the ETA came up I could not see Abingdon. It was slightly hazy, and then I did the worst thing, I wandered about in the air trying to find it. At last I decided I would stop and ask, and soon an obliging large and flat grass field came into view. I duly landed and touched down almost on top of a dozing fox which hurriedly departed.

Not seeing anybody I got out of the Tiger Moth and then met some children who told me that Abingdon was about seven miles away. I walked back to the aeroplane, donned my parachute and then pondered how to start the engine on my own and with no chocks. Suddenly I remembered that I had once seen someone swing a propeller from behind so, although being rather cumbersome wearing Sidcot suit and parachute, I turned on the engine switches, opened the throttle slightly, and took up my position between the leading edge of the lower wing and the propeller. I gave it one or two swings but still being warm, the engine refused to oblige. Ah! I thought, a little more throttle is needed, and got back to the cockpit and slightly opened it.

I repeated this laborious pantomime about three times, and at the next swing the engine burst enthusiastically into life at what may well have been about half throttle. The aircraft waddled aimlessly off, and I desperately tried to get back to the switches, only to get my parachute pack wedged against the rigging wires.

The waddle speed was fairly constant: we were nowhere near airborne, but after some distance the wheels must have hit a clump of grass or some uneven obstruction and the Tiger Moth stood very neatly on her nose, the propeller immediately becoming nothing better than quality firewood.

Discarding my parachute I then had about a half mile trudge, wearing my Sidcot, to a largish house where I hoped to find a telephone. By now my thoughts were becoming almost adventurous and I was conjuring up visions of meeting a glamorous blonde etc., but it was not to be. I found the house alright but the sole occupant was a mean, wizened old lady, who grudgingly let me use the telephone and made me pay for my call. On instructions from Hatfield I walked back and waited by the aeroplane. They were going to fly a new propeller out to me. In about two hours a School Tiger Moth appeared, circled the field twice and landed. The aircraft was being flown by George Cox, one of the School instructors and a pilot from Royal Flying Corps days, and in the back seat was Maintenance Manager Sid Weedon, sitting with a propeller between his knees, sticking vertically out of the cockpit. It was soon fitted, engine run up, and I was told to take off and circle the field and wait for George to join me. All this went according to plan and I followed him back to Hatfield to land in the failing light of a February evening."

Tiger Moth L6936 (3571), was involved in a collision with Hawker Hind K6669 at Prestwick on 23 June 1939. The pilot of the Hind, surprised by the sudden appearance of a Tiger Moth under his nose, confused his engine ignition and bomb release switches and flipped the wrong one, fortunately without dropping live cookies and blowing everyone up.

The entry into RAF service of Tiger Moth N6972 (82210), was less than auspicious. Delivered from Hatfield to Brize Norton on an English summer's day, 19 July 1939, the aircraft taxied onto a wet and slippery tarmac where she was hit by a gust. The ferry pilot could do nothing except wait for the inevitable as the aircraft skated over the surface and collided with a pair of petrol bowsers, watched by the ground crew who claimed the aircraft had arrived unexpectedly.

Although badly damaged N6972 was taken onto the books the following day but was not allocated to 18 EFTS Fairoaks until 22 November 1940. There, school, life was full of incident. N6972 was waiting to take off on 11 April 1942 when another Tiger Moth, T5718 (83439), landing in poor visibility, undershot and, fortunately for all concerned, collided with just the wingtips. Only four days later a 16 year old civilian was injured during a propeller swinging incident which caused the Station Rules to be re-written. N6972 landed in a field at Effingham on 4 April 1945 and hit a post which caused the undercarriage to collapse. The pilot claimed he had been forced to land to satisfy the call of nature and the station medical officer confirmed that the pilot did have a bladder problem and the claim was probably genuine. The aircraft was retrieved and temporarily housed in a blister hangar at the bottom end of the airfield alongside NL828 (86286), when a Bristol Beaufighter MkX, NE347, operating with 455 Squadron, landed on the short runway in a light wind, skidded on the grass due to heavy braking, and collided with the hangar. N6972 survived the ordeal and after repairs continued to fly for another two years when she was downgraded to an Instructional Airframe (6317M). On 1 August 1947 she left Newcastle on board the SS *Bonn*, bound for Oslo, a gift to the Royal Norwegian Air Force Collection at Gardermoen Air Force Base.

The wheel tracks in the grass indicate that this Tiger Moth may have run through a patch of wet ground causing her to deviate and stand on her nose, bending her metal propeller and no doubt shock loading the engine. *deHMC Archive*

In the quasi-camouflage scheme of the day, Tiger Moth G-ADGT was very much nose down at Sywell on 31 May 1939. The rig on the right is defuelling the petrol tank while the civilian ground crew decide how best the aircraft could be moved.
deHMC Archive

Ben French had been involved with Tiger Moths at Hatfield's Reserve School from 1936 by which time the new type had already joined the establishment. In the autumn of 1939 when the aircraft were eventually forced to admit they were in the pay of the military and took on coats of camouflage to disguise their distinguished colours of maroon and silver, Ben French and his colleagues were obliged to apply the first coverings using brushes and buckets of dope without dismantling any parts of the aircraft, such was the urgency. The undersides of the lower wings were painted by engineers lying on their backs on the hangar floor underneath the trestled airframes.

It was the duty of the Flying School's senior engineers each evening to taxy aircraft into their dispersed positions around the aerodrome and at Hatfield a favourite site was close by the shelter of a wooded area on the northern boundary. The practice was not without its local perils as Ben French explained:

"Dispersing the Tiger Moths gave rise to some fast taxiing with tail up and only when the undercarriage began to bounce did warning bells ring and it was time to throttle back. At that time a ridge ran across the aerodrome and it was imperative that speed was reduced before going over the top. With no brakes, a ditch and a wire fence awaited the unwary.

We had an engineer, Fred, an ex Royal Flying Corps mechanic. To us youngsters Fred was ancient and so short in stature that when sitting in the cockpit he could hardly reach the rudder pedals and could not see over the coaming. It was during one of our taxiing trips when I was in formation with another engineer that we were overtaken by a Tiger Moth on our starboard side, apparently pilotless and going at great speed. Suddenly the cockpit door dropped and we were greeted with a grinning Fred giving us a two finger salute. In his jollity Fred had forgotten the ridge and as we taxied over the top we saw Fred having switched off the engine, endeavouring to evacuate the cockpit to throw himself over the tail. Unable to do so his machine careered on towards two already parked aircraft. There was a loud crunching noise as the port and starboard wings took the tops off the rudders of the parked pair, causing extensive damage to all three.

Fred claimed the throttle had stuck but the excuse was not accepted and after spending unpaid overtime in trying to reduce the extent of the damage, assisted by some of his colleagues, Fred was handed his cards and shown out of the gate."

In 2003 Tiger Moth G-ADGT was a welcome visitor to the de Havilland Moth Club's annual Rally at Woburn when she was painted in a pseudo First World War colour scheme with her impressment serial stencilled on the fin.
Roger Birchall

At most if not all flying schools across the wartime Tiger Moth world the ground engineers were permitted to taxi aircraft as required. It was not unknown for them to travel at a speed which allowed a brief hop. *RAAF Museum*

Extreme caution is required when taxying a Tiger Moth on a hard surface, especially an aeroplane fitted with brakes and a tailwheel. In addition to the broken propeller and possible shock loading to the engine, the nose and chin cowlings will be bent and the front cylinder rocker box cover crushed. *Tom Sumner*

Pilots for the Fleet Air Arm were trained at civilian managed, RAF operated Elementary Schools assigned for the purpose such as No 14 EFTS at Elmdon where this shot was taken. These young men can be identified as prospective naval pilots by the cut of their uniform shirts showing underneath their white scarves. *deHMC Archive*

Engineers at 14 EFTS Elmdon where recruits for the Fleet Air Arm were trained were also encouraged to disperse their Tiger Moths in the face of occasional hit and run attacks by lone enemy aircraft roaming the Midlands. Malcolm Carlisle flew his first solo at Elmdon although he was not allowed to log it as he was a civilian in a Service aircraft and the wheels should have remained on the ground:

"When we heard the alert, factory workers downed tools and took to the shelters. Myself and a few colleagues, instructors and senior pupils, would scramble the parked Tiger Moths to disperse them around the airfield boundary. Engineers soon became dab hands at high speed taxiing and after a number of such trips we had our tails up and ran on the mainwheels. We then progressed further by lifting the aircraft slightly off the ground! Our unorthodox taxiing seemed to go unobserved except for one instance when we tried a return in Vee formation, and that manoeuvre earned us a blast from our Chief."

All thoughts of the war must have been far from the minds of two RAF officers as they enjoyed a spot of recreational flying in their Tiger Moth in the late afternoon sunshine of a day in mid-October 1939, meandering over the Firth of Forth. What subsequently occurred after a heavy aircraft buzzed them was described by A B Austin in his wartime salute to RAF Fighter Command:

"Probably the other pilot was being sportive. Entering into the fun of the thing, the pilot of the Tiger Moth dived on the big black aeroplane, zoomed up and dived again. It was rather like a wren playing tig with a hawk. But the stranger pilot did not seem to be so playful after all. Indeed he appeared to be

Tiger Moth R5130 was used by her manufacturer for publicity shots when she was not engaged at Hatfield in flight tests on behalf of Air Transport Auxiliary pilot selection procedures.
de Havilland Aircraft Company

moody, even a vicious fellow. As the Tiger Moth dived, something spat out of the black fellow's tail, and bullets whined past. Startled, the Tiger Moth turned sharply away, whilst the German bomber disappeared into a cloud. Probably the German crew were puzzled about the behaviour of the little British aeroplane which dived in true fighter fashion, and yet did not bother to fire."

All the lights that were permitted to burn were suddenly extinguished in Henley-on-Thames one night early in 1940 as the result of a Tiger Moth pilot parachuting onto the overground mains supply cable. The aircraft had been engaged in a night exercise from Woodley and was using the Relief Landing Ground (RLG) near Shiplake. The ailerons had locked when a drive chain jumped off its sprocket in the wing box and jammed the system.

The problem had occurred before and several modifications were made to British built Tiger Moths to improve the aileron control system, including Mods 56, 101, 125 and 138. Wing boxes built into Australian-made wings were never changed from the original design. Not until May 1945, at the request of the Ministry of Aircraft Production, was Modification 134 raised, to seal the aileron gearbox and improve inspection facilities. The reasoning, said MAP, was quite simple: fifteen cases of foreign bodies entering or being left in the aileron gearbox had been reported; jamming of the aileron and loss of control were the results!

On 12 March 1940 a pupil and his instructor were engaged in aerobatic training at 3,000 ft near Mangere in New Zealand. Going inverted during the demonstration of a slow roll, the instructor checked forward on his stick when the flange at the lower end of the handgrip caught behind the cord attached to the safety harness spring clip, withdrawing the locking pin. The straps were released instantly and to the horror of the pupil the instructor fell out of the aircraft. Contrary to training policy elsewhere, parachutes were not carried as standard equipment at the time of this incident. When parachutes were later issued as a matter of routine, the RNZAF considered the seat anchorage to be inadequate and modification NZ106 dated 12 November 1941 was raised in an effort to remedy the perceived deficiency.

A pupil at 2 EFTS Ashburton, South Island, was engaged in an aerobatic sortie with an instructor in 1943 when he was asked to check the security of his Sutton harness, a standard procedure. He released the triangular wire locking device, rearranged the straps and was just refitting the wire lock when the instructor asked if he was ready. Without thinking he answered 'yes' at which point the aircraft was flipped onto her back and the pupil fell out. He descended 3,000ft by parachute only to be blown by a gusting wind into a barbed wire fence where he sustained his only injury of the day.

Civilian contractor W Mumford repaired RAF Tiger Moths in a hangar sited just outside the boundary of Roborough Aerodrome, Plymouth. Visible in the mouth of the hangar is a visiting Heston Phoenix. *via Dick Gliddon*

During the early 'fifties, an Australian pilot in a borrowed civilian aeroplane was flying inverted along the top of a square loop when a safety harness clip shot earthwards past his startled eyes. Instinctively he grabbed the seat at the same time as pulling hard back on the stick, causing the Tiger Moth to half loop and return to level flight. When he was calm enough to run his hand along the harness webbing he discovered the clip was still firmly in its place and the one that had fallen out must have been carelessly dropped down inside the bowels of the aircraft, unreported, where it had lain concealed until revealing itself at the most opportune but inappropriate time.

Thirty years later, a fire extinguisher fell out of the cockpit of a British based Tiger Moth during an inverted manoeuvre. The incident was considered serious enough to result in a full accident enquiry, not on behalf of the owner of the empty field into which the device harmlessly fell, but in respect of what might have been the outcome if the pilot of the Tiger Moth, who was wearing a protective helmet, had been incapacitated as a result of collision with the unguided missile.

Mary de Bunsen learned to fly at Woodley and her first solo was on an overcast day in November 1930 when she guided a Cirrus II Moth, G-EBUS, around the circuit. She flew several other Moth types during the next ten years and in the frantic summer of 1940 was a member of the London Fire Brigade when she volunteered for duties as a ferry pilot with the Air Transport Auxiliary (ATA).

On 19 June 1940 Mary de Bunsen failed her ATA selection flight test undertaken on Tiger Moth R5130 (83012), operating from Hatfield, due to a condition described by her examiner as 'rusty, very rusty', and she returned to her duties at the fire station. Within three weeks she had been contracted to collect civil Tiger Moth G-AFZD (82595), from Barton where the aeroplane had been accepted into the Northern Aviation School and Club less than a year before, and deliver her to Witney. By her own account the trip was memorable in that she was uncertain of her position for almost half the two hour journey; the Air Ministry refused her any proper maps and had cancelled her preferred routing just prior to take-off. And it was her first solo flight for 364 days. The Tiger Moth had been acquired by brokers W S Shackleton and the nearly new G-AFZD was militarised and shipped to the South African Air Force as '1547' the following September.

In August 1940 Mary de Bunsen became Chief Test Pilot to Lundy and Atlantic Coast Airlines, a Civilian Repair Unit (CRU) based in Devonshire and contracted to specialise in Tiger Moth maintenance and repair. In her diary for 17 August, she wrote:

> "All pilots who are not maimed, halt and blind being usefully employed elsewhere, I am the only pilot on the premises and my pronouncements seem to carry considerable weight. I have done seventy nine hours and forty minutes solo in the past ten years. I wonder how you test aeroplanes? Test this one on the principle that if it and I come down together in one piece, the aeroplane is all right. Ten minutes later: report aircraft nose heavy, but everybody seems delighted with what, it appears, is their first effort. "They said we could not rig a Tiger Moth etc etc.," they told me. I feel tempted to reply, "they said I could not fly one!" From now on, all Tiger Moths inspire me with the greatest confidence."

RAAF Tiger Moth A17-114, damaged at 8 EFTS Narrandera on 6 December 1940, was routed to the Clyde Engineering Co Pty Ltd, at Granville, NSW, a civilian organisation which worked on a wide range of military aircraft during the war and continued into the immediate years of peace. *Bruce Winley*

A railway siding into the premises of the Clyde Engineering Co at Granville was used for regular deliveries of Tiger Moths damaged as a result of their daily toil amongst the flying training schools. Major repairs were carried out at three other establishments including the de Havilland factory at Mascot. *Bruce Winley*

Having become far less 'rusty', Mary de Bunsen was accepted into the ATA in October 1941 and a little over two years later was ferrying DH.98 Mosquitos.

A single bomb fell onto the hard standing by the 14 EFTS hangar at Elmdon early in the war but instead of exploding on contact it ricocheted into the middle of the grass aerodrome and harmlessly blew a hole in the ground. One engineer expressed thanks for his salvation by suggesting with great seriousness that he had been spared in order to continue stitching and patching the fabric on the school's Tiger Moths. To sound the all-clear, the duty officer strode to the middle of the tarmac with a Very pistol which he raised to full elevation and fired. Many eyes watched the coloured ball of flame as it soared skyward and then descended, still blazing. Unerringly, it fell into the rear cockpit of a parked Tiger Moth which was soon a mass of flame.

The thrill of a first solo was, in the opinion of a pupil at 15 EFTS Carlisle, something to be savoured and exploited to the maximum. He made the excuse that a slightly imperfect three-point landing after his first solo circuit had prompted him to go around. During his second approach the pilot became aware that the layout of the airfield and boundary appeared to have changed and he was only sure of his own position by the reassuring sight of the hangars and parked aeroplanes where he thought they ought to be. After landing and a ticking off by his instructor, the pilot discovered that in the short time while he was airborne, dummy hedges and shadows had been painted on the grass as part of an overall camouflage plan which had nearly caught him out.

Flying from 18 EFTS Fairoaks in July 1940, just after take-off Richard Davies and his instructor spotted a parachute in an adjacent field, attached to what appeared to be a cylinder. They circled and flew low over the object then returned to base to report their sighting. Later that afternoon while waiting for another sortie the assembled crews witnessed a tremendous explosion. The object over which the Tiger Moth had made several low, slow passes in the morning had been a land mine dropped during the night and fitted with a delayed action fuse.

Polish pilots at play but with serious intent. Tiger Moth T5631 supporting two air gunners in addition to her normal complement at No 25 EFTS Hucknall. *via Jacek Mainka*

Although the uncertainty of British weather was an important ingredient in the establishment of major flying training facilities overseas a considerable amount was carried out from the wartime schools already established in Great Britain. Operating on a murky day No 25 EFTS at Hucknall was a centre for Polish pilots. *via Jacek Mainka*

Operating with No 1 School of Army Co-operation at Old Sarum, N6856 (82111), was engaged in a triangular cross country flight around the Marlborough Downs on 27 September 1940, an area not renowned for navigational landmarks. The pilot, an escapee from Poland, became unsure of his position and when attempting a precautionary landing at Frobury Farm, Kingsclere, he became temporarily confused and fully opened the throttle on landing, driving the aeroplane full tilt into a hedge. He explained later that throttles on Polish Air Force aircraft operated in the reverse sense. The aircraft was repaired at nearby Witney and banished to Perth where she remained operational with 11 EFTS until declared surplus in 1952.

N6856 was civilianised as G-ANLR and later operated by a co-ownership Group as a glider tug, instructional machine and tourer. She was booked to be flown during a Battle of Britain display at Wyton in September 1963 with a soldier standing in the front cockpit, restrained by a specially adapted long harness, firing blank cartridges as part of a spoof shooting demonstration. During the take-off run the soldier stood up but knocked off the ignition switches and the unexpected return to earth precipitated a bounce from which the aircraft cartwheeled and turned over. In a replay of her Service days G-ANLR was landed in a Norfolk field in April 1966 to allow the captain to ask his whereabouts and although the landing was completely successful and the required information identified him as being only a few miles from his destination, the aircraft veered into a hedge when attempting to take off again and was substantially damaged.

In 1968 a survey of the Seaplane Club's Tiger Moth G-AIVW (83135), revealed a heavily corroded fuselage. The storeman at Rollason's hangar at Croydon had just the thing as a replacement, and wheeled in the complete fuselage of G-ANLR. The rejuvenated Sea Tiger enjoyed another fourteen years of a unique lifestyle on the south coast of England until August 1982 when, in murky conditions which merged sky with the surface of the sea, she hit the water at Rye, Sussex, during a turn at low level, and the salvaged remains were rebuilt for static display at the museum organised by the Robertsbridge Aviation Society.

When a survey revealed that the fuselage of Sea Tiger G-AIVW was subject to salt water corrosion, the remedy was to replace it with the fuselage of Sea Tiger G-AIVW! (One of them was G-ANLR.) *M J Hooks*

When first unveiled Sea Tiger G-AIVW was painted yellow overall. The aircraft was trial rigged with her ex-Aeronca Sedan floats in the Rollason Aircraft hangar at Croydon in 1963. *David Welch*

With covered accommodation used almost exclusively for maintenance, military Tiger Moths were mostly left out in the weather and in Great Britain the threat of invasion or a surprise attack on airfields needed to be countered by night guards posted among the picket lines. At Sywell, Hatfield and other establishments, scrap cars were towed out onto the airfield at night to act as mobile obstructions and pupil pilots were detailed off as guards and issued with ancient rifles complete with bayonets, but no ammunition. During one particular period at Sywell it was believed aircraft were being sabotaged when each morning a number of innocent Tiger Moths were found with slashes in the fabric-covered under-surface of the top mainplanes. Only after thorough investigation was it realised that the damage was being caused by bayonet tips when rifles were carried over the shoulders of the defending troops.

An all night guard utilising the services of reluctant pupil pilots was mounted at 15 EFTS Carlisle where 'armed patrols' were also undertaken without the benefit of ammunition. During storm conditions one night the guards could only watch as Tiger Moths picketed nose to wind, dragged their wing restraints out of the ground but, still secured by the tail took off and landed on their backs. One pilot clung on to a propeller as the Tiger Moth was lifted bodily into the air but let go just before the aircraft flipped over. About a third of the fleet was damaged that night before further assistance arrived from the main camp and by morning it could be seen that a number of aircraft had suffered, not only from the effects of the wind, but also from the efforts of the ground crews when attempting to claw them out of their airborne positions.

To prevent tearing of their dural tie-down brackets which could result in their release in high winds, Tiger Moths in service with the RNZAF were fitted with a modification which replaced the original fittings with an alternative design made from mild steel. Inspection of fourteen aircraft damaged during a storm at 2 EFTS Ashburton on 1 February 1943 revealed that none of the pickets had failed. Three aircraft were written off and another three severely damaged. As a further result plans for additional hangarage were immediately authorised.

Pity the poor ground crew working all hours to present serviceable aircraft when training was an urgent necessity. Engineers at 21 EFTS Booker, an airfield at high elevation on the edge of the Chiltern Hills in Buckinghamshire, worked through the winter of 1940 carrying out daily inspections in an unheated T-type hangar, muffled up to their eyebrows in layers of clothing. Outside, the airfield was covered in snow and frost as the Tiger Moths were trundled to the tarmac ready for engine runs. The cold got into the engines and the propellers were hard to pull over. Rather than sit in the aircraft the engineer in control of the switches stood alongside the cockpit with head and shoulders tucked well inside. When the engine fired and began running he would adjust the throttle to a fast tickover, tighten the friction nut and stand well clear of what was an icy blast.

N6532 (3845), was with 22 EFTS Cambridge when operating from Bottisham on 18 May 1941. The pilot removed his leather gauntlet to make a throttle adjustment but the silk inner on his left hand picked up in the quadrant and while trying to disentangle it with his right hand, the aircraft stalled and crashed. After extensive repairs completed on site the aircraft remained at Cambridge until sold as surplus to the Darlington and District Aero Club in 1954. Registered as G-ANTS, but remaining unconverted, the dismantled airframe was acquired for the Strathallan Collection in 1968, and an assembly of parts catalogued as G-ANTS was sold at the slimming-down auction conducted at Strathallan in June 1981.

In a partially restored condition the aircraft was re-sold to Sweden in September 1991 but meanwhile, following the decision to close the museum altogether, a further clearout at Strathallan yielded another fuselage clearly marked 'G-ANTS' which was sold at a second auction in 1985 and disappeared into obscurity.

During the early days of BBC Television a children's programme followed the fortunes of a young lad looking over the fence at Tiger Moths operating at Fairoaks. He wanted to be a pilot and had studied all he could about flying from books and magazines. A friendly instructor noting how often the lad was a visitor offered him the opportunity of a quick circuit. During the flight the instructor removed his gauntlet to adjust the trimmer and his silk inner snagged in the quadrant. The only possible solution to achieve a satisfactory ending to the programme was to allow the young pupil to be talked through a landing which he achieved admirably on all three points, almost.

Hatfield-built N6457 (3787), was delivered into storage at Dumfries in November 1938 but when 34 ERFTS was established at Southend on 16 January the following year she was posted hundreds of miles south again. By October the aircraft was back at Hatfield, operating with 1 EFTS. Flying near Alconbury on 16 September 1941, the pilot became unsure of his position and in an effort to locate familiar landmarks began a search pattern during which the aircraft ran out of fuel and crashed as a consequence of a misjudgement of the forced landing. At the subsequent enquiry it transpired that the aircraft's clock was broken and that the flight endurance had been stretched to almost three hours. In addition the pilot had been operating without a map; he had not been issued with one due to a critical shortage in supply!

On detachment to 17 EFTS Peterborough late in 1941 Ben French was called upon to change a propeller on a Tiger Moth which had landed away at the new aerodrome at Wing in Buckinghamshire. An instructor had taken the aeroplane 'home for the weekend' but had had the misfortune to taxy off the runway and into a hidden gully running alongside, breaking the propeller and denting the cowlings in all the usual places. Ben French was chauffeured to Wing in a Tiger Moth with the replacement propeller strapped to the side of the fuselage and the near certainty that it would fit. Probably, everyone had heard the story of the pilot who flew a DH.60 Moth to Australia with a spare propeller lashed to the fuselage side and was fortunate not to have needed it whilst en-route. Reaching Australia unscathed, he discovered that the spacing of the bolt holes in the hub was different from those on his engine, and as an emergency replacement the propeller was completely useless!

After landing and without brakes Ben French's Tiger Moth rolled down the new runway which was soon to host Vickers Wellingtons on circuit training. The engineer was then required by his pilot to render assistance on the wingtip to help taxy back to dispersal. Having found the victim of the gully the breathless white knight was able to get on with his job: remove the broken propeller and its hub; clock the crankshaft (was it bent?) change the front rockerbox cover which was squashed, dress out the bottom cowling, fit the new propeller, check the tracking and run the engine, pack up and fly back to Peterborough. It was all in a day's work, completely routine, but these were unusual times. What excited Ben French most was that during his unscheduled trip he came to realise how much effort the war was taking for at no time during the flight was he out of sight of a newly constructed aerodrome.

Back at Peterborough on 24 February 1942 the civilian ground crews were subjected to a verbal explosion by the Commanding Officer when their uncoordinated handling managed to persuade the pilot of L6936 (3571), to taxy into parked Tiger Moth T7356 (83666). Had he been there the following advice might have been offered by an accomplished Tiger Moth pilot with experience of operating the type in all conditions in most parts of the world:

"It is seldom realised that steering the aircraft is down to the helpers when there is wing tip assistance. If you are wing-walking a Tiger Moth watch the rudder and you will get a good idea where the pilot wants to go!"

In 1943, L6936 was one of a number of Tiger Moths selected for conversion to Queen Bee configuration and the aircraft was moved to the Pilotless Aircraft Unit at Manorbier in September. Although not actually converted she suffered 'substantial damage' in November which took a month to repair in Barnstaple and she subsequently returned to training duties with 21 EFTS at Booker from January 1944. The aircraft survived the war and civilianised as G-ANPK she was counted down, but not out, after a well publicised attack on a sea wall during a joyflight from Clacton in 1996. She is believed to be one of only four survivors of the 30 civil specification aircraft bought by the Air Ministry off the Hatfield line in 1937.

For reference purposes, aircraft accident reports were usually copied to the Ministry of Aircraft Production (MAP). One such, originally addressed to the Commanding Officer of 6 Flying Instructor School (FIS) Staverton, concerned the accident to a Tiger Moth in February 1942 and was cited by the MAP recipient as one of the finest examples of the art of aircraft accident reporting he had encountered during his very long career:

"I was ordered to carry out exercises with Pilot Officer X, and after spending some time on the circuit, we went away from the aerodrome to practice aerobatics. After both of us had carried out a considerable number of rolls, loops and rolls off the top, the aeroplane started to do a series of dives, stalls and stall turns, starting at about 2,500ft to 2,000ft and gradually getting lower and lower. At this time I thought Pilot Officer X was piloting the aircraft and although I did not like the manoeuvres that were being carried out, at that altitude anyway, as he was an officer and already had his flying badge, which I had not, and moreover had, I knew, flown many more advanced types than I had, I assumed he knew what he was doing and accordingly sat tight.

As he several times said he did not like doing crazy flying of this description near the ground and I was still under the impression that he was flying the machine, for some reason I got the impression that he was trying to scare me and consequently just sat in front and said nothing, as I was waiting for him to get tired of what I thought was just an exhibition of unauthorised low flying for my benefit.

Eventually the aeroplane hit a hedge and crashed. I was out first and whilst trying to assist Pilot Officer X, I was astounded to hear him blaming me for the accident, and told him so. As he was, and I believe still is, under the impression that I had been piloting the aeroplane at the time, he naturally thought I was trying to put the blame on him. I also jumped to the conclusion that he was trying to put the blame on me and as a result we spent the following two hours not speaking to each other very much.

I telephoned Worcester Aerodrome and spoke to Squadron Leader Y and in view of this misunderstanding with Pilot Officer X was reluctant to discuss the matter over the telephone, but on being pressed, stated what I believed at that time, that the accident was due to 'low flying'. Later I spoke to Squadron Leader Z and again stated that I was reluctant to discuss the matter until I had an opportunity for an interview with him. After I had arranged for a police guard for the aeroplane, Mr A brought us home in a van in which he had been sent to pick us up.

The quickest way to recover a lightly damaged fuselage is to trailer it back to base behind a tractor unit. Note that the rudder of Tiger Moth T6179 shows all the indications of a turn-over and that the hole in the fuselage fabric aft of the roundel is evidence that the first aid kit has been removed. *via Dr Ken Ellwood*

While in the van and just prior to arriving at Staverton, the thought crossed my mind that possibly neither of us had been piloting the aeroplane during the twenty minutes preceding the accident, during which times the stalls and dives had been going on. I mentioned this fact to Pilot Officer X after he had seen the medical officer, and he not unnaturally, being under the impression that I had first of all tried to blame him, does not hold the view that this was the case. I should like to state that I was definitely not using the controls during the time that these dives and stalls were made, and that I do not now hold the opinion that Pilot Officer X was either. I think personally that the accident was caused because it did not occur to either of us that the other was not piloting the aeroplane, and because we were both under the impression that the other was showing off.

I would also like to make it quite clear in order to exonerate completely Pilot Officer X, that I was in the front cockpit and therefore, though of lower rank, nominally in charge of the aeroplane. It was for this reason that I carried out the telephoning and arranging for the guard afterwards."

N6924 (82168), had been involved in a number of skirmishes since posting to 22 EFTS Cambridge in September 1939. Mostly these were forced landings due to pilot disorientation but on 27 June 1942 her pupil pilot ignored a red light on finals to land at night at Caxton Gibbet RLG and bumped into N6971 (82209), which was ahead of him. N6924 was operating near Northampton on 10 February 1943 when the solo pilot saw a Lockheed P-38 Lightning catch fire in the air, followed shortly after by the sight of the pilot baling out and descending by parachute only to land in a tree. The Tiger Moth was immediately put down in an adjacent field with the thoughts of her pilot tuned to the prospect of rendering all possible assistance but the aircraft ran into soft earth and only succeeded in standing on her nose, hopefully out of sight of the Lightning pilot who was left suspended in his harness. Following more landing damage sustained at Caxton Gibbet in June and repaired by Lundy and Atlantic Coast Airlines, the grandiose and deliberately confusing title of the CRU in Barnstaple, N6924 served until 1945 with two Polish squadrons operating North American P-51 Mustangs: No 316 at Friston and Coltishall and No 306 at Andrewsfield. Sold in 1951 and registered G-APHZ in 1957, the aircraft was converted into the ninth Thruxton Jackaroo in 1958 and operated initially as a cropspraying demonstrator. Sold in Canada after the owner emigrated there in 1970, the Jackaroo was fitted with a forward raked and braked DH.82C undercarriage, and is maintained in concours condition at Guelph.

The pilot of DE715 (85645), taxiing on tarmac in strong winds at 16 EFTS Burnaston in June 1942, waved away the wing walkers and was promptly blown into Miles Magister V1074. Post war when part of the establishment of 12 RFS at Filton, the same aeroplane, flown by a pilot who was unsure of his position and suffering from severe airsickness in turbulent conditions, put down at the first aerodrome to come into view: it was Exeter and unfamiliar territory. Too exhausted to await assistance after landing, DE715 was taxied slowly towards habitation until a gust picked her up and blew her over.

Donald Smith was posted away from the Supermarine Spitfire Vs of 72 Squadron in July 1942 and was required to travel just a few miles from his former base at Biggin Hill to join 116 Squadron whose Detachment at Croydon was operating Tiger Moths and Airspeed Oxfords in support of gun and searchlight calibration duties. Set courses at heights up to 10,000ft were flown as determined by signals displayed on the ground, after which the cold and tedium of the whole exercise was tempered by the occasional chance to land back at Croydon, having slipped round the famous control tower, to touch down and stop within the confines of the concrete apron.

Returning from an East Anglian sortie one afternoon the weather closed in, obliterating all signs of Croydon Aerodrome, the control tower and even the local cooling towers which were used as an outstanding landmark. A few snatched glimpses of the ground revealed nothing familiar until Donald Smith suddenly spotted two Tiger Moths parked on a grass airfield. He spiralled down to discover he was over Hanworth and while taxiing in after an uneventful landing the engine coughed and stopped. This sortie had lasted over two and a half hours, and the fuel tank had run dry.

Under similar conditions a 116 Squadron Tiger Moth flown by a Canadian bad weather specialist, Nobby Clark, was heard overhead Croydon but the engine note diminished as the aircraft appeared to head towards the west, leaving those on the ground in no doubt that he had diverted. In conditions of low and lowering cloud and poor horizontal visibility all further flying was abandoned. Half an hour after most other pilots had settled into the mess, Nobby Clark appeared in full flying kit with a story that he had flown over a railway station and by counting the number of platforms had deduced it was East Croydon from where he had followed the road to the airfield. Gliding in to land on the side furthest from control nobody was aware of his safe arrival after which the fog settled and he could not see to taxy. Abandoning the aircraft in the middle of the airfield another successful mission by 116 Squadron had been completed on foot.

Fog too was one of the problems experienced during winter training at Kirton in Lindsey on the east coast of Lincolnshire. Bob Palmer was airborne for a half hour session of steep turns when his instructor observed red Very flares being fired off from the control tower and the reason was soon obvious as both pilots saw a wall of sea fog rolling inland at amazing speed. The instructor immediately took control, dived for the airfield and put down nearly into wind, to be enveloped in swirling vapour as soon as the run back to dispersal was completed. Later arrivals were not so lucky and several aircraft were stranded on the airfield. Taxiing the Tiger Moths in fog with the constant need to swing the tail to ensure some modicum of forward visibility resulted in crews getting hopelessly disorientated. They were forced to switch off the engines and listen for the approach of help in the form of the station Jeep, and hopefully not another Tiger Moth which might collide on the ground or even worse, attempt to land on top of them.

Following a number of fatal mid-air collisions in New Zealand all trainee pilots were further encouraged to maintain a sharp lookout at all times. After Tiger Moths NZ778 (DHNZ28) and NZ1411 (DHA497) from 3 EFTS Harewood collided and crashed on 25 July 1942 Training Command issued an order that all Tiger Moths still operating in their FAFAI camouflage colours were to be repainted in their original bright yellow, a scheme that endured until the end of the war.

Whilst waiting for American light aircraft types to be delivered from the USA, at least sixteen Tiger Moths were loaned to the United States 8th Army Air Force in Great Britain between 1942-1945, principally for communications duties, although some degree of 'orientation' and 'recreational' flying was enjoyed. The aircraft retained their RAF camouflage and serial numbers, but the fuselage roundel was changed to a star in a circle or a star and bar insignia, and some were repainted with dark green upper surfaces (olive drab) and neutral grey undersides.

Not surprisingly, the loaned fleet was involved in a number of incidents and several aircraft were lost. DE826 (85724), allocated to the 'Mighty Eighth' on 12 October 1942, was damaged in an accident at Membury only five days later and written off following a crash near Wadebridge, Cornwall on 4 April 1943, when operating from Heston. It was usual for USAAF pilots with Observation or Reconnaissance Groups waiting for the delivery of their long-range fighters to be temporarily attached to RAF squadrons and at least one Membury-based pilot flew Tiger Moths for local familiarisation followed by Spitfire Mk VIs with 66 Squadron at Perranporth, escorting bomber raids to the Brest Peninsula. DE826, seemingly a long way from home, might well have been supporting the detachment.

DE745 (85675), was officially allocated to 336 Squadron USAAF on 7 October 1942, but was actually on charge with the 353rd Fighter Group at Goxhill in February 1943 and named *Dorothy* when a squadron P.47 put down in an East Anglian cabbage field. The unit commander, Colonel Duncan, landed DE745 alongside the victim without incident but on take-off managed to turn the Tiger Moth upside down causing considerable damage and embarrassment, after which the benign Wizard of Oz titling was changed to *El Pisstopho Jr*.

The detachment of DE935 (85806), to Membury lasted three days before her first accident and barely six weeks before her second. She was returned to the RAF in January 1943, shipped to South Africa and lost at sea on 1 April. DE932 (85803), was deployed to Warton in August 1943 and in October forced landed near Stockton, out of fuel, and was written off. DE933 (85804), was repaired after her third accident in May 1943 but was returned to the RAF in August, converted to an instructional airframe and vanished into the system. Five more were lost in 1943, three in 1944 and one the following year. Two other aircraft known to have been returned to the RAF are DE262 (85308), which was allocated to 3 EFTS Shellingford on 3 August 1944 and written off on 3 September, and DE560 (85527), which joined 11 EFTS Perth in November 1944 and exactly a year later, stalled and crashed during forced landing practice.

Although the USAAF operation of Tiger Moths both in Great Britain and, to a lesser degree in Australia, was organised through official channels there is every possibility that aircraft were liberally swapped amongst host units. A senior USAAF officer admitted long after the war to knowing of 'Reverse Lend Lease' agreements sealed with a couple of bottles of whisky, including one deal which resulted in a pilot securing a Rolls-Royce built Merlin engine for his North American P-51 Mustang.

One of those stories which may have been propagated from a basic element of truth was spread amongst the students undergoing grading at No 4 EFTS Brough in 1942. A wheel which allegedly fell out of the sky near a police station was identified as coming from a Tiger Moth. Having no wireless communication two instructors at the local EFTS took off with the wheel in a Tiger Moth in an effort to intercept the subject aircraft in the circuit and warn the pilot of the problem. As the instructors left the ground a wheel detached from their aeroplane. Unaware of their own situation they sought and found their quarry and held up the wheel to the amazement of the solo

From USAF Station 366, RAF Metfield, Suffolk in 1943, an American pilot from the 353rd Fighter Group prepares for a trip in a camouflaged Tiger Moth bearing the Stars and Bars of the USAAF and eyes and teeth of a ferocious beast. *via Colonel Sid Tucker*

Four American airmen of the 353rd Fighter Group based at RAF Metfield, Suffolk with their loaned Tiger Moth in 1943. Of the group two were later killed in action, another taken prisoner or war and the fourth survived and retired to Florida. *via Colonel Sid Tucker*

A 'communications' Tiger Moth serialled in the DE700 series, complete with shark's teeth, a steely eye, and USAAF fuselage insignia, photographed at RAF Metfield in 1943. Having completed 300 hours in P-47s, USAAF pilot Herbert Field was due for posting, but with D-Day imminent, he volunteered for an extension of service and was killed in action on 7 June 1944. *via Colonel Sid Tucker*

student who wondered how this other aircraft could be carrying a wheel on board having lost one from the chassis. Both aircraft made successful landings, the student's adjudged to have been better than the other. The loss of the wheels was attributed to corrosion of the axles. Almost immediately notices appeared at dispersal urging aircrew to cease forthwith their habit of relieving themselves on the undercarriage and to use the latrine which was soon to be provided.

In 1942, 18 EFTS Fairoaks was the scene of a near disaster featuring a Tiger Moth, details of which were not released until some time later. According to the official reports the aircraft had been operating in an authorised low flying area when the cloud ceiling suddenly dropped to 200ft, requiring the Tiger Moth to be climbed up into the overcast to enable it to clear a range of hills between its present position, presumed to be south of the South Downs, and her base which, for security reasons, the censor would not allow to be identified. During transition the Tiger Moth hit a suspended barrage balloon with its wheels; the fabric bag was punctured by the propeller and escaping hydrogen gas ignited against the hot exhaust from the Gipsy Major engine.

The starboard side of the empennage of a Tiger Moth that suffered the effects of burning hydrogen when the aircraft attempted to touch down on a barrage balloon flying above a cloud layer south of Fairoaks Aerodrome in 1942. *Flight*

Instantly enveloped in a ball of fire, fabric on the starboard upper trailing edge inboard of the interplane strut, starboard lower trailing edge inclusive of the aileron, and complete upper surfaces of the starboard tailplane and elevator was burned off. The flames were extinguished only by an instinctive and violent sideslip to port in an effort to keep them away from the crew and the petrol tank as much as anything. Finding that the aircraft continued to fly, albeit with crossed controls, the crew elected to return to base where the Tiger Moth was landed normally.

The coincidence of the descent onto a golf course of a blazing barrage balloon and the appearance of a heavily singed Tiger Moth landing at a local aerodrome had to be explained. The release of the story, as told, placated those for whom it was intended and attracted welcome publicity for the amazing survivability of the aeroplane. But in reality, and behind closed doors, it was admitted that the crew of a Tiger Moth operating above a cloud layer had spotted the silvery manifestation of a balloon, suspended and apparently motionless and, hidden from all observation by the furry carpet of vapour, they had indulged in the well known practice of airborne spot landing.

On this occasion the 'landing' had been firm or slightly off target. Fortunately, although the balloon had been ruptured and exploded, all had survived. T6188 (84636), the aircraft involved, was repaired and remained part of the establishment at Fairoaks until finally struck off charge in May 1950.

On the other side of the world fire took hold of Tiger Moth NZ819 (DHNZ69), whilst standing at rest at 2 EFTS Ashburton on 8 November 1942. A spark from the chimney of a traction engine passing along the adjoining public road set fire to the dry summer grass and the aeroplane was a victim of the conflagration which rapidly swept across the dispersal.

Why was a pilot landing DE615 (85569), into a 40kt wind at Fairlop in October 1942? Having touched down he waved away the handlers, took off again, landed on another runway and was promptly blown over. When the pilot was carpeted by his Commanding Officer he was reprimanded against a charge of taking off (again) without permission!

Pity the pilot of DE315 (85349), taxiing in a gusting wind at 25 EFTS Hucknall in February 1945 who thought a main wheel must have dropped into a hole. The moment he climbed out to investigate he could only watch in dumb horror as the aeroplane was lifted bodily by the wind and turned onto her back.

For a comparison of wind speeds against experience the following is a reasonable summary devised by a many-houred Tiger Moth pilot who, as a licensed engineer, was well practised in the art of repairing them:

0-5 kts: Suitable for all, especially if the wind is straight down the runway.
5-10 kts: Suitable for all but be alert for the possibility of wind shear.
10-15 kts: Suitable for experienced Tiger Moth pilots and low time pilots providing the wind is not gusting.
15-20 kts: Start to watch it. The aircraft rocks on the ground and slats pop out if they are left unlocked. Operate into wind only. When you taxy the aircraft, get help.
20-25 kts with gusts: Now you have your hands (and feet) fully occupied. There is a good chance of being blown onto a wing tip. Get help.
25-30 kts: A situation for aces, idiots and emergencies only. Put the aeroplane back in the shed. It should not have been outside anyway.
30 plus kts: Get a quote in advance for major damage repairs.

Painted in an early camouflage style one of a number of Tiger Moths allocated to RAF squadrons as hacks, her tyres caked in clay, picketed but otherwise unprotected. *via Murray Peden*

Tiger Moth N6932 was allocated to 87 Squadron in June 1940 operating Hurricanes from Exeter with detachments at Hullavington and Bibury. The officer on the left is wearing a revolver holster. The aircraft crashed on take-off from Charmy Down in March 1942 and was replaced by another in June. *via Mike Davies*

198 Squadron had formed at Digby on December 8 1942 with thirteen Hawker Typhoons and one Hawker Hurricane but only the Hurricane was serviceable. Two weeks later, with aircraft positioning to and from maintenance facilities, the squadron was joined by Tiger Moth T7271 (83770). For the remainder of the month the aircraft was used to ferry pilots and spares but on 21 January 21 1943, at 100ft just after take off from Digby to follow the Typhoons to their new posting at Ouston, T7271 spun off a turn and was demolished injuring the pilot and squadron Intelligence Officer travelling as passenger. She was replaced by DE765 (85679), which arrived at Ouston on 9 February, posted in from an itinerant Supermarine Spitfire Vc equipped 312 Squadron, and continued with a round of pilot and spares ferrying as the squadron continued to change bases and experience problems with serviceability.

The squadron's first Commanding Officer, Sqn Ldr J W Villa, was credited with acquiring the Tiger Moth and is on record as saying that whenever a new pilot joined the squadron he would be sent up to familiarise himself with local geography. All new pilots could fly the Tiger Moth: almost none of them had any experience on Typhoons so they could learn the local layout without having to worry about flying a still unfamiliar aircraft.

DE765 was lost on 5 September 1943 when she ditched into the Thames Estuary near Margate as the result of engine failure when returning to Manston after a ferry trip to Martlesham Heath. DE779 arrived as a replacement on 29 September 1943 and remained on paper charge until she was administratively posted to 14 EFTS at Elmdon in August 1944, but by then 198 Squadron had been fighting in France for two months and much had changed.

The Hawker Typhoon 1Bs of 181 Squadron spent almost the whole of June 1943 at Appledram, a forward airfield close to the eastern extremities of Chichester Harbour. When taxying their warhorses to and from the runway the squadron pilots soon realised that an abundance of game, mostly partridge, took absolutely no notice of them but were off at high speed at the sight of a man strolling around the dispersals. A communications Tiger Moth was enlisted into the task of supplying supplemental rations and while the aircraft was taxied from the front cockpit the occupant of the rear seat brandished a loaded shotgun. Results were not spectacular as on uneven ground the soft-sprung undercarriage created a poor platform for gunnery. Performance was slowly improving with practice when on 3 July 1943 the squadron was ordered to pack its tents and relocate to the barren acres of Romney Marsh. The game birds of Appledram were left to multiply in quiet isolation for less than a year before five squadrons of Supermarine Spitfire IXs descended upon them.

At 28 EFTS Wolverhampton in 1944 the instructors were coping with groups of Iraqi, Iranian and Turkish students, all under some pressure from their respective governments to achieve distinction. Somebody discovered that while the British Government was responsible for the costs of training Turkish pilots, Turkish navigators were being funded by the Luftwaffe.

It was a Turkish officer who landed Tiger Moth '98' after an exercise prescribed for spinning and aerobatics, and who was completely bemused when his propeller flew off the hub as he applied power to taxi cross-wind. The pilot was so astonished at the lack of performance that he sat for several minutes behind the engine, still rattling under power, before a member of the emergency services switched off the ignition. Despite a comprehensive review nobody could determine the reason why all eight hub bolts had sheared until a chance remark made by a visiting Boulton and Paul test pilot led to a complete revelation. He had been testing a locally-built Barracuda, flying level at 180mph, when his aircraft had been subjected to a fighter style attack by a Tiger Moth which had broken away in a dive at an estimated speed of about 200mph. On the nose of the Tiger Moth the test pilot distinctly remembered reading a unit code: '98'. The Turkish officer later confessed to an irrational mock attack on what he had believed to be an enemy aircraft. Apart from the engine change the unit Engineering Officer immediately ordered a second and thorough inspection of the airframe which failed to reveal any further obvious indication of damage or stress.

Alex Smith was stationed at RAF Northolt awaiting call-up for aircrew training towards the end of the war when the system had already created a surplus and recruits were being found a diversity of alternative things to do just to mark time. The Station Commander volunteered all such chaps to plant vegetables between the runways and alongside the perimeter track, and to keep their enthusiasm at fever pitch all plantings were logged: 1,000 cabbages entitled each volunteer to an hour's flight in the station Tiger Moth.

During his hour of entitlement, Alex Smith was flown via Ruislip Lido, where the wheels were subjected to their obligatory skim of the water's surface, and on towards Heston by which time the visibility had deteriorated to such a degree that the pilot elected to land at the first airfield which hove into view. After touchdown both pilot and passenger were astonished at their encounter with so much contractor's plant and mounds of sand and gravel, and were even more alarmed as they climbed out of the aircraft to see a party of workmen advancing towards them with anything but a welcoming attitude. All was revealed soon enough; the Tiger Moth had touched down in the middle of the expansion of RAF Heathrow, soon to be London Airport and the world's busiest international terminal. The next movement by a Tiger Moth at Heathrow was twenty years later when G-AMIU (83228), an aircraft purchased as a tug for the British European Airways' Silver Wing Gliding Club, was overhauled at the Corporation's engineering base and afterwards flown out, non radio, to her base at Booker.

Returning to Southampton from Ceylon late in 1945, troops from all three services were embarked on an ancient Royal Mail ship which had hardly cleared the dockside at Colombo before it was subjected to a series of low level attacks by a Tiger Moth. The pilot, identified as the Wing Commander Flying, and his bomb aimer were both observed to be wearing full mess kit and assumed to have recently left the all-night farewell party. The aircraft bombed the ship with tins of 'tickler', Royal Navy cigarette tobacco, attached to yards of bunting which carried rude messages. There was only one direct hit but the exercise was appreciated by everyone.

In order to move a Tiger Moth single handed, the most efficient way is to lift the rear of the aircraft by the tailplane strut at least to normal shoulder height, at which point she is balanced on her main wheels and can be manoeuvred quite easily on level ground. In this configuration on a rough surface, or particularly where an up-slope is encountered, the load becomes marginal for an ordinary mortal but is still a perfectly reasonable proposition for two people.

Turkish pilots were trained by the RAF at No 28 EFTS Wolverhampton whilst their navigating colleagues enjoyed the hospitality of the Luftwaffe. The Turkish trainee in this picture attends to the needs of the press photographer as briefed but the young RAF instructor shows a greater interest in activity in the circuit. *deHMC Archive*

Tiger Moth N6754 (82032), had served as a training aircraft since allocation to 18 EFTS at Fairoaks in October 1939 and from June 1947 she was part of the Cambridge University Air Squadron (CUAS) fleet lodging with 22 RFS at Teversham. During the night of 16 January 1948, a man later identified as an escaped German Prisoner of War, broke into the hangar and moved the aircraft nearest to the door, N6754, onto the apron outside. It was his intention to position the Tiger Moth as far from the buildings as possible to allow time to familiarise himself with the aircraft, start and warm the engine, and take-off at first light, creating no unnecessary attention. The plan might have worked had it not been for growing fatigue and loss of orientation and a gust of wind which unbalanced the arrangement. The following day in the cold light of a January morning the CUAS engineers were astonished to find N6754 lying on her back in the middle of the aerodrome. Repaired and maintained in service until 1953 the aircraft emigrated to New Zealand the following year but within two days of the completion of major work at Rotorua on 31 March 1981 the hangar burned down allowing only a few small parts to be salvaged from the ashes.

A sister Tiger Moth from the same Hatfield batch created in the early summer of 1939, N6797 (82067), was another survivor of wartime training released to the civil market in 1953. Sold to the Association of British Aero Clubs (ABAC) on behalf of the Defford Aero Club for a mere £25, the aircraft was rough rigged at Cosford and flown home to RAE Defford where she was registered G-ANEH in September 1953, and qualified for a Certificate of Airworthiness

Left and below: During her last scheduled landing in Uruguayan Military service Tiger Moth B2-603 suffered a collapsed port undercarriage on 16 June 1948 putting all the weight onto the port lower wing and probably, but not obviously, cracking the rear spar. *via George Boubeta*

After the war the RAF offered aircrew training to ex members of the Air Training Corps during their two year period of National Service and the first to take up the offer and fly solo was this group at No 7 FTS Cottesmore. Following demobilisation the one-time cadets were promised continuation training with the RAFVR or the Royal Auxiliary Air Force. *Flight*

under the hand of club engineer Cyril Pugh in July 1954. At the same time the Club bought a second Tiger Moth from Cosford at a price of £75. R5065 (82960), had logged test flight hours only following a complete overhaul. In 1950, the Club had purchased four Tiger Moths from Sandown, Isle of Wight, at £60 the lot, from which two good aircraft were rebuilt and eventually sold.

Following incidents with a number of subsequent owners, G-ANEH was discovered in a semi derelict condition in a barn near Kemble in 1968 by none other than Cyril Pugh who took ownership in December that year and undertook a complete rebuild in the gliding club hangar at Nympsfield where he was then resident engineer. On 6 May 1973 with the part time restoration of G-ANEH about 75% complete, some guttersnipe thought it incredibly amusing to set the hangar on fire and, as a consequence, just like her old stablemate 82032, Tiger Moth 82067 was reduced to a collection of parts heavily singed round the edges. Also lost in the fire was the gliding club's own Tiger Moth G-AODX (83437), salvaged parts of which later were sold to the USA. As a rebuilding project G-ANEH passed through a number of hands and proved a financial nightmare to her owners particularly when a restoration company collapsed taking all the up-front funds with it, but the programme endured and the aircraft was finally completed by Ben and Jan Cooper at the Newbury Aeroplane Company in 1995 to an outstanding concours condition.

During a Battle of Britain flying display at Ternhill on 18 September 1948, Tiger Moth T6774 (85061), a resident aircraft with 6 FTS, was conducting a mock attack on a cardboard fort when the luggage locker door flapped open, distracting the pilot who subsequently flew into the ground but managed to recover to land on the one remaining wheel. The aircraft was declared a write-off, sold to Wolverhampton Flying Club and registered G-ALNA in April 1949. In January 1986, having suffered a traumatic civil life, the aircraft was reported to have suffered a rudder control problem and had involuntarily sideslipped into a flooded gravel pit near Clacton.

The occupants were rescued with difficulty from the sheer sided workings by a man walking his dog who heard cries for help. The aeroplane was rescued too, dried out and restored to airworthiness.

DF159 (85908), a 1943 Morris Motors model, was scheduled to spend the first year of her life in a 15 MU Purgatory Store before erection and test at Cowley and issue to a training system already in contraction. As part of the establishment of 1 Radio School, Cranwell, DF159 was operating from Spitalgate (Grantham) in July 1951 on what was officially described as 'ground strafing practice', but the pilot took off with a faulty intercom, the occupant of the front seat clutching a lapful of primed flourbag bombs. During the first run in towards the target the front doors were let down to permit visual signals to be given to the pilot but some of the flour which had escaped from the bombs blew up into his face causing loss of control at low level. The port lower wing struck an RAF Regiment officer who was standing near the target judging hits, injuring his thigh, but with a damaged mainplane and pasty faced pilot the aircraft was landed safely at Saltby. In 1955, registered G-AOAA, 85908 was the first Tiger Moth to be assigned to the fleet of the Tiger Club at Croydon, and was later converted to become *The Deacon,* one of the unique quartet of Super Tigers, much refined to boost the aerobatic qualities of the basic aeroplane.

Tiger Moth DE141 (85212), was based at RAF Coltishall during the summer of 1952, appropriately enough in the care of 141 Squadron. When not operating their Gloster Meteor NF.11s, the squadron pilots were encouraged to use the aeroplane to hone their basic flying skills and were permitted to take DE141 away for weekends at a charge of 5s.0d, payable to squadron funds. Everybody agreed that this was a splendid arrangement and enjoyed by many, but things were too good to last. While inspecting a cereal crop from low level on 22 July 1952 the undercarriage became entangled with the ripening ears and the flying career of DE141 came to an abrupt end. The pilot escaped the crash and his subsequent court marshal unscathed, but the unit funds and weekends away were destined never to be the same.

Flushed with the exuberance that can only be the result of captaining a Tiger Moth at the age of 17, an Air Training Corps cadet flying under the provisions of an RAF Flying Scholarship scheme in 1957, overstepped the mark near Petersfield, Hampshire, after which he was prosecuted for flying below 500ft (fined £5), and for 'flying an aeroplane in a reckless manner' for which he was fined a further £5. These indiscretions were highlighted only because the Tiger Moth was damaged when it collided with the ground.

The Royal Navy was a quietly prolific user of Tiger Moths and apart from supplying the RAF with an example for their Museum at Hendon after the original exhibit suffered an arson attack, even before the facility had been opened to the public, the Senior Service bought back four aircraft from the civil market long after the type had been declared obsolete. The Tiger Moths were to join others already on strength to provide air experience flying at minimum cost to officer cadets at Plymouth and during their summer camping expeditions to Scotland. As part of the Air Day organised at Lossiemouth in 1959 a Tiger Moth Air Race was scheduled, each aircraft carrying a coloured pennant mounted on the tail skid, and a Wren in the front seat wearing a coloured jumper to match. After three laps the aircraft were to land to allow the girls to jump out and race through an obstacle course to reach the control tower. The rules for the race permitted full power until the leader was overtaken, at which point the engine was throttled back to 1,800rpm until in due course the new leader was passed.

On the day all went well with the three Tiger Moth entrants until at the end of the race it was time to land as near to the control tower as possible. Only then was it realised that the prospective touchdown area was meshed with lengths of anchor cable, all part of the arrester training system. No undercarriages were lost but the ladies had a longer sprint than had been anticipated.

At a little over 17 years of age, Paul Barton was flying a Tiger Moth at Cambridge, the beneficiary of an RAF Flying Scholarship, although he later transferred allegiance and retired after a successful career as a pilot in the Fleet Air Arm. On his solo cross-country he reached Luton safely, but a change in the wind on the second leg to White Waltham put him off track and he landed in what proved to be a rough surfaced field in order to ask the way. The firm three pointer broke off the tailskid although he was not aware of that until after a take-off which scraped the top of the surrounding trees, and a downwind landing at White Waltham where he mis-read the windsock and found taxiing the aircraft more difficult than he could remember.

The lack of brakes on his Tiger Moth was forgotten as he approached the fuel pumps:

"A veritable brainstorm of a decision, the pumps being surrounded by a concrete apron. Moreover, this apron sloped ever so gently down to a set of gates in the airfield perimeter fence beyond which lay a public highway. Once on the apron there was, like the engineer's big wheel, no way of stopping it. So off we trundled down the slope with a depressing inevitability that totally scuppered my previous euphoria. Luckily though, the gates were open and there was nothing immediately in the way, so there seemed little point in adopting the standard emergency procedure (jump out) and in any case we were soon going rather too fast. Luckily, the laws of gravity, having been gently responsible, with me, for starting this debacle, elected to terminate it by means of the camber in the road, which is where we stopped, right in the middle. So there, like a lemon, I sat in my flying machine, holding up the traffic until help arrived.

As a precaution I joined the Fleet Air Arm to continue my flying career as a helicopter pilot. The Navy seemed to have a rather more liberal understanding of the foibles of the youthful aviator than most; besides, it was obviously going to be very much easier to stop and ask the way!"

Taxying downwind on concrete with a steerable tail trolley under the skid requires an officer or two to act as brakes. Royal Navy Tiger Moth T8191 wearing the Culdrose code, striking down at Yeovilton. *deHMC Archive*

The caption attached to this photograph of a camouflaged T8191 in an 'unusual attitude' reads: 'The Tiger Moth was not designed for arrested landings and with the barbed wire firmly wrapped round the port undercarriage, the old girl came to an abrupt halt and tipped gracefully onto her nose.' *HMS Heron*

CHAPTER ELEVEN

European Variations on a Proven Theme

Norway proved to be a good customer for de Havilland products and in 1930 the government owned aircraft factory at Kjeller near Oslo (Haerens Flyfabrikk) negotiated a licence for production of the DH.60M, known in military parlance as the 'Standard Moth', after which ten aircraft were constructed the following year.

Welcomed as a visitor to Stag Lane in 1931, Norwegian Army Air Force Capt Richard Clason was invited to fly the new DH.82 with the result that he recommended to his superiors that no more 'Standard Moths' should be built and that efforts should be concentrated on the DH.82 Tiger Moth instead. He was particularly impressed by the versatility of the aircraft in the military roles of reconnaissance and observation as much as the type's primary function as a basic trainer.

In February 1932 it was announced that an agreement between the de Havilland Aircraft Company Ltd. and the Norwegian Government, acting on behalf of the State Military Aircraft Factory at Kjeller, would result in licence production of the DH.60M being discontinued in favour of local manufacture of seventeen DH.82 Tiger Moths, for each of which British built Gipsy III engines would be supplied from Stag Lane. Information provided to the press spoke only of 'training duties', a description which covered most military prospects in addition to circuits and bumps.

The de Havilland licence had been procured at a fee of almost 16,000 Norwegian Kroner (Nkr) and every effort was made to build the aircraft as economically as possible. Much of the DH.60M production tooling could be used again for the manufacture of DH.82 parts, with little or no modification, although an investment of Nkr 14,500 was necessary for additional jigging.

All seventeen licensed aircraft were completed by the summer of 1933 at a total manufacturing cost of Nkr 215,348 plus an additional Nkr 132,320 spent with the de Havilland Aircraft Company's Engine Division for the supply of twenty Gipsy III engines. The entire fleet was paraded at Kjeller before allocation to duties: thirteen were scheduled for the Army Air Force Flying School and some other operational units before 1 July 1933, two would join the Flying School after 1 July and two more were to be retained for use by the factory as communications, liaison and development aircraft. Kjeller issued build numbers 149-165 to which the Army Air Force allocated serials 127-159 but using only the odd numbers in sequence; even numbers were reserved for the Naval Air Force. Before delivery of the DH.82 Tiger Moths the Norwegian Government voted funds for manufacture of a further twenty aircraft to be built at Kjeller to the DH.82A specification.

These new machines were to take second place to a batch of ten Fokker C.V-D and C.V-E reconnaissance and bomber aircraft under construction at Kjeller, but the de Havilland design was given priority when the military immersed itself in indecision regarding the choice of a suitable engine for the Fokker airframes. However, all aeroplane construction was substantially interrupted in 1934 when the authorities decided in favour of a major programme of factory repair and refurbishment, very much with a view to creating modern facilities for the future mass production of a new fighter. It is also suspected that an extended trainer production schedule was necessary to maintain continuity until the site was again fully functional and the fighter project firmly on the shop floor.

Norwegian Army Air Force DH.82 Tiger Moth 159 was fitted with a float chassis and tested by the Norwegian Navy in a series of trials totalling twenty two flying hours in 1934. As a prospective seaplane trainer the type was rejected as unsuitable for naval service. *Kjeller Flyhistoriske Forening*

An allocation of funds was made to purchase Gipsy III engines for the DH.82A fleet but negotiations with Stag Lane proved difficult and de Havilland refused to consider lowering their contract price. It was probably part of a preconceived business strategy for, with the Gipsy III soon to make way for the Gipsy Major, the Norwegian Government found they were offered a better deal on the new engine. The contract called for just twenty units to be delivered, one for each airframe, and no extras for reserve. In February 1935 the Inspector General of the Army Air Force announced that when the twenty aircraft were complete in the spring, three years after the line was laid down, six aircraft would be allocated to the Army Air Force Flying School at Kjeller, ten to the operational units at Kjeller and the remaining four to Vaernes, the military base near Trondheim.

The DH.82A line was identified by build numbers 171-190 and Army Air Force serials 161-199 were allocated, again using odd numbers only. Having described the DH.60M as the 'Standard Moth', the DH.82A was to be known somewhat confusingly as the 'Moth Major' to distinguish it from the Gipsy III powered DH.82. Allowing for revised jigging, each of the new aircraft had cost a little under Nkr 19,000, about 10% per unit less than the DH.82, essentially a function of lower pre-production costs. A further financial saving per aircraft was made by the decision not to fit leading edge slats, thus depriving the Handley Page Aircraft Company of a potentially handsome royalty.

The Norwegian military were strong proponents of the de Havilland philosophy of a 'one type trainer' as indicated by their widespread deployment of the Tiger Moth. In addition to a single seat operational trainer experimentally equipped with a machine gun fitted over the front cockpit, the winter exercises at Kongsvinger in 1934 unveiled DH.82 No 129 (150), in the role of bomber, with a rack of four under-fuselage bombs, each of which could be released individually. Zeiss camera guns were fitted to several aircraft in addition to long range fuel tankage of ten, twenty or even thirty five gallons capacity installed in the front cockpit, the greater endurance requiring larger capacity oil tanks to be fitted to aircraft with the Gipsy III engine.

Standing on her ski chassis, Norwegian DH.82 Tiger Moth 129 is fitted with a concrete practice bomb. A rack underneath the fuselage floor was designed to carry four bombs of up to 10kg each. *Kjeller Flyhistoriske Forening*

Blind flying panels and hoods were standard for instrument training which continued throughout the year and night flying equipment included a wind driven generator fixed to the undercarriage V strut and an accumulator in the luggage locker. Although not equipped with landing lights night landings were accomplished with the aid of floodlit touch down zones, rather than flarepaths, which could be seen at high altitude from very long distances.

On behalf of the Department of Meteorology at the University of Oslo, the Flying School at Kjeller provided facilities for research and data collection. Beginning in June 1933, Capt Normann, Commanding Officer, flew DH.82 No 149 (160) several times a week to altitudes in excess of 15,000ft. In recognition of the conditions faced during these ascents the pilot's cockpit was fitted with a turn indicator and a fore and aft level, while barographs were strapped to the interplane struts. The role was assumed by DH.82A No 163 (172), for six months from September 1936, and DH.82 No 151 (161) later in 1937.

On 29 March 1936 Norwegian built DH.60M LN-BAE (139), of the Widerøes Flying School, formerly Army Air Force No 111, was written off after an accident at Grorud. As replacement the Widerøes school was offered Army Air Force DH.60M No 109 (138), which was registered LN-BAT in their name at the company's Oslo base on 7 April, only eight days after the accident. As No 109 had been transferred from the Army Air Force Flying School at Kjeller, an organisation which now needed its own replacement, DH.82 No 157 (164), one of the two factory communications aircraft, was nominated.

The sale of DH.60M No 109 had raised Nkr 7,300, money which was paid to the factory account. In consequence a single new DH.82A Tiger Moth was commissioned on 2 April 1936 and a Gipsy Major engine was delivered from England on 30 September. The new Tiger Moth (193), was allocated Army Air Force serial 201, fitted with a metal propeller which produced a distinctive sound, mainwheel brakes and a castoring tailwheel. She was the 38th and last of the type to be built locally. No 201 was delivered across the workshop floor on 1 October 1937, largely for use by the Commanding Officer of the Factory, Capt Eckhoff. The improved stopping capability was welcomed during the autumn of 1939 when No 201 operated from an abbreviated strip at Stavern when on detachment to tug targets for anti-aircraft gunnery practice.

The Kjeller factory had suffered its share of difficulties spawned by incorrect drawings but mostly the errors had been identified and corrected before the DH.82A was put into production. In December 1934 several spare sets of front fuselage side frames were constructed and following the demise of the first Norwegian-built DH.82A No 161 (171), after a crash at Aurland on 29 July 1935 and with only ninety five hours logged, the Gipsy Major engine was removed and installed in No 159 (165), the second of the factory's DH.82 communicators, during the Autumn of 1936.

During the engine change the opportunity was taken to upgrade the aeroplane for the personal convenience of the Inspector General of the Army Air Force, Col Trygve Klingenberg, an officer who had been left with a stiff leg following an accident as a young pilot. The rudder bar was modified to accept a clamp on one side instead of a conventional pedal, an arrangement which allowed the Colonel to pull with his good leg in addition to pushing as normal, and to retain complete authority with otherwise standard controls.

On 27 May 1937 Col Klingenberg led seven Tiger Moths and four Standard Moths from Kjeller to the opening of the new airfield at Sola but weather conditions were so bad that only two aircraft arrived. Two Standard Moths, No 107 and No 117 crashed en route, one of the pilots being killed when he baled out. Lieutenants Hansen and Mohn parachuted from Tiger Moth 183 (182), and the aircraft crashed at Eidsfoss.

Tiger Moth No 159 had been the subject of marine investigations in 1934 when she had been loaned to the Naval Air Force for evaluation as a float-equipped trainer. Purchase of a pair of Short Bros floats had been sanctioned in November 1933 and in February 1934 Lt K Ostby flew the ski-equipped No 159 from a snow covered Kjeller to Lake Borrevannet where the float chassis was fitted. Trials were completed at the Norwegian naval base at Karljohansvaern where after almost twenty two hours flight time the Naval Air Force pronounced

Sporting the colours of the Norwegian Army Air Force in use until 1940, Tiger Moths LN-KFT and LN-MAX flown by Morten Myhr and Anders Håkensen in close harmony at the air display at Lista Airfield on the south west coast of Norway in July 2010. *Sten Arne Brunsby*

that the type was not suitable for its purposes. No 159 was flown back to Kjeller, alighting on the river Nitelva which normally flowed half a mile from the airfield, but which in May 1934 was in flood, creating a lake immediately adjacent to the airfield buildings.

The Kjeller factory had been responsible for the design and manufacture of skis for all Norwegian military aircraft since January 1916 when flight trials had been conducted on a locally-built Maurice Farman MF.7 Longhorn (Kjeller FF.1). The first director of Kjeller Flyfabrikk, Capt Einar Sem-Jacobsen, had adapted a 'domestic' ski and fitted one pair to each side of the FF.1 with remarkable results. As a matter of course all Norwegian land-based military aircraft later operated during the six month long winters on skis designed, developed and manufactured at Kjeller. The Tiger Moths were provided with two types of narrow width skis with round or squared-off ends, fore and aft, or a broader laminated ski which was less likely to 'straighten out', a configuration which could cause embarrassment on touchdown. When equipped with skis Tiger Moths were restricted to a maximum diving speed of 165mph. With the exception of laminated skis all others were smeared with Tento, a proprietary wax, and some were fitted with bullet shaped aerodynamic fairings to help lessen the drag.

Operating on snow covered ice with a ski-equipped aircraft was hazardous, even for experienced pilots, until the engineers devised a simple but very effective solution. By bolting a steel strip to the outer edges of each ski they created skates on which the aircraft could, with practice, be controlled on the slippery surface with both verve and precision.

During the summer months the cast iron tailskid shoe would wear thin due to the abrasive nature of dry grass runway surfaces or concrete hard standings and taxy tracks. Loose or wet ground was easily excavated by the ploughing qualities of the skid as it fulfilled its primary functions of steering and braking. Trials proved that leaving the winter kit's mini-ski on the tailskid arm all through the summer, in preference to the iron shoe, not only preserved runway surfaces with very little difference in braking capacity, but reduced the frequency of attention and replacement.

On 20 June 1938 DH.82 Tiger Moth No 135 (153), on the strength of the flying school at Kjeller, took off on a routine exercise crewed by two trainees, Åge Kvil and Even Berger, each with about 140 hours flying time. They flew to a remote area near to the village of Svinndal over which they commenced a series of low level aerobatic manoeuvres witnessed by many of the local farmers. Birger Kolbjørnsen described seeing what might have been an attempted stall turn which was never completed as the aircraft stalled, went out of control and, with the engine at full power, crashed into a stand of trees. The wreckage was quickly cleared away by the military whose court of enquiry into the accident failed to reach a conclusion except to suggest that the probable cause was due to careless manoeuvres at a low height. In 2013, seventy five years later, small pieces of wreckage were uncovered by a local historian, Dan Engebretsen, who was given a file of photographs of the crashed aircraft taken by a friend's father on the day of the accident and which had been stored away ever since.

Tiger Moths flew as target tugs in support of the anti-aircraft schools and the experience was later put to good effect when towing gliders or advertising banners. In the reconnaissance role during the Russo-Finnish War of 1939-1940, the aircraft routinely patrolled the country's northern borders in defence of Norway's neutrality.

To ensure uninterrupted operations under the severest winter weather conditions oil was drained from the engines immediately on shut down after the last flight of the day and heated almost to boiling point before the tanks were replenished. To ensure there was no misunderstanding oilless engines were placarded with red triangles and both pilots and engineers were required to sign log books before attempting to start up. When aircraft were required on a stand-by basis in severe weather the nose of the aircraft was shrouded by a Dalli Apparatus under which heating elements, the size and shape of a brick and housed in a perforated container, were suspended below the engine. Three elements were sufficient to maintain warmth in the bay for twelve hours. An alternative system was the provision of heat by a small portable furnace from which hot air was fed into the cowlings along flexible ducting. Apart from these precautions, and the choice of landing gear appropriate to the surface conditions, there were no concessions to the climate.

For the crews it was necessary to be dressed in fur lined boots, flying suits, helmets and gloves, with face masks to prevent frost bite. Operating under such conditions the inadequacy of the fuselage width was revealed when pilots were obliged to fly with the cockpit doors hinged down in order to improve shoulder space, but it was not until after the winter exercises of 1938 that serious thought was given to the procurement of a training aircraft fitted with a canopy, and then only in preparation for the arrival of the new Gloster Gladiator fighters as much as anything else.

DH.82A Tiger Moths No 183 (182) and No 185 (183), were modified at Kjeller in 1935 to carry a machine gun but only on a temporary basis. Experience gathered from these and previous installations led two Air Force officers to develop a new system of gun synchronisation driven by the engine camshaft and in preference to other hydraulically operated arrangements which were prone to leakage. The synchronisation was proven by firing a bullet from a Colt .303 machine gun, mounted with a sight above the front cockpit, through a hole in one blade of the propeller, which had itself been fitted several degrees off its normal orientation.

The system was installed on DH.82A Tiger Moth No 165 (173), which was used for gunnery training by student pilots in the summer and experienced officers during winter exercises. The Army Air Force was pleased enough to award the two inventors an extraordinary payment for their work and funded conversion of another four aircraft in the winter of 1939. No 165 was detached to the Jagervingen, (Fighter Flight), operating their Gloster Gladiators from Fornebu in the spring of 1940 where she was destroyed by enemy bombing on 9 April. The other four aircraft had already been disarmed in support of the spring pilot training programme at a time when they were needed most of all.

Several other Tiger Moths were early casualties of the German invasion, destroyed in bombing raids at Sola and Fornebu. At Kjeller it is estimated that five Tiger Moths were on station with two fighter units and a further three Tiger Moths and three DH.60M Moths were in the factory undergoing maintenance and repairs. No 171 is known to have been destroyed on the ground and another Tiger Moth took off in the dark but collided with a Fokker C.V-E. At first light No 167 and No 175 had left Kjeller and landed at Steinfjorden. The previous day, fifteen Tiger Moths of the Army Air Force Flying School had been flown to Oyeren where they landed on the ice and were immediately camouflaged. On 10 April at dawn they flew to Rena leaving behind one immobilised machine whose engine could not be started. Later that evening the Army High Command ordered the aircraft to move to Nordre Osen in the eastern province of Hedmark, close to the Swedish border, where a gathering of twenty three aircraft was hidden in woodlands along the edge of Lake Ossjoen.

The Norwegian Army Air Force fitted machine guns to six Tiger Moths which were used for gunnery practice on a seasonal basis dependant on the experience of the pilots. The guns and magazines were fitted into the front cockpits which retained their normal instrumentation and Gosport systems. *Colonel Knut Kinne*

Below: Five DH.82A Tiger Moths of the Norwegian Army Air Force operating from a frozen lake during pre-war manoeuvres in northern Norway. 189 escaped to Sweden on 15 April 1940; 185 was lost in a crash in southern Norway on 20 April 1940; 181, 187 and 191 continued to fight in the north until 7 June 1940. *via B Olsen*

In 1970 during a stay with friends at Koppang, American Tiger Moth owner Bill King was introduced to a local farmer called Guttu who said that in April 1940 his house had been used as the Headquarters of the Training Wing and that one of his fields had been occupied by Tiger Moths painted white. Two of the aircraft had crashed. In his barn Mr Guttu revealed a complete rudder and two port lower mainplanes, all of Norwegian manufacture. He confirmed that the Germans had removed the fuselages and engines. He donated the parts to the Norwegian Aviation Historical Society and they were quickly removed to Oslo.

Following a decision to evacuate the Flying School aircraft to Sweden, seven Tiger Moths accompanied by four Fokkers flew north again to Horrmundssjoen on 15 April, but one aircraft became detached from the main group during a heavy snowstorm and landed on a small frozen lake; another touched down in a bog and was later recovered in a dismantled condition, eventually joining the other six at Ostersund in Sweden where they had arrived on 18 April.

First of the Kjeller built DH.82 Tiger Moths, Army Air Force 127, was tested on aerodynamically shaped skis during the winter of 1933.
Kjeller Flyhistoriske Forening

At a surface temperature of at best minus 18°C, ice thickness is considered sufficient to support the weight of an aircraft. Norwegian Tiger Moths LN-BDM and LN-MAX landed on a frozen lake surface near Oslo in March 2001 where they were filmed for the Discovery Channel.
Arild O Krosby

Below: The dark green scheme of the pre war Norwegian Army Air Force was broken only by national insignia carried at the tail and wing tips. LN-MAX, masquerading as Army Air Force '127', can be identified as a post-war import by the carriage of spin strakes.
Ivar Windingstad

The seven escapees were DH.82s Nos 127, 131, 137, 151 and 157, and DH.82As No 163 and 185, all of which took civil letters on the Swedish register and continued operating much as before in the varied roles of trainer, target and glider tug. In April 1971, DH.82 SE-ANL (No 151), was acquired by the Norwegian Aviation Historical Society (NFF) and returned for permanent display at the Military Museum established at Akershus Castle, Oslo.

On 16 April 1940 Group R was formed in southern Norway to which all available aircraft were attached and on whose behalf the remaining Tiger Moths were extensively used for communications duties. In support of an attempt by four Tiger Moths to escape through northern Norway to Finland in June 1940 each had been hurriedly disguised as a civil aircraft but only one, No 159 (165), posted to the Army Air Force Flying School in July 1937, was successful, carrying the markings LN-BDD. The aircraft subsequently saw service with the Finnish Air Force as MO-159.

DH.82 Tiger Moth No 145 (158), had spent her entire career with the operational unit at Vaernes and had recorded 1,814 flying hours by December 1939. On 28 April 1940 the aircraft was located at Lake Lesjaskog when civilian pilot Conrad Mohr and mechanic Arne Akersveen were granted permission to fly her north but the engine failed just north of Dombås and she was wrecked when she force

Tiger Moth 189 was built at Kjeller in 1935 and in 1940 escaped across the border to Sweden where she remained airworthy until 1962 flying under Swedish registry as SE-ALP. The aircraft was returned to Norway in 1997 and rebuilt at Kjeller from where she made a second maiden flight in 2005. *Colonel Knut Kinne*

landed in a plantation at Dovrefjell mountain. Although some parts were collected and hidden the substantial remains of the aircraft were not finally recovered by local inhabitants until 1990 by which time the engine had long since disappeared but was traced to a local farm in 1993, the same Gipsy Major engine installed on manufacture at Kjeller. Plans to restore No 145 to static display standard by the local War Memorial Group lost momentum and in October 2009 the project was transferred to a group of enthusiasts led by Eivind Svenningsen rebuilding a Fieseler Storch at Fetsund. Much of the original structure that survived has been grafted into a static model intended for local exhibition at Dombås where the aircraft will be displayed in her 1940 standard winter camouflage mounted on a ski undercarriage.

Once the fighting in southern Norway had stopped German forces took control of all surviving aircraft. DH.82 No 129 (150), was dismantled at the flying school at Lesja and removed from the site; the engine and fuselage of DH.82A No 187 (184), which had crashed during take-off from Koppang in April were also confiscated. A published photograph of a scrapped aircraft dump at an unknown Norwegian airfield taken some time after the start of the German occupation shows what appears to be the relatively intact rear end of Tiger Moth No 183 (182) in the background, an aircraft which had crashed in bad weather during delivery to Sola on 27 May 1937.

Norwegian Army Air Force Tiger Moth 145 on conventional undercarriage at Elvegårdsmoen, north of Narvik, in August 1933. The dark green colour applied to wings and fuselage blended with forested background but not snow. *via Eivind Svenningsen*

Conrad Mohr with Norwegian Army Air Force Tiger Moth 145 in a winterised colour scheme after the aircraft force landed in a plantation at Dovrefjell mountain, north of Dombås in April 1940. *via Bill Mohr*

Painted in Luftwaffe colours and bearing military code GM+OS this DH.82 Tiger Moth was photographed at Kjeller where she appeared to be in airworthy condition. Her original identity and ultimate fate are unknown. *via Jan van den Heuvel*

de Havilland DH.82A Tiger Moth, MO-159, LeLv26, Finnish Air Force, 1943. Oliivinvihre (Olive Green) upper surfaces and Vaaleanharmaa (Very Light Grey) undersides. Underside of wingtips and fuselage band in Yellow. Codes in black. National markings in six positions. *Artwork ©Richard Caruana, 1:72 scale*

Four civil registered Norwegian Tiger Moths were gathered into formation during the local flying day organised at Kjeller Airfield near Oslo in September 2013. *via Marius Håkensen*

At least one DH.82 was photographed at Kjeller painted in full Luftwaffe colours bearing the code GM+OS, but her previous identity and subsequent fate are unknown. The aircraft was fitted with a windy ASI on the port front interplane strut and rear doors with the cutaway modification to accommodate the arms of the blind flying hood, indications, perhaps, that she was of de Havilland manufacture.

The Norwegian Tiger Moths and others confiscated in Denmark were not the only examples to see wartime service with the Luftwaffe. Some of the aircraft abandoned in France by 81 Squadron in 1940 were made serviceable and flown in German markings at least until the lack of spares rendered the situation untenable. Four civil registered Tiger Moths based at the Austrian Air Force Air Training School at Parndorf in October 1939 were reallocated to Flying School A/B24 at Olmutz where at least one is known to have been written off in a landing accident during training operations that continued until October 1940. It was a situation immersed in irony bearing in mind the opinions expressed on the suitability of the Tiger Moth to de Havilland's Austrian agent, Nikolaus von Eltz, in 1936.

Sweden

Cementing their good relations with the de Havilland Company through Swedish agent Sven Blomberg of Aero Material in Stockholm, also acting as de Havilland representative in Latvia and Finland, the Swedish Air Force bought ten of the first batch of twelve DH.60T Moth Trainers during the summer of 1931. Ordered on their behalf by the Flygstyreisen office in Stockholm, and redesignated as type Sk.9, serials allocated were Fv5103 to Fv5112. It was almost inevitable that as a major customer for de Havilland products the Air Force would progress to newer models as they became available and following the emergence of the DH.82 Tiger Moth as a next step development from their still new Sk.9s, the type was soon subject to serious investigation.

Following demonstration of DH.60T Tiger Moth G-ABNJ by Hubert Broad at Barkarby in December 1931 and subsequent purchase of that aircraft, orders were placed with Stag Lane for a June 1932 delivery of twelve DH.82 Tiger Moths with Gipsy III engines. These would be classified together with G-ABNJ, formally taken on Swedish Air Force charge as Fv6562 on 9 February 1932, as type Sk.11. Aircraft 3108-3115 and 3138-3141 would become Fv5563-Fv5568 and Fv5591-Fv5596 respectively. In the event, delivery was spread through the year 1932: 3108 and 3109 arrived during the last week of April while 3110 and 3111 were delivered on 6 May. 3112-3115 were received in the middle of July, and the final four, 3138-3141, were not taken on charge until 25 October.

Four of the aircraft, 3112-3115, had been ordered by Aero Material as civil aeroplanes (SE-ADE to SE-ADH), for a reason directed by budgetary constraints and alternative methods of funding or some associated political rationale. Following delivery all were cancelled from the civil register and allocated the Air Force serials Fv5567, Fv5568, Fv5591 and Fv5592.

The new aircraft were posted to the 5th Air Corps Flying School at Ljungbyhed near Malmö where they were used for *ab initio* work during courses which included 170 hours of elementary and advanced flying training spread over a twelve month period. Markings carried on the aircraft changed progressively between 1932 and 1944 and it was as 4-74 that aircraft 3139 crashed at Bydalen in March 1945 with

Stag Lane built DH.82 Tiger Moth 5563, type Sk.11 of the Royal Swedish Air Force, on floats at Vasteras Centrala Flygverkstaden (CVV), a Tiger Moth repair station which licence-built the rival Focke Wulf Stieglitz (Sk.12) between 1939 and 1945. *via Mats Roth*

Painted in the colours of a Royal Swedish Air Force DH.82A Tiger Moth (SK11A) as delivered in 1933, '6550' is in reality SE-AMG, ex-RAF, built by Morris Motors and registered in Sweden in 1988. *Lars Lundin*

DH.82 Tiger Moth SE-ADF was delivered new to Sweden in 1932 and immediately taken on charge by the Air Force as 5568. Registered SE-ATI in 1947, the aircraft was operated as a glider tug by the Royal Swedish Aero Club. Original registration SE-ADF was restored in June 1987. This aircraft is the world's oldest surviving Tiger Moth of any marque and is maintained in airworthy condition. *KSAK*

2,062 hours flight time logged in thirteen years. The very substantial remains were sold and the parts stored until 1997 when they were rediscovered by Mats Roth and transferred to the Aeronautical Engineering College at Vasteras for restoration to airworthy condition.

Fv568 (3113), survived two major accidents during her Air Force career, but was sold in an airworthy condition in February 1947 and registered SE-ATI to Hans Peterson at Orsa who occasionally operated her on a float chassis. In April 1949 the aircraft was acquired by the Royal Swedish Aero Club (KSAK) for glider tugging duties at the Central Gliding School, Alleberg, and remained operational in that capacity until 1985 when she underwent a major overhaul and restoration to her original Air Force configuration. By consent of the authorities the 1932 registration letters SE-ADF were reallocated in June 1987 and, painted in her wartime colours, panzergra (nearly black) and orange, the aircraft took up residence at the Alleberg Gliding Museum near Falkoping where she is maintained in airworthy condition.

In the mid 1930s it was customary for Sweden to build under licence most of the aircraft required for her own defence forces, a practice which enabled the Services to match airframes with appropriate engines of their own defined choice. Apart from the Tiger Moth and Raab Katzenstein, a single seater used for advanced training and fitted with a Walter Castor engine, all other operational aircraft were matched to Bristol Aeroplane Company engines built in Sweden by NOHAB at Trollhättan.

While de Havilland were experiencing an increase in demand for the Tiger Moth there was a selective willingness to permit local production and it was agreed that three additional DH.82s ordered by the Swedish military were to be built under licence by Aktiebolaget Svenska Jarnvagsverkstaderna (ASJA) at Linkoping. Allocated build numbers 38-40 and military serials Fv597-Fv599, the three aircraft were taken on charge on 15 March 1935.

First military Moth to be lost was Fv6562 (1727), the DH.60T Tiger Moth delivered after Hubert Broad's demonstrations in December 1931. The aircraft crashed on 16 April 1934 after 631 flying hours and was struck off charge on 10 July. Next to suffer was Fv5595 (3140), which crashed at Ugerupsfalter on 20 September 1934 and was struck off on 16 October with even less recorded time at 593 hours. By 6 September 1935, Fv5567 (3112), had accumulated 1,010 hours when she came to grief at Eket, and was judged to be a total loss on 4 October.

Although the military serial numbers remained unaltered (a four digit number in black was displayed alongside the fuselage insignia on the otherwise all silver scheme, except for national colours of blue and yellow worn as vertical rudder stripes, the M/32 system), after 1935 all the aircraft adopted and displayed code numbers indicating to which Air Corps each belonged. By far the most numerous was '5-' when the majority of Tiger Moths were employed for basic training duties at 5th Air Corps, Ljungbyhed, but in later life the survivors were scattered through other divisions, and allotments had reached '18-' by 1944. Colours changed to the high visibility red and yellow in 1935 (M/35); low visibility panzergra/armour grey and orange in 1940 (M/40), with dark green replacing the near black panzergra in 1944 (M/44).

With the introduction of the improved Tiger Moth airframe married to the Gipsy Major engine early in 1933 it was apparent that any further production at Linkoping would need to be to the DH.82A standard. Subsequently, an order for ten such aircraft was placed with ASJA with delivery scheduled for the summer of 1935, the first to be taken on charge only two months after the last Sk.11. The new aircraft were designated Sk.11A and build positions 41-50 were allocated with Air Force serial numbers Fv519, Fv520 and Fv511-Fv518.

ASJA designed a number of improvements to cater for all-year operation in a widely variable and generally harsh environment. Pickup points for a float chassis were included as standard and several aircraft were eventually operated in this configuration, including the Sk.11s imported from Stag Lane. Pilots were advised that should engine failure occur when operating float equipped aircraft over snow covered territory an enforced landing should be treated like any other marine touchdown and was likely to be much smoother and relatively uncomplicated, providing there were no obstacles. Brackets were also fitted to enable a pair of skis to be carried along each fuselage side, a most practical measure born from experience to help crews cope with landings, scheduled or otherwise, away from base.

The Sk.11A retained the simple rubber block in compression system for main undercarriage damping, rejecting the greater complication of the steel multi spring Dowty legs introduced with the British DH.82A, and spin strakes were not fitted either during manufacture or retrospectively. Navigation lights were not carried but an electrics panel accommodated on the re-designed instrument board controlled a pitot heater and variable throat venturi. Windscreens were redesigned to hold safety glass panels without the complications of brass channel edging.

It was not until the Royal Swedish Air Force was well into its third full season of winter operations with the Tiger Moth that complaints were fed back to Hatfield via Hugh Buckingham that, amongst other observations, instructors believed the cockpits were too small for comfortable operation in heavy protective clothing. Undeterred, in 1936 ASJA was contracted by the authorities to complete a second

Swedish-built Tiger Moth Sk.11A Fv.553 was retired from Air Force duties in 1952 and took up glider tugging at Alleberg as SE-BYL until 1960 when she was withdrawn and stored. Acquired by Peter Billing and painted in pre-war Swedish Air Force markings as 5-20 she flew again in 1988 and was sold early in 1997 to Kenneth Ohrn ('Eagle'). *Geoffrey Perrior*

batch of ten Sk.11As in parallel with the twelve Focke Wulf 44 Stieglitz which had been ordered in December, just as Hugh Buckingham had signalled as a real probability a year previously.

Ten Gipsy Major engines were ordered from Stag Lane by Aero Material between December 1936 and June 1937 to coincide with the second batch of Sk.11A, Nos Fv509-Fv510, Fv546-Fv550, Fv553 and Fv589-Fv590 (66-75)), delivered in January 1937 (5), February (2) and June (3). Meanwhile, the first Sk.11A taken on charge, Fv511 (43), had flown only seventy seven hours between 21 May 1935 and 10 January 1936, when she came to grief at Barkarby.

The arrival at Ljungbyhed of the Stieglitz, Sk.12 on the Air Force inventory and licence manufactured by Vasteras Centrala Flygverkstaden (CVV) at Vasteras in the same factory where most Tiger Moth overhauls and repairs were completed, released a number of the surviving Sk.11 and Sk.11As from training to other duties, and they were subsequently distributed amongst Air Corps' bases to be employed as communications aircraft and glider tugs.

de Havilland SK11a (DH.82A) Tiger Moth, 5-3, Swedish Air Force, 1935. Yellow overall with red trim. Codes in black, with '3' repeated on engine cowling. National markings in black and white in six positions. *Artwork ©Richard Caruana, 1:72 scale*

Originally a British registered glider tug based at Lasham, '5882' was sold to Sweden and from there to the USA in 1977. Painted in the high visibility colour scheme (M/35) adopted by the Royal Swedish Air Force for trainer aircraft before the Second World War, the aircraft is registered N85882 and is based in Florida. *Lars de Jounge*

Following in the wake of chivalry when a gentleman picked up a dropped handkerchief, one time Royal Swedish Air Force jet fighter pilot Par Cederqvist has demonstrated the gentle art many times flying Tiger Moth SE-CWG. Once part of the establishment of White Waltham's de Havilland Reserve School, the aircraft was sold to Sweden in 1963. *via Par Cederqvist*

Fv515 (47), remained in service until January 1952 when she was sold and registered SE-BYM. Operated by the Stockholm and Roslagen Aero Clubs, the aircraft was sold to SAAB in 1965, refurbished and repainted in the pre-war M/35 high visibility colour scheme, and in 1984 was put on permanent display in the Royal Swedish Air Force Museum at Malmslatt variously marked Fv.515, 5-15, 5-20 and F5-19.

Fv517 (49), was struck off charge in March 1948 with a total of 1,561 hours flown in thirteen years. The remains of the aircraft were discovered in poor condition in a boathouse near Stockholm by Mats Roth who also traced the wings of Fv599 (40), which had been operated by the Skovde Aero Club since sale to the KVAK in May 1958. Rebuilt and registered with personalised letters SE-AMR in 1986, '49' flew from Vasteras in September 1985 painted in the M/40 wartime scheme of panzergra and orange carrying code F1-72.

Sk.11A Fv553 (73), was retired from Air Force communications duties in November 1952 and together with Fv550 (72), was sold to the KSAK's Central Gliding School at Alleberg. Registered SE-BYL in May 1953 the aircraft was withdrawn from service in 1960, stored, and eventually sold to Peter Billing at Lidingo in 1983. The fuselage was sent to England in 1986 for restoration by Henry Labouchere at Langham and returned to Sweden where, painted in M/35 colours, the post restoration flight on locally rebuilt wings took place on 4 April 1988. Sold to Kenneth Ohrn the aircraft crashed on landing at Nisshyttan on 14 September 1997 and the wreck was moved to Vasteras for rebuilding.

In May 1938, a year after local production of the Sk.12 began, the Swedish Air Force advised de Havilland that it had no requirement for any further Tiger Moths and that licensed production at Linkoping would not be continued. By a strange coincidence notes and photographs covering Tiger Moth operations with the Swedish Air Force had only just been sent by de Havilland's Public Relations Department to Leonard Bridgman, respected staff member of *The Aeroplane* and Editor of *Janes*, to assist in compilation of an article on behalf of the American magazine *Popular Aviation*.

Following cancellation of the licence Aero Material received a request from KSAK for details of price and delivery for five Tiger Moths to be supplied from Hatfield for distribution amongst affiliated Clubs. The resultant offer was not pursued, almost certainly for reasons of delivery position rather than price. Ultimately, the Club was obliged to wait until 7 May 1942 when a Norwegian-built refugee Tiger Moth (164), was assigned to the Club as SE-ALK which crashed a year and two days later. Another Norwegian-built Tiger Moth (172), was posted in as SE-ALM in July 1942 and survived to become a permanent exhibit at the Alleberg Museum. The two aircraft had been authorised for transfer to the Swedish civil register during the war following contact with and agreement from the Norwegian Government which had set up in exile in England. The Club acquired additional Tiger Moths in 1947 (1), 1952 (2) and 1958 (2).

Above: Panzergra and Orange (M/40), the adopted wartime colours for Royal Swedish Air Force training aircraft, applied to SE-AMR, Swedish built SK.11A No 49, which served in the military between 1935 and 1948. *Steve Barnes*

Left: Wearing her wartime training colours the Swedish-built Sk.11A Tiger Moth SE-AMR, ex military Fv.517, was discovered in a boathouse near Stockholm during the late 1970s and rebuilt by Mats Roth at Vasteras. She was one of three Swedish registered Tiger Moths to visit the International Moth Rally at Woburn in August 1997. *Ian Oliver*

In 1953, the Norwegian Norsk Aero Club (NAK) bought Tiger Moth SE-AWO from Birger Nilsson at Falkoping, Sweden, a DH.82 (Sk.11) built in May 1935 by ASJA at Linkoping as works number 44. The aircraft had served with the 6th, 7th and 8th Air Corps but carrying serial Fv.512 had been retired from operations with the 5th Air Corps at Ljungbyhed on 23 May 1947 having reached 2,000 airframe hours. Registered to NAK as LN-TVB on 19 August 1953 and operated as a glider tug, the aircraft was sold to the Royal Norwegian Air Force in December 1955 and NAK was commissioned by the new owners to manage the aircraft on their behalf. The arrangement worked well until 14 June 1958 when, during a glider towing sortie at Jarlsberg, the aircraft ran out of fuel and was almost destroyed in the subsequent forced landing. The Air Force advertised the wreckage for sale on 16 October but emphasised the impossibility of restoring any part of the salvage to airworthy condition, after which she disappeared without trace.

In July 1938, ASJA test pilot Lennart Segerqvist paid a courtesy visit to Hatfield but there was to be no more Tiger Moth production from the erstwhile railway factory at Linkoping for him to fly. Sven Blomberg, the de Havilland agent with Aero Material, was appointed General Representative for Sweden, Norway and Denmark in 1946 and was closely involved with the introduction of DH.100 Vampires into the region in the early post-war years. He was also actively concerned with the inauguration of the Swedish National Aircraft Factory, Svenska Aeroplan AB (SAAB), which took over the facilities once employed as the Tiger Moth factory at Linkoping.

In a Swedish winter it is best to take the opportunity to fly when it stops snowing. At Skå Edeby airfield on New Year's Day 2006 Tiger Moth SE-AMI was flown for 30 minutes by Åke Kjellgren while Gunnar Elmgren and Lars Gustavsson hardly noticed the cold. *Jarl Sundgren*

Portugal

Through the efforts of the de Havilland agent in Portugal, Carlos Bleck, aided by the demonstration flying of Christopher Clarkson, the Portuguese Government selected the Tiger Moth as a replacement training aircraft for the Aeronáutica Militar Portuguesa in preference to the Avro 631 Cadet and Caproni Ca.100. They purchased a DH.60T Tiger Moth, G-ABPH (1732), and a DH.82, G-ABSK (1796), for evaluation purposes in December 1931 followed by DH.82As 3159-3169 and 3212-3221, ordered by the Ministry of War, Lisbon, and delivered from Hatfield without serial numbers applied, in 1933 and 1934. A further batch of eight aircraft, 3645-3652, was delivered at the beginning of 1938, consigned to Oficinas Gerais de Material Aeronáutico (OGMA), the government aircraft factory at Alverca.

During manufacture of the eight Portuguese Tiger Moths at Hatfield in December 1937 the factory was visited by a delegation of military officers from OGMA, led by Major Beja, whose brief was to study manufacturing facilities and requirements. The de Havilland Company had previously signed a licence agreement with OGMA and at the time of the visit to England home-based production had already begun.

Stag Lane was somewhat embarrassed to receive an order for twelve Gipsy Major engines in March 1938 as their production capacity was allocated for the next three months, but the Engine Division promised to endeavour to supply at the rate of four engines a month from June. In the event Stag Lane despatched seven engines in June and five in July.

A second batch of Tiger Moths was laid down at Alverca early in 1939 and an order was placed with Stag Lane for the supply of ten Gipsy Major engines, eight of which were delivered a month later. Production at OGMA continued until 1952 and eventually reached a total of ninety one aircraft which were allocated works' numbers P01-P91.

Most Tiger Moths were employed as basic trainers in the Military Aeronautical School at Sintra but a few were delivered as hacks to operational squadrons. Although the Portuguese military took on charge about 150 Tiger Moths in total it is estimated that never more than between thirty and fifty aircraft were ever in commission at one time and many of those built by OGMA were as replacements.

As a neutral country during the Second World War Portugal was at liberty to organise military supplies from whichever source it saw fit and in September 1943 the British Government supplied twenty new Tiger Moths from stock, eleven of which were delivered to Lisbon on board the SS *Empire Moonrise* on 7 October 1943 and nine by the SS *Empire Nightingale* on the same date. These were followed by a further order for ten, all of which were despatched from Liverpool on board the SS *City of Lancaster*, reaching Lisbon on 9 December 1944. These shipments were intended for the central training school of Aviação Naval (Portuguese Navy Aviation) at Aveiro. Not all the aircraft were put into immediate service and several were reported to have remained in their delivery crates for more than ten years and according to official records only twenty aircraft were issued with Navy serials, T-1 to T-20. It is known that during the Second World War the Portuguese Army Headquarters in Mozambique operated a fleet of Tiger Moths serialled 1-9 but their origin and eventual fate is unrecorded.

The DH.82 Tiger Moth displayed at the Museu do Ar at Alverca, and painted in 1934 military colours with serial '111' displayed on the sides of the engine cowlings, is based on parts of some of the first ten aircraft delivered from Hatfield and one other unidentified airframe is held in storage. A Tiger Moth marked '119' but also carrying the misapplied RAF serial 'LN928', was returned to flying condition on behalf of the Air Force Historic Flight in 2002. The aircraft was painted in colours carefully researched to represent a 1943 naval association but local historians confirm she was not the original NL928 (86371), as that aircraft would have been delivered in December 1944 with spin strakes, but rather an assemblage of donated parts. During a test flight from Sintra in December 2004 with

Marked as '111' when displayed in the Portuguese Air Force Museum at Alverca, this Tiger Moth was constructed from parts taken from some of the first ten aircraft delivered from Hatfield. *via Stuart Howe*

Painted to represent a Portuguese Tiger Moth with wartime naval associations, a composite aircraft was constructed for the Historic Flight at Sintra based on NL928 although the serial applied actually read LN928. During a test flight from Sintra in December 2004 the aircraft crashed probably when attempting a forced landing. *Luis Tavares*

Above and below: Delegates to the NATO 'Tiger Meet' hosted by Portugal at Beja Aerodrome in May 1996 were greeted by an aircraft wearing code '102' and other titling, restored to airworthiness for the Portuguese Air Force Historic Flight by the OGMA factory in February 1989. *Luis Tavares*

the base commander in the front seat, the aircraft crashed, probably during an attempted forced landing as the result of engine failure, killing the passenger and injuring the pilot.

In July 1952 the Força Aérea Portuguesa was created by amalgamation of the Aviação Naval and the Aeronáutica Militar and in 1955 the Tiger Moth was phased out in favour of the Chipmunk. Tiger Moths T-10 and T-11 did not appear within the new serial allocations. Many were sold cheaply or donated freely to flying clubs but the attrition rate was high and most blame was placed on the lack of experienced engineers. Between 1957 and 1961, thirty nine civil Tiger Moths were registered in Continental Portugal and nine in Mozambique of which sixteen quoted manufacturer's serial numbers allocated by OGMA, and four were identified as wartime imports from Great Britain. Twelve others were registered against numbers from a new series originated following major rebuilding or repair. One of these, DHTM.3A, believed to be P01, the first licence-built Tiger Moth, was registered CS-AEF to the Aero Club de Porto in 1957 but the registration was cancelled in 1970 when the aircraft appeared in the Portuguese Air Force Museum painted with serial '102'. Moved to storage at Sintra in 1978 and to the OGMA factory in February 1989, the Tiger Moth was restored to airworthy condition on behalf of the Portuguese Air Force Historic Flight. On 20 May 1996, '102' represented the host country at Beja Aerodrome during the regular NATO Forces' 'Tiger Meet', and carried an ungainly legend, triple banked in large capital letters along the length of the fuselage: 'Once a Tiger ... Always a Tiger!'

Tiger Moth G-AKUE was built by OGMA (P.68) and operated by the Portuguese Air Force in East Africa until 1961. She was sold to South Africa in 1969 and ten years later arrived in Great Britain with owner Roy Godwin. The aircraft was damaged in a take-off accident from a Welsh strip in 1989 and not returned to airworthiness until 2001. *via David Welch*

Portuguese built Tiger Moth P.12 was civilianised as CS-AFC in 1959 after service with the Air Force, and suffered a number of major mishaps before relegation to storage on behalf of the Museum at Alverca. *deHMC Archive*

CHAPTER TWELVE

Adventure in Canada

The proposal to establish a Canadian branch of the de Havilland Aircraft Company grew after a visit to Stag Lane in 1927 by Captain Roy Maxwell, acting on behalf of the Ontario Provincial Government. He was permitted to fly a conventional Cirrus powered DH.60 Moth and, acting upon his suggestion, the company made hurried arrangements with Short Bros at Rochester to fit a DH.60 with a float chassis and to fly trials from the river Medway. The subsequent purchase of four Cirrus Moths by the Ontario Provincial Government to be employed as fire spotters, and their immediate and popular acceptance, was reason enough for Business Director Francis St Barbe to travel to the Dominion that same year to investigate future prospects.

The result of St Barbe's visit was that in January 1928 Bob Loader arrived in Toronto, sent out from Stag Lane with a brief to set up the de Havilland Aircraft of Canada Ltd., a task which he quickly and efficiently achieved. By February a disused warehouse had been acquired at Mount Dennis to act as a reception and storage facility for dismantled DH.60 Moths which were already en route from London in their packing cases, accompanied by Arthur Robins

RCAF 8905, part of the middle third of the last batch of 350 DH.82C Tiger Moths delivered to the RCAF between March and September 1942. Production averaged fifty one aircraft per month throughout the run and had peaked at seventy five aircraft per month at the end of 1941. *deHMC Archive*

carrying the necessary lore and experience on a temporary posting from his duties in the Stag Lane erecting shop. By March the company was fully incorporated and a small aerodrome had been established at de Lesseps Field on part of the home estate of Frank Tretheway, an enthusiastic member of the Toronto Flying Club. A total of sixty two Moths had been processed and sold by the new company by the end of 1928, a level of business which warranted a change of premises and, in the spring of 1929, work began on the erection of buildings and preparation of an aerodrome site at Downsview which was ready to be occupied in September.

The company continued to flourish and booked sales of the DH.61 Giant Moth, considerately re-engined to accept a Pratt and Whitney Wasp radial, an engine well known, liked and respected in the region. Competition from other manufacturers was fierce which forced de Havilland into adapting their designs to cope more realistically with the Canadian environment, especially the winter conditions. In 1931 the company lost an order for twenty primary trainers required by the Royal Canadian Air Force to the Fleet Fawn, an aircraft of American origin assembled in Canada, and which in many respects St Barbe admitted was better than the DH.60M. When in 1936 the RCAF was still struggling to understand what a Gipsy Major powered Tiger Moth really was, they bought another ten Fawns and further increased their establishment after that. Sales prospects

169

The Royal Canadian Air Force was a good customer for the DH.60M Moth but its declaration that it would buy no more aircraft until the improvement of emergency escape procedures for the instructor had been addressed was the catalyst for radical reform of the configuration. *deHMC Archive*

of the DH.80 Puss Moth were also facing a severe challenge from Stinson who were offering a 215hp four seater equipped with electric starter, tailwheel and brakes for less than £1,000.

Drawing on his operational experience and an increasing exposure to competing designs the Director of the RCAF advised St Barbe during a second business visit in April and May 1931 (homeward bound to England at the end of his world tour) that following their 1929 order for thirty four DH.60Ms, to be used as primary trainers at Camp Borden, the Air Force would buy no further DH.60 Moths for training until and unless both emergency egress and the view from the front cockpit were improved. The message was clear and echoed those same precise sentiments being expressed at home. At Stag Lane the re-engineered DH.60T Tiger Moth emerged from its corner of the workshop only five months later with both issues largely resolved.

The 1931 Christmas letter distributed to shareholders in the Canadian Company and signed by the Chairman of the board, W R Parker, drew attention to their new model:

"The Tiger Moth is a new type of training machine which has been specially designed to meet the requirements of the Royal Canadian Air Force, and from the tests which have been completed, your Directors are satisfied that this should prove another successful type to be added to the Company's lines."

During his report to the Annual General Meeting of the de Havilland Aircraft of Canada Ltd., held on 8 January 1932, Bob Loader, introduced against his North American title as Company Vice President, praised the virtues of the Puss Moth and Bert Hinkler's flight to England, announced that Downsview was to become the Canadian centre for Bellanca aircraft production and refurbishment, and that three other manufacturers in Canada had chosen Gipsy engines. He ended his review by saying:

"We have recently demonstrated to the Dominion Government a new type of training aircraft known as the Tiger Moth, which we believe to be definitely superior to any other craft for similar duties in existence. This type has already been purchased in quantity by the RAF and the possibility of it being accepted as the standard training type is, I understand, exceedingly encouraging."

Canada's first Tiger Moth was one of the eight aircraft built to the DH.60T Tiger Moth specification: G-ABNI (1726). The British registration was cancelled in June 1931 and she was shipped to Toronto where she became CF-APL in September and known affectionately as *'Apple'*. Operated by the company as a demonstrator on both a wheeled undercarriage and floats, the aircraft was acquired by Leigh Capreol, the company test pilot, when he left Downsview in 1933 as part of an economy measure and set up a charter business on the Toronto waterfront partnered by Chuck and Jack Austin. Test piloting duties subsequently became the responsibility of the versatile Alan Lee Murray, an Australian by birth, who had arrived from England in 1933 to assume the post of General Manager in succession to Bob Loader who returned to promotional activities with the Business Office at Stag Lane.

The *'Apple'* subsequently passed to Walter Deisher, a private owner based in Ottawa before sale to the Toronto Flying Club and ultimate donation in 1942 to the Central Technical School in Toronto, where the airframe was eventually scrapped. It was hardly the 'exceedingly encouraging' start which Bob Loader and his chairman had anticipated at the end of 1931, and it was not until August 1935 that the Canadian company took delivery of another Tiger Moth from England, a fully developed DH.82A.

The first Tiger Moth delivered to Canada was a type DH.60T, G-ABNI, registered CF-APL in September 1931 and known to the workforce as *'Apple'*. Note the configuration of the open front cockpit door. *Bombardier Aerospace*

With DH.82A Tiger Moth RCAF 238 (ex CF-AVG) supplied from Hatfield and locally built RCAF 240 (C302) standing by, preparations are made at Downsview to launch DH.82A (Can) RCAF 239 (C301), on her maiden flight four days before Christmas, 1937. *Fred Hotson*

A view of a Canadianised DH.82A which highlights some of the features adopted to create the 'C' model: low chord steel interplane struts; lagged oil tank with new filler and drain necks; rudder cable shroud; new instrument panels and canopy with sliding mechanism. The blind flying curtain can just be seen folded down on the starboard side of the rear canopy. It was deployed by the pupil who pulled it up and over his head, the curtain running on two rails which followed the contours of the canopy frame. *Don Long*

Build No 3348 was a conventional model but with an extra fuel tank installed on the floor of the front cockpit and a plumbed system which permitted sustained inverted flight. Intended as a new demonstrator for the British company she had been built with a batch of aeroplanes scheduled for the Reserve Schools and modified for aerobatics at the approved higher gross weight of 1,770lb. The registration letters G-ADHA were allocated but never carried. In 1984 at a time when the British registration authorities were more generous and flexible in their attitude to vintage aircraft, the letters were re-allocated to a DH.83 Fox Moth imported into England from the USA. The aeroplane had been a direct export to New Zealand exactly fifty years previously and was in need of a 'period' registration. In Canada the national letters CF-AVG were issued to 3348 on 24 August 1935.

Having taken heed and 'winterised' the open cockpit DH.60 Moth, and generally adapted the type to the Canadian environment, there were more than several who were astonished to find that 3348 had been built to European standards and delivered with no apparent attempt to offer any form of winter protection. A sliding canopy was soon fitted which replaced both conventional windscreens and was found to be generally easier to install due to the revised geometry of the centre section. In this configuration CF-AVG was widely demonstrated by Lee Murray; included in his itinerary was the RCAF in Ottawa and at Camp Borden, and every flying club within a reasonable radius.

In the wake of his tour Lee Murray was officially advised that although the new aircraft met all the criteria laid down by the Air Force there was no budget to buy a single one and only four sales in total resulted from the exercise. The quartet was despatched from Hatfield in July 1936 less engines which were to be installed at Downsview together with sliding canopies, and each aircraft was subsequently registered to the Department of National Defence for operations by the flying clubs at Moose Jaw (3478/CF-CBR), Calgary (3481/CF-CBS), Hamilton (3479/CF-CBT) and Kingston (3480/CF-CBU). CF-CBR was donated to the Director of Youth Training in 1941 and CF-CBS went to Saskatoon Technical College in the same year, both re-classified as ground instructional airframes. CF-CBT was destroyed by a fire which originated in the engine compartment as the aircraft was being started at Hamilton on 16 April 1940. CF-CBU remained a civil registered aircraft throughout the war, transferring from Kingston to Toronto Flying Club in January 1941 and to the Department of Transport the following October. In May 1944 she was operating in Winnipeg and from 1946 in Arborg, Manitoba. Landing on snow at Elliott Lake on 20 February 1946 she overturned and was abandoned on site. CF-AVG continued in use for occasional demonstrations but spent more time as a company communications aeroplane in and around the Province.

In May 1936 after a three year commitment, Lee Murray returned to England to take up the position of General Manager at Hatfield. He was replaced in that same capacity at Downsview by Phillip Garratt, a Toronto-born man who had been studying medicine at the outbreak of the First World War when he elected to become a fighter pilot instead. Although he owned a chemical company, Phil Garratt had

de Havilland Canada completely redesigned the engine cowling, reducing the number of panels from five to three, providing engineers with almost unrestricted access to all parts of the engine and accessories. The idea was not copied across to production elsewhere. *Neil Davidson*

been recruited as an occasional test and demonstration pilot for de Havilland in Canada but showed such enthusiasm and determination that he had been invited to join the board of directors in 1935.

The new General Manager immediately campaigned to sell demonstrator CF-AVG to the Air Force at a price of $5,000, insisting that the aircraft had been respecified to meet their particular requirements and already had cost the company $6,000. Four months of correspondence finally resulted in recognition and appreciation by Ottawa that the new aircraft was fitted with the Gipsy Major engine, an improved version of the Gipsy III, an example of which they already held in reserve for a Puss Moth. To save money the Air Force suggested that they might fit their spare Gipsy III if the Tiger Moth airframe alone could be secured for a reasonable sum. Before the matter could be pursued Phil Garratt received a letter from the Director of Contracts dated 24 September 1936 in which he stated the concern held by some elements of the Air Force, who still believed they were faced with acquiring a single engine of a new design.

Phil Garratt was still convinced that the Tiger Moth should become a primary trainer with the RCAF which added more Fleet biplanes to its inventory early in 1937. His persuasive lobbying of Ottawa, discussion on design improvements and offer to build the aircraft in Toronto, resulted in the issue of specification C/11/36. A contract for the supply of twenty eight Tiger Moths was signed on 12 March 1937. The order itemised twenty seven brand new aircraft built to the basic British DH.82A design but re-engineered locally to conform to the issued specification, and to be known as type DH.82A(Can) Tiger Moth. Demonstrator CF-AVG was included in the contract as the twenty eighth aircraft, but first it was completely disassembled for every part to be drawn and used as working patterns.

Don Long was promoted Chief Designer and W E Ledingham was hired as his assistant only three days after the contract signature, to be joined on the programme by Peter Gooch on 3 May. CF-AVG was nominally accepted on behalf of the Air Force and immediately returned to Downsview for remodelling. To provide essential assistance a complete set of working drawings was received from Hatfield on 14 May.

Under Don Long's experienced eye the Drawing Office called up its considerable knowledge gained as the result of Moth operations throughout the Dominion during the previous ten years. Unlike some customers who required multi-role Moths the RCAF expected their Tiger Moths to be used only as primary trainers but on wheeled or ski equipped undercarriages and in variable climatic conditions. The main changes which led the transition from DH.82A to DH.82A(Can) were listed by the Chief Designer:

> "Wide plywood walkways located on lower wings adjacent to each side of the fuselage, finished with a granulated cork non slip surface.
> Plywood leading edges on the upper surfaces of both lower mainplanes.
> Re-inforced hand holds at the tip bow position on both lower mainplanes.
> Mass balanced ailerons.
> Streamline section steel interplane struts replacing the wider chord wooden struts.
> A covering of 2in thick Dunlopillo foam rubber over the instrument panel faces to act as crashpads in preference to a headroll.
> A new canopy, similar to that fitted locally to the imported DH.82A Tiger Moths, but with an aluminium frame rather than steel tubing, ball bearing track rollers and a transparent fairing built into the rear-most of the three sections. That section deployed over the rear seat included provision for a blind flying curtain."

DH.82A(Can) Tiger Moth No C327, registered CF-BNF in September 1940, was the flying test bed for the Menasco D-4 Pirate. Re-engined with a Gipsy Major, she became Phil Garratt's personal transport. In 1971 the aircraft was rebuilt by Watt Martin to open cockpit configuration. *Watt Martin*

As a complete unit fitted to the aircraft, the canopy employed 838 individual parts in its manufacture. With the canopy slipped to what would be its normal rearmost position on the ground it was not possible to provide an external door to the luggage locker and provision for access was made through the headrest in the rear cockpit.

> "A cockpit heating system fed from a muff on the long exhaust tailpipe.
> A differential action built into the elevator spring trimming system to improve feel.
> Fire extinguisher, watch holder and document pouch all provided against standard RCAF specification.
> Engine cowling to be constructed in three pieces only rather than five, a nose bowl and the remainder opening from a central hinge line running fore and aft along the top cowling, permitting instant access to left, right and underside of the engine.
> Enlarged filler necks with quick action caps on fuel and oil tanks and with an enlarged drain on the oil tank to be fitted with quilted lagging for winter protection, easily removed for more temperate conditions.
> Fuel tank vent and bonding tabs to standard RCAF specification.
> Installation of a Borden Safety Harness, also designed to RCAF specification, comprising two shoulder harness straps attached to a transverse cable, but joining at the crutch position from where a single strap was attached to another transverse cable at floor level.
> Heavy duty main undercarriage axles to cope with conversion for operations on skis."

The new Tiger Moth line was identified with build numbers C301-C330 to accommodate thirty airframes. CF-AVG (British built No 3348) was allocated RCAF serial 238; C301-C320 became RCAF 239-258 and C322-C326, RCAF 275-279. Positions C321, C327 and C329 were built as civil aircraft, CF-CFJ, CF-BNF and CF-BNC respectively. C328 and C330 were never completed as whole aeroplanes and may have been sacrificed as test specimens.

At lunchtime on 21 December 1937, a miserably cold day and with the aerodrome covered in snow, Phil Garratt test flew RCAF 239, (C301), operating from the rear seat and dressed unobtrusively in his city overcoat and trilby hat. From contract to first flight the programme had consumed less than ten months, and 239 was delivered to the RCAF at Trenton, at that time Canada's newest and biggest flying base, on 18 January 1938. The remainder of the order followed as agreed and was complete by 12 April.

In her new guise as RCAF 238, Hatfield's No 3348 was taken on military charge on 28 February 1938 but by June 1939 had been civil registered CF-CGZ on behalf of the Department of National Defence. Until May 1941, when she re-mustered into the Air Force, the Tiger Moth was operated for approximately six months each by the Aero Club of British Columbia, Edmonton and Northern Alberta Aero Club, and Moose Jaw Flying Club. In February 1944 she was finally struck off the inventory having been reduced to spare parts at No 6 Repair Depot, Trenton.

CF-CFJ (C321), was fitted with a Gipsy III engine and delivered to the Kitchener-Waterloo Flying Club in February 1938 on behalf of the Department of Transport. Transferred to the Toronto Flying Club in December 1940, ownership passed through several Ontario based organisations until November 1946 when the registration was cancelled as 'lapsed'.

CF-BNC (C329), was registered to the manufacturer in October 1939 and delivered to their flight hangar at Downsview on 7 May 1940. In June the aircraft was sold to the Hamilton Flying Club where she remained until 1951. Last registered to a private owner in Toronto, the C of A lapsed in June 1955 and the allocation was finally cancelled two years later.

At lunchtime on 21 December 1937 General Manager Phil Garratt completed the first flight of the prototype DH.82A(Can) bearing RCAF serial 239. *Fred Hotson*

The third production DH.82A(Can) Tiger Moth, RCAF 241 (C303), was quickly introduced to the flight test programme, taking advantage of the seasonal conditions to explore the type's performance with a ski undercarriage. *Don Long*

A team of ladies active during the taping of a port upper wing. The hinge brackets for the leading edge slats are clearly visible. *Bombardier Aerospace*

Having established a production base Phil Garratt was keen to ensure that the Air Force purchased more Tiger Moths in preference to any other type, especially as Ottawa had declared early in 1938 that following delivery of the first order, no more RCAF DH.60 Moth aircraft would be overhauled or rebuilt, neither would Gipsy I or Gipsy II engines be reconditioned once they had become time expired. The creation of a workshop at Downsview which was accepting Gipsy Major engines supplied in kit form from Stag Lane had ensured that the engine situation was well catered for. Nine sets of Gipsy Major components had been despatched from England in July 1937 followed by six more in August.

A general review of the situation surrounding Canadian-built Tiger Moths appeared in the February 1938 edition of *the de Havilland Gazette:*

"Without sacrificing the essential characteristics of the Tiger Moth as a trainer of up-to-date orthodoxy, several interesting detail modifications have been introduced to suit Canadian conditions. The aircraft have interchangeable wheel, ski or float chassis and must operate as efficiently and conveniently in the severest cold of winter as in the heat of summer.

A sliding transparent coupe top affords cabin protection without restricting vision or ease of exit, and incorporates a blind flying hood of instant actuation. The instrument panels cater for all primary and blind flying instruction and are covered with moulded rubber pads for protection in the event of minor accident. The special RCAF fighting harness is fitted in both cockpits. Trim has to cover all conditions of summer and winter operations and a differential spring loading on the elevator control affords a comfortable longitudinal trim, thumb operated ratchet levers being provided in both cockpits for trimming the tail.

The ventilation system supplies heated air to the cockpits in winter or cool air in summer, and another special winter provision consists of quickly attachable masks and covers to reduce the amount of engine cooling and oil tank cooling.

For convenient maintenance, particularly in seaplane use, a three piece engine cowling similar to that used on the Dragonfly has been adopted. The tanks have quick acting bayonet filler caps and there is a special cap to expedite oil draining in winter. A pressure type fire extinguisher in the engine bay may be operated from either cockpit or from outside the aircraft at a point convenient to the person cranking the engine.

Once the new facilities at Downsview were available and space was plentiful, each of the aircraft of the March 1937 contract could be rigged in situ. One of the three civil aircraft called up and allocated a late production slot, CF-BNF (C327), is on the left of the picture ahead of the fleet. *Bombardier Aerospace*

"The contract for the new Tiger Moths was secured in March last, and since then all the jigs and tools have been built and the entire aircraft have been constructed there, the only imported items being standard parts such as bolts, instruments and wheels. The Gipsy Major I engines have been assembled and tested in Toronto.

The staff has lately been increased, two new hangars have enlarged the factory, and new plant including sheet metal formers and machines, has been installed, while the older welding and finishing shops, stores, airframe and engine assembly departments have been much augmented."

With no immediate sign of a further order from the Canadian Government and Hatfield under pressure from the Air Ministry to supply Tiger Moths at an increased rate, Phil Garratt's suggestion that his under utilised works might assist the process was welcomed in England, subject to certain conditions. The result was that 200 Tiger Moth fuselages were built at Downsview and shipped to Hatfield between the autumn of 1938 and mid summer 1939 which helped to maintain the workforce until the substantial new orders began to flow early in 1940.

For a country that was supplying a high proportion of the sitka spruce timber that was being fashioned into wooden aeroplane components the reasoning behind the choice of steel interplane struts for the Canadian-built Tiger Moth has often been queried. There is nearly always a simple answer, provided in this case by de Havilland Canada historian Fred Hotson:

"I was the one who built the jigs for the struts and ran off the first sets. The final decision to change from wood to steel was made by Engineering and as I was doing the centre section struts anyway I felt it more economical at the time and it was quite a simple procedure.

We manufactured quite a few hand-made wooden struts before that for Moth overhauls etc., but the move to metal had a lot to do with our shop capabilities at the time. The wood-shop was upgrading to making spars and had all they could handle. In the metal shop we were more flexible and soon had some very fine welders on staff."

Perhaps it was a lack of awareness that their new trainer was equipped with a canopy that led an unknown RCAF hand to pen an ode to the biplane:

It's a practical craft, a biplane,
Its beauty is not all that you gain,
The upper wing's gift
Is additional lift,
Besides which
It keeps out the rain.

Having got production of the Canadianised DH.82A under way as the DH.82A (Can), the Downsview Drawing Office sought to add even more refinements. A significant improvement was provided by the installation of cable operated Bendix mainwheel brakes, a system identical to that employed on the Puss Moth, and a fully castoring tailwheel with pneumatic tyre. The brake was activated by a hand lever fitted in both cockpits and mechanically modulated by the rudder pedals for steering on the ground. The undercarriage radius rods were shortened to permit revision of the angle of the compression legs, sweeping them forward, guarding against any tendency for the aircraft to lift her tail when brakes were applied. The decking between the cockpits was reduced in radius and height, a change which, when combined with smaller instrument panels enabled direct forward vision from the rear seat. A revised suite of instruments, sourced from the USA and of reduced diameter, were recessed into the foam rubber covered panels and their layout was completely changed.

This shot into the front cockpit of a DH.82C illustrates how a new instrument array was embedded into a foam rubber facia which acted as a crash pad. The contour of the middle decking was revised to allow the pilot in the rear seat a better forward view when the canopy was closed. *via Blake Reid*

Two open cockpit and camouflaged Tiger Moths flying together in Canada. The aircraft nearer the camera is a DH.82A with a tailwheel. The further aircraft is identified as a DH.82C by virtue of her forward raked main undercarriage and thinner chord steel interplane struts. *via Jerry Fotheringham*

The tail wheel assembly of the 'C' model was constructed along identical lines to the basic skid. Steering on the ground was assisted by a pair of ears bolted through the reinforced lower front member of the rudder. *deHMC Archive*

A view of a Menasco engine installed in a DH.82C airframe. The most obvious difference is the propeller which is clearly designed for right hand rotation.
via Blake Reid

The apparent difficulties experienced with the elevator trimmer fitted to the DH.82B at Hatfield in 1939 clearly did not deter Don Long and his design team and a tab was set into the trailing edge of both elevators to which mass balances were introduced, indeed there is likely to have been an interchange of information. The trimmer was capable of precision setting by finger tip control of a small lever which could be exercised in either cockpit.

Before delivery to Hamilton Flying Club in June 1940, Tiger Moth CF-BNC (C329), had been used by de Havilland as a test vehicle for both brakes and trimmer but the first serious brake trials were credited to the third of the civilian DH.82A(Can) aircraft, C327, which was first flown as an unregistered test aircraft by Phil Garratt on 9 December 1938 and as CF-BNF was to continue in service for some time as an important company trials machine.

The improvements to the DH.82A(Can) were exploited by the installation of the upgraded engine developed at Canada's request, the Gipsy Major IC, rated at 140hp for take-off as compared with 122hp for the basic Gipsy Major I, and to which the Air Force insisted on fitting a pressure system fire extinguisher. Another user specified requirement was for battery powered navigation and signalling lamps and modifications to the canopy which would permit it to be jettisoned. Although de Havilland argued that the canopy rolled back very satisfactorily to allow either occupant freedom to step over the side, the modification programme was insisted upon and proved to be extremely awkward and frustrating to satisfy.

Following the delivery of the last DH.82A (Can) on 12 April 1939 and completion of the sub-contracted fuselages for England, the factory closed down the Tiger Moth line having still not received the 100 aeroplane order for which engines had already been delivered in anticipation. Downsview accepted an unexpected contract from the Air Force to refurbish twelve DH.60 Moths which were afterwards to be supplied to civilian flying clubs as part of a government sponsored training scheme. The job allowed the entire workforce to be maintained without layoff and as the last overhauled DH.60 was delivered in August the Dominion found itself only days short of involvement in a world war.

The British Commonwealth Air Training Plan was announced on 10 December 1939 and in February 1940 the de Havilland Aircraft of Canada Ltd. received a government order to supply 404 Tiger Moths embodying all the modifications and improvements which had been authorised under specification AP/3/39. The number of aircraft exactly equalled an order recently placed with Fleet for their Canadian-built Finch trainer. The new type designation was to be DH.82C Tiger Moth, 'C' for Canada, and owing no allegiance whatever to the system of identification which had been established elsewhere. The first aircraft built to the specification, RCAF 4001, (C331), was erected almost immediately, flown by Bruce Douglas on 12 March and handed over to the RCAF on 10 April 1940.

Until the submarine menace in the North Atlantic had been largely addressed, the shipping of materials and supplies in easterly or westerly directions was hazardous, and the Canadian company quickly realised how dangerous their situation could become should they find themselves isolated from their sole source of engine supply. Propellers were the least problem, supplied from Laidlaw in Toronto and 'S and S' in Winnipeg. On mainland North America they sought and found an alternative powerplant: the D-4 Pirate engine designed and built by the Menasco Manufacturing Company of Los Angeles, California.

During the 1930s de Havilland engines were in daily use all over the world, supported by a thriving airframe industry and first rate publicity machine. Overseen by Frank Halford's enthusiastic and capable design team and the boundless energies of the Business Director, output was substantial and profitable. Now the Canadian company's concern was that an interruption of the supply line, for whatever reason, could result in a factory full of engineless airframes.

In England in 1936, Phillips and Powis, Reading-based manufacturers of Miles aircraft designs, realised that as far as their powerplant requirements were concerned de Havilland held a virtual monopoly and could vary speed of supply, price and development potential at will. The success of the Miles Hawk (and Percival Gull) range of touring and racing aeroplanes had boosted the image of the Gipsy engine whilst simultaneously posing a threat to the airframe designs of de Havilland's own business which some commentators were beginning to believe were looking rather dated.

At Woodley Aerodrome the Miles design team was looking for improved engine performance which they believed, wrongly, was not a priority at Stag Lane, and in seeking greater independence approached Menasco in California with a view not only to using their engines, but to building the range under licence in England. Examples of 'B' and 'C' series engines were delivered to Woodley during the year and plans were agreed to import American manufacturing jigs and tools. Al Menasco, Chairman of his company, visited the Phillips and Powis factory on at least two occasions in 1936, accompanied by a C-4 Pirate engine on the first visit. In July 1937, with licences signed, contracts placed with suppliers and construction of an engine test rig all but complete, Charles Powis suddenly resigned from his board following a dispute over policy and the Menasco company was advised shortly after that the project was to be terminated. Phillips and Powis continued to work on their Hawk Trainer, soon to be built in hundreds for the RAF as the Gipsy Major powered Magister, and early in 1938 Al Menasco too resigned from office in Los Angeles and enlisted in the United States Army Air Force.

There was some irony in the contact now made between a company bearing the de Havilland name and an engine supplier who might have caused commercial embarrassment in England. On offer to Phil Garratt in 1940 was an engine from the Menasco D series, the -4 Pirate, physically similar and with a performance almost identical to the Gipsy Major IC. The D-4 Pirate was rated at 130 hp on take-off: 10hp and 100rpm less than the Gipsy Major IC and complete with all accessories was heavier by about 50lb. Distinguished by a crankcase of stove enamelled dark blue, both air and ground crew needed to be aware that the propeller rotation was American industry standard, turning in the opposite sense from the Gipsy Major which rotated in an anti-clockwise direction (Left Hand Tractor) when viewed from the cockpit. The first Menasco installation (of a C4 model) was made in Downsview's development aircraft CF-BNF (C327), and test flying by Bruce Douglas began on 30 June 1940.

Shortly before flying the Menasco powered Tiger Moth Bruce Douglas flew trials with the single blade Everel propeller designed by Walter W Everal of Lancaster, Pennsylvania. The propeller had been fitted to a Taylor Cub in 1937 and flown on a 3,000 mile test. "The Everel single blade propeller is a statically and dynamically balanced unit, the blade being balanced by a suitable counterweight. The line passing through the centre of gravity of the blade and centre of gravity of the counterweight passes through the centre of rotation." The propeller was of the automatic variable pitch type, changing pitch with the increase in rpm, seeking its own optimum pitch for climb and cruise, and was claimed to be of much greater efficiency than the orthodox two blade propeller.

At the time of the trials Fred Hotson was in charge of aerodrome services at Downsview and fitted the Everel blade to the aircraft which he says "sure looked funny!"

> "Swinging it was hard work, flipping it over from the front, switches off, mostly two compressions until the blade was in the swinging position. Then it was 'switches on', swinging from behind, again and again, until the engine caught. The sound on take-off was quite different from the regular propeller."

Bruce Douglas found the Everel propeller offered no advantage in performance and neither did the Toronto Flying Club when similar trials were undertaken on a DH.60M Moth immediately after. Although flight tests were conducted on a number of different airframe and engine types and on a Piper Cub in England, there was some interest but the scheme was never generally accepted.

Deliveries of the 404 DH.82Cs ordered in February 1940, some fitted with Gipsy Major IC engines provided by the British Ministry of Aircraft Production, began on 10 April 1940 (RCAF 4001-4404, C331-C734), and all had been placed on charge by 12 March 1941 at which time further contracts were already under discussion.

Ten aircraft with Menasco Pirate engines ordered for delivery between 15 May and 11 June 1941 were redesignated DH.82C2 by de Havilland and Menasco Moth by the Air Force (RCAF 4935-4944, C735-C744). The continuing supply of engines from Stag Lane promoted orders for another 428 DH.82C specification aircraft (RCAF 4946-5175, C745-C974; RCAF 5800-5824, C975-C999, and RCAF 5825-5999, C1128-C1302), which were delivered progressively from April to December 1941. These followed a second batch of Menasco Moths which had entered service as wireless trainers in the first half of 1941 (RCAF 4810-4812, 4830-4934 and 4945, C1000-C1127), excepting airframes C1125 and C1126 which were not completed and may have been siphoned off for test purposes or donated to effect major structural repairs elsewhere.

When DH.82A Tiger Moth No 3348 was delivered to Canada in 1935 the aircraft was equipped with Handley Page slots and it was agreed that these devices should be fitted to the first batch of DH.82A (Can) Tiger Moths and subsequently to the 404 DH.82C aircraft ordered by the RCAF in February 1940. Equally, it was agreed that the second batch of 428 aircraft ordered for delivery from April 1941 would not be fitted with slots and that those already supplied would have them removed. None of the aircraft eventually offered for sale as war surplus appear to have retained them.

DH.82C Tiger Moth 4398 built in about February 1941 showing the two sliding portions of the canopy at the back end of the guide rails. Imagine flying the aeroplane with the canopy hard against the fin. *via Murray Peden*

This batch of DH.82C Tiger Moths under construction at Downsview was taken onto RCAF charge from late in 1941. 5935 was transported by surface to the Reserve Depot at Calgary, erected and air delivered to 33 EFTS Caron on 6 January 1942. *Bert Davis*

DH.82C4 Menasco Moth 4861, built as a wireless trainer and powered by the Menasco D-4 Pirate engine, a type chosen as insurance against potential losses of imported British built Gipsy Major engines. A tell-tale sign of a Menasco engine under the cowling was the obvious right hand rotation of the propeller. *Gerald F Schwam*

The wireless trainers were designated DH.82C4 (Menasco Moth II) and appeared ideally suited to their task on account of the engine driven generator system. The rear cockpit was stripped of its instrument panel, crash protection and inter-cockpit decking, and received instead a complement of obsolescent wireless equipment shipped from Great Britain, complete with wind-up trailing aerials. For their specified task the aircraft were overloaded and under powered and, although they served with the four wireless schools at St. Hubert, Guelph, Winnipeg and Calgary, all were replaced as soon as practicable and converted back to standard Menasco Moth trainers. In order to salvage some credibility, a Gipsy Major IC Wireless Trainer designated DH.82C3 had been proposed but never progressed beyond initial planning.

The Menasco development aircraft CF-BNF (C327), was registered to Leavens Brothers Air Services of Toronto on 7 September 1940, a company chosen by Ottawa to operate a major repair and service centre for the Tiger Moth. Leavens Brothers converted CF-BNF back to Gipsy Major power and in September 1941 she was re-registered to the de Havilland Aircraft of Canada Ltd. at Postal Station L, Toronto, where she became the personal transport of General Manager Phil Garratt. Sold in January 1948, the sixth owner from 18 January 1957, but for only six months, was again Leavens Bros. of Toronto. Sold twice more, to owners in Hamilton and Exeter, the aircraft was acquired by Frank Ball of St. Mary's, Ontario in November 1962 who preserved her in airworthy condition in the open cockpit configuration of an original and unique DH.82A(Can). After more than thirty five years of ownership the aircraft was sold to Dr John Burson in Carrollton, Georgia, USA, and registered N6387T to him in 1999, later N82CQ. In May 2005 the aircraft suffered engine failure on take-off from Gum Creek, hit a power line and crashed back on the airfield. A year later she was sold to Harry Schoning at Palm Desert, California and rebuilt in a canopied DH.82C configuration. Painted yellow and black and carrying her original Canadian letters, the aircraft was offered for sale in 2012.

Menasco Moths in service at the flying training schools were generally not popular due to their comparatively poor performance and flight characteristics which differed from the more numerous DH.82C as a result of the opposite rotation of the engine. Following the second contracted batch no further Menasco Moths were ordered and the next 200 aircraft, manufactured under the Mutual Aid programme on behalf of the United States Government, were all specified to receive the Gipsy Major IC. These 200 aircraft were scheduled for operations by the United States Army Air Force, although exactly where is not clear. For induction into the American military, the DH.82C became the Pursuit Trainer type PT-24 and, anticipating full integration, the Air Service Command at Wright Field published a preliminary manual: 'Operation and Maintenance Instructions, Model PT-24 Airplane' dated 10 February 1942. The designated aircraft (C1303-C1502) were allocated USAAF serial numbers 42-964 to 42-1163 and each manufacturer's plate affixed to the fuselage carried the concise individual details including a date of clearance for test.

The complexity of economic agreements cast in wartime and tied firmly to political decisions concocted far away from aeroplane factories and flying training schools meant that the PT-24s were never to wear Uncle Sam's colours. Before delivery the whole consignment was donated to the Air Training Plan, which might have been the intention all along, and were allocated RAF serial numbers FE100-FE266 and FH618-FH650, running consecutively. In turn the RAF reconsigned the fleet as an integral part of the Air Training Plan and in the field the aircraft wore the standard yellow and black trainer colours of the RCAF with serials 1100-1299 stencilled on their sides. Deliveries began on Christmas Eve 1941 and the last aircraft, C1502/42-1163/FH650/1299, was signed off from Downsview on 23 March 1942 and delivered on 8 April.

A further 350 DH.82C Tiger Moths were delivered to the RCAF commencing on 3 March 1942 and ending with the last on 9 September: RCAF 3842-3991 (C1503-C1652), RCAF 8851-8999 (C1653-C1801), and RCAF 9645-9695 (C1802-C1825 plus C1827-C1853). Airframe C1826 was not completed and may have been extracted from the line and grafted onto a damaged aircraft as part of a major repair.

From April 1940 until September 1942 the factory at Downsview maintained an average output of fifty one Tiger Moths per month, reaching a peak of seventy five complete aircraft per month at the end of 1941. With Tiger Moth production likely to be in decline from that heady time a contract first for the assembly of imported Avro Anson aircraft previously used by the RAF in Great Britain, then gradual introduction to complete manufacture of new Ansons, a standard twin trainer for the Air Training Plan, had been accepted. By 1943 the Mosquito was soaking up huge productive effort, aided and abetted by Fred Plumb and Douglas Hunter, part of the team who had nurtured the first Tiger Moth at Stag Lane twelve years previously. Downsview built 1,549 Tiger Moth airframes in addition to the kits sent to Hatfield. Phil Garratt and his team could feel completely satisfied that their early and persistent lobbying had paid off.

DH.82C Tiger Moth CF-BNF was employed by the manufacturer for trials purposes and was flown with a Menasco engine and in open cockpit configuration. The aircraft has been restored to her original specification by Harry Schoning at Palm Desert in California. *Harry Schoning*

The United States Government ordered 200 DH.82C Tiger Moths under the Mutual Aid Program in 1942. Designated PT-24 the aircraft were allocated USAAF serial numbers but all were re-assigned to the RAF and in turn and before delivery, to the RCAF in whose markings they were absorbed into the training system in Canada. *Bert Davis*

From within the last batch of twenty DH.82C Tiger Moths built at Downsview in August 1942, 9680 (C1838), fitted with a conventional undercarriage, cruises over a snowscape stretching as far as the eye can see. Note the bird attacking the engine cowling. *via Watt Martin*

CHAPTER THIRTEEN

Industry for the Antipodes

The Australian branch of the de Havilland Aircraft Company, the de Havilland Aircraft Pty. Ltd., was incorporated in Victoria on 7 March 1927 following a visit to the country by Major Hereward de Havilland the previous year. Stag Lane had decided that in order to improve and promote exports it was imperative to offer a good local after-sales service and the Australian Dominion was considered to be rich in prospects.

The business was established in a rat infested warehouse in South Melbourne and prospered until the recessionary times beginning in 1929, after which sales gradually declined and a number of customers, especially outback farmers hit by the poor state of the economy and exacerbated by drought conditions, approached the company in the hope of selling back their aircraft.

The heightened aviation activity observed in New South Wales, in and around Sydney, tempted the company to relocate and purpose-built premises were erected at Mascot Aerodrome. New machine tools were installed, the investment reckoned to offset the cost of transporting every manufactured part from England but, more importantly, establishing a local skills base which was considered

Tiger Moths off production at Mascot awaiting flight test and allocation, mid-1940. The man who painted the company name on the hangar facade needed a good measuring stick and a steady nerve. *RAAF Museum*

essential for future development. Metal fittings and wooden wings were produced immediately after the new factory was opened in February 1931 but the complexity of jigging for welded steel tube structures encouraged the continuing import of fuselages from the parent company, for the time being.

During his world tour of de Havilland outposts in 1931 Francis St Barbe had met Major Alan Murray Jones at the Australian Directorate of Civil Aviation. The two men had established an immediate rapport and Murray Jones was soon offered the post of Managing Director of the Sydney based company, a move which released Hereward de Havilland to return to England where he became a development pilot and production trouble shooter at Hatfield. Murray Jones was to prove a competent production test pilot and capable administrator.

The Mascot works was soon busy not only with sales, servicing and assembly of DH.60 Moths but was also in receipt from England of DH.83 Fox Moths, DH.84 Dragons and DH.86s, commercial transport aircraft which assisted in bridging the gap in the private owner market left by the lingering effects of the depression.

Some of the Australian aero clubs recognised the advantages of the new Tiger Moth but were not prolific customers for the type even after British export authority had been approved. The first aircraft received, VH-UTD (3320), was not registered until May 1935, sold

Australia's first civil registered DH.82A Tiger Moth, VH-UTD *Halcyon,* imported by the Newcastle Aero Club in 1935, photographed at Broken Hill in 1938. *via Neville Parnell*

to the Newcastle Aero Club, a major flying training organisation still today closely associated with the type. The aircraft was named *Halcyon* during a ceremony at District Park Aerodrome attended by 2,000 people on 3 June. Would the crowd have believed that the 1,000th Tiger Moth to be assembled in Australia would roll out of the factory at Mascot only seven years later? A17-565 was a gifted aeroplane, purchased for £1,200 by the good folk of Kuringai, NSW, and the centre-piece of a ceremony in which she was handed over to the RAAF by Lady Zara Gowrie, wife of the Governor General.

Two more Tiger Moths VH-UVZ (3508,) and VH-UXC (3515), were received late in 1936 respectively for Airflite Ltd., a training organisation based at Mascot, and the Whyalla Aero Club situated in South Australia. The Royal Aero Club of New South Wales received VH-UYJ, VH-UYK and VH-UYL (3593, 3598 and 3600), in August and September 1937, which were followed by a pair for the Royal Victorian Aero Club at Essendon, VH-UYP (3622), and VH-UYR (3621), in November. Two Tiger Moths marked VH-UYO and VH-UYP were photographed for a Melbourne newspaper flying in close harmony over the mouth of the Yarra river a few days later at which time it was noticed that the letters VH-UYO, prominently displayed near the camera, had been allocated to a DH.87B Hornet Moth five months previously. The Tiger Moth should have been masked for painting as VH-UYR, a situation that was quickly remedied. Another for Newcastle, VH-UYQ (3623), was also delivered in November and seven further Tiger Moths were imported from Hatfield, erratically spread through 1938, before the persistence of Murray Jones was rewarded with receipt of the first major government order.

In common with the economic juggling practised by many governments pre-war, the aero clubs were considered to be useful in that most could provide cheap rate basic flying training and a financial inducement sponsored at official level could dictate their choice of equipment. Australia was no exception and early in 1940 many clubs and schools operating mostly DH.60 Moths, and the handful of Tiger Moths, were formally contracted to provide elementary training to RAAF pilot recruits. Due to difficulties with the administration of payments, not to mention RAAF dissatisfaction with the quality of some instruction, the arrangement was cancelled the following April and by August all the aircraft had been impressed and absorbed into the rapidly expanding network of the RAAF's own Elementary Flying Training Schools (EFTS).

As a logical progression from its still strong association with the DH.60 Moth, of which seventy four had been delivered to the Air Force between 1926 and 1936, and a further forty eight civil aircraft impressed into service in 1940, de Havilland Australia lobbied hard to interest the RAAF in standardising on a new basic trainer by purchasing versatile DH.82A Tiger Moths. In spite of their efforts the Avro 643 Cadet was chosen instead after an evaluation which had included the Tiger Moth, a type rejected on the grounds that at £1,000

The 'new' VH-UTD is the former A17-322 which was sold by the RAAF in 1946 and which spent some time as a crop sprayer until she was withdrawn in 1965. A number of hands were involved in rebuilding from 1988 but a serious programme was not started until 2007 by Ray Windred and Brian Zeederberg at Luskintyre where she completed her post-restoration flight in April 2009. *Brian Zeederberg*

Much publicity surrounded the roll-out of the 1,000th Tiger Moth assembled by de Havilland at Mascot, not to be confused with the 1,000th aircraft manufactured on site which appears not to have been recognised at all. A17-565 was finished in a foliage green and earth brown camouflage scheme with yellow undersides and broad band around the rear fuselage. *via Richard Dent*

each less engine, plus a 5% commission demanded by the business office at Mascot, it was too expensive. Moreover, its performance was inferior and delivery quoted at twenty weeks was almost twice as long. The de Havilland Company had also made it clear that they would not entertain the thought of building the Tiger Moth in Australia until a minimum of thirty six aircraft had been imported from Great Britain. Paradoxically, a total of thirty four Avro Cadets was delivered between 1935 and 1939 but the order for an additional twenty aircraft was cancelled and the negotiated licence to build the type in Australia was never taken up.

Two major de Havilland presentations had been parried before 21 November 1938 on which date the Australian Air Board at last placed an order (A37202), for twenty Tiger Moths, its first for an 'Australian-built' aeroplane of any type, at a total cost of £33,660. The deal allowed for fuselages to be imported from England and these were despatched from Hatfield in January 1939 (6); February (6) and March (8). Wings and empennage were to be built at Mascot where Gipsy Major Series II engines manufactured at Stag Lane would be installed and the aircraft assembled, test flown and cleared by the Australian authorities.

Coincident with assessments made in Canada, Australia believed operation of the Tiger Moth would benefit from the advantages of the Gipsy Major Series II engine but without a controllable pitch airscrew. Twenty such engines had been ordered from Stag Lane in November 1938 with the intention of fitting them into the British-made fuselages, probably with metal propellers which had also been a specification raised in Canada in July 1938, but the de Havilland Engine Division had already announced that production of the Series II was to be discontinued, on a temporary basis, and no further business would be sought. The last few orders which were honoured included a pair required by Handley Page for their experimental HP.75 tailless pusher. In the event several more engines were built and eight Gipsy Major Series II engines were despatched to Australia in February 1939 with eight more in March. Following incorporation of a number of Hatfield-approved modifications to accommodate the additional ancillaries on the back of the crankcase, the engines were installed into the imported Tiger Moth airframes at Mascot.

Fuselages supplied by Hatfield were identified by de Havilland in England as build numbers 82555 to 82574, to which Mascot added their own identities DHA1 to DHA20, and the RAAF allocated serial numbers A17-1 to A17-20, the 17th aircraft type to have been included in their inventory. Murray Jones made the first test flight of A17-1 from Mascot on 8 May 1939 and she was delivered into RAAF charge at Richmond eight days later. The aircraft was extensively used for training until February 1942 when she crashed at Maryborough in Queensland while in service with No 3 Wireless Air Gunner School (WAGS). All twenty aircraft had been delivered to the RAAF by October 1939, thirteen by the outbreak of war and, apart from some initial use by communications squadrons, each aircraft was used almost exclusively thereafter for elementary training purposes. The experience was survived by fifteen of the original fleet, all of which were sold into the civil market in 1946 and 1947 with the exception of A17-11 (82565/DHA11). This aircraft was converted into an Instructional Airframe as early as October 1940 and used by various technical establishments based at Wagga Wagga until June 1957. Currently registered VH-DBE, the aircraft has been based in Queensland since 1967.

Having secured their first RAAF Tiger Moth order de Havilland pressed for more, not only on the grounds that the world was re-arming but in an attempt to maintain continuity of supplies and the expertise of labour. Their approaches were answered with an order for fifty DH.94 Moth Minors placed by the Department of Supply in October 1939 on the grounds that there was now a serious shortage of trainer aircraft and the Moth Minors could be provided quickly. The majority of these (A21-1 to A21-50) were delivered in March and April 1940, mostly as kits of unfinished aircraft hastily evacuated from Hatfield at the beginning of the year together with all production jigs and tooling. In the event only thirty nine aircraft were constructed from the imported material plus a further three built locally from scratch using materials entirely sourced in Australia.

Recognition of the inevitable resulted in an order for a further 350 Tiger Moths and 500 engines being placed on 10 October 1939, a month after the outbreak of war. All were to be built locally, the Gipsy Major engines manufactured in Australia under the terms of a licence already held by the Commonwealth Aircraft Corporation. The

A17-1, first of a twenty aircraft contract for the RAAF, assembled at Mascot using fuselages imported from Hatfield, Gipsy Major engines from Stag Lane, and wings and tail units built locally. The aircraft was delivered into RAAF care at Richmond in May 1939. *Robert Veitch*

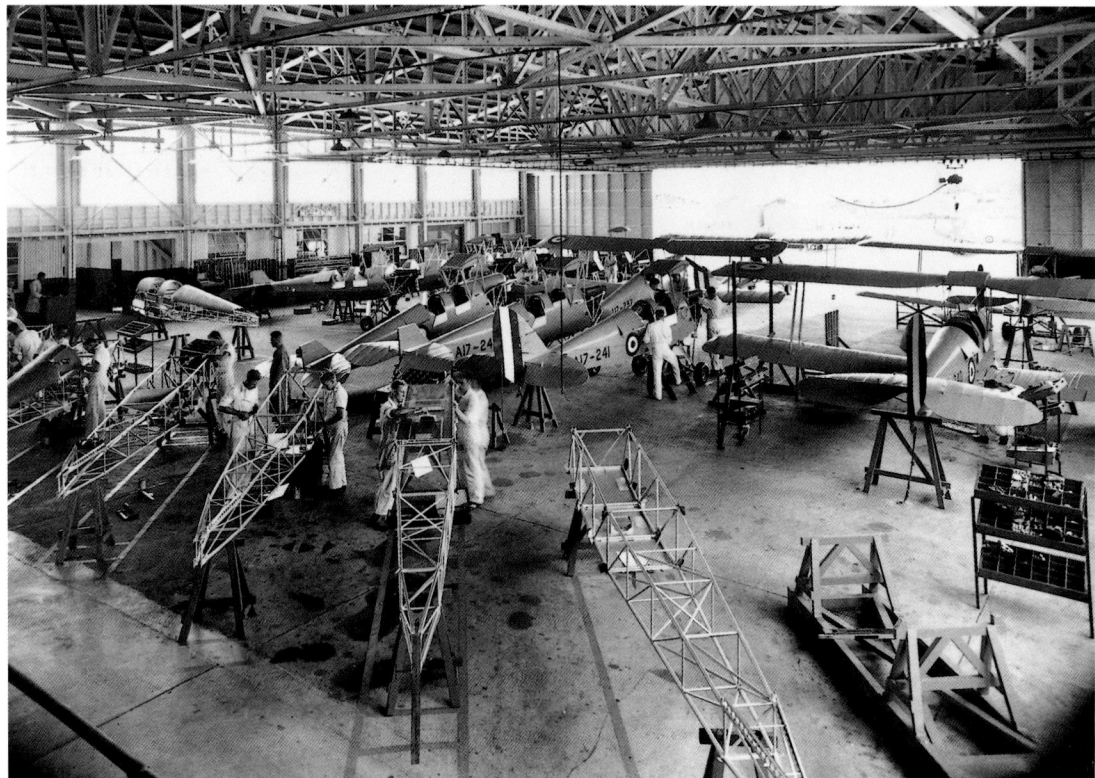

Steady progress evident at Mascot in January 1941. Note that vertical rudder stripes were still being applied as part of the RAAF insignia at this date. *via British Aerospace*

total order was valued at £800,000 and the aircraft were to equip nine additional Elementary Schools established under the provisions of the Empire Air Training Scheme (EATS).

While de Havilland Aircraft Pty. Ltd. was re-organising itself and expanding into leased facilities at Mascot previously used by Australian National Airways and Butler Air Transport, and arranging for supplies from sub contractors who would soon number 150, the British Government sanctioned release of 100 new Tiger Moths from Reserve stocks against an order for the RAAF which were shipped to Australia in batches: twenty five aircraft (all 'N' serials) arrived between February and March 1940; forty one ('R' serials) were taken on charge in June and July. The thirty four aircraft ('T' serials) which were delivered between July and September were near to the last production from Hatfield before the line was finally relocated to Morris Motors.

Eighty aircraft were routed to No 1 Air Depot (AD) Laverton near Melbourne and twenty to No 2 AD Richmond, north of Sydney, from where they were mostly air delivered with the exception of five which were simply transferred in their packing cases to Adelaide; twenty others were redirected in a similar condition to Tasmania. A pair of Laverton imports, N6901 (82145), and N6905 (82149), were nominated to be Instructional Airframes and posted to the Engineering School at Ascot Vale on 24 February.

Although these 100 aircraft were generally regarded as a gift from the British Government, a theory strengthened by the fact that all retained their RAF serial numbers, not until after the war when asset realisation was being encouraged, was it revealed that the Australian Government had paid for the aircraft, but 200 Gipsy Major engines had been gifted as assistance towards early completion of indigenous airframes. Although the ebb and flow of war caused agreements to be made and frequently cancelled or re-negotiated, at the commencement of the EATS programme it had been expected that Great Britain would supply or provide funding for 223 CAC Wirraways, 336 Fairey Battles, 591 Avro Ansons and 486 Tiger Moths. By the end of the conflict the RAAF had taken on charge 1,028 Ansons and 861 Tiger Moths, of which 712 were built at Mascot.

Bruce Winley, an engineer with 5 EFTS at Narromine, was given occasional instructional flights at the station, but during his previous posting with 2 EFTS at Archerfield, and before the training scheme was in full cry, there were more instructors than pupils and he was taught to a standard at which he was permitted to fly solo in a civil registered DH.60 Moth. Bruce Winley was resident at Narromine when at least four British-built Tiger Moths joined B Flight in September 1940. While the locally built aircraft were all-over yellow the RAF Tiger Moths were in camouflage, and being of slightly lighter construction offered better performance at the cost of a greater risk of ground handling damage.

A feature which was quickly appreciated by instructors engaged on night flying tuition was that the British aircraft all had wing tip and rudder lighting installed in addition to the downward facing identification lamp, whereas the locally produced aircraft were fitted only with quartered lights at the root end of the port upper mainplanes. Electrical power was provided by an accumulator clamped to the floor aft of the front cockpit rudder bar pivot. About one third of each School's aircraft establishment was fitted out for night flying and the battery boxes were fitted by the groundcrew only when the aircraft were detailed off for operations after dark. At 7 EFTS Western Junction, Tasmania, the British aircraft were described as being 'religiously reserved' for night flying training in preference to the Australian models which, during night circuits, were described as being 'perspectively inferior'.

Landing lights as such were not carried on military Tiger Moths although they had been fitted to one aircraft supplied from Hatfield to a British private owner pre-war and several others had been delivered to the Government of India. If it proved necessary for the pilot of a night flying Tiger Moth to illuminate the ground around him, usually as the result of an imminent forced landing, he fired off a Holt flare suspended under the lower wings from a spring loaded bracket mounted below the front interplane strut. The flares were similar in appearance to large Roman candle-like fireworks, had the same disadvantage of a once-only performance, and were electrically

This shot taken at No 2 EFTS Archerfield in 1940 almost shows DH.82A Tiger Moth N9135, one of the 100 British built aircraft delivered in 1940 in an effort to boost local establishments. The aircraft retains her RAF serial and colour scheme. The British aircraft were much preferred for night flying due to what was considered a superior system of navigation lights. *via Robert Veitch*

activated from two push buttons placed alongside the Morse tapper on the starboard wall of the rear cockpit. The units were a standard fit on almost all operational and night-flying biplanes of the day and the intensity of the burning flare was shielded from the pilot's view by a simple fore and aft blanking plate which doubled as a flame guard to prevent the wing fabric from catching alight.

Working to maximum capacity in its enlarged facilities at Stag Lane, the de Havilland Engine Division was only just coping with orders for Gipsy Major engines for home-produced Tiger Moths and Miles Magisters, and was now required to continue the large scale supply of Canada, New Zealand and Australia. Some of the workforce had even queried their value to the war effort and had had to be reminded that without initial training there would be no new pilots to operate the more aggressive machines. Canada was already researching the Menasco engine and although New Zealand would always be reliant on imports from somewhere, Australian industry was thought capable, with assistance, of building a creditable monthly output of Gipsy Major engines using its existing resources and without the benefit of sophisticated equipment routinely available to accelerate processes and procedures within the British industrial base.

In October 1935 the Commonwealth Government had announced its intention of entering into aircraft manufacturing through the Department of Aircraft Production and exactly two years later the de Havilland Aircraft Company licensed the Commonwealth Aircraft Corporation (CAC) of Melbourne to build Gipsy Major Series I and Series II engines. Coincidentally, a licence had been offered to Japan although that seemed less likely to materialise as rights to build the French Renault engine had already been secured for a quarter of de Havilland's requisite £20,000 fee. The Australian licence was extremely modest in comparison at £2,500 with an additional annual service fee of £250, and de Havilland were pleased to have had the opportunity of entertaining CAC's new production manager, Mr Shipper, straight from Pratt and Whitney in the USA, during a planned visit to Stag Lane.

The licence was not activated until November 1939 after the order for 500 Gipsy Major I engines was placed by the Australian Government and in January 1940 General Motors (Holdens) Ltd., a major shareholder in CAC, was appointed co-ordinating contractors for engine manufacture with the brief that production standard engines should be available for installation in Mascot-built Tiger Moths as quickly as possible. It was fortunate that Holdens were still in business; the company had recorded losses of £600,000 in 1930-1931 and a further £200,000 during the next 18 months and remained solvent only by the intervention of the parent company, General Motors, supporting it from the USA.

It was a challenge. The Australian automotive industry was based on units of Imperial measurement whereas, with its origins in French Renault powerplants dating from the First World War, the Gipsy range, historically, was founded on the metric system. Before there was the remotest chance of production every drawing and specification had to be closely examined: 41,500 dimensions required conversion, and where identical materials were not available the closest alternative specification needed sourcing and testing for approval.

Apart from the difficulties experienced with the differences in units of measurement and the necessary adaptations to tooling and manufacturing equipment, some of the drawings were found to be

Above and below: Mike Stacy went to great lengths to establish the specification of the original delivery colours of his Tiger Moth N9140, civil registered VH-ABL, and publication of his research resulted in an improvement in the overall standard of aircraft finished in the style of the period. Airframe upgrades over the years have deleted the external navigation lights and replaced the pitot head with an Australian version. *Mike Stacy*

already obsolete; others had not been amended or upgraded since they were provided when the licence agreement was drawn up in 1935. Literal interpretation was made more precarious when it was discovered that some aspects referred only to the special needs of the Tiger Moth Seaplane and Queen Bee.

To assist Holdens two de Havilland engineers were seconded from Stag Lane and arrived with a pair of production Gipsy Major engines, both of which were subsequently dismantled, one complete set of parts being retained by Holdens while the other was fragmented and distributed amongst the fifty seven approved sub-contractors as appropriate.

There was no time to source, order and await delivery of imported equipment to improve the efficiency of manufacturing and especially inspection processes, and whatever specialist tooling was required was designed and built locally. Each contracted supplier eventually provided twenty sets of component parts from which just two were selected, one to be maintained by Holdens for reference and the other for return to the manufacturer as a master pattern.

Less than three months into the massive effort of Australianising the programme the Australian Government, through the Air Department, expressed their concern that the cost of locally built Gipsy Major engines was going to be unacceptably high, and suggested that their preference would be for a continuation of supply from Great Britain. At an Air Council meeting held in London on 26 February 1940, the Air Department officially requested a quotation for the urgent supply of 500 engines. The arrangements made with General Motors had not allowed sufficiently for the immensity of the pre-manufacturing preparation required. Meanwhile, de Havilland at Mascot were expecting the first 100 locally-built engines to be delivered at the rate of twenty per month from April 1940.

In reply to their enquiry the Air Department was advised that the major limitation on engine manufacture was in the machining of the crankshaft. To ease pressure on British production, de Havilland had agreed that from October 1940 the Standard Motor Company would build twenty Gipsy Major engines per month, rising to 100 per month by February 1941, subcontracting production of crankshaft, camshaft and propeller hub to Austin Motors. Although the manufacturing and assembly techniques for automotive engines were not the same as those currently practised by the aircraft industry, discussions on the matter between de Havilland, Standard and Austin had resulted in a complete and satisfactory agreement.

Holdens were aware of the situation concerning crankshafts as confirmed by a report published by the Aviation Historical Society of Australia in 1981:

> "Crankshaft machining of the type required was an unknown art in Australia. Overseas, the job was done on special crankshaft lathes. Here it was done on motor car engine reconditioning equipment. The machining dimensions were extremely critical; the crankshaft itself was so relatively flexible that intricate fixtures were needed to ensure absolute rigidity during machining. The finished shafts had to be held to extremely close limits of dynamic balance, to measure which it was necessary to import a crankshaft balancing machine, which, incidentally, was the only specialist machine imported for the whole job. In the machining, the weight of the forging was reduced from 70lb to 32lb. The crankshaft final check required 250 measurements, and some surfaces, such as journals, would have at least ten to twelve checks made of each dimension."

From the end of 1939, de Havilland had been supplying parts directly to Holdens in an effort to expedite production. By March 1940 one hundred complete crankshafts had been shipped together with 430 blank forgings for machining locally. By agreement, 50 camshafts, 500 carburettors, 510 pairs of BTH magnetos and all necessary ball bearings had already been despatched. "The relief from any further obligation to supply parts would be of immediate and substantial benefit to home production" declared the Air Council.

All parties having expressed their views and pending a decision from Australia all further shipments of engine parts were suspended. On 16 March 1940 the Air Department announced that it had elected to continue with domestic manufacture.

In Great Britain, the proposed supply of engines from Standard Motors never did materialise. At the very last moment, the Ministry of Aircraft Production decided that the facilities could be better allocated "to projects with a higher priority."

Seven months after the start of the programme the first test engine was assembled at Holdens' plant at Fishermans Bend near Melbourne where, due to the major differences in drawings, production techniques and some material specifications, a full fifty hour running type test was considered necessary. It was essential to establish absolute credibility, for in service in Australia or in southern Africa or India or elsewhere, the Australian parts had, in every way, to be interchangeable and compatible with those manufactured and supplied from any other source.

The first of 1,300 Holdens-built engines costing about £610 each was installed in RAAF Tiger Moths at Mascot in December 1940 and the whole of the batch of eighteen aircraft exported to the Governments of India and Burma in January 1941 was similarly fitted. One enduring difference was the decision to fit Bendix-Scintilla magnetos, imported from the United States, which were considered superior to the standard BTH magnetos retained for production at Stag Lane.

On introduction in 1932 the overhaul period for a Gipsy Major I was 450 hours, extended to 750 hours in July 1933 and to 1,000 hours in August 1937. A year after the introduction to service of the Holdens engines, the British Air Ministry announced that the life had been extended to 1,260 hours with no intermediate top overhauls and in May 1945 this was again extended to the unprecedented figure of 1,500 hours. One reporter was prompted to write:

> "This quite exceptional figure represents about double the overhaul period for the average aero engine, and that despite the fact that the Gipsy Major operates under the most arduous conditions that aviation can impose on a power unit, the conditions of the elementary flying schools which involve endless repetitions of taking off, climbing on full power, gliding, taxiing and cooling down, this embodying a great deal of handling by inexperienced pupils. Its faithful dependability has meant much to the building up of their confidence in the air."

Delivery of the first DH.82A Tiger Moth to be wholly constructed in Australia was accomplished on 21 June 1940 when A17-25 (DHA21), was taken on charge at 2 AD Richmond. Allocated to 5 EFTS at Narromine on 12 July 1940, A17-25 worked until August 1944 when she was overhauled at Mascot then consigned to storage at Bankstown and later Cootamundra. In February 1946 the aircraft was sold to the Royal Queensland Aero Club at Archerfield, Brisbane, but their £250 investment was damaged beyond economical repair at Toowoomba on 13 October, only six months after registration as VH-AQC.

The first Tiger Moth wholly constructed in Australia, A17-21, was delivered to the RAAF in June 1940. In this photograph taken at Mascot, A17-31 in the foreground is complete but less rudder. Activity in assembling other fuselages appears to be less than frenetic. *de Havilland Aircraft Company*

Dennis Peck's Tiger Moth VH-DWP is an amalgam of parts gathered over sixteen years and displaying serial A17-240 is painted in the 1941 RAAF style of camouflage with yellow trainer bands and Pacific Area roundels. The aircraft was restored by Matt Webber and his team at Luskintyre in 2012.
Motty's Aviation Photography

Alan Murray Jones had recognised the need for an Australian based propeller industry and, with the approval of the parent company following another visit by Francis St Barbe in 1938, a new factory was established at Alexandria, NSW, which opened for production of wooden blades in March 1940 and was also to host the company's administrative offices.

The threat of war and disruption of supplies had encouraged Mascot to stock up on raw materials and spare parts to the extent of having an estimated two year's provisions on hand by September 1939, a far sighted policy which provided an essential buffer before total self-sufficiency could be achieved. As the training programme ground inexorably on and aeroplanes were heavily utilised and frequently damaged, some of the civil Maintenance and Repair Units established across the country suffered constant shortages of spare parts and were often forced to rob one aircraft in order to establish serviceability of another. The Australian Aircraft Production Commission provided additional space at Mascot purely for the overhaul of RAAF aircraft and in which five Tiger Moths were destroyed by fire on 3 May 1944, although a considerable number of parts were salvaged and recycled. Additional facilities were developed at Alexandria where all component metal work was subsequently completed.

In June 1940, as the result of a conference to determine future training needs, de Havilland was authorised to order raw materials for a further 300 airframes, and Holdens to provide seventy five spare engines, figures based on what proved to be the pessimistic recalculation of wastage estimated at an annual rate of ninety aircraft and seventy two engines. The package was valued at more than £570,000 within which the utilisation of existing jigs and tools was expected to reduce the unit cost of an airframe to £1,170 and an engine to £500.

To complement the four second-hand Tiger Moths supplied to the Netherlands East Indies by British aircraft broker W S Shackleton late in 1940, four more (DHA 141, 143, 144 and 145), were supplied from Mascot in October 1940 after representations at government level. On arrival in Batavia the aircraft were painted blue and, joined by the British imports in a red colour scheme and four Bückers painted white, they flew a combined formation at an air display representing the colours of the Dutch flag.

Throughout the Netherlands East Indies the flying club movement was heavily supported by the government, operating in the capacity of a civil reserve. In view of the world situation and, very much in accord with what was being practised elsewhere, the scheme was considered ready for necessary and immediate expansion. A formal request for more Australian-built aircraft was rejected early in 1941 on the grounds that all production was allocated, but in March and April 1941 the delivery of forty eight aircraft was approved, one of which, PK-BPP (DHA507), was to be supplied with provision for the attachment of a float chassis. By September 1941, approval for a total of sixty two Tiger Moths for export to the East Indies had been granted.

Following Japan's entry into the war in December 1941 many of the Dutch colony's training aircraft had been consolidated into an intense flying programme conducted at Tasik Malaja, but plans for their continued operation from there were abandoned when the islands were invaded by Japanese forces. With no shipping space available for evacuation the fleet was ordered by the Dutch authorities to be destroyed. Six Tiger Moths were hastily dismantled at Surabaya where they were in store prior to formal acceptance by the Naval Air School and the anticipated delivery of Edo floats from the United States. The aircraft were hurriedly loaded on board the SS *Tjinegara* which sailed on 19 February bound for Adelaide, South Australia. Although records of the original identities of the six had become confused, all were adopted by the RAAF, allocated serials A17-621 to A17-626, and operated by 1 EFTS at Parafield, a school which specialised in the training of pilot candidates of Dutch extraction.

The Prime Minister of Australia, Robert Menzies, led a mission to London in January 1941, part of whose purpose was to encourage the British Government to increase its purchase of Australian war supplies. These were already considerable and involved almost everything from felt and serge cloth despatched directly to Egypt, to bombs, machine guns, ammunition, tank tracks and food shipped to Great Britain. Whilst Robert Menzies was in London, on 4 February Tiger Moth R5182 (83044), forced landed near Greenvale, Victoria, whilst operating with 3 EFTS from Essendon. The pilot was unhurt and later travelled to England to train as a fighter pilot on Hurricanes and Spitfires. His name was John Gray Gorton and twenty seven years later he, too, became Prime Minister of Australia.

The aircraft industry in Australia was developing along proven lines and although no major complaints had been received in England, a complex industrial programme to build the Bristol Beaufort in considerable numbers was already running late due, allegedly, to many of the drawings supplied by the Bristol Aeroplane Company containing gross inaccuracies. One report said that many of the notes on the drawings, such as could be read, carried so much mis-information that they were best ignored. Prior to the Prime Minister's visit to London his office had been in contact with the Air Ministry to offer Australian assistance to the Tiger Moth programme. In September 1940 London received an appreciation that the Mascot factory would complete its current order book for 650 Tiger Moths by the end of 1941 and that by early the following year planned production would exceed all anticipated requirements. The report surmised that in view of the British Government's possible needs, there was every justification to authorise de Havilland Australia to proceed with the manufacture of at least another 200 Tiger Moths, plus spare parts.

At the end of November 1940, the Air Ministry advised the Australian Air Board that it would be prepared to take twenty five Tiger Moths per month after the end of April 1941, and if a higher rate of production was possible the additional aircraft would be gladly accepted for delivery to flying schools situated in Africa and the East. It was made clear that Great Britain could not provide engines, nor could it assist with the provision of any factory equipment, machine tools or personnel. Five weeks later, Australia replied that providing an early decision was taken with respect to materials, Mascot would be capable of supplying 420 Tiger Moths for export in 1941 and a further 650 in 1942, all to be fitted with Holdens-built engines.

By 31 December 1940 Mascot had delivered 208 aircraft and production reached ten Tiger Moths per week, a rate which they believed possible to raise by half as much again. Stag Lane had delivered 200 engines; 500 were on order from General Motors (Holdens) from whom eighty nine had been received. Manufacture was now at the rate of forty engines per month, a figure which de Havilland said could easily be increased.

The provision of Tiger Moths from the Southern Hemisphere to the schools of the expanding Empire Air Training Scheme in Africa, together with reinforcement of the Air Force in India, would lift the pressure off production of training aircraft in Great Britain and the associated shipping requirements, resources which could be immediately released to other urgent needs. It was even suggested early in March 1941 that with Australia's development of an indigenous 'Intermediate Trainer', the RAAF might be persuaded to release additional Tiger Moths from the home based schools. In the meantime the whole of the 420 aircraft output promised for export delivery in 1941 could be absorbed, agreed the Air Ministry, plus any additional machines that might be manufactured after the RAAF demand had been satisfied.

Of major concern was the provision of aircraft quality timber and plywood, neither spruce nor birch being native to the Dominion. The likely repercussions from an interrupted supply had been identified more than ten years previously during which time a programme of progressive investigation into the properties of some thirty native species had been conducted. Although not as ideal as spruce, hoop pine and bunya pine were available in commercial quantities: both had good properties but also deficiencies which could only be accommodated through detail redesign in an effort to redress the loss of strength. Scented satinwood was chosen for the manufacture of plywood as its qualities were almost the equal of birch, and the estimated annual availability of 2,000,000sq ft could all be released to the standard required for airworthiness. In the event, with the careful distribution of supplies amongst different ships and convoys the arrival in Australia of regular and sufficient supplies made the fallback onto alternative materials unnecessary. Meanwhile, concerns about the supply of imported aircraft quality Grade A spruce, specified as main spar stock had been ameliorated to some extent by the approval of Grade B spruce (Modification 59) and multi-laminated spars (Modification 80), following detailed analysis and trials started at Hatfield in 1940 in an effort to use every available cubic inch.

Aircraft allocated to the Empire Air Training Scheme in Southern Rhodesia were operated on behalf of the Royal Air Force by the Southern Rhodesia Air Force, and retained RAF serial numbers; those directed to South Africa were part of an alternative policy and adopted SAAF serials.

In order to supplement British deliveries and to guard against major loss and damage caused by submarine warfare, the effects of which had already been amply demonstrated, Australian-built Tiger Moths were added to the Southern African inventory. In July 1941 contract 1279/C.23(c) was placed by the British Government with the de Havilland Company at Mascot for the 420 aircraft which had been the subject of debate the previous year although the proposed export number was reduced to 395 of which 214 were actually shipped to South Africa, ninety four of them further despatched up the railway line from Durban to Southern Rhodesia. The first consignment of aircraft was ready for shipment from Sydney in August 1941 but were delayed and not processed through the port facilities at Durban until 8 December. These were allocated RAF serial numbers but their notification to the appropriate office at Mascot had been lost and the aircraft were received bearing their build numbers as identities, shortly to be replaced by SAAF serials for those remaining in South Africa and a corrected RAF allocation on arrival in Southern Rhodesia.

Tiger Moth production at Mascot had been continuous from June 1940, reaching a peak of two aircraft per day by March 1941. Following assessment of training and home defence needs a further sixty four airframes were ordered in August 1941 at an estimated cost of £1,200 each.

In the circuit at RAF Heany in 1949, Australian built aircraft DHA 542 first delivered to the RATG in Bulawayo in 1943. The Tiger Moth arrived ahead of her confirmed RAF serial (DX453) and became Machine No 542 (MC542) an identity which was maintained until sold in 1952 when she was locally registered as VP-YJK. *David Vernon*

Built at Mascot in June 1942, A17-558 led a fairly standard life until July 1945 when she was removed from reserve storage at Benalla to serve with the Netherlands East Indies Personnel and Equipment Pool, then based at Canberra. *Robert Veitch*

de Havilland DH82A Tiger Moth Mk II, A17-358/58, No 1 Air Observer School RAAF, Cootamundra, 1943. Earth Brown and Foliage Green upper surfaces with Trainer Yellow undersides. Trainer Yellow cowling, rear fuselage band and chordwise bands above top wings. Serial and code in black. National markings in six positions. Although roundels are in blue and white, the fin still carries the original three-colour flash. *Artwork ©Richard Caruana, 1:72 scale*

Japan's entry into the war in December 1941 had caused a deal of reappraisal and resulted in termination of the export of Tiger Moths to southern Africa. Some of the eighty aircraft ready for shipment were stored in and around Sydney for up to two years pending a decision on their future. Eighteen of these were released from May 1942 for use by the United States Forces in Australia pending delivery of their own communications types, and the remainder was absorbed into RAAF service, obviating the immediate need for further manufacture at Mascot. When the line closed in August 1942, temporarily as it happened, the de Havilland Company had assembled and delivered 1,035 aircraft.

It is probable that the photograph of this unidentified Tiger Moth painted in USAAF colours was taken in Australasia. The Avro Anson seen in the background is painted with RAAF Pacific Area roundels but what of the B.17 at left? *via General Mike Carns*

The Tiger Moths loaned to the United States 5th Air Force were identified only by their Mascot build numbers and were painted in matt 'foliage' green, displaying a white American star on either side of the fuselage. One (DHA907), was returned to RAAF service in August 1945 and another (DHA964), was loaned to the RAAF for a seven month detachment with 36 Squadron at Garbutt from August 1943. Apart from the loss of DHA963, which suffered a mid-air collision with a Bell P-39 Airacobra in September 1942, the fate of the remaining fifteen aircraft is unknown.

A further eight Tiger Moths were allocated late in 1942. DHA917 was damaged during transit through Brisbane in December the following year and DHA918 was seemingly cannibalised on site to provide spares and then abandoned to the administrative machinations of the RAAF's No 1 Technical Supply Depot. DHA917 eventually served in New Guinea with an American fighter squadron and was later adopted by a bomber group, but her ultimate fate is unknown. DHA1044 was damaged during her positioning flight to Archerfield in November 1942 and was never officially handed over. Nothing is recorded concerning the operational careers of the other five.

Transferred to local use was DHA870, intended to be DX838 in southern Africa but taken on to the RAAF inventory as A17-640. The aircraft crashed on take-off from Mascot on 20 August 1943 at the start of her delivery flight to the nearby Air Park at Bankstown and her arrival there was delayed by some eleven weeks. A17-640 later remained in service with the RAAF until 1956 when she was sold for agricultural use after which she was recovered from long term storage in Western Australia in 1990, registered VH-NMD to John Markham and restored by Lyn Forster.

In September 1944 the Mascot line was re-opened to provide a further 60 Tiger Moths at a cost of about £1,200 each, assessed as necessary by a review which had been adopted over two years previously. The new production at Mascot was authorised in spite of an offer to supply Tiger Moths from Great Britain where, for some months already, Morris Motors had been delivering aircraft straight into store. By February 1945, thirty five of the new Australian aircraft had been delivered but the remainder of the order was subsequently cancelled on the grounds that all training was being run down and the aircraft were simply not required.

The Aviation Historical Society of Australia reported in 1982 that the last Mascot aircraft, A17-759 (DHA1090), undergoing overhaul, had been found to carry an inscription scribbled onto the ply beneath a cockpit panel: "The last of the tribe. W Sullivan. 3/1/1945." A17-759 was delivered to 2 AD at Richmond on 5 February 1945 and remained in active service until 1957 before sale to the Royal Victorian Aero Club at Moorabin. Registered VH-COA and painted in RAAF Pacific area colours, apart from one year 2008/2009, the aircraft has been based near Canberra since 1981, the 1,070th and what might have been the last all-Australian aeroplane of the 1,090 Tiger Moths assembled at Mascot.

In November 1943, 700 Tiger Moths were listed on the RAAF inventory and 648 remained when peace was finally declared in 1945. The last two remaining in service, A17-671 (DHA821), part of a frustrated delivery to southern Africa, and A17-616 (DHA1051), an aircraft paid for by residents of the shire of Oxley, were sold on 23 April 1959. DHA821 was registered VH-SNP to Townsville Aero Club in Queensland and was last reported with a private owner at Tully to whom the letters VH-CEE were allocated in 1995. DHA1051 simply disappeared into the civil system and was probably used as a source of spares.

Very much a standard Tiger Moth, equipped with a tailskid but no mainwheel brakes, an inverted oil or fuel system or a self starter, aircraft manufactured in Australia were subject to a number of modifications some of which, like the aspirations of their Canadian cousins, were an inspired attempt to hold the local environment at bay, or to improve the technical and safety standing of the aeroplane by subtle changes which the Mascot management were ordered to incorporate via Technical Orders issued by the RAAF Directorate of Technical Services.

Principal modifications to the basic DH.82A Tiger Moth design for aircraft constructed by de Havilland Aircraft Pty. Ltd. at Mascot, or incorporated into post-war civil aircraft at the instigation of the Australian Airworthiness Authorities, were many and varied but none was incorporated into wartime production at Cowley or Rongotai.

> The leading edges of all wings, except at the slat position of the port and starboard upper, have a plywood skin glued to ribs and riblets extending back to the front spar.
> Main undercarriage legs carry a check cable to prevent the oleo from slipping out (and down) in the event of a collapse of the internal structure. This is particularly valid in the case of an undercarriage damaged during the course of a landing from which the aircraft is in a position to 'go around'.
> Aluminium alloy fork ends fitted as standard to both ends of the main undercarriage shock struts were changed to steel to permit operations at an increased all-up weight.

de Havilland DH.82A Tiger Moth Mk II, A17-616/BF-Z, No 5 Squadron (Army Co-Operation) RAAF, Mareeba (Queensland), summer 1943. Earth Brown and Foliage Green upper surfaces with Sky Blue undersides. Serial in black, codes in Neutral Grey. National markings in six positions. *Artwork ©Richard Caruana, 1:72 scale*

Main wheel hub blanks are fitted on both inner and outer faces as standard to minimise ingress of foreign matter at the bearing.

The instrument panel is restrained on rubber 'Lord' shock absorbing mounts.

Fore and aft levels (inclinometers) are fitted as standard instrumentation and were retained following an RAF modification which deleted them.

The oil pressure is read directly from the oil gallery on the crankcase rather than from a banjo fitting at the rear of the engine.

An American round type oil pressure gauge is used in preference to the vertical type, standard on most British built aircraft of the time from Avro Lancasters to Supermarine Spitfires.

Tachometer drive cables are routed through the port side of the fuselage front bulkhead rather than the starboard side.

A fail safe latch is fitted to the fuel on/off cock operating rod giving a positive indication of the fuel on/off position and resistance to the prospect of the cock vibrating into the closed or semi-closed (restricted fuel flow) position.

Front cockpit cover plate to blank off the control box position when the front control column is removed.

Rear floor inspection panel reprofiled.

The lead mass balance weight is deleted from the leading edge of the rudder.

Port and starboard aileron control cables are continuous from the operating lever under the cockpit floor to the sprocket in the wing box. The RAF modification which introduced short cables from the operating lever to join long cables at the wing root was not copied.

Port and starboard aileron control boxes were retained at the standard of the original oblong design, prior to RAF modifications.

Aileron crank reprofiled to prevent cable chafing.

The engine air intake position on the starboard engine cowling is fitted with a removable Vokes filter element.

The fuel filter is fitted to the port side of the engine bay.

The engine cowling starboard panel was re-profiled.

Stub exhaust pipes were fitted in preference to standard branch manifold.

The engine oil breather pipe is extended to the bottom of the port undercarriage radius rod and deflects oil overflow away from the underside of the fuselage floor.

The oil tank fitted to bearers on the fuselage port side is retained by quick release straps rather than a system of bolts passing through a peripheral flange, and is less liable to cracking.

Two additional fuel drain cocks, (a new total of three) are fitted to the underside of the centre section fuel tank.

The starboard side venturi tube serving the front cockpit is mounted on the forward arm of the inverted 'V' centre section strut rather than bolted to the wooden cowl.

A night flying quartered navigation light is fitted to the root end of the port upper mainplane in preference to lights on the tips of each upper wing and rudder.

Straight style pitot head in preference to the modified (kinked) RAF version, Mk VII.

Deletion of the external fuselage drainage cover plate above the position of the rudder cable joint with the rear rudder bar extension pieces.

All ex-factory metalwork supplied in silver finish rather than green or grey.

A footrest is built into the starboard side fuselage frame at the position of the lower longeron, directly under the rear cockpit door. This was deleted from British-built aircraft as part of the upgrade from DH.82 to DH.82A in 1933.

Geometry for the Sutton harness lower strap fixing points was revised and a new cable system introduced to pick up the rear seat shoulder harness.

Kicking boards are fixed to port and starboard fuselage frames, inboard, adjacent to both front and rear rudder pedal positions.

Spacer units are fitted at the base of the rudder to improve the interface of the steering plates and the castoring tailskid, to assist with directional control during taxiing.

None of the local modifications was ever fed into the British line at Cowley where the aeroplane was regarded simply as a repetitive production job, receptive only to the minimum number of essential modifications and changes as dictated by the design authority at Hatfield. Under British direction a fuel cock locking device was introduced as a mandatory modification (TNS 34), in March 1999; as the result of an accident owners were reminded about the control box cover plate to be fitted in the event that the control column was removed (TNS 36), in August 2000 and increased strength shoulder harness restraint cables were called up as a mandatory modification (TNS 37), at the same date.

Above: The last Tiger Moth to come off the line at Mascot was A17-759. The aircraft was found to have a message written on a panel dated 3 January 1945 describing her as 'the last of the tribe.' *Stuart Saunders*

Left: Wearing the last colour scheme to be applied to RAAF Tiger Moths, A17-640 is based in Western Australia and carries her civil registration VH-NMD under the tailplane. *Ian Brackley via David Welch*

CHAPTER FOURTEEN

Honeymoon in New Zealand

In May 1931 Francis St Barbe completed a twenty week world tour in his position of Business Director on behalf of the de Havilland Aircraft Company Ltd., during which he visited clubs and private owners, associated companies and agents in the course of travelling 22,000 miles by ship, 6,000 miles by air and 3,000 miles by train. On his return to England he was pleased to report to the board that the whole exercise had cost the company not more than £950.

Furthest from Stag Lane was his visit to New Zealand agent Douglas Mill whose business, the Air Survey and Transport Company, employed four engineers at their base at Hobsonville near Auckland, a New Zealand Permanent Air Force (NZPAF) station with seaplane facilities attached. Francis St Barbe was delighted with what he saw: the servicing arrangements, spare parts supply, and ability to cope with anything up to and including major repairs. "I am satisfied that our affairs are in very good hands," he reported. He was also pleased to add that during his eight day stay he had flown over 900 miles around North Island in the agent's demonstration DH.80 Puss Moth, and that all his official expenses had been met by Mr Mill. "My visit to New Zealand did not cost the company one penny," he wrote gratifyingly.

Due to the initial limit imposed on the supply of civil Tiger Moths from Stag Lane and Hatfield by military precedence, it was not until July 1937 that the company could acknowledge its first order for the

Tiger Moth ZK-AIA was exported from Hatfield to New Zealand in 1938 and registered ZK-AGI. She was photographed in January 2006 when operating from Bridge Pa Aerodrome. The New Zealand authorities had some time previously agreed that aircraft incapable of international flight from the country had no need to carry national identity letters. Tim Whittaker

type from New Zealand, booked to F D Mill. Two aircraft were required and ZK-AFN (3629), and ZK-AFO (3630), were subsequently shipped in October on board the SS *Port Campbell*. Reaching Auckland on 20 December they were delivered to Hobsonville, erected, inspected, test flown on 12 January and fully inspected again by the authorities in view of their differences from a standard DH.60 Moth which was familiar to them, finally reaching the Auckland Aero Club on 15 February 1938.

At the suggestion of what from 1 April 1937 had become the Royal New Zealand Air Force, a revised scheme of training for Civil Reservists and Air Force direct entrants was introduced which progressed each stream, very much on the lines of the British Elementary and Reserve Flying Training School (ERFTS) system, through an existing and efficiently organised civil club channel to A licence standard. One hundred pupils were to be trained each year under contracts let from April 1937. A year earlier, four military DH.60 Moths had been transferred to civil clubs to assist with *ab initio* training of pilots destined for the Air Force and, in August 1937, the government introduced an interest free loan scheme, with repayments spread over three years, to encourage clubs to buy the most modern and appropriate equipment. The delivery of Tiger Moths ZK-AFN and ZK-AFO to Auckland in February 1938 was a direct result of this initiative.

ZK-AFN survived her subsequent war time-enforced Air Force career as NZ719 and was sold in February 1947 to W H Johns of New Plymouth, where she was operated by the local Aero Club under a new identity: ZK-AOL. The aircraft suffered engine failure near Mangere and crashed on 10 January 1959, sustaining damage considered uneconomical to repair. Stablemate ZK-AFO, the first Tiger Moth ever to fly in New Zealand, also reluctantly joined the military and as NZ720 had no distance to travel to enrol with the Flying Instructors' School (FIS) at Hobsonville where she spent her entire war service. Issued as a free gift to Hawera Aero Club in June 1948, the registration ZK-ASA was allocated but the aircraft was not used and in April 1950 she was sold for agricultural conversion to Air Contracts of Masterton with whom she survived a catalogue of near terminal disasters. Passing to Aerial Advertising at Nelson in 1957, ZK-ASA was withdrawn after her final flight on 13 April 1958, having logged 7,203 flying hours. Dismantled and stored, the aircraft was acquired by John Galpin of Te Puke in August 1981 after his own Tiger Moth ZK-BFG (82032), had been destroyed in a hangar fire at Rotorua. In November 1981. Registration letters ZK-AFO were re-allocated, and the aircraft embarked on a long programme of restoration to airworthiness until the project was abandoned and the registration cancelled in 2009.

Less blind flying hood, the price of a 1938 model Tiger Moth delivered to New Zealand was quoted at £1,547.10s.0d. Under the government's loan scheme by August 1939 Auckland Aero Club's monthly repayment for ZK-AFO amounted to a few shillings less than £40. Seven more aircraft ordered by Air Survey, despatched from Hatfield in November and December 1937 (3638-3644), and delivered in February 1938, collectively cost £7,680, just over £2 each more than the published list price. The price tag of £1,708 affixed to the Marlborough Aero Club's ZK-AHH (82052), a one-off order placed by the Air Survey and Transport Company in 1939, probably reflected Francis St. Barbe's exclusive right to call the tune.

ZK-AFU (3641), and ZK-AGE (3654), delivered to the Middle Districts Aero Club early in 1938 were lost when the Club's new hangar at Milson burned down on 17 February 1939. The engine of ZK-AFX (3644), scheduled for the Western Federated Flying Club, failed shortly after take-off on a test flight from Hobsonville on 28 February 1938 and ditched in the harbour. The airframe was written off but the engine was salvaged, overhauled and installed in Percival Gull NZ572. Just after take-off from Hobsonville on 18 July 1940 the engine failed again and the aircraft was fatally wounded in the forced landing. The pilot, Flt Lt E F Harvie RNZAF, was later to become Chief Inspector of Accidents.

By 3 September 1939 a total of twenty one Tiger Moths were in use by New Zealand's civil clubs. Three others, ZK-AHO, ZK-AHM and ZK-AHR (82230-82232), were painted in civil colours and awaiting delivery from Hobsonville but following declaration of war adopted military marks instead and were diverted straight into the Air Force as NZ716, NZ714 and NZ715 respectively.

With the country on a war footing all flying club equipment was requisitioned and the aircraft previously provided against 'free loans' were compulsorily purchased by the government. Following inspection an agreed level of compensation was due, the figures dependent to some extent on the amount of the loan left outstanding.

Since her introduction the Tiger Moth had proved herself to be almost ideally suited to New Zealand's training requirements and, with an established base at Hobsonville offering service and support, the Air Force decided it would happily standardise all its primary training needs on the type.

In his 1931 report to the board, de Havilland's Business Director clearly stated his opinion of future prospects: "We can be fairly satisfied that we shall get the lion's share of the business in New Zealand." Based on that judgement, the satisfactory performance of the overseas companies, and the extended supply line even beyond Australia which would always be subject to possible disruption, Alan Butler, Chairman of the Company, announced at the 19th Annual General Meeting on 7 February 1939 that a de Havilland Associated Company was to be established in the Dominion of New Zealand, with new offices and workshops situated near Wellington.

Hugh Buckingham, one time de Havilland Aeronautical Technical School student and later a company sales and demonstration pilot, was married on 30 March 1939 and a few days later with his new bride, Pamela, was on board the RMS *Queen Mary* taking a first class passage to New York, a wedding present from his employer. He took the opportunity to fly a Moth at the Canadian branch in Toronto before travelling overland to Los Angeles to board the SS *Maraquesa* on 26 April, bound for Australia and New Zealand. At the age of twenty nine he was to take up duties as General Manager of the newly created de Havilland Aircraft Company of New Zealand.

The firm had been registered in Wellington on 6 March 1939, the sixth de Havilland overseas company, while the General Manager was still en-route, and followed initial organisation by Francis St Barbe paying a second visit during which he must have closely liaised with

Hatfield exported Tiger Moth No 3795 to New Zealand in 1938 where she was registered ZK-AGZ to Western Federated Flying Club at New Plymouth. She was re-registered ZK-ALK after wartime impressment and was fitted with a canopy.
via David Welch

Rongotai Aerodrome, Wellington, New Zealand. The new de Havilland factory was set in scenic conditions but with little between it and Antarctica was wind-swept and cold. *Hugh Buckingham*

Martin Sharp developed a distinctive 'house style' for de Havilland Company publications and promotions based on the 'Times Roman' typeface, somewhat different from the fashionable 'Broadway' type, used on the facade at Rongotai. The streaming flags enforce the reputation of 'Windy Wellington'. *Hugh Buckingham*

the Air Survey & Transport Company, detailing Hatfield's intentions. All but one of the 20,000 shares were to be held by the parent company; the odd one was registered to Major Alan Murray Jones, Managing Director of the Australian company, with a brief to lend a helping hand in addition to keeping a fatherly eye. Murray Jones was in Wellington on 28 March to review progress pending the arrival of Hugh Buckingham and on 24 May construction of a new 200ft by 100ft workshop was commenced at Rongotai Aerodrome, Wellington.

Writing in *The Aeroplane*, Editor C G Grey expressed his tacit support of the venture and particularly that of the new General Manager. "He is well known as a demonstration pilot and has flown all over Europe on the company's business. He is well liked everywhere he has been. He should do great things."

According to Alan Vause, an early employee who had transferred locally from Wellington Aero Club, it was hard to believe this was considered the ideal place at which to produce a large number of light training biplanes, on the eastern boundary of Rongotai Aerodrome, wide open to the frequent southerly gales ripping in straight from Antarctica. The new building had few windows: the main light source was through the glazed North Light Truss roofing, quite correctly facing south and away from the sun, but as a result the shop floor was dark, miserable and freezing in the winter. It was believed locally that the building and layout had been designed in Great Britain against a misconceived understanding of Southern Hemisphere geography and after the first year it was found necessary to install a substantial heating system just to provide basic warmth.

The policy of the new company dictated by Hatfield was clear:

> "Give the close attention and service to the Dominion Government, the air lines and other commercial undertakings, the flying clubs, schools and private owners which are demanded in the present growing state of civil and military aviation in the Dominion and which must be governed very largely by the policy of the New Zealand Government."

The first business was to be construction of Moth Minors and Tiger Moths for local distribution, working initially under the direction of eight staff posted on a temporary basis from England, including John Johnston who was to take up the position of Work's Manager, Jack Balls, in charge of metalwork production, Fred Betts, woodworking department, and Bill Gilbert. Ted Whitehouse arrived later to set up the jigs for making fuselage frames and to instruct some of the workforce, including a number of pretty girls, in the art of welding.

To begin with the factory relied on Hatfield for the supply of almost everything but gradually became self reliant. The exceptions were proprietary items: wheels, tyres, instruments, rigging wires, some specialist airframe parts, windscreens and Gipsy Major engines.

Negotiations between the de Havilland Company and the New Zealand Government had already resulted in the understanding that additional Tiger Moths would be required for the RNZAF but due to the economic situation as much local input as practicable would be necessary. Total manufacture in New Zealand was the obvious answer and the prospects had been further discussed during a visit by the United Kingdom Air Mission in April 1939, soon after incorporation of the business. Hugh Buckingham was aware that following the Munich Crisis of 1938, de Havilland had been advised by the British Air Ministry to initiate Tiger Moth assembly at suitable overseas 'dispersed' sites and the coincidental establishment of pre-war production in Canada, Australia and now New Zealand was probably beyond the projection of normal commercial strategy.

Only nine weeks after de Havilland had sanctioned construction of the new factory at Rongotai, the Prime Minister of New Zealand, Rt. Hon. Michael Savage MP, announced to Parliament that the government had agreed to order 100 Tiger Moths at a total delivered cost of £155,000, all aircraft to be manufactured at Wellington, the last aircraft to be delivered by February 1941. The timing of the announcement may have been unexpected as a temporary halt to the factory building programme at Rongotai had been called while plans were urgently approved to add a further 5,000 sq ft of floor space. Makeshift office and workshop accommodation was temporarily secured in municipal facilities themselves awaiting completion.

To initiate the 100 aircraft contract it was intended to import batches of partially assembled aircraft kits from Hatfield and to complete them to civilian standards for *ab initio* pilot training on behalf of the Air Force, a function which would continue to be undertaken by the flying clubs. In the event, and as a result of changed circumstances, all Tiger Moth work at Rongotai would prove to be for exclusive sale and delivery directly to the RNZAF.

Hugh Buckingham's voyage to Wellington had been broken by a visit to the Australian company at Mascot where he took the opportunity to tour the local area in a demonstrator Puss Moth in addition to test flying several new production Tiger Moths. Following arrival at Rongotai he flew Percival P.10 Vega Gull to Palmerston North on 20 October, recording the flight under civil registration ZK-AFI, although officially the aircraft had been requisitioned from the Wellington Aero Club on 15 September and allocated Air Force serial NZ571. He retraced his steps some days later in a Waco UOC Custom, logged as ZK-AEL, yet another aircraft from the Wellington Club fleet, impressed as NZ575, and based locally under the auspices of the Rongotai Communications Flight. From the beginning of November he made a number of test flights and local visits in DH.94 Moth Minor ZK-AHL, an aircraft sent from England in August intended for his personal use but also destined to join the military as NZ595.

On 22 December 1939, as the finishing touches were still being applied to the factory, Hugh Buckingham, known as 'Jimmy' since Stag Lane days, but answering to 'Hughie' in his new post, took off from Rongotai for a twenty five minute test flight in Tiger Moth NZ740 (82296). This aircraft was amongst the first batch of twelve (82294-82298; 82344-82347 and 82393-82394), to be sent from Hatfield which had simply to be unpacked, erected, inspected and test flown. Serial numbers NZ738-NZ749 were allocated on arrival, but not in any particular sequence. By the end of January, NZ738-NZ743 had been tested, and on 9 February, 'Hughie' flew NZ744, NZ747 (twice), NZ748 and NZ749.

Not until 8 March 1940 was NZ746 tested, and NZ745 was left for the twenty seven year old Peter de Havilland, Geoffrey's middle son, to tackle as an introduction to his new role as production test pilot, a position which he filled between April 1940 and early 1942. Peter de Havilland's arrival was to allow the General Manager administrative breathing space but Hugh Buckingham remained in test flying practice throughout the period, airborne in DH.94 Moth Minors ZK-AHJ (94061) and ZK-AHN (94071), in March 1940, both delivered from Hatfield against orders placed on an agency basis by the Air Survey and Transport Company. Neither aircraft retained its civil letters for long: both were impressed into military service as NZ591 and NZ592, and were flown as such by the General Manager on 8 and 16 April respectively, although on both occasions he logged their type identity as 'Tiger Moth'.

Refuelling time at 3 EFTS Harewood for a gaggle of RNZAF Tiger Moths of mixed parentage: part built at Hatfield or wholly built at Rongotai. Once declared surplus the three aircraft nearest the camera went to civil flying clubs in New Zealand. *RNZAF Ohakea*

In order to expedite pilot training while the production facilities at Rongotai were still being organised, the British Government gifted ninety new Tiger Moths manufactured at Hatfield against pre-war contracts for the Strategic Reserve, in a fashion similar to the 100 aircraft shipped to the Royal Australian Air Force. Unlike the RAAF who retained the original RAF serial numbers, the RNZAF allocated its own identities and over a period of several months post-delivery, obliterated the standard RAF green and brown camouflage scheme, known affectionately in some quarters as 'slime and sewage', with an overall coat of familiar 'Trainer Yellow' or 'Sunshine Yellow' to quote its proper identity, until the FAFAI scheme called for further temporary changes.

The first batch of aircraft from England was despatched from 36 Maintenance Unit (MU) Sealand and arrived on board the SS *Somerset* in April 1940. Six were transported directly to the RNZAF base at New Plymouth where they were erected and flight tested. Although the aircraft were unloaded in random order, RNZAF serial numbers were applied in strict sequence as each was processed, the New Plymouth aircraft becoming NZ851-NZ856, respectively ex-RAF N9456, N9142, N9457, N9185, N9183 and N9410. These were followed at approximately monthly intervals by more new aircraft drawn from reserve storage at various RAF MUs in England, delivered on board the freighters *Rangitane*, *Wairangi*, *Rangitikei*, *Rangitata* and *Opawa*. RNZAF serial allocations for ex-RAF 'N' and 'R' aircraft continued consecutively from NZ857 to NZ900; and from NZ656 to NZ689 for all 'T' serialled aircraft later supplied direct from the Morris Motors' factory at Cowley.

Hugh Buckingham test flew the first of the ex-RAF aircraft routed to Rongotai, N9249 (82350/NZ857), on 30 April, followed by the next six, (NZ858-NZ863), all within the first week of May, after which the job became the sole responsibility of Peter de Havilland, 'Pete the Pilot' as he was affectionately known. A similar job of erection and test flying was required for the entire fleet of eight Tiger Moths formerly with the London Aeroplane Club which had ceased operations at Hatfield following the embargo on civil flying imposed on the outbreak of war. The well-used aircraft were all shipped directly to Wellington where they were prepared for service with the RNZAF as NZ730-NZ737, and taken on charge between 9 June and 16 August 1940. Integrated in the erecting shop with the brand new camouflaged aeroplanes arriving from England, they appear to have been allocated a lower priority in view of the greater amount of pre-delivery preparation required by each, and were found space in the system when available manpower permitted. According to the engineers who received them, working under the direction of Chief Inspector Bill Brazier, the London Club aircraft had every appearance of being packed up immediately after a day's flying and were still streaked with oil and generous plumes of Hatfield mud. With the influx of dismantled aircraft just requiring assembly and rigging, arrangements were made for an overspill to be accommodated in the Centennial Exhibition Buildings on the opposite side of Rongotai Aerodrome, where the de Havilland Aircraft Company had planned to be a major independent exhibitor earlier in the year.

Above: G-ADUK of the London Aeroplane Club flying in the vicinity of Hatfield Aerodrome. The whole of the Club fleet was sold to New Zealand in 1940 and arrived spattered with aerodrome mud and engine oil. *de Havilland Aircraft Company*

Right: It was fortunate that the Centennial Exhibition Buildings were both adjacent, suitable and available for Tiger Moth overflow. Note the DH.94 Moth Minor in the right foreground, and the port wings of a DH.90 Dragonfly. *deHMC Archive*

The second batch of twelve Tiger Moths to be assembled from Hatfield kits was ready in July: NZ751-NZ762. Five of the aircraft (82395-82397 and 82713-82714), had been sent from England complete with engines, but the remaining seven (82715 and 82836-82841), were scheduled to be united with part of a consignment of twenty one Gipsy Major engines which had arrived in February as an anticipated prelude to greater participation in the local manufacturing programme.

The allocation of RNZAF serial numbers was again completely haphazard, and further confusion was caused when the factory allocated local build numbers (DHNZ1-DHNZ12), again on an apparently indiscriminate basis, on the grounds that all the wooden parts of the mainplanes together with dope and fabric work (Stage A of the local production programme), had been completed on site. These twelve aircraft were regarded as the first part of the order for 100 home-produced Tiger Moths announced to Parliament on 1 August 1939, and were called up against de Havilland's internal contract reference 8200.

New Zealand's first aircraft recognised as having a significant percentage of local content was NZ762 (DHNZ12), which was taken on charge by the Air Force on 18 July 1940. In spite of being the last of that DHNZ build allocation, it was the first aircraft to be completed to delivery standard. NZ751 was test flown by 'Hughie' Buckingham on 25 July and handed over four days later. NZ755 and NZ757 were flown by the General Manager on 20 and 21 August respectively, but the Air Force acceptance date for NZ755 is quoted as 1 August 1940 which adds to the uncertainty of the identities.

Sleuthing by Cliff Jenks and David Phillips trying to identify Air Force serials and build positions against Hatfield's allocation has met with limited success:

NZ751 (DHNZ1) 82713
NZ752 (DHNZ2) 82840?
NZ753 (DHNZ3) 82714
NZ754 (DHNZ4) unknown
NZ755 (DHNZ5) 82836?
NZ756 (DHNZ6) 82397
NZ757 (DHNZ7) 82395
NZ758 (DHNZ8) 82396
NZ759 (DHNZ9) 82841?
NZ760 (DHNZ10) unknown
NZ761 (DHNZ11) 82838?
NZ762 (DHNZ12) unknown

Stage B of New Zealand's coordinated building schedule covered the second batch of twelve unassembled kits, (82944-82949 and 83077-83082), all received engineless from Hatfield which, in an ordered sequence (had the manager waved a big stick?) were allocated local build numbers DHNZ13-DHNZ24, and Air Force serials NZ763-NZ774. In addition to the mainplane woodwork, Stage B required Rongotai to build control surfaces and to provide all metal parts for the wings with the exception of drag struts, internal bracing wires and fabricated wiring plates. Hugh Buckingham considered the step forward to be of considerable significance and test flew the first aircraft, NZ763, on 11 September.

The problem of raw material supply in a non-industrialised country with few natural resources was only solved by staking a complete reliance on imports. Although local timber sources were investigated none was found to be satisfactory and baulks of spruce and ash, sheets of plywood, round, square and streamline section steel tube, plate and bar, fabric and even certain ingredients for the manufacture of dope were all secured from sources in Great Britain and Australia. Stocks of raw materials were consistently maintained to a 'more than adequate' level for the programme in hand and new supplies always managed to get through. Apart from one centre section cross spar which indulged in a brief flirtation with an American specification round tube, later found to be below strength and necessitating some subtle re-design, all Tiger Moth production at Rongotai complied with material specifications already tried and tested elsewhere.

Tiger Moth NZ680 (83532), operating from 4 EFTS at Whenuapai, was aerobatting at 3,000ft over Otahuhu, Auckland on 6 March 1941, when a front flying wire failed, a wing folded and disintegrated and the aircraft spun into the ground. Investigation found the wire carried a manufacturing fault and all Tiger Moths were immediately inspected.

Fuselage tie rods fitted to British models were specified with an 8mm cut metric thread, the pitch of which had been changed after early production to one of increased fineness, and supplies were manufactured in Great Britain and shipped to Wellington. On an occasion when stocks had run surprisingly low, possibly due to a loss during shipping, rods were imported with an urgency from Mascot and fitted on production. Tie rods manufactured in Australia were supplied with a 5/16 BSF thread. It was necessary for all to be aware of the difference.

During aerobatics at Kaiapoi on 11 September 1941 what was later described as 'faulty workmanship during maintenance', caused a port wing of Tiger Moth NZ883 (82889), to fold back at an angle of about 45°. The instructor ordered abandonment and baled out but the pupil released his parachute harness in error for his Sutton and went down with the aeroplane. The NCO responsible for the maintenance at 3 EFTS Harewood was court martialled.

Flying low over the sea or a beach has its attractions especially if the sun is warm and the pilot keeps an eye on the height of the rollers. ZK-BUO was caught frollicking near Daroaville, New Zealand in the hands of Simon Spencer-Bower. *via Henry Labouchere*

Fuselages under construction at Rongotai with most of the component parts readily at hand. In the background the factory appears to be well occupied with work in progress. *Hugh Buckingham*

A posed photograph of fuselages at an advanced stage in construction. It was necessary to lift each completed unit off the workbench for the fabric stage before assembly of a new structure could be started. *Hugh Buckingham*

The metamorphosis of the DH.60 to the DH.82 had resulted in a conglomeration at fuselage joint 'H' where undercarriage and wing attachment points were in close proximity. The forged attachment brackets were secured by a pair of tie rods spaced either side of a substantial lateral compression tube. Heavy landings could distort the tie rods but in constant Service use many may have been replaced before their ultimate life was reached although the manufacturer never published anything to suggest either the tie rods or any other part of a Tiger Moth airframe were of limited life.

During the routine inspection of a heavily used civilian aircraft in England in 1998 a nut dropped onto the hangar floor within which was found the threaded end of a tie rod. Immediate close inspection of all Tiger Moths was followed by the issue of TNS 29 which placed a mandatory calendar life on all tie rods or a restriction on hours flown, whichever came sooner. Thus was introduced the first lifed component part in a Tiger Moth airframe.

In December 2013 a pleasure flying Tiger Moth broke up in mid-air near Brisbane and the sequence was filmed by an on-board video camera. Although at the time of writing no final report had been published by the accident investigators failure of the tie rods was strongly suspected as a contributory cause. It is believed those fitted to the aircraft had not been manufactured strictly to the de Havilland drawing specification with the result that from 21 March 2014 all aircraft were subject to immediate inspection and removal of any rods supplied by the same manufacturer. The loss of the aircraft and its two occupants was a hard reminder that the Tiger Moth and her forebears had been designed and tested by a skilled team at the top of their profession and every one of their decisions had been made only after considerable reasoning and agreement.

Hatfield supplied 'unassembled' airframes 83202-83207 'less engines' and Morris Motors shipped all major component parts for the next eighteen bare fuselages (83379-83396), to which Rongotai added their own identification DHNZ25-DHNZ48, Air Force serials running consecutively from NZ775 to NZ798. The first twelve were completed to production Stage C (all as previously agreed plus Rongotai's responsibility for the engine cowlings), and the last twelve conformed to the requirements of Stage D which added a locally built centre section with fuel tank, and the complete chassis system (undercarriage), with the exception of the tailskid.

Stages E and F were phased-in during construction of the next fifty two aircraft which bore only local build numbers. DHNZ49-DHNZ60 (NZ799-NZ810), represented Stage E which called for manufacture of the whole fuselage frame including controls, control box, top deckings (cowls), seats, instrument boards, bulkheads, oil tank and pipe connections, ignition wiring, external fittings, exhaust manifold and engine installation kit. By Stage F, apart from non-de Havilland proprietary items, special forgings, castings and pressings which included items such as seats (imported from Australia), the whole aircraft was to be a product of the Wellington factory. This coalescence was first met by NZ811 (DHNZ61), which was subject to a thirty minute test flight by the General Manager, to his great satisfaction and delight, on 19 April 1941. Much had been achieved in a short time by a small team working up from nothing but a green field site.

While the remainder of contract 8200 was being fulfilled, NZ812-NZ850, (DHNZ62-DHNZ100), with the last aircraft accepted by the military on 24 October 1941, it was recognised that the provisioning programme which progressively had been losing time was eight months behind schedule. In an effort to alleviate some of the shortfall Hugh Buckingham made exploratory contact with his Australian shareholder, Alan Murray Jones, at the Mascot factory. The result was the supply by Australia of component parts which were integrated into New Zealand production from March 1941, followed by the provision of twenty complete aircraft, NZ1401-1420, (DHA487-DHA506). The Australian-built Tiger Moths were erected at Rongotai just as the last of the first batch of home-produced aircraft were being assembled and, apart from their Air Force serials, adopted no amended form of builder's identity to cause the same degree of confusion afforded to earlier imports from England.

Aircraft consigned from Mascot had arrived with ten spare engines, Australian-built Gipsy Majors manufactured by General Motors (Holdens). At a package price of £42,000, the twenty aircraft and spares were more expensive per unit than the local product, but the British Government agreed to contribute 50% of the total cost as part of their obligation to the Empire Air Training Scheme (EATS).

Above: Stage D of the development of New Zealand production included one of the most complicated parts of a Tiger Moth, the centre section petrol tank. *RNZAF Ohakea*

Left: New Zealand elected to build standard pattern engine cowlings for its Tiger Moths rather than follow the Canadian example which was less complicated. *RNZAF Ohakea*

The last of the first batch of New Zealand built Tiger Moths under final assembly in September 1941, eight months behind schedule. Ready erected is NZ1404, one of twenty Tiger Moths purchased from de Havilland Australia in an effort to redress the shortfall on deliveries. *Hugh Buckingham*

Right: NZ1415 was one of twenty complete aircraft imported from Australia in 1941 in an effort to speed up supply to the schools. *deHMC Archive*

Below: Hugh Buckingham set up a propeller workshop in the former Electrolux factory at Evans Bay which was capable of the manufacture or repair of propellers for all the aircraft types likely to find their way through the factory at Rongotai. *Hugh Buckingham*

Before the days of copy lathes and computer aided design and manufacture, each propeller blade was produced by hand to the highest degree of accuracy. The laminations were cut against patterns and carefully glued together. Final balance was often achieved by the application of one lick of varnish at the tip of a blade. *Hugh Buckingham*

A central maintenance, repair and support facility for Tiger Moths was established in the unheated wooden Centennial Exhibition Building where all floorspace was quickly allocated. The aircraft second from the right in this pictures is NZ671, an aircraft built by Morris Motors and seemingly all in one piece. *Hugh Buckingham*

Hugh Buckingham continued to share test flying duties but on a much reduced scale, concentrating instead on the establishment of aircraft and engine overhaul facilities, raising staff levels from the initial sixty to about 400, and converting the old Electrolux factory at Evans Bay into a first class propeller workshop capable of manufacturing wooden blades for all airframe types scheduled to pass through the Rongotai overhaul and repair process, including the ubiquitous Airspeed Oxford and Supermarine Walrus.

The engine overhaul facility was to play a vital part in maintaining the flow of aircraft for, apart from a small residual stock of new engines which had been previously delivered from Stag Lane, and an almost similar number supplied from Australia, most airframe production from 1942 until the last aircraft built in 1944, relied on re-lifed engines acquired from many sources including service write-offs, estimated at a monthly wastage rate of three airframes and two engines. So vital was the business of repair and overhaul that the de Havilland Aircraft Company of New Zealand expanded into the unheated but elegant Centennial Exhibition Buildings on a permanent basis and recruited extra civilian staff not only to relieve local pressure on Air Force maintenance shops but to create one centrally located Tiger Moth support facility. Initially the overhaul schedule imposed at 1,000 hours flying time reduced a Tiger Moth airframe to a pile of component parts, each of which was examined in minute detail. It was a curious course of action for an establishment cradled with British expertise since no such policy was ever encouraged by de Havilland's Service Department or implemented at military Maintenance Units anywhere.

It was soon realised that in the best interests of time and economy much less dismantling combined with systematic visual inspection was entirely satisfactory as the costs involved under the 'strip and overhaul' policy were greater than manufacture of a new aeroplane. By September 1944 the airframe overhaul life had been extended progressively and by degrees to reach 1,600 hours.

It may have been due partly to the extravagance of the original policy which caused Hatfield to issue a first rebuke to their General Manager in New Zealand, but the final straw perhaps, concerned Hugh Buckingham's attempt to beautify the factory surrounds by planting daffodil bulbs. Having seen a number of different varieties in flower he had unwittingly chosen one which he considered outstanding and ordered 500 bulbs, only to discover after planting that they were a rare species, a factor reflected in their price. Quite embarrassed, the invoice for £1,500 was forwarded with apologetic trepidation to Hatfield where upon receipt Company Secretary Wilfred Nixon was said to be 'very unhappy'. Meanwhile, 'Hughie' Buckingham awaited arrival of the storm he knew was brewing.

Having established a fully functional and competent industrial organisation from a standing start which he led from the front, Hugh Buckingham test flew the last of the Australian supplied aircraft, NZ1420 (DHA506), on New Year's Eve 1941, and three overhauled Tiger Moths the following week. On 19 January 1942 he made a final flight around the local area in Miles M.11 Whitney Straight NZ579, the impressed ZK-AFG, late of the Wellington Aero Club, before returning to England but certainly not into obscurity. Hugh Buckingham, a well-liked de Havilland personality from the early Moth days at Stag Lane, remained with the company and continued flying on its behalf until 1951, succeeding Aubrey Burke as Executive Director of the de Havilland Engine Company in 1955 and remaining at its head until his retirement. Forty years after his departure from New Zealand he could still chuckle over the outrageous cost of the prize-winning daffodil bulbs.

The new General Manager appointed for Rongotai was Nicholas Higgs, New Zealand's Technical Representative for Bristol Aeroplane Company engines since 1939. Other members of the original Hatfield team had already left and Peter de Havilland also returned to England at this time to join brothers Geoffrey Jnr and John who were fully engaged with Mosquito work at Hatfield. Test flying duties at Rongotai were delegated to John Neave, recruited from flying DH.83 Fox Moths for Air Travel (NZ) Ltd. to and from primitive strips along the West Coast. His was to be a daily diet of new and reconditioned Tiger Moths until the end of the war when he left the company to take up the position of Chief Flying Instructor with the Canterbury Aero Club.

There had never been serious technical difficulties with any new Tiger Moths manufactured at Rongotai but during Neave's time one batch of aircraft was fitted with carburettors carrying an insert made necessary to salvage them from a manufacturing error committed elsewhere. Although the results of test bed and ground running all proved satisfactory, on at least three occasions the insert came loose in the air, generally during the climb out immediately after take-off, causing the engine to shut down. It was only the pilot's skill on each occasion that allowed the aircraft to be landed deadstick back on the aerodrome.

A further thirty six Tiger Moths were ordered early in 1942 (DHNZ101-DHNZ136), which were scheduled for delivery at the rate of three aircraft per month from the beginning of March, although signature of the contract was delayed until April. Wearing serial numbers NZ1426-NZ1456, the order was satisfied by November 1942 although NZ1447 (DHNZ127), accepted onto Air Force charge at Rongotai on 8 October, never did reach her destination at Harewood. Flying in a strong north westerly wind on 28 October, conditions had become increasingly turbulent on the leeward coast of Motunau Island, North Canterbury, and the pilot descended to 200ft to seek relief. There was none and during

With an obligatory white silk scarf streaming behind, Des Strong's New Zealand-built Tiger Moth ZK-BMY was part of a three biplane circus act at the Vintage Aviator flying display at Hood Aerodrome near Masterton, north of Wellington, in April 2012. *John Mounce*

The unmistakable figure of John Neave clad in long leather coat, preparing for another day's work testing Tiger Moths. In the background, some of the twenty aircraft imported from Australia and erected at Rongotai late in 1941.
RNZAF Museum

the climb to regain altitude the aircraft became uncontrollable and fell inverted into the sea. The pilot swam ashore and the Tiger Moth minus her engine remained afloat long enough to be salvaged, but was written-off after inspection as a complete loss. On 6 May 1943 delivery of the first of a further batch of thirty six aircraft ordered under government contract A/129/42 was commenced, DHNZ137-DHNZ172, serialled NZ1457-NZ1492, and in July 1943 a further thirty six were contracted for delivery at the agreed rate of three aircraft per month throughout 1944.

Rongotai's dependence on imported parts whose local manufacture had never been contemplated (streamline wires, castings and forgings), was challenged when severe shortages were experienced towards the end of 1943 due to late deliveries, principally from Mascot; the same lack of supplies that was delaying numerous repair jobs across Australia. Some new aircraft at Rongotai were only completed to a standard to permit acceptance as a result of robbing spares from dismantled aircraft awaiting repair or overhaul.

As the 1942 programme slipped further back, contract A/129/42 was terminated following delivery of only twenty seven aircraft. The July contract (A/132/43) specifying thirty six deliveries in 1944 was cancelled completely. Only following extreme administrative effort was the production programme re-scheduled; the aircraft were still required and consequently an entirely new contract was drawn up in February 1944. A/133/44 called for forty five Tiger Moths, essentially the residue of the earlier contracts, to be delivered by 3 December that year. These were to include the nine aircraft originally scheduled to become NZ1484-NZ1492 (DHNZ164-DHNZ172), plus NZ1493-NZ1528 (DHNZ173-DHNZ209). The realisation that Air Force serials NZ1501-NZ1528 duplicated those previously allocated to extinct Hawker Hinds resulted in substitution of serials NZ1601-NZ1628. Now, with the gradual reduction in the training programme and an attrition rate lower than forecast, the final twenty seven aircraft of contract A/133/44 were cancelled in September 1944 leaving the last of the Wellington-built Tiger Moths, NZ1493-NZ1500 and NZ1601 (DHNZ173-DHNZ181), to be taken on to Air Force charge by the end of February 1945.

Tiger Moths built at Rongotai were essentially the same as those created from identical drawings held at Hatfield, Cowley and Mascot. The New Zealand-built aircraft were more akin to the British product; improvements spawned at Mascot, practical and genuine, were not adopted at Rongotai even after New Zealand's experience of assembling Tiger Moths manufactured in Australia when they were able to enjoy the unique benefit of direct comparison between those and others supplied from sources in Great Britain.

The British spin strake, over which the RAF had made such strong representation, had been thoroughly investigated at Farnborough and Boscombe Down, trials which had been followed by a massive 'on production' and retrofit programme, but was never copied across to Australia or New Zealand where, essentially, the same aeroplanes were occupied by exactly the same commitments, even to the extent of carrying bomb racks. Details of the strakes were studied by the New Zealand factory late in 1941 and a set was fitted to a Tiger Moth and flight tested by John Neave early in 1942, but upon his recommendation the modification was considered unnecessary and was never fitted to production aircraft. Assessment of the British spinning trials, however, did result in universal removal of aileron mass balance weights.

Tiger Moth NZ1486 was one of the aircraft built against the last contract placed in 1944 after renegotiation due to slippage on delivery dates. In the event only twenty of the forty five aircraft order were delivered.
RNZAF Museum

Surplus aircraft that could not be flown away from an RAF MU after their sale had to be collected by road within a strict limit of time. This fuselage for the future G-ANKC was delivered to the Rollason hangar at Croydon on the back of a surplus army lorry. *deHMC Archive*

CHAPTER FIFTEEN

Going for a Song

Total war is as much about resources, logistics and economics as it is to the politics, brutality and destruction. Supplies, services and support required to defeat the enemy must be provided almost regardless of cost although accounts are dutifully and meticulously maintained in appropriate quarters. Long before any cessation of hostilities plans will be laid by the optimists and realists of both sides engaged in the conflict, designed to cope with the continuation of trade, commerce and the freedom to prosper after the enforced interruption. Much of the legion of artefacts and miscellaneous equipment salvaged from the material requirements of sustained modern warfare is readily adaptable to civil use following a return to peace and stability. The victor, witnessing the signature of the vanquished, could so easily become the unwitting victim of economic suicide were not the return to peace and normality managed with as much tactical care as direction of the greatest battle.

As early as 1944 the British, Canadian and American Governments were engaged in delicate discussions in Washington aiming to establish a post-war policy for the ordered disposal of thousands of aircraft in a manner politically acceptable to all parties, which did not flood the world markets with state of the art technology at insane prices, yet provided opportunities for refurbishment, operation and maintenance without degrading the prospects for future research, design and manufacture.

Each camp in Washington harboured a vested interest. The Americans had a near monopoly of large transport aircraft whilst Great Britain had a major input in bombers and fighters, sharing a common interest in training aircraft with her Commonwealth partners and the USA. In 1944, with the war not won, Lend-Lease aircraft were still being provided by the United States. Intransigence on the part of the British Government during discussions concerning surplus disposals could affect currently agreed and future aid, it was believed.

A view developed on the British side that suggested separate rules should be applied to aircraft bought outright rather than leased, loaned or borrowed. "Why not scrap all surplus aircraft and have done with it?" was a bold new line tabled by the British Secretary of State for Air, Sir Archibald Sinclair. There would be little financial return from such an exercise but it had merit, and would obviate the need for expensive care and storage facilities. But if a total scrapping policy was not the answer, what proportion of the surplus should be retained to guard against future emergencies, also to guarantee that closed lines for staple types, like the Tiger Moth trainer, would not need to be re-activated?

The equation was complicated and grounds for endless debate in the corridors of power. In Great Britain, implementation of whatever agreement was reached was to be the prerogative of the Ministry of Aircraft Production (MAP), rather than the Air Ministry, although in practice situations and solutions never were clear cut and sharp inter-departmental exchanges resulted when ill defined boundaries were thought to have been transgressed.

The scene at Scone Aerodrome, Perth, immediately after the war, when the Tiger Moths of 11 EFTS were transiting from camouflage to all-over yellow, unlike the hangars. Some aircraft still carried letters identifying their 'Flight' within the school. *via M J Hooks*

Emphasis was placed on the interpretation of two reports published almost simultaneously in the USA. On 26 June 1944, the War Contracts Sub Committee to the Committee on Military Affairs published its paper, 'Disposal of Surplus Aircraft and Major Components Thereof' which was followed by what became known as the Clayton Report: 'Report on Surplus Aircraft Disposal, submitted by Surplus Aircraft Advisory Sub Committee to William L Clayton, Administrator, Surplus War Property Administration, Office of War Mobilisation'.

The Clayton Report carried a wide ranging and balanced view of the whole matter and provided reasoned argument for construction of all the equations, but it was binding on nobody. On behalf of the MAP, the Air Ministry had on 22 May 1944 contacted its Washington delegates before either American report had been released, requesting them to investigate claims made in the British weekly magazine *The Aeroplane*, that the United States authorities had announced they were shortly to put up for sale 5,000 war surplus training aircraft from a total of about 12,000 aircraft eventually to be offered to the market. The report stated that 3,200 aircraft had already been declared surplus, of which 1,823 were trainer and liaison types of twenty one different models, and sales would be organised against a bidding process open, initially at least, only to citizens of the United States.

The British delegation was reminded that "current practice is to break down surplus RAF aircraft," but they were advised that "we are now considering holding on to Tiger Moths and Magisters for post-war individuals and clubs, and are taking soundings as to possible bids for such aircraft from Empire or European countries."

At the beginning of June 1944, Canada announced that due to a reduction in the training programme they intended to offer surplus aircraft first to the British Government and then to other Dominions. An agreement was already in place with the United States that neither would flood the other with surplus equipment. There was no prospect that the British Government would be interested in buying Tiger Moths having itself declared a surplus of 150 aircraft with a further 300 (plus 150 Magisters) to be released by the end of 1944, leaving 2,050 in service or in store! At the same time, an Air Ministry survey identified 600 Tiger Moths available in Canada, 660 in Australia, 235 in New Zealand, 580 in South Africa, 290 in India and a further 228 in Southern Rhodesia.

Canada was also anxious to dispose of 200 Fairchild Cornells built locally for shipment to South Africa and which the SAAF had refused to accept on the grounds that, unlike the Tiger Moth which might itself have been marginal, performance of the wooden winged Cornell was not compatible with a hot, high altitude environment, a rejection which had embarrassed the Canadians very considerably.

In a move generally accepted as being within the framework of agreements reached in Washington, the United States formally announced in July the release of 11,450 surplus aircraft for private sale within the USA, and on 23 July the Air Ministry confirmed the Canadian Government's proposal to sell 600 DH.82C Tiger Moths into the world market, phased at 100 aircraft per month for the next six months. This news had reached the MAP via Francis St Barbe at Hatfield whose intelligence had been gathered from the heart of the Dominion: "The theory is that the good market for surplus war stocks will not last very long. If the government waits for a Conference with the United Nations, the opportunity will be lost."

The Director General of Civil Aviation (DGCA), Sir William Hildred, expressed his view that of the 450 Tiger Moths and 150 Miles Magisters due to be declared surplus by the RAF from 1 January 1945, a total of 200-300 aircraft (of which it was suggested 75-100 ought to be Magisters), should be retained for sale to allied governments, export to the colonies or sale to private owners and clubs within the British Isles. The remainder would be scrapped. As responsible selling agents, the MAP urged him to discuss the plan with the Americans, especially as 500 Cornells which had been obtained under Lend-Lease (Mutual Aid Canada), were still serving in Southern Rhodesia and India.

With the gradual deceleration of the Joint Air Training Scheme, in mid-June 1944 South Africa declared it would have a surplus of fifty Tiger Moths from early 1945, and the Rhodesian Air Training Group (RATG) announced from Salisbury that it had declared 118 Tiger Moths surplus with immediate effect. RATG suggested selling the aircraft at £100 each: "There was no covered accommodation for them and they would rapidly deteriorate if left too long in open storage." The advice offered from London was to sell immediately at any reasonable price, preferably within Africa, and whatever was left over should be scrapped. RATG was also directed not to offer any assistance for sale of surplus Cornells.

Confusion in the British approach to the still fluid disposals policy was revealed by the Air Ministry on 23 September. MAP suggested that the Air Ministry had given permission for British Government owned aircraft damaged in South Africa to an assessment level of Category A (repairable on site), to be broken down. The Air Ministry replied politely that this report was not true. Although the normal policy on redundant aircraft was to break down, no decision on the South African based aircraft had yet been made. But some action would shortly be demanded, and following a gathering of all interested parties at the first formal meeting of the Aircraft Disposal Committee held in London on 1 November 1944, the Joint American Secretariat in Washington was cabled with the following statement, classified as 'Top Secret':

London. 8 November 1944.
To Joint American Secretariat Washington. Re Class C light aircraft.
"Light aircraft manufacturers share the view that judicious sales (ex-military) in the immediate post-war period will encourage future personal and flying club demand. Particularly so for types out of production due training cutback. We may have need of these to meet genuine civil demands until new civil types are developed. Careful watch to ensure surplus sales do not endanger new development – watch disposals in Third countries. Price and quality control required calculated to ensure the emergence of only genuine demands, to discourage speculative purchase, and to prevent the release of ill conditioned aircraft likely to discredit the manufacturer and set back the prospects for private flying. We doubt whether sale by auction is likely to achieve this."

A better than anticipated wastage rate, improvements in the fortunes of the Allies, and the efficiency with which the training schools were producing qualified aircrew, caused an inevitable reduction in the training programme from early 1944. Although a revision to the length of an EFTS course was a ploy previously used in the control of output, an overall reduction of 40% capacity was sought resulting in the closure of 25 EFTS Belvedere, near Salisbury, Southern Rhodesia in November 1944 and consequent redundancies in the fleet.

The first attempt by the Rhodesian Air Training Group (RATG) Headquarters to sell a surplus Tiger Moth was under guidance from London and dragged on for six months. In October 1944, the Air Ministry (not MAP who should have been approached), cleared RATG to sell one Tiger Moth to the Southern Rhodesia Air Service Communications Squadron. It later transpired that this was for the government's Medical Officer of Health to enable him to reach outlying districts more expeditiously.

Guidance as to price was based on the original contract agreement with de Havilland which covered a new aircraft delivered in Great Britain, quoted as £1,310, a figure itemised as £880 for the airframe and £430 for the engine. RATG were advised to deduct 10% of the new price to cover the cost of a complete overhaul or one thousandth of the new price for every hour flown since the last complete overhaul. It took ten weeks for the significance of the resultant offer price of £866.15s.8d to filter through Salisbury's bureaucratic system, but the reply was much as expected in view of the fact that RATG and MAP had previously advocated quick sales for reasonable prices, and were on record as quoting £100 as a realistic expectation.

"It is not considered that the cost bears fair relation to its value under present circumstances, and the price is unacceptable to the Southern Rhodesia Government. Opportunity will be taken of the presence in the UK of AOC RATG, Air Vice-Marshal Sir Charles Meredith, to negotiate transfer on a different basis."

Reacting less quickly than might have been expected to defuse an embarrassing situation, the Air Ministry replied on 3 February 1945 suggesting that the subject aircraft should be taken from store and put to immediate good use. If the transfer of the aircraft was not catered for in the course of more comprehensive arrangements, the cost would be guaranteed at not more than £400. As the majority of the RATG aircraft were eventually sold by tender or cut up for scrap, the British Government had no mass transfer within which to shade handover of the Medical Officer's Tiger Moth, and in spite of 'Billy' Meredith's intervention in London, £400 was the sum duly paid.

News quickly spread throughout southern and East Africa that Tiger Moths (and a large number of Avro Ansons) had been declared surplus in Southern Rhodesia, and enquiries began to flow through to RATG who passed them to MAP in London for approval. The number of Tiger Moths declared surplus rose to 138 on 13 April 1945, and on the advice received from MAP, a minimum price of £500 each was requested, as standing. RATG was ordered not to get involved in any form of overhaul agreement with purchasers. MAP believed the aircraft were less liable to be transported out of the region if the initial purchase price was maintained at a high level, and the origin of most enquiries encouraged this view. Misr enquired after a batch of aircraft for their Flying Institute in Cairo; two aircraft in use, SU-ABX and SU-ABY (3597/3608), had been exported from Hatfield in 1937 and although six more were added to the fleet in 1944 they were recruited more conveniently from the Mediterranean Allied Air Force (MAAF). The Aero Club of East Africa asked for quotations as did the Government of Mozambique, Quelimane Aero Club in Portuguese East Africa, and the Emperor of Ethiopia.

The supply of cheap war-surplus aircraft was still of major concern to the manufacturers and even though Hatfield had not built a Tiger Moth since 1940, and de Havilland had no plans for light aircraft in the immediate post-war era, except perhaps a replacement for their own Tiger Moth, MAP sought the views of the company's Business Director

DX709 'AZ' of 4 FTS Heany in 1948. The aircraft was supplied from Australia in 1944 against a British Government contract and was written off after a crash on the last day of 1951. There may have been some creativity during her time in Southern Rhodesia for the aircraft is fitted with spin strakes, navigation lights on the top wings and a British style oil tank. *David Vernon*

at a meeting in his Hatfield office on 16 April 1945. Francis St Barbe stated his opinion that the manufacturers should have a greater say in the disposal of their products and as to the suggestion that Tiger Moths should be issued free of charge to flying clubs he was totally opposed. He believed the price for a weary Tiger Moth in Southern Rhodesia might be about £200, but no encouragement should be offered to assist with their transport, least of all back to Great Britain.

When Colonel Rod Douglas of de Havilland's South African Associated Company was in London a few weeks later, it was suggested that if the re-sale prospects of the Southern Rhodesia Tiger Moths were bright; he would consider setting up a refurbishment centre in which case he might be tempted to make an offer for the entire stock. Meanwhile, RATG reported that the condition of the aircraft was rapidly deteriorating and on 11 May, nineteen were withdrawn from sale and scrapped. MAP made urgent contact with their Air Mission representatives in South Africa requesting an immediate survey of the remaining stock. The report received on 16 June grouped the surviving 119 aircraft into three categories: twenty two were said to be in good condition with an average utilisation of 600 hours each; forty five were fair having accumulated about 1500 hours and the remaining fifty two were described as 'indifferent', mostly due to weathered fabric.

As the Government Disposals Office in Salisbury had offered no help and shown no interest, and there was no local working facility capable of overhauling the aircraft, MAP's suggestion that in order to protect the reputation of the manufacturer and provide the most valuable option to purchasers, only the best aircraft should be offered for sale, and this should be accomplished by tender.

With the acknowledge of Colonel Douglas a target price of £250 per aircraft was to be sought, and the names and addresses of all purchasers were to be supplied to de Havilland in Johannesburg for their follow-up offer of technical assistance and provision of spares.

The sale was widely advertised in Africa but, by agreement, not in South Africa, and forty four tender forms were distributed including one to the de Havilland Company who eventually decided not to bid. The sealed offers were opened on 4 October 1945 and resulted in seventy six firm bids for forty five aircraft from twenty prospective clients ranging from local citizens and aero clubs to the Governor General of Mozambique. Only twenty three bids topped £250 posted against fifteen individual aircraft, bids ranging from £50 (thirteen hours run on the engine) and £100 (twenty five minutes run on the engine), both with high airframe hours, to £425 which was probably too high for EM741 (85972), with almost 900 hours on the airframe and over 330 on the engine. For £350 the Governor General of Mozambique bought EM786 (86003), with fewer than 190 hours total time since delivery.

Built in Australia and operated by the Air Forces of South Africa and Southern Rhodesia, VP-YNV was registered to the Civil Aviation Flying Club in Salisbury, but not until 1956. This photograph was taken at Bindura in 1965. In 1984 she was transferred to Zimbabwean marks but was sold to South Africa in 2000. *deHMC Archive*

Before the bid process was closed MAP received notice of interest in 'a large number' of Tiger Moths which were required in Chile, but 4 October came and went without receipt of an offer. However, in April 1946 a request for twenty Tiger Moths for Chile was received in London and rejected by one of the many proliferating civil service committees on the grounds of non-availability, and eventually a number of Miles Magisters was acquired instead.

The Emperor of Ethiopia did not bid either, but arrangements were made for the private sale of two aircraft which were airlifted to Addis Ababa on 16 November and erected there. Four more Tiger Moths were later sent from Great Britain: two aircraft, EM857 and EM858 (85059/85060), were supplied from RAF storage on 22 and 15 November 1945 respectively. BB675 (3402), and T7338 (83864), were amongst twenty aircraft, probably damaged, bought by the de Havilland Company through MAP in England for refurbishment and resale. Following overhaul at Witney they were delivered to Addis Ababa on 6 November 1946 and both served with the Imperial Ethiopian Air Force before joining the Imperial Ethiopian Aero Club in 1949 and subsequently were written off in 1950 and 1952.

A week after the Southern Rhodesia bids had been reviewed RATG Headquarters received a visit from the proprietor of Spencer's Airways and Garage, Victoria Falls. Mr E H Spencer's total offer of £950, bid against nine individual aircraft and ranging from £50 to £150, had not been successful. He asked for favourable consideration of his plan to buy all thirty unsold aircraft, no matter what condition, all of which would be completely dismantled and re-worked to as-new condition by his team. As good a case as he pleaded the decision, which was referred back from London, was not in his favour and no bulk deal was ever agreed. Spencer's Airways were later credited with purchase of four unidentified Tiger Moths, three of which the company itself advertised for sale by tender in June 1947 (VP-YEA, VP-YEB and VP-YEC), all said to be in an unconverted state, whilst the fourth, VP-YDY, was offered only as a source of spare parts.

At the end of 1945, Schreiner and Company, an aircraft trading business based in The Hague, approached RATG directly enquiring after ten aircraft on behalf of the Dutch Government who were seeking to equip a new training school shortly to be established in the Netherlands. RATG advised Schreiner on 14 January 1946 that another batch of 'ancient' aircraft ("five years old and with about 1,500 hours logged") was currently available against tender. The unofficial reserve level was about £200 per lot but RATG warned that each aircraft would cost £150 to dismantle and pack, plus £50 to despatch by rail to a South African port, plus shipping to Europe. Copies of the correspondence were sent to MAP in London who confirmed that the Director of Civil Aviation in the Netherlands had already been in contact with them, and that a deal for twelve ex-RAF Tiger Moths was being negotiated.

Sale of the second batch of thirty seven surplus RATG aircraft resulted in twenty seven contracts which raised £5,087, but eight aircraft were withdrawn and retained by the RAF. Another pair was considered not to match the quality criteria, and both were scrapped.

One contented customer provided cheer for the de Havilland publicity department: Australian built '538', having somehow escaped the scrapping policy with 2,232 hours recorded on the airframe and a little over 300 hours on the engine, was sold to J H Forsythe of Gatooma for £150 and registered VP-YEE on 20 March 1946. A need to attend two conferences in South Africa combined with a touring holiday did not synchronise well with the aircraft's limited range, but the Shell company laid down petrol stocks at various staging fields "where servicing facilities no longer existed." Later reports indicated that "in the course of their flight, Mr and Mrs Forsythe landed at twenty six towns and villages and were able to see much more of the natural beauty and wild life of the country than would have been possible in the same time by other forms of transport. The total cost of the trip, including landing and hangarage, amounted to £46.10s.6d. Customs formalities were simple except at Durban where forms in sextuplicate were required." Less than a year after the adventure the registration was cancelled on the grounds that the aircraft had been "withdrawn from use."

In 1946 MAP was redefined as part of the new Ministry of Supply (MoS) and in Southern Rhodesia RATG, having trained 7,600 pilots and 2,300 navigators, bomb aimers and air gunners, reformed on a reduced scale as the Air Training Wing (ATW), later to revert to its original title. An early task was to supervise disposal of a further fifty one Tiger Moths. In July 1946 six aircraft, each with a spare engine, were sold to the Southern Rhodesia Government at a price which was quoted as being 'slightly less than 1/12th book value'. ATW had been requested to negotiate sale of four others to local flying clubs 'on best terms' but minimum values of £100 per aircraft and £20 per spare engine were expected to be generated.

The remaining forty one aircraft were, at the suggestion of the Air Ministry, to be offered in conjunction with the new Ministry of Civil Aviation (MCA), to flying clubs in Great Britain, provided packing and transport for each aircraft was covered by the purchasers. Even the MoS regarded this suggestion as one of acute optimism and likely to achieve nothing. Did the Air Ministry not realise the difficulties involved with individual inspection in and transport from southern Africa, and were they not aware that during the course of the next four years, their own policy would declare 1,000 British based Tiger Moths redundant?

It seems unlikely that this third batch of aircraft, all high time and badly deteriorated due to poor local storage conditions, ever did raise much interest. The previous sales had virtually saturated what was a very limited regional market but one within which South Africa was not immediately included due to the practicalities and politics of her own disposals. As no reports of a major catastrophe have ever been uncovered, notification that the forty five Tiger Moths struck off charge on 28 October 1948 as having been "destroyed by fire" almost certainly points to them being scrapped and burned, and probably well before that date which merely tidied the paperwork.

VP-YEP was built in Australia and sold from the SRAF in 1956. By 1958 she was operational with the Mashonaland Flying Club in Salisbury but her fate is unrecorded. *Liz Elliot via Mitch Stirling*

The 100 hand picked Tiger Moths which arrived in Rhodesia from Benoni in October 1946 were allocated to 4 FTS Heany and 5 FTS Thornhill. These were part of the Air Ministry's declared need for 200 high quality aircraft which were extracted from the expired JATS Agreement in South Africa, and replaced aircraft which had already been sold or relegated to scrap. Several of these which were delivered as 'urgent replacements' had been sold by the following July. The remaining 100 Tiger Moths were shipped across the Indian Ocean from Cape Town and into the care of the Hindustan Aircraft Company at Bangalore.

The slimming down of the training system resulted in a total of just eighty eight Tiger Moths remaining on the ATW's inventory under RAF control from the end of 1948, to which a further twenty two were added, shipped from RAF stocks in Great Britain, arriving as a trickle throughout 1950, an expansion almost certainly made with an eye on the political situation in Europe and Korea. The number was gradually eroded until July 1952 when the survivors were finally withdrawn. The CFI at Heany, Squadron Leader Hyland-Smith, inadvertently helped to get the numbers down on 27 July 1948 during practice for a crazy flying display. The station was due to open to the

The propeller seems to have survived this turnover of Tiger Moth T8257 unless its lack of rotation was the cause of a forced landing that did not end well. The aircraft was delivered from England late in 1950 when she was fitted with spin strakes. She was written off as the result of an accident in July 1951 although it seems unlikely to have been this one. *deHMC Archive*

Decorated with a witch, a black cat and a broomstick, this Tiger Moth of the Southern Rhodesia Air Force was one of a fleet in service at Cranbourne in 1954 when Rhodesian nationals were trained to fly during a five month 'Short Service Course'. *Jerry Dunn*

public a few days later and what more exciting than a Tiger Moth in unusual attitudes close to the ground? Operating from the front cockpit of EM843 (86045), the CFI dug the tip of the starboard lower wing into the ground during a tight turn at no altitude near the control tower, injuring himself and his bemused wireless mechanic passenger in the rear cockpit, and fatally wounding the aeroplane.

During the period 1948-1952, forty nine Tiger Moths were scrapped or mostly crashed, twenty four of those in 1951 alone. Nine aircraft had been sold to the Southern Rhodesia Government in 1948/49 to which a further seven were added in 1952. On final withdrawal, six went to the Kenyan Government and seventeen were sold locally to various civilian enterprises. The Southern Rhodesia Air Force continued to use Tiger Moths in its own right at Cranbourne until the end of 1955, and the survivors were sold into the civil market in January and February the following year.

As the Second World War appeared to be turning in favour of the Allies, the British policy of breaking down aircraft surplus to military requirements was beginning to cause concern amongst pre-war owners and operators whose light aircraft assets had been requisitioned in 1939. Geoffrey Alington, signing himself 'Chief Test Pilot, Elmdon', enquired of the Air Ministry in August 1944 whether he could expect the early release of aircraft which had been the property of his company before the war, and which with many others had been in store at Kemble almost ever since. He was advised in December that the aircraft were essentially redundant government property, the scrapping policy was still in effect, that 'Moth Dragon, Moth 60 and Moth Puss' had been scheduled for breaking down and work had already started on Moth Dragon. Not until the end of 1945 was the policy adopted of selling off surplus aircraft in a state where they could be returned to flying condition, and from December of that year the 147 survivors of

As an 18 year old cadet, Jerry Dunn attended No 6 Short Service Course conducted by the Southern Rhodesia Air Force at Cranbourne between April and August 1954. During his subsequent service career he delivered de Havilland Vampires from Hatfield and retired as the Chief Pilot of Air Botswana. *Jerry Dunn*

the 1,017 impressed civil aircraft were put up for public view and tender at Kemble, Cosford and Aston Down.

Throughout the summer of 1944 Commander Harold Perrin, Secretary of the Royal Aero Club, had been involved with the Air Ministry, Ministry of Aircraft Production (MAP), the Society of British Aircraft Constructors (SBAC) General Council, and his own Private Flying Committee, addressing the prospects for post-war private and club flying. In May 1944 a Joint Committee agreed that light aircraft of a suitable type should not be scrapped but rather handed back free of cost to the parent designing company who would undertake any necessary reconditioning in order to qualify for a Certificate of Airworthiness (C of A). The 'free of cost to the designers' provision was perhaps what caused the SBAC to approve and to modify any concerns which Francis St Barbe for the de Havilland Company may have expressed about plans for a suggested free of cost issue to flying clubs and similar organisations. The Committee agreed that selected surplus aircraft types which would meet the immediate post-war requirement, and the price which owners and operators might realistically be expected to pay were: Auster £100; Tiger Moth £125; Magister £125; Proctor £200; Dominie, Oxford and Anson £500.

Early the following year, Perrin's group advised MAP that the Air Ministry had told them that from March 1945 in excess of 178 Magisters would be declared surplus together with a substantial number of Austers, but no Tiger Moths would be released in quantity until a new RAF trainer was available "in a year or so." To emphasise their opinion, the Air Ministry were even signalling a potential need to import training aircraft from the USA. The threat was countered by the Treasury who reminded MAP that the Air Ministry was already suggesting the British Government should give away its half share of the Tiger Moths based in South Africa, that surplus aircraft were already for sale in Southern Rhodesia, and that the first of 600 Canadian owned Tiger Moths were about to be offered for sale on the world market.

The Air Ministry reacted by confirming that within the British Isles there were no surplus Tiger Moths, but supposing a new elementary trainer was in production by mid-1947, and no schools were to be relocated to Great Britain from Canada or Southern Rhodesia, then perhaps 100 Tiger Moths could be available then with more to follow at a later date. If Elementary Schools were to be re-located then some of the 250 South African based Tiger Moths expected to remain on strength after disposal of 505 surplus machines, might be headed for British bases. Stocks of Tiger Moths in use or in store, they admitted, as of 1 March 1945 amounted to 2,273.

In 1944 the British Government had sanctioned the delivery of sixty five new Tiger Moths to French Air Force flying schools operating in Algeria and Morocco and all were shipped in May and June. In September the following year six new aircraft were transferred from the Mediterranean Allied Air Force (MAAF) and delivered into store at Casablanca. As occupying forces were cleared out of France four Tiger Moths were allocated to the RAF's 'Training Delegation to France' late in 1944 all of which were transferred to the French military in June 1945.

Until France's own manufacturing industry was in a position to cope with the country's post-war demands, 1,383 ex RAF aircraft were to be sold to the French military under the terms of the Hartemann Agreement signed in November 1945. The first consignment, comprising training and communications aircraft, was scheduled for delivery from the following January: 160 Tiger Moths were to be flown to mainland France by June 1946 drawn from the 896 declared to be in store in Great Britain at the turn of the year. The French aircraft were brand new, manufactured by Morris Motors between the latter part of 1943 and mid-1944 when they had been dismantled and placed in purgatory storage in the most suitable requisitioned premises in and around Oxford. Upon sale they were recalled to Cowley, inspected and modified where necessary before being test flown and delivered to one of the designated Tiger Moth Maintenance Units (MU) at Aston Down, Colerne, Little Rissington and Llandow. Gathered in small groups at airfields in the West Country, Dunkeswell, Pershore and St Mawgan, the aircraft were flown by pilots of 16 Ferry Unit to Romorantin near Paris, and Châteauroux, for acceptance and allocation to establishments within the Armée de l'Air.

A batch of aircraft transiting through Buc on 23 March 1946 was hit by an overnight storm and ten Tiger Moths were damaged after dragging their pickets and colliding with one another on the ground. The RAF sent a repair party with spares but some aircraft were delayed in reaching their destination at Romorantin until after mid-April.

In September 1946 the Royal Navy aircraft carrier HMS *Colossus* was in North African waters in process of handover to the French Navy. The ship was already flying the tricolore and had adopted the name '*Arromanches*'. Fifteen airworthy Tiger Moths were loaded on board whose destination was the French Ecole de Pilotage Elementaire at Cognac. The carrier set sail for Toulon and when within range each of the Tiger Moths was flown off by a fighter pilot who landed at the Naval Air Station at Cuers.

de Havilland DH.82A Tiger Moth, '5', EC 2/595, Vichy French Air Force, Tong (French Indochina), 1941. Silver overall with yellow/red engine cowling, red spinner and rear fuselage, fin and elevators. Horizontal white stripe along fuselage and another vertical around rear fuselage. Serial black, roundels in six positions with those on fuselage being outlined in white. Artwork ©Richard Caruana, 1:72 scale

Flight hours of Tiger Moths operating with the French military at the end of the war were relatively slight. Following controlled release into the civil market, white registration letters were applied to show against the 'as delivered' camouflage background. Note how the bottom of the rudder of F-BGCG has been cut away to cope with glider towing gear. *via Stan Roberts*

Minimal use appears to have been made of the aircraft in North Africa or at Cognac and by June 1949 it was estimated that 130 Tiger Moths were in store, eighty at Orleans-Saran and fifty after transfer from Cognac to Châteauroux. A plan to utilise them as Air Observation Posts by the army was abandoned as was their allocation to civilian flying clubs as the nucleus of an Air Force Reserve.

The SALS (Service de l'Aviation Légère et Sportive) was established in the late 1940s as an agency of the Ministère des Transports to direct and encourage the rebirth of France's civil aviation and aero club movement. The stored Tiger Moths were officially retired from military service and put at the disposition of the SALS in June and July 1951.

Of the 135 aircraft in total received by SALS, four were considered beyond reasonable repair and were retained at St. Cyr and broken up as spares; the others were allocated to clubs all over France, mostly free of charge.

In 1955 ten aircraft were made subject of 'Contrats de Cession', and were cancelled from the system through attrition. By 1966 the surviving aircraft were very outdated and shabby although high quality Gipsy Major engine maintenance continued to be provided by Boudoin Aviation, a company based near Paris. Several of the aircraft were known not to have flown for some years and it was decided to dispose of them. The fifty four survivors were withdrawn in May and June 1966 and transferred for a nominal ten Francs to the Service de Domaines, a government body whose responsibilities include the disposal of surplus public property in the private market, usually by auction or tender. However, the aircraft remained registered in the names of their operators until all restrictions on their disposal were lifted in the early 1970s and the clubs mostly took one of two options: scrappage or, mostly, private sale.

To confound all previous belief in the Air Ministry's statement that there would be no surplus Tiger Moths in Great Britain before mid-1947, in addition to the deliveries to France twenty aircraft were allocated to the Yugoslav Training Flight in January and February 1945, delivered to 222 MU High Ercall, and packed for passage by ship from Glasgow Docks to Brindisi in southern Italy. The aircraft were unloaded and erected on the dockside in company with lines of Spitfires, then simply pushed a short distance to the aerodrome which was immediately adjacent. RAF markings had been obliterated prior to despatch from England and Yugoslav mechanics quickly overlaid national stars and fin flashes onto the camouflaged background with a squirt from their paint guns, working in the open air.

The political situation in Yugoslavia was volatile. The Tiger Moths were flown across the Strait of Otranto to their new base at Zemunik to join ten North American Harvards where they were officially listed as operational from 26 April. The ship ferrying additional support material had been forced to sail from Brindisi on 28 March to beat a politically imposed deadline and consequently was obliged to leave behind 1,500 cases of spares and other equipment including two Link Trainers which could not be loaded in time.

The RAF Element was briefed to train selected Yugoslav Air Force pilots to be instructors on the Tiger Moths, converting them onto the

F-BGDD was released from French military service in 1951 and was operated by the Aero Club d'Arcachon. The universally adopted standard colour scheme was silver overall with minimal black trim and usually some identification of previous history painted on the rudder. *deHMC Archive*

de Havilland DH.82A Tiger Moth Mk II, 0802/NM-150, Yugoslav Air Force. Ocean Grey and Dark Green upper surfaces with Trainer Yellow undersides. Serials in Night. National markings in four wing positions. *Artwork ©Richard Caruana, 1:72 scale*

Harvard as soon as practicable, and then supervising the first intakes of Yugoslav pupils. Some of the Yugoslav instructors had not flown for several years having been prisoners of war, while others had had recent experience as fighter pilots in Messerschmitt Bf109s. The RAF personnel were not much impressed with the general situation. Apart from having to leave valuable equipment in Italy, since frozen by the Italian authorities, fifty sets of Gosport tubes had to be sent out from England as a personally addressed gift to prevent their confiscation in Brindisi. Inspection Schedules for the Tiger Moths had to be translated from English but by the middle of June it was found that much of the work called up in the schedules was unnecessary or simply incorrect due to the total lack of technical appreciation on the part of the interpreter.

On 16 June, whilst erecting a hangar, the Yugoslav mechanics managed to drop a door onto a parked Tiger Moth, bending the tip bow of the port upper mainplane. To the astonishment of the senior RAF engineer, under the direction of a Yugoslav officer, the mechanics produced a large hammer and set about correcting the situation, saying that once bent back into shape the tip would be bound with tape and all would be well. The RAF engineer insisted that the wing be removed and the tip bow replaced with a new part, during the course of which repair it was discovered that the internal bracing had gone loose and the wing had to be re-rigged.

In spite of the broken Tiger Moth, the fleet managed 493 hours instructor conversion in June and once pupil training commenced on 3 July, 640 hours were flown that month. Relations between the RAF and their hosts were always under strain, especially over the matter of who owned what. When at the beginning of the pupil programme fuel was said to be very scarce, an RAF officer stumbled upon a stock of 27,000 gallons of 100 octane petrol which had been hidden on the airfield under the pretext that it really belonged to another unit.

A delivery of Tiger Moths from the southern Italian port of Brindisi to the Yugoslav Air Force was made across the Strait of Otranto to Zemunik. The Tiger Moths were assembled on the dockside where national insignia was applied and the aircraft manhandled to the local aerodrome for test flying. *IWM*

The Zemunik flying instructors made their first solo conversion flights on the Harvards on 16 July 1945 and two aircraft were badly damaged in wheels up landings during the first hour. Two Tiger Moths sustained damage in a storm which raged through the site on 31 July. One aircraft suffered a bent centre section strut and another was torn from its pickets and thrown 40ft into the air, crashing down as a pile of wreckage. RAF opinion was that the aircraft was a write off but the local engineers insisted that it could and would be rebuilt. The British officers were unsure about ownership of the aircraft although they wore Yugoslav national markings and believed they were in no position to argue, a situation made no easier by a rumour that all the aircraft were shortly to be flown to Belgrade. When clarification was requested through official channels, the British Commander was advised not to raise any objections.

The end of the operations at Zemunik came swiftly. In a situation of fast deteriorating relations between the RAF and local commanders, a Tiger Moth with one of the best instructors and a pupil went missing on an early morning flight on 8 August and in spite of an intensive air search the aircraft was not found due to the fact that the crew had defected to Italy! The following day, 351 (Yugoslav) Squadron arrived with thirteen Hawker Hurricane IVs from their base at Prkos, and two days later the RAF Element was asked to withdraw as quickly as possible but to leave all their transport. The unit Jeep had already mysteriously disappeared from inside a guarded and locked compound. On 15 August pilots from 351 Squadron flew all the serviceable Harvards to Zagreb and the following day nine Tiger Moths took off for an undisclosed destination. Two days after that the RAF Element withdrew.

What happened to the Tiger Moths after they left Zemunik is unclear. All are believed to have been allocated local serial numbers and a list dated June 1945 identifies survivors as 'Aircraft 1-6; 12-14; 16; 18-23 and 25-30', a total of twenty one. Another list dated July fills in all the gaps with the exclusion of '8' and '15', deletes '22' and adds '31'. Post war seven aircraft are known to have been transferred to the Yugoslavian civil register and one, YU-CHX (86470), was donated to the Musej Yugoslovenskog Vazouhplovsta at Surcin Airport, Belgrade, where she was erroneously repainted with Air Force serial '0802' rather than the correct identity 'JRV0902'.

Within the RAF a Belgian Initial Training School had been established at Snitterfield on 1 January 1944, moving from overcrowded accommodation at Goring on Thames. In October the unit relocated to Snailwell where the brief was "to provide disciplinary, technical and aircrew training for Belgian personnel." On 20 February 1945, four new Tiger Moths were delivered from Aston Down together with a further eight from Llandow. The flying element moved to the previously designated satellite airfield at Bottisham on 23 November, and within a year thirty one additional Tiger Moths had been delivered, all formally sold to the Belgian Government, and which eventually relocated to Belgium where they took up military markings. Very much in parallel with their neighbours in the Netherlands, many of the Belgian Air Force Tiger Moths were later transferred to the Belgian State Flying School and sixteen survivors were issued with civil identities (OO-EVA to OO-EVM, OO-EVO, OO-EVP and OO-EVR), in 1958.

Exactly a year after the first joint meeting between the Royal Aero Club, MAP, Air Ministry and SBAC, by May 1945 Commander Perrin was in a position to report that dormant civil flying clubs and schools had been roused to respond to his enquiries about post-war equipment. He confirmed there was no interest in Magisters but had noted a requirement for 156 Tiger Moths for British clubs together with six for Ceylon and twenty four for Kenya, plus twenty Dominies. The Air Ministry had had a substantial change of view on pricing and tabled a proposal that the cost to clubs should be no greater than 25% of the original selling price, in the case of the Tiger Moth about £350 or almost three times as much as indicated twelve months previously. Perhaps somebody had discovered that when the thirty civil registered Tiger Moths had been requisitioned from the British clubs pre-war, compensation of between £550 and £1,200 each had been paid to the owners.

Displayed as Belgian Air Force Tiger Moth 'T-24' at the Air Museum in Florennes, this aircraft had served her entire post-war life as a civil registered trainer with the Belgian State Flying School. She was withdrawn from operations in 1971 and presented to the Museum in 1975. *Barry Dowsett*

OO-SOF was typical of the many civilian conversions for export completed by W A Rollason at Croydon: neat, tidy and silver overall. This aircraft was ordered on behalf of the Belgian national airline Sabena in 1952 and after two decades of training airline pilots was withdrawn from use and cancelled. *M J Hooks*

Tiger Moth G-AHNX flying over a placid summer scene in 1946. Within a few years the grass acreage and modest clubhouse were swamped under the relentless development of Luton Airport. *deHMC Archive*

The end of the war in Europe in May 1945 triggered further prodding of the Air Ministry, this time by the civilian contractors responsible for operating the Elementary Flying Training Schools (EFTS). Both Airwork and Marshall of Cambridge had reported large numbers of apparently unemployed Tiger Moths standing on their airfields and the Air Ministry was obliged to advise the MAP that although considerable numbers of elementary trainers were 'at present' not in use, they would be withdrawn into Aircraft Storage Units (ASU) in the near future.

> "It is not possible to have any of these unemployed Tiger Moths declared surplus to combined military requirements as the existing stocks will have to meet all RAF requirements until the new elementary trainer is available. The date when the new elementary trainer will be in service is still an unknown factor. It may be months before Flying Training Command is re-equipped and before then a large number of training schools will have to be formed (probably) to deal with the intake of personnel under the National Service Act after the defeat of Japan.
> When the new trainer is approved and a definite rate of production is known it will be possible for the Director of Organisation to recast his requirements, and if it then appears that there will be after all a surplus of Tiger Moths, immediate action will be taken to have them cleared and transferred to you for disposal."

The first post-war civilian registration of a British Tiger Moth was G-AGRA (86173), ex-RAF NL690, sold to the Ministry of Civil Aviation (MCA) in July 1945, and which was pre-registered to the Minister on 30 June for operation by the MCA Flying Unit based at Croydon. The Ministry also acquired NL905 which was registered to them as G-AGRB on the same date. Marshall's Flying School at Cambridge was the first wholly civil, non-government organisation post-war to register Tiger Moths. In January 1946 they were allocated G-AGYU (DE208/85265), G-AGYV (N6751/82029), G-AGYW (N6544/3857), and G-AGZY (N9176/82287).

Sir Arthur Marshall recalled how the return of civilian flying in Great Britain was celebrated on 1 January 1946:

> "The first civilian flying pupil for six years to leave the ground on a training flight in the UK took off in Tiger Moth G-ACDG at nine o'clock on that Tuesday morning, the newly restored freedom of the air was nine hours old. The pupil was Lady Alice Bragg, Mayor of Cambridge and the instructor, Sqn Ldr Leslie Worsdell DFC, an apprentice flying instructor at Cambridge in 1936 who had returned after a distinguished wartime operational career with the RAF. A number of other pupils were in the air on that first day, and the first British 'A' Licence after the war was obtained at Cambridge on 6 January."

On 26 January 2008 the Marshall Group organised a special gathering of Tiger Moths at Cambridge Airport to celebrate the delivery of the

Painted pale blue, G-AGYU sporting tasteful and rounded civil registration letters anticipating post-war trade on behalf of the Marshall Company at Cambridge. *Richard Riding*

first Tiger Moth to 22 ERFTS exactly seventy years previously. During the war years 22 EFTS trained over 20,000 pilots for the RAF and operated 200 Tiger Moths from Teversham, Clyffe Pypard, Bottisham and Caxton Gibbett. The company's proud record which it doubted anyone could equal was that Tiger Moths had operated from its Cambridge airfield providing flying instruction on an unbroken daily basis for a continuous seventy year period.

Harold Perrin's determined efforts on behalf of the British civil aeroplane clubs bore fruit early in 1946 when the Ministry of Civil Aviation promulgated its views on the release and allocation of surplus military light aircraft. The Parliamentary Secretary announced in the House of Commons on 24 January that 100 surplus light aircraft would be offered for sale on favourable terms to 'genuine' flying clubs which would need to satisfy certain conditions. The 100 aircraft were to be sold at a special low price, the offer would not be repeated, was additional to, but separate from, any other sales of surplus material, and there would be no prospect of an additional operating subsidy.

It was proposed that the 100 aircraft would be composed of sixty three Miles Magisters and thirty seven Austers, but Perrin's enquiries had already established beyond doubt that the club preference would be for Tiger Moths. Coincidental with this affirmation the Ministry was advised of 100 RAF Tiger Moths in store, all lightly damaged, but immediately available for disposal due to the contraction of repair facilities. The constituent numbers of the MCA's offer were accordingly modified to read sixty Tiger Moths, thirty Austers and only ten Magisters.

A precise definition of the eligibility of applicants as 'flying clubs' and the need to supervise their subsequent operations and business transactions was considered a difficult prospect, but it was decided that if aircraft distribution was to be the responsibility of the General Council of Associated Light Aeroplane Clubs, the representative body for club flying, they would be in the best position to adjudicate whether any bidding organisation was genuine. The General Council would be expected to exercise authority in monitoring all conditions which the Ministry of Aviation were attaching to the sale:

1. The aircraft must be used exclusively for club flying for the benefit of club members. The aircraft must not be used for charter or other forms of commercial flying or aerial work save instructional flying for club members.
2. The aircraft should be placed in use within a reasonable period of time according to the judgement of the General Council.
3. The ownership of the aircraft should be vested in the General Council or its constituent clubs.
4. The aircraft should not be hired or resold except to clubs which have been admitted to membership of the General Council and are vouched for by the Council as genuine flying clubs. The approval of the General Council should be required to the hire or resale of the aircraft.

After extensive negotiations the batch of surplus aircraft purchased by the Royal Aero Club in 1946 included T6745 which was immediately registered to the London Aeroplane Club at Panshanger. She was written off as the result of a forced landing in Hatfield Park in 1952. *deHMC Archive*

The Midland Bank Flying Club operated three ex-RAF Tiger Moths at Fairoaks from July 1946, replacing one that was written off in 1948, but by October 1949 the adventure had come to an end and all the aircraft were sold. The young 'bank clerk' second from the right went on to complete a commercial licence and spent his career with British European Airways. *deHMC Archive*

In recognition of the fact that fifty associated clubs could be interested in taking a share of the spoils, the Air Ministry was prepared to vary (increase) the numbers of each aircraft type on offer, all of which would be additional to those already subject to the current round of competitive tendering.

Applicants were reminded that the aircraft would need to be collected from store within a reasonable time scale and against an 'as is, where is' policy. Spares were not included in the scheme, but supplies were readily available and each club was expected to make its own arrangements. All additional costs of transport, refurbishment and certification would also fall on them.

The estimated average market value of the aircraft was quoted at £250 but under the Ministry scheme a nominal price of £50 was asked for each, irrespective of type, location or condition. Pre-sale inspection was not exactly encouraged, but limited access to RAF storage sites by nominated parties acting on behalf of the General Council was agreed.

The Royal Aero Club proposed that it should purchase all 100 aircraft for £5,000, completing final payment within three months of the approval or alternatively it would guarantee purchase by the General Council. What resulted was a combination of both. During 1946, from April to August, thirty two Tiger Moths were credited with 'sale' directly to the Royal Aero Club and from the end of May, five were sold to the Association of British Aero Clubs (ABAC), the new name adopted by the General Council following its annual general meeting on 20 February. All these aircraft were subsequently re-registered in the name of the recipients and in many cases within months of obtaining civil certification had been resold within the flying club movement, or to more commercially orientated flying 'schools' who were already well established with Tiger Moths as their standard training type.

With the war finally over and the difficult transition to peace under way the RAF was faced with a fleet of 22,000 military aircraft in Great Britain, a number that was actually increasing as production contracts for the latest marques were honoured. Two contraction plans initiated by the Air Staff in September and December 1945 reduced the RAF's wartime squadrons from 350 to 206 under a scheme scheduled for completion by the last day of March 1946. All other units were similarly affected including the flying training schools and, under difficult immediate post-war administrative conditions, a massive programme of storage, sale and reclamation was embarked upon, made correspondingly more complicated and urgent as some of the storage units were themselves scheduled for closure.

Foreign sales, subject to government approval, were encouraged, not only to alleviate the storage problem and to recover at least a fraction of the costs, but as a means of securing a foothold for supporting services and future exports. The regeneration of friendly Air Forces could be controlled by gifts dealt straight from the political hand, and it was a device used to good effect.

Tiger Moth 86051 (ex-RAF EM849), is credited as the first post-war club aircraft. She was registered G-AHDD to Huntingdon Aviation on 21 February 1946 (one of four), and was operated by the Luton Flying Club for two years. In 1950 she was owned by the Birmingham based 'Yellow Air Taxis' and in 1952 was registered to Chipperfield's Circus and Zoo. During her delivery flight to a new owner in West Germany in August 1955, the aircraft crashed while taking off from Calais and the wreckage was delivered by surface as a source of spare parts for her replacement.

During this period of planned post-war military contraction the British Government sold more Tiger Moths to a number of overseas air arms. Between October 1947 and February 1948, thirteen Tiger Moths ex-stock were shipped from Birkenhead to the Burmese National Air Force; twelve new and twelve used aircraft were delivered to the Royal Hellenic Air Force between February 1947 and September 1949, satisfying an order which had been in prospect under different conditions since 1938. The Government of Iraq took fifteen new aircraft between May and July 1947, having lost most of its Air Force to RAF action during the war. Eleven years later six of the consignment were sold to the Lebanese Air Force for Air Observation duties. Malaya, a country much familiar with the performance of the Tiger Moth, accepted eighteen used aircraft for its Auxiliary Air Force as a counter to the Emergency situation over a four year period from November 1949.

The Air Ministry's grudging assertions in March 1945 that 100 surplus Tiger Moths might be available from mid 1947, subject to the international movement or not of military flying schools and the expected availability of a new elementary trainer, had clearly been overtaken by events and the pressing need to reduce stocks of stored aircraft now that a selective scrapping, reclaim and selling policy had been agreed.

When discussing the situation in April 1946, MAP had confirmed with the Air Ministry that the Air Council's Director of Organisation was fully aware of the requests received in London following the advertised release of Tiger Moths in Southern Rhodesia. These requirements now amounted to twelve civil aircraft for the Dutch Government, fifty six for the Dutch military, eight for Afghanistan, twenty for Chile, four for Ethiopia, three for Trans Jordan and one for Ceylon.

MAP revealed that seventy nine Tiger Moths were expected to be declared surplus shortly, belonging to RAF units both within the British Isles and stationed overseas. From these, consideration would be given to satisfying the Dutch military order and also the twenty aircraft required by Chile, although that prospect had been temporarily blocked by a Civil Service committee. The Afghanistan enquiry should be covered by aircraft supplied from South Africa, suggested MAP. Only seven days after expressing this opinion the same department signed an agreement with the Government of Afghanistan for the supply of eight Tiger Moths already stationed in India. From a batch of aircraft purchased specifically for overhaul and resale, and which might have been stored near White Waltham during the summer of 1946, de Havilland did supply two aircraft to Ethiopia, T7338 (83864), and BB675 (3402), the former G-ADOI, but provided nothing for Ceylon. Two aircraft were sold to the Arab Legion Air Force in Amman on 26 April 1946: NM156 (86476), and NM205 (86513), which became T-201 and T-200 respectively, and later TJ-AAG and TJ-AAF with the Arab Airways Flying Club before they both were sold to the RAF Amman Flying Club in 1956.

The Dutch military did eventually take delivery of all their fifty six Tiger Moths: thirty six aircraft drawn from RAF storage were air delivered between 22 July and 26 August 1946, and a further twenty were ferried as one consignment across the North Sea, dismantled and packed onto the SS *Ponto*, sailing from Dagenham Docks on 12 February 1947. These were scheduled to be held in reserve but were integrated into the commissioned fleet between September 1947 and August 1948.

The shipment on the SS *Ponto* included the last Tiger Moth to be built at Cowley: PG746 (86632). Having graced MUs at Wroughton, Llandow and Sealand between July 1944 and September 1946, PG746 took on Royal Netherlands Air Force markings A-49 and led a varied life until March 1959 when she joined the Navy as VU-103, a serial amended to '002' the following October. By the time she was withdrawn from use in December 1965 the aircraft had accumulated only 1,348 hours, but corrosion had been discovered in the fuselage frame and by order of the Navy some parts were donated to the Kooy Gliding Club operating from the naval air station near Den Helder, and the remainder of the aircraft, along with '001' (86589), was burned.

An agreement between the British and Saudi Arabian Governments in 1946 resulted in the establishment of a Training Mission, to be based at Taif, operating an Avro XIX and two Tiger Moths for training Saudi nationals to 'A' licence standard with the prospect of selected pupils travelling to England to qualify for their 'B' licence and navigation qualifications. The scheme was contracted to BOAC and under the title 'British Civil Air Training Mission to Saudi Arabia' was to last for two years at a cost of £84,500. BOAC decided that it was already over committed and the contract was transferred to Airwork Ltd., an organisation much more suited to such opportunities.

Painted in the scheme applied to the fifty six Tiger Moths delivered to the Royal Netherlands Air Force from RAF stocks in 1946, PG712 was one them before sale from the military in 1962, registration as PH-CSL and mandatory civil modifications which included the Fokker tail. *Sjors van Dam*

TJ-AAF, *Beni Kinnanab* of the Arab Airways Flying Club, was sold to the RAF Amman Flying Club in 1956 but probably never flew under their ownership. *deHMC Archive*

The two Tiger Moths, G-AITH (85525), and G-AITI (84000), had been registered to the Middlesex Flying Club at Denham in November 1946, purchased through the Royal Aero Club scheme, but both were re-registered to the Airwork Flying Club in August and July 1947 respectively after qualification for their Cs of A. The aircraft were shipped to Jeddah on board the SS *Lycaon* on 13 September from where they were collected by instructors Lt Cdr Herbert Bromwich and Sqn Ldr P H Herbert and ferried to their new base at the historic Hawiya Airfield, eighteen miles from Taif where training began in primitive conditions on 16 November. Due to the nature of the Mission the aircraft were to remain under British registry.

A third Tiger Moth was added in August 1948, G-AKCM (83303), originally registered to BOAC in support of the Mission contract in August 1947 but transferred to Airwork in September with whom she qualified for her C of A in February 1948. By early the following year seventeen of the nineteen trainees at Hawiya had flown solo but on 2 February G-AITH was wrecked by a solo student during unauthorised low flying and was replaced by G-AKCG (DHA124). In a surprising move in August 1947 this aircraft had been purchased from Australia by the Scottish Flying Club in Glasgow and operated by them at Perth until June 1949 when she was acquired by Airwork and shipped to Jeddah. During unloading the crate was dropped by the crane and the aircraft damaged.

The Mission contract was extended in May 1949 until the end of September 1950 by which time an agreed valuation had been placed on the assets and the British registrations of Tiger Moths G-AITI, G-AKCG and G-AKCM were cancelled in October after local sale. Shortly afterwards both G-AITI and G-AKCG were destroyed when their hangar collapsed at Hawiya and although G-AKCM escaped damage she disappeared into oblivion.

A Tiger Moth not included in the original de Havilland package, NM187 (86495), joined Arab Airways Association in August 1946 as TJ-AAH and was damaged in a desert landing on 16 January 1949. Although she was in Arab Airways' colours she was actually owned by the Arab Legion under Glubb Pasha. The accident report was submitted by the pilot, Captain Fred Terry, to the General Technical Manager of Arab Airways, Captain Sanders. Azraq is some fifty miles due east of Amman and the Azraq Marshes offered winter facilities to wild duck escaping south from the Prippet Marshes in Russia. Members of the Arab Legion were partial to wild duck and a ground party had gone ahead to the Marshes by station wagon. Fred Terry followed in the Tiger Moth to act as 'beater'.

All yellow Tiger Moths wearing the post-war codes of 1 EFTS, Flying Training Command, on parade at Panshanger in 1948. *Don Stoneham*

"The aircraft was flown to Azraq in fair weather conditions on Sunday 16 January 1949. Approximately half an hour after touching down, 0930hrs, a sand storm arose with winds gusting from 50 to 60mph.

It was decided to stay with the aircraft, check it and take the necessary precautions to prevent damage until some such time as the storm showed signs of abating, and then attempt a move to some form of shelter or picketing position. For approximately one hour the aircraft remained on the open mud flats, and with the aid of Mrs Sanders and Mr Herron we were able to prevent damage.

The storm had by now shown a slight decrease in intensity, whereupon we were able to move the aircraft to the extreme edge of the mud flats and picket her to bushes. She remained in this position until 1500hrs when it was decided after consultation with Captain Sanders that the lesser of two evils had to be chosen, ie. either to leave the aircraft unattended and without picketing precautions being taken of sufficient quality to stand up to a sandstorm which was again increasing in violence, or, get the aircraft if possible to safe hangarage at Amman.

On an assumption of two hours thirty minutes duration and having already flown for one hour ten minutes, we decided to refuel to the extent of four and a half gallons which was carried as spare petrol in the accompanying car. This was carried out with difficulty owing to the lack of a filter and the high wind, with the result that not more than two gallons approximately went into the tank.

On this assumption we calculated the aircraft's duration now to be approximately one hour thirty five minutes, and at 1540hrs we set course for Amman in rather bad weather conditions. For one hour we were flying in a sandstorm with visibility reduced at times at 100-200 yards. We eventually flew out of the sand and encountered low cloud and extremely poor visibility, rain and a calculation of drift to the extent of about 25 degrees.

In the interests of our safety I decided a forced landing was necessary to prevent loss of life and even more severe damage to the aircraft by continuing the flight with a shortage of petrol and the possibility of making a landing with a dead stick, in darkness and without knowledge of the terrain beneath. By this time we had been airborne for one hour and twenty five minutes, leaving a ten minute endurance, and at the same time having a none too reliable petrol gauge showing almost nil.

Bearing all these facts in mind I chose the most suitable field available near habitation, ie. a railway station, and carried out a forced landing. Shortly after the landing run the aircraft's wheels became bogged in soft ploughed soil, causing it to slew to starboard and come to rest on its nose. Subsequent inspection during remaining light showed a collapsed starboard undercarriage leg and broken propeller."

To add insult to injury and in spite of all the precautions TJ-AAH was blown onto her back during the night even though an Arab Legion guard had been posted to remain in the rear cockpit. The aircraft was repaired and re-registered TJ-AAW but was destroyed on 9 May 1951 as the result of a hangar fire at Amman.

Taking into account the aircraft separately purchased by tender, approximately 130 ex-RAF Tiger Moths were registered in Great Britain alone in 1946, in addition to those bought as sources of spares, sold abroad, or broken down for scrap. At the end of the war, Dick Gliddon, Chief Engineer at W Mumford, a specialist Tiger Moth repair centre dispersed to Plymouth, was told to cut up all unserviceable aircraft into pieces that would fit inside a standard forty

A trio of all-yellow Tiger Moths from No 28 EFTS, Flying Training Command, near Wolverhampton in 1946. In addition to a four letter code each aircraft carries a unit number on the engine cowling. *Charles Hastings Winch*

Post-war members of the Glider Pilot Regiment continued to train on Tiger Moths operated by No 21 EFTS at Booker including DE606 which by 1949 had acquired her silver scheme with yellow trainer bands. Ease of handling on a hard surface is considerably improved by adequate pressure in the tyres and a two man team. *Jim Hutchings DFM*

gallon oil drum. The following three years were thin on British disposals as the European political situation was again uncertain, the Malayan Emergency was developing and by 1950 the United Nations was fighting a war in Korea. British civil registrations allocated to Tiger Moths during that time, however, showed an increasing trend from about twenty to fifty per annum, the higher total being reached when the RAF's new trainer appeared at last.

On his desk in the offices of the de Havilland Aircraft of Canada, Wsiewolod Jakimiuk had been doodling with ideas for a new, low wing monoplane since 1943; ideas which would become reality on 22 May 1946 when the company's first independent design, the DHC.1 Chipmunk, was flown by Pat Fillingham at Downsview where, subsequently, 218 aircraft were built. Phil Garratt was hoping it could be his second Tiger Moth. The Anglicised version of the Chipmunk went into production at Hatfield in 1950 and then at Chester, several years later than anticipated when the fate of the Tiger Moths in Southern Rhodesia was being debated in 1944.

The entry of the Chipmunk into service with the Royal Air Force released more than eighty Tiger Moths onto the British register in 1951, but teething troubles with the new type and consequent delays caused concern and probably accounted for there being only one Tiger Moth release in 1952. No 2 Reserve Flying School (RFS) based at Barton re-equipped with Chipmunks in January 1951 but had converted back to Tiger Moths by the following December and maintained the type until disbandment in February 1953. Two other units, 8 RFS Woodley and 22 RFS Cambridge continued to operate Tiger Moths in parallel with Chipmunks from April 1950, and two more, 7 RFS Desford and 25 RFS Wolverhampton never took delivery of the 'replacement' aircraft before they were disbanded.

In times of national emergency, the 'Cook and Butcher's Air Force' had had to do as it was ordered, but in a country racked with post-war shortages, controls and a new level of virulent bureaucratic interference, civilian pilots now were willingly prepared to pay hard earned cash to continue to experience the privilege of Tiger Moth flight.

Aircraft and staff of the London University Air Squadron photographed on what is evidently a cold day in April 1950, illustrating no unity in flying clothing. *The Aeroplane*

Maurice Marsh responded to an advertisement placed in a local newspaper by the Coventry Aero Group, and in February 1950 presented himself at a snow covered Baginton Aerodrome for a trial lesson, travelling the twelve miles from his home by train and bus instead of bicycle due to the weather. Outside the club hangar he made his first acquaintance with Tiger Moth G-AHKZ (83636), a surplus aircraft released in May 1946, and which, now called *Barbie*, was rocking on the frozen grass in a bitter easterly wind.

"The CFI welcomed me, took my money and saw the necessary forms signed before handing me over to a friendly, weather beaten character. George looked after Armstrong Whitworth company aircraft in his working hours and Club aircraft when off duty. He was very concerned that he could only find an oversized flying suit for me and no boots. I was not worried and wondered what all the fuss was about. Eventually, I was installed in the rear cockpit of G-AHKZ wondering whether the seat belt would stand the tension George had pulled on or whether there would be a sudden crack and I should find myself sitting on the frozen grass. The CFI climbed in and chatted to me about switches on and off, and then repeated the process to George. The engine started, creating a freezing draught. We rattled across the frozen turf and after more interesting explanations, were soon climbing over the A45.

It was obvious now that an Arctic wind was diving into the front cockpit and whistling out of the rear. A good percentage of the airflow was taking an alternative route via the legs of my flying suit and out through the neck. As I got colder and colder I realised what had concerned George. I paid less and less attention to the friendly chat from the front as I concentrated on survival. I think I held the stick for a while and remember something about ailerons, but I was really trying to calculate how many minutes more I could survive, and how much of the flight remained. Fortunately, the state of hyperthermia had not yet been invented, so I was still alive when we landed. Somehow, I was extracted from the aircraft and stood for a while to allow the cold east wind to thaw me out."

Before the Second World War, John Isaacs had helped to build some of the first Supermarine Spitfires by hand and living near Southampton had joined the Hampshire Aeroplane Club at Eastleigh on a wintry morning in 1951:

"I found the CFI, Reg Langridge, reclining in the instructors' office, chair tilted and his feet on the desk. He greeted my request to be converted to open cockpit Tiger Moth flying with singular lack of enthusiasm: his rounded jovial face resumed its friendly normality when I added that I did not necessarily wish to fly on that cold day. Like the instructors at Thruxton, he had learned to fly with the Civil Air Guard before joining the RAF as an instructor on Tiger Moths. He had also served with Bomber Command on Avro Lancasters and then flown on the Berlin Airlift.

So in the fullness of time, like thousands before me, I flew circuits and bumps from the Tiger Moth's rear cockpit. The tired club parachutes, used to pad the bucket seats, did not inspire confidence and I never strapped one on to my backside without recalling the Cagney bush pilot film in which his associate accidentally pulled the ripcord, thereby releasing a month's dirty laundry."

A celebration of the 21st anniversary of the formal issue of a Certificate of Airworthiness to the DH.82 Tiger Moth (4 March 1932), was arranged at Denham Aerodrome in 1953. The event was intended to be a show of strength if not gratitude by the clubs, nearly all equipped now

DE474 in the employ of Reserve Command at Burnaston in about 1950. It is possible to single-handedly manoeuvre a Tiger Moth on the apron provided there is no great upward slope and the groundcrew is both tall and strong. The secret is to get the aircraft to the point of balance on the mainwheels. *Charles Waterfall*

Tiger Moths in the post-war silver scheme of Cambridge University Air Squadron, part of Reserve Command, managed by the Marshall Company at Cambridge. *Marshall Aerospace*

Reserve Command Tiger Moths awaiting trade at Burnaston in 1951. *Charles Waterfall*

A miserable day in March 1953 at Denham Aerodrome where it was planned to celebrate the 21st anniversary of the civil certification of the 'A' model Tiger Moth. Very few parties attended, but the RAF Element of the Army's EFTS at Middle Wallop did their best to raise a smile, (or was it a frown?) with EM879 'BD-T'. *de Havilland Aircraft Company*

with 'new' training aeroplanes acquired for very little financial outlay and not much effort. Unfortunately, acting with every good intention, the organisers chose Saturday, 7 March as the date for the party, a day blessed with winter mist and cloud and seasonal average temperatures. Fewer than twenty aircraft attended of which Tiger Moths were rare; the chosen date was five months prior to the mass public sales. Only two teams entered the inter-club competitions, one from the RAF element of the British Army's Elementary Flying Training School at Middle Wallop, and the other from the London Aeroplane Club at Panshanger. One of the Middle Wallop Tiger Moths, EM879 'BD-T' (86081), arrived covered in graffiti and fake patches, with bandaged struts, the tattiest instrument hood that could be found on the establishment, and was parked with lines of washing strung along the fuselage side. Intended to be a light hearted and humorous gesture, it was hardly a fanfare to the dawn of the new age of opportunity which had been so eagerly anticipated.

Having resolved the problems with their new elementary trainer, RAF storage units were finally encouraged to turn out their residual holdings of Tiger Moths and in 1953 at least 380 aircraft were transferred to the category of 'Non Effective Stock'. The RAF now had a choice of which disposal technique to apply: outright scrapping, recovery of parts or onward sale. Fortunately, the majority of aircraft were offered for sale and the public was invited to visit Cosford, Hullavington and Lyneham on 18 August 1953 and to deposit individual bids on 222 aircraft. The RAF wanted the storage space and the Treasury needed the funds; it was a situation tailor made for bargain hunters and finally broke down the high expectation on prices adopted by the Air Ministry and the Ministry of Supply (MoS).

The degree of public interest showed without doubt that the market was far from saturated; rather it was still hungry and that at least vindicated the disposal policies adopted by the British Government before the end of the European war. It was also a stark reminder of the lack of a suitable new light aeroplane for the clubs and private owners. The protectionist attitudes adopted by Francis St Barbe and SBAC were hollow: there was nothing left to defend.

In November 1945 it was realised that some of the pre-war civil aircraft types would be difficult to maintain due to an absence of spares, manufacturing jigs and in some cases drawings and technical records, destroyed inadvertently or otherwise during the hectic activity of more imperative wartime programmes. Already limited stocks of spares had

Packing spares was often undertaken as homework by groups of friends as part of the war effort. The standard and style of packing was very strictly supervised and depended on the nature of the spare and its destination. This group of homeworkers was active in July 1945. The de Havilland Company continued to make Tiger Moth spares for some years after the end of the war whilst waiting for the Chipmunk to come into service. *deHMC Archive*

de Havilland DH.82A Tiger Moth Mk II, DE709/BD-X, Army Air Corps Centre (British Army Elementary Flying Training School), Middle Wallop, 1955. Silver overall with yellow bands around rear fuselage and chordwise above the top wings and below the bottom wings. Codes and serials in black. Roundels in six position. Red spinner front and wheel hubs. The aircraft went to Australia and is stored pending rebuild in Victoria. *Artwork ©Richard Caruana, 1:72 scale*

Damage caused by a heavy landing in a Tiger Moth was nearly always the same: the bottom of the fuselage front side frame would be bowed and cause obvious wrinkling of the fabric at the wing root and the centre section rigging would go slack. In the case of G-AHIZ at Panshanger the landing has been severe enough to bend a centre section strut and distort the entire cabane structure. *deHMC Archive*

been largely consumed in keeping the impressed aircraft airworthy, after which airframes were broken down to 'produce'. Particularly badly affected were all models of the DH.60 Moth, Puss, Fox, Leopard and Hornet Moths, the Moth Minor, Dragon, Dragonfly and DH.86; no spare parts for the Gipsy Minor engine were available without cannibalisation. A crumb of comfort was supposedly offered by the assertion that "some Tiger Moth fittings are interchangeable with those of the DH.60G Moth, and Australian Dragons can still be served by the Sydney company."

de Havilland issued a statement from Hatfield in April 1948 claiming quite categorically that as the Tiger Moth "is likely to remain in world-wide service in considerable numbers for some years to come," they would continue to manufacture spares for the aircraft until the end of 1949. However, in reply to a Parliamentary question posed on 19 June 1950 the Minister of Supply, Labour MP George Strauss, replied that in the previous twelve months 239 Tiger Moths had been broken up by civilian contractors for the recovery of components and spares and a further eighty one by the Royal Air Force with the same object. This situation resulted in de Havilland maintaining their spares provisioning into the early 1950s due to the late delivery of the Chipmunk and unexpected retention of the Tiger Moth in RAF service. It also assured the purchasers of aircraft at the major sales events of 1953 that enormous quantities of packaged spares would be released from store upon which to draw for years ahead.

The majority of the aircraft released from 1950 and later were perfectly serviceable, and mostly their silver doped wings and fuselages, 'aluminium' in official parlance, were adorned with broad yellow bands to indicate their recent training role, together with national insignia, unit badges and codes. It was still something of a shock to bureaucratic minds that military aircraft in airworthy condition were being sold to civilians and capable of delivery by air rather than in tattered chunks destined for the smelter.

Once the formalities of bids and acceptances had been acknowledged and monies paid, those aircraft scheduled for air delivery were allocated civilian registrations based on whatever documentary evidence could be provided. This sometimes resulted in confusion as to which serial numbers identified what, and the pre-war civil identities of impressed aircraft dressed in military clothing were occasionally forgotten.

It was necessary for the civil letters to be worn for the duration of the ferry flight to wherever 'demilitarisation' was to take place and for the most part these were crudely applied on the fuselage sides using black paint, daubed with a three inch brush. To add the ultimate indignity, the once proud national insignia was blotted out using the same brush and bucket, encouraging varying degrees of perverted artistry.

Formation take off, all pilots solo. The lead aircraft, T6066, spent her last years in the RAF as part of No 1 Grading Unit in Lincolnshire. She was sold to Christchurch Aero Club in 1953. The photograph was originally commissioned to illustrate a magazine article on the design of aircraft undercarriage legs. *deHMC Archive*

Above: Collected from RAF Maintenance Units by recruited volunteers, some auctioned Tiger Moths were airworthy and were flown into Croydon Airport immediately after sale. Civil markings daubed on their fuselage sides, remained until overhaul. Unlike some previously civil registered aircraft BB748 was recognised as the pre-war G-ADIB of the de Havilland Reserve School. *deHMC Archive*

Left: A Sunbeam and a Triumph motorcycle with other classics in the Rollason hangar at Croydon Airport. Loose stacked wings accompany a selection of very shabby fuselages, illustrating a variety of colour schemes and application of military markings, evidence of some aircraft being withdrawn and stored at various times during their military careers. *Richard Riding*

Above: Almost every available parking space at Croydon Airport was occupied by Tiger Moths in varying states of undress during the height of the influx in the early 1950s. *Norman Rivett*

Stripping the military colours off W7955 revealed a pre-war civil identity, G-AFGT, an aircraft originally based at Luton. Although new letters, G-AMEA, were allocated the original registration was restored only to be cancelled in 1951 when she was sold to the Royal Thai Navy. *Charles Holland*

Somewhat greater care than usual has been taken to cover the military markings DE454 and replace them with civil registration G-ANIW on fuselage sides and upper wing prior to delivery to the Darlington and District Aero Club at Croft. Immediately following the issue of a civil certificate in June 1954 the aircraft was sold to New Zealand. *Raymond Rayner*

In the sealed bid auctions some organisations and groups made offers for entire blocks of lot numbers and substantial quantities were sold in single transactions. It was not uncommon post delivery for aircraft to be immediately advertised for sale 'as standing', often in a bid to satisfy previously disappointed clients and make a quick profit. By the time of the last mass sales in 1953 potential bidders realised what good deals were being offered and the flying clubs recognised this was their final opportunity to acquire cheap equipment. The Association of British Aero Clubs (ABAC) placed bids on behalf of constituent members to bring order to the system and to save them the embarrassment of bidding against one another. W A Rollason bought heavily against anticipated demand at home and overseas as did the Wiltshire School of Flying, Hants and Sussex Aviation, Muir and Adie, Marshall Flying Services, Peacock, Aerocontacts and several smaller groups and individuals. As part of the sale conditions, none of the aircraft could be sold directly to overseas customers.

Ted Hawes, Managing Director of Hants and Sussex Aviation Ltd. based at Portsmouth, wrote the following in his history of the company:

"The cornerstone of our initial engineering policy was to refurbish complete aircraft, mostly purchased from military surplus, to the highest possible standard. Our refurbished (overhauled) specification involved a complete re-fabric of the airframe, the complete overhaul of the engine to zero hours together with all instruments and radio equipment if fitted. Tiger Moths were purchased from the RAF Disposal Branch at £50 each or thereabouts. Certainly we expected to pick and choose a Tiger Moth for £50 and would not pay that sort of money unless the aircraft was in fully serviceable and flying condition. On one occasion we purchased over 100 of them in one job lot at £5.00 each. This particular batch had been dismantled and were partly cannibalised, lying at 38 MU Llandow, fifteen miles west of Cardiff. They were transported by road and this task was carried out entirely by my brother and myself using one of our old army trucks towing an extraordinarily long lightweight trailer. There was no bridge across the river Severn in those days and it was a very arduous task to drive a cumbersome truck and trailer combination literally seven days a week from Portsmouth to Wales via Gloucester. We worked from dawn until dusk and finally became completely exhausted."

The consignment had to be cleared from the MU against a deadline which clearly was not going to be met and Ted Hawes arranged to stockpile aircraft in a field outside the perimeter of the RAF station from where they could be collected under less frenetic circumstances. Even this proved to be arduous and eventually about thirty aircraft were abandoned and burned on site. The majority of the purchase was delivered to Portsmouth:

ZK-BAA was registered to Garnham Aviation at Taihape in April 1952 and operated as a crop sprayer and later a glider tug at Ohakea. Sold to Hants and Sussex Aviation in March 1951 she had been overhauled and sold by July the same year. *John King*

At one time almost every aero club hangar in Great Britain housed an ex-RAF Tiger Moth purchased for civilianisation or as a source of spares. Such was the fate of the former T5842 whose new registration letters G-ANDK have been crudely daubed over RAF insignia while the engineering staff at White Waltham have removed the engine and undercarriage and opened up the fuselage fabric for inspection of the lower longerons. *David Welch*

The attempts to obliterate military insignia on what were now civil registered aircraft varied from half-hearted to the disrespectful but in most cases the correct civil letters were applied to the appropriate airframes. Confusion was later caused by the new owners misreading or misunderstanding airframe and engine serials when applying formally for registration and certification. *deHMC Archive*

Surplus Tiger Moths air delivered to Croydon were picketed in the open and whatever covers were available used to protect engines and cockpits. The application of a civil registration of a minimum size was obligatory if the aircraft were ferried. To minimise space wings were soon removed to covered storage and fuselages gathered closely together in rows. *deHMC Archive*

Three surplus Tiger Moths stored in a barn at Ratcliffe, Leicestershire on the last day of 1955, all fully equipped for night flying. The photographer was offered his pick of any one for £100 or all three for £250. *Charles Waterfall*

"With several hundred Tiger Moth wings stacked on the airfield we were selling these 'as-is, where-is' at £1.10s.0d each or £4.0s.0d for a set of four. Customers sorted out what they wanted and carted these away on trailers. Our standard re-furbished Tiger Moth (when ordered in pairs), including an Export Certificate of Airworthiness was sold for exactly £400 each."

The restriction on direct sale to overseas parties resulted in Lots 1, 4, 5, 10 and 23 offered for sale at 9 MU Cosford early in 1954 being acquired for a total price of £355 by Derby Aviation, bidding on behalf of the Norwegian Aero Club (NAK), and who converted them to civilian status at Burnaston. The first aircraft to be certificated, LN-BDO (85738), was flown to Oslo in thirteen hours during the last three days of June 1954, and the remaining aircraft, LN-BDL (3443), LN-BDM (85294), and LN-BDN (85328), were all collected by members of the Drammen Flyklubb in the autumn. LN-BDP (82229), was not converted and eventually was delivered by surface as a source of spare parts.

The restriction on direct sale of surplus Tiger Moths to overseas customers opened the way for agency deals and four aircraft were secured by Derby Aviation on behalf of the Norwegian Aero Club. LN-BDM was collected by members of the Drammen Flyklubb in the autumn of 1954. *deHMC Archive*

LN-BDM was one of two Tiger Moths filmed operating from an ice covered lake near Oslo for a television documentary to be broadcast on the Discovery Channel. *Arild O Krosby*

Painted with a Viking longboat on the fuselage and a headrest fitted for the rear cockpit, LN-BDM was sometime configured as a single seater and employed as a glider tug. *deHMC Archive*

The notorious faked photograph of Tiger Moth LN-BDN, presenting her as a three seater, which caused the Norwegian authorities to pack bags and initiate a field investigation, hurriedly followed by a large invoice. *via K Hagby*

LN-BDO ran out of fuel due to an inaccurate assessment of consumption when towing a banner over Skallum near Oslo on 13 September 1959 and was badly damaged in the forced landing. LN-BDM was employed as a glider tug and in 1959 was offered to Sweden in exchange for a Norwegian built aircraft then on the Swedish civil register, but the deal was rejected. LN-BDL was written off at Steinsfjorden in 1956 and LN-BDN which was damaged at Trondheim was rebuilt using parts of the dismantled LN-BDO.

Early in 1955, members of the Norsk Teknisk Hogskole Flying Club at Trondheim applied for a Certificate of Airworthiness for LN-BDN, then owned by Jens Rolfsen, and submitted to the authorities a faked photograph showing the aircraft in a three seat tandem layout. The Civil Aviation Department was horrified and immediately sent an inspector to Trondheim having advised the club that such major structural alterations required a spectacular degree of approval paperwork. But the last laugh was with the authorities who submitted a substantial invoice to cover their expenses.

A view held in some quarters that ex-surplus aircraft were bought for almost nothing, sprayed silver, and passed on at great profit was entirely false. RAF Tiger Moth R4878 (82795), was acquired by W A Rollason in November 1953 and placed in store at Croydon. Pending sale to West Germany the aircraft was issued with British civil registration G-AOBP in April 1955, a necessary qualification to see the aircraft through overhaul, certification for export and test flying. In many such similar cases the registration letters were temporarily chalked or laid out in masking tape on the fuselage side and the new national identity added only with the finishing touches to the colour scheme.

R4878 was a Hatfield product of January 1940 and her first posting had been to 1 EFTS, following which she served at Wolverhampton and Cranwell before she was tagged with the label declaring her obsolete following service with 6 RFS at Sywell. Along the way she had acquired mainplanes and control surfaces manufactured, repaired or overhauled by de Havilland, Morris Motors, Taylorcraft and at least two other civilian contractors. According to the Rollason worksheets all these items were "opened up, cleaned down and inspected, attachments checked, all structure inspected, rectifications carried out as necessary, centre section inspected and re-rigged."

In the aftermath of Hurricane 'Ike' in September 2008, the custodians of the Lone Star Flight Museum at Galveston, Texas were faced with this awful scene: Tiger Moth N9714, donated by the late Roger Sherron, in too close a proximity to other exhibits and surrounded by most of the roof. *Texas Aviation Hall of Fame*

And so the thoroughness continued:

> "Undercarriage: removed, dismantled, cleaned, inspected, wheels and assemblies serviced, rectifications carried out as necessary. Flying controls: all cables removed, cleaned, inspected, reprotected and replaced. All pivots, bearings and pulleys cleaned. Controls re-trued to manufacturer's requirements, movements checked and recorded. Duplicate inspection carried out. Fuel and oil system: tanks removed, inspected and pressure tested. Fuel and oil lines tested. Systems assembled and fuel flow carried out. Engine installation: firewall and bearers cleaned, inspected and reprotected. Engine No 85142 installed. Propeller BA7588 fitted. Engine run carried out. Tail skid: overhauled. Instruments: overhauled (or tested or certified) and fitted. General: all struts and wires cleaned and inspected. Mainplanes, ailerons and tail unit assembled to machine, rigged to manufacturer's specification and figures recorded. Serviceable fire extinguisher fitted. Aircraft sprayed to required scheme. Machine weighed and C of G calculated. Machine test flown and reported as satisfactory."

The mass turnout of ex-RAF Tiger Moths revealed one strange quirk in the Air Ministry's specification for the aeroplane. Each luggage locker door was fitted with a high specification Yale and Towne No 2277 mortice lock and it is probable that every one across the fleet used the same key. It would have been an impossible task for any EFTS Engineering Officer to cope with tracking a different key for each individual lock, especially as aircraft were often rotated for maintenance, overhaul or repair. How often and under what circumstances would it have been necessary for lockers to be locked? Few seemed to query the fact that no keys were provided when the aircraft were delivered to their new civilian owners.

Viscount Yves le Gallais led a proposal to supply many additional Tiger Moths to civilian clubs in France and he purchased 198 surplus aircraft which were registered to his British agent, Croydon based A J Whittemore (Aeradio) Ltd., a company incorporated on 17 January 1952 with an address at Biggin Hill. The bulk purchase deserved special treatment by the authorities and rumours suggested that the unit price might have been as little as £20 each. The airworthy aircraft, about 130, were ferried to Croydon by freelancing civilian pilots and picketed out with fitted cockpit, engine and propeller covers where these were available. In almost every case wings were removed and where space permitted, fuselages shifted under cover.

A good way of moving a Tiger Moth by road in the southern hemisphere is to employ a special lorry with a long, low flatbed and secure side panels. Tiger Moth ZK-BCO had been stored at Wanaka for eight years until sold to a syndicate in 2006 and transported to their base airfield for a thorough inspection and overhaul. *Shane Gaughan*

The first batch of overhauled French registered Tiger Moths, each painted silver overall with black lettering, was ferried from Croydon to Le Touquet on 30 May 1954. For some considerable time after, lines of dismantled aircraft stood wheel by wheel on almost every square inch of hard standing at Croydon, a situation exacerbated by the French contract running only to a fraction of the anticipated numbers, the French SALS organisation having already placed more than 100 Tiger Moths with clubs at no charge or for only a nominal fee. In the British climate some airframes at Croydon deteriorated sufficiently to be declared scrap while at least two went missing, believed to have been stolen. Whittemore eventually disposed of their surplus; many were absorbed on site, mainly by the Rollason company who became probably the world's biggest and most enduring supplier of Tiger Moths and spare parts, continuing their business for over forty years.

The purchase of aeroplanes at anything between £20 and £50 in 1953, together with new engines in manufacturer's delivery crates at £5, provided scope for a complete overhaul, often including new fabric on the fuselage at least, and a repaint, for re-sale with a profit at a price of less than £600. Some dealers were more than happy merely to turn round their wares at a simple 100% mark up or to offer basic services:

> "May 31 1954. We now confirm that we can supply a de Havilland Tiger Moth 82A without a Certificate of Airworthiness for £100. Naturally this price does not include the plane being delivered to your area, but arrangements can be made at the approximate cost of six shillings per mile, including loading and unloading, but not fitting of wings on completion.
>
> The particular aircraft we are offering has approximately 1,000 hours on the engine and therefore should you wish to make it airworthy at any time in the future the engine still has approximately 500 hours to run.
>
> Regarding your query about the instruments supplied we are prepared to include in this price the complete range of instruments as set out in the original Air Ministry specification. Should you wish to have the machine painted, this service can be carried out before delivery at the approximate cost of £20. Should you have any further queries the writer will be pleased to discuss the whole matter more fully on the telephone."

Some of the bigger dealers directed their advertising at specific markets and were particularly interested in the export trade to New Zealand where a positive requirement had been identified. Ex-surplus purchase prices, and material and labour costs for overhaul, were virtually identical, the sale prices reflecting how much or how little work had been applied during the civil conversion. A £5 undercut here and there was significant when prices were at such standardised levels, and was just about the only avenue open to creative competition.

Aerocontacts, operating from Gatwick Airport in 1951, directed their attentions at Australia, a country which had recently absorbed over 500 surplus Tiger Moths from its own resources:

> "By despatching aircraft in pairs we are able to quote the following unit prices. With 12 months' Certificate of Airworthiness and engine under 200 hours, £610 each; with engine nil hours since overhaul, £650 each; with new fuselage bag and engine with nil hours since overhaul £750.
>
> 12 months' Certificate of Airworthiness means that the machine has received a first class complete overhaul in our own shops immediately prior to despatch and each machine proudly bears our own name plate which is becoming known as a badge of excellence. There are Tiger Moths and Tiger Moths, but there is only one standard which we will recognise, and that is the highest.

A proposal to air deliver G-AXBZ from Belfast to Norfolk across the Irish Sea in January 2003 was vetoed in favour of the employment of a special lorry with a long, low flatbed and secure side panels. It was necessary to splay the undercarriage to lower the tank below the level of the roof. *Bill Cleyndert*

We are offering a reduction of 10% on quoted list prices of Tiger Moth spares."

Early in 1956 W A Rollason, which changed its name to Rollason Aircraft and Engines Ltd. in 1957, produced a small brochure which carried a description of the Tiger Moth in terms of construction, leading particulars and performance. It was far from any recognised attempt at a hard sell. Almost apologetically a small leaflet, not much bigger than a pair of cloakroom tickets, was slipped inside reminding potential customers that completely rebuilt Tiger Moths with zero-houred engines were still available at £900 each. Readers were invited to write to Croydon Aerodrome or to telephone the office to enquire about the attractive HP terms.

Tiger Moth T6825 was sold to French Somaliland in 1958 and was operated by the Djibouti Aero Club until 1960. By 1966 she had been acquired by a group operating in the heat of Aden but was returned to Great Britain in 1973 and stored with a number of repatriated helicopters in a barn in Hertfordshire where she was discovered and returned to airworthiness as G-APLU. *via Mike Vaisey*

de Havilland Gipsy Major I engines, nil hours since complete overhaul, £155 or if ordered in pairs, £150 each."

In January 1954 the Rollason company wrote to a number of prospective customers in New Zealand:

"If all the big stores in England can hold January sales, why cannot we? It is with the greatest pleasure, therefore, that as a result of price slashing, we are able to make the following unprecedented offers. But before you read on, remember the old slogan, First come, First Served! So, place your orders early.
A quantity of DH Gipsy Major Series I engines with test bed hours only since complete overhaul, internally and externally inhibited, packed, shipped and insured, CIF main New Zealand port, delivery to docks seven days. £145 each.
A small number of DH Tiger Moth aircraft, with airframe hours less than 250 since new, reconditioned throughout, complete with full dual control and blind flying instruments in both cockpits. All modifications complete. DH Gipsy Major engines with zero hours since complete overhaul. Twelve months' C of A. Dismantled, packed, shipped and insured CIF main New Zealand port. Delivery to packers three weeks from order. £1170 per pair.

The pastoral scene. A summer's day in England. Far from the heat of the Horn of Africa and Aden, Tiger Moth G-APLU and an ancient Morris car in a hay field near Glastonbury in 2006. Both vehicles might have been manufactured in the same factory. *Mike Vaisey*

Tiger Moth G-ANBW was overhauled at Croydon in 1953 and converted as a crop sprayer following sale to Thames Aerial Topdressing in New Zealand. Registered ZK-BFF she passed through the glider tug stage into private ownership. Acquired by John and Gloria Pheasant in 1978 she flew again in 2005 and is named 'Foxy Lady'. *John King*

Although the aeroplanes were relatively cheap to buy and to operate, the financial facts of life for impecunious groups of enthusiastic aviators were still harsh. Southport Aero Club had paid £250 in 1955 for Tiger Moth G-ANOD (84588), an aircraft whose second registered civil owner, Hon. Peter Vanneck, was destined to become Lord Mayor of London in 1977. Assistance with the purchase price had been in the form of a loan from the Kemsley Flying Trust, and the aircraft was collected from Honiley Airfield on 9 November 1955 by David Vernon. Mist and darkness necessitated a precautionary landing near Wrexham where the aircraft was tied to a telegraph pole and left in charge of the local constable. The pilot went home to his bed by train, returning next morning to effect the delivery. G-ANOD was operated with great enthusiasm from Southport Beach at Hesketh Park but the club could not raise sufficient cash to pay for the C of A renewal and G-ANOD was flown south to Kidlington and sold to Peter Clifford Aviation for £109. Peter Clifford only wanted the engine, which was removed and resold, while the airframe went by road to Christchurch to begin another life.

Believed to be the last operational Tiger Moth on RAF charge, T6056 (84547), spent from December 1943 to May 1950 in store with 10 MU at Hullavington before release to RAF Benson Station Flight. She was posted in a similar capacity to RAF Waddington at the end of 1951 until withdrawn to 9 MU Cosford in November 1954. A year later she was sold to the 61 Squadron Flying Group at Upwood and registered G-AOES, passing to No 600 (City of London) Squadron Flying Group at Biggin Hill in 1958. The aeroplane led an adventurous life until 1999 when she was badly damaged at Baxterley where it is hoped she will be restored.

Harold Perrin's report to authority in May 1945 that quantified 156 Tiger Moths as the post-war requirement by British flying clubs proved to be fairly accurate, but once surplus aeroplanes began to trade through the system more than twice as many could be found in daily operation in Great Britain. Employed by clubs and registered co-ownership groups, an affiliation to the Royal Aero Club qualified them for a healthy rebate on their petrol bills, a small concession from the government who viewed the drawback as an economic method of maintaining links with the most basic 'reserve'. Commercial rates for a Tiger Moth until the mid 1950s was rarely more than £4.10s.0d per flying hour, wet, and seemed to increase only after the approval to import American light aircraft was granted, a limitation imposed by the British Treasury to preserve the country's post-war dollar reserves. Lifting the prohibition spelled the end of the Tiger Moth as a serious club training aeroplane. Gliding clubs who used the aircraft extensively gradually abandoned them too, replacing them with a range of types more efficient in the climb and less costly to operate and maintain.

Very few institutions operating under government authority may have the desire but not the funds to maintain most out-of-service aircraft in airworthy condition, although there are exceptions. With a growing number of privately owned but military marked Tiger Moths available for exhibition and display flying, the world's biggest one-time operators, the RAF, RAAF and RCAF, elected not to maintain airworthy models of their own. The Fleet Air Arm Museum at Yeovilton exhibits an aircraft painted to represent G-ABUL, one of Alan Cobham's pre-war display machines, in recognition of the support provided to them by Sir Alan's company, Flight Refuelling Ltd. The aircraft is, in reality, the former T7291 (83805), sold into

T6056 is reputed to be the last operational Tiger Moth in RAF service. In 1955 she was registered to the 61 Squadron Flying Group and based at RAF Upwood. Owned and flown by Ken Broomfield G-AOES took part in the de Havilland Moth Club's Charity Flying Weekend at Old Warden in 1994 but was wrecked when landing at Baxterley in 1999. *Stan Roberts*

German priest Father Paul Schulte, a First World War fighter pilot, organised a flying training school for young people at Bonn-Hangelar in 1955 and fifteen Tiger Moths were air delivered as a formation from Thruxton, an event worthy of recording by the newsreels of the day. *Eric Brorup*

One of the Tiger Moths delivered to Paul Schulte's flying school at Bonn-Hangelar in 1955 was D-EDAN which was acquired by Hartmut Hesse in Munich in 1991 and re-registered D-EHHT. During the winter of 2010/2011 she took up residence at the Deutsches Museum Flugwerft Schleissheim near Munich. *Tom Singfield*

To fly a civil aircraft in military markings in Great Britain it was once necessary to carry conventionally sized civil letters too. Later the rules were changed to permit removal of the civil identification providing it was displayed on a plate near the cockpit and the military had no objection. Tiger Moth G-AZGZ conformed meticulously to the known rules when she was expensively repainted but her owner was later threatened with prosecution unless either the civil letters or military serial was removed. The military option won. *Terry Burke*

To fly a civil registered, ex military aircraft in military markings in Great Britain it is necessary to seek military approval and pay a fee. Tiger Moth G-AOGR could have offered either of two military marks and the additional factor that her owner was a serving Wing Commander.

The final colour scheme adopted by the last Tiger Moths operational with the Royal Navy was silver overall with the addition of then fashionable peel-off 'day-glo' tape, stuck on to engine cowlings, rear fuselage and fin. *Mike Longden*

the civilian market in 1953 to become G-AOXG. She was one of four civil registered Tiger Moths purchased by the Royal Navy in July 1956 as part of an expansion of Britannia Flight at Plymouth, operated on behalf of the Royal Naval College at Dartmouth, and was allocated a new military serial, XL717. On retirement from active duty the aircraft was presented to the FAA Museum for permanent static display. The Royal Navy did retire their last working Tiger Moth, T8191 (84483), to the Historic Aircraft Flight at Yeovilton but with limited funds and the insatiable appetite of other rarer aircraft, T8191 was placed in store from 1987 until sold at public auction in November 1994. After years of inactivity the aircraft was acquired by an ex-Royal Navy observer, Kevin Crumplin, in 2013 and, following a complete overhaul, is scheduled to join his Tiger Moth flying school at Henstridge in Dorset.

During her time with the Royal Navy Historic Aircraft Flight, Tiger Moth T8191 was operated in a naval camouflage scheme of two tones of grey with yellow undersides, not the most inconspicuous when operating over the browns and greens of the rolling British countryside. *R J Wilson*

de Havilland DH.82A Tiger Moth, PG-712/2, Royal Netherlands Air Force, 1946. Dark Earth and Dark Green upper surfaces with Trainer Yellow undersides. Serial in black, code '2' on engine cowling in white. National markings in six positions. Kept in flying condition the aircraft is registered PH-CSL. *Artwork ©Richard Caruana, 1:72 scale*

The Royal New Zealand Air Force Museum locally built Tiger Moth NZ1481 (DHNZ161), on static display, painted to represent NZ825 (DHNZ75), whilst the real NZ825, civil registered ZK-AIB, was under restoration to flying condition at Mandeville for many years until the project was suspended in 2001. The Museum's Historical Flight maintain in airworthy condition an ex-RAF aircraft, T5763 (83492), shipped to Wellington in November 1940 and taken on RNZAF charge as NZ662. Following a post-war career in agriculture and an assignment in Fiji, the aircraft was sold to the Flight in 1985 and has been maintained in airworthy condition since 1987 at Wigram and more recently at Ohakea.

The Historic Flight of the Royal New Zealand Air Force maintains Tiger Moth NZ662 in airworthy condition at Ohakea. The aircraft was sold as surplus in 1946 and bought back in 1985. *deHMC Archive*

The Historical Flight of the Royal Netherlands Air Force has been custodian of Tiger Moth PH-TYG (82535), at Gilze Rijen since 1986. The aircraft has been the subject of several extensive overhauls and although of British civil parentage has been painted in full Dutch military colours using identity A-12 and later A-57.

What is now the Canada Aviation and Space Museum at Rockliffe, Ottawa, inherited two DH.82C Tiger Moths from the National Museum of Science and Technology in 1967. CF-FGL (DHC724), repainted with her former RCAF serial 4394, is a Gipsy Major powered static exhibit while DH.82C2 4861 (DHC1052), is maintained in airworthy condition as a rare surviving example of the type with a Menasco engine.

India, a vast sub-continent with strong Tiger Moth connections dating from before the Second World War, appropriately maintains at least one aircraft in airworthy condition with the Indian Air Force Museum at Palam near Delhi. Cowley-built DE893 (85778), was shipped to South Africa in March 1943 and served with the SAAF as 2492. She was one of the aircraft selected in 1946 for transfer to India, arriving at Bangalore in February 1947 and, following overhaul by Hindustan Aircraft, joined the Indian Air Force as HU-512. In April 1963 the aircraft was registered VT-DPK to the Government of India, Civil Aviation Department, Madras, but the allocation was cancelled in 1991 and the aircraft reappeared in airworthy condition with the Indian Air Force Historic Flight.

Following a major refurbishment at Gilze Rijen the Tiger Moth operated by the Royal Netherlands Air Force Historical Flight, PH-TYG, was operational in 2009 wearing a new colour scheme, test flown by Ton Hendriks who first flew a Tiger Moth in 1946. *Ben Ullings*

Blending into a background of parkland and mature oak trees Tiger Moth PH-TYG circles to land at Woburn Abbey in 1994. The aircraft is painted in the finite camouflage colours of the Royal Netherlands Air Force with yellow upper surfaces to the lower mainplanes. *Pim van Dam*

In March 2011 a decision was made to return the aircraft to pristine condition with the aim of appearing at the 80th anniversary celebrations of the Indian Air Force planned for Hindon Air Force Base on 8 October 2013. HU-512 was dismantled in India and carried to England where a number of companies bestowed their particular skills. In order to qualify for a Certificate of Airworthiness the registration G-CGYN was allocated to allow a test flying programme at Leicester which was completed in September before she returned to 'steal the show' at Hindon.

Air Marshal Barry Grayson learned to fly on Tiger Moths at Point Cook and upon his retirement as Chief of the Air Staff, Royal Australian Air Force, in 1994, he chose to leave the Service on board Tiger Moth VH-SSK (DHA885). Painted in her previous RAAF colours as A17-468, the pristine aircraft was on temporary loan to the RAAF Museum at Point Cook but was withdrawn by her owner early in 1998 after sustaining damage in a careless ground handling incident.

Chile improved her internal communications in the 1920s with a fleet of DH.60 Moths engaged on aero-postal duties and in 1998 the Air Force Museum began a search for an airworthy example to complement the static aircraft already displayed in Santiago. In 1987 the Museum made a successful bid instead for British based DH.82A Tiger Moth G-BACK (85879), which had unexpectedly been offered for sale. The aircraft was airlifted by Chilean Air Force Lockheed Hercules from Hurn Airport in December 1987 and has been maintained in airworthy condition at Santiago ever since. Painted in RAF camouflage bearing serial DF130, she was listed as a civil aircraft, CC-DMC, to the National Aeronautical Collection in 1995 and on 23 March 1998 was part of a formation of nine vintage aircraft which proudly flew past the President of Chile at the opening of the biennial FIDAE airshow.

Tiger Moth HU512 of the Indian Air Force Historic Flight underwent a major refurbishment in England in preparation for her appearance at Air Force Day organised at Hindon Air Force Base on 8 October 2012 from where it was reported that she was the star of the show. *deHMC Archive*

It was necessary for Indian Air Force Historic Flight Tiger Moth HU512 to take up British civil registry in 2012 to permit flight testing at Leicester Aerodrome after which her IAF markings and insignia were applied and she was airlifted home. *Paul Kirby*

CHAPTER SIXTEEN

Resisting the Change

de Havilland's Associated Company in South Africa had been responsible for the import of almost sixty Tiger Moths pre-war, mostly complete, but occasionally received less engines which were ordered independently and fitted at the company's premises on the historic aerodrome at Baragwanath near Johannesburg. In the main these aircraft were scheduled for flying clubs where they were used as primary trainers and amongst the first were ZS-AIL, ZS-AIM and ZS-AIN, (3525, 3526 and 3522), operated from Baragwanath in the red and silver colours of the Johannesburg Light Plane Club. All three were impressed into the South African Air Force in 1940.

In 1935 and with an eye on events in Abyssinia as much as Europe, the South African Government decided to accelerate modernisation of the country's defence plans. A contract was written for the light aeroplane clubs to provide courses of fifty hours elementary flying training for pilots who would then progress to the Air Force's Central Flying School (CFS) for advanced training. It was intended to produce 1,000 qualified pilots by 1942 and each club was required to standardise on equipment by selecting one of four basic aircraft types: Ryan ST-A, Miles Hawk, Miles Magister and DH.82A Tiger Moth.

The scheme became effective in 1937 and resulted in orders for thirty Tiger Moths to be shipped from Hatfield, but the SAAF reported adversely on the quality of club instruction although pilots were generally 'improved' by their subsequent courses at CFS. For purposes of administration nine clubs were issued identifying numbers (1-9) as component parts of the collective Transvaal Air Training Squadron (TATS) in March 1937, but these had been amended by October 1938 when the more appropriately named Union Air Training Group (UATG) took over and expanded into thirteen 'Flights', all operating civil registered aircraft. At the same time the fifty hours training was extended to seventy hours before the new pilots were posted to a network of Air Schools operated by the Air Force.

Coincident with the CFS move to Tempe near Bloemfontein in May 1940, the SAAF decided that its standard elementary trainer would be the Tiger Moth. The decision followed impressment of about 250 assorted light commercial, school, club and privately owned aircraft of some sixty different types or marques. The UATG Flights were subsequently disbanded and all elementary flying training was consolidated under control of the new SAAF Flying Training Command at seven established Air Schools.

The substantial reorganisation was partly due to South Africa's conditional agreement to take an active part in the Empire Air Training Scheme (EATS), which had been the subject of debate since October 1938. On 6 September 1939, fifty new Tiger Moths from the RAF's Home Reserve were allocated for shipment to South Africa. The aircraft were flown to Sealand, dismantled, packed and despatched by sea in five separate shipments between January and April 1940. On arrival the camouflage schemes were oversprayed with trainer yellow, and each aircraft was allocated a SAAF serial number. Allocation appears to have been very much against the order in which the fuselages were unpacked and set up to receive their newly painted wings.

Coastal Patrol Flights under the sunny skies of the Southern Hemisphere could hardly have been more different from the atrocious conditions suffered by the British crews in 1939. Steve Harris flying ZS-AAP over the breakers near Port Alfred in January 2010. *Cliff Reynolds*

Although primarily intended for the training of South African nationals to operate within the confines of their own continent, the RAF was anxious to expand its own aircrew training programmes and agreement was reached in January 1940 to allow British nationals resident in South Africa to be trained, but under SAAF control. A further sixty Tiger Moths were despatched from England between 7 January and 8 March 1941, all brand new aircraft packed and shipped directly from the Morris Motors factory at Cowley, with just a few minutes flight test time recorded in their logbooks.

A new Agreement was signed in June 1940 under the title 'Joint Air Training Plan' (JATP), allowing British cadets to train in South Africa for RAF service, while permitting a gradual expansion and the introduction of seven Elementary Flying Training Schools (EFTS). The 'Joint Air Training Scheme' (JATS) was defined in June 1941, for which South Africa would provide airfields, fuel, oil and facilities while the British Government would be responsible for all instructors and staff, aircraft, spares and training equipment. In addition to the Tiger Moth, selected aircraft types were Miles Master, Hawker Hurricane, Airspeed Oxford and Avro Anson, all shipped from Great Britain. A general shortage of aircraft meant that some Elementary Schools had to share and operated with only thirty six aircraft instead of the agreed establishment of forty eight until deliveries caught up.

By July 1941 SAAF training units for every discipline were involved in JATS and a number of South African Government owned aircraft had been added, mostly obsolete Avro and Hawker biplanes. From December, training capacity began to exceed demand and resources were offered to train aircrew principally from Belgium, Poland, Greece and Yugoslavia. As more RAF recruits arrived some local protest groups with grudges held since the Boer War were moved to commit murderous acts of sabotage on unguarded aircraft with the result that some stations put up standing patrols to fly around the airfield perimeter to observe movement of people or vehicles on the otherwise nearly deserted approach roads.

Eight Air Depots (AD) were established by August 1941 to cope better with the continuing delivery of aircraft, each with responsibility for specific types. No 4 AD at Lyttelton was assigned to the reception of Tiger Moths and Miles Masters. Shipments from Morris Motors were recorded every month from January to October 1941 and during the ten month period 250 new aircraft were accepted through Cape Town.

Forty Tiger Moths shipped in April 1941 and more than twenty in July were lost at sea due to enemy action, part of the 15% losses being suffered on all shipping destined for South Africa. Six of the eight aircraft despatched on 12 October 1941 were later recorded as being "badly corroded due to immersion in sea water and considered beyond repair." Their ship had run aground near Cape Town and suffered a flooded hold. As a counter to the losses Tiger Moths manufactured in Australia were imported via Durban from December. Between February and June 1943, a further fifty six Tiger Moths were delivered to Cape Town from Great Britain, including for the first time, ten reconditioned aircraft, a few of which were to be included with most consignments shipped during that period.

With the training machine well established the Director of Coastal Air Force called a conference in December 1941 to identify the assistance which might be expected from the Schools by the coastal squadrons in protection of the extensive coastline. The result was that by April 1942, thirty Reserve Squadrons had been formed with Nos 1-7 Air Schools constituting 101-107 Reserve Squadrons, complete with their own administration and their Tiger Moths designated 'Light Bomber'. Apart from isolated incidents of a type expected on any wartime coastline the main concern was fear of a possible invasion by Japanese forces following the attack on Pearl Harbor. By December 1943 the threat was believed to have diminished and a sufficient number of operational squadrons had been raised to tackle resistance on a more permanent and professional basis.

In February 1944, 200 Canadian-built Fairchild Cornells were allocated to South Africa as a Tiger Moth replacement following a trend started in Canada and a pair of aircraft was delivered for trials on loan from RATG in Southern Rhodesia. These two, 15266 and 15271, were operated as part of the Communications Flight of 24 Group based at Zwartkop Air Station during March and April 1944, and found little favour with pilots or engineers. The replacement aircraft was considered to be underpowered, especially for flying training duties at the elementary schools situated in the Highveld, locations specifically chosen on account of their weather record. They were also considered 'bland' and 'viceless' and consequently not ideally suited to the training role. The SAAF preferred the Tiger Moth and refused to accept its intended replacement.

With Canadian production geared up, and Southern Rhodesia's reluctant acceptance of the Cornell, one compromise solution was to move seemingly redundant Tiger Moths from RATG to South Africa. In March 1944, twenty six Tiger Moths were transferred south followed by forty three on 31 May and a final twelve on 14 June. In addition, nine new Australian-built aircraft were diverted to Lyttelton rather than continuing on their rail journey to Bulawayo, and a quartet of Tiger Moths from Kenya's Auxiliary Air Unit (KAAU) arrived in March: a final tally of ninety four. But there was consternation at the condition of some arrivals which had evidently spent considerable time picketed in the weather. As a result of post-delivery surveys, eleven Tiger Moths were immediately scrapped.

In spite of the constant build-up of complete aeroplanes from RAF Maintenance Units, from Cowley and Mascot, and later from RATG and Kenya, there was, or appeared to be, in concert with all other types a constant shortage of spare parts for Tiger Moth airframes and especially for Gipsy Major engines. Always in demand were Tiger Moth mainplanes, the victims of poor ground handling, taxiing accidents, ground loops and nose-overs following bounced landings. Rising to the occasion at the request of the Director General of War Supplies was G H Starck who alleviated the problem by converted his furniture factory in The Cape to the remanufacture and repair of wooden wings.

Potentially more serious was the shortage of engine parts caused, to a large degree, by excessive wear, the result of the hot, dry and dusty aerodrome surfaces. During take-off and landing the Tiger Moth's tailskid spoon cut furrows in the topsoil, ripping out the binding grass and creating clouds of gritty dust. Other aircraft taking off flew through the debris which was ingested by the engines, causing excessive wear in carburettors and cylinders. Australian-built aircraft were fitted with Vokes air filters attached externally to the intake on the starboard side cowling, but the British aircraft had no such luxury until they were fitted as an extra precaution on site. The problem was equally bad for aircraft attempting to land when, in addition to the suspension of abrasive particles, visibility was impaired by clouds of dust generated by aircraft on the roll.

The situation was considered serious enough to warrant a detailed study of aerodrome surfaces, a task undertaken by the South African Engineer Corps (Aerodromes and Maintenance) in conjunction with the Directorate of Aerodromes and Works. Experiments with eighty five different types of grass were conducted on plots at Wonderboom, but with constant over-utilisation the situation was never completely resolved. The best solution was to try a small wheel in place of the skid, designed and trialled at 62 AS Bloemfontein, and which eventually became the standard fit on all JATS tailskid equipped aircraft. Pilots were urged to exercise extra caution when taxiing, however, as the mainwheels still were not fitted with brakes.

Continuous efforts and organisational refinements resulted in peak output of aircrew achieved late in 1943 and maintained into 1944 when, with the war outlook appearing to be brighter for the Allies, the pace was allowed to slacken off. No 1 Air School at Baragwanath, home of de Havilland (South Africa) Pty. Ltd., was closed down on

The sheer inelegance of the giant serial numbers meant there was no room for a fuselage roundel on some SAAF Tiger Moths. 4608 was delivered from Great Britain in March 1943 and departed for India in July 1946. Note the tailwheel in lieu of a skid and the absence of spin strakes.
Maurice Kelly

Bearing 'high visibility' serial 2471, this Tiger Moth was received by the South African Air Force from RAF stocks in June 1942 and survived to be part of the post war consignment despatched to India in 1946.
Maurice Kelly

29 February 1944 having peaked with an establishment of fifty eight Tiger Moths in July 1943. During the previous four years the school had been a willing custodian of de Havilland types having also operated Hornet Moth, Moth Major and DH.60 Moth, all disguised under military colours.

The mixture of high adventure, bravado and boredom was by no means unique to the trainee pilots and instructors of JATS, although South African weather was probably a contributing factor in some of the high jinks. To inspire their pupils to greater levels of confidence it was reported that on some occasions instructors would climb out of their cockpits in mid-air and inch along the line of the lower wing front spar until they reached the interplane strut, from which position they would view the passing scrubland from varying heights. A similar story was told of an instructor in Australia and another in Great Britain, operating with 21 EFTS Booker, who told his pupil to hold the aircraft steady at which point he would climb out onto one lower wing and then the other, advising the pupil that he was checking the rigging to ensure it was safely attached prior to initiating an aerobatic routine.

But it was the overconfidence of some trainees which led them to inspect the ground, and often buildings and people, from too low a level. To help identify miscreants, for one yellow Tiger Moth looked exactly like another yellow Tiger Moth, and stem a rising tide of accidents, JATS aircraft were painted with serial numbers on fuselage sides and underneath the wings, as large as could decently and practically be accommodated. A similar ploy was adopted in Canada, and for the same reasons. The Tiger Moths of No 2 AS Randfontein carried a giant '2' on the top surface of the port upper mainplane, and the school identification on the starboard upper, both of which could be easily read on a banking aircraft from some distance.

Two indulgences of the Benoni flying instructors were to run the Tiger Moth's mainwheels along the straight dirt roads, creeping up behind an unsuspecting vehicle until the aircraft filled the rear view mirror, and then to hop over the top and disappear at low level, possibly to run a tip of one lower mainplane along the surface of the water in a local stream.

Sqn Ldr W L Woodward AFC was posted in as CFI at No 7 AS Kroonstad in November 1941. Having survived the hardships of a soldier in the First World War he joined the RAF on a five year commission in 1919 and then flew civil aircraft until re-enlisting in August 1939. The press hounds picked up the scent when it was revealed that on account of his age (and experience), King's Regulations had been altered to allow him to continue instructing and much was made of the fact that his talents might otherwise have been lost when, in 1942, an interview was published under the heading 'The Oldest Instructor in The Empire':

> "People who are good horsemen almost invariably make good pilots. I noticed that when I started out as an instructor and it is still the same today. The syllabus of training is similar in outline to what it was in the early days, but it is now more thorough and of course there are more things to think about. More than 50% of the flying accidents at training schools are

A favourite ploy of bored instructors was to fly low along a road behind a car before breaking off and disappearing via a local feature. In 2013 and on behalf of the Johannesburg Light Plane Club, Courtney Watson and Tiger Moth ZS-UKW were invited to play with a replica 1930 Alfa Romeo Monza. *Richard Webb, Camera Stuff*

caused by disregarding regulations. Usually the cause is over confidence on the part of the inexperienced pilot; over confidence which breeds a certain carelessness and makes him boast to himself: I need not worry about this or that regulation! A good pilot takes no unnecessary chances! A much smaller percentage of accidents owe their cause to errors of judgement or other mistakes by the pilot. A very small number of accidents can be traced to aircraft weaknesses or failure."

A popular story told at No 5 AS Witbank concerned a pupil pilot who had damaged a Tiger Moth during the course of normal flying training and in consequence suffered an artificially dramatic tirade from his instructor during which the pupil was threatened with having to pay for a new aeroplane. At a time when cheque books were still a fantasy of most young men's imagination, the pupil is alleged to have drawn one from an inside pocket and with pen raised calmly asked for how much and to whom the cheque should be made payable.

The difficulties of adapting to high temperatures, high altitude and a reduced aircraft performance, especially for pupils who had begun their training in Great Britain, were sometimes demonstrated in spectacular fashion. Having flown solo on one occasion at Sealand, Paul Goddard's second solo was at Benoni where he rounded out too high and in spite of a rapid application of full power hit the ground hard and bounced back into the circuit. The aircraft continued to fly but the engine revs were high, there was a deal of vibration, the altimeter was stuck at 500ft, two holes had appeared in the lower wings, and there was no acceleration. Having persuaded the aircraft around to finals, dismissing the thought of ditching in a local lake, the aircraft made a successful touch down but taxiing back to dispersal was an effort. After shut down, investigation revealed six inches missing from each propeller blade, the tips having been fired through both lower wings, and the crankshaft was bent. During the subsequent interview with his Flight Commander, Paul Goddard, who later took up Holy Orders, was admonished for breaking the aeroplane but congratulated for managing to fly it in a 'thoroughly unairworthy condition'.

The urgent need for 'acclimatisation' was later recognised by the establishment early in 1943 of No 2 Pilot Despatch Centre (PDC) at Nigel and No 3 PDC at Standerton, with the aim of providing a four week period of refresher training, but there was never enough equipment or instructional personnel to run both centres at anything approaching an ideal capacity.

Exercising over the appropriately named Mud Bay, British Columbia, Bill Teague and DH.82A Tiger Moth C-GWET *'Old Harry'*, an aircraft which emigrated from South Africa with her owner in 1976. *Terry Elgood from DH.82C CF-ATG*

A variation on the standard RAF training colours was decided when ZU-EEG was rebuilt following damage incurred during a forced landing in 2005. The South African ZU identification recognises the aircraft's vintage classification. *Ian Popplewell*

ZS-NWJ is a composite aircraft created by the Strecker family, famous for Tiger Moth activities since the end of the Second World War. In 1998 the aircraft carried the abbreviated registration G-AAB for appearance in a film. *Miles Sutherland*

Records were as accurately maintained as practicable, including the civil impressments lists but excluding prospective deliveries known to have been lost at sea, a total of ninety three aircraft. The South African Air Force can be credited with the receipt of 698 Tiger Moths of British or Australian origin of which 238 were struck off charge before the Joint Air Training Scheme was concluded on 8 March 1946.

The reduced demand for pilots from 1944 allowed many aircraft to be withdrawn from service and positioned for storage at Air Depots. While the SAAF considered its future the fate of the aircraft was being discussed 6,000 miles away in London from December 1945 by Committees constituted by delegates from the MAP, Air Ministry, Treasury and Dominion Offices. While there had already been hectic activity surrounding surplus disposals in Southern Rhodesia and apparent confusion over the policy covering RAF stocks held in Great Britain, the South African question needed quiet diplomacy. Under the terms of the Agreement setting up JATS both sides had accepted that upon termination there would be a physical division of residual aircraft and equipment rather than cash apportionment from sales. Such an understanding would, therefore, lead to neither side demanding or suggesting minimum sale prices as elsewhere. The British Government was free to extract its allocated stock leaving the South African authorities to raise whatever cash they could from sale of the remainder, where and how they liked, to help offset the cost of aerodromes, buildings and facilities.

The fluctuation of fortunes and requirements since the Agreement was signed was now seen to have blurred the issue. A number of aircraft had undoubtedly been shipped to South Africa to help build a strategic reserve, and had now become indistinguishable from those declared surplus from JATS. London was concerned that if much was made of this issue when apportioning individual aircraft, the South African Government might retaliate by imposing high charges for storage and maintenance on all aircraft declared redundant.

Chris Langeveld airborne on the first post restoration flight of his Tiger Moth ZS-DNP on 18 May 2010. The flight took place at Stellenbosch Airfield in the shadow of 'The Helderberg' mountain around which a layer of cloud had started to develop. *Richard Greeff*

A suggestion made to a South African Mission visiting London in August 1945 that the Dominion might be offered the whole of the British share of surplus aircraft at a price of £100,000 had not been further discussed at the Mission's own request. Since then, the cessation of Lend-Lease supplies from the USA had caused the Air Ministry to consider withdrawal of 200 Tiger Moths from South Africa for training purposes in 'other theatres' and the sum of £100,000 was, therefore, no longer appropriate.

Of the 460 Tiger Moths declared still to be operational, many were known to be in a 'well used' condition, and the prospect of the RAF hand-picking the 200 best examples was thought not to be diplomatic. South Africa had already declared an interest in maintaining a Tiger Moth fleet for its own defence training needs and there was growing friction over the proposed withdrawal to Great Britain of 300 North American Harvards supplied under Lend-Lease, and not included under the Agreement's clause covering JATS proportional division. The SAAF had hoped to secure these aircraft at little cost for their own use but, as events moved on, 280 Harvards were shipped back to open storage in Great Britain where most of them were eventually scrapped.

It is not clear whether the MAP or Air Ministry did have a specific destination in mind for its anticipated share of South African based Tiger Moths, but apart from a return to Great Britain it seems likely that India was the intended target possibly to stave off any prospect of further foreign competition, evidence of which was being flagged up by RAF Commands in the sub-continent during the summer of 1945. It was London's decision to vest full rights of negotiation with their people on the spot, the British Air Liaison Mission (BALM). They were to propose South African purchase of the whole of the residual stock less the 200 Tiger Moths and to report back to MAP before accepting any offer. In addition, and to support the selected aircraft, London asked for fifty spare Gipsy Major engines from a stock believed to number 240, spares to service 250 engines, and two fifths of all Tiger Moth airframe spares. It was appreciated that the best of the engines would already be fitted to the aircraft in service. In confirming that no other British owned aircraft would be withdrawn, the MAP were signalling their willingness to permit disposal of all other assets in situ, a decision made on the grounds of practicality and convenience as much as economics.

Tiger Moths were gradually withdrawn from the Air Schools between February and September 1944 and placed in storage at a number of sites: Waterkloof, Germiston, Baragwanath, Benoni, Nigel, Vereeniging, Potchefstroom, Witbank and Kroonstad, sometimes at their own home station but all under the general administration of No 15 AD with headquarters at Zwartkop. As more aircraft were received, especially towards the end of 1945 when Air Depots themselves were being closed and covered accommodation became scarce, Tiger Moths were stored with their mainplanes stowed alongside the fuselage, while a few had their engines removed.

From February 1946 the fate of most of the SAAF Tiger Moths was decided. The Air Ministry was allotted their 200 aircraft: 100 were drawn from storage and flown to Cape Town, dismantled and transferred by sea to India progressively from July, when they were delivered to the Hindustan Aircraft Company at Bangalore. Several were modified for night flying before they left their Air Depots in South Africa and Hindustan's main task was to prepare them for local service with the Indian Air Force who later released large numbers which were civil registered on behalf of the government for the creation of a 'Reserve' through subsidised flying clubs.

The SAAF selected 100 Tiger Moths in February 1946 for post-war service with the Central Flying School at Dunnottar from where several were sold in August 1948 at £4.10s.0d each. It was in the wake of requirements to clear storage areas and close expensive facilities as quickly as possible that nightmare stories originated: forty seven Avro Ansons sold to a company in Port Elizabeth at £2.0s.0d each; the thirty seven aircraft sold without engines were cleared at exactly half that amount. In retrospect the £6.0s.0d. each paid for serviceable Curtiss Kittyhawk IVs might still be considered a bargain, although the buyer was in the scrap metal business.

The RAF took their second batch of 100 Tiger Moths from store in April 1946 and they were delivered in September and October to the Air Training Wing in Southern Rhodesia, replacing the aircraft which had themselves been declared surplus and sold in batches from 1944. The replacements were gathered at Benoni and flown north to equip Nos 4 and 5 Flying Training Schools at Heany and Thornhill.

The South African War Stores Disposal Board sanctioned release of Tiger Moths as surplus to requirements only after the RAF's selection for India and Rhodesia had been satisfied and sales by auction were held at many of the Air Depots in June 1946 and July 1947. Prices varied between £40 and £85 with several at £50 and the occasional extravagance such as SAAF 2152 (84435), which was sold from Benoni on 2 June 1946 for £125.

SAAF 579 (84197), was retired from No 7 AS Kroonstad on 18 December 1944 and placed in store on the same airfield. She was moved to Witbank on 1 October 1945 and later the same month transferred to Germiston where she was expected to be tagged as one of the 'RAF 100 aircraft', probably scheduled for Southern Rhodesia. On inspection the aircraft was rejected and remained in store until she was moved again, to Vereeniging, on 14 June 1947, and sold the

The ordered scene at 3 Air Depot, Cape Town in 1946, as some of the 100 RAF aircraft selected for a passage to India were gathered together ready for packing. *W T Blick*

Australian-built ZS-VIG operated with the RAF and in civil markings in Southern Rhodesia and Zimbabwe, and in military and civil ownership in South Africa. Her most recent upgrade was by Brian Zeederberg and Ian Popplewell from until she flew again from Krugersdorp from 1985 to October 2005. *Ian Popplewell*

Left and below: One time RATG Tiger Moth T6529, VP-YJV was sold to L R Nicholson in Salisbury in 1952 and ended her career in unrecorded circumstances with the Mashonaland Flying Club at Mount Hampden in October 1957.
Liz Elliot via Mitch Stirling

Pastel blue is not a colour much associated with Tiger Moths, but operating under the sunlit skyscape of South Africa, Tiger Moth ZS-DNG, ex SAAF and of Australian origin, proves colour and airframe are in complete harmony. In September 2000 she was sold to a new owner at Kilimanjaro International Airport, Tanzania. *Dave Becker*

following month. In November 1950, 84197 took up civil markings ZS-DEU under the ownership of H E Fourie at Brixton, and following an engine overhaul by Bok Strecker, and a new red and silver paint scheme, she was flown on 7 March 1951. Several owners later in 1959, ZS-DEU was standing at Windhoek in what appeared to be an abandoned condition. A pilot from 28 Squadron, a member of the SAAF's Defence Flying Club (DFC), was told by a local airline engineer that the current owner would be pleased to present the aircraft to the Club. This intelligence was relayed to the Committee who sent a club engineer to inspect and dismantle the aircraft. Almost coincidentally, an empty transport aircraft passing through Windhoek was bound for the DFC's main base at Swartkop and, not wishing to miss the opportunity, all four wings and the propeller were loaded on board and safely delivered.

Enter Mr M L Greenberg of Benoni, wondering where he might find the rest of the aeroplane he had just bought from Mr Friedrich Bohnemeier: ZS-DEU. It came as quite a shock to discover that the wings had been flown to Swartkop and Mr Greenberg politely asked the DFC to send him £300 or return the missing parts. Equally diplomatically, the Club secretary replied from a position of great embarrassment that he was empowered to offer £50 for the whole aeroplane or £25 for the four wings. "Should you find this unacceptable," he wrote, "we will return the mainplanes, reassemble the aircraft and park it where it was found." The offer was refused, but to avoid any further embarrassment a deal was struck in which the SAAF agreed to fly the fuselage of ZS-DEU from Windhoek to join the wings at Swartkop from where the whole would be available for collection by the new owner. In addition the DFC was willing to offer a veritable collection of spare parts and compensation for legal expenses of £12.10s.0d.

Following sale of the Disposal Board's declared surpluses of 1946-1948, CFS absorbed all the remainder until they released a batch of Tiger Moths in 1955, several of which were disposed of as scrap but subsequently appeared on the civil register. CFS made a final break with the type in June 1956 when the last aircraft were sold to the SAAF Aero Club, possibly for as much as £25 each, following the Club's successful bid of £5 for an engineless airframe in 1951.

INDIA

To stimulate and support the export trade the de Havilland Aircraft Company had opened a branch office in Karachi in 1928 to handle increasing sales of the DH.60 Moth, and before the war some privately owned Tiger Moths were shipped to India together with several intended for use by the flying clubs acting in the capacity of a government sponsored reserve.

More civil registered Tiger Moths were imported at the beginning of the war following an order placed with Hatfield by the Indian Government. The aircraft were subsequently built by Morris Motors and test flown at Cowley wearing civil registrations in September and October 1940. The twenty seven aircraft order, VT-AMI to VT-ANI, had been built in seven small batches integrated with RAF orders, taking build positions between 83571 and 83746. After delivery, a handful of the aircraft was impressed and military serial numbers allocated. A few others met well-documented ends, but the majority were simply cancelled from the civil register against no known fate but were probably just withdrawn from use and stored in a completely worn-out condition.

In addition to the Indian Government receiving second hand civil Tiger Moths in 1940 supplied by British aircraft broker W S Shackleton, the British Government re-equipped the Bristol Aeroplane Company's 10 EFTS when it relocated from Yatesbury to Weston-super-Mare in September 1940, after despatching the whole of their previous fleet to India where the aircraft took up consecutive civil letters in the block VT-ANU to VT-AOP. An additional thirty three Tiger Moths were supplied as civil registered aircraft from de Havilland Australia between January and August 1941, DHA237-249; 252-254; 361-368; 370-376 and 508-517. All were delivered via the RAF Depot at Karachi with the exception of DHA252-254 which avoided the perilous voyage round the southern tip of India and were delivered directly to the Madras Flying Club as VT-ANN, VT-ANQ and VT-ANO. Of the Karachi imports, DHA370 became VT-AQE, but was later allocated military marks LR236, and was operated by the Royal Indian Air Force Volunteer Reserve with No 1 Coastal Defence Flight (CDF) at St. Thomas Mount, Madras.

Civil marked Tiger Moths of the Bristol Flying School lined up at Filton Aerodrome where the newly whitewashed headquarters building of No 2 ERFTS reflects a style familiar at similar establishments. All the aircraft of the company's sister No 10 EFTS at Yatesbury were despatched to India in 1940. *Bristol Aeroplane Company*

Thirty three Tiger Moths, a trio of Hawker Harts, 3,000 tons of cement, 175 tons of tobacco, ten horses and a brand new Rolls-Royce listed as a Silver Phantom were part of the cargo of the SS *Breda*, a 7,000 ton Dutch ship operated during the war by the P & O Shipping Company. She had loaded at Southend with goods bound for Mombasa, Bombay and Karachi, and departed on 12 December 1940 to rendezvous with a convoy forming at the Lynn of Lorn near Oban in Scotland. Whilst marshalling there, the unprotected ships were attacked by two Luftwaffe Heinkel He111 bombers on 22 December 1940, and the *Breda*, badly damaged by blast from a bomb which exploded in the water alongside, was towed into the protection of Ardmucknish Bay where she sank in 100ft of water.

Although a salvage effort was attempted both before and after the ship went down, the aircraft cargo was not recovered although the horses and the Rolls-Royce were. The Tiger Moths are believed to have been scheduled originally for delivery to Kenya which would explain the call at Mombasa, but the manifest suggests the aircraft and spares were consigned to the RAF in India.

In 1975, part of the wreck was explored by members of the Royal Navy's Air Command Sub Aqua Club, more in hope than in anticipation of confirming the rumour that the thirty three Tiger Moths had all been packed in watertight containers, and were accompanied by a clutch of spare Gipsy Major engines. The expedition did find the remains of seven Tiger Moth fuselages, free standing and completely corroded, plus some engines but no sign of the Harts. As evidence of their underwater adventure a number of heavily protected Gipsy Major induction manifolds was brought to the surface and presented to the Royal Navy Historic Aircraft Flight at Yeovilton where, underneath the grease and oiled wrapping, they were found to be in perfect order.

Several of the 208 new production Tiger Moths sent from Great Britain in RAF markings to India during 1943 and 1944 adopted civil letters on arrival and were operated by flying clubs on behalf of the government. Unlike the losses suffered by shipments to South Africa, apart from those on the SS *Breda*, only one Tiger Moth, DE238 (85284), en-route to India in March 1943, is believed to have been lost at sea. British deliveries were routed to Bombay where the aircraft were collected from the docks alongside crated Hawker Hurricanes and carried by tank transporters to Santa Cruz Airport, about ten miles from Juhu, where Tata Industries had been contracted to assemble them. The Tiger Moths were test flown and subsequently collected from Santa Cruz by Service ferry pilots from 229 Group and air delivered into the vastness of the sub-continent.

Although some Tiger Moth spares were manufactured in India on behalf of the de Havilland Company a plan for production of 239 new Tiger Moths in Bombay was not proceeded with and RAF serials in the BS and BT blocks which had been set aside were neither taken up nor re-allocated to another type. Although there is no record of Tiger Moths being supplied directly to the Indian Air Force before the war, in March 1940 five IAF Tiger Moths were presented to the press at the Risalpur Training School. The 'K' letter in the serial numbers (K1778, K1780, K1782, K1783 and K1784), had been

This photograph of straked Tiger Moth EM875 was taken after August 1943 when she arrived in India. Had the camera been at a slightly different angle it would have been possible to count how many Tiger Moths, Harvards and Spitfires were on parade. *Armed Forces Information Office*

applied erroneously instead of 'T' when the aircraft were taken on charge by the IAF, a fact which led to much historical confusion. The 'donor' of 'K1778' was found to be the Delhi Flying Club to whom she had been delivered from Hatfield as VT-ALE (82580), in the spring of 1939 and it is likely that the other aircraft on parade were from similar sources.

To some extent the aircraft at Risalpur pre-empted the post-war RAF training markings by carrying broad yellow bands around the rear fuselages, but were otherwise painted silver overall. Later, all military marked Tiger Moths operating in India took up standard brown and green camouflage, although the civil registered machines maintained an overall scheme of insipid yellow.

The Indian authorities were keen to impress upon 1939's correspondents that due to a rapidly developing expansion scheme, scores of volunteers from all ethnic backgrounds would be selected and trained to the highest standards enjoyed by pilots in the Royal Air Force. To speed the training of Indian pilots courses were later arranged in Great Britain, and the ERFTS which had been closed down at Gravesend on the outbreak of war was reformed as 20 EFTS for the purpose at Yeadon, operating Tiger Moths between March 1941 and January 1942.

The varied operational life of an RAF Tiger Moth in India was identified by Reginald Sansome in his book *The Bamboo Workshop*, the history of the RAF's Repair and Salvage Units (RSU) in India and Burma between 1941 and 1946. The type was used by nearly all units for the transfer of supplies and personnel, collection of urgently needed spares, and for locating aircraft reported to have put down in otherwise totally inaccessible areas. Damage reports and surveys were quickly executed by Technical Officers flown in to and out of the nearest convenient clearings, movements ripe for their own accident potential.

A Hawker Hurricane had forced landed near Kaladan early in 1944 and the Technical Officer of No 3 RSU flew out from Dhoapalong in the unit's Tiger Moth to inspect the casualty, landing as close to the scene as was possible. During his survey a flight of RAF Dakotas arrived overhead and proceeded to drop supplies to the local army garrison, unaware of the camouflaged Tiger Moth dispersed below. The aircraft was struck squarely on the starboard upper mainplane by what her beleaguered pilot described as "a crate of bully beef." The rations fell right through the wing, shearing a mainspar, and the container embedded itself in the starboard lower. The pilot managed to return to base after hitching a ride with an army convoy and the Tiger Moth was later recovered by his own Salvage Unit.

When a mobile detachment arrived at the scene of a reported Supermarine Spitfire crash near Pyingaung, they found a second, unreported Spitfire lying alongside the first in a much better condition, and having dismantled and removed what could be reasonably expected, they set off back to base. On the banks of the Chindwin river they came across an abandoned Tiger Moth. The effects of the forced landing were evident in a fractured rear fuselage and a lower wing which had been torn off, but space was found on the Chevrolet transporter to carry the remains, including a valuable Gipsy Major engine. Due to a shortage of trained engineers and tradesmen, and an enormous increase in activity, technical surveys were of necessity very harsh, and more aircraft were categorised as non-repairable than might normally have been the case. The rescued Tiger Moth became a bonus supply of spare parts.

No 3 RSU's own Tiger Moth, NL708 (86191), described as being 'rather battered', was exchanged for a North American Harvard 2B, FS988, following a visit by Flying and Engineering Group Liaison Officers early in 1945. NL708 was flown away for servicing elsewhere and was one of the fourteen aircraft which survived to be presented to the newly independent Indian Air Force in October 1947.

Indian Air Force officer cadet pilots awaiting inspection at a passing out parade in May 1943. All the aircraft carry Indian civil registration letters. *deHMC Archive*

On 26 May 1945 Geoff Hulett, a pilot with Ferry Flight, Trichinopoly, was delivering Republic Thunderbolt Mk1 FL781 to his base from Yellahanka. FL781, like all RAF P.47s operating in India, had been disembarked at Madras from where the aircraft were ferried to designated units for modification to RAF standards, and then on to squadrons re-equipping from Hurricanes and Spitfires. He was operating via Arkonam which was a refuelling stop and where a tyre check put one unserviceable. Due to a general shortage there were no spares held on site but a signal classifying FL781 as 'AOG' resulted in the promise of one for the next day. AOG, 'Aircraft on Ground', was and still is the internationally recognised term demanding the highest priority for the provision of spares. Geoff Hulett explains what happened next:

"This was a set-back as a party was planned at Trichinopoly for that night: it was the monthly allocation of whisky and I needed to be there. As I had been an instructor on Tiger Moths in Southern Rhodesia an approach to the Station Engineering Officer brought forward the offer of a Tiger Moth, NL720 (86203), to be returned next day on collecting the T'bolt. NL720 was fitted with a long range tank, a five gallon oil drum, and I recruited a passenger to do the pumping from the front cockpit. An hour out and it was time to top up the gravity fed tank but the fuel would not flow. Perhaps it was an air lock that a roll or a loop would correct. No luck there so I started a gentle climb to gain height and then throttled back to eke out the fuel remaining and prepared for a long glide if necessary.
Twenty four miles out from Trichy and two hours and fifteen minutes into the flight the engine coughed and then stopped. All those training sessions on 'glide approach and landing' came to mind but they never included landing in a paddy field where the water resistance can be a hazard even with a three point landing .Result: nose in the mud. A bullock cart to the nearest village and a telephone call brought out the rescue gang many hours later and much, much too late for the party! A signal to Group brought forward the information that this aircraft was not on its books and they demanded details. A Court of Enquiry followed after which I was no longer welcome in Arkonam. Many Engineering Officers in India, it transpired, had built up aircraft from salvaged bits and learned to fly on them. NL720 was no exception. I gave flying lessons to one engineer on a salvaged Piper Cub.
Unknown to us some RAF police were working in the hangar masquerading as fitters, recording our comings and goings, the amount of fuel used etc. That led to another Court of Enquiry!"

No 1 RSU (India) was established at Asanol, about 120 miles from Calcutta in February 1941, and amongst the Vickers Wellingtons, Bristol Blenheims and Westland Lysanders rotating through the unit for regular servicing and repair were sundry communications aircraft including Tiger Moths. At least one of these aircraft was always unofficially available to the Chief Technical Officer (CTO) for duty as a unit hack and, on 11 May 1941, a Tiger Moth was despatched to Ranchi to collect spares and other essential supplies. During their return to Asanol the crew sighted what was not an uncommon local phenomenon in the form of a dust storm. On this occasion the swirl appeared to be of great intensity and heading straight for the airfield. Although the Tiger Moth was landed expeditiously there was insufficient time to warn each dispersal to take protective measures and during its ten minute passage what had become a fully developed cyclone caused considerable damage to seven Blenheims, a Wellington and a Hurricane which flew unaided after being lifted off its trestles. The Tiger Moth later was found about a mile from where she had been parked, lying upside down with a buckled undercarriage and four broken wings: a total loss.

Not all accidents and incidents were attributable to enemy action or the sometimes precarious state of the weather. After months of work the repair units were occasionally witness to accidents involving their most recent charges. Tiger Moth Z-02 of the Burmese Volunteer Air Force (BVAF), operating on behalf of 221 Group Communications Flight, was lost at Asanol on 6 September 1942. The engine stopped and the aircraft dived into the ground from 100ft immediately after take-off for a routine air test. The pilot and his passenger were injured but the Tiger Moth was written off.

The BVAF operated four Tiger Moths, two built in Australia (DHA250/251), and two British-built examples which had been exported from Hatfield as civil machines early in 1940, XY-AAB (82874) and XY-AAC (82875). The two Australian aircraft became Z-03 and Z-04 from January 1941 on delivery to the Defence Department in Rangoon but were transferred to the RAF's 224 Group Communications Flight in 1942 and both were written off in landing accidents at Dum Dum, Calcutta, in July and September that same year. It is not known which markings were taken up by the two British built machines, but to complete the elimination of the quartet, Z-01 crashed into the sea as the result of running her wheels into sand dunes after take off from Cox's Bazaar in June 1943.

When a Dakota forced landed near Manmon on 14 March 1944 the Commanding Officer of 132 RSU, together with the unit's test pilot, flew into the site from Imphal in Tiger Moth DE725 (85655), with the object of surveying the transport and assessing the possibility of flying her out. The Tiger Moth was official unit property, a new aircraft, and between them the crew contrived to wreck her on landing, leaving them both stranded and without communication. The pair subsequently took three days to get back to base by walking, fording rivers, commandeering mules and riding in an army Jeep, before collection by Dakota from Tamu. The following day, much to their chagrin, 132 RSU was advised that the stranded Dakota and the wrecked Tiger Moth had both been destroyed during target practice by one of the locally based Hurricane squadrons.

In May 1943, Squadron Leader Frank Godber finished an operational tour on Consolidated Catalinas and was posted to command RAF Vizagapatam, a large base situated between Calcutta and Madras, and which with the associated port facilities was being prepared for prospective operations against Japan. Apart from the airfield which accommodated no aircraft, the Commander was responsible for two additional aerodromes, a wireless unit and several radar sites, and in order to expedite his inspections was supplied with Tiger Moth DE372 (85401), from the Communications Flight of the Air Force Headquarters at Bangalore.

"This Tiger Moth was my delight and it was not long before the Navy and the Army saw that it could be useful as well. Of course it had no wireless so the Navy made me some canvas purses with snap fasteners on them and three feet of coloured bunting to make them easy to see.

The radar stations were beginning to get blips out to sea which they could not explain. Accordingly they would telephone me and give me a bearing and distance which could be twenty miles out to sea. I would drive down to the airfield, take-off in the Tiger Moth and fly to the radar site and thence down the bearing looking for possible radar reflectors. Usually they turned out to be close gatherings of the local open fishing boats in sufficient quantity to show up on radar. On returning towards the coast I wrote details of the sighting on my note pad, put it in a purse and as I passed over the Senior Naval Officer's headquarters by the harbour, I threw the purse down on the forecourt whence a rating would retrieve it.

In February 1944 things got more dramatic. My old squadron commander, Group Captain G A V Clayton happened to be visiting me at the time and we had a high ranking crew in a low powered aircraft doing what can only be described as operational flying. I remember trying to get an MTB to follow me to a torpedoed ship and the following day went out to inspect an oil slick from a submarine, suspected sunk after the torpedo attack."

A dusty looking Tiger Moth, EM918, on charge with the Indian Air Force at Comilla in August 1944, complete with primed Holt flares under the wings.
Howard Levy

The exact fate of DE372 is unrecorded, but she was struck off charge on the last day of October 1946 and was not one of the aircraft transferred to the new Indian Air Force or to the Indian Government as a civil aircraft.

The subject of disposal of RAF Tiger Moths in India was raised at the Air Ministry during a meeting on 8 August 1944 with Sir Frederick Tymms, Director General of Civil Aviation in India (DGCA). Sir Frederick suggested that the flying club movement might require upwards of 100 Tiger Moths if the sale price was pitched at the right level. Five of the original ten pre-war clubs remained operational, working for the government and lending their facilities to effect overhaul and repair. The five dormant clubs would probably regenerate once peace returned to the region and equipment for civil flying was available.

The Indian Government had formulated no policy on surpluses and in spite of the formation of an Indian Disposals Board (IDB) it was thought the government owned very little war material itself which would fall into the category for disposal. The DGCA believed that the possibility that RAF Tiger Moths might be declared surplus in India was a fact that should be brought to the immediate attention of the government, and he even toyed with the prospect of some being delivered into club hands before the formal declaration of an armistice.

Having been provoked by the Ministry of Aircraft Production (MAP), the Air Ministry confirmed from London its long established position in a statement issued on 11 May 1945 indicating that the prospect of a surplus situation developing amongst Tiger Moths in India would only be realised as the result of re-equipment with Fairchild Cornells, and unless and until that decision was taken it was not possible to confirm any sort of figure. By 13 July 1945 the Air Ministry had mellowed very slightly as the result of an approach by the Government of Afghanistan, forwarded through official channels in India.

Afghanistan required a number of trainer aircraft and the Air Staff had ruled out the Miles Magister as being unsuitable, leaving open the prospect for the sale of eight Tiger Moths. The Air Ministry decided it could, after all, release this number of aircraft without need of replacement, and the sale should have priority over any civilian sales in India which might have been under consideration. They assumed there would be no diplomatic or political objection as the Indian Government was aware of the request. MAP, who as primary selling agency should have been involved from the beginning of negotiations, was advised that the agreed price would have to hold good for future sales to the Indian Government, but should not be seen as setting the standard for genuine civil sales in India.

Some thought had been given to providing Afghanistan with aircraft from the surplus in South Africa, but this was countered by a suggestion that they might be supplied from the RAF pool in North Africa, from where they could be delivered by air. But the geographical proximity of India made it the ideal and logical donor once the politicking had been resolved and eight aircraft from RAF storage in India were sold, but not until 25 April 1946. The fact that three of the Tiger Moths carried sequential RAF serial numbers, NL962/3/4, (86394/5/6), must fuel speculation that they were from stock having never been assigned. Two others, DE572 (85539) and EM986 (86169), had been delivered new to the RAF in India although no subsequent allocation to a unit can be traced unlike EM780 (85997), which had been listed in service with 1 EFTS (India) at Begumpet.

The day following the London meeting with India's DGCA, Headquarters Air Command South East Asia (ACSEA) signalled the Air Ministry to the effect that they could not release any Tiger Moths. Sir Frederick Tymms was still hopeful of a supply of ex-service aircraft to the flying clubs and confirmed his view that the 100 Tiger Moths already owned by the Government of India had been "flown to the limit" and were probably not suitable for economical conversion and operation as true civil aeroplanes.

Prompted, possibly, by the DGCA's further enquiries, ACSEA signalled again on 5 August with their own suggested alternative. Having re-emphasised that they had no surplus 'serviceable' Tiger Moths, they advised that the Command had loaned thirty Tiger Moths to civilian flying clubs primarily to provide targets for silent anti-aircraft gunnery practice, and added that it was open to question whether these thirty were currently being used for the furtherance of the war effort. DGCA was requested to provide confirmation that he would be willing to accept transfer of these aircraft and to accept full responsibility for their future maintenance.

At the same time, and perhaps guided by impishness as much as genuine curiosity, ACSEA asked to be provided with details of condition and price of the Tiger Moths it understood were currently being offered in southern Africa. ACSEA's reference was probably to the aircraft being advertised in Rhodesia rather than South Africa, although plans for the extraction of 100 Tiger Moths from South Africa were almost certainly being mooted in London at the time. In the event, their transfer was not to be until July 1946, and then was principally on behalf of the Indian Air Force.

Although ACSEA was adamant that under existing responsibilities it could not afford to release a single Tiger Moth, with the exception of the special offer to DGCA, Headquarters of Base Air Forces in Delhi showed concern for the operation of the disposal procedure as practised. On 29 September 1945 they advised the British Secretary of State for Air, The Viscount Stansgate, that already some sixty three surplus American aircraft had been disposed of in the India/Burma/China theatre by the United States Foreign Liquidation Commission. All British sales were referenced through the MAP and Air Ministry in London, and the system was too cumbersome. Unless there was greater flexibility, "it will be too late," they advised.

Attrition continued to account for some of the scattered fleet. Ferrying a Tiger Moth across India in the summer of 1946 with a passenger in the front cockpit Derek Piggott was approaching Agra when the Gipsy Major engine failed, having given some reasonable warning of doing so. The pilot overshot his selected field and the wheels of the aircraft hit the bund of a paddy field, arresting the landing run within 30ft but forcing the aircraft onto her nose. Although the obvious damage seemed relatively slight the sergeant in charge of the salvage party who arrived complete with Queen Mary transporter was more sceptical. His initial diagnosis after assessing the strains, stresses and visible breakages, was that the Tiger Moth was probably a write-off and that the pilot should have set it alight to have saved everybody a lot of trouble. Much to the surprise of the Tiger Moth crew the salvage party cut the aircraft into manageable pieces and threw them all down the shaft of a disused well.

Far from being a disposal centre, India became a net importer of Tiger Moths after the conclusion of the Japanese war and there was much administrative tidying to arrange following Independence and Partition on 15 August 1947. Twenty civil aircraft which had been impressed into RAF service were handed over to the Indian Air Force, although in most cases their original identities had been lost. On 25 September 1947, twenty seven RAF Tiger Moths were transferred to the IAF followed by fourteen more at the end of October. That this was largely a paper exercise is confirmed by the fact that two of the October transfers, DE357 (85379), and NL708 (86191), had already been placed on the Indian civil register as VT-ASL and VT-ATP respectively in March and December 1945.

Seven aircraft from the RAF contingent in the sub continent were transferred to the Pakistan Air Force in September 1947 and a year later six more were added, all second hand civil aircraft sourced in Great Britain by dealers W S Shackleton. Although consigned to the Pakistan Government the aircraft were almost certainly scheduled for duty with the Air Force and their civil status was a tidy manner in which to comply

Australian-built Tiger Moth DHA 409 which was exported to India in 1949 and was last used as an instructional airframe. In 2002, after a three year negotiation, the aircraft was shipped to Canada and offered for sale from storage at Abbotsford. *Cham Gill*

with some diplomatic nicety. In 1948, a further twenty four Tiger Moths were supplied, purchased from RAF home stocks by de Havilland, refurbished at Witney, and shipped in May to Karachi.

Of the 207 British-built Tiger Moths landed for RAF use in wartime India, discounting transfers to the Air Forces of India, Pakistan and Afghanistan, 150 aeroplanes were struck off charge without any formal statement of circumstances. Of sixteen exceptions one aircraft is known to have been donated to the Hindustan Aircraft factory at Bangalore, where almost certainly this unidentified example was used as an educational tool for the Hindustan workforce, soon to be the recipient of 100 Tiger Moths shipped from South Africa.

Some of the other 'struck off' aircraft appeared on the Indian civil register. EM846 (86048), which served with 1 EFTS (India) was supposedly on strength with Air Command South East Asia on 30 August 1945, yet she had been registered VT-ARP to the Government of India in October 1943. The aircraft was transferred to the Madras Flying Club in June 1946, cancelled in September 1959, rebuilt in August 1971 and re-registered VT-EBP against a new builder's identity: MFC-01-1971. Parts from three other aircraft, one believed to be a Jackaroo, and the engine from a fourth, were all used for the 'rebuild' which must have been comprehensive. Airworthiness was followed by sale to Canada as CF-EIO in 1972, but the aircraft passed south of the border in 1974 and was registered G-BDVI to a British owner living in Texas. The aircraft arrived in England in 1977, but negotiations over a property deal fell through and she returned to Texas to become N982JG with a new owner in Houston in 1985. In 1997 she returned to Canada to be rebuilt by Watt Martin for owner Adam Smuszkowicz in Toronto to whom she was registered CF-RTX in 1998.

The Indian imports from South Africa had been gathered together in Cape Town, half of a 200 strong hand picked selection from the RAF's residual share of the assets of the Joint Air Training Scheme: eighty eight British built airframes and twelve of Australian origin. Although officially transferred from South Africa in July 1946, some at least of the 100 aircraft did not arrive in India until the end of February 1947 and were credited to the Hindustan Aircraft Company only from 27 November, a series of delays which might be attributed to the massive and rapid administrative changes occurring in the country.

The aircraft were overhauled at Bangalore and slowly fed into the IAF system from which the first were released to civilian use as early as 1948, and replaced in turn, many finding their way into club use in batches during 1956, 1959 and throughout the early 1960s. About thirty civilian aircraft can subsequently be identified as originating from within the South African shipment, at least three of which were of Australian manufacture. In Indian Air Force use all these aircraft were allocated 'HU' serials, but later overhaul outside the military was often the cause for substitution of revised identities. This was a practice common among the flying clubs who allocated tags based on the initial letters of the club name, the date, and a numerical count of all overhaul and rebuild/repair projects previously put through their shops. Frequently, overhaul could be defined as rigging an amalgam of parts essential to the creation of a new aeroplane with a new identity in a new logbook.

In 1947, Hangar 10 at Chakeri Air Force Base, famous as the last resting place for hundreds of Consolidated Liberators, was in receipt of numerous Tiger Moths which arrived from all over the sub-continent, delivered in a dismantled and often damaged condition on board Air Force Dakotas. From the best parts, whole aircraft were reconstructed, painted yellow overall, and delivered into the care of the Indian Air Force at 1 EFTS Begumpet and 2 EFTS Jodphur. The Tiger Moths were of mixed British and Australian manufacture in the EM, NL and DG serial batches, although there is evidence that some of the pre-war civilian aircraft impressed into RAF service in 1941 with serials in the DP range, were still active at 2 EFTS, operating in Indian military markings.

Most of the aircraft operated by the flying clubs were flown at heavily subsidised rates by civilians aiming for a career with the Air Force or the airlines and in late 1946 the government took whole page advertisements in national newspapers encouraging people to apply for flying training. Although in the flying clubs there was no distinction between Indian nationals and Europeans, immediately after Independence and without warning, the flying rates for non-nationals were raised by 500%, indicating, perhaps, the level of subsidy that was being paid.

The remains of an unidentified Tiger Moth fuselage bearing traces of code '20' on the engine cowling were discovered at the Hyderabad Public School in 2011 where it is believed she had stood for 40 years. The deflated tyres are still attached to the wheel rims. *Aidan Curley*

Derelict Tiger Moth VT-DBM was discovered at the Behala Flying Club near Calcutta by Colonel Amardeep Sidhu and in 2007 was acquired by Indian Army Aviation and restored to static display condition for their museum at Maharashtra. In 2008 she was moved to Bangalore for restoration to airworthiness for the Indian Army Historic Flight with the assistance of Hindustan Aeronautics. *via Brigadier Amardeep Sidhu*

A first attempt at building a missing rudder for Indian Army Historic Flight Tiger Moth VT-DBM resulted in some dismay at the new shape which was later corrected. *via Brigadier Amardeep Sidhu*

Morris Motors-built Tiger Moth T6376 served with the SAAF and at the end of the war was one of the two hundred examples hand picked by the British Government for shipment to India where she served with the Indian Air Force. Civilianised and operated on behalf of the Indian Government by the Madhya Pradesh Flying Club she was damaged on landing at Indore in 1962, cancelled from the register in 1995, and acquired by John Markham in Perth, Western Australia in 2011

The climate encouraged pilots to fly in a relaxed manner, often wearing short sleeved, open necked shirts, and the civilian accident rate steadily rose, largely due to unauthorised low flying, often resulting in fatalities. In an effort to stop the practice instructors randomly hid barographs on board which could be scrutinised on return and the culprits subjected to disciplinary action. The long and unspoilt beaches of southern India were a temptation for the pilots of the Madras Flying Club and on 16 August 1952, VT-AMC (3664), a used aircraft supplied from England by W S Shackleton in March 1940, was comprehensively wrecked when it hit the beach and turned over. The two club members on board were not seriously hurt but afterwards each admitted that they thought the other was in command. One said that his admiration for the other's daring was suddenly shattered by the crash.

Not all incidents occurred at low level: VT-DBZ (84258), was another W S Shackleton import, this time from ex-RAF stocks held in England, shipped after Independence, joining the Bengal Flying Club at Barrackpore in July 1949. The aircraft made news when a collision with a soaring vulture on 5 April 1952 demolished a large portion of the port upper wing. Repairs were effected and the aircraft remained in service until December 1955 when she was written off in a landing accident at Calcutta.

A Tiger Moth registered VT-DGA to the Madhya Pradesh Flying Club in February 1952 quoted her previous identity as 'Indian Air Force' and builder's number CPF/FU/79. The aircraft subsequently passed to the Nagpur Flying Club and may have suffered an accident for a further major rebuild was recorded in 1955 during the course of which substantial parts of the following aircraft were grafted on: VT-CUL (DHA883) and VT-CUJ (DHA890), both of which had been exported from the Newcastle Aero Club in Australia in 1948; Indian Air Force HU861, later VT-DEQ, origin unknown, written off in 1951; VT-DDQ (84477), ex T8185 from South Africa, written off in July 1958; VT-DDN (85453) ex DE457 from South Africa, not reported as cancelled; VT-DDO (85517) ex DE550 from South Africa, written off in August 1957 and VT-CUF (85526) ex DE559 from South Africa, written off in 1952.

Several of the donor aircraft remained operational after the rebuilding schedule of 1955 in which case each would have become net recipients of parts from other sources to make up the deficiency! Although cancellation dates are often those quoted purely for administrative convenience, some write-off dates are attributable to documented accidents. Laid up in 1966, VT-DGA was one of many

A trio of time expired Tiger Moths all registered to the Indian Government, VT-DOX, VT-DOZ and VT-DPB, parked on a weed infested concrete apron at Madras. Painted yellow overall with green 'trainer bands' the three aircraft were part of the consignment purchased by Doug Arnold and delivered to England in 1979. *Bob Wall*

Tiger Moths offered for sale by an Indian based aircraft sales agency, Vintair, which targeted Europe, the USA and Canada. Most of their Tiger Moth stock was scattered around the sub continent, the aircraft staked out open to the weather, with time expired engines. VT-DGA was surveyed in 1978 by an engineer flown out especially from England as the result of which the aircraft was shipped back to Yorkshire. Following a period of storage, registration G-BHUM was allocated in June 1980 and the aircraft rebuilt in Lincolnshire from 1983 to qualify for a Certificate of Airworthiness in May 1984.

As part of a deal involving the purchase of abandoned and decoy Supermarine Spitfires, twelve whole Tiger Moths and a vast collection of new spare parts were offered for sale in India in 1979. One airframe in poor condition was donated to a childrens' playground but the remainder was shipped to storage at Shipdham Aerodrome, Norfolk, and although little effort was made to supply complete aircraft to the market the huge volume of spares satisfied customers on a global scale for several years until the not insubstantial remains were sold as a single lot to a consortium based in South Africa. Distributed amongst the membership the parts resulted in the appearance of a number of refurbished aircraft which had lain dormant and incomplete for many years.

In other parts of the world unaffected by the passage of the war disposal of ex-military aircraft was generally due to the types having outlived their usefulness and their unquestioned fate was delivery to a scrapyard. The eighteen aircraft fleet of the Uruguayan Military Aeronautics, established in three waves since the first deliveries in 1935, had been reduced to just three when the order for their withdrawal was signed in 1948. The decision was largely based on the difficulties of procurement and cost of spares which had already resulted in some degree of cannibalisation, in addition to the loss of function to the big fleets of American imports.

The last three Tiger Moths in the inventory were 600 (3312), 604 (3619), and 606 (3313), and an enquiry as to their history, condition and opportunity for sale was delivered to the military authorities by Charles Chalking on 8 August 1948. Within a few days Mr Chalking had received a reply to the effect that the aircraft were not for sale. In December the General Director of Military Aeronautics, Colonel Oscar Sanchez, asked the General Inspector of the Army to investigate how the three Tiger Moths could be ceded to civilian flying clubs but in January 1949, after consultation with various departments of the Army, the Superintendent of Arms opposed the proposal alleging ethical reasons and principals and the possible ramifications of donating obsolete material for civilian use.

Further consultation with levels of officialdom in the Civil Aviation Directorate resulted in their decision on 17 May 1949 to support the suggestion of civilianisation and on 3 June the views of the sporting institutions were sought which resulted in positive replies from twenty two aero clubs. In October opinion within the army had swung back against the proposals and on 8 November, over a year since the first enquiries, the General Director of Military Aeronautics ordered that the three aircraft be scrapped.

Meanwhile, Tiger Moth 601 (3617), which had been grounded at Durazno since July 1948 with suspected structural deformation was cleared by an engineer and on 18 May 1949 was flown to Boiso Lanza, the last flight of the type in military service, where she was broken up for scrap. One aircraft, devoid of any identifying marks, was saved in recognition of the country's aviation history and presented to the Aeronautical Museum of Uruguay where it languished, untouched, for decades, narrowly missing incineration in the disastrous fire which swept through the museum in December 1997. Work by volunteers to restore her to static display condition continues.

In 1977 Yorkshire farmer and enthusiast for all things mechanical, Graham Towers, despatched an engineer to Nagpur to inspect VT-DGA, an aircraft selected by the RAF from SAAF resources for despatch to India at the end of the Second World War. The aircraft was rebuilt at Wyberton and issued with a British C of A in 1985. *Charles Holland*

G-BHUM ventures out only when weather conditions are considered to be ideal and forecast to remain so for the duration. *Malcolm Barratt*

Above: Ex-Indian Tiger Moth VT-DOW standing in the snow at Felthorpe in March 1981 where as G-BINH she was the leased property of the local Flying Group. Badly smashed during low level aerobatics only a month later, she was rebuilt probably using an ex-India fuselage, but crashed again after engine failure in 1984 and was written off. *Gordon Poulter*

Part of the collection of eleven complete aircraft and tons of spares that had arrived at Shipdham in England from India during the late 1970s, part of a deal which included abandoned decoy Spitfires. Most airframes were painted yellow overall with 'green trainer bands' and all were civil registered. *Peter Bish*

CHAPTER SEVENTEEN

The Great Commonwealth Rundown

When Australia declared war on Germany on 3 September 1939 the RAAF had thirteen Tiger Moths on charge ten of which were allocated to operational squadrons. On the day the EATS Agreement was announced in London on 10 October 1939, the Australian Government approved a submission by the Air Board for £800,000 to be spent on 350 Tiger Moths and 500 engines to be manufactured in Australia. In his book *The DH.82A Tiger Moth in Australia*, Julian Forsyth explains the next step:

> "On 22 November 1939 with the RAAF completely mobilised with all squadrons at war stations, Ministerial approval was given for the training of RAAF aircrew at eleven aero clubs and commercial flying schools in all States except Tasmania. All of these organisations were equipped with DH.60 Moths and some with Tiger Moths.
> The civil training school programme was to be short lived, however. In April 1940, because the financial basis of the scheme presented difficulties, and some aspects of training were considered unsatisfactory, the scheme was abandoned in favour of the RAAF's own rapidly expanding training regime. The expansion had seen the RAAF take over thirty nine civil aerodromes for training in addition to using space at five capital city airports."

Australian-built Tiger Moth N176TM painted in pseudo RAAF markings as A17-177 flying over the south west side of Patillas, Puerto Rico on 25 May 2002. Flown by Bill Norris with his son William Jr as passenger, the photograph was taken by David Norris flying the family's Piper Cub.

By December 1940 nine EFTS had been established across the country with a further three added in 1941. Including the overseas elements operating in support of communications and casualty evacuation Tiger Moths eventually were attached to 207 RAAF units, establishments and organisations.

The Australian solution to its post-war surplus aircraft situation was quite straightforward: if the aircraft was likely to qualify for a civil Certificate of Airworthiness it could be sold but if not, it was scrapped. The authorities decided that the ex-RAAF DH.84 Dragons could be sold but would only qualify for a restricted certificate; Airspeed Oxfords on the other hand would not be accepted as civil aircraft and the entire fleet was scheduled for the bonfire.

With the war not yet concluded the Australian Government established in November 1944 a Commonwealth Disposals Commission (CDC) acting under the direction of the Minister of Supply and Shipping. Their brief was to arrange ordered disposal of all war surplus materials and to fix realistic levels of pricing. The Commission made full use of the press and broadcasting media to publicise its activities and was genuinely surprised at what they regarded as the exceptional public interest, particularly in the sale of aircraft.

The first 100 aircraft were offered for sale by public tender in February 1945 and included a variety of types from Tiger Moth to 'three engined flying boats'. DH.94 Moth Minors and Tiger Moths raised between £100 and £200 each, the government actively encouraging sale to stimulate private and club flying. Pre-war, only 200 light aircraft had been registered in Australia, but in the first fourteen months of their brief the Commission sold 340 with many more still held in storage.

Sale of TIGER MOTHS at exceptionally low prices

● If you want one or more 2-seater planes for pleasure, personal travel, or club or business use, here is an outstanding opportunity. The Commonwealth has numerous used Tiger Moths for disposal at Air Force Stations in all States. Full, detailed data of the serviceability and fixed sale price of each machine is placed in your hands as a preliminary on enquiry. Prices vary according to condition between £300 and £500. (List price of a similar machine new on today's market would be about £1,800.) Write or call at the address below for full details.
REGIONAL MANAGER,
Commonwealth Disposals Commission,
"London House,"
321 Murray Street,
Perth, W.A.

ALSO ENGINES
Used Gipsy Major Engines are also offered separately at prices varying according to condition, maximum being £150 for good used condition. The aviation industry knows the fame of the Gipsy Major for reliability, low petrol consumption, and ease of servicing.

The CDC's pricing policy hardened due partly to the strong demand and also, following advice from the British Government's Ministry of Aircraft Production (MAP) Liaison Officer in Australia, Air Commodore E R Pearce, that his masters were expecting between £250 and £500 for the Tiger Moths declared surplus in Southern Rhodesia. Pearce was asked by London to consult with de Havilland at Mascot and to elicit their views.

To provide every would-be purchaser with equal priority in obtaining a particular aircraft, should they live in the outback or the middle of Melbourne, a system was introduced linked to the date and time the bid had been lodged and recorded at the despatching Post Office. It assured equality of opportunity but was time consuming and some later sales were conducted by auction held at the storage sites.

The maximum price for a Tiger Moth, the CDC decided, should be £500, but administration and structure of the pricing policy was to be generous and flexible. Discounts were to be granted to government subsidised aero clubs, air ambulance services and religious organisations which worked in the outback. It was also agreed that concessions would be available to what were described as 'reputable speculators' who were prepared to buy 'considerable numbers' of aircraft, thus saving on sales administration.

The Empire Air Training Scheme (EATS) came to a formal conclusion on 31 March 1945 at which time the British Government waived all rights and interest in the residual value of British owned aircraft stationed in Australia, although they insisted that Australia would pay for any aircraft or item of equipment contributed to the Scheme at British expense which was diverted outside the continuing Air Training Organisation within the next twelve months, subject to the return of any stock required by the RAF. At the end of the requisite period in April 1946, a naive official at the Air Ministry in London advised the Ministry of Supply (MoS) as successor to the MAP, that 100 Tiger Moths had been shipped to Australia between June and September 1940 as part of the British contribution towards establishing the EATS, and as the RAAF was holding 639 Tiger Moths the Air Ministry was unable to distinguish between the British and Australian owned aircraft. Having not been advised otherwise, the official was forced to assume that all 100 British supplied aircraft remained accountable. Had it been realised that the British Tiger Moths had retained their RAF serial numbers in Australia the headcount would have been quickly achieved. Two thirds of the original force had disappeared anyway, victims of five years of the attritional nature of intensive flying training.

The Air Ministry also advised MoS that the RAF had no requirement for any of the British owned aircraft in Australia to be returned to Great Britain and, as the Australian Air Board had decided to scrap all surplus aircraft thought not to have an immediate post-war civil or military future, the Ministry had offered no objection to a policy of breaking down in situ.

The matter of the 100 British supplied Tiger Moths was still rankling with one section of the Air Ministry which was determined to balance the books. On 14 May 1946 an official request was made to RAAF Overseas Headquarters (based in London) to determine the fate of the aircraft, even though the British Government had already relinquished further claim. The reply received on 16 July came as quite a surprise: of the 100 aircraft despatched in 1940 only thirty eight had survived. Furthermore, the whole of the consignment had been ordered and paid for by the Australian Government; the aircraft were not British property at all. "Please refer to Indent 758," the Air Ministry was advised! The only gift had been in the supply of 200 British-built Gipsy Major engines and British Government funding for a further 124 built in Australia. The Air Ministry dutifully acknowledged receipt of the information and apologised for any inconvenience their enquiry may have caused.

In June 1945 the MAP in London signalled Air Commodore Pearce that twenty Tiger Moths in Australia which somebody had identified as the property of the British Government, were to be included in the disposals. Would he confirm that the CDC could act as agents for the sale; could they arrange for the aircraft to be reconditioned; what was the state of the aircraft and were there any other known surpluses? Pearce was reminded that an agreement with the manufacturers dictated that only aircraft in good condition were to be offered for sale, providing also they were supported by an adequate spares backup. Not surprisingly, the answer was that the CDC could not act as selling or reconditioning agent: it was busy enough selling its own assets as they lay.

The Salvation Army had taken delivery in August 1945 of the first Tiger Moth to be civilianised from surplus RAAF stock after the war. With a 'fixed' registration, VH-ASA (DHA976), the aircraft had been purchased for £468 from storage at Point Cook thanks to a donation from Red Shield units in Melbourne and, following civil conversion by the approved regional Tiger Moth centre, Victorian and Interstate Airways at Essendon, she was flown around his 'parish', the northern districts of Western Australia and the Northern Territories, by Salvation Army Captain Victor Pederson. He would regularly call at Darwin to pass time with the engineers working in the oppressive heat of the hangars and always carried a fold-up bicycle in the front cockpit which he used to good effect on the many substantial and remote airfields when visiting his congregation.

The aircraft was lost under bizarre circumstances on 14 January 1947. VH-ASA had forced landed in the Cambridge Gulf, north west of Wyndham, Western Australia. The pilot lit a signal fire in the hope of attracting the attention of a searching RAAF Dakota but the

The first Tiger Moth to be civilianised from RAAF surplus stock after the Second World War was VH-ASA, acquired by the Salvation Army for £468 from Point Cook and flown by Captain Victor Pederson until she was destroyed by fire in bizarre circumstances in Western Australia. *deHMC Archive*

spinifex grass allowed the fire to work its way back against the wind and engulf the aeroplane. A replacement Tiger Moth, VH-BJD (DHA 1034), was borrowed from Ben Hingston in Darwin at an agreed price of £1.00 per flying hour until the Salvation Army purchased her for £400 in November 1951. She was forced landed due to a stuck exhaust valve near the Katherine river and taken by road to Darwin where in July 1955 she was exchanged for an Auster Autocar.

Cycling freedom was enjoyed in the less arid countryside of Southern England twenty years afterwards. Bill Hardy, a professor at Reading University, would fly south in the Calleva Group's Tiger Moth G-APRX (85302), operating from a small strip near Newbury, and land in a Dorset field near Shaftesbury where his daughter was at school. Her chums might have been surprised (the first time) after being told that her father was flying down for the day, to see a besuited gentleman wearing a black beret appear at the school gates on a fold-up bicycle.

The CDC offered a further 200 Tiger Moths for sale in February 1946, with bids expected up to the maximum value of £500. Provision was also made to offer forty eight spare Gipsy Major engines: those with full life to be offered at £150, the price declining in proportion to the recorded hours and general condition. Seven years later, during the final acts of removing the Tiger Moth from the RAF inventory in Great Britain, brand new, zero time Gipsy Major engines were reportedly selling at between £5 and £20 each.

During 1946, 170 ex-RAAF Tiger Moths were added to the Australian civil register with 154 more in 1947, 52 in 1948 and 23 in 1949. The clubs organised themselves much as they had in Great Britain and the Australian Associated Aero Club bid successfully for 116 aircraft on behalf of constituent members. Total sales of ex-RAAF Tiger Moths between 1945 and 1949 amounted to 525 aircraft, 357 being released in 1946 alone. Until 1953, at least eighty five aircraft were reported to have been sold out of Australia going mostly to India (thirty seven confirmed) and New Zealand (twenty two confirmed), in the main exported by the Newcastle Aero Club and Kingsford Smith Aviation Services who are believed jointly to have handled about fifty single shipments.

The Australian authorities went to considerable lengths to ensure that prospective purchasers of fifty four Tiger Moths and twenty one Gipsy Major engines scheduled for sale by auction at Western Junction, Tasmania on 18 May 1946, were well acquainted with detail and fact. In addition to the stock lists which had been circulated on request, catalogues were available from the Woolgrowers Agency Co. Ltd. of Hobart, and attendees were advised that the auctioneers had arranged special buses from Launceston and reservations (2s.6d return) were to be made with them.

Help was also available to purchasers. Petrol coupons were supplied by the Civil Aviation Department on presentation of sale receipts and the new owners were positively encouraged to fly home.

Built at Mascot in August 1940 for the RAAF, A17-63 served initially at Tamworth and later Narromine. She was sold for £100 in September 1946 but remained in store and unconverted until a certificate of airworthiness was issued in November 1990. *David Freeman*

In March 2011 a celebration of the 90th anniversary of the formation of the Royal Australian Air Force involved a flying 'Pilgrimage' through some of the bases used during the Second World War. Tiger Moth VH-AWA, the former A17-692, was acquired by the RAAF Museum in 2006 and is maintained in flying condition at Point Cook. At the end of the tour she was photographed leaving Temora for home. *Michael Wignall*

For those expecting to cross the Bass Strait heading for Melbourne and beyond there were special preconditions: the aircraft had to be in possession of either a civil Certificate of Airworthiness issued in Tasmania, or an authorisation for the ferry flight signed on the spot by a Department representative. Pilots were only permitted to fly solo; all departing aircraft were expected to fly in groups which would be escorted by an RAAF Catalina.

Ten days prior to the sale the CDC announced that an additional twenty five Tiger Moths were to be included in the auction, aircraft which had been intended for the RAAF Reserve, and were all serviceable. Eleven of the new lots had flown less than fifty hours since complete overhaul and one, A17-731 (DHA1062), which was sold to a local owner for £300, had only eighteen hours logged from manufacture. As VH-AUI this aircraft was operated by the Tasmanian Aero Club until 1954 when she was sold to the mainland and converted for agricultural use.

A further forty eight Tiger Moths (and sixty Consolidated Catalinas) were offered for sale in October 1946, all lying at bases scattered across the country. The CDC urged potential buyers to inspect the aircraft and advised them that copies of survey reports ("however, it is regretted that these surveys are not complete") were available for perusal at the Commission's offices in each state capital. On this occasion sale was to be against a fixed price dependent upon the condition of each individual machine, based on the maximum value of £500 for an aircraft considered to be in excellent condition. A priced list of lots was available along with the summarised survey sheets and sales were to be made on the basis of first formal application received, the system originally notified to London in 1945.

What the Commission described as "probably the last opportunity for the public to obtain one of these popular machines," was the announcement in November 1947 of sale of a further twelve Tiger Moths lying at Temora, Bairnsdale and Tamworth. They were to be added to the more than 520 Tiger Moths already handled and their condition was described as being only 'fair' without summarising hours as had been customary. A further twenty five aircraft were to be released in 1948 but as far as the Commission was concerned, when the bids closed at 2.00pm on Friday 5 December 1947, they could be satisfied that the year and their task were ending with another 130 Tiger Moths in private circulation, and almost £73,500 in the bank. The CDC had worked efficiently and fairly; aircraft had been sold from twenty nine sites scattered all over the country as the result of fifteen separate invitations to the public to bid.

The disposal of Tiger Moth and Gipsy Major spares was handled separately from the main aircraft sales and huge quantities were released into the market to satisfy the needs of the private owners, clubs and soon, an almost insatiable demand by the agricultural operators. They quickly realised the potential of the just adequate but cheap and plentiful Tiger Moth, an aircraft which became an essential tool for the industry in Australia and New Zealand. Harry Wallace bought twenty seven tons of engine and airframe spares at an auction in Sydney, although that was only part of the inventory, and he continued to satisfy the demands of his clients from his store at Moorabbin for over forty years.

In 1948 the de Havilland Company was pleased to afford publicity to the fact that the Royal Aero Club of New South Wales had a membership of 700 and was flying more than 3,500 hours per year

Built as A17-746 in 1944 and sold into the civil market in 1954, VH-CEJ (sometime VH-CES) was cancelled in 1966 and extensively rebuilt by Bob Miles using all new parts. The aircraft qualified for Public Transport certification in 1983 and was enrolled into a joyriding career at Moorabbin. *Keith Jose*

Barry Hills and his Australian manufactured Tiger Moth VH-AUZ in the back yard of his house near Adelaide, June 1998. *Barry Hills*

operating twenty eight Tiger Moths, two taper-wing DH.87A Hornet Moths, a DH.85 Leopard Moth and a DH.84 Dragon. Freely available petrol supplies were regarded by commentators in Great Britain as a significant factor in the encouragement of such levels of activity.

A spot check on 31 July 1951 revealed that at 235, Tiger Moths represented 33% of all aircraft registered in Australia on that date. The restoration of commercial operations across the country resulted in a steady increase in the number of civil aircraft and a similar check conducted on 31 May 1959 revealed that 314 Tiger Moths were active, one in four of the total.

For a country awash with surplus aircraft and tempting offers filtering into the system from suppliers in England, Australian Aircraft Sales, a company based at Mascot, provided a sufficiency of brand new Tiger Moth spares to allow Airwork Co Pty. Ltd. to build four complete aircraft at Archerfield: VH-AWH (AW/TC/1), in April 1957; VH-AWJ (AW/A/16) and VH-WPP (AW/A/17), in March and June 1958, and VH-AWM (AW/A/20), in September 1959. Lawrence Engineering and Sales Pty. Ltd. of Camden built a Tiger Moth from all new spares and registered her as VH-KRW (LES 1), in February 1959. By June 1962 the company had registered its eleventh and last new construction when VH-CRA (LES 11), was listed to Nigel Rogers of Corfield in Queensland. All of these aircraft were treated as 'normal' DH.82A Tiger Moths by the Australian Airworthiness Authorities of the day and operated on unrestricted Certificates of Airworthiness, an acceptance that was to become an issue when one of their number was sold to Great Britain.

From his strip at Yarra Glen, Victoria, Dr Barry Walters flew Tiger Moth VH-PME for many years in a single handed operation for which purpose he designed and built a special platform for refuelling purposes. The rig incorporates a 450 litre fuel store and is positioned by a Mini Moke. The aircraft is winched into position by cables attached to the axles. *Dr Barry Walters*

Offering greater comfort than a standard windscreen yet more flexibility than complete enclosure, this moulded unit with streamlined headrest was fitted to Australian built Tiger Moth VH-AUK at Griffith, NSW in 1974. *N K Daw*

At the end of the day. The last ten RAAF training Tiger Moths in their post-war silver with yellow bands assembled at Point Cook on 9 January 1957. The aircraft flew in formation to Tocumwal for disposal. *RAAF*

The building of the first of the new aircraft coincided with release of the last RAAF Tiger Moths; ten operational aircraft were flown from the RAAF College at Point Cook to Tocumwal on 9 January 1957 for disposal. Each civilian purchaser was required to acknowledge that sale of the Tiger Moths was conditional on their immediate availability for military requisition in times of national emergency.

NEW ZEALAND

The declaration of war between Great Britain and Germany meant that in New Zealand in 1939 an interim War Training Scheme was organised with the task of streaming 650 pilots and 650 observers and air gunners a year through three Elementary Flying Training Schools for service with the RAF. Cliff Jenks and David Phillips outlined the situation in their book *New Zealand Tiger Moths*:

> "As the only suitable aircraft available to equip these schools were twenty one Tiger Moths, twenty two Gipsy Moths, two Miles Magisters and three Miles Hawks (with three more Tiger Moths en-route from England) it was possible to authorise only two schools at half strength, plus a flying instructors school. The latter unit received priority as there were only thirty nine fully qualified instructors in the country and twenty eight assistant instructors. Consequently the first RNZAF Tiger Moths to be put to work were the Auckland

Aero Club's six machines at Mangere. There on 10 September 1939 the Flying Instructors School officially came into being."

No 1 EFTS began operations at Taieri, Dunedin, on 16 October 1939 with a fleet of sixteen Tiger Moths of which thirteen were impressed Club aeroplanes and three brand new imports. On 14 November No 2 EFTS opened at Bell Block, New Plymouth with a mixture of ex club DH.60 Moths and Miles Hawks and Magisters. In December the New Zealand Government increased its offer of training and agreed to the supply of 880 fully trained pilots per year plus a further 520 pilots, 546 navigators and 936 air gunners whose initial training would be in New Zealand but completed in Canada.

After Nos 1 and 2 EFTS were up to full strength, No 3 was formed from May 1940 at Christchurch Airport, Harewood, with No 4 following in December at Whenuapai, a new operational station near Auckland.

Possibly unique to any nation during the Second World War the Royal New Zealand Air Force organised a 'Touring Flight' for members of the Air Training Corps as described in the History of the ATC by R.G. Williams DFC.

"In 1943 it was felt that there was an urgent need to provide more interesting instruction for ATC cadets to retain interest and to build up the numbers of recruits required for aircrew intakes. Approval was granted by the Chief of the Air Staff on 21 April 1943 for allocation of aircraft and personnel to the following establishments: five Tiger Moths, five General Duties officers, one Flight mechanic and one Rigger.

Originally it was provided that one aircraft was to be stationed at both Mangere (Auckland) and Rongotai (Wellington) and the remaining three to be constantly on tour but soon after commencement it was considered more desirable to be banded into one unit. All machines of the Touring Flight were distinctive in their colourings: fuselage and engine cowling blue-grey, wings, empennage and undercarriage training yellow. In addition to usual Service roundels, Air Training Corps insignia appeared on both sides of the fuselage and was in black upon a yellow background.

The mode of operation of the flight was on the following lines: an itinerary was arranged for at least two months ahead and copies posted to all units concerned in order to allow cadets to be organised accordingly. Ground staff attached to the flight would proceed ahead of the aircraft in practically all cases, transported in a van which was fitted out for the purpose of doing maintenance work on the aircraft. The van also contained two bunks to be used for sleeping accommodation, most necessary as often the aircraft were picketed down in open paddocks and it was necessary for two members of the staff to remain on guard overnight.

The aircraft would arrive and commence cadet flying practically straight away. Each cadet would be given a ten minute flight. At the conclusion of flying an aerobatic display would be given by one of the machines. Every endeavour was made to induce parents and intending cadets to visit the aerodrome.

Every cadet was offered a bonus flight for each new recruit introduced to his unit. Bonus certificates were issued and payable when the Touring Flight visited his district and some cadets would have up to two and three hours flying owing to him.

In August 1944 a directive was received from the CAS disbanding the Touring Flight on the grounds that with the change in picture on recruiting for the RNZAF the pre-entry training in the ATC was no longer of paramount importance. This decision had a very bad effect on the morale of the ATC and after strong representations were put forward to the Air Department verbal authority was given to re-instate the Flight which continued with its good work until it was finally disbanded in August 1945. It is estimated that just on 20,000 flights had been provided for cadets."

An aircraft of the New Zealand Air Training Corps Touring Flight during a change over of cadets. The resident pilots sat in the front seat and acted in the instructional role. *RNZAF Museum*

Tiger Moths of the RNZAF awaiting their visit from the 'oiler'. Unusually, serial numbers and codes applied by stencil, have not been 'filled in'. Note the aircraft log temporarily suspended below the chin cowling of '43'. *deHMC Archive*

Although there is no definitive list of aircraft allocated to the Touring Flight it is believed a total of ten aircraft were used including, in 1944, NZ732 (3426), the previous G-ADUK, exported after close of flying one day by the London Aeroplane Club at Hatfield. NZ818 (DHNZ68), NZ847 (DHNZ97) and NZ854 (82302), were all fitted with a sliding canopy and NZ859 (82341), with a hinged lid.

At the time of the Japanese surrender in August 1945 the Royal New Zealand Air Force could account for 232 Tiger Moths on the inventory, many of which where in store at Taieri or Woodbourne. During conduct of the wartime training programme 103 aircraft had been written off whilst tutoring over 7,000 pilots to elementary standard and beyond.

The peacetime Air Force requirements indicated that about 180 Tiger Moths could be declared surplus and an initial list of 114 aircraft was provided for action by the New Zealand Government's disposal agency, the War Assets Realisation Board (WARB). An additional fifteen Tiger Moths were set aside for presentation to flying clubs as compensation for aircraft requisitioned at the beginning of the Second World War.

The New Zealand Air Department took note of the surveys conducted by the Royal New Zealand Aero Club (RNZAC) which suggested that the country's aero clubs could accommodate between them about sixty Tiger Moths, and arrangements were made for the systematic overhaul of that number with a fixed selling price in mind of £450 each, a figure negotiated down from £800 which had been the original suggestion. To establish the system four aircraft were flown from Taieri to the de Havilland factory at Rongotai in August 1945 where on 25 September 1946, part of the Centennial Exhibition Buildings previously used as a maintenance and storage facility was destroyed by fire. Lost in the blaze were NZ732 (3426) and NZ826 (DHNZ76), Tiger Moths undergoing scheduled maintenance and then, by some irony, attached to the Forest Fire Patrol based at Rotorua, a Howard DGA operated by the United States' Legation, a pair of instructional airframes and eighteen engines.

The Forest Fire Patrol operated on behalf of the State Forest Service (SFS) on a seasonal basis between January 1943 and April 1948 and used a number of different aircraft types including an Oxford, Harvard and Fox Moth. The Tiger Moth was considered the most versatile in spite of the carriage of a heavy radio and intercom equipment together with observer in the front cockpit and a wind driven generator inset into the leading edge of the port lower mainplane, all contributing to a maximum cruising speed of between 65 and 70mph. The dual controls were removed and screened ignition fitted together with electrically bonded flying surfaces. After the loss of the two aircraft in the fire at Rongotai they were replaced by three others: NZ1421 (DHNZ101), NZ1462 (DHNZ142) and NZ1473 (DHNZ153). Pilots, who were committed to regular practice in short field landings every week, reported having to use full throttle for much of the time and it was a struggle operating in 25-30mph headwinds common in summer.

Flying low over the sea has always held a compulsive attraction, and when the sun is shining and sand conditions are ideal, a friendly shadow will dance along too. Tiger Moth ZK-BRM inspecting the surf in New Zealand. *Gordon Bain*

Coastal flying can be more relaxed when miles of deserted sandy beaches stretch ahead. Sheer cliffs rising from a ribbon of shoreline provide an awesome backdrop and demand concentration. Tiger Moth ZK-BRM, her pilot sensibly equipped with a Mae-West, operating off the coast of South Island, New Zealand. *Gordon Bain*

Surplus stock, now identified to the WARB as ninety eight Tiger Moths, was sold very much in line with proceedings elsewhere, and against a graduated scale of condition were offered for tender as lying, with fixed reserve prices ranging from £30 to £330. When the list closed on 9 December 1946, only twenty aircraft had been sold for between £35 and £235 each. A number of private sales reduced the unsold number to seventy four to which the Air Force added a further declared surplus of fourteen. A second tender operation which closed in May 1947 resulted in only seventeen of the eighty eight aircraft on offer being sold, and a serious storage problem to be faced.

The first of the de Havilland overhauled Tiger Moths, ZK-AIC (82263), a survivor of the wartime shipments from Great Britain, was delivered to the New Plymouth Aero Club and on 11 January 1946 inaugurated civil flying in New Zealand following the end of the Second World War. Before the turn of the year, sixteen clubs were in operation having received fifty seven machines. From April 1946, the £450 aircraft were also available from Aircraft Service (NZ) Ltd. and Airwork (NZ) Ltd. at Mangere and Harewood, all delivered in the standard scheme of trainer yellow overall, except by special request.

Aircraft in storage at April 1947 were re-assessed for a further sale by tender but in view of the poor public attitude displayed the previous December and in the face of opposition from the aero clubs, the idea was abandoned. In October 1947 the Minister of Defence was prevailed upon to donate forty two Tiger Moths, free of charge, to the RNZAC for re-issue to deserving organisations. Although there was no purchase cost, £20 per aeroplane was charged for assembly and rigging ex-storage, plus sixpence per mile air delivery by Air Force pilots. Even at these bargain prices there were objections, and perhaps with reason. The 'free' aircraft would be delivered with no civil certification which would become the responsibility of the recipients, and at their own cost. Assuming no major problems the engineering work and subsequent paper chase was expected to average some £200 per aircraft. Following a £450 invoice received for the overhaul and civil certification of one Tiger Moth some of the clubs maintained they could not afford the burden and their gifted aircraft were re-sold or stored for later disposal, used as a fallback reserve or even a source of free spares.

Although the rate of delivery was slow and only twenty eight 'free' aircraft had been provided by May 1949 the system was working and must have caused distress to those in the industry, especially in Great Britain, who had expressed strong reservations against any suggestion of free issue. Perhaps the New Zealand Government was not aware of such objections or believed they were too far from the centre of the argument because a year after the first allocation a further nineteen aircraft were gifted to the RNZAC. These could not be air delivered due, it was claimed, to a shortage of Air Force personnel although it was widely believed that their condition was such that it precluded anything but delivery by surface transport anyway. All the free issue aircraft had been distributed by 1950 and at the end of the following year twenty seven clubs were active with almost 130 Tiger Moths in service.

The RNZAF was the last of the Commonwealth Air Forces to operate Tiger Moths in the primary training role. Nine aircraft were sold by tender in 1955 and the final eleven by August 1956. NZ1421 (NZ101), went to Aircraft Engineering Co. of NZ Ltd. for £425 and NZ1453 (NZ133), was converted to the status of Instructional Airframe and allocated to No 4 Technical Training School (TTS) at Woodbourne in September. The average price of £363 paid for the aircraft sold into the commercial market reflected the diminished public interest in the last disposal. Two damaged aircraft, NZ1425 (NZ105), which had crashed at Taieri on 19 October 1954 and NZ1427 (NZ107), which suffered an accident on the same site in March 1955, were sold for £42 and £25 respectively, almost certainly as sources of spare parts. While the aero clubs were now beginning to seek more modern equipment the agricultural industry was almost insatiable and remained a net importer of Tiger Moths from specialist suppliers overseas.

RNZAF Tiger Moths receiving fuel at the start of another training day. The aircraft closest to the camera, NZ741, was sold to Middle Districts Aero Club in 1946 but crashed in 1954, a year after joining the Waikato Aero Club at Oparau. *RNZAF Museum*

CANADA

Under the Terms of Agreement for the Empire Air Training Scheme signed in Canada on 17 December 1939, the Canadian Government was to provide facilities to train Canadian, British, Australian and New Zealand aircrews, for which the British Government would supply the estimated requirement of 3,540 aircraft.

Pre-war, the civil flying clubs had provided elementary training for the Royal Canadian Air Force, and to avoid delay in commencing the EATS, clubs were called upon to supply flying instructors and ground staff while operating under the jurisdiction of the RCAF. Although airfield construction made a good start, commencement of the flying programme proper was seen by local observers as lethargic.

During the summer of 1940, with Canadian approval, the Air Ministry moved a number of RAF Service Flying Training Schools (SFTS) from Great Britain to Canada, a policy that was opposed by many including some Cabinet Ministers who believed the units should remain at home as a second line of defence and new schools should be raised as a 'reserve'.

Repositioning of the schools was physically ponderous, but by the end of 1940, four SFTS were in commission. All flying instruction was given and received by RAF personnel, although administration was a Canadian responsibility. Having seen the system into operation, Canada offered to accept more RAF schools in addition to the thirty six EATS facilities which had been established by the end of 1940, but on the condition that training aircraft should be of local manufacture.

Discussion on the merits of transferring Elementary Flying Training Schools to Canada had been high on the agenda since 1939 when the expenses surrounding an average 25% wastage rate had

Hard packed snow under a bright blue sky and two long lines of DH.82C Tiger Moths several of which are fitted with ski undercarriages. *deHMC Archive*

A civilian ground crew jesting with the solo pilot of a DH.82C with the canopy slipped to the rear of its limit of travel. Note the unconventional chocks, necessary when working on a snowy surface. *deHMC Archive*

been sufficient to rule out the prospect and provide added impetus to the introduction of the Grading system.

With the establishment of the SFTS network in Canada, and continuous training possible in the same country, new RAF elementary units were opened from June 1941: 31 EFTS Calgary (later De Winton), 32 EFTS Swift Current (later Bowden), 33 EFTS Caron, 34 EFTS Assiniboia, 35 EFTS Neepawa and 36 EFTS Pearce.

Nos 31 and 32 EFTS were established with Boeing PT-17 Stearman, but even with a cockpit canopy the type was unsuited to the extremes of climate suffered on the Canadian Prairies and all were eventually replaced by locally-built DH.82C Tiger Moths.

Following Japan's unexpected entry into the war from December 1941 a major review of air training policy in North America was undertaken at a conference held in Ottawa in May 1942 which extended its remit to cover all Commonwealth training on a global scale. The result was signature on 1 July of a revised Agreement valid until 31 March 1945, under which the administration of all RAF and EATS schools in Canada would be merged and transferred to the RCAF under a new umbrella: The British Commonwealth Air Training Plan (BCATP). All the RAF Elementary Flying Training Schools were to be operated on a daily basis by civilian contractors, much as the EATS schools already were, although all flying instruction would be provided by RAF personnel. DH.82C Tiger Moths were operational at twenty three Canadian based EFTS from 1940, in addition to four Wireless Schools, replacing Fleet Finches at eight, an aircraft which had at one time appeared to pose a serious threat to the Tiger Moth in Canada.

Having delivered 1,520 'C' models between April 1940 and September 1942, the Canadian Government was already well advanced in seeking a replacement, eventually choosing the Fairchild PT-26 Cornell, a wooden, low-winged monoplane manufactured in Canada under the United States' Mutual Aid Program, and introduced to the elementary schools from November 1942. The re-equipment process worked progressively through the system until June 1944, replacing Tiger Moths at eleven stations. Of the remaining twelve schools, six were disbanded during the summer of 1942, pre-Cornell, and the other six retained Tiger Moths until BCATP was, effectively, closed down in 1944.

The Assistant CFI at 33 EFTS Caron early in 1942 was Leslie Gosling, a pilot who had trained on DH.60 Moths in the 1920s with the London Aeroplane Club at Stag Lane. His personal aircraft, RCAF1120 (DHC1323), carried a skull and crossbones on the black engine cowling, intended, he thought, to deter over-confident pupils about to take their CFI test. After Leslie Gosling nosed the aircraft into a snowbank while taxiing, the death's head disappeared and was quickly replaced by a figure of an ostrich with its head in the sand, and a legend: *The Gostrich*. After 1120 was posted to 31 EFTS De Winton, replaced in January 1943 by a Cornell, she was flown by pupil pilot Roy Day who had successfully passed through his Grading exercise on Tiger Moths with No 4 EFTS at Brough. After the war, in 1949, Leslie Gosling was captain of a British South American Airways Avro York freighter operating Heathrow to British Guiana; the First Officer was Roy Day, having graduated from RAF Lancasters and who later became a senior captain with British Airways.

In stark contrast to the heat and dust of Southern Africa which attacked and degraded fabric and engines, and the dampness of Great Britain, the Canadian aircraft, which mostly were obliged to remain picketed in the open when not in use, were ravaged by snow and savage low temperatures which were more acceptably tolerable when the sky was blue due to the dry nature of the atmosphere. Used to such regular conditions, aircrew and groundcrew all dressed suitably for the season. Thick coats were especially necessary when in strong, freezing wind conditions, any attempt was made to prepare Tiger Moths which were literally flying at the end of their tethering wires. In high winds pupils would fly twenty minutes downwind and leave forty minutes to claw their way back to base.

RCAF Tiger Moth 1120 was the personal mount of Leslie Gosling, Assistant CFI at 33 EFTS in 1942. The aircraft carried the skull and crossbones motif on the engine cowling as a deterrent to over confident pupils. *Leslie Gosling*

DH.82C 4032 exhibiting a seemingly distressed bottom edge of the rudder during service at 6 EFTS Prince Albert. Taken on charge in May 1940 she was struck off at the end of 1941 following an accident in September. *deHMC Archive*

Trainee pilots in Canada were equipped with flying gear the same as their contemporaries elsewhere. Although the DH.82C was fitted with a cockpit heater extremes of cold and the risk of losing a canopy ensured the full kit was worn all the time. *deHMC Archive*

The familiar scene: a pupil waits while the refuelling truck services the line at No 3 Flying Instructor School, Arnprior, Ontario where 8965 was based from 1942 until 1945. Civilianised in 1948 the aircraft is currently on display in the Aviation Museum at Greenfield, Iowa. *Murray Peden*

Tiger Moth ZS-CTN was registered to Vintage Aero Services at Empangeni in 1985 and was based at Krugersdorp in 1987. *deHMC Archive*

On 6 August 1987 static electricity caused ZS-CTN to catch fire in her hangar at Krugersdorp. Although the aircraft was quickly pushed out of the hangar she was almost completely gutted before the fire service had time to react. *Ted Phelps*

Although the large fixed windscreen offered a high level of protection flying a DH.82C with no canopy was compared to sitting in a bath. Spinning the aircraft in this configuration caused some concern over her ability to recover. *deHMC Archive*

When the temperature on the ground was recorded at -50°F, all flights were restricted to a maximum duration of sixty minutes. At lower temperatures, flying was cancelled and some instructors would place thermometers outside their bedroom windows to give them warning of the morning's likely agenda.

At 20 EFTS Oshawa in 1941 a 'weather-wash out day' had resulted in the unusual situation of all sixty of the school aircraft being crowded into one hangar. While one engineer was employed in draining fuel another decided to check the magnetos on the same aircraft with the almost inevitable result that it caught fire. Bill Marsh, a seventeen year old working on the flight line prior to training as a pilot, remembered that the hangar was evacuated in a new record time. Before the fire was brought under control six aircraft had been destroyed and several others badly damaged.

The danger of working with petrol in a hot climate was illustrated on 3 August 1987 when engineer Ted Phelps was draining fuel from the tank of Tiger Moth ZS-CTN (86006), at Krugersdorp in South Africa in pursuit of a foreign body which was believed to be the cause of a leak at the water drain tap. Ted Phelps was wearing overalls made from synthetic fabric and in the hot, dry hangar environment a charge of static electricity jumped between the engineer and a steel engine bearer which caused the draining petrol stream to ignite and the fuel tank to explode. The burning aircraft was quickly removed from the hangar but the developed conflagration was already beyond the capacity of the local fire extinguishers and ZS-CTN was severely damaged.

The sliding canopy of the DH.82C was a great protector from the weather but on pleasant days one half could be slipped back on its rails. The type could be flown solo from either seat, although the rear position was the one usually occupied in this configuration. It was also possible to fly the aircraft with no canopy at all, relying on the adequately wide front windscreen for total protection. Pilots who operated in this configuration likened it to flying in a bath, but the practice was not acceptable to the military users and mostly was reserved for youthful experimentation after the war.

The canopy shielded hidden dangers too. Operating from 19 EFTS Vinden during the establishment's first winter, 1941/1942, one pupil was unlucky enough to lose his entire canopy when flying aerobatics. The aircraft was remarkably undamaged but the pupil's unprotected face subsequently suffered frostbite to cheeks and nose. It was to be a not uncommon occurrence. The canopy was held in the closed position by two Pirelli webbing straps fixed over studs attached to the front windscreen and any aerobatic manoeuvre with the canopy partially or accidentally open was not recommended. Part of the solo pre-flight check was to ensure that the canopy was clipped shut.

Operating at 31 EFTS De Winton in January 1943 and flying solo from the rear seat, Roy Day found after thirty minutes flight on a calm day that his canopy had become unlatched and was tending to creep back along its rails. Attempting to hold it closed by placing flat hands on the side panels caused extreme discomfort, even though the pilot was wearing the equipment of the day: silk inners, woolly gloves and leather gauntlets.

At Caron a pupil pilot flying solo experienced a situation when the sliding hood jumped its tracks and became lodged on the rear fuselage, limiting movement of the rudder and elevators. Although standing instructions were that the aircraft should be abandoned in the face of obvious control difficulties the pilot found he had sufficient movement to coax the aircraft into a low level circuit and flew past the tower at 60ft in the hope of raising the alert prior to what would be an awkward landing. There being absolutely no sign of recognition of his plight by activation of the emergency services he eased the aircraft into a long final approach and precarious touchdown only after which did somebody on the ground ring the alarm at which point the aircraft was quickly surrounded by a horde of ambulances, fire engines and would-be rescuers.

Giving every appearance of being a standard, open cockpit Tiger Moth, the large tailwheel, raked undercarriage and steel interplane struts betray Otto Dietrich's CF-DHA as a conversion from DH.82C to DH.82A configuration. *Otto Dietrich*

Flying a DH.82C solo from the rear seat it was difficult to stop the front canopy from sliding back if the retaining straps ceased to function. On a very cold day it was more than a distraction. *deHMC Archive*

Shortly after the first DH.82C Tiger Moths were delivered by school instructors from the No 10 Air Depot at Calgary to 33 EFTS Caron in December 1941 a serious accident occurred which was attributed to exhaust fumes entering the cockpit. For a time in 1942 all Tiger Moths operating from Caron did so with the rear portion of the cockpit canopy removed. John Pearson was detailed to fly an engineer carrying gas detection apparatus and on 4 February 1942, with both parts of the canopy firmly closed, they trundled around the sky in a series of one hour trials, adopting a variety of flying attitudes. Without knowledge of any official results Pearson was posted away but as there was no further reported trouble with suspected exhaust leakage the theory was that the accident had occurred to a rogue aircraft, probably with a cracked heater muff. Thomas Madigan who arrived at 33 EFTS early in 1943 and heard about the accident realised the problem had been solved when he found that all the Tiger Moths had been replaced with Cornells.

Instead of clearing snow from grass or hard runways the winter temperatures permitted it to be rolled and hard packed and for wheeled operations to continue as usual with pupil pilots needing to make neat judgements when landing between the markers. The icy surfaces often resulted in completely uncontrollable but elegant ground loops, with the occasional loss of an undercarriage, but the wheeled chassis configuration was much preferred. A downside at De Winton was when a Chinook wind started blowing in from the Pacific and across the Rocky Mountains which could quickly raise local temperatures by up to 30°F, converting rolled surfaces into lakes of slush. Under such conditions De Winton's remedy was to cancel flying and send everybody on leave until civilian contractors had cleared the operational surfaces.

Tom Payne trained on DH.82C Tiger Moths at 35 EFTS Neepawa from late 1942:

RCAF DH.82C 4329 operating from 33 EFTS Caron over a snow covered landscape with the rear canopy open, possibly during the exhaust fume scare. In compensation, the pilot has his fleecy collar turned up and is favouring sunglasses rather than goggles. *John Pearson*

One of the perils of a forced landing on a conventional undercarriage in deep snow. 4043 was part of the establishment of No 6 EFTS at Prince Albert in March 1941 when she suffered an accident which resulted in her reduction to scrap. *deHMC Archive*

Civilian contractor Northern Cartage was employed to recover less badly damaged aircraft on behalf of No 31 EFTS Calgary. Wings were racked on the flatbed and the fuselage towed home on her mainwheels. Note the steam locomotive just visible above the bonnet of the lorry. *deHMC Archive*

"To most of us cross wind operations were an essential part of our course. Whilst we had the 'luxury' of a cockpit canopy we also had brakes and a tail wheel instead of a skid. This was because at Neepawa we operated from hard runways, not grass, so being able to 'line up into wind' for take-off and landing was not an option.

Usually the wind was near enough in line but when it became stronger, more often than not it was some 15 to 20 degrees across the runway. If from the left, things were manageable due to the right swing tendency, but when from the right then it was quite 'hairy'.

The worst problems were in the late winter/early spring when there was snow to contend with. The very efficient snow blowers/ploughs cleared the runways and taxy paths but piled it high along the sides of them. At Neepawa the runway appeared as a black groove in a white plain. The height of the snow banks on each side of the runway was around five to six feet high, enough so you could not see over them from the cockpit. Whilst it felt like a headwind coming straight at you, immediately the Tiger Moth got above the protection of the walls you were literally moved sideways.

Take off was hard enough but landing was more difficult. In a strong wind it was full throttle to the threshold, no attempt at three pointers, just ensuring enough speed to keep rudder control. Immediately below the level of the walls of snow it was a different world. One instructor was able to take-off, throttle back and get blown backwards, then approach and land without crossing any of the airfield's boundaries.

No 8 Repair Depot, Winnipeg. Piles of DH.82C Tiger Moth fuselages, less engines and undercarriages, soon to be turned into scrap. *Lloyd Carbert*

This shot of DH.82C Tiger Moth C-FGTU about to touch down illustrates the lie of the undercarriage when weight is taken off the wheels. *Eric Dumigan*

In better weather I had an experience that made my subsequent pre-flight inspections more careful. I was on solo aerobatics when the aircraft seemed to develop a mind of its own half way through a slow roll. Having recovered and resumed level flight after losing some 2,000ft I carefully went through all the controls. I had walked round the aeroplane, checking the movements of ailerons, elevator, rudder etc., but had not noticed that some of the cable connections had been secured by rounds of thin wire.

The port aileron had become disconnected from the control cables; it did not move when I moved the stick; when slowing down it hung like a flap. After experimenting with speeds and use of rudder I beat-up the Control Tower, the approved manner to alert them that I had a problem as we did not have wireless. I made my circuit and approach with very flat turns, did a wheelie landing holding a fairly straight line along the runway, returning to the apron without further incident. The problem was that only thin 3 amp fuse wire had been used to make the connection instead of the more robust 30 amp which had been used on all the other points. I was told that a lack of brass turnbuckles forced the ground crews to improvise.

Another less fortunate trainee pilot had a heavy landing at night. He came to a halt but could not taxy away. Alerted by the blocked runway the crash crew found that the undercarriage had collapsed and the aeroplane was sitting on its wheel hubs. A length of rope was placed round each wheel while a 'tug of war' team each side pulled away and the undercarriage sprang open allowing the aircraft to taxy back to the apron. She was checked and available for flying next morning, presumably with thicker wire holding the undercarriage assembly."

Blake Reid taxying a DH.82C Tiger Moth in which the forward view is still strictly limited requiring the pilot to lean into the propeller slipstream, not unpleasant on a hot day. The radius of the sides of the middle cowl (decking) was redesigned to improve the view from the rear seat. *Blake Reid*

Following a period of snow a rapid thaw could set in at Neepawa within the endurance of a short cross country flight, and touching down on a conventional undercarriage the wheels would break through the top of the mushy surface arresting the aircraft almost within its own length. From such a predicament taxiing back to dispersal was quite impossible and it was an uncomfortable walk for any pilot not wearing regulation boots.

In February 1943 some Tiger Moths were fitted with skis, a new challenge to pilot and instructor alike, and a configuration in which it was difficult to taxy on anything less than take-off power. Progress

DH.82C Tiger Moth C-FGTU (RCAF 4319), was restored to airworthiness in 1996 and is employed in Canada on a Public Transport certificate as a professional joyrider. This view illustrates maximum extension of the oleos when not loaded and the bulk of the heater muff surrounding the long exhaust pipe. *Eric Dumigan*

DH82C Tiger Moth 4108 on skis at No 6 EFTS Prince Albert during the winter of 1940/1941 showing the stabilising unit attached to the tail ski fitted in place of the wheel. The aircraft was damaged in July 1941 and written off the following month. *deHMC Archive*

was erratic when attempting to travel in a straight line in any appreciable crosswind and if one ski hit a watery patch the aircraft tended to rotate like a wounded fly until it could be broken free. Once airborne the leading edges of the skis stabilised in a neutral position but the vibration and noise were considered to be unacceptable.

By the end of 1943 further expansion of the RAF was believed to be unnecessary in favour of resources directed towards the Army, and a revised Agreement was signed in February 1944 to reduce the size of the BCATP which resulted in six elementary schools receiving an almost immediate notice of closure. The overall rundown of the training programme was effected with great rapidity and in July 1944 all eager recruits at 20 EFTS Oshawa were paraded and advised that they would be permitted twelve hours dual instruction but no solo time. Most hours were preciously recorded in note books as official flying logs never were provided.

Canada's War Assets Corporation (WAC) took administrative charge of each establishment's aircraft following receipt of approval for their disposal, a declaration passed down through the appropriate command structure, at which time the stock was offered for sale. Many of the Tiger Moths declared surplus in 1944 did not reach new civilian owners until well into 1945, possibly as a result of official procrastination or prolonged political discussion concerning the declared intent of the government to offer 600 surplus DH.82C Tiger Moths to the world market at the rate of 100 aircraft per month. In the event overseas' sales were very limited: a pair went to Israel and six were sold to Iceland in 1945, via an American agent working out of New Jersey.

The Icelandic aircraft were all registered between July and October 1945, and apart from minor alterations to the colour schemes which included stencilling civil registration letters on the fuselage sides, they were operated in standard Canadian configuration by the Cumulus Flying School in Reykjavik and the Akureyrar Flying School at Akureyri in the north of the island. TF-KAV (DHC1822), was operated as a tug by the Iceland Gliding Club at Reykjavik but crashed on take-off from Sandskeid in September 1952. The aircraft was rebuilt by July 1954 but remained in commission only for one more year before her last flight in August 1955. TF-KAV was placed in store for eight years but was finally burned in 1963.

Three other aircraft were written off, one each year in 1952, 1954 and 1959. TF-KBE (DHC1353), was sold to Sweden in 1961 but was never registered there. TF-KBD (DHC1407), was stored following non renewal of her C of A in July 1955, and remained in Iceland after acquisition by an expatriate owner living in Alaska and later Texas. In December 1987, TF-KBD was sold to new owners in Akureyri for restoration to airworthy condition. A seventh DH.82C Tiger Moth, TF-ABC was registered in July 1946, although her previous Canadian identity was misquoted. Operated by the Cumulus Flying School from July 1947, and painted all over bright red with large white 'rounded' style registration letters on the fuselage sides, the aircraft crashed on the ice-covered Lake Ellidavatn in February the following year, and was not repaired.

Left: Ski equipped RCAF DH.82C Tiger Moth 5173 at 10 EFTS Pendleton, warming up against snow chocks while the low sun betrays the presence of the groundcrew and their camera. *via Watt Martin*

Below: DH.82C Tiger Moth CF-FUG moored on Lake Winnebago sporting a pair of Edo floats. Originally fitted with a Menasco engine in RCAF service, the aircraft had accumulated only 762 hours between March 1941 and her sale in October 1946. *Howard Levy*

Only a tiny fraction of surplus DH.82C Tiger Moths were exported. TF-KAD was sold to the flying school at Akureyri in Iceland in 1945. She was acquired by new owners in Reykjavik in May 1959 but crashed at Langarvatn shortly afterwards. *deHMC Archive*

Bearing the legend 'Spirit of Sky Harbour' DH.82C Tiger Moth C-GCVE (RCAF 4198), was rebuilt in December 1986 for John Hindmarsh, and based at Goderich on the same site where the owner had been a resident Tiger Moth instructor with 12 EFTS in 1944. *Martin Lee*

In November 1944 two private pilots from Havana, Domingo Newhall and Juan Benito Viera, both expressed their interest to the Canadian Government Trade Commission in Cuba in each acquiring a DH.82C Tiger Moth and on 19 February 1945 the WAC completed sales orders for ex-RCAF 3966 (DHC1627), and 5987 (DHC1290), to be sold at US$1,000 each and to be civil registered as ND1032 and ND1033 respectively. Clearance details for the delivery flight south from St. Johns, PQ were precise and included the requirement for prior notification of American military authorities and observance of all civil Air Regulations. The two aircraft left Montreal on 4 March and routed via Burlington, Albany, Newark, Washington DC, Richmond, Raleigh, Charleston, Jacksonville, Vero Beach and Key West. ND1032 arrived in Havana on 14 March but ND1033 sustained minor undercarriage damage as the result of a forced landing at Jacksonville and followed on some days later. Nothing further is known of their activities in Cuba or their later history.

By August 1945 the WAC was credited with the sale of 389 Tiger Moths each with a spare engine and sufficient parts to keep the aircraft serviceable, it was estimated, for two years. The sales raised $2,400,000, an average sum per aircraft far in excess of any demanded elsewhere. The Royal Canadian Flying Clubs Association bought 200 Tiger Moths on behalf of its twenty two constituent members, and sold them on at cost.

All the Menasco engined Tiger Moths were scrapped except for a handful as were some fitted with high time Gipsy Majors. Following removal of engine, instruments and wheels from unsold aircraft, fuselages were piled up and burned, often within the boundary of their base airfield, several of which became storage units after operational flying had ceased. Officially struck off charge on 23 January 1945, fifty DH.82C Tiger Moths bearing construction plates identifying them as PT-24s of the United States Army Air Force, were destroyed in this manner at Goderich, former home of 12 EFTS. The unit was disbanded on 14 July 1944 having operated only Tiger Moths since March 1942, when Fleet Finches had been displaced. The dump site became a haven for souvenir hunters over the years especially during the winter when it was more easily accessible by ski. It was a regular attraction for John Hindmarsh, a former instructor at Goderich who still lived locally and kept his own imported DH.82A Tiger Moth on the same airfield until, as he put it, he flew it into the only tall tree in the Province.

In August 1941 Gordon Jones commenced his RCAF flight training at No 5 EFTS High River, Alberta, during which time he flew about ten sorties in Tiger Moth 1214 (DHC1417). Having qualified for his wings he was sent on a course at Trenton and in August 1942, at the age of nineteen, was posted back to High River as a flying instructor, remaining there after the Tiger Moths were replaced by Cornells in November 1942. He was disappointed not to have been posted to an operational squadron overseas but remained in Canada as an instructor until the end of the war when he took up farming on land near High River, eventually opening a flying school there. In 1984 he discovered that RCAF Tiger Moth 1214 had survived the war and was registered CF-CIX to an owner in Edmonton. Ten years later he bought the aircraft, returned her to High River and flew her on a regular basis until his death at the age of 91 in September 2013 when the aircraft was willed to the Bomber Command Museum at Nanton.

DHC 1348 was built under contract to the US Government as a PT-24 in 1942 and allocated a USAAF serial, 42-1009. In the politics of war she was reallocated to the RAF as FE145 but served with the RCAF as 1145 at No 34 EFTS Assiniboia until sold as surplus and registered CF-DHS. *Dick Pallett*

C-GTAL is one of the very few DH.82C Tiger Moths not to be painted in the yellow and black livery carried throughout their service careers. The aircraft was recovered from long term storage at the Western Canadian Aviation Museum in 2007 and delivered to her new owners at Saskatoon the following year. *Doug Tomlinson*

DH.82C Tiger Moth C-GMFT, an outdoor exhibit sharing space with assorted vehicles at the Museum of Flight and Transportation in British Columbia, experiencing a heavy accumulation of snow during a winter storm on Canada's Pacific coast. *Ed Zalesky*

Due to the post-war expansion of Canadian naval aviation it was decided that all advanced technical training, previously provided by the Royal Navy in England, would be conducted at home and the Royal Canadian Navy's School of Naval Aircraft Maintenance (SNAM) was established at the RCAF Station at Dartmouth in April 1948. An unforeseen time lapse resulted in a requirement for sample airframes for use as training aids by the SNAM and Fleet Requirements Unit 743 (FRU) being satisfied by the acquisition of three ex-RCAF aircraft sold by the CDC into civil ownership in 1945. CF-CJG (DHC887), CF-CJH (DHC1667), and CF-CJJ (DHC813), all fully airworthy, were purchased by the Canadian Commercial Corporation of Ottawa in May 1948. The decision was queried by those who recognised that in the same year the RCN retired six Fairey Swordfish already based at Dartmouth and which were burned on site.

CF-CJG carried Royal Canadian Navy markings and retained her previous military colour scheme and serial 5088 although this was not displayed. She was systematically dismantled and rebuilt by naval engineers some of whom were rewarded by a test flight for which the canopy was not fitted. The aircraft was struck off charge as early as January 1949 and probably scrapped. CF-CJH was last used as a teaching aid in 1950 after which the aircraft was stored at Shearwater. In 1954 she was restored to airworthiness and maintained so until 1957 when she was withdrawn and sold to RCAF Chaplain Fr John MacGillivray. Re-painted blue and white with red trim and registered CF-IVO she was flown extensively until 1965 when she was donated to the Experimental Aircraft Association (EAA) in Wisconsin and registered N667EA.

The third Naval Tiger Moth, the one-time RCAF 8865 and CF-CJJ, was employed by the FRU to provide air experience to naval personnel which she did until October 1949 using the callsign VG-TFA, a group of letters derived from the Naval Air Arm (VG), FRU (TF) and aircraft code (A). In March 1950 she was sold to the first of a series of owners with a military connection until acquired by the Quebec Soaring Club in September 1955. The following August she stalled off a slow turn after dropping a glider tow-rope at low level, hit the ground at Ancienne Lorette and was damaged beyond repair.

DH.82A Tiger Moth C-GSTP force-landed into standing maize in 2011 and although of 1943 manufacture her owners decided during repairs to repaint her into a 1940 military scheme. An efficiently run repair programme was completed for her to be flown again on 26 May 2012. *Robin Tripp*

DH.82C Tiger Moth NX82LN was converted into a 'A' model by Gar Williams between 1987 and 1991 for owner Loran Nordgren and is based at Viroqua, Wisconsin. The steel interplane struts are the most evident clue to ancestry. *Loran Nordgren*

For about 37 years the former PT-24/DH.82C Tiger Moth 1263 was stored in a barn at Saskatoon. In 1982 she was acquired by Doug Robertson in anticipation of a three year restoration programme although the first flight in her new open cockpit configuration was not achieved until 7 October 2012. *Doug Robertson*

Right: Masquerading as a Royal Navy 'A' model Tiger Moth at Old Rhinebeck, New York, for many years, DH.82C N8731R, formerly RCAF 9690, was one of the last batch of DH.82Cs delivered in September 1942 to the new home of 10 EFTS at Pendleton. The aircraft flew only 580 hours with the RCAF before sale into the civil market in July 1945. *deHMC Archive*

Below: Tiger Moth N4030E is a Canadian built 'C' version instantly identified by the narrow chord steel interplane struts, raked landing gear and large tailwheel. *Art Armstrong*

CHAPTER EIGHTEEN

Back to the Drawing Board

Built as a basic training aeroplane capable of performing the complete repertoire of standard aerobatic manoeuvres, it was unfair to expect the Tiger Moth to become a serious contender in post-war civilian competitions, especially those organised at national and international level. Competitive flying required something infinitely better than what became known, perhaps unkindly, as a 'cooking Tiger' and, although the Super Tiger prolonged the type's active participation, Tiger Moth aerobatics increasingly became the preserve of the dedicated 'amateur' and simple manoeuvres were flown to maintain the skills or just for fun. However, for commercial operators, Tiger Moth joyrides produced extra revenue when the pilot was commissioned to sail effortlessly round in a loop, else frighten the uninitiated when slow rolling through the inverted, accompanied by the faltering sounds of a fuel starved engine and the shower of detritus released from the cockpit floor. Pencil cameras fixed at strategic positions recorded every last detail.

Inevitably, the docile nature of the Tiger Moth as an aerobatic platform was used to best advantage. At the 1975 Air Day organised by the Royal Navy at Yeovilton, Heron Flight's Tiger Moth T8191 (84483), was flown by Lt Cmdr Pete Sheppard in an aerobatic routine

The Author's Tiger Moth G-AZZZ during an aerobatic sequence flown by Desmond Penrose at Halton in 2010. The aircraft is painted to represent the DH.60G Moth G-AAAA owned by Captain Geoffrey de Havilland in 1928. *Steve Le-Vien*

which included thirty two consecutive loops. Intoxicated by the effort the pilot promised to fly thirty five loops the following year in celebration of his birthday, but not as a reflection of his age. During the de Havilland Moth Club's annual Woburn Abbey Rally in 1986, Henry Labouchere raised a substantial sum of money for charity by flying continuous loops for a ninety second period in his Australian-built Tiger Moth G-BEWN (DHA952), and managed ten complete manoeuvres before the whistle blew. It was an exhausting exercise not only for the pilot and those watching, but especially for the spectators who had pledged cash for each completed loop.

The structural integrity of the Tiger Moth was tested in South Africa in 1971 where it was claimed an aircraft had been successfully pushed through an outside loop with the engine switched off!

Innovation could have its drawbacks. During the Lockheed Trophy in 1956, John Pothecary attempted an inverted falling leaf in Christchurch Aero Club's G-ANPL (85624), a manoeuvre which cost him 800ft and an admission afterwards that it could be the cause of structural damage and was not, therefore, recommended for Tiger Moths.

A great exponent of the erect falling leaf was Air Commodore Allen Wheeler, one of the investigating pilots of the wartime spinning trials at Boscombe Down and Farnborough. Less than a year before his death on 1 January 1984 at the age of 80, Allen Wheeler was seen effortlessly aerobatting his Tiger Moth G-ADGV (3340), in the sky above Old Warden Aerodrome.

A well flown aerobatic routine should exert no undue strain on engine or airframe, and a flowing sequence is a delight to behold. As part of his 1993 'Assessment' of the Tiger Moth, RAAF test pilot Tony Morris flew each of the basic manoeuvres with which the aircraft is most closely associated:

> "Generally, the Tiger Moth required large control column and pedal deflections to fly acceptable aerobatics, as the control power available, especially laterally, is quite low. Engine thrust, even at maximum power, is also low, and a high power setting is normally required. 1,950rpm was used for this evaluation, although a higher power setting can be used if necessary, within the engine limitations."

Loop: entry speed for the loop was 100 kias, (knots indicated air speed), which required lowering the nose below the horizon. As the airspeed increased from cruise toward 100 kias with 1,950rpm set, and a fixed pitch propeller, the throttle required a small reduction to ensure the engine did not exceed the limiting rpm. At 100 kias, the control column was moved centrally aft to commence a pitch rotation. As the nose pitched up, constant aft longitudinal stick pressure was required to ensure the pitching motion continued smoothly and sufficient airspeed remained to complete the manoeuvre without 'falling out' of the loop. Small rudder inputs were required as the airspeed decreased and increased throughout the loop.

Slow roll: entry speed for the slow roll was 95 kias. The roll was commenced by applying almost full aileron in the required direction, and introducing a small amount of rudder in the same direction as the roll. This application of rudder was required to assist the roll, as the lateral control circuit was designed such that at full lateral control deflection, only the up going aileron was deflected. The application of opposite rudder, as is required in some other aircraft to prevent nose drop, effectively cancelled out the rolling moment generated by the aileron and the roll ceased mid-manoeuvre, with the nose dropping rapidly. As the aircraft continued rolling towards the inverted position, forward longitudinal stick was required to prevent excessive nose drop. Past the 270 degree roll position, the amount of lateral control column was decreased to maintain a constant roll rate.

Stall turn: the minimum recommended speed for entry to the stall turn is 70 kias. The pull to the vertical was straightforward, with good visual cues available at the wing to ensure a level pull. Having achieved the vertical position, power was maintained, to give rudder authority, and as the airspeed decreased rudder in the desired direction was introduced such that full rudder was achieved at the point where the aircraft had almost stopped its climb. As the aircraft pivoted about the inner wing, a small amount of outboard aileron was required to keep a vertical attitude. The aircraft nose continued to slice down, and as the vertical position neared, a small 'check' with rudder was applied to ensure the nose did not transition past the vertical position. The power could then be reduced if required. A recovery to level flight was then simply affected.

Barrel roll: the entry speed for the barrel roll was 100 kias. The entry attitude and initial pull-up were similar to those required for the loop. As the nose rose to the 45 degree position above the horizon, aileron in the required direction of roll was introduced, and the aft stick force maintained. The nose was then 'flown', using continuous roll and pitch, to a previously identified 90 degrees reference point, such that at the wings level, inverted attitude, the nose was pointing at this feature.

Part of the dispensation from the Air Navigation Order permitting this British registered Tiger Moth to fly under the hoop at the Woburn Abbey Moth Rally in 1997, was clearance to operate the aircraft to a minimum height of three feet above ground level. *Darryl Cott*

Tiger Moth G-ANMY is operated on a commercial basis by ex RAF fighter pilot Robin Russell who offers training from *ab initio* to licence standard in addition to advanced training and air display routines. *Terry Burke*

In the air a Tiger Moth is in her element but manoeuvring on the ground requires co-ordination of a different kind not the least of which is the ability to recruit volunteers who know where to push, and where not to. *Mick Bajcar*

Anders Håkensen flew an aerobatic sequence in Norwegian Tiger Moth LN-BDM at Skå-Edeby in Sweden in June 2007. The occasion was to mark the 75th birthday of the world's oldest Tiger Moth, DH.82 SE-ADF, built at Stag Lane and delivered to Sweden in June 1932. *Bo Haggkvist*

Desmond Penrose flew his last public air display in Tiger Moth G-AZZZ during the de Havilland Moth Club's annual Charity Flying Weekend at RAF Halton in June 2010. *Steve Le-Vien*

From this position, roll and pitch were continued as the nose fell below the horizon, and the aircraft returned to the wings-level, upright attitude pointed at the original feature. To maintain a constant roll rate during the manoeuvre, variation of the aileron input was required as the airspeed decreased during the climb and increased during the dive.

Roll off the top: entry speed for the half roll off the top of a loop was 118 kias, requiring a moderate nose-down attitude. The initial pull-up required more aft control column force than the loop, to ensure sufficient airspeed was available to complete the roll. As for the loop, the force needed to be maintained positively until an attitude just short of the inverted position was achieved, with wings level. At this position, which was adopted to cater for the nose drop during the half-roll, a positive check forward was required to prevent further nose drop. The roll was then commenced, using full deflection aileron, assisted by a small amount of rudder in the same direction, which also had the benefit of minimising nose drop.

In-flight re-start: occasionally during manoeuvres with low forward airspeed and a low power setting, such as a spin, the engine rpm would decay, and on one occasion the propeller stopped completely. This is understood to be a phenomenon associated with a new or 'tight' engine, or with an incorrect idle setting. In an attempt to airstart the engine, the aircraft was dived to 125 kias, requiring a steep nose down attitude. When this did not turn the propeller, a recovery to level flight using 2-3 'g' provided sufficient force to restart the engine. The total altitude loss required to restart the engine varied with airspeed; in the worst case, starting with an airspeed of 40 kias, the altitude loss required to dive, start the engine and recover to level flight was approximately 1,000ft. After further evaluation of this

Richard Brougham's Tiger Moth VH-DDA was registered in his name on New Year's Day 2009 and was photographed exercising overhead Luskintyre Airfield on 12 May. *Wayne Brown*

characteristic, it was found that occasionally increasing airspeed to 125 kias alone would restart the engine; on other occasions a positive application of 'g' was required.

Sixty years after instructing at 28 EFTS Oshawa in Canada from September 1943, Charles Cornish could still remember the 'patter' associated with demonstrating how to deal with an engine fire and restarting the motor in the air:

> "Here we are at 5,000ft agl and the engine is on fire. We pull the fuel lever to 'off' and open the throttle fully to use up the fuel in the carburettor.....When the engine stops we switch off the magneto switches.....and assume the gliding attitude.....noting that with the propeller windmilling the nose is slightly lower than usual to maintain the correct gliding speed.....we bring the aircraft to the stall.....and the propeller stops. We re-trim into the glide noting that the attitude is once again more nose down to maintain correct gliding speed.....got that?
>
> We recover to straight and level and will now restart the engine.....fuel 'on'.....switches 'on'.....throttle one third open.....a steep diving turn to check below and then nose right down to build up the speed to about 120mph when the propeller will turn and the engine start.....ease out of the dive and bring back the revs to cruise. Nothing to it is there? But you do not attempt that on your own except in the very unlikely event of the engine stopping while carrying out aerobatics. I can see you in the mirror. Why are you looking so pale?"

In 1984, the de Havilland Moth Club in association with the London auction house, Christie's, sponsored an international Tiger Moth aerobatic competition with a difference. Each of the major Tiger Moth owning countries who agreed to be represented were requested to fly local heats to choose a national candidate and all the winners were subsequently invited to England to compete in the finals during the Club's annual rally at Woburn Abbey in August 1985. Pilots from Australia, New Zealand, South Africa, the United States and Great Britain spent several days at Old Warden Aerodrome practising on the aircraft each was to fly at Woburn, G-AVPJ (86322), kindly loaned by Robin Livett soon after the aircraft had been rebuilt following her dunking in the river Trent. It was an ironic twist that the British competitor, Barry Tempest, had been the pilot on that occasion too.

The Christie's competition revealed a remarkable level of consistency between pilots familiar with the Tiger Moth's aerobatic capabilities and who knew exactly how to exploit them. Brian Zeederberg from South Africa was a worthy winner, taking the Christie's Trophy, while Dick Nell from Australia was awarded the BAe146 Trophy for the best freestyle sequence displayed after the competition proper.

CANOPIES

As the result of a difficult flight home to England from North Africa in an open cockpit DH.60 Moth in 1928, after which Mrs Louie de Havilland is believed to have suggested the idea, the de Havilland Company converted several DH.60G Moths into Coupe Moths by building superstructures over the cockpits which were subject to many modifications as the result of in-service experience. Generally, the configuration proved to be unpopular, especially amongst those who were more used to flying with their heads in the air who found the coupe tops engendered a feeling of claustrophobia, especially amongst the ladies. Most were re-converted to open cockpits, including Captain Geoffrey de Havilland's personal DH.60G Moth, G-AAAA, which had been used as the prototype.

In Canada, some DH.60 Moths and later DH.82 type Tiger Moths were 'winterised', a procedure which usually involved the addition of a cockpit canopy and the inclusion of other necessities in the pursuit of comfort. The DH.82C Tiger Moth was the ultimate model. What powerful force directed some post-war owners of DH.82C model Tiger Moths to abandon their sliding canopies and heaters, and 'convert' their aeroplanes to open cockpit configuration, complete with brass framed windscreens and built-in draughts? The lure of the open cockpit is ever present, and a Canadian summer provides just as great an opportunity for shirt sleeved enjoyment high above the madding crowd as anywhere. Canopies fitted to Canadian Tiger Moths were essentially in aid of comfort with a bonus in efficiency due to the elimination of some drag, but at the expense of extra weight and a battle with the authorised limits for the centre of gravity (CG). Field performance was generally improved.

In New Zealand six Tiger Moths were modified at Rongotai in 1943/1944 to accept either a permanent hinged or sliding canopy structure for aircraft allocated to the New Zealand Air Training Corps Touring Flight. Transiting was more comfortable for the staff pilots but taxiing the aircraft called for even extra vigilance with no view immediately ahead as usual and with only limited vision through the side panels, a situation demanding energetic use of the rudder bar. For ATC cadets often flying for the first time a comfortable cockpit was a gentle baptism but then there was no requirement to dress up with leather jacket, helmet and goggles which surely was all part of the ritual, although most cadets, and pilots, still did.

During the conversion programme contact was made both with Hatfield and Downsview seeking assurances on CG positions and allowable locker loads due to the redistribution of fuselage weight. It was not possible to read Canada's limits directly across to the New Zealand-built DH.82A although Downsview's advice was that with their own canopied aeroplane it was wise never to exceed a maximum load of 40lb in the locker. Rongotai's signal to Hatfield was more specific quoting a CG position with canopy of 28.9in when loaded to 1,700lb, a figure achieved on paper with two crew but only half oil and petrol capacity, a position way aft of the approved limit in normal configuration. New Zealand's figures also indicated that with two crew, or a pilot operating solo from the rear seat, no load was permissible in the locker although 60lb could be carried if the front seat only was occupied.

John Neave, de Havilland New Zealand's resident test pilot, flew Tiger Moth NZ859 (82341), with an early design of side-hinged canopy in August 1944. The style proved more popular than the sliding versions similar to the Canadian design which had been tried previously and not only provided a quieter cockpit but was immune to partial or total loss in flight. The trial canopy fitted to NZ859 was later improved by adding six times the area of Perspex in the rear window and incorporating sliding panels in the port side for ventilation and 'clear view'.

Rongotai capitalised on their design post-war by selling drawings or offering to fit canopies in their works at an installed price of £50 if the job was completed during qualification for a Certificate of Airworthiness (C of A), but more than twice that if booked in at any other time. The Civil Aviation Department insisted on a series of flight tests, including spinning with strakes, and John Neave was called upon to complete these with ZK-ANG (82429), in March 1947. By May 1950 the aircraft had been converted again: sold by the owner for agricultural use.

In addition to the Rongotai canopies (Mod DH/33), at least four other designs were approved within New Zealand which are known to have been fitted to twenty four locally registered Tiger Moths, plus others based in Australia. One aircraft owned personally by John Neave in 1947, ZK-ANE (82230), was configured with a canopy covering an enlarged rear cockpit only and fitted with a strengthened floor in a stripped out front cockpit which was faired over. The aircraft operated as an aerial seed-sower and between 1948 and 1951 as a freighter for the transportation of crayfish and whitebait from the west coast to Dunedin. A seat could be fitted in the front compartment if

Photographed in April 1977 when based in Queensland, the bright red fuselage of Australian built Tiger Moth VH-BRM highlights the minimum structure and maximum glazing of the canopy, all of which was subsequently removed. *Peter Keating*

Royal New Zealand Air Force Tiger Moth NZ859 with the early design of side hinged canopy, photographed at Ohakea in August 1944. *RNZAF*

It would be easy to misconstrue the intentions of Spanish Tiger Moth EC-AHY, but the bomb shaped devices under each lower mainplane are streamlined canisters designed for carriage and mid-air dispersal of nothing more sinister than leaflets. *via John Pothecary*

Yellow and black Tiger Moth ZK-AKE was delivered to the New Plymouth Aero Club in 1946 and was operational in about 1949. The canopy, based on the DH.82C and offering excellent all-round visibility from both seats, had been fitted when the aircraft was in service with the RNZAF as NZ818. She was sold for agricultural use in 1951. *Ed Coates Collection*

Once owned by John Neave, test pilot for the de Havilland Aircraft Co of New Zealand, ZK-ANE was fitted with streamlined windscreens at both cockpits, and a sliding canopy over the rear seat. At one time the aircraft was modified with a strengthened floor to act as a freighter. *via A J Jackson*

necessary, accommodated under a detachable decking with a windscreen from a DH.94 Moth Minor already mounted.

A canopy was fitted at Croydon to the 'Taxi Tiger' G-AOXS (85425), in 1957 although the comfort was reserved for the passenger occupying the front seat. It was another inspired development by Rollason Aircraft, in all probability, very few fares would have been carried as the aircraft was extensively raced and rallied by the Tiger Club in whose hands she hit a tree during an aerobatic sortie overhead Dungate Farm near Reigate in February 1960.

At least four other Tiger Moths were fitted with canopies in post-war Britain, all custom made and all removed by subsequent owners. In 1952, G-AIZF (83635), was converted to carry a sliding canopy by H M Woodhams, an early employee with the de Havilland Company at Stag Lane in 1920, later a director of Sir W G Armstrong Whitworth Aircraft at Baginton where the design was finalised and the job completed. The glazing had long since been removed before an agricultural career began in 1958 and ended in 1964 after numerous misadventures.

G-ANRN (83133), carried a canopy until it was cut off at Swanton Morley in October 1979. On 1 December the aircraft was ferried to Odiham on a day described by her pilot, Garry Bisshopp,

Above and below: Universal Flying Services converted Tiger Moth G-AOXS into a 'Tiger Taxi' at Fairoaks in 1957, enclosing only the front (passenger) cockpit. The aircraft spent more time displaying with the Tiger Club than ever carrying fares. *deHMC Archive*

Chapter 18 — Back to the Drawing Board

Above and below: A sliding canopy was designed and built by Sir W G Armstrong Whitworth Aircraft Ltd and fitted to DH.82A Tiger Moth G-AIZF at Baginton in 1952. The aircraft operated at Stapleford Tawney until 1958 when she was sold and converted for agricultural use. She was flown in a single seat open cockpit configuration until February 1964 when she was damaged beyond economical repair when spraying a field in Northamptonshire. *via Ken Pye*

Tiger Moth G-ANSA was converted by Doug Bianchi at White Waltham and fitted with a side-hinged canopy, long exhaust pipe and mainwheel spats. *David Welch*

One of the dilapidated ex-ATA hangars at White Waltham plays backdrop to canopied Tiger Moth G-ANSA. Unless checked on a regular basis spats on aircraft operating from grass runways tend to clog with mud which can exert a braking effect when not always required. *John Osborne*

as 'desperately cold', which forced him to land at Old Warden en-route in an attempt to thaw out. In the hands of her new owner, Jonathan Elwes, G-ANRN was later to make spectacularly long open cockpit flights from England to Gibraltar and North Africa, Moscow and the North Cape and two return visits from England to the Crimea.

Sold as scrap ex-RAF Tiger Moth N6944 (82194), was acquired by Doug Bianchi's Personal Plane Services at White Waltham in May 1954 and, civilianised as G-ANSA, qualified for a C of A complete with mainwheel spats and an elaborate canopy a year later. In March 1958 the aircraft was retrieved from the river Mersey by the New Brighton Lifeboat.

Engineer Chris Roberts and his commercial pilot wife Claire initiated their own charter company, 'Chrisair', in August 1957 with Tiger Moth G-AHVU (84728). Fitted with a canopy and operated from a number of sites in the Midlands, southern England and the West Country, the Tiger Moth ranged deep into Europe aided by a long range tank and wobble pump activated by the occupant of the front seat. Replaced by a DH.84 Dragon and DH.85 Leopard Moth, the Tiger Moth almost joined the agricultural business in 1963 but entered a long period of storage at Farnborough and Chessington where she lost contact with her canopy and 'boudoir style' interior decor. She was delivered to Richard Parker at Denham in 1986, joining a collection of

military training aircraft and painted in a fully researched, early RAF camouflage scheme, an initiative by Geoff Masterton not immediately recognised for its value by many unfamiliar with pre-war history.

Some of the Tiger Moths operated by the National Flying School from various sites around Belgium were fitted with canopies to improve all-weather comfort, as were a few Stampe SV-4s, all arrangements modelled on the Canadian DH.82C's three piece design built on a very light framework.

In Australia canopies were most popular immediately after the end of the Tiger Moth's agricultural career when hinged styles similar to those developed in wartime New Zealand were rivalled only by complete sliding systems removed from surplus CAC Wacketts, an almost perfect match requiring relatively little engineering.

The 1,000th Tiger Moth assembled at Mascot, A17-565 (DHA1000), had returned to the mainland from a tour of duty in New Guinea in 1944 and was placed in storage at Cootamundra where she was recommended for conversion to spares in March 1946. The order was never confirmed and although sold in 1948, registration VH-FBR was not allocated until ten years later. Dutifully serving in the agricultural role for three years the aircraft flew only twenty hours with an owner at Kelso between 1961 and 1964 during which time a New Zealand style canopy was added. In that configuration VH-FBR was sold to the USA and registered N17565 in July 1971, and G-BCRD to British resident Richard Dent in November 1974. Both owner and aeroplane relocated to Switzerland in 1978 and registration HB-UPP was adopted the following year after which the aircraft was dismantled and stored until the bold decision was reached to convert her to her

Above: Welcome aboard. Captain Claire Roberts with the Chrisair Tiger Moth Taxi G-AHVU at Luton Airport in the company of classic period airline types. *Chris Roberts*

Right: Welcome aboard. Captain Claire Roberts waiting for her passenger to board for a trip from Luton Airport. Reminiscent of early commercial aviation there was no cover for the pilot. The passenger was tasked with pumping fuel from the long-range tank. *Chris Roberts*

original RAAF specification. The first step was achieved by the simple expedient of taking a handsaw to the top decking, and the subsequent removal of 132lb of structural weight to create a new nimbleness in open cockpit Alpine revelry.

Harry Schoning had trained on Chipmunks in Canada before going to war in Korea and had retired from captaining a B.727 on Pacific routes to concentrate on rebuilding and flying Tiger Moths. He particularly enjoyed very long cross-country exercises at high altitude for which a DH.82A Tiger Moth was hardly suited.

> "Why would anyone want to put a canopy on a Tiger Moth? Actually my reason was to make a trip back to Oshkosh (from southern California) a comfortable one. In 2002, DH.82A Tiger Moth N3549 (86554) was fitted with a canopy. The view out of the sides is just great and the sliding mechanism works well on strong rails. There are two intermediary stops between full open and closed; the whole assembly is overbuilt and can sustain 350kts. When I flew with the canopy fully open I put my hand up to feel if there was any heavy wind loading and found that the windscreen seemed to deflect most of the air around it.
>
> With the canopy closed at about 1,900rpm I am close to 100mph IAS on the internal ASI and 97mph IAS on the windy unit. At 1,800rpm I am cruising at about 90mph. I tried slow flying to see if the canopy restricted any airflow over the rudder and all seems well."

A pleasing study of Chrisair Tiger Moth Taxi G-AHVU just airborne, showing the extended exhaust pipe, neat spats and a low profile canopy which allowed a minimum of headroom for the occupant of either cockpit. *Chris Roberts*

Tiger Moth VH-BRM was fitted with a sliding canopy in the style of a DH.82C and was at one time based at Berwick in Victoria. *David Welch*

Not a place for a forced landing. HB-UPP, the 1,000th Tiger Moth assembled in Australia, reached Switzerland via the USA and Great Britain and with some trepidation was detached from her heavy canopy but not her colour scheme. *Eric Gandet*

The canopy fitted to VH-AQU blends in well with the front fuselage, due in particular, perhaps, to the absence of a large set of registration letters. Canopies were never universally accepted and nearly all were later removed. *deHMC Archive*

Australian built, British registered and resident in Switzerland, Tiger Moth G-BCRD was re-covered with lacquered lightweight fabric in 1976 at the beginning of an eight year sojourn in the USA. The Wackett canopy remained undisturbed for some years after her move to Europe. *Richard Dent*

Harry Schoning trained on Chipmunks in Canada to become a fighter pilot in the Korean War. His conversion of the rear cockpit of Tiger Moth N5446 into that resembling a Spitfire still allows for the aircraft to be flown as a two-seater when the occasion demands. *Harry Schoning*

The rear cockpit of Tiger Moth N5446 has been configured as closely as practicable to that of a Spitfire for owner John Burson in California. Not unnaturally the aircraft is referred to as a Spitmoth. *Harry Schoning*

A large bubble canopy was fitted to the rear cockpit of Tiger Moth N5446 when she was restored by Harry Schoning in California and flown via Lethbridge in Canada to Oshkosh in 2009. The configuration photographed from this angle does present a racy appearance while the cockpit layout and instrumentation replicates that of a Spitfire. *Nigel Hitchman*

In July 2009 Harry Schoning fitted an identical canopy to Dr John Burson's Georgia based Tiger Moth N5446 (DHA434), one of the very first Tiger Moths exported from Australia to the USA in 1968 and which caused the Australian authorities to impose an export ban on vintage aircraft for fear of losing their entire heritage. A major difference between N5446 and the earlier conversion of N3549 was that the new canopy enclosed a rear cockpit fully instrumented to a Spitfire specification and the aircraft immediately became known as the 'Spitmoth'.

SEAPLANE

Although largely rejected as a suitable candidate for serious investment as a seaplane trainer in the early 1930s, ten years later with war raging all round half a dozen Tiger Moths were miraculously repatriated to Australia from the Dutch East Indies prior to entering service, immediately available for no other reason than that they were stored awaiting delivery of floats from the United States. They were quickly loaded on board critically scarce shipping space and whisked away from the danger posed by advancing Japanese armies. Unlike the DH.60 which, as a series, was well endowed with supplies of floats and operated fitted with them in many parts of the pre-war world, few Tiger Moths ever took to the water other than in isolation.

Late in 1960 a group of British based marine aviation enthusiasts led by Air Commodore G J Christopher Paul, Secretary General of The Air League, proposed the formation of a Seaplane Club and at a formal meeting held on 20 January 1961 the Club was officially constituted under a committee chaired by Britain's foremost seaplane pilot, John Lankester Parker.

Recruitment of members and raising of funds to secure a suitable aircraft, support equipment, staff and facilities, probably to be based at Gillingham on the river Medway, was too slow and the committee eventually persuaded the altruistic Norman Jones to donate a Tiger Moth from the still comfortably stocked Rollason store at Croydon. The airframe was to be mated with a pair of Edo 2000 floats which had been imported from Canada the previous year. Norman Jones contributed G-AIVW (83135), an aircraft acquired after the damage inflicted during a heavy landing at Woolsington in September 1959 had proved too expensive for the Newcastle Aero Club to repair. G-AIVW, released by the RAF late in 1946, had earned a reputation as a very fast racing aircraft in the hands of the manager of Newcastle Airport, Jimmy Denyer. In the 1958 King's Cup Air Race he flew the Tiger Moth into first place at an average speed of 118.5mph.

Sea Tiger G-AIVW being refuelled off the shingle beach at Lee on Solent on a cold day in September 1965. Constant vigilance was necessary to ensure she stayed afloat in the shallow water. *Cliff Barnett*

Painted yellow overall with matching parallel cheat lines on fuselage and floats, G-AIVW was christened *Oswald Short* as recognition of the pioneer's generous launch donation of £500, and was first flown from Lee on Solent on 20 July 1963 by Christopher Paul. Initial utilisation was poor due to limited facilities and indifferent weather and by the following year and in debt, the Seaplane Club's brief excursion had been absorbed as the Seaplane Section of the Tiger Club.

The change of status coincided with a move to the sheltered acres of Castle Water, a disused fresh water gravel working and watersports centre near Rye, where G-AIVW, officially designated a 'Tiger Moth Seaplane', became universally known as the Sea Tiger.

A quick release system for the conventional land undercarriage was designed and fitted which allowed G-AIVW to be flown from a short grass strip alongside the water at Rye for periodic checks at Redhill and it was there in 1968 that the enemy of all seaplanes was discovered: incurable corrosion in the tubular fuselage frame. A new fuselage was substituted, that of the repairable G-ANLR (82111), and the opportunity was taken to repaint the airframe and floats a mellow maroon and silver.

The level of skills required to fly a Tiger Moth accurately were magnified in the Sea Tiger. To begin with it was necessary to learn how to launch and retrieve/beach the relatively frail aeroplane, let alone how to taxy on a medium which was itself subject to ebb and flow, wind and tide. The Sea Tiger flew herself off the water at 41kts IAS and was allowed the luxury of a climb at 44kts to 15ft where level acceleration to 60kts was required prior to further manoeuvring.

Perhaps the declared unsuitability of the aircraft for training pilots in the 1930s was a result of not attempting to increase fin and rudder area to compensate for the additional side area of the floats. This reduced the tendency to weathercock when on the surface of the water but caused directional instability in the air when heavy rudder pressure was required to overcome the additional linkage to the water rudders.

Tiger Moth G-ANLR looking smart with an 'all-weather' rear windscreen at Rochester in 1963. The aircraft took a tumble at Syderstone, Norfolk in 1966 and parts were grafted onto the Sea Tiger G-AIVW to replace corroded frames. *David Welch*

Flown by Concorde pilot Steve Bohill-Smith Tiger Moth G-AOBX flies past Halton House, the Officers' Mess at RAF Halton, during a de Havilland Moth Club Charity Flying Weekend in June 2007. The house has been the setting for a number of major film productions. *via Steve Bohill Smith photographed from DH.84 Dragon G-ECAN*

Tiger Moth G-AOBX flown by Steve Bohill-Smith over Highclere Castle during a fund-raising event for 'Help for Heroes' on mid-Summer Day 2011. *Candice Bauval*

Christopher Paul remembers that general handling was considered 'clumsy' and that response to control input was delayed. Stalling was to be avoided because at the point of stall, the floats, at the increased angle of attack, provided a good deal of lift forward of the normal C of G to a point where even full forward stick could no longer get the nose down. Speed was critical when approaching for touch down and in gliding turns.

Alighting at a faster than intended speed at Frenchman's Creek, Rye, on 14 July 1973, the floats dug into the water and G-AIVW overturned, floating upside down until salvaged and subsequently dried out and repaired. In view of the operating conditions, but guided by the small band of enthusiastic and knowledgeable instructors and volunteer helpers, there were remarkably few incidents but on 27 August 1982, off Silver Sands, Camber, G-AIVW slipped out of a low turn in poor visibility and was wrecked when she hit the sea. A marginal operation at the start, the Sea Tiger enterprise had been sustained for almost twenty years.

In 1975 Tiger Moth G-AOBX (83653), was fitted with a set of Short floats originally designed for a DH.83 Fox Moth and which used a reverse chassis geometry when compared with G-AIVW. She was successfully operated for several seasons from a disused gravel pit within hailing distance of Heathrow Airport by Leisure Sport accompanied by other waterborne types, included amongst which for site dressing were non flying replicas of famous pre-war racing seaplanes. The business was an early attempt to 'theme' a water orientated leisure facility, but a change of management saw all the marine aviation interests sold off and G-AOBX resumed her career on a conventional undercarriage.

Both G-AIVW and G-AOBX proved that the weak points on a Tiger Moth Seaplane were the front fuselage side frames and to prevent unnecessary damage the strength of these became the limiting factor when assessing whether the condition of the water was conducive to operations. Engine mounting bolts also required careful inspection after heavy loadings or when a seaplane alighted untidily with some degree of sideways component.

By 1980 Hannu Riihela's Finnish based 'Experimental' Tiger Moth OH-XLA, fitted with a 180hp Lycoming engine, had been placed on a set of GRP floats and struts for which much useful data had been supplied by Rollason Aircraft, the gear adding over 200lb to the empty weight. OH-XLA suffered from a rear C of G limit which restricted use of the luggage locker to little more than the carriage of mooring ropes, but these mostly were left attached to the front chassis struts and allowed to trail free and ready for instant deployment on touchdown.

With GRP floats the aircraft was operated at a maximum weight of 1,984lb and overload flight trials revealed nothing sinister at 2,050lb. Directional stability was found to be far from ideal when floats were attached and plans were prepared for the addition of a ventral fin but the aircraft was taken out of the water before the likely benefits resulting from such an experiment could be assessed and during the winter operated on skis instead.

The 180hp Lycoming engine fitted to Hannu Riihela's much modified Finnish Tiger Moth OH-XLA provided a phenomenal improvement in climb performance amongst much else, but after 30 years remains the only such conversion in the world. *Hannu Riihela*

Previously registered OH-ELA, a 1951 import from Great Britain, the rebuilt Tiger Moth was obliged to carry 'Experimental' identification OH-XLA from 1977 due to the major modifications incorporated, none of which was acknowledged by the British Design Authority. In addition to the Lycoming engine, some undercarriage components and electrics were sourced from a Beech Musketeer. *M J Hooks*

Lycoming powered Tiger Moth OH-XLA was configured for wheel and ski undercarriage, as a glider tug and lake hopping floatplane by her creator, Hannu Riihela, during his four years of operation following restoration. *Hannu Riihela*

Below: Blue sky, green trees, yellow Tiger Moth on a deep carpet of white snow. The ski tracks after landing appear to be only as long as the fuselage. Experimental Tiger Moth OH-XLA on a frozen lake in Finland. *Hannu Riihela*

In Canada where some outposts survived solely through communications and re-supply by aircraft, float equipped Tiger Moths found little favour before, during or after the war. One of the rare exponents of the Tiger Moth Seaplane was Watt Martin who in 1947 fitted a set of Short floats originally supplied for a DH.60M Moth, to DH.82C Tiger Moth CF-DGC (DHC1020). The aircraft had been sold from No 8 Service Flying Training School (SFTS) Moncton in 1946, with only 860 hours logged, to a civilian owner in Muskoka. Watt Martin bought the Seaplane himself in 1954 and kept her for the next ten years. By the summer of 1958 CF-DGC was on Edo 1835 floats with Jack Arnold at Brantford.

In 1950, DH.82C CF-CKW (DHC1636), was converted onto Edo floats at Mount Hope from where she was launched off the main runway from a purpose built dolly, a conventional operation in Seaplane circles but one requiring a long, hard runway. Watt Martin acquired the wreck of DH.82C CF-CKF (DHC1593), in 1966, an aircraft which had been damaged at Buttonville Airport during the passage of Hurricane Hazel. In between rebuilding and maintaining Moths for his customers, CF-CKF was returned to airworthiness by 1985, fitted with Edo 1835 floats and a standard wooden propeller in place of the more favoured Fairey Reed. Operated from Timmins, CF-CKF flew from numerous small lakes in the area to provide support for a film being shot on behalf of Expo 86 soon to be hosted in Vancouver.

In the hands of a skilled pilot Watt Martin demonstrated the ease with which a Tiger Moth Seaplane could be landed on lush grass, provided touchdown was completed with absolutely no hint of drift, when CF-CKF was positioned back to the workshops at Milton on 30 September 1985.

After airline captain Willie Gerdes moved from South Africa to live in England he was joined in 1981 by Tiger Moth ZS-BCU (85028), which he had owned since 1960. The aircraft was issued with the personalised registration G-ERDS in July 1994 and based at Lee on Solent. Willie Gerdes had long considered fitting floats and it was during his enforced stay in Rome in 1998 with engine problems when en-route to Australia that he met Stefano Rusconi who had access to a pair of Edo 1835 floats. A deal was done and the floats and chassis parts were delivered to England where, with the aid of a dummy front fuselage, all the necessary parts, aided by location of the correct drawings, were assembled. On her conventional undercarriage G-ERDS was flown to White Waltham where a trial fitting of the floats and beaching gear was completed ahead of weighing and a survey by the CAA. After the floats were replaced by the conventional gear she was returned to Lee on Solent to await an opportunity to make a test flight. On 12 December 2001 she became the first British registered Tiger Moth to employ Slick magnetos under a recently approved modification designed by Ed Clark in California.

Although none of the world's military air arms favoured the Tiger Moth as a seaplane trainer, since the early 1950s Watt Martin flew a number of DH.82C Tiger Moths on floats without incident. CF-CKF was spotted with a pair of floats originally designed for a DH.60 Moth, operating from Lake Puslinch, Ontario, in September 1985. *Jack McNulty*

At the end of the 1985 summer season, float equipped DH.82C Tiger Moth CF-CKF was flown to his hangar/workshop at Milton, Ontario, by Watt Martin in readiness for conversion to wheel or ski undercarriage. Wind conditions on 30 September were ideal for the floatplane to be landed on the grass without any sign of fuss, bother or incredulity on the part of the pilot. *Watt Martin*

Once the snow laden storms have passed through, the temporary exposure of clear blue skies, unlimited visibility and a stable air mass entice aviators aloft, provided the aeroplanes are properly shod. Watt Martin's DH.82C Tiger Moth CF-CKF in a blue and yellow colour scheme, February 1978. *Watt Martin*

Tiger Moth Seaplane G-ERDS on Edo 1835 floats taking off from Eagle's Nest in Florida in 2002. "After applying full power and holding the stick back the pilot waits for maximum rise. Now, with the stick neutral and the aircraft on the step she will fly off in this attitude at about 42mph." *Tom Beck*

G-ERDS was shipped to Florida just before Christmas 2001 where a number of local familiarisation trips were flown before the float chassis was fitted and she undertook a first thirty minute test flight on 20 February 2002, followed by another the following day. In April Willie Gerdes flew his seaplane to the "Sun 'n Fun splash in" at Lake Parker, a ninety minute flight via Jack Brown's seaplane base for fuel, where G-ERDS was awarded the prize for the best 'fabric covered seaplane'.

An unexpected addition to the floatplane fraternity was Tiger Moth N41DH (84734), an aircraft registered against the personal ownership of William Arthur Rollason in September 1946 before sale to the Netherlands only two months later and passage to the USA in 1971. N41DH was hangared at Amana Airfield, Iowa, during the severe flooding suffered by the American mid-west in the summer of 1993. In anticipation the Tiger Moth had been jacked up and when the hangar flooded to knee height only the lower halves of the mainwheels were left submerged in the invasive brown goo. By placing a long wooden beam under the fuselage, as parallel as possible with the wing leading edges, and borrowing a pair of styrofoam blocks from a local marina, then attaching an inflatable children's toy to the tailwheel, the Tiger Moth became buoyant. A security fence around the airport buildings blocked the direct route to high ground so the aircraft was floated a short distance down the main runway, around the fence, through a neighbour's back yard and out onto a dry street. As the mainwheels protruded a few inches below the flotation blocks, N41DH was 'beached' on sloping ground. The problem of high guard-rails on a local canal bridge was overcome by borrowing a flatbed truck from the municipal depot and winching the aircraft onto its back for the journey through the town to a suitable local highway. With no shortage of volunteers to stop traffic, N41DH took off from the temporary runway headed for higher ground safe from the wet.

INVERTED

To celebrate the 25th Anniversary of Louis Blériot's successful flight across the English Channel in 1909, Geoffrey Tyson flew DH.82 Tiger Moth G-ABUL (3107), from Lympne to Calais on 25 July 1934. With the aid of the 'de Havilland inverted system', the entire sixteen minute flight was made upside down, a celebration worthy of front page news. The 50th Anniversary of the Blériot crossing was marked in similar style but with less public adoration when Elwyn McAully flew Tiger Moth G-ANZZ (85834), inverted from Lympne to Le Touquet in June 1959. Perhaps the second of these anniversary flights was the more significant. Geoffrey Tyson was flying a relatively new aeroplane, surrounded by manufacturer's support and an inverted fuel and oil system which had been designed, manufactured, flight tested and developed by de Havilland specifically for the RAF.

In 1957, through the good offices and financial support of Norman Jones and his controlling interest in Rollason Aircraft, the Tiger Club was born. As a result of efforts to help British pilots compete more equally in top level aerobatic competition, there evolved the Super Tiger, complete with a re-incarnation of the manufacturer's tried and tested inverted system, but minus the massive industry and service support of pre-war days.

The 'inverted' system had been flown in Tiger Moth G-ANSH (86320), at Croydon in 1957. An otherwise standard aircraft operated by the Fairoaks Aero Club, another arm of Norman Jones' business interests, G-ANSH had crashed during an air race at Whitchurch in 1955 and was subsequently rebuilt by Rollason into a lightweight aircraft in a search for improved aerobatic performance. The inverted system was a straight copy made from the original de Havilland drawings but all the hardware, including the undercarriage mounted air pump, had to be won or manufactured. A description appeared in *The Aeroplane* on 7 June at the beginning of the 1957 display season:

Above and Right: In anticipation of severe flooding in Iowa in 1993, Tiger Moth N41DH was jacked up in her hangar and fitted with floatation devices. After the deluge she was navigated to high ground. The top of the airport security fence is just visible in this picture. The recovery team was prepared to tow the Tiger Moth with the canoe if the water proved too deep for their waders. After N41DH reached higher ground she was flown off a public highway. *John R Tiffany*

The second of the Super Tigers for the Tiger Club was G-ANZZ, *'The Archbishop'*. After a long period of inactivity in 2013 she was converted back to a standard two seater for a new career as a joyrider.

"The system is based on the use of a small pressurised fuel tank in the front cockpit. A small Rotherham airscrew-driven air pump mounted on the undercarriage struts provides a pressurised air feed to the tank and to the rear cockpit. At the cockpit the air supply again splits, one branch passing to atmosphere via a Vickers on/off cock and the other to a pressure relief valve. With the Vickers cock closed, the fuel tank is pressurised to 2½ psi, at which value a relief valve starts to blow off. A pressure gauge, tapped from the tank, shows the tank pressure.

With the tank pressurised, fuel is forced along the third tapping from the tank, to a standard Tiger Moth on/off cock mounted adjacent to the engine. For inverted flight, this is opened from the cockpit, allowing the fuel to proceed to the carburettor where it is injected into the choke section via a special metering jet.

For the lubrication system, arrangements have to be made to scavenge the oil which drains to the crankcase top cover with the engine inverted. This is achieved by drilling the top cover webs to allow the oil to drain to the rear of the engine where an additional oil pump has been fitted. This re-directs the oil into the inlet of the main oil feed pump, the oil in this instance thus completely by-passing the oil tank. The crank-case breather pipe, which previously had been fitted where the additional oil pump is now situated, has therefore been repositioned to the front of the crankcase. The oil tank vent is also modified to use a longer pipe, such that it vents to atmosphere at a point 'higher' than the tank oil level when inverted."

Identified only by his initials, author Ken Fulton, a graduate of the de Havilland Aeronautical Technical School, had been flown in G-ANSH by Peter Langstone, a pilot contracted by Rollason Aircraft to complete the trials. Following the technical description, Ken Fulton briefly outlined his experience:

"During our flight, three inverted runs were made, the longest of these being for just under two minutes. On such occasions, the phrase 'time flies' seems less than apposite, and the second hand on one's watch appears to take its lead from the minute hand. In the welcome process of rolling out, the engine procedure is the reverse of the preparation for inversion, except that again the throttle has to be closed an amount to obviate the possibility of overspeeding."

What Ken Fulton's dispatch did not reveal was that during the three inverted passes fuel leaking from the additional tank strapped to the floor between his legs dripped constantly, rather in the manner of a Chinese water torture, but with even more sinister prospects.

In spite of all the design and testing the pilots who flew G-ANSH in serious competition were critical of the inverted system which they regarded as clumsy and difficult and distracting to operate. Placarded instructions were carried as a reminder of the essential sequence:

Ensure mixture (altitude) lever is in rear position.
Run engine at 1,900rpm or above.
Move change-over cock to vertical position, wait until engine misfires then move mixture lever to forward position.
When changing rpm keep throttle lever ahead of mixture lever during both closing and opening.

The selection of the Normal System could be achieved at any engine speed simply by moving the change-over cock back to the horizontal position.

It was also the contention of some that however much effort had been made to reduce weight, the aircraft was seriously underpowered for satisfactory execution of some of the advanced manoeuvres increasingly expected to be within a competitor's basic ability.

David Phillips, who flew G-ANSH in the 1957 Lockheed Trophy competition at Baginton, was faced with the prospect of attempting an outside loop but apprehension caused him to forget to tighten his shoulder harness before he pushed forward and he duly lifted off his seat. It may have been the tiniest fraction of an inch but the sensation, even to an experienced pilot like David Phillips, momentarily caused him to believe he was in imminent danger of involuntarily leaving the cockpit.

Bill Tomkins, a farmer from Apethorpe in Northamptonshire, had owned a civil registered Gloster Gamecock between the wars and entered the second Lockheed Aerobatic Trophy competition in July 1956 in his modified Tiger Moth G-AHRC. Believed to have been ex RAF T6064 (84555), there was some doubt about her real identity, confused even further in 1954 when she had been repaired after turning over when being started. The damaged fuselage of 'G-AHRC' was spotted in the famous Coley's scrapyard near Heathrow in May 1955 by which time she was airborne again in somebody else's clothes.

G-AHRC's inverted fuel system was quite simple: the aircraft was modified to accept a four gallon petrol tank attached to the cockpit side of the front bulkhead from which a pair of SU electric pumps provided fuel to an additional jet in the carburettor. During the modification programme at Sywell, and in an effort to improve the qualities of inverted flight, extended leading edges were fitted to the undersurface of both upper mainplanes between the root end and the front interplane strut, together with revised symmetrical leading edges on both lower wings,

Bill Tomkins' freestyle sequence flown in the eliminating rounds of the Lockheed Trophy was later described as "a semi aerobatic display of rock and roll flying," which was not good enough for him to qualify for the finals. In 1968, following her return to standard configuration, G-AHRC was sold to Charles Boddington, a pilot renowned for the quality of his aerobatic flying and precision in front of the film cameras and a member of the Barnstormers Flying Circus. G-AHRC was one of four aircraft travelling home in loose formation across the Irish Sea from Dublin in conditions of low cloud and poor visibility in August 1971 when she stalled off a tight turn and spun into the sea off Anglesey when attempting to avoid one of the aircraft accompanying her. The wrecked Tiger Moth quickly sank but Barnstormer pilot Jack Morton and his passenger released themselves and were circled by the other aircraft until they were rescued six minutes after the impact by a helicopter scrambled from Valley.

SUPER TIGER

The Rollason team's experience with the inverted system and lightweight but otherwise standard G-ANSH was developed into the first of a quartet of aircraft which quickly became known as a 'Super Tiger', G-APDZ (83699), in April 1958. The Super Tiger airframe was that of a standard aircraft considerably cleaned up, most noticeably by removal of the centre section fuel tank which was repositioned to the front cockpit and faired over. The leading edge slats and hinge mechanism were removed, rear cockpit door reprofiled and glued into the closed position, and a tiny windscreen substituted for the standard heavy brass frame.

Although a hard leading edge was not immediately applied to improve the contour of the wing the quartet of Super Tiger aircraft were fitted with modified wings at some stage although their eventual withdrawal from serious competitive aerobatics meant that damaged wings were usually replaced with standard units. Unlike the Tiger Club's other workhorses lightweight synthetic fabric covering was used, and the elevator surface area increased by 10%. Additional power was provided by installation of a 145hp Gipsy Major IC engine turning a Fairey Reed, fixed pitch metal propeller, after which the undercarriage-mounted, independent air pump was deleted.

In all other respects, apart perhaps from the leather stirrups attached to the rudder pedals, the 'Super Tiger' was pure Tiger Moth and remained registered so as a basic 'type'. G-APDZ was named *The Bishop* in deference to the Club's Chief Flying Instructor, C Nepean Bishop, 'Bish', still devoted to light aeroplanes after thirty years and thousands of circuits as a wartime flying instructor in Southern Rhodesia. *The Bishop* was followed by a trio all taking an ecclesiastical line: G-ANZZ (85834), in 1959 was almost inevitably *The Archbishop*, followed by two aircraft in 1965, G-AOAA (85908), *The Deacon* and G-ANMZ (85588), *The Canon*. G-AOAA, the longest survivor in Super Tiger configuration, was eventually outclassed in her aerobatic proclivities and spent most of her last operational seasons as a hired-out glider tug. Following a landing accident at Redhill in 1989 G-AOAA was acquired in 1990 by one of her former pilots, Roger Brookhouse. The aircraft was involved in a number of frustrated attempts at restoration but by 2013 had moved into the care of Chiltern Classic Flight at Turweston to undergo a thorough survey prior to the commencement of a programme to return her to her original Super Tiger specification.

As a prelude to the 1960 World Aerobatic Championships in Bratislava, the Tiger Club suggested that it might prepare a trio of Super Tigers which they referred to as 'Bishop Tiger Moths', and offer each of six candidate pilots fifty hours' aerobatic flight training. Following selection the three best pilots would be considered to constitute the nucleus of an official British Team. The total cost of the exercise including positioning and maintenance of the three 'Bishop' aeroplanes was estimated at £5,000 and in May 1960 a correspondent with *The Aeroplane* wrote: "The Tiger Club poses the question where the money should come from without suggesting any possible answers!"

Following such initiative the Club must have been considerably disheartened to read that the Czech Government was offering contestants the opportunity to lease Zlin Z.226 trainers at a cost of about £200 for ten days, inclusive of fuel, servicing, insurance, practice and competition flying. A trio of British pilots did participate in the competition with a 'Bishop' Tiger Moth, but were totally outclassed and managed to fill the last three places in the list of twenty nine international competitors.

The first of the Super Tigers which appeared in 1957 was G-APDZ, 'The Bishop'. Although every bit a Tiger Moth this shot illustrates the clean line of the fuselage, top wings and cabane. *deHMC Archive*

A rare photograph of three Super Tigers displaying identical colour layout flying a tied-together formation at White Waltham. In choppy conditions the trio experienced a tape-break for the first time; although most demanding on pilot concentration all other shows were completed successfully. *via Lewis Benjamin*

Super Tiger G-AOAA *'The Deacon'* was the last of the quartet to remain operational. She could be flown as a single seater or, with some adjustment, a two seat aircraft. Note the pick-up brackets for the 'Stand on Wing' rig near the leading edge of the centre section. *deHMC Archive*

Super Tiger G-ANMZ *'The Canon'* was immortalised in print when, with Lewis Benjamin on board, she was much photographed as she spun into the ground from low level during an air display at Sywell in July 1963. Repaired with Rollason magic she was fatally injured when she crashed at Challock during a glider tugging sortie in May 1969. *deHMC Archive*

The special tank-carrying rig attached to the centre section pick up points of a Super Tiger, used when the front seat tank was removed. The fuel on/off cock was operated by string which was fed into the rear cockpit: two strands for fuel on and a single strand for off. *deHMC Archive*

In order to carry a lightweight passenger in a sling seat rigged in the front cockpit where it displaced the fuel tank, Super Tiger G-AOAA was fitted with a standard tank on a rig fixed to pick up points for the Stand on Wing platform in the old centre section. It was fairly crude but practical and effective. *Richard Riding*

Peter Jackson and his brother David completed the overhaul of their Tiger Moth G-ANZU (3583), in 1974, one of the small batch of civil aircraft purchased off the Hatfield line by an animated Air Ministry in 1937, allocated serial L6938 and converted to the contemporary military specification. With the aircraft Peter Jackson became an accomplished racing and aerobatic pilot and recognised how basic improvements could be made with the use of modern technology. Using the resources and skills within his company, Specialised Mouldings Limited, whose output ranged from bodies for Formula 1 racing cars to static display replicas of fighter jets, each requiring great precision, Peter Jackson built up a 'new' Tiger Moth, G-BPAJ, based on the core of G-AOIX (83472). All tubular frameworks were protected internally and externally and the use of composite materials for engine cowlings, seats, fuselage deckings, fairings and fillets resulted in lighter weight components with a hard, glass-smooth finish impervious to wear, cracking and corrosion. What became known as the 'High Technology Tiger Moth' was flown by CAA test pilot Bob Cole from Stukeley Airfield in Huntingdon on 11 June 1991 and immediately qualified for a C of A as a standard Tiger Moth.

In view of the non-committal opinions aired over several years by senior aerodynamicists when asked about the degradation in performance suffered as a result of sweeping the wings during gestation of the first Tiger Moth without realigning the R.A.F. Section 15 (modified) ribs, an Australian owner, Les Penna, took the opportunity to investigate. During the construction of a Tiger Moth airframe made from all new parts in 1970, VH-ULC (LP.5), "only the instruments and engine had ever flown before," he said, Les Penna built wings with ribs fixed parallel to the longitudinal axis, a job he had been contemplating for some considerable time. After forty years of speculation many of the questions could now be answered but after all the effort the greatest benefit was gained, he considered, as a result of improving the drag and reducing the weight by leaving off the 20lb encumbrance of the leading edge slats and associated operating mechanisms.

The aircraft was slightly out of rig and had flown only about twenty hours when VH-ULC was acquired from the Penna estate by David Cordy in 2006, an owner who had his own views after experiencing such a fundamental change to one of the Tiger Moth's most debated features:

The skeletal fuselage of Peter Jackson's High Technology Tiger Moth G-BPAJ which incorporated cowlings, deckings and a miscellany of other non-structural parts made from modern synthetic materials in the form of Kevlar and carbon fibre. Metal parts were protected with finishes resistant to almost any known attacker. *Specialised Mouldings*

In 1970 Les Penna built a new Tiger Moth from all original parts and, as a matter of curiosity to judge any advantages in performance, manufactured wings with the ribs aligned with the centreline of the aircraft. His own opinion after flights tests was that the biggest improvement was made by his decision not to fit slats but current owner David Cordy disagrees. *Les Penna*

Peter Jackson flying his High Technology Tiger Moth G-BPAJ at the International Moth Rally at Woburn Abbey in 2006. *Philip Stevens*

It would be hard to tell the difference between a Tiger Moth built by the de Havilland Aircraft Company at Mascot and Les Penna's creation from all new Tiger Moth spare parts. Under the fabric covering even the unique realignment of the wing ribs would not be immediately obvious. The current owner of VH-ULC claims the aircraft is substantially faster than aircraft with wings of conventional construction. *David Welch*

In the summer of 1998, New York based Mike Maniatis fitted spats to the mainwheels of his black and silver Tiger Moth N9410. The spats add an aristocratic air although no great advantage in performance. Their addition to the airframe was a mere trifle to Mike Maniatis who has also built a DH.71 Tiger Moth and a DH.60GIII Moth Major from scratch. *Mike Maniatis*

"I bought VH-ULC after I wore out Tiger Moth VH-AIP. The new aeroplane is fitted with a 145hp Gipsy Major 1C engine and a 5ft 1in pitch cruising propeller as opposed to my previous 130hp engine and 4ft 11in propeller. The wings do not have ply leading edges and are not fitted with slats. She cruises in the high eighties compared with VH-AIP's high seventies and climbs like a homesick angel. It is difficult to know what contribution the wings alone make to her performance given the other deviations from 'standard' and the fact that she is a very clean airframe. However, I have flown a number of other Tiger Moths over the years including some fitted with 145hp engines and none has seemed as fast as VH-ULC. She also hangs on when landing, more like an aircraft with slats deployed. I suspect that the realigned ribs do make a difference to overall performance."

TNS 32

Tiger Moth VH-TMK, an aircraft of uncertain origin, was flying an aerobatic routine over Wellard, some thirty five miles south of Perth, Western Australia, on 28 February 1998 when the starboard upper wing failed and the aircraft crashed at Mundijong. The repercussions of the accident were felt almost immediately when the Design Authority responsible for the Tiger Moth, British Aerospace (BAe), after consultation with interested parties including close association with the de Havilland Moth Club's Technical Support Group, published Technical News Sheet 32 Issue 1, which introduced an interim prohibition on aerobatics and spinning by any Moth aircraft type previously authorised for such manoeuvres, pending the results of the accident investigation.

In Australia the enquiry became the responsibility of the Bureau of Air Safety Investigation (BASI) conducted with the fullest co-operation from BAe and whose report was published in mid-1999. Their investigations revealed that VH-TMK had been damaged in 1991 and again in 1993 and the report was critical of the standard and degree of inspection and repair and subsequent failure to diagnose and correct bad flying characteristics. Although there was no logbook record a replacement spar, which may have been distressed due to long exposure to very high temperatures whilst in storage, had been fitted into the wing at some time. Post crash inspection indicated that the front spar had been significantly weakened around the interplane strut attachment point by the effects of fungal decay and a partially de-bonded doubler. It was considered that additional contributory factors may have been poor rigging, an egg-shaped loop flown at lower than normal aerobatic height which may have resulted in the pilot applying a higher g-force to effect recovery and the possibility that the leading edge slats were not locked closed.

The Bureau reported that it was looking into a perceived safety deficiency involving the airworthiness of wooden structural components in passenger carrying aircraft. "This deficiency relates to the quality assurance, repair and on-going maintenance of wooden structure aircraft," it said.

TNS 32 was re-issued (Issue 2) and introduced detailed visual inspection requirements for the wooden wing and tail unit structures of the biplane and strut-braced monoplane Moth types. Enhanced access provision was added to the fabric covering schemes to facilitate such inspections. Satisfactory findings enabled reinstatement of aerobatic and spinning clearances where applicable to type but in all cases an ongoing three yearly major inspection interval was imposed.

After in-depth negotiations between the de Havilland Moth Club and British Aerospace, soon to become BAE Systems, it was agreed that a new company should be established in 2000, de Havilland Support Ltd. (DHSL), with a brief to deliver Continuing Airworthiness services as the formal Type Design Organisation (TDO) for civil-certificated de Havilland legacy aeroplanes. The company would be appropriately staffed and managed and focussed on their appointed task without outside distraction.

In order to review and possibly alleviate what many Moth owners considered were draconian measures introduced by BAe's TNS 32 it was necessary to compile a file of evidence based on international experience spread over several inspection cycles. In December 2008 DHSL published TNS 32 at Issue 3:

> "The worldwide results from ten years of such inspections have now been reviewed by de Havilland Support Ltd. It was concluded that a fixed frequency and scope of re-inspection is incompatible with the diverse restoration standards, styles of usage, climatic and hangarage conditions that are experienced in practice. TNS 32 has, therefore, been revised at Issue 3 to promote an evidence-based approach to the depth of structural inspection. At the same time, improved guidance is provided to help in the identification of damage or deterioration in the wooden primary structure of Moth aircraft."

Prior to the establishment of de Havilland Support Ltd., with their expert staff housed together with all appropriate and original technical records in historic facilities at Duxford, as a result of incidents in the field the Tiger Moth airframe was subject to two major changes. The old design of Sutton harness was subjected to a maximum calendar life and had to be replaced by an alternative approved system on a regular basis and the life of fuselage tie rods, the threaded ends of which could be damaged by heavy landings, were aligned to a schedule of hours flown or calendar dates which triggered a mandatory replacement, a major engineering task. With an aging aeroplane now under closer scrutiny these were the first ever changes which introduced lifed airframe parts.

In most countries of the world civil registered Tiger Moths were operated under the rules and regulations determined by the nationally administered scheme for the issue of a Certificate of Airworthiness, in almost every case taking their lead from British approvals. In the USA owners were offered a choice between a C of A in the 'Standard' category or in the more flexible but limiting 'Experimental' category. With no Tiger Moth ever certificated in the USA pre-war and, with an increasing rate of acquisition from the 1960s, to allow US registered aircraft to qualify for a Standard Category C of A it was necessary for the authorities to issue a Type Approval. This is often a long and expensive process with all costs borne by the first applicant. In the case of the Tiger Moth all technical records were available and in 1969 an American Type Approval was issued in the name of film actor Cliff Robertson who had imported three British built Tiger Moths acquired in England in 1965. The US authorities demanded a separate Approval for aircraft of Australian origin which was later issued to Leo Gay acting as import agent for aircraft being shipped by the Sydney based Hendon Aeroplane Company. Although several Canadian DH.82C Tiger Moths were registered in the USA no owner ever applied for a Type Approval and the DH.82C has remained in the 'Experimental' category.

Apart from the USA and due to the availability of technical data and support through approved organisations from the original designers, via company amalgamations to the formation of de Havilland Support Ltd. in 2000, Tiger Moths of British, Australian and New Zealand manufacture were obliged to operate to the standards of a Certificate of Airworthiness. In Australia the Tiger Moth airframes assembled post-war from unused component parts were accepted as new aeroplanes with individual build numbers allocated by their constructors and issued with Cs of A.

In Great Britain the airworthiness authorities took a different view. When Wally Cubitt of Norfolk Aerial Spraying wanted to construct a Tiger Moth from all original parts in the early 1980s he was advised that the issue of a C of A would not be possible and provided that each step of construction and all parts used were scrutinised and approved by British Aerospace, the resulting aircraft would be allowed to operate only on a 'Permit to Fly', as was Concorde in her early days. The issue of a Permit would influence her maintenance programme and place limitations on her use. The result was a Tiger Moth registered G-BJZF in March 1982 (NAS-100), which was almost immediately offered for sale at a premium price in a belief that the Permit was more valuable than a C of A, and she eventually moved to a new base at a centre of Tiger Moth activity at Sywell when the price differential was recognised as invalid.

Australian Tiger Moth VH-KRW (LES-1), was sold to a new owner in Great Britain in 1998 and was delivered to Tilbury Docks in a container in August 1999. Although the aircraft, a post war construction from new parts, had arrived with a valid Export C of A, the British authorities refused to offer anything but a Permit and the aircraft was subjected to a comprehensive and costly overhaul spread over three years.

Above: G-BJZF was constructed from all-original Tiger Moth parts by Wally Cubitt under the tight supervision of both British Aerospace, inheritor of de Havilland records, and the CAA. Subsequent paint schemes did not appeal to most enthusiasts of the marque, nor the 'go-faster' style of registration. In 2014 the aircraft was sold to a new lady owner in the USA. *Marcus Lodge*

Left: One of a trio of DH.82A Tiger Moths once owned by actor Cliff Robertson whose initiative resulted in the aircraft qualifying for Type Approval in the USA, N524R was operational in California carrying an impressive avionics suite and a strobe mounted on the rear decking. The aircraft was sold at auction in 2013, acquired by a museum in Anaheim and grounded. *via Bill Lusk*

In 1959 G-PWBE was constructed from all-new Tiger Moth parts by Lawrence Engineering of Camden, NSW, Australia where she was permitted to operate on a Certificate of Airworthiness, a fact denied by the CAA when the aircraft was purchased by a British owner in 1999. She was instead an early candidate for a Permit to Fly, a category of airworthiness which was eventually opened to all British registered Tiger Moths as the result of a major policy change in 2012. *David Welch*

Built from unairworthy parts and carrying the letters G-MAZY in remembrance of team leader Harry Hodgson's late wife, this Tiger Moth was assembled by the Cotswold Aviation Society for display at the Newark Air Museum. The whole of the port side has been left without fabric to permit visitors to inspect the structure. *Harry Hodgson*

The replica Tiger Moth built by Darci Assis in Brazil and painted in military colours with serial 2-1-2 is displayed at the Brazilian Museum of Naval Aviation. *Darci Assis*

Following a major change in policy by de Havilland Support and the British CAA, an agreement was reached that allowed, subject to certain conditions, British registered Tiger Moths to be operated on the Permit system from 31 March 2012 but with the option of maintaining a C of A. As most of the subject aircraft were privately owned and non commercial many migrated to the Permit, balancing the limitations against what they anticipated to be a less bureaucratic and more amenable system of administration.

REPLICAS

With a glut of tired old Tiger Moths on the world market post-war, the incidence of their demise at bonfire parties and similar celebrations was only to be expected. When genuine demand began to rise again and outstrip supply values increased to a level at which every hangar roof was scoured for the treasure that might have been long abandoned in the rafters.

The refinement of microlights quickly led to an American designed biplane, the Fisher R80 Tiger Moth, described in the company brochure as having "the historic looks of the Tiger Moth. An 80% replica of yesterday's aircraft with today's technology."

At Ivanovo in the former Soviet Union, Sergei Mazny built a Tiger Moth entirely from wood. A skilled model maker and regular supplier of 1/10 scale productions for the Soviet Air Force Museum, Sergei Mazny constructed the whole aircraft with the aid of magazine articles, photographs and some sketchy plans gleaned from aero-modelling journals and papers. Last heard of in 1993 the airframe was substantially complete with a Walter Minor M332 engine ready for installation and the builder anxious to visit western owners to glean first hand practical data.

Recognising the need for conservation of airworthy parts, in 1997 Harold Carlaw built from scratch a full size DH.82C 'Tiger Moth lookalike' using commercial materials, intended as a children's plaything at touring country fairs. When not on the road, the 'Tiger Moth' was exhibited at the military museum at Campbellford, Ontario.

Unlike the authorities in Uruguay, in 1947 the Brazilian Air Force had no qualms in donating its remaining Tiger Moth stock to the civil clubs and by the mid-sixties PP-DLL (3329), was registered to the Clube de Planadores Albatroz at Porto Alegre where flying instructor Darcy Assis maintained her in airworthy condition using parts donated from other aircraft. In 1973 PP-DLL was transferred to the Aerospace Museum at Campo dos Afonsos in Rio de Janeiro and in 1987 she was re-registered PP-ZTM and returned to flight at Osório where she was badly damaged but lack of funds prevented her restoration.

In 1969 at the request of the Brazilian Navy Museum, Darcy Assis began the construction of a replica Tiger Moth with the aid of data and manuals supplied over several years from Hatfield. The project incorporated a number of genuine Tiger Moth parts acquired for the purpose and was fitted with one of the small number of Gipsy Major engines manufactured by Alfa Romeo. She was completed in 1998 after which Mr Assis volunteered that he would consider building a batch of airframes for museum static display but in May 2005 he suffered a heart attack and died on board a commercial flight. Painted in Brazilian Navy colours and carrying serial number 2-1-2 the replica aircraft is hangared at the naval base at Pedro da Aldeia, eighty miles east of Rio de Janeiro, where she is used as a static exhibit on ceremonial occasions and was a feature of the 96th anniversary celebrations of the Service held at Cabo Frio in August 2012.

The remains of the damaged PP-ZTM and a pool of spare parts were sold by the Assis family and currently the aircraft is under restoration to airworthy condition by Jose Fonseca in Maringa.

CHAPTER NINETEEN

The Grand Tourists

Given that the brochure figure for ultimate range of a Gipsy Major powered DH.82A Tiger Moth Landplane is 279 statute miles, it is perhaps all the more remarkable that, mostly post-war, the vehicle chosen with which to undertake long distance commemorative flights should be a Tiger Moth. But perhaps not! In another age many pilots would have flown a DH.60 Moth modified for the purpose for the majority of the many flights linking Great Britain with all parts of the Empire: Africa, India, Australia and New Zealand. Post war almost all the en-route servicing facilities established by the de Havilland Company had disappeared and some international boundaries had been redrawn and now displayed notices which invited travellers to 'keep out' or 'go around!'

In the late Twentieth Century there was still adventure in flying a vintage biplane which was already fifty years older than most of the aircraft which had pioneered the trails. It was an affordable and meaningful challenge to fly against the elements, a task requiring physical and mental preparation and courage not to mention patience and diplomacy to cope with plans increasingly frustrated by bureaucratic reluctance or indifference. Mere delivery flights within the continental masses of Australia and North America have spawned tales of adventure and grit and aircraft not modified for long distance flying have required frequent refuelling stops and, in an age of change, careful route and logistical planning.

A trio of Tiger Moths flying over Victoria Falls in April 2011, the ultimate goal of the Botswana Moth Safari which began from Krugersdorp in South Africa and involved six Tiger Moths, a Hornet Moth and supporting cast. *via Courtney Watson*

Tiger Moth G-ANRF (83748), had once belonged to Air Commodore Allen Wheeler while still a serving officer at Boscombe Down. He used the aeroplane to commute between there, where flight research probed daily at the frontiers of man's knowledge, and Old Warden, where Allen Wheeler was Aviation Trustee of The Shuttleworth Collection, a unique flying museum of yesterday's technology. In December 1974 G-ANRF was acquired by a farmer's son from East Sussex. As an English Electric Lightning pilot with 56(F) Squadron RAF, Flt Lt David Cyster was able to sample both ends of the flying spectrum. During a tour as an instructor on Hawker Hunters at Valley he conceived the idea of a Bert Hinkler commemorative flight to Australia. In some secrecy, G-ANRF was modified to accept extra fuel and oil tanks, radio, pilot comforters and other equipment considered necessary by the authorities. Much of the preparation was completed by Basil Carlin at Barton and G-ANRF was teased out briefly at Valley before positioning to the British Aerospace Harrier flight test aerodrome at Dunsfold in Surrey.

Nagging fuel leaks and last minute electrical problems were cured by British Aerospace engineers who worked throughout the night. In spite of the frost and fog which enveloped the whole of southern England and the near continent, David Cyster was able to take-off on schedule early on the morning of Tuesday, 7 February 1978, flight planning direct to Marseille. The seventy nine gallons of petrol on board raised the endurance of G-ANRF to 10.5 hours, assuming that the tripled oil capacity was sufficient.

Fifty years after the birth of the Gipsy engine, it was left to an American engineer and Moth owner, Ed Clark, to develop a piston

David Cyster boarding Tiger Moth G-ANRF at Dunsfold before dawn on 7 February 1978, destination Australia. *via BAE Systems*

Below: On a foggy, frosty morning, 7 February 1978, David Cyster taxies out at Dunsfold prior to taking off for Marseille and on to Australia. *Philip Birtles*

Bottom: The Royal Air Force PR machine ensured the world was kept advised of Flight Lieutenant David Cyster's progress on his flight to Australia but it was pure chance that his arrival in Bahrain coincided with that of the scheduled British Airways' Concorde. *via David Cyster*

David Cyster taxies G-ANRF in to a tumultuous welcome at the Qantas Engineering Base at Kingsford Smith Airport, Mascot, NSW, on 22 March 1978 at the end of his flight from England, the first ever to be achieved in a Tiger Moth. *Neville Parnell*

ring system which reduced the engine's unkindly 'dripsy' reputation and factually prodigious thirst for oil to almost nothing at all. Perhaps more than any other single modification, the reduction in oil consumption opened up whole new areas for exploitation whilst restoring the ultimate endurance to the carriage of maximum fuel.

Although David Cyster's flight to Australia was in tribute to his hero Bert Hinkler, and undertaken in a private capacity, the strength of the RAF's publicity machine ensured that regular media coverage kept the world advised of Flt Lt Cyster's progress until the aircraft arrived safely in Darwin on 11 March, officially greeted from a watching Lockheed C-130 Hercules 21,000ft above. Eleven days later, demonstrating the size of the continent, *Headwind* (a name coined by the media and not recognised by the owner), touched down at the old Mascot Aerodrome, now Sydney's Kingsford Smith Airport, at the end of her epic voyage, the first Tiger Moth ever to fly from England to Australia.

G-ANRF returned to Great Britain as air cargo and following a number of air display appearances in 1978 to satisfy contractual obligations to sponsors the Tiger Moth was flown back to Barton for re-conversion to standard configuration. Following engine overhaul by Peter Franklin at White Waltham G-ANRF, crewed by David Cyster and his wife Cherry, was declared winner of the de Havilland Moth Club's *Famous Grouse Moth Rally*, Hatfield to Strathallan, in July 1979. *Headwind's* Australia flight and the Famous Grouse victory were both well covered in classic BBC Television documentary films. In recognition of Shell's association with the Australia flight, on the 20th anniversary of the epic G-ANRF was the central feature of the Shell exhibition stand at the 1998 Farnborough Air Show.

Tiger Moth G-ASET (86247), an aircraft owned in England by Dr Jeremy Johnston emigrated with him to Vancouver in 1972. As CF-FDQ the aircraft was aerobatted and toured extensively, aided by a Rollason installed long range tank and inverted fuel system. A growing family necessitated replacement of the Tiger Moth by a classic Beech Staggerwing and in 1984 86247 became N775NL, a personalisation of her original RAF serial NL775, following sale to Alan Lapidus in New York. The delivery flight which involved crossing the Rocky Mountains at 13,000ft was successfully accomplished by the new owner with Gerry Schwam, Chairman of the American Moth Club, acting as navigator, and also generated some impressive statistics: 3,000 statute miles covered in thirty six flying hours and twenty six stops to uplift thirty six quarts of oil and 270 gallons of fuel.

Long range fuel tanks had been a standard option on Tiger Moths since the earliest days of the Persian exports from Stag Lane and, usually, were tailored to fit under the top decking (cowl) between the front cockpit instrument panel and the engine bulkhead. Fuel was transferred by hand-operated 'wobble pump' to the standard tank in the centre section from where it was fed to the engine by gravity. Due to the distances involved when routinely flying in Australia, many aircraft based there acquired long range tanks at some time in their early civilian life assuming none was fitted during their military service. One pilot operating in Victoria had a shock soon after take-off when he discovered flames licking round his right boot and he subsequently discovered that the fabric covering around the starboard lower wing root and adjacent fuselage frame had been burned away. The aircraft had recently acquired a long range tank and the fuel vent had been positioned close to a stack exhaust. With great presence of mind the pilot immediately pumped fuel into the main tank to prevent further venting and extinguished the flames by diving at 120kts.

Morris-built Tiger Moth 86069, an ex-Indian aircraft sold to Canada in 1972, was registered N6353 the following year and rebuilt in Massachusetts, remaining in the state until 1987 when she was sold to Bud Molloy in Texas. The hilarious tale of her delivery as recounted by pilot Bob Remonte ended with a few vital statistics: 1,885 statute miles; twenty six hours flight time; six days and twenty six quarts of oil. Through the international network of the de Havilland Moth Club, member Arthur Whitlock realised that 86069 was the one time VT-ARQ, the aircraft in which he had flown

Wearing blue and white chequerboard markings to illustrate her one time attachment to 19(F) Squadron RAF when operating Gloster Meteor F.4s from Church Fenton in 1951, DH.82A Tiger Moth C-FFDQ emigrated to Canada with owner Dr Jeremy Johnston in 1972 and was aerobatted extensively until a growing family necessitated her replacement in 1984 by a Beech Staggerwing. *via Jeremy Johnston*

An illustration which defines a new meaning to the terms 'minimum safe altitude' and 'having faith in the donkey': Neil Davidson flying his DH.82C Tiger Moth CF-COR overhead the Rocky Mountains whilst operating out of Marysville, British Columbia in 2000. *via Neil Davidson*

Wearing her ex-RAF serial on the fuselage and US civil registration on her rudder, Tiger Moth N6353 was registered in India and Canada before sale to the USA in 1973. Owner Bud Molloy permitted Arthur Whitlock to fly her in April 1997, fifty years after his first solo in her in India. *Bud Malloy*

Airborne from Motueka on 17 January 1988, Boyd Munro and his Tiger Moth prize, ZK-BLQ, en route to Auckland during the first leg of their mostly overwater delivery flight from New Zealand to Sydney, Australia. *John King*

his first solo at Madras on 17 March 1947. Courtesy of the new owner Arthur Whitlock, by now a retired airline captain, flew 86069 again on 14 April 1997 and entered the *Guinness Book of Records, Aircraft Facts and Feats*, having created a world record in consideration of fifty years between solo flights in the same aircraft.

In order to celebrate the Golden Jubilee of Christchurch International Airport, New Zealand, in 1987, a committee was formed to organise an air race from Singapore to Christchurch. Advertised as the 'The Last Great Air Race', contestants were expected to cross the line during a spectacular air show. First prize was notified as a fully restored Tiger Moth, quoted to be worth 'around $NZ45,000'. From the allocated prize fund the committee purchased ZK-BLQ (84120), which many observers believed was bought at too high a price considering its poor condition, leaving very little resource to improve it. Registration ZK-PDL was allocated in February 1987 in deference to the main sponsors, PDL Industries, and a former de Havilland engineer, Charlie Liddell, refurbished the aircraft which was painted white and handed over to Christchurch dignitaries at a ceremony at Hobsonville. Flown by John MacDonald, ZK-PDL then began an exhaustive publicity tour which included dropping 2,000 tennis balls over South Bagley Park on 12 March, part of the 'PDL Goldair Big Prize Drop' when collected balls were redeemable against free gifts.

The Air Race itself was the subject of much controversy, the prize being awarded to Boyd Munro from Australia who had entered and flown a 'Panther Navajo'. The prize aircraft was registered in his name on 15 January 1988, reverting to the original letters, ZK-BLQ. Following meticulous preparations, which included provision for an additional sixty four gallons of petrol and four gallons of oil accommodated in tanks in the front cockpit. The aircraft was flown home to Australia in six sectors starting on 17 January, the last three of which involved long crossings of the Tasman Sea: Te Kao to Norfolk Island, 456nm; Norfolk Island to Lord Howe Island 482nm and Lord Howe Island to Sydney, 490nm. For company the Tiger Moth was shadowed during the entire journey by Boyd Munro's own circling Piper Navajo. In case of engine failure the plan was for the pilot to bale out and descend into the sea by parachute from which predicament he would be picked up by rescue craft, rather than risk ditching the biplane with its fixed undercarriage. Exhaustive enquiries around the world had failed to discover a pilot with knowledge or experience of ditching a Tiger Moth in the ocean. Safe landfall in Australia was celebrated by a quick inspection of the underside of Sydney Harbour Bridge.

Following a pleasant social evening in Johannesburg, a group of Tiger Moth owners, pilots, engineers and supporters picked up on a

The only Tiger Moth currently registered in Botswana, A2-PIX took part in the 2011 Moth Safari to Victoria Falls flown by Brett and Stan Warren. The aircraft was part of the consignment delivered from India to England in 1979, and resold to South Africa for rebuild in 1999.
via Courtney Watson

casual suggestion and organised a flight of three Tiger Moths into the Okavango Delta region of Botswana, setting off in April 1988. Supported for the outward journey by two other aircraft carrying supplies and press reporters on behalf of the sponsors, and a cross country vehicle loaded with emergency fuel stocks, the three Tiger Moths, ZS-CKX (84869), ZS-DKY (85636), and ZS-DHR (82262), covered 1,600 miles in eleven days, flying over jungle, plains, salt pans and swamps. All three British-built aircraft had been operated by the SAAF, and ZS-DHR, taken on charge in March 1940, was the oldest airworthy Tiger Moth in South Africa, taking a break from filming in her most recent appearance in *Brutal Glory*. Two years after the adventure, ZS-CKX was dismantled and packed for emigration with her owner to Canada, but in 1991 she was out of the box again and receiving maintenance at Rand.

In March 1996, a further expedition into the Okavango was mounted from Pietersburg, when four British built Tiger Moths, all ex-SAAF imports from 1941 and 1943, pressed on to fly over Victoria Falls on 8 April: ZS-BGL (84221), ZS-BGN (84864), ZS-BXB (82709), and ZS-DNI (84454). During the flight home, operating via southern Zimbabwe, ZS-DNI broke a throttle linkage at Gwanda, home of the country's only operational Tiger Moth, and owner Ray Hollins was happy to donate the essential part on short term loan. The adventure was recorded on film and copies were made available from the Tiger Moth Club of South Africa under the title *'A Tiger Moth Safari'*.

The film was seen by sixteen year old Courtney Watson who had graduated to flying his father's Tiger Moth ZS-UKW (84412), and considered that by 2011 it was time for a repeat performance but on a more lavish scale and to be branded as the 'Tiger Moth Botswana Safari'. As a result in April 2011, during the Easter holiday, the local participants were joined by three Tiger Moths and a Hornet Moth shipped out from Europe for what one of the most experienced British pilots later described as 'my best flights ever'. Undeterred by distance, weather, shortage of facilities and fuel the expedition's eleven aircraft flew over stunning scenery from Krugersdorp via many adventures to overhead the Victoria Falls and back again. For the European element it was necessary to continue south to Scottburgh Airfield where their four aircraft had been erected and now were to be dismantled and containerised for the overland journey to Durban docks. After much investigation Scottburgh had been selected as base camp due to its close proximity to Durban, reducing the road journey to an absolute minimum, but the downside was that the distance from there to Krugersdorp was 600 miles and the positioning flights necessitated crossing the Drakensberg Mountains twice, routing through the van Reenens Pass at 8,000ft. There were no dramas and from the thousands of photographs and miles of film Courtney Watson was able to produce a vast printed tome and another spectacular DVD.

A Tiger Moth has charisma. the aeroplane is not the butt of cheap jibes at the hands of the airfield jokers, neither will she ever be. Put three Tiger Moth owners together in London and announce that they will fly to Moscow, and the world stops to take notice. Jonathan Elwes had travelled extensively in his Tiger Moth G-ANRN (83133), long before plans were conceived for the Moscow flight in 1989 and three crossings of the High Alps, trips to Gibraltar and North Africa and to Finland, the Arctic Circle and North Cape in 1984 had proved that anything was possible providing that preparation was thorough.

Courtney Watson flying the family Tiger Moth ZS-UKW overhead the Victoria Falls during the Botswana Moth Safari in 2011. *via Courtney Watson*

Flying long distance into sparsely populated areas calls for a degree of logistical pre-planning and it was necessary to dump barrels of Avgas for the participants in the Botswana Moth Safari in 2011. Roy Watson hand pumps fuel into the 25 gallon tank fitted to family Tiger Moth ZS-UKW at one of the critical locations along the route. *via Henry Labouchere*

Obviously but discreetly placarded with details of their sponsors, the Glasmoth Trio fly in close formation, each with a Russian navigator in the front cockpit.
The Glasmoth Trio

During a fourteen month programme of investigation and persistence a formula for the Moscow expedition was crystallised centring on the Tiger Moth as a privately owned vintage aeroplane of high reputation. The flight was to be regarded as one of a purely touring nature, for which category all prospective applicants were made aware that every previous entreaty made to Moscow since 1932 had been refused although a British registered Zlin Z.526 Trener and two Stampe SV-4s had been granted permission to fly to Moscow in 1966 as competitors in the World Aerobatic Championships.

With the most astonishingly appropriate timing, and in the light of a continuing thaw in East-West relations, the culture of 'Glasnost' quickly was re-interpreted as 'Glasmoth' and when April 1989 was declared to be British-Soviet trade month it provided the ideal peg on which to hang the project. The release from a Russian prison of Mathias Rust, a young German pilot who had landed his Cessna 172 in Red Square on 28 May 1987, was regarded as a friendly gesture and subsequently the pressure from Jonathan Elwes increased. All correspondence, submitted in Russian, now sought permission not only for his own aircraft but for two additional Tiger Moths to fly in company and suggesting that each should carry a Russian navigator. Eventually, the long awaited answer came from Moscow: "Approval granted."

Selection of the two additional Tiger Moth pilots was the matter of careful consideration. Not only was it vital that the team members were all compatible, they had to be reliable diplomats too, quite apart from a basic ability to provide and fly a Tiger Moth in almost all imaginable conditions, and have the facility to cope with any unforeseen eventuality, especially serious delay. Nicholas Parkhouse, a young surgeon, experienced Tiger Moth pilot and aerobatic competition winner, joined the team with G-ANOH (86040), an aircraft with family associations since 1966. He was followed by Roger Fiennes, businessman and genial wit, with G-BALX (82103), the last Rollason Aircraft Company civil conversion completed at Fairoaks in 1973.

There was much to organise before the trio left England, including confirmation of the return routing which was to be different from the outward journey. Aided by joint sponsorship from the *Daily Mail* and London based asset management concern, James Capel, finance, communication and reliable administration was established and the plans were given maximum exposure in the media. Anatoly Gorbatov, one of the three Russian navigators, paid a short visit to England to meet the pilots and complete various formalities such as confirming the size of boots and measurements for the specially tailored flying suits to be worn by him and his colleagues. All three navigators were on hand in England prior to the early April departure and were to remain with the Tiger Moths until they touched down back at White Waltham at the end of the adventure: Anatoly Gorbatov flew with Jonathan Elwes; Sasha Zaitzev with Nick Parkhouse and Roger Fiennes was crewed with Andrei Izmailov, navigator on Mathias Rust's Cessna repatriation flight to Denmark.

Under glowering skies on Friday, 7 April 1989, the assembled guests at White Waltham waved away the trio who took-off on their first leg to Wevelgem in Belgium. That same night they were in Aachen and on Saturday slept in Prague. During the afternoon of the following Friday, 14 April, they were poised to leave Kaluga bound for Moscow. Roger Fiennes penned his thoughts:

> "Inbound from Briansk we landed, refuelled and re-started our engines. The control tower reported fog en-route. We stopped engines and waited, for four hours. I played chess in a ramshackle hut with an old babushka and lost quite heavily, so I was glad when the word came that the authorities had reduced the minima for Sheremetyevo to 150 metres ceiling and 1,000 metres horizontal visibility.
> We re-routed to avoid hills, electric pylons and other obstructions, took off and were soon in close to IMC conditions. Surely we must turn back? No, we pressed on, barely able at times to remain in visual contact with each other. We flew over forest, just above the tops of the trees poking through the ground mist and bumping our heads on the cloud. Just when the conditions seemed impossible we found a river valley and followed it for almost half an hour. I had no idea where we were, and neither did my navigator.
> We came across a road straight as an arrow: it lead to

Moscow. None too soon the suburbs of the city could be seen in the murky distance. We descended to below 300ft and picked up the ring road which we followed around the city. I could see into the flats of the high rise buildings and people waved to us as we passed.

All traffic had been stopped at the airport but our eyes were skinned for high tension cables that we knew surrounded the city. Without warning we were there, flying a 300ft vic formation, passing over the VIP terminal. Another low level circuit in echelon, a break and stream landing and we were down. I for one was not sorry.

I did not notice the welcome: just held the flowers that were thrust at me and gulped down the champagne offered until my head sang. We hugged our wives and gave thanks to our Gods."

On 19 April 1998, Roger Fiennes flew his Tiger Moth from Headcorn in Kent to France for lunch, an exercise which he had enjoyed on several previous occasions. He left Dieppe for the return leg and headed out over the French coast on a direct track for Headcorn, a water crossing of seventy miles. Following a routine radio call giving an estimated time at mid-Channel nothing more was heard from G-BALX and the aircraft did not arrive in England. In spite of an intensive air and sea search, no trace of the Tiger Moth or her pilot was ever found.

Always looking for an opportunity Jonathan Elwes decided that Tiger Moths should be involved with the commemorative events being planned to mark the 150th anniversary of the Crimean War (1854-1855) and in particular the famous Charge of the Light Brigade during the Battle of Balaclava on 25 October 1854. After what appeared to be a promising start, following negotiations with Ukrainian officials which would have seen five Tiger Moths flying the route of the charge, the expected permissions did not materialise and the project was put on hold. A year later permission was granted for Jonathan Elwes and Anatoly Gorbatov, his Russian navigator for the 'Glasmoth' trip to Moscow in 1989, to fly Tiger Moth G-ANRN plus an escorting Robin Aiglon to the Crimean capital of Simferopol. From there it was a mere three miles to the scene of the attack in 1854 and 151 years after the event the charge was commemorated by a lone Tiger Moth flying from its interplane struts the colours of the 11th Hussars and 4th Light Dragoons.

Jonathan Elwes was still keen to fly the route of the charge with five Tiger Moths, each representing one of the five regiments which took part, and in 2008 negotiations were reopened at a high diplomatic level. Five years later and following debate in the Ukrainian Parliament and subsequent redrafting of laws concerning light aeroplanes, clearance was approved. This time the fleet consisted of twenty one aircraft operating under the umbrella of the Air Squadron including five Tiger Moths although one starting from Europe went unserviceable en-route and in spite of best efforts to repair or replace was forced to withdraw. And then there were four: G-ANRN plus G-ANRF (83748), David Cyster; G-AOGR (84566), Rupert Clark and G-APMX (85645), Ralph Hubbard. The Tiger Moths left England in late June and after 1,800 miles and twenty hours flying spread over ten days and through some savage Central European weather, they charged the Russian guns, each aircraft flying a regimental colour. Their passage along the North Valley was accompanied by orchestrated explosions underneath them and gunfire directed from across the valley. It was yet another of Jonathan Elwes' Tiger Moth missions accomplished in spectacular style.

Brian Edwards sent his heavily dismantled, bright yellow Tiger Moth VH-HPH ('1375'), *Matilda,* to England early in 1990 and she was re-assembled at the Royal Aircraft Establishment (RAE) Bedford. *Matilda* had been created from an amalgam of parts by Murray Griffiths at Deniliquin and registered in August 1988.

Jonathan Elwes in position to refuel Tiger Moth G-ANRN at Rivne during the Air Squadron's visit to Ukraine in 2013. Jonathan's daughter Tatiana poses for the camera with Ocsana, the local interpreter allocated to the party. *Rupert Clark*

During his long flights around Europe Jonathan Elwes discovered that the correct grades of petrol were not always available at aerodromes and some cautious manoeuvring off site was often called for, taking the aeroplane to the source rather than risking the use of cans with an unknown history. *Jonathan Elwes*

Tiger Moth G-AOGR parked next to the Russian 'Bear' at the Ukraine National Aviation Museum at Zuliany Airfield, Kiev during transit of the Air Squadron in 2013. *Rupert Clark*

The Tiger Moth fleet which was part of the Air Squadron visit to Ukraine in 2013, dressed with appropriate regimental colours prior to their commemoration of the Charge of the Light Brigade. *Jonathan Elwes*

Brian Edwards' father had been lost when captaining an RAF Avro Lancaster out of Binbrook on 3 July 1943 and his family was cared for in Australia by Legacy, a charitable organisation which provided assistance and education. The 1990 flight, planned to start appropriately from Binbrook, was Brian Edwards' effort to raise funds on behalf of the charity.

On the morning of 2 March 1990 VH-HPH took off from the old bomber base in Lincolnshire bound for Perth, Western Australia, but only two hours into the flight and a few minutes short of crossing the English south coast, the crankshaft in the Gipsy Major engine snapped. The propeller, full of energy, flew off and collided with the structure of the starboard upper mainplane causing major spar damage before careering off into oblivion. The aircraft was further damaged when the undercarriage partially collapsed during the forced landing at Gillham Lane Farm near Smarden in Kent and again during recovery to Headcorn Aerodrome. News of the disaster was broadcast throughout the media, reprofiling what had otherwise been a very quiet and dignified departure.

Dismayed by the story Michael Vaisey immediately flew to Kent in his own Tiger Moth G-APLU (85094), and by enlisting the assistance of other members of the de Havilland Moth Club, VH-HPH was removed to Hatfield where repairs were effected by volunteers and a replacement engine borrowed, overhauled and fitted, all with great urgency in an attempt to maintain validity of the diplomatic and overflight clearances. Twenty days after the engine failure Brian Edwards resumed his journey when he left Hatfield on 22 March and on 12 May was greeted by 16,000 enthusiastic supporters when he landed at Langley Park, an historic old aerodrome site situated in the heart of the city of Perth. The flight raised A$50,000 for Legacy which was topped up through sales of *The Matilda Mission*, a blow by blow account of the journey as logged by the pilot and in honour of which Brian Edwards was appointed to the Order of Australia.

More funds were raised in 1993. Starting on 26 September, *Matilda* circumnavigated Australia in a thirty six day anti-clockwise circuit which began at Jandakot and finished at Langley Park on Australia Day. Their arrival was greeted by an RAAF formation aerobatic team and confirmation that not only had Brian Edwards beaten the record for the 7,000 mile journey, set at forty four days by a Fairey IIID Seaplane in 1924, but during the course of his lectures and meetings organised for stopovers around the country at seventy one aerodromes, he and *Matilda* jointly had raised a further A$70,000 for Legacy.

In preparation for the World Vintage Air Rally starting from White Waltham Airfield, west of London, in March 1990, destination Sydney, N524R (85332), was modified on behalf of owner Bill Lusk at Chino, California, and sent by container to England. In view of the long sector distances involved in the Rally and the requirement to carry two crew together with a long list of mandatory equipment, the aircraft was clearly expected to be heavy: an additional seventy gallons of fuel were carried in two auxiliary tanks fitted in the front cockpit; navigational equipment included a Mode C transponder, DME, VOR, ADF, Comms radio and Magellan Nav 500 GPS. A combination strobe and navigation light system was installed on the tips of the upper mainplanes and to carry the electrical loads a 35 amp belt-driven alternator was connected to the back cover of the Gipsy Major engine. N524R left White Waltham on schedule on 25 March 1990 flown by Bill Lusk and fellow American Tiger Moth owner, Lars de Jounge but, due to windshear and strong cross winds encountered during the first landing at Le Touquet, the undercarriage collapsed on touchdown and the dream was shattered along with the propeller.

Tiger Moth HB-UCJ (DHA737), the former ZS-DND, left Johannesburg in February 1993 en route for Switzerland and having travelled the length of Africa, stalled, spun and hit the ground 115 miles north of Addis Ababa probably as the result of inattention when

Brian Edwards and his Tiger Moth VH-HPH, 'Matilda' whose flight from Binbrook in Lincolnshire to Perth, Western Australia nearly ended before it had begun due to catastrophic engine failure on 2 March 1990. *via Brian Edwards*

The city centre at Perth, Western Australia, was a welcome sight for Brian Edwards when, with a suitable escort, he arrived on 12 May 1990 after his solo flight from England, to be greeted by 16,000 people. *via Brian Edwards*

Tiger Moth N524R was fitted with a miscellany of navigation and safety equipment to comply with the rules set for the World Vintage Air Rally, England to Australia, in March 1990. During her first landing in crosswind conditions in France N524R suffered an undercarriage collapse. *Paul Robinson*

operating a heavy aircraft in searing temperatures and high altitudes. Misinterpretation of the graduations on the air speed indicator (ASI) may have been a contributing factor. The wrecked aircraft was returned to South Africa for long term restoration during which the ASI was scheduled to be changed but during the journey by transporter all the original instruments were stolen.

The 'Farmhand Appeal' was established in August 1994 to raise urgently needed funds to assist Australian farmers battling against what in some areas was the worst drought ever recorded. Nick Gerathy, an experienced fifteen year old pilot living in Queensland, too young to fly solo or to drive a car, raised more than A$40,000 for the cause by attracting sponsorship and publicity when he crewed Tiger Moth VH-UVB (DHA91), on a 3,800 mile adventure involving sixty three refuelling stops during fouteen days. The Tiger Moth had been loaned by Barry Hempel of Archerfield, Brisbane, and the trip began on 24 September, returning to Archerfield on 8 October, during which time Nick Gerathy was accompanied by flying instructor Paul Mikkelsen. The only delays experienced were all weather related: three hours were lost at Parafield when they were forced to return due to en route conditions; 45kt winds and dust storms were encountered at Dubbo, but the greatest irony for a drought inspired flight was the disruption caused at Glen Innes by waves of impenetrable squally rain.

In February 1996 Tiger Moth G-ASKP (3889), was climbing out of Brindisi and over the sea when the number one big end bearing failed, and the connecting rod punched a hole in the side of the crankcase. The damaged Gipsy Major engine, tough and resilient, maintained sufficient power to allow G-ASKP to return to the coast in a gradual descent and a controlled emergency landing within the confines of a live Italian Air Force bombing range, from where she was later retrieved by courtesy of a United States Air Force helicopter. At the time of the failure the aircraft had been heading for Greece and on to Cape Town, commemorating Alan Cobham's survey flight made on behalf of Imperial Airways in a DH.50 in 1926.

Repaired at Redhill and booked to appear in a film sequence for *The Famous Five* being shot at a narrow airstrip in Gloucestershire the following September, G-ASKP ran off the landing area in a strong crosswind, possibly due to a punctured tyre, slipped down an old railway embankment and overturned.

A more successful London to Cape Town flight occurred in 1961 when the newly overhauled G-ARMS (85698), was sold to a South African customer, Paget Bellin, who flew her from Croydon, attempting to establish a record for aircraft in the under 1,000kg category. The Tiger Moth left England on 14 May and arrived safely in Cape Town on 25 May, but only two days later whilst flying home along the east coast route from Youngfield Aerodrome, Cape Town to Greytown, Natal, he stopped for fuel at George. On departure Paget Bellin was goaded into providing an exhibition of low level aerobatics at which he was very inexperienced and during which G-ARMS failed to recover fully from a loop, hit a tree, and was wrecked.

Tiger Moth VH-UVB was loaned to Nick Gerathy in 1994 for a charity fund raising flight in Queensland which covered 3,800 miles over fourteen days and included sixty three refuelling stops. *Russell Broadie*

Tiger Moth VH-UVB was rebuilt in 1990 by Barry Hempel at Archerfield, Brisbane, using the wreck of VH-ARW as the core. The aircraft had been acquired from the RAAF in 1946 by the Cape York Aero Club at Cairns but was probably not airworthy until 1950 when she was owned by the North Queensland Aero Club, also at Cairns and where she was based until 1957. *Russell Broadie*

The unfortunate G-ASKP which was blown off the side of an abandoned railway track at Westbury-sub-Mendip in September 1996 due to a combination of factors probably including a punctured tyre. A friend crashed the pilot's car on the same day. *deHMC Archive*

A very rare shot of Tiger Moth G-ARMS at Redhill during Paget Bellin's working-up programme prior to his flight to South Africa in May 1961. *Mike Longden*

Marked with her former British registration in a modern go-faster style, this aircraft is currently ZS-XRF owned by Rodger Foster and rebuilt from a long stored wreck. *Rodger Foster*

Tiger Moth VH-GVA (DHA1014), was previously VH-GVE, but the amended letters were allocated on request in 1961 to reflect the identity of her new owners, Goulburn Valley Aero Club. In 1984 the aircraft was painted white overall and took the starring role in a delightful family film *Tail of a Tiger* shot at Bankstown and given wide distribution, later to be shown on television around the world. Under the ownership of Ray Vuillermin who had learned to fly on the aircraft, and later was to instruct on her, VH-GVA was one of only three Tiger Moths in Australia to hold approval for carriage of the Stand on Wing (SOW) rig.

In 1993 VH-GVA was acquired by John Fisher with the express intention of flying her from England (London) to Australia (Sydney). In preparation for the flight, John Fisher planned long solo sectors to calibrate the fuel and navigation systems, flying from Maitland Aerodrome, Newcastle to Perth and back again, and later a return trip from Maitland to Alice Springs. On 24 August 1995, during a period of familiarisation, VH-GVA jumped her chocks on start-up and taxied for 100 yards at high speed with the owner in hot pursuit, before turning over. Repairs were effected for test flying to begin on 21 December 1995, and five days later VH-GVA left on the westbound sector of her transcontinental proving flight to Perth. Fifteen days later the Tiger Moth was back at Maitland and arrangements were made to ship her to England from where, after local flying and a special guest appearance at the de Havilland Moth Club Rally at Woburn Abbey in August 1996, she would fly home.

Following a great send-off from White Waltham on 1 September and accompanied by the de Havilland Moth Club Diamond Nine Formation Team as far as the English south coast, all ten Tiger Moths featured in a sea front air display. For all his meticulous planning, world wide support and assistance, nobody could have envisaged the delays inflicted almost immediately on John Fisher by ferocious storms raging in the south of France. With his schedule soon in tatters he discovered that apart from appalling weather, bureaucracy became his greatest enemy, together with dangerous situations created by unimaginative Air Traffic Controllers. Apart from cash which opened some doors, he discovered that his next greatest assets were the gold epaulettes and airline style cap which hastened his movements through many others.

VH-GVA, still covered in messages applied before her England-Australia epic journey in 1996, was flown by John Fisher during the Pilgrimage tour in March 2011 celebrating the 90th anniversary of the founding of the Royal Australian Air Force. *Michael Wignall*

John Fisher with his Tiger Moth VH-GVA at the International Moth Rally at Woburn Abbey in August 1996. He left White Waltham for Australia on 1 September and was escorted as far as the South Coast of England by the de Havilland Moth Club's Diamond Nine formation team. *Geoffrey Perrior*

In spite of flying extremely long sectors of up to nine hours duration the aircraft took thirty days to reach Darwin and another seven after that before arrival in Sydney. VH-GVA was welcomed there by officials from 'Canteen', a teenage cancer charity, who were to receive substantial sponsorship funds raised by John Fisher's pugnacious forty two day epic.

Ten years after his epic journey, John Fisher, a man of great resourcefulness, was well advanced in establishing a vintage aviation museum at his base airfield at Maryborough, Victoria, with a strong de Havilland content and plans for lectures and meetings. On the evening of 27 January 2012, with David Oxley, President of the Maryborough Aero Club as passenger, he elected to give Tiger Moth VH-GVA an airing. During the take-off roll the engine failed to develop full power, possibly due to a restricted fuel flow, and the aircraft hit a tree during an attempt to climb and crashed into the ground, killing both occupants.

West Australian land agent Barry Markham acquired Tiger Moth DHA1088 in 1989, almost thirty years after the aeroplane had been substantially damaged and written off during service with the Royal Newcastle Aero Club. One of the last RAAF Tiger Moths (A17-757), to be sold out of the Service she was registered VH-RNQ in 1955 but the letters were cancelled in July 1960 following her crash at Port MacQuarie.

Rebuilt by Ray Windred at Luskintyre and registered VH-NOV in October 1991, Barry Markham flew her home to Perth a year later taking eight days to cover the twenty nine sectors. In an effort to raise funds for the Royal Flying Doctor Service and commemorate the flight in August 1933 from Perth to Croydon by West Australian Jimmy Woods in DH.60 Moth VH-UPD, Barry Markham was given a rousing send off by 2,000 spectators when he left Langley Park on 26 April 1998, headed for England.

VH-NOV arrived at Cambridge on 24 June having been airborne for 172 hours on the thirty five legs during forty five of the sixty elapsed days as planned, running ahead of fierce tropical storms, a political revolution in Indonesia and nuclear test explosions in India and Pakistan. In achieving his great ambition, Barry Markham became the first Tiger Moth pilot to complete the westbound route, flying 'uphill' into the prevailing wind and weather. Modifications to VH-NOV included permitted operations at a maximum gross weight of 2,004lb (910kg), the luxury of mainwheel brakes and a steerable tailwheel which helped considerably when manoeuvring at major international airports. Long range fuel, 69.5 gallons, was carried in the same front fuselage tanks previously fitted to VH-HPH during her west-east transit, generously loaned for the occasion by Brian Edwards, and range had been estimated on a fuel burn of seven gallons per hour travelling at 50kts. However, had plans worked differently, Barry Markham might have been recognised only as the first *solo* Tiger Moth flight along the route. A plan for three Tiger Moths of the Royal Aero Club of New South Wales to fly in formation from Australia to England was announced in April 1939. Scheduled to arrive on the opening day of Birmingham's new airport on 8 July the ceremonies at Elmdon were completed without them.

Wiltshire based strawberry farmer Norman Parry had long nurtured a dream to fly from England to Australia in his Mascot built Tiger Moth G-BPHR (DHA45). An accomplished glider pilot equipped with the necessary grit and determination, Norman Parry left a private strip near Reading on 20 September 1998, transiting via White Waltham to refuel to maximum capacity, and intending to rendezvous in France with a second Australia-bound Tiger Moth, G-ERDS (85028). A third aircraft was not airworthy in time and remained in England.

Persistent engine problems suffered by G-ERDS caused Willie Gerdes and his wife to abandon their flight having struggled as far as Rome and after some weeks delay the aircraft was ferried back to England. Norman Parry continued on his own but slipped further behind his already flexible schedule, delayed by technical problems and bad weather. Lines of communication were maintained with British based engineer Ben Borsberry, along which vital supplies and spares were shipped together with much advice for 'on the spot' maintenance and repair.

Unlike Barry Markham's east-west flight which had run ahead of weather and political disturbance, Norman Parry coincided with the worst of both. Severe delays were caused by storms and bureaucracy exacerbated by expired overflight clearances, spare parts held without reason by Customs, theft of money and a series of significant engine problems. However, the ambition was achieved when G-BPHR finally touched down at Kununurra in northern-most Western

Barry Markham left Langley Park Aerodrome, Perth in Tiger Moth VH-NOV on 26 April 1998 and arrived at Cambridge on 24 June, the first and only pilot to fly a Tiger Moth 'against the wind' from Australia to England. *Paul Falconer West*

Barry Markham and VH-NOV in France before embarking on the final leg of their journey from Australia to England. The aircraft was sighted near Royston and escorted into Cambridge by a flight of Moths to the sound of popping champagne corks. *Michael Gibbs*

Australia on New Year's Day 1999 at which point the pilot decided it was time to return home: there was a farm to run! Persuaded otherwise he continued on to Newcastle where he arrived on 12 January to be met by, amongst other enthusiasts, John Fisher, well aware of the emotions behind the tired expression. There was some good news too: locally based Tiger Moth VH-KRW (LES-1) had just been sold to a new owner in Great Britain and there was space in the shipping container for two dismantled aeroplanes.

Not dismayed by the problems of a long distance solo flight in a Tiger Moth Norman Parry left England in September 2006 bound for Durban, South Africa. Initially the front cockpit of Tiger Moth G-BPHR was occupied by fellow owner, John Baxter, but following arrival in Brindisi the party was joined by engineer Ben Borsberry, who had flown commercially from London, and a thirty two gallon fuel tank which had arrived by road. Converted into a single seater the aircraft left Brindisi headed east to Crete before crossing the Mediterranean to Alexandria. As usual a private flight passing through the area was subject to long bureaucratic delays and monumental landing, parking and handling charges but in spite of the frustration the flight proceeded via Khartoum to Juba in Southern Sudan where, shortly after landing and whilst considering the implications of an electrical systems failure, G-BPHR was attacked by a line squall which appeared from nowhere. Hit by a 50kt gust the aircraft dragged her concrete tie downs along a wet runway until she was arrested by a metal tank trap which damaged a wing tip but wrecked the starboard elevator.

Following communications with his fellow owners and consideration of all the possibilities it was decided that Norman Parry would fly commercially to Nairobi to await the arrival of a replacement elevator sent from England. He returned to Juba with the new part classified as hand luggage and tidied up the aeroplane but with the realisation that a flight through to Durban was now not possible. Through more poor weather he flew with difficulty to Nairobi where he was all but arrested for allegedly violating the conditions of his entry into Kenyan airspace and was accused of being a spy. Following advice that he would be best off by routing on to Mombasa, help was available there to dismantle and crate the aircraft ready for shipment home. Travelling over twenty eight sectors totalling 4,680 miles in seventy two hours flight time the aircraft had burned 460 gallons of fuel of various qualities. The huge adventure was not quite finished: her container was mistakenly offloaded at Rotterdam and only traced by the efforts of her owners.

A special fuel tank designed to provide maximum capacity of thirty two gallons when fitted into the front cockpit of Tiger Moth G-BPHR was installed by Ben Borsberry at Brindisi prior to departure for Durban. *John Baxter*

G-BPHR during engine and fuel checks conducted by Norman Parry at Brindisi in September 1998 following installation of the long range tank in the front cockpit. *John Baxter*

G-BPHR picketed in the Sudan where the authorities provided tie-down facilities and a mobile fire extinguisher. *Norman Parry*

Norman Parry's flight from London to Durban was rudely interrupted at Juba in Southern Sudan when G-BPHR was attacked by a line squall and blown against a tank trap, demolishing the starboard elevator. *Norman Parry*

The coming of the new millennium was recognised by the Tiger Moth Club of New Zealand who organised a Millennium Vintage Air Rally in February 2000. A fleet of vintage aircraft were to fly from North Cape, at the north of North Island, to Bluff, near Invercargill, at the southern extremity of South Island. Amongst the fifty four aircraft entered, twenty one were Tiger Moths including three from England whose crews overcame the bureaucracy, the hassle and the unexpected, not to mention the physical gymnastics involved in dismantling, packing and shipping vintage aeroplanes half way round the world. The southbound trip mostly along the east coast was spread over ten days and ended with a dinner at *The Moth* restaurant at Mandeville Aerodrome when a mass of prizes and awards were presented. An English visitor who had travelled as a passenger on an accompanying Dragon Rapide, Clive Abbott, later wrote: "The organisers had done a superb job, the Rally had been great fun and was a unique opportunity to socialise with a very friendly and generous bunch of 'vintage' aviators. I would not have missed it for anything. I hope they do not wait ten years before having another one."

Above: Having decided there was little option but to abandon his planned flight to Durban, Norman Parry flew from Nairobi to Mombasa where the aircraft was dismantled and packed into a container which was offloaded in Rotterdam in error. *via Norman Parry*

Once carrying the red and silver livery of the London Transport Flying Club and based at Fairoaks, Tiger Moth G-AIIZ was purchased by David Baker, son of the Club's retired CFI, and shipped to Hong Kong where this photograph was taken from an aero club Cessna 182 flown by Ray Hanna in September 1976. *via David Baker*

On retirement from his colonial posting, David Baker's plans to fly G-AIIZ from Hong Kong to England, possibly in company with another Tiger Moth, were shelved and eventually the aircraft arrived at London Gatwick as palletised cargo on the main deck of a Cathay Pacific Boeing 747 Freighter. *David Lipson*

If one civil aircraft in the world is more deserving and demanding of attention than a yellow Tiger Moth, it is Concorde, a machine of enduring majesty, beauty and immense power. Steve Bohill-Smith, co-pilot of Concorde and captain of Tiger Moth G-ANFM, led some of his friends to Manston on 11th May 1991 as part of the Tiger Moth's Diamond Jubilee celebrations. *Gordon Bain*

The Tiger Moth Club of South Africa generated enough enthusiasm for an event in the opposite direction four years later with sixty entries including ten from Europe but the chosen schedule of late February, picked to ensure the best weather, coincided with the worst summer in living memory which resulted in a fragmented but still enjoyable event.

Organisers of long range races and rallies which cross national borders are obliged to ensure that a minimum level of navigation and emergency equipment is carried. For most modern aircraft contemplating taking part in a race from England to Australia the requirements offer little challenge but when Roger Pullen entered Tiger Moth G-AHVV (86123), into the 2001 Australia Race, like Bill Lusk's entry with Tiger Moth N524R in the 1990 event, the 1931 cockpit and equipment design and specification needed serious revision.

The aircraft was scheduled to carry sixty four gallons of fuel and just over four gallons of oil enabling a still air range of 705nm with no reserves and an endurance of almost nine and a half hours. The rear instrument panel was extended in depth to accommodate a revised suite of instruments fitted with smaller diameter faces and requiring a shortening of the rear control column. An avionics tray was situated under the luggage locker behind the rear seat and a battery box mounted on the control box was charged by an air-driven turbo-alternator fitted between the undercarriage legs.

Unlike Bill Lusk's entry which left England on schedule but collapsed her undercarriage on first contact with foreign soil, the work programme for G-AHVV proved to be so extreme that she was not signed off until 15 May 2001, ten months after initiation and two months after the race had been won, and even then with not the whole of the intended package installed. In October 2002 G-AHVV clipped trees when landing at a private strip near Winchester incurring

In 1995 Tiger Moth G-ANKL was shipped to New Zealand where she was overhauled by the Croydon Aircraft Company and sold to new owners in Portland, Oregon. Registered N82TM the aircraft was painted as NC82TM and delivered in a container on 15 June 2000. *Ted Millar*

A small fleet of British registered Tiger Moths joined the Vintage Air Rally organised by the Tiger Moth Club of New Zealand in February 2004. Experience proved that by splaying the main undercarriage sufficient height was lost to enable the aircraft to be packed into a standard shipping container with no disruption to the critical rigging of the centre section. *Henry Labouchere*

Tiger Moth G-AOJK flown by Bob Willies was one of ten aircraft shipped from Europe to be part of the 2004 Vintage Rally organised by the Tiger Moth Club of New Zealand. The event co-incided with one of the worst periods of autumn weather the country had experienced. *via Henry Labouchere*

Tiger Moth G-AHVV was modified to accept instrumentation and avionics to comply with the rules of the England-Australia Air Race in 2001. The design and installation was so protracted that the race had been won long before G-AHVV was ready for test flying. *Roger Pullen*

During the celebrations in Hampshire in 2010 to mark the centenary of the first successful flight by Geoffrey de Havilland this unique gathering of long distance Moth pilots was caught in de Havilland Field at the village of Crux Easton. Norman Parry, David Cyster and John Fisher had all flown Tiger Moths along the route; in 1974 Tim Williams accompanied by Henry Labouchere flew Puss Moth G-AAZP from Mildenhall to Melbourne. *Hope Knight*

Tiger Moth G-AHVV was acquired by Ace Flight Training in 2005 and employed as a joyrider at Dunkeswell in Devon She became famous after suffering an engine failure on take off on 14 September 2008 and the textbook forced landing was captured on the obligatory on-board video the recording of which appeared almost immediately on the internet. During the landing roll the port lower wingtip hit a cow which is seen completing a loop in the background. The cow was unhurt; the Tiger Moth suffered some damage. *Roger Pullen*

considerable damage including a collapsed undercarriage but she was repaired and sold to become a professional joyrider in the West Country. She became an international celebrity through the medium of the internet when on 14 September 2008 she force landed due to engine failure immediately after take-off from Dunkeswell. The whole of the sequence had been filmed by an on-board video camera. During the text-book landing G-AHVV collided with a cow which could be seen flick-rolling in the background as the aircraft slowed to a stop. The cow was uninjured and the Tiger Moth was repaired.

In their DH.82C Tiger Moth the Canadians had incorporated Bendix mainwheel brakes and a fully castoring tailwheel neither of which was incorporated into mass manufacture elsewhere. Operating a standard Tiger Moth from a large grass field was exactly what the type had been designed to do but as aerodromes grew larger, busier and more commercial and hard runways and taxiways became the norm, where there was no alternative it was prudent for aeroplane owners to consider modifications. Basic parking brakes fitted to the mainwheel hubs gradually gave way to fully functional taxy braking systems, mostly fitted to aircraft based in the USA and Australia, almost all custom designed and based on heel or toe application associated with the rudder pedals and linked to the wheels by cable

Long distance flights by Tiger Moth invariably necessitate transit of airfields with acres of concrete upon which brakeless aeroplanes with standard tailskids are a hazard. 4X-AAA is fitted with a tailwheel and brakes as a practical precaution against conflict with a parked airliner or a hangar door. *via Aharon Sagi*

At some time during her civilian career Australian Tiger Moth VH-AJG was fitted with a Canadian style undercarriage and tailwheel, possibly when she was used by the Bathurst Soaring Group in 1966. The aircraft which was seen at the old RAAF training airfield at Temora in 1991 suffered a number of major accidents during her time and was finally written off in 2002. *David Welch*

Most of the major changes which resulted in the definitive DH.82C were in the fuselage which can be more easily assessed without wings: engine cowlings, raked and braked undercarriage, long tailpipe, missing in this shot of C-FATG, lagged oil tank, canopy, tailwheel and elevator trim tabs. The basic construction of the fuselage is almost identical to the 'A' version. *deHMC Archive*

The result of allowing a Tiger Moth to be walk-taxied on concrete close to an obstruction. The 'pilot in command' inadvertently opened the throttle and the aircraft accelerated away. *Peter Walpole*

Only the tailwheels superimposed against the high cumulus point to the location of these two 'RAF' Tiger Moths being in the United States rather than the United Kingdom. Bob Curtin and Walt Kessler once formed part of a show trio in Wisconsin where paved runways necessitated that Tiger Moths be fitted with tailwheels and mainwheel brakes. *via Walt Kessler*

Tiger Moth VH-AJV suffered this embarrassment through her inability to stop (no brakes!) before the grass ran out during landing at Orange, NSW in 1953 and she nosed down into a mud filled culvert. The aircraft was retrieved, washed and repaired and flew again. *J A Burns*

or even hydraulic lines. One enterprising Swiss owner fitted a tailwheel before mainwheel brakes and learned that the only way to stop on a hard runway with a downhill slope was by colliding with an immovable object, in his case an expensive helicopter.

There have been many other plans for long-distance flights! As early as 1972 an Indian commercial pilot, Captain Dalzit Singh from Chandigarh, owner of Tiger Moth VT-DBX (83044), advertised for a photographer or journalist to join him for a proposed round-the-world flight and to split the costs. Nothing further was heard although VT-DBX was last reported to be stored in Germany.

G-AHUF (86221), together with two other Tiger Moths was to have been presented to the press at White Waltham in April 2000 to announce a flight to Cape Town. On each of about 150 short sectors it was planned to carry a celebrity in an effort to raise funds for charity. The trio was scheduled to leave England on 10 October but nothing further was heard and later the charitable status of the organisation was queried and eventually cancelled by the appropriate authorities.

Tiger Moth G-ALRI (83350), was acquired in 2003 with the intention of celebrating the 75th anniversary of Francis Chichester's 1929 flight from London to Sydney the following year. In a manner similar to G-AHVV, the aeroplane was fitted with an extensive instrument and avionics suite and media coverage promoted the idea of the 'Chichester Challenge' to raise funds for a Francis Chichester Flying Scholarship. The joint promoters became involved in other things: one entered politics and after a false start was elected as a British Member of Parliament. There was no grand departure and in 2007 G-ALRI was sold to a flying club in Thailand to whom she was delivered in a container.

A Tiger Moth restored in New Zealand gets her tail up at Chalmington Manor, in rural Dorset, England. Out of picture at left the ground slopes steeply down, requiring all arrivals to be uphill, finely judged and towards the house. *Gordon Bain*

CHAPTER TWENTY

The Agriculturalists

The stimulation and protection of crops is one of the fundamentals of farming and good agro-industrial economics and the potential of using aircraft to fertilise or apply protective chemicals over a vast acreage was recognised in the USA during the 1920s when Louisiana cotton plantations and Californian fruit farms were 'dusted' by low flying 'bug-smashers'. The first recorded use of 'agricultural aviation' was in 1921 when a Curtiss Jenny spread lead arsenate dust on an infestation of caterpillars in Ohio. In England at the same time a de Havilland Hire Service DH.9 was involved in similar work in Kent until the poisonous nature of its cargo was appreciated and there is some evidence to suggest that at least one DH.60 Moth was used between the wars for aerial application in the USA, an image having appeared on a calendar published by the Union Carbide Company.

No details have survived of the system which would have spread 'Paris Green' from RAF Tiger Moths onto invading troops had the various levels of the Banquet programme become operational in Great Britain in 1940. It may have been as simple as the pilot pouring the fluid over the side of the cockpit, but is likely to have been a little more sophisticated and involved a venturi let into the fuselage floor. Neither can details be found of the spraying gear fitted to RAF Tiger Moth N9275 (82376), which was positioned to Halton in June 1941 and, following a seven week stay, departed via 47 MU Sealand to 24 MU Ternhill in August where 'anti-malaria spraying apparatus' was fitted.

A moment in the working life of Tiger Moth G-ANFP at her two foot operating altitude. Until alternative methods were developed human field markers were faced with this view of low level Tiger Moth operations as a routine. J Blake

In September she was despatched to Takoradi in what was then the Gold Coast of West Africa. Details of her mission, local operation and eventual fate of the aircraft are unknown.

In New Zealand, soon after the First World War when returning soldiers sought to earn themselves a living from previously unallocated land, the idea of harnessing aviation to the fertilisation of land was dismissed at government level as 'impractical' in spite of growing evidence from overseas that exactly the reverse was true. Advocates of the system cited numerous examples of progress made elsewhere; a forty five acre potato crop in Lincolnshire had been sprayed from the air in twenty nine minutes, a job which would have taken at least two days of backbreaking effort if working on the surface.

The breakthrough did not come until 1941 when a Public Works Department employee, flying a government owned Miles Whitney Straight, used his initiative to redress a situation caused by weather and sowed 375 acres with lupins in two days by pouring bags of seed at a predetermined rate down a perforated pipe held out of the cabin window. Although admonished by his superiors the practicability of aerial agriculture was established and official trials were sponsored using a 75 Squadron Grumman Avenger with a hopper installed in the torpedo compartment.

The first New Zealand trials of an agricultural Tiger Moth were in March 1949 when, in an attempt to reduce the rabbit population, the front seat passenger of ZK-ASO (83533), poured poison pellets through a funnel let into the floor. In May, ZK-ASO was fitted with a hopper of 400lb carrying capacity and, flown by John Brazier, serviced

Between 1954 and 1957 Tiger Moth ZS-DEC was one of three used for crop spraying in South Africa. Pre war experiments in aerial agriculture had been successful using a Dragon Rapide but post war the opportunity seems not to have been taken to harness the hundreds of surplus Tiger Moths in a manner exploited to good effect in Australia and New Zealand. *via Pat Evans*

A grader blade type spreader was fitted to Tiger Moths of Airwork (NZ) Ltd and used for dropping poisoned carrot cubes for rabbit control or superphosphate powder. *deHMC Archive*

sixty four acres in the first recorded hour of such commercial activity in the country, spreading three tons of superphosphate on Sir Heaton Rhodes' property at Tai Tapu during the course of sixteen flights.

Once the benefits of agricultural aviation had been fully recognised in Australia, New Zealand, Canada, Great Britain and, to a limited extent in South Africa, it was the Tiger Moth that promoted her own virtues: cheap to buy, maintain and operate, available in large numbers with a healthy spares backup, and engineers and pilots ready, willing and experienced. Converted locally as an evolving improvisation, each scheme approved on its own merits, the Tiger Moth laid the foundation for a whole new industry, only withdrawing as more efficient purpose-built aircraft were gradually introduced.

In nearly all Tiger Moth agricultural conversions it was usual for the front cockpit to be stripped out to accommodate a hopper or a tank, depending on the business role: spraying, dusting, top dressing, spreading, seeding etc. Distribution of the load was achieved either through a specially designed venturi under the floor or spraybars or atomisers mounted on the lower wings activated by wind driven pumps often attached to the undercarriage. Operationally, the aircraft were pushed to the limit, and beyond. Fine pitch propellers were essential for getting out of some of the tiny and unprepared landing strips most conveniently situated for working sites, and flying for days or weeks at a time away from base was known to cause memory lapse when engine and airframe hours were finally logged.

Before daily operations commenced it was essential that the spray bar equipment be calibrated and, using a basic formula which included airspeed and width of the swathe, given a known system pressure it was possible to calculate the spraying duration based on an ideal output measured in gallons per acre. Spray droplet size was critical too: coarse droplets would not wet all the crop, but too fine a measure and the spray would drift and evaporate.

British company Micronair, an associate of Isle of Wight-based Crop Culture Ltd., a business founded by Jim McMahon, John Britten and Desmond Norman, developed a rotary atomiser which, using a system of spar saddle plates, was bolted onto the top surface of a Tiger Moth's lower wings. Liquid chemical was fed into a rotating drum and expelled by centrifugal force through a gauze cylinder where it was broken into droplets to form a spray. A major advantage of the system was that droplets were of uniform size, a feature controlled by the drum's rotational speed, governed by simply adjusting the blade pitch of the air-driven fans.

Doing the business in 1976. Equipped with full span spray bars and a wind driven pressure pump, Hap Neville demonstrates stripped down 'Ag-Tiger' ZK-ANL, the last working example in the world. The Tiger Moth boosted the promotion of practical agricultural aviation and secured for many surplus aircraft a whole new career. *R L Ewing*

The Britten-Norman rotary atomiser picked up on the rear spar of the lower mainplanes. Feed pipes ran inside the wing. Rotary atomisation was considered to be by far the most economical method of dispensing liquid chemical. *Richard Riding*

The elaborate wind driven pumping system fitted to Tiger Moth G-AOAD. In agricultural operations free wind power was always selected to drive the systems in preference to any other energy source. *Richard Riding*

Tiger Moth G-AOAD was chosen to demonstrate the Britten-Norman rotary atomiser during a conference at the Woodstock Research Centre, Kent in October 1957. The dispensers were set to yield one gallon of chemical per acre. *via Hugh Scanlan*

The corrosive nature of some cargoes caused a few operators to remove fabric covering from the rear fuselage to facilitate cleaning and inspection of the tubular steel structure. The practice was condoned in Australia where the undressed aircraft were known as 'bare bum Tigers', but the configuration was not approved in New Zealand and at least one operator was grounded by the authorities for flying with no fabric on the underbelly of the rear fuselage and loose covers attached to the sides of the frame by baler wire. The lack of fabric resulted in an altered spin recovery technique and, due to the general nature of the configuration, a complete ban on any form of intentional aerobatics. An approved modification to replace all fuselage fabric with plywood panels screwed to a false wooden framework found no favour.

In September 1947 only three of the surviving nine Tiger Moths with the Uruguayan military at Boiso Lanza were airworthy, 600 (3312), 603 (3618), and 613 (3616), and they and six pilots were enrolled into the task of combating swarms of locusts which arrived in the north east region of the country every year, crossing the border from Brazil. The three Tiger Moths were each fitted with a tank tailored to occupy the rear cockpit and the discharge through a chute in the floor was controlled by a rudimentary mechanism operated by the pilot in the front seat. Tiger Moth 613 was written off at Boiso Lanza after an accident there on 14 October and 600 was lost at Mazangano on 18 December. Following a long overhaul the fleet was joined by 605 (3311), in December.

In Uruguay the military fitted a tank in the rear cockpit of E-600 and some others and insecticide was exhausted through a rudimentary chute let into the floor and controlled by the pilot operating from the front seat. *Aeronautical Museum Collection*

The business end of the spreader box fitted to Tiger Moth G-AKXG at Panshanger during the early 1950s. Note the fairings fitted between wing root ends and fuselage lower longerons. *The Aeroplane*

It was common practice for undeclared cattle to be driven across the dry frontier with Brazil and in 1948 the Uruguayan Government ordered Military Aeronautics to raise patrols to be flown by Tiger Moths operating from Durazno. On 15 May 602 (3310), became entangled in a wire fence when attempting to take-off from Tacuarembo; on 2 June 611 (3614), overturned after losing power on take-off and, ten days later 603 (3618), hit an anthill when landing in the wrong field 300 yards inside Brazilian territory at Guaviyu. All three aircraft were subsequently withdrawn. Tiger Moths 601 (3617), 604 (3619), and 606 (3313), also were allocated to the patrols until the end of June 1948 when they were replaced by PT-19s and both 604 and 606 were withdrawn for use on their return to Boiso Lanza.

In post-war Canada ski-equipped DH.82C Tiger Moths were used to hunt wolves when the animals could be easily tracked in the snow and shot at with rifles fired from the back seat during low level passes. In New Zealand pioneer crop spraying pilot Ron Bush was asked by Otago sheep farmers to assist in tracking a dog which had been worrying their flocks. The dog was duly found during a brief airborne reconnaissance and driven towards a wall of local residents all armed to the teeth. Sensing a trap the dog changed direction and headed towards cover but not to be outsmarted Ron Bush dived down and hit the dog with a mainwheel, killing it instantly, bending the undercarriage leg and damaging the wing leading edge in the process. Forced to land straight ahead the Tiger Moth suffered further injury but the farming community was so pleased to see the headless body of their enemy that they carried a hat around the district and raised sufficient funds to pay for the repairs.

As an agricultural tool the DH.82C Tiger Moth found only moderate favour in Canada due to limited capacity and the enormity of the acreage to be treated but, they were cheap to buy and to operate until largely replaced by the Stearman. About a dozen aircraft were converted: the canopy removed and a hopper fitted into the front cockpit space.

As an experiment in New Zealand, Temple Martin fitted a pair of external spray tanks to the underfloor 'bomb rack' position of Tiger Moth ZK-AIX in December 1949, but after only one job the tanks were removed and discarded. *Temple Martin*

Above: In Canada in 1949 DH.82C Tiger Moth sprayer CF-CIE was converted by Skyway Air Services of British Columbia onto a float undercarriage when it was necessary to position the aircraft into areas where it was more efficient to operate from water. *Skyway Air Services*

Right: After her working life was considered at an end one time sprayer CF-DAL was allowed to go derelict but she was later acquired by the Reynolds Museum in Wetaskiwin. *deHMC Archive*

Skyway Air Services of White Rock BC flew converted DH.82C Tiger Moths in support of anti-mosquito operations from 1949 distributing copious quantities of DDT. A serious infestation at the huge Kemano Dam project resulted in CF-CIE (DHC986), being despatched north along the Pacific coast to Kitimat, operating on floats. The aircraft remained in service until 1957 when she was withdrawn and in 1966 was donated to the British Columbia Farm Machinery and Agricultural Museum at Fort Langley BC, where she is currently on display.

Frank Young began agricultural operations in Alberta in May 1952 with CF-CJP (DHC1398), and gained useful publicity by employing Mary Wilcox who had learned to fly at the age of sixteen in Altoona, Pennsylvania, and was soon working on up to 950 acres a day. A second aircraft, CF-DAL (DHC644), was added in November and in July 1954 Frank Young and Mary Wilcox jointly formed Skyspray of Canada Ltd. CF-CJP crashed while spraying at Bassano, Alberta in June 1957 and CF-DAL was cancelled in March 1958, neither being replaced. The derelict fuselage of CF-DAL complete with engine was acquired from Calgary by the Reynolds Museum at Wetaskiwin, Alberta in 1979 and returned to airworthy condition in her original RCAF specification in November 1984.

Even with its fine pitch propeller, at normal loaded weight the agricultural Tiger Moth suffered a lack of climb performance, especially when operating in hot, high conditions. The deficiency was countered to some extent by the type's good slow speed handling and manoeuvrability, but its carrying capacity in terms of both volume and weight was considered barely adequate to be economical.

Following a series of tests in New Zealand, representation to de Havilland in England, and a period of trial operations with selected modified aircraft, the maximum all-up take-off weight was gradually increased from the standard category 1,825lb to 2,190lb. Part of the argument for an increase had been to divide the declared tonnage dropped by the number of logged sorties. The answer was a rough indication that almost all take-offs were over the legal maximum anyway, and no spate of structural failures had been reported. By 1955 the bureaucrats had established themselves as regulators of the industry and decided that unless the Tiger Moth could comply with a new load-dump safety regulation, their maximum all-up weight would revert to standard.

In Australia, similar increases in take-off weight reached a maximum of 2,000lb and the Department of Civil Aviation (DCA), produced a take-off weight graph which had reached issue five by June 1962, worthy of any multi-jet Flight Manual, recognising not only the more obvious parameters of take-off distances, altitude, shade temperature and wind component, but laying heavy emphasis on runway slope and the effect of grass, long or short, wet or dry. All performance was assumed on the basis of a propeller of 4.33ft pitch or finer, and a Gipsy Major engine operating at full throttle.

Peter Charles methodically landed his agricultural Tiger Moth on an Australian farm strip and at taxy speed with the engine idling bumped the skid over a hidden tree stump causing the tail to lift and the propeller to strike the ground, breaking the tip of one blade. Hundreds of miles from base, what to do? Peter Charles cut off the damaged tip with a hacksaw, then an equal amount from the undamaged blade. The engine ran smoothly enough on the ground and then in the air, so the spraying continued uninterrupted for a week and without any noticeable loss of performance, until the replacement propeller was delivered into the district by railway.

During a mineral survey flight west of Alice Springs on 25 October 1950, Tiger Moth VH-ARN (DHA97), landed at Lake Hopkins but a wheel went through the salt crust during a turn and fifteen inches was broken off the end of each propeller blade. The pilot, Kurt Johannsen and his business partner Jimmy Prince, chipped away at the blade ends with a tomahawk to effect a good balance. Refitted to the aircraft the Tiger Moth staggered into the air with the Gipsy Major engine rotating at 3,300rpm and barely maintained a height of six feet until Kurt Johannsen saw eagles thermalling. Following their example he managed to climb to about 300ft where he was able to throttle back to 2,700rpm and struggle back to base camp where he collected another Tiger Moth for the trip to Lake Hopkins to rescue Jimmy Prince. The reduced diameter propeller was saved and later presented to the Alice Springs Aviation Museum.

When moving around from one contract to another, much of the support equipment was transferred by surface, but occasionally it was necessary to carry it by Tiger Moth. The loading door to the hopper was nearly always too small to allow pumps and hoses to be carried inside and the remedy was to wrap the hoses around the lower wing root and carry the pump in the luggage locker where it put the CG well outside the approved limits. Holding the stick hard forward was considered acceptable for short duration flights and the problem was alleviated to some extent by the practice of lashing the pilot's personal kit to the root end confluence of rigging wires.

A number of reported accidents were thought to have had similar causes, possibly due to carburettor icing, although test flights conducted in known icing conditions in New Zealand proved negative. Failures of Sutton harnesses, a style of restraint regarded purely as a military requirement for aerobatic training, resulted in the type's replacement in both New Zealand and Australia where a much improved system of strap anchorage was also introduced.

The only obvious clue to the previous life-style enjoyed by seemingly conventional Tiger Moth VH-SSI is the roll-over pylon or truss, fitted as a mandatory requirement to all Australian registered 'Ag Tigers' fairly late in the types' agricultural career. *deHMC Archive*

Constructed from all new spares by Lawrence Engineering and Sales of Camden in 1960 and registered to Mitair Agricultural Aviation as VH-MIT, this Tiger Moth was fitted with a protective cabin, later removed when the aircraft was overhauled and prepared for commercial joyriding. *Gerome Gleeson*

In May 1961 the Australian DCA announced that turn-over trusses were to be fitted to all agricultural Tiger Moths registered in the country. This involved bolting a welded tube pylon onto the fuselage frame at four points just behind the rear cockpit, an imaginary line running through the top of which, and roughly parallel with the rear decking, would coincide with the top of the rudder spar. The purpose was to protect the pilot's head in case of a turn over and some operators took the opportunity to build an additional light framework around the pylon, creating a protective cabin with a large windscreen of the type later found on purpose-built agricultural aircraft. In New Zealand, a simple modification to save weight and drag was to reduce the depth of the rear top decking from a position immediately aft of the cockpit, the advantage balanced against the loss of protection to the pilot in case of a roll over.

On a miserable day in March 1959 hundreds of farmers and officials from the National Agricultural Advisory Service and the British Sugar Corporation assembled as guests of Fisons Pest Control at Bexwell Aerodrome in Norfolk, there to witness a demonstration of all the currently available types of agricultural aeroplanes and helicopters. Three Tiger Moths equipped with spray bars or venturis which were included in the flying demonstrations were singled out by the press for their special attraction of being cheap to buy and to operate. "Despite winds that gusted up to 15kts the pilots achieved their object by bringing the succession of aircraft past the enclosure low, slowly and with extreme accuracy," wrote J W R Taylor for *The Aeroplane*.

Operators from all over the world were bidders for the annual round of contracts let to spray cotton in Egypt and the Sudan, and British companies often survived the European winter on income generated by their North African adventures. Due to the urgency of complying with contract dates, or the panic call to battle without delay against a damaging infestation, some Tiger Moths travelled to the cotton fields in the holds of freighter aircraft but more usually small gaggles of agriculturists would fly out on the long haul via the South of France, Italy and Tunisia to follow the Mediterranean coast heading east.

Long range fuel was carried in the hopper, which was fitted with rubber liners for the purpose, and transferred to the top tank by hand operated wobble pump. In this configuration it was not unknown for the endurance to be increased to twelve hours, within which sectors of eight hours would be flown without landing.

Prior to Ed Clark's engine modifications which dramatically reduced oil consumption, a doubling of the oil capacity was often insufficient to cope with fuel range and additional oil supplies were carried in cans stowed in the cockpit. Various methods were adopted for re-oiling in flight, one of which was remembered by Jim Birnie:

> "The oil filler was routed to the dashboard, taming it with a cork, and assuaging the Gipsy's thirst by removing this item,

In 2012 Tiger Moth VH-BGG was retrieved from long term storage for restoration in Queensland. Her agricultural ancestry is illustrated by the turn-over truss that was still fitted after the aircraft had been returned to two seat configuration. *Adam Cramb*

Tiger Moth G-ANCT fitted with a quartet of atomisers, demonstrating the emergency dump facility, a mandatory requirement for all agriculturists operating at high weight and low level. *deHMC Archive*

Right: It was customary for crop spraying Tiger Moths to be flown from England to the Sudan on a seasonal basis except in cases of emergency when they would be dismantled and air lifted. In this shot John Freeman is in transit towards Khartoum with Tiger Moth G-ADGT, heading back to her British base at the end of the contract. *via Dennis Neville*

> inserting a funnel and upending a two gallon can into it, manipulating the whole clear of the ignition switches whilst flying by knee pressure."

Operating basic aeroplanes with tailskids and no brakes on transit through major international airports laid out with miles of concrete taxiways and aprons was uninviting too:

> "Well do I remember the sight of three Tiger Moths taxiing on the main tarmac at Cairo Airport, throttles set, hopefully, to a sensible taxy speed, with the three pilots outside the aircraft leaning heavily on the fin area and straining to maintain some sort of direction against a very brisk, playful crosswind, the while passing a row of Comets, Tu104s, etc., all positioned beautifully for a ghastly debacle."

This method of taxying, which was considerably safer than trying to control the aircraft from the cockpit without the assistance of wing-walkers, especially in any condition of wind, was employed by all the pilots during their transit stops when flying between England and Australia when the wear suffered by tailskid spoons was considerable. Walk-taxiing was severely frowned upon at some large airfields where apron controllers were unaware they were witnessing a largely lost art.

A hazard of a more unexpected nature was encountered by Peter Charles when operating in the rural idyll of Somerset. He thought little of a loud bang which occurred at the commencement of a spray run, but after landing he discovered a number of small holes in the fabric of the starboard mainplanes. Later in the day he heard two more loud reports and felt a scattering of shotgun pellets as they hit the aircraft. Locating the culprit in an adjoining field, Peter Charles flew slowly towards him at 30ft.

> "As I approached he raised the shotgun and emptied both barrels at me. Momentarily I was shocked, then angry. As I passed over him I pulled the dump lever and emptied yellow dyed spray all over him. Two months later a man was charged with unlawfully shooting at an aircraft, an offence for which he was found guilty and fined £20."

Birdstrikes have always been a hazard to aerial applicators and Peter Charles was forced to make an emergency landing in elephant grass in Tiger Moth G-AMVF after a bird struck shattered the propeller when operating in the Sudan. *via Dennis Neville*

Tiger Moth G-ADGT was converted for agricultural operations by Hants and Sussex Aviation in 1957 and operated in the role for ten years. The aircraft is fitted with spin strakes and stub exhausts but no slats. She became a joy rider in 2002 and joined the Tiger Club at Headcorn in 2008. *deHMC Archive*

It is perfectly safe to walk-taxi a brakeless Tiger Moth, especially across wide expanses of concrete. Pilot Jorgen Skov Nielsen can easily steer OY-ECH at Roskilde Airport by leaning against the fuselage and has immediate access to throttle and ignition switches. *Thorbjorn Brunander Sund*

Spray nozzles required adjustment for each individual job to ensure that the flow rate and droplet size were most ideally set for the task. Expert calibration accurately determined the volume of chemical deposited per acre. *Bill Bowker*

One of the most active British operators was Bill Bowker's Farm Aviation Services, born from the financial wreckage of a concern which had gone broke after converting Tiger Moth G-AMTO (84655), to take a hopper, the same aeroplane soloed by Bill Bowker at Panshanger on 25 August 1953 while a student at the de Havilland Aeronautical Technical School. He and two partners managed to raise enough money to liberate two Tiger Moths from the Receivers and to start their own business on a farm strip near Hitchin in the winter of 1959:

> "Three seasons later we could say that we had developed systems for operating a fleet, now grown to three Tiger Moths, with a minimum of personnel, maximum mobility and efficiency of application. To do this involved designing a venturi spreader for solid materials which was powerful enough to give a wide swathe and so avoid striping of the crop because of uneven application. Also loading equipment which was light, mobile, and required only one operator, and a system of field marking using disposable fluorescent paper cylinders instead of expensive and unreliable human beings, had to be evolved. By these means the company succeeded in doing as good and reliable a job as English weather permits, and staying in business where others had fallen by the wayside or abandoned British work as hopelessly uneconomic.
>
> With techniques perfected and ways found to deal with most of the muddles, which can only occur in a contract service involving vehicles and aeroplanes loose in a large slice of central and southern England, the aeroplanes soon became the limiting factor in developing the enterprise. Once airborne the Tiger Moth, when suitably equipped and flown, did an excellent job, but apart from having too small a payload it was draughty and uncomfortable for the pilot and difficult to manoeuvre on the ground. Its antique though lovely appearance was the subject of increasing prejudice on the part of the customers."

Farm Aviation turned away from Tiger Moths and became associated, fittingly, with the agricultural version of the DHC.1 Chipmunk, but it was to be a sad farewell. Having every intention of giving G-AMTO an honourable retirement and returning her to her original configuration with which Bill Bowker was familiar, to his eternal shame he broke her beyond economical repair at Upwell, near Ely, while taking-off on almost her last spraying sortie on 22 July 1965.

Adrian Deverell, passionate supporter of the Tiger Moth through a lifetime's association with Rollason Aircraft and the Tiger Club, defended the type against the Chipmunk which in the 1950s was still considered an upstart. He quoted the case of a taxiing mishap in which a Tiger Moth and a Chipmunk had sustained precisely the same damage to propeller, port wing spar and leading edge. The Tiger Moth was returned to service in less than two days whereas the Chipmunk was unserviceable for more than two weeks. The cost of labour and materials to repair the Tiger Moth was only 8% of the bill for the Chipmunk.

Loading the aircraft required maximum deposit in the minimum time and each operator designed equipment equal and appropriate to the task. Great care was required on the part of the driver due to the geometry of the structure and the risk of colliding with vulnerable parts of the fragile airframe. *Bill Bowker*

There was very little room for manoeuvre when loading the hopper of a Tiger Moth, most of which was achieved with the engine running during a rapid turn-round. *deHMC Archive*

The dexterity of the loader driver was all important in hastening the turnround of the applicator who shut down the engine only when refuelling was necessary. Care was essential not to damage the aeroplane or to lose load to the slipstream. Tiger Moth ZK-AIE operating at Northland in April 1953. *via Janic Geelan*

At one time the identity of the operator was allowed to be more important than the size and positioning of the registration letters. Tiger Moth G-APPN in pristine condition suffered but recovered from a number of major accidents between 1959 and 1964. Rebuilt in military markings in 2001 she was delivered to a Spanish museum in 2004. *deHMC Archive*

After retirement ZK-AJO was maintained in airworthy condition by James Aviation as a reminder of how the release of military surplus Tiger Moths fuelled and accelerated the growth of the agricultural aviation business in New Zealand immediately after the end of the Second World War. *Norman Eastaff*

Unceremoniously dumped outside the hangars of the former RAAF Base Uranquinty after losing her undercarriage and rearranging the spray bars when landing there on 8 December 1964, VH-ACJ was stored for 20 years before transfer to a new owner at Berwick. *Neville Parnell*

Elsewhere, the writing was on the wall. On 6 November 1962 the Australian Minister for Civil Aviation, Mr Shane Paltridge, announced in Canberra that Tiger Moth aircraft would be banned from use in aerial agricultural work from 31 December 1965, a time scale considered sufficient for the acquisition of other more suitable aircraft types. One of the reasons for the ban was a quoted accident rate "three to four times higher than that of more modern aircraft engaged in low flying agricultural work." Accepting the ban but not the reasoning, Tiger Moth supporters analysed the Australian civil register to discover 220 commercially operated Tiger Moths, outnumbering the nearest rival by 5:1, and the 'one' spent little time at modest speed at zero altitude.

In New Zealand a total of 210 Tiger Moths was engaged in aerial work reaching a peak in the mid 1950s and reducing to just fifteen by 1963. Revered and respected, the agricultural Tiger Moth earned her place in history and the museums of the world. Although New Zealand's first conversion, ZK-ASO (83533), was written off in April 1957, her Australian counterpart VH-PCB (DHA41), survived to the end. Cancelled in October 1964, the aircraft was donated for permanent exhibition with the Walcha Historical Society of New South Wales.

James Aviation, one time operators of a fleet of eleven agricultural Tiger Moths, had owned ZK-AJO (DHA489), for ten years from October 1949, and repurchased her in August 1966. Retired to the company hangar at Hamilton in 1981 and maintained in airworthy condition as a permanent reminder of how it all began, ZK-AJO is credited with 6,914 hours of agricultural flying in addition to her Air Force and club service, during which time she spread 13,393 tons of fertiliser and lime, 42,000lb of seed, and sprayed 9,274 acres. Gross earnings until retirement amounted to £56,000 or about 160 times her military surplus value.

In recognition of the sterling efforts of agricultural Tiger Moths operating in New Zealand, the country's Postal Authority issued a 50c stamp in 1993 depicting a yellow Tiger Moth mounted on a plume of dispersing 'super'. The series, of which the 50c stamp was a part, celebrated notable events determined by decade and the 'Aerial Topdressing' titling of the Tiger Moth was listed under the banner of the 1940s, which it most certainly was, but only just.

In 1953 a hopper system had been designed, manufactured and tested by Jim McMahon, a flying instructor employed at the Herts and Essex Aero Club at Broxbourne in England, all neatly packaged inside Tiger Moth G-ALZA (83589). The aircraft was sold to New Zealand immediately after flight trials and certification and registered ZK-BAH but her sterling service ended in 1967 when she collided with a hillside. Rebuilt in 1986 she was acquired by Murray Miers who learned to fly and completed all that was necessary to qualify for his commercial licence entirely on that aeroplane, thought to be the last New Zealand based pilot ever to do so. In 1990 Murray Miers sold the Tiger Moth locally and moved to Zaire to establish a flourishing aerial agriculture business of his own.

The legacy of the Tiger Moth's agricultural era is the consolidation of a new industry from which some of the original and surviving jewels of the trade have been handed on for safe keeping to an appreciative new generation. For some time, assets from early agricultural businesses were still turning up in relatively inaccessible areas in Australia where they once fell by the wayside and were not considered worthy of salvage. In 1989, a collection of redundant 'Ag Tigers' was released from over twenty years of storage in Western Australia: fourteen fuselages, seventy three wings, eighteen engines plus a treasure trove of assorted spare parts. Included as a bonus was a DH.83 Fox Moth once operated by the Royal Flying Doctor Service.

Tiger Moths served the British agricultural industry faithfully and well for many years until the advent of more efficient tractor-drawn farm equipment suited to the relatively small nature of the fields and which quickly proved that crop spraying by fixed wing aircraft was no longer economic. However, the country maintained its position at the forefront of invention and development of aerial spraying and spreading technology and equipment, and is still a net exporter to those countries where the only practical and most economic treatment of vast acreage or otherwise inaccessible areas can only be bestowed through the wonders of aviation.

VH-NWM was one of a number of ex agricultural airframes released from long-term store in Western Australia, the majority of which were delivered to Luskintyre for restoration to standard configuration by Ray Windred and later Matthew Webber. *Motty's Aviation Photographs*

In perfect harmony a pair of Tiger Moths in the last training colour scheme worn by RAAF aircraft are pictured flying near RAAF Base Point Cook where they operate as joyriders. *Garry Herne*

CHAPTER TWENTY ONE

All in a Day's Work

Air racing has been a competitive sport ever since it was discovered that one aeroplane could fly faster, or further, than another, and entrepreneurial sportsmen or publicity seeking newspaper proprietors were persuaded to put up crocks of gold as wagers or prizes. Most prolific of the British based private owner types during the 1920s, the DH.60 Moth featured heavily in high profile, closed circuit racing for relatively small money prizes although the majority of entrants flew in these closely contested events for the sport, honour and recognition rather than any cash reward.

It was the numerical superiority of Tiger Moths in Great Britain during the 1950s that did much to re-stimulate some of the pre-war interest. Races between many aeroplanes of the same type would be won on merit: the degree of polishing and honing would be complemented only by the skill of the pilot and his ability to confuse the handicappers. There was no need to devote energy to sealing the gaps and fairing the strut ends, or to streamlining the cockpit and fitting tiny mainwheels in order to minimise the drag, all features employed during the 1920s. Skill in rounding pylons and assessing the best conditions for wind and drift at high or low level in a well rigged aeroplane with crisp controls and a good engine would determine the winners.

A disadvantage to racing a privately owned Tiger Moth was that the engine needed to be run at nearly full throttle in the heats, to defeat the best endeavours of the handicappers, then in the finals at full throttle all the way. A broken engine was expensive to replace and a raced engine, unless maintained to the peak of perfection, soon lost its edge. Club owned and maintained aeroplanes were fair game: cash prizes and kudos for the organisation and no expensive maintenance charges for the competing pilot.

One of the first post-war race meetings held in Great Britain was at Lympne in 1947 which featured five Tiger Moths in a Scratch Race run over four laps of a ten mile course and was won by Fred Kirk in G-AINW (83011). The Tiger Moth was sold to India the following year and was lost in 1958 when an Indian Air Force Vampire collided with her hangar. At the same Lympne meeting John Cunningham could only manage sixth place in the High Speed Handicap, in spite of achieving 494.63mph in

de Havilland test pilot Pat Fillingham climbing aboard the London Aeroplane Club's G-AHXC at Lympne in August 1948 in preparation for a Tiger Moth Air Race. *via British Aerospace*

Below: The pastoral scene: air racing in Great Britain during the 1950s. The starter, wearing a lounge suit, waves away the Tiger Moth which had been restrained from applying too much throttle while the pilot of the Hawker Aircraft Company's 'vintage collection' Tomtit pays attention. *The Aeroplane*

A typical line up at the start of a Tiger Moth race during the annual jamboree that was the National Air Races at Coventry in the early 1960s. Jackaroos were classified as 'Tiger Moths' but when flown solo had a better performance. *Richard Riding*

a DH.100 Vampire F.1, but Pat Fillingham set up a new 100km closed circuit record of 178.33mph with the de Havilland Aeronautical Technical School's TK2, G-ADNO. In August the following year, Pat Fillingham won the Tiger Moth Race at Lympne flying G-AHXC (85032), at 86mph, although John Cunningham's Vampire, this time an F.3, rose to second place in the High Speed Handicap, beaten by a Supermarine Spitfire Mk VIII two seat trainer.

Unlike the 'mock' air races which perambulate gently around a closed circuit in the style of a demented formation, or 'handicap' races with so many different types involved and the single seat ultra-light enjoying as great a chance of victory as the speed twin taking off half an hour behind, races limited to Tiger Moths only generated great rivalry and high emotion. A first wave of perhaps six Tiger Moths in a field of ten or twelve taking off with the same handicap time and in line abreast, diving for the first pylon turn, was a sight worth beholding. Who could ignore the sound of six Gipsy Major engines at full throttle rotating their assortment of wooden and metal propellers of differing pitch and diameter, each selected with infinite care? The choice of propeller was one of the few physical variations between otherwise standard machines that could greatly influence performance.

Tiger Moths have been competitors in, if not winners of, most of the recognised and prestigious air races. Jimmy Denyer's winning speed of 118.5mph flying Tiger Moth G-AIVW (83135), in the 1958 King's Cup Air Race was bettered by Dennis Hartas in G-ANZZ (85834), when he won the de Havilland Tiger Moth Challenge Trophy in 1962 at 120.5mph, a feat which contributed to his award of the Royal Aero Club Jubilee Trophy and British Air Racing Championship for that year.

Lewis Benjamin was offered friendly advice by the future Air Racing Champion before the 1959 National Air Races at Baginton in which 'Benjy' was scheduled to make his racing debut flying his favourite Tiger Moth, G-APRA (85347). His total racing qualification was, as he put it, a Competitor's Licence which he had been awarded for asking. The friendly advice of course was to fly as fast as possible all the way but the novice racer soon discovered that although he won the first heat by miles, he was handicapped out of the rest of the meeting. Following further advice from seasoned campaigners the Tiger Moth's tyres were pumped up hard in an effort to reduce ground rolling distance on take-off, 'hard' spark plugs were fitted and 'thinner' oil. But it was to no avail and, apart from the experience of legitimate low level flying at high speed through gateways and between trees, Lewis Benjamin's first racing season ended without further success.

Since Tiger Moths, and especially their Gipsy Major engines, have largely become privately funded icons, 'Air Racing' for the type has taken on a different meaning. In 1977 Bill Hitchcock organised the first *'Great Tiger Moth Air Race'* centred on the Royal Newcastle Aero Club at Maitland, New South Wales. The early sponsors inadvisedly and inaccurately promoted the event as the world's first Tiger Moth race and thirty seven aircraft took part, but the 'race' was really an intensive two day time-trial around Sydney and the Hunter Valley, and the winner was decided on a mix of navigational ability, time keeping and fuel conservation, rather than blind throttle bending. A lack of regular and guaranteed sponsorship prevented the Great Race from becoming a biennial event as originally intended but a total of twelve races were run between 1977 and 2014.

A very similar exercise took place in Great Britain in 1979, organised by the de Havilland Moth Club, when Matthew Gloag and Son, purveyors of Famous Grouse Scotch Whisky, sponsored forty one Tiger Moths, seven DH.87B Hornet Moths, and a mixed fleet of supporting aircraft including four DH.89A Dragon Rapides and a DH.114 Heron, in an event sold to the media as *'The Famous Grouse Tiger Moth Air Race'*.

The aircraft flew from Hatfield by way of Hucknall and Sunderland to Strathallan in Perthshire, and the winner was decided against parameters very much in parallel with those laid down in Australia. It was appropriate, perhaps, that David Cyster and his wife Cherry, flying Tiger Moth G-ANRF (83748), carried off the Grouse Trophy and a gallon jar of the sponsor's product which over thirty years later remained unopened. The tenth anniversary of the 'Grouse Rally', as the event inevitably became known, operated around a curtailed circuit including Old Warden and Duxford due to the closure of both Strathallan and Sunderland in the intervening years. Desecration of the Hatfield site itself in 1994 and closure of Hucknall in 2013 ensures that the 1979 Grouse Rally will remain special and totally unique.

Perhaps one of the most challenging races in which Tiger Moths have been involved, and which really was a no-holds-barred all-out race with time as the principal challenger, was the *Daily Mail*, London (Marble Arch) to Paris (Arc de Triomphe) Air Race organised between 13 and 23 July 1959, celebrating Louis Blériot's 1909 crossing of the English Channel. The Race stimulated the imagination of all: competitors, officials, Customs, Immigration, airlines, travel agencies, Air Forces, the media and sponsors. Every type of vehicle was featured: high powered motorcycles, formula racing and veteran

Considered to be a very fast standard Tiger Moth, G-AIVW was a regular entrant for the National Air Races. Based at Newcastle Airport, this photograph was taken at the end of the 1950 racing season and before the aircraft was sold, later to become the Sea Tiger.
Raymond Rayner

In the 'pits' at the Royal Newcastle Aero Club, Maitland, New South Wales where competitors gathered in 1978 for the locally organised 'Great Tiger Moth Air Race', in reality a test of navigational skills and fuel economy. *Bill Hitchcock*

Charlie Miller and his Tiger Moth VH-CES taking off from Port Macquarie during the second Great Tiger Moth Air Race in October 1978. Note the elaborate reprofiling of the cockpit surrounds. *Neville Parnell*

When the crew of G-AYUX reported at home base prior to joining the Famous Grouse Rally at Hatfield in June 1979, they found the Tiger Moth's rudder had been damaged in her hangar. Astonishingly, the local maintenance organisation had a complete unit overhauled to the red dope stage in their stores. *deHMC Archive*

cars, helicopters, hovercraft, jet airliners, bombers and military fighters operating at low level, not to mention pedal cycles, fold-up scooters and running shoes. Hugh Tansley chose a motorised lawn mower for the journey from Central London to Croydon, and from Toussous to the Arc, averaging 3.5mph on these sections. The Croydon-Lympne-Toussous sectors were accomplished in Tiger Moth G-ACDC (3177), flown by Lewis Benjamin whose contribution was included in Hugh Tansley's overall time of ten hours and forty four minutes. Using a combination of a fast motorcycle and RAF Hawker Hunter, the winner completed the course in less than half an hour.

Neil Stevens purchased Tiger Moth ZK-AWB (DHA635), in 1968 and she was shipped from New Zealand to Vancouver where registration CF-XNR was allocated in September in advance of taking part in the *Daily Mail's* next aviation spectacular the following year, a Transatlantic Air Race. After leaving the top of the Empire State Building in New York the rules stated that the deadline by which entrants must clock in at the Post Office Tower in London was midnight on 11 May 1969.

The aircraft was modified to include a seventy five gallon fuel tank in the front cockpit together with an extra oil tank, new compasses and artificial horizons, transistorised ADFs, portable VHF and HF sets and a pair of twelve volt batteries. A life raft, lifejackets, wet suits, beacon and emergency supplies were to be carried on board. Somewhat optimistically, after leaving home base at Vancouver, the planned route was blandly declared to be Moncton, Labrador, Greenland, Iceland and London.

On the eve of the 1979 Famous Grouse Rally, Hatfield to Strathallan, part of the fleet drawn up at Hatfield Aerodrome. The buildings on the left are the first private owner hangars built in 1930, and in the distance, the classrooms, offices and hangars constructed for the Reserve Flying School. *Philip Birtles*

The participants in the Famous Grouse Rally drawn up at Hatfield in June 1979. The large building at left, 'the aluminium shed', now listed and protected, was erected as the Flight Test Shed for the DH.106 Comet airliner programme and is unique. The Clubhouse and squash courts built for the London Aeroplane Club in 1930 stand alongside the tree and marquee on the right. *deHMC Archive*

The Famous Grouse Rally fleet safely assembled at Strathallan Castle together with a number of local visitors and the Royal Navy Lynx helicopter which accompanied the stream along the route from Hatfield. *deHMC Archive*

Tiger Moth N5050 was an entrant in the 1969 Transatlantic Air Race although the crew travelled by scheduled jet service and still won a prize. *Ritchie Rasmussen*

Bill Maynell's Tiger Moth G-ANEL was a familiar sight on the British air racing scene for many seasons. Once all silver she lived through a camouflage period and is currently red and silver and living in the South of France. *via Jaap Niestadt*

The dismantled N5050 on a trailer which was driven 3,651 miles from Vancouver to Moncton only to be declared unairworthy on arrival. *deHMC Archive*

Anthony James in his Tiger Moth VH-ALC, an ex-RAF aeroplane shipped to Australia in 1940, gradually losing his race with Graeme Lowe in a 1936 Alta at Mangalore Aerodrome in April 1986. The Tiger Moth was later sold to a German owner but was badly damaged in transit when its trailer overturned and rolled into a ditch. *via Anthony James*

With the entrant's preparation funding running out Harry McPhee offered his services and, with the help of a local radio station, additional funding and logistical support was provided but the team was well behind schedule. It was decided that Harry McPhee would position the aircraft from Vancouver to Moncton where she would be collected by Neil Stevens who would fly her to New York to register and then back to Moncton. During take-off from a grass runway at Bellingham Airfield, (close to Vancouver but actually in Washington state), the heavily laden aircraft hit a mud patch and ground-looped, damaging a wing and breaking the propeller which was replaced by another found hanging over a mantel-piece in Seattle. The Tiger Moth was dismantled, loaded onto a trailer and with the help of a relief driver driven to Moncton, a distance of 3,651 miles, in eighty six hours, where an engineer declared that two fuselage longerons were damaged and could not be repaired within the time remaining.

The two pilots travelled by train to Montreal, wearing their flying kit and clutching the Tiger Moth's propeller, where they caught a BOAC 707 service to Prestwick. There they were met by Bill Maynell and his Tiger Moth G-ANEL (82333), who flew Neil Stevens to Denham to rendezvous with Harry McPhee who had driven south. The two arrived in London as pillion passengers on a pair of high-powered motorcycles and clocked in on the 33rd floor of the Post Office Tower. Next morning they were advised they had won their category: 'the most meritorious effort by a non-winning entry from the Commonwealth'.

The crew said after the race they would raise funds to repair CF-XNR and make the Atlantic crossing against their original flight plan, and soon, but they never did. Although delivered to Neil Stevens in Vancouver, according to official records the New Zealand registration had been cancelled on sale to a new owner in the USA and before the race, in February 1969, she was registered N5050 to Clayton Henley in Idaho who may have loaned her for the Atlantic crossing. The Canadian markings were never carried but were not cancelled until 1981. Currently registered N17440 to reflect her ex-RAAF serial, the aircraft is currently owned by Mike Harris and based in Wisconsin.

To settle an argument about the relative merits of racing cars and small aircraft a pint of beer was put up as a wager at Sunderland Flying Club in May 1964 when Tiger Moth G-AREH (85287), was entered in competition against a Lotus Ford 23B to travel the length of Usworth's 1,500 yard runway. Operating unfavourably into wind the Tiger Moth started her challenge in the airborne position but from a standing start the Lotus had achieved over 100mph within ten seconds and accelerated away to take the trophy with relative ease.

Placings were identical in a similar challenge mounted at Mangalore Aerodrome near Sydney on 13 April 1986. The quarter mile dash was a competition between Anthony James, representing the Antique Aeroplane Association of Australia and flying his British built Tiger Moth VH-ALC (82360), one of the 1940 imports, and Graeme Lowe of the Historic Racing Car Register of Australia, who was driving a 1936, two litre, supercharged, twin OHC Alta, described as being 'very fast'. Predictably the Tiger Moth got off to a flying start and climbed to her racing height of 5ft but the driver of the car kept his boot pressed hard down and slowly overhauled the Tiger Moth to win by a short head.

During the 1950s and 1960s almost every gliding club in Europe employed a Tiger Moth as a tug but as the needs of gliders and sailplanes became more demanding the type was gradually phased out. *deHMC Archive*

GLIDER TUGGING

In post-war civil life Australian glider pilot Fred Hoinville was one of the first to be approved for towing club gliders with his ex-RAAF Tiger Moths VH-AIU (DHA398) and later VH-AYY (DHA214), the famous *Brolga*. On 27 September 1951, Fred Hoinville left Bankstown in VH-AYY with a Grunau Baby in tow scheduled to be delivered to Toowoomba, 500 miles away, a trip estimated to take two days divided into four sectors and flying at 60kts. A telephone line was attached to the tow rope to enable the Tiger Moth pilot to communicate with Bob Muller the glider pilot, but the exhaust note of the Gipsy Major, combined with the wind noise in the open cockpit, neutralised an already weak tone and Bob Muller fell back on the tried and tested method of hand signals transmitted with the aid of a table tennis bat.

The flight progressed through conditions of extreme turbulence, low cloudbase and at one point a pall of smoke which rose to 6,000ft from a succession of huge forest fires. In order to circumvent the worst of the smoke the linked pair was forced to fly directly into sun where all the problems of keeping in station and with the tow line taught were magnified by the blinding orange ball on the horizon. An unexpected headwind had cut the groundspeed after a period of rapid progress and within twenty miles of his destination, having unexpectedly travelled almost 500 miles in the one day, Fred Hoinville decided it would be safer to land rather than risk the prospect of running out of fuel. With a tail down attitude due to the presence of the glider the fuel gauge was considered to be unreliable although on estimates about thirty minutes' worth of fuel was believed still to be in the tank. An unexpected problem soon arose as described by Fred Hoinville in his book *Halfway to Heaven*:

> "It was sad to have to land so close to our goal, but the risk of going on was not justified. I selected a nice large, flat paddock alongside a farmhouse on a main road and waggled *Brolga's* wings in a signal to Bob Muller. He released the rope and circled down into the paddock. I dropped the rope beside him and trundled in too. *Brolga* landed smoothly but seemed to stop rather short.

Tiger Moth G-AMLF climbing away from Husbands Bosworth Airfield in September 1968 with a heavy single seater sailplane in tow. A glider pilot maintains his ideal position by referencing the top wings of the Tiger Moth to the horizon. *Alfred Jenks*

A Tiger Moth on the roll under what appears to be good soaring conditions with a high performance sailplane of three times the wingspan in tow. More efficient and quieter tugs gradually took over. *Michael Dressler*

SE-ANL just taking up slack on a snow covered runway in Sweden was built in Norway and escaped to neutral Sweden in April 1940. The aircraft was sold back to Norway in 1971 for display in a museum in Oslo. *deHMC Archive*

I stepped out into six inches of soft, gooey Queensland black soil, wet as a swamp. It was unbelievable. Here in this drought scorched land, how the dickens did the field get wet? We had landed in Bill Becker's barley field, at the township of Cambooya, fifteen miles from Toowoomba. Bill arrived smartly and solved our mystery. There had been a small local storm on the previous night and alone in all Queensland the barley paddock had got a soaking.

Within five minutes about twenty helpers arrived, dragged the two aircraft to the end of the field, got some fuel, and passed on all the latest radio reports. All Queensland and almost all Australia were following our unusual flight with interest and goodwill. Everybody knew about us and was desperately anxious to help us along. In a few minutes we were ready to go again. We had covered over 500 miles in one day and had only fifteen to go, with half an hour of light left. We climbed in, waved good-bye, and I opened the throttle. *Brolga* strained mightily, took up a little slack in the rope, and then stopped, tail up but wheels not moving.

Sadly and sheepishly we scrambled out again. We guessed what had happened. The Grunau had a special pair of tiny solid rubber wheels mounted on the skid. These had sunk into the mud and made a really efficient anchor. Racing against the sunset we got out our tools and whipped the wheels and axle off and tried again. No luck. The skid this time pushed up a mound of mud ahead of the glider. We were stuck. There was not time to take down a part of the fence to get out into the road tonight. We dragged the aircraft back to the fence and tied them down finding great difficulty in driving the pegs into the hard earth. The end of the field had missed the heaviest rain and although the top two inches were soft the rest was like a rock."

The epic journey was completed the following day after a 30ft section of wire fence was removed which enabled both aircraft to be pushed through onto a straight road three miles long. Twelve minutes after take-off the Tiger Moth and its towed cargo was overhead Toowoomba Gliding Club.

Almost a year after the Toowoomba delivery, Fred Hoinville's Tiger Moth towed a pair of gliders simultaneously from Camden to Dubbo, a distance of about 200 miles, and recorded the first double tow ever attempted in Australia.

Throughout post-war Europe many civil and military gliding clubs and schools relied on Tiger Moth tugs as launch vehicles, apart from basic flying training and agricultural work, perhaps, the most universal of all tasks with which the aircraft was ever charged. In Scandinavia, the ability to tug targets and gliders had been a primary operational requirement since the Tiger Moth was introduced to service during the 1930s yet this flexibility was not recognised as a selling point and was never exploited in pre-war marketing.

Earliest records lodged with the British airworthiness authorities show that clearance was granted by an Airworthiness Approval Note in March 1947 to permit Helliwells and Marshall's Flying School to tow gliders with Tiger Moths, subject to the following basic limitations which were imposed at that time:

> Maximum glider weight 650lb (but satisfactory flight trials were completed with gliders weighing 660lb, 680lb and 730lb).
> Breaking strain of towrope (or weak link), 8 cwt.
> Towing speed, 70mph.

In 1953, the British Ministry of Supply (MoS) initiated Modification 145, possibly in respect of the minimal number of Tiger Moths scheduled to remain in service with the Royal Navy or even as support for many of the ex RAF aircraft sold to overseas governments. Mod 145 introduced the MoS request to equip the Tiger Moth Mk II for glider towing duties, and made provision for the installation of an 'Ottley' release hook and associated controls. Engineers were advised that they were expected to provide all parts necessary for the modification by making them on site with the exception of the release hook which could be supplied ex stock by Ottley Motors Ltd. At first glance a simple exercise, the job was estimated to take about a week per engineer, per aircraft.

Sold from 9 MU Cosford in one of the first post-war surplus disposal sales, T6901 (85130), was re-sold to the Netherlands and registered PH-UAW in May 1947. The aircraft hit a glider towing cable while taxiing at Hilversum in August 1956 and in 1963 she collided with a banner towing cable while airborne at Eelde. The cable end snaked into the cockpit and wrapped itself around the pilot's hands; the aircraft was comprehensively demolished when she subsequently landed without proper assistance. The wreckage was sold, rebuilt into a Tiger Moth in single seat configuration at Rotterdam and, with a new identity, PH-AAB, embarked upon a career as a banner tug along the coast. Within a year she was in a ditch at Zestienhoven. The aircraft had picked up the banner at too slow a speed, failed to lift it off the ground, failed to release it too and had slowly subsided back to earth.

Banners had to be carefully laid out on the ground in a manner which allowed them to be peeled back on themselves once the aircraft's tow hook had engaged on a suspended wire strop, thereby gently feeding in the drag rather than attempting a snatch. Any other method of pick up with the limited power available to a Tiger Moth would have been impossible. As a precaution against snagging the suspended strop with the main undercarriage a light cable deflection system was designed utilising the axles, the top fixing of the undercarriage radius rods, and the underside of the front cowling as anchorages.

Charity, one of the fleet of three Tiger Moth tugs maintained by the London Gliding Club at Dunstable in the early 1960s. Two were later damaged by fire in the hangar situated underneath the unique art-deco clubhouse. *John Ellis*

Tiger Moth PH-BIS was fitted with a light tubular framework picking up on undercarriage and engine mounting as a precaution against a misjudged cable snatch when employed for banner towing. *via Herman Dekker*

In 1977 Finnish PiK glider designer Hannu Riihela opted for a readily available 180hp Lycoming 0-360 engine when rebuilding his Tiger Moth OH-XLA, resulting in a phenomenal increase in all-round performance. *Hannu Riihela*

During a banner towing flight in formation with another aircraft in July 1964, the pilot of Tiger Moth PH-UVC (84638), realised his banner had become entangled with that towed by the other aircraft and, during a manoeuvre intended to help them disengage, one tow cable broke leaving PH-UVC in command of both. Even at full power the Tiger Moth could not maintain height or speed and, unable to cast off the tow, was forced to land in a bulb field where she nosed over unceremoniously in the rich topsoil.

With the exception of an Italian Tiger Moth and another on long-term restoration in Germany whose motive power was temporarily supplied by an Alfa Romeo licence-built Gipsy Major engine, and similarly a Brazilian replica, it is believed that without exception all other airframes have only been mated to the Gipsy Major engine (of several different marques) or the Menasco Pirate. In 1970, Hannu Riihela, Finnish designer of world class PiK sailplanes, acquired the mortal remains of OH-ELA (85167), a British export of 1951 which was badly damaged at Hollola in 1954 when operating on skis and subsequently placed in store.

Hannu Riihela completely rebuilt the aircraft using alternative parts when originals could not be located and, having no Gipsy Major engine, installed a close-cowled Lycoming 0-360 delivering 180hp, complete with self starter and generator. First flown on 29 April 1977 by Pekka Parssinen, the improvement in performance was phenomenal: from a 200ft take-off run a climb rate of 1,500fpm was achieved. Not surprisingly the aircraft was used for launching PiK sailplanes and was also operated on floats and skis. Later sold to a group of airline pilots, the aircraft spent a season suspended from the ceiling of the gentleman's outfitting section of a Helsinki department store.

Standard Tiger Moths have been employed by many gliding clubs to provide aero tows to customers at the end of a 200ft nylon rope, and much of the economy of the operation was in the art of getting back down again as quickly as possible. The benefits of reduction in airborne time due to the methods employed were often outweighed by the cost of engine repairs. A full throttle climb followed by the rapid cooling experienced in a power off descent many times in an hour was not the best way to treat a Gipsy Major engine.

Lewis Benjamin earned some free flying by offering Tiger Club Tiger Moths to gliding clubs, and the occasions proved to be very competitive as well as financially rewarding:

"It was not that glider towing was dull, but any journey could be more exciting if, whilst on the way down, you could also have some fun. There was an element of competition amongst the tug pilots not only to see who could be down the quickest, but who could best entertain the others en route.

We normally lost our tow around 2,000ft and it was soon proved that the fastest way down without tangling the rope was to spin the Tiger Moth. The routine was to cast off, close the throttle and whip the nose up for a bit more altitude, then boot on rudder at the right moment and start counting the turns. Five turns in a spin were plenty and all too soon you found yourself at 700ft or so, nicely placed for the run in. An acknowledged variation was a slow roll either way, but no one ever attempted a loop because we believed the rope might curl around and foul the controls. Just for the record we were wrong; others have done it since.

There were two schools of thought too about releasing the rope after the tow and prior to landing. The first was a slow run in at 30ft, to release the rope and, if possible, plonk it neatly in front of the next glider all ready for the hook up. The second, because some thought the extra circuit, no matter how brief, a waste of valuable time, was to land with the rope still attached. One's landing had to be so short, that all one had to do, at least in theory, when one rolled to a stop, was to move the glider forward a few feet to hook up. The trouble was that since the prudent glider pilot wanted as long a run as possible he would position his machine as near to the hedge as he could, and the Tiger Moth's landing run had to be very short indeed.

It is a simple fact that the slower one flew, and the aircraft could be encouraged to fly very slowly, the more the end of the rope would dangle, aided and abetted by the metal clip at the end. To drag the rope through a tree or a hedge could prove disastrous. On one of my earlier trips I misjudged everything and dragged my rope not only through a hedge but between a couple having a picnic at the field's edge. The hook whipped away the cloth and goodies as neatly as any conjuror. The two were so shattered by this disappearing act that by the time I got there to apologise, they had fled."

JOYRIDING

In whichever country there had been military Tiger Moths during the Second World War, come the peace and almost every civil aerodrome boasted a club owned example, rocking gently in any breeze as she stood head to wind on the grass between flights, the Gipsy Major engine tinkling erratically as it gradually cooled, the aromatics of hot oil and petrol fumes mingling with other unique aeroplane smells. But more than fifty years after the Tiger Moth was training citizens of the Empire to fly in times of crisis, and the Tiger Moth became too outmoded for the clubs, a whole industry grew up providing 'trial lessons' and 'joyrides'. The businesses became particularly well established in Australia where the climate has much in its favour when harnessing commercial enterprise to outdoor activity, but in New Zealand, the USA and Great Britain also the public was actively encouraged to play a fuller part by accepting the extra trappings of fleecy lined jacket, shunned by those in the know, and satirical white scarf, in addition to the essential and traditional helmet and goggles.

The customers who flocked to the booking offices knew that a flight in a Tiger Moth, (aerobatics optional and at extra cost), was special and significant, and was much more than a mere circuit in an open cockpit biplane. The young men who flew Supermarine Spitfires and Avro Lancasters and Handley Page Halifaxes and all those legendary wartime aeroplanes learned to fly on the Tiger Moth, did they not? Fifty years after the great conflict many of those once young pilots wished to renew acquaintance, or to fly again in celebration of

An electrically driven hoist designed and built by Geoff Bray specifically for use with Tiger Moths and Chipmunks was employed for several seasons of Charity Joyriding by de Havilland Moth Club volunteers and enabled passengers with limited or no mobility to be safely lifted in and out of cockpits which would otherwise have been totally inaccessible. *Peter Hambrook*

Given care and attention by the handlers and the precision of positioning by the operator of the hoist, it was possible to thread a seriously disabled passenger into the front seat of a Tiger Moth and to ensure they were comfortable and secure. On some occasions passengers so enjoyed their experience that they asked to go round again. Lifting them out of the aeroplane took skill and patience until they were safely seated back in their own transport. *Geoff Collins*

VH-DHK is operated as a full time joyrider from Torquay in Victoria. An invitation to fly in a Moth is painted across the span of the lower wings and a contact telephone number on the underside of the starboard upper. *Graham Hyslop*

For more than twenty years VH-WAP was operated as a professional joyrider by Bruce McGarvie from Surfers Paradise on the Sunshine Coast of Queensland although few surfers are visible in this picture. *Stuart Howe*

Painted in military markings with Polish Air Force insignia, Jacek Mainka's Polish based Tiger Moth retains her British registration G-AFVE as a matter of practical convenience whilst remaining on a full Certificate of Airworthiness. *via Jacek Mainka*

a special birthday or anniversary. Children and grand-children were encouraged to fly to experience what dad or grand-dad once did. The first jet pilots learned to fly in Tiger Moths; also the Reservists whose units retained the aeroplane into the 1950s. Many of the first generation of Concorde pilots learned their skills on Tiger Moths too.

In 1998 Commander Philip Shaw MVO, RN, a helicopter instructor who had taught HRH Prince Andrew to operate the Sea King and who was a regular pilot with the Royal Navy Historic Flight based at Yeovilton, and owner of Tiger Moth G-AFVE (83720), completed a civilian flying instructor course on his own aircraft which was maintained on the then applicable Public Transport category Certificate of Airworthiness. Subsequently, 'Phil' Shaw was awarded a contract with the Defence Research Agency (DERA), for his Tiger Moth to be flown as part of their 'handling' syllabus by pilots attending the Empire Test Pilots School at Boscombe Down, one of the greatest compliments to the training abilities of the aircraft.

PARACHUTES

In December 1937 the Austrian designer Joseph Eschner demonstrated his rapid deployment parachute to a select group at Ford in Sussex, jumping from 300ft. In July 1938 he was invited to be part of the air display organised in celebration of the official opening of Luton Airport when the jump height from Luton Flying Club's Tiger Moth G-AFGT (3681), flown by Eric 'Jock' Bonar, was reported as 150ft.

A parachutist in free fall having stepped off the trailing edge of a Tiger Moth's starboard lower wing with sufficient time and space to miss the tailplane. *via Gerry Schwam*

In the immediate post-war era the development of parachuting as a sport, rather than a pure military necessity, often featured a Tiger Moth as a launch vehicle. The front cockpit was insufficiently large to accommodate a jumper with both seat parachute and a chest mounted reserve but providing the front stick was removed the jumper could crouch on the seat with their head out one side and their bottom out the other. There was a strong liklihood that during manoeuvres to exit the cockpit the jumper might inadvertently knock off the ignition switches on the port side, leaving the pilot in a state of some embarrassment, but aircraft in regular use were often fitted with a switch guard as a defence.

As a sport parachutist one has to have a head for heights, especially when climbing out of the front seat of an open cockpit biplane. Note exit has been made on the starboard side; the ignition switches are situated on the decking on the port side. *via Gerry Schwam*

In a relaxed mood in Australia parachutist number twenty three waits for the signal to start up and taxy, showing every sign that he will leave the aircraft on the port side. The front ignition switches are already in the 'on' position. *deHMC Archive*

Under the terms of the Permission granted by the British authorities in compliance with the Air Navigation Order, aircraft were approved on an individual basis to drop parachutists subject to the following conditions:

a. The pilot must occupy the rear cockpit.
b. The front cockpit control column must be removed.
c. The parachutist must occupy the front cockpit and exit to starboard.
d. At the time of dropping the wings must be level and airspeed between 60 and 80mph IAS.

Julie Hanks smiles for the camera as she steps off the wing of Tiger Moth G-AGZZ over Wiltshire whilst pilot Charlie Shea-Simonds looks on approvingly. *via Charlie Shea-Simonds*

When Charles Shea-Simonds applied in a private capacity for permission to drop parachutists from his own Tiger Moth G-AGZZ (DHA926), not influenced by his standing as Vice-President of the British Parachute Association (BPA), Pilot Examiner and Private Pilot Licence X Examiner, he was advised that in addition to the existing limitations it was expected that:

1. The front rudder bar must be disconnected and the rudder bar connecting rod removed.
2. The front cockpit entry door (starboard) must be removed.

A gentle letter to the appropriate Aviation Division ensured that common sense prevailed, and the requirement to meet the additional conditions was withdrawn.

When dropping from a Tiger Moth the normal practice was for pilot and jumper to confirm the beginning of the run-in at which time the parachutist would stand up on the seat using the centre section struts for assistance, and perch half in and half out of the cockpit, in the slipstream, to ensure the best view for the final positioning. There was no necessity to open the door which could be comfortably straddled. Buffeting was considerable such that speed was often reduced to less than 60mph, irrespective of what it said in the Permission, reducing further to just above the stall with a little power on to aid stability at the moment of departure. Facing the tail the jumper would dive off or facing forward merely step backwards off the walkway. In the 1950s and 1960s it was the done thing for the aircraft to follow the parachute down, exercising a degree of mother hen protection should the jumper descend into some unexpected predicament, when the Tiger Moth would be overhead to mark the spot and ready to summon assistance if necessary.

RAF surplus Tiger Moth DE313 (85347), was sold as Lot 166 from 10 MU Hullavington in 1953 and delivered into the W A Rollason hangar at Croydon. In an effort to offer the best

Stepping backwards off the trailing edge of the starboard lower mainplane of a Tiger Moth a sport parachutist is in the ideal position to free fall. Steve Plank, dropping away from Pete Colman's throttled G-AKXS, tidied the aeroplane and closed the front cockpit door during the run in towards the drop zone. *Peter Jackson*

opportunities for jumping, especially during the conviviality of the Tiger Club's regular air displays of the late 1950s, the Club's founding father, Norman Jones, now owner of Rollason Aircraft, arranged for DE313, registered G-APRA from June 1959, to be converted with the specific intention of providing airborne assistance to parachutists. G-APRA was named *Sue Burges* in honour of Great Britain's leading lady sport parachutist of the day.

Modifications to the airframe included the removal of controls and compass bracketry from the front cockpit, fitment of a streamlined forward windscreen and a grab-handle on the starboard side of the fuselage. The starboard front door was removed and the exposed sill rounded and padded; the starboard walkway was widened, and a transparent panel some twelve inches square let into the trailing edge.

Right: Sue Burges wearing the classical kit of a sport parachutist of the 1960s clambers aboard Tiger Moth G-AODS at Fairoaks. The pose gives a good indication of how little room there would be in the front cockpit of a Tiger Moth when wearing the parachute pack. *deHMC Archive*

Below: Sue Burges on the narrow starboard walkway of Tiger Moth G-ANPB and stabilising herself with the aid of the decking prior to jumping. Most parachutists favoured leaving the wing when facing forwards. *deHMC Archive*

Rollason Aircraft converted Tiger Moth G-APRA especially for parachuting. Named the *Sue Burges* the front doors were removed and the sills padded, a grab handle was fitted on the centre decking and a transparent panel let into the starboard lower wing. *via Lewis Benjamin*

Flown by Lewis Benjamin, with Sue Burges as a temporary passenger, G-APRA was positioned from Croydon to Stapleford Tawney on 10 May 1959 for her first operational sortie, and with the intention of attempting to take the national free fall record past the one minute barrier. Sue Burges was dropped from 10,500ft over Stapleford in conditions of rising wind and developing cumulus, but her descent ended in disaster when she was blown into an oak tree and sustained serious injuries from which, fortunately, she made a full recovery.

With wires and struts to grasp the Tiger Moth was an ideal, steady platform from which to drop, a pure vindication of how the manufacturer had acceded to the specifier's exacting 'escape' requirements laid down in 1930. When parachutes became more directionally controllable and efficient due to rapid technical development, the sporting skydiver's quest was for an aircraft that could climb higher, faster and with a greater load ensuring the type was relegated to occasional guest appearances only.

SKYWRITING

Writing slogans or messages in the sky using smoke from aircraft equipped with the necessary equipment is an invention of the immediate post First World War era when nimble ex-scouts were modified for the purpose. In more recent times smoke generation for aerobatic performances by civilian singletons or teams of military jets has become a visual enhancement of standard expectation. Probably in all history, only one Tiger Moth has been involved professionally in skywriting and that in 1952 when Fred Hoinville's VH-AYY (DHA214), was the first and only licensed performer in Australia.

Influenced by the size and orientation of the target towards which the message was directed, the cloud situation, position of the sun, thermal activity and wind shift, VH-AYY would operate at heights between 12,000ft and 17,000ft and in some areas, notably over Sydney, the pilot would liaise with research meteorologists who had set up programmes to track the smoke drift on behalf of studies into clear air movements. At such heights a message in smoke can be clearly read within a radius of twenty miles covering 1,200 square miles, can be placed within ten miles of the target without loss of clarity and, depending on the stability of the atmosphere, may linger overhead or drift intact for up to thirty minutes before decaying.

The employed system of smoke generation, apart from the use of firework-like smoke candles which are totally inappropriate for sky writing, has always centred on the injection of smoke-oil or diesel fuel into a hot engine exhaust where it vaporises into billowing white smoke, coloured as required by the addition of concentrated dyes. On

The advantage of a formation leader not smoking is evident in these shots of the Italian Tiger Moth Team *'Le Tigri'* during their participation at the Redhill Air Show in July 1987 when their European tour was sponsored by an Italian furniture manufacturer. Smoke generation of such generously billowing proportions is generally difficult to achieve from an engine the size of a Gipsy Major even when operating at full throttle. *Barbara Setterfield*

Tiger Moth VH-FAS smoking heartily against the seafront cityscape of Perth, Western Australia. *Paul Falconer-West*

opening the Tiger Moth's smoke-oil control valve, Fred Hoinville's aircraft immediately generated a huge plume of white smoke which just as easily and completely was cut off when the valve was closed. For total consistency in smoke quality it was necessary to operate at full throttle to achieve and maintain maximum exhaust temperature, only one of the deciding factors in determining that smoke trails should be laid in the horizontal, rather than the vertical plane.

How does a pilot maintain orientation during a skywriting exercise? Fred Hoinville explained:

"It is impossible to steer by compass. Once I start writing the compass will be two laps behind all the way. Even a gyro compass is no use; it would topple and stop working on the vertical turns. I must steer by eye alone. Today it can be done only by using the sun. It is 2.00pm and the sun is very high in the sky, so it will not be easy. I must fly towards the sun and towards the shadow of my head on the instrument panel for a rough west-east line. For north-south I must line up the sun with the aileron hinges either side. That sounds simple enough but it is not, for when you are coming out of a vertical turn, with fifteen other things to do also, finding your head shadow and centring it where the instrument panel would be if you were flying level is a bit like doing a crossword puzzle while making a 100 yard sprint.

When operating over Sydney the bay water was useful to me at times for observing my work as I did it. The smoke would not cast a shadow on the land, but on the grey-brown water near the city, where the muddy river stained the sea, the letters showed up very clearly. Although they still read back to front to me, the shadows gave me a perfect picture as I wrote. It was this, and some photographs, that amazed me by revealing to me the sharpness of the right angles which the Tiger Moth drew in writing such letters as L or E, using vertical turns. I had expected to see corners that were rounded somewhat, for it does not seem possible for any aircraft to change direction by 90° without some skid on the corner, yet the smoke is angled as sharply as though traced with a square.

Telling people that the letters are half a mile long does not impress them half as much as saying that one letter is the same size as six Sydney Harbour bridges piled one on top of the other, or two and a half times as high as the Empire State Building, or three times as high as the Eiffel Tower, but somewhat less enduring."

On the occasion that Fred Hoinville sprained his ankle by falling over a chock when moving his Tiger Moth out of the hangar, he decided he should have a deputy pilot, and lined up a suitable candidate:

"He was a first class pilot, but he had never tackled anything like skywriting before. He had two attempts and got utterly lost each time. His letters varied from very small to enormous in size, and from west to south east in direction, and either overlapped or were six miles apart. Apart from these minor points he was not bad. He got a little confused at one point halfway through the test, after he had unconsciously changed direction by 90°, and proceeded to write the next bit over the top of the first. Shortly after that he lost all sight of the smoke and could not find it again. He landed and I showed him the sketches of his progress. We had a good laugh together and he went and got a job as an airline pilot instead."

AIRCRAFT CARRIERS

During its Service life the Royal Navy operated just over 100 Tiger Moths from land bases in a wide variety of roles and some of them managed to put to sea. T6808 (85077), an aircraft delivered new into Admiralty charge with 785 Squadron in December 1941, and during attachment to 768 Squadron, swung to port, went over the side and crashed into the sea during deck landing practice on HMS *Ravager*, a training vessel cruising off the Scottish coast on 7 May 1944. Early in the war, Fleet Air Arm pilots having learned to fly on Tiger Moths at Elementary Schools dedicated to the Senior Service but under the administrative and operational care of the RAF, often undertook both dummy and live deck landing instruction in requisitioned DH.60 Moths painted in Navy colours. Mike Lithgow, a naval pupil at 20 ERFTS Gravesend was one who later completed Advanced Training, again with the RAF, flying North American Harvards and Fairey Battles at Netheravon. As a post-war test pilot with Supermarine he was to travel considerably faster in the prototype Swift F.4, WK198, on 25 September 1953, when establishing a world air speed record of 737.3mph. Only eighteen days earlier, Neville Duke, Hawker's Chief Test Pilot, trained on Tiger Moths with 13 EFTS at White Waltham in 1940, had raised the record to 727.6mph in his all-red Hawker Hunter Mk 3, WB188.

Above: Before technology changed everything forever the Batsman was a vital aid to landing aircraft on a carrier. The visit by Plymouth-based Tiger Moths to HMS *Eagle* provided practical experience to all elements of the ship's crew. *Royal Navy*

Mystery aircraft. Loaded on board HMS *Pursuer* at Durban in 1945, this Australian built Tiger Moth apparently carrying no identification, returned with the carrier to the Clyde where she was flown off and never seen again. *Eric Morton*

Of the 460 Tiger Moths on charge with the South African Air Force (SAAF) in September 1945, the RAF drew off their 200, possibly 210, and about 220 were civil registered locally during the early post-war years. The others were victims of accidents, scrapping and reduction to spares, or were simply numbers mislaid in the overburdened administrative system. Where, for example, did the Tiger Moth that appeared on board the Royal Navy aircraft carrier HMS *Pursuer* come from?

The ship had been refitting in Durban between May and June 1945 in readiness for *Operation Zipper*, the planned invasion of Malaya, during which the carrier's Grumman Hellcats of 898 Squadron, Fleet Air Arm, were to provide air cover. The Tiger Moth appeared on board packed in a crate along with boxes of aircraft compasses and a consignment of rifles. The compasses and firearms were returned from whence they came by order of the Captain, but the aircraft stayed, believed to have been 'liberated' from a salvage yard. Durban was certainly the port through which Australian imports were received and perhaps this example just arrived late, or missed the train, or perhaps she was damaged on unloading, her paperwork was missing or she was simply forgotten and left behind.

However, this aeroplane was not fitted with navigation lights or spin strakes, the interplane struts appeared to be non-standard and she exhibited square-cut doors in the rear cockpit and a small venturi mounted on the side of the front fuselage clues, perhaps, that might indicate she had been a pre-war civil aircraft impressed into service. Apart from a dubious fuselage roundel and a fin flash, which may have been based on Pacific Area specification, there were no other markings. Had she been a ground instructional airframe?

By the time the refit was completed the Japanese war was over and 898 Squadron left HMS *Pursuer* which became a Headquarters and Communications vessel. The Tiger Moth was unpacked and erected on deck where she was thoroughly checked and once at sea was test flown, an exercise which required the ship to reduce speed to allow the aircraft to land on. At some stage during the flight programme the propeller was broken and for the remainder of the voyage to the Clyde the Tiger Moth was stowed below decks. On arrival in Scotland she was fitted with a new propeller scrounged from an unknown source, and flown away, disappearing into obscurity, and never to be recorded on any official list.

Under the command of her new Captain, Robert Dickson DSO RN, the Royal Navy aircraft carrier HMS *Theseus* left Glasgow on 21 February 1947 bound for New Zealand. On board, on the hangar deck, she carried the Seafires of 804 Squadron and Fireflies of 812 Squadron whilst lashed down as deck cargo were thirty Seafires scheduled for transfer to HMS *Glory* which was already in Eastern waters. The ship was Captain Dickson's first association with naval aviation with the result that he considered he should learn to fly. When HMS *Theseus* cast off she carried with her, amongst the fighter aircraft, an air-sea rescue Sea Otter and Tiger Moth, BB858 (3389), the former G-ADOY, operated by Reid and Sigrist at Desford until her change of colours on impressment in 1939. Following time spent at 7 EFTS Desford and elsewhere in store or under repair, she was transferred to the Royal Navy in July 1943 and served at Yeovilton and with Eastleigh Station Flight between January and July 1946 after which her next recorded appearance was in Scotland when she was loaded on board the carrier.

It is not clear where Captain Dickson learned to fly or when but one of his ship's company believes it was in Ceylon after the deck cargo had been cleared away and the ship's two operational squadrons had flown off to HMS *Bambara*, the Naval Air Station at Trincomalee, on 15 March 1947. BB858 was certainly exercised in Ceylon for 'Montague', a name bestowed by the Captain, suffered engine failure on take-off on 25 March and was forced landed on a beach in Malay Cove from where she was recovered to the ship and repaired. During this operation BB858 was painted royal blue overall with yellow interplane and cabane struts and undercarriage with a large *Theseus* crest applied on the upper fuselage sides between front and rear cockpits. The scheme mirrored that carried by the ship's Sea Otter.

A Sea Fury, Fireflies and Tiger Moth BB858 drawn up on the flight deck of HMS *Theseus* as she arrives in Auckland in August 1947. Note the landing T painted on the deck at bow and stern. *via John King*

Captain Robert Dickson RN in shirtsleeve order in the cockpit of Tiger Moth BB858. The aircraft was painted royal blue after an accident in Ceylon and carried the crest of HMS *Theseus* on the fuselage sides. *via John King*

To fly naval aircraft BB858 into the RNZAF base at Whenuapai in August 1947, the New Zealand authorities required her commander to apply for a civilian pilot's certificate. The aircraft had been painted royal blue during repairs following an accident in Ceylon. *via John King*

Drawn up on the flight deck of HMS *Theseus* as she arrived in Auckland in August 1947 were Tiger Moth BB858, the Admiral's Barge, Fireflies and a Sea Fury. All the aircraft were flown off before the ship docked. *via John King*

Watched with interest by all the usual gawpers on the island, Captain Robert Dickson takes off from HMS *Theseus* in his royal blue Tiger Moth BB858 which he named 'Montague'. To fly the aircraft on shore in New Zealand the captain had to apply for a civil pilot's licence. *via John King*

de Havilland DH.82A Tiger Moth T.2 W7957/ GP-2C, ex G-AFST, impressed on 15 January 1940 of 727 Naval Air Squadron FAA, Gosport, 1950. Trainer Yellow overall with all lettering in black. Serial repeated below wings. Post-war style roundels in six positions. *Artwork ©Richard Caruana, 1:72 scale*

HMS *Eagle*, working-up in the Western Approaches after a major refit during the summer of 1964, was host on two occasions to Tiger Moths of the Royal Naval College's Britannia Flight operating out of Plymouth. *Royal Navy*

The carrier continued her voyage to Australia and *Montague* was regularly flown when *Theseus* was at slow speed close to port, never in the open sea. On 15 July the operational squadrons flew demonstrations off Melbourne when BB858 was flown by Commander Robert Everett RAN, son of Australia's first Navy Board member, and the press commented on the fact that the aircraft was off the flight deck and climbing away after a run of 20ft.

The operational squadrons suffered a series of accidents off Melbourne and Sydney and by the time the ship arrived at Brisbane on 8 August all aircraft had been grounded pending some serious training exercises scheduled for New Zealand. HMS *Theseus* arrived in Wellington on 23 August and on Saturday 30 August all aircraft were flown off to the RNZAF Station at Whenuapai before the ship docked at Auckland. Tiger Moth BB858 also flew to Whenuapai for which Captain Dickson was required to apply for a Private Pilot's Licence issued by the New Zealand Air Department in Wellington, an interesting requirement as he was flying a military aircraft but was not a qualified military pilot and appeared to have no valid British civil licence. His New Zealand licence was issued on 27 August 1947 stating his address as HMS *Theseus*, was valid for a year and authorised him to fly 'Type DH.82'. The captain's medical was dated the same day but the documents were not signed by the holder nor renewed in 1948.

After a vigorous working-up session 804 and 812 Squadrons and the Tiger Moth were the centrepiece of an Air Pageant held at Whenuapai on 13 September before re-embarking and setting sail for the Soloman Islands, the Far East and home.

When HMS *Theseus* arrived back in the Clyde early in 1948 she had a pair of Tiger Moths on board. The Royal Navy was allocated ten locally manufactured Tiger Moths for use in and around Australia in 1945. A17-84 (DHA81), was delivered to the Senior Service at HMS *Nabberley* (Bankstown Airfield) in November where the serial number was inadvertently amended to read 'A1784', following which, with the run-down of British forces in the Pacific Region, she was shipped to HMS *Nabcatcher* (Kai Tak, Hong Kong) and taken on charge by 721 Squadron, a Fleet Requirements Unit, in August 1946.

A1784 was embarked on HMS *Theseus* in November 1947 during the ship's return voyage to the Clyde. She was carried through to Scotland and, following overhaul at Donibristle, was operated by a number of units at Royal Naval Air Stations across the country. In June 1958 she failed to remain airborne after take-off when taking part in the Navy Day Display at HMS *Gamecock* (Bramcote Airfield) and crashed into the car park alongside Air Traffic Control. Struck off charge her mortal remains were last reported at Lossiemouth in 1962.

Nothing further is known of the history of BB858 except that she was officially struck off charge at Donibristle in February 1949, a year after returning from her cruise to the opposite side of the world.

The Royal Navy aircraft carrier HMS *Eagle* was working up in the Western Channel following a major refit at Devonport when a plot was hatched between naval officers attached to Britannia Flight, Royal Naval College Dartmouth, to visit the ship by Tiger Moth, and to appraise the Wardroom facilities. Approval was sought from Their Lordships of the Admiralty, and willingly gifted, with the result that NL879 (86322), and three other Tiger Moths operating from the Flight's base at Roborough, BB814 (82187), BB694 (3340), and XL714 (84566), all touched down on HMS *Eagle's* expansive flight deck on 20 June 1964. Conditions were ideal but following good naval practise short lengths of knotted rope had been looped through the tie-down eyes to ease deck handling should the need arise. While the crews availed themselves of the ship's hospitality, the Tiger Moths provided practical handling experience for the deck parties, including striking down onto the capacious hangar deck with the aid of the hydraulic lift. A second visit was successfully accomplished on 1 July 1964 immediately after which NL879 was officially transferred to the Royal Air Force College Flying Club at Cranwell although she was not delivered for another three years, taking up her civil letters G-AVPJ in June 1967.

An observer on board HMS *Eagle* later reported that another visit was paid in 1967 and on departure the ground speed of the Tiger Moth was less than that of the ship necessitating the aircraft to turn to starboard to avoid conflict with the island. In fact a right turn would have brought the aircraft face to face with the island or at least into the area of severe turbulence created by the superstructure.

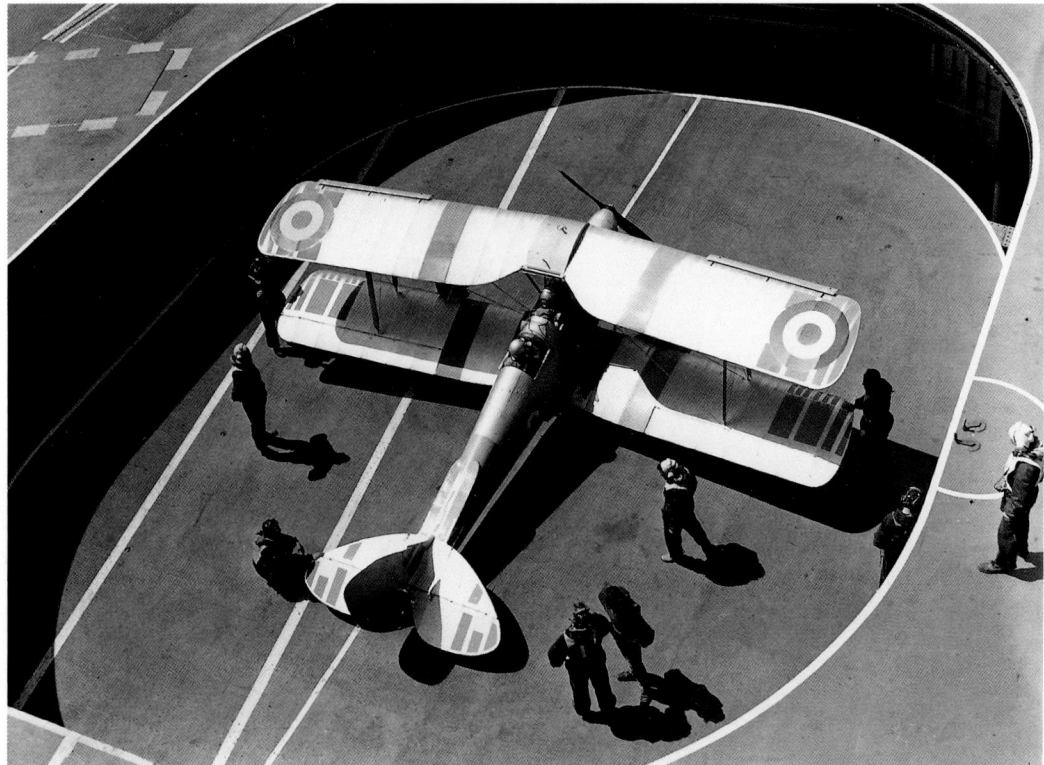

The visit to HMS *Eagle* was a serious exercise to provide practical handling experience for the flight deck crew. In this photograph, one of the visitors is seen striking down in order to de-man out of the wind. *Royal Navy*

A trio of Royal Navy Tiger Moths with crews on board preparing to leave HMS *Eagle* following their visit in 1964 and return to their land base at Plymouth. *Royal Navy*

BB814 was posted to Arbroath in 1966 to serve as a tug on behalf of the Condor Gliding Club, and during the summer added a large letter 'H' to her mundane livery to commemorate her deck landing on HMS *Hermes* on 23 June that year. Restored to her pre-war civil identity as G-AFWI in 1972, the aircraft continued her tugging career for a further ten years on behalf of the Portsmouth Naval Gliding Club at Lee on Solent until sold into the private ownership of two Royal Navy officers.

Right: Only the style of flying kit distinguishes this picture of Naval Air Cadets Bruce Hutton and Pete Frame at Plymouth in 1961 from all who had gone before. Bruce Hutton went on to a career on fast jets, through airline operations and back to Tiger Moths as a joyride pilot. *via Bruce Hutton*

Below: Gawpers on the flying bridge of HMS *Eagle* in June 1964 had the perfect opportunity to compare the arrival techniques of each visiting Tiger Moth. *Royal Navy*

The arrival of Tiger Moths on board HMS *Eagle* in 1964 provided valuable handling experience for the deck party, every member of which had a defined duty. *Royal Navy*

Royal Navy Tiger Moth BB814 at RAF Linton on Ouse thought to be on the occasion of a Wings Parade. The aircraft was sold to a group of Royal Navy officers and took up her old civil registration of G-AFWI when she was enrolled as a glider tug at Lee on Solent. *deHMC Archive*

CHAPTER TWENTY TWO

Front Page News

During the communist insurgency in Malaya in the early 1950s, the Malayan Government enlisted the aid of civilian flying clubs to act in the capacity of couriers, taxi drivers and observers. Members of the Kuala Lumpur Flying Club volunteered their piloting services together with a trio of club Tiger Moths, VR-RBA (DHA25), and VR-RBB (DHA444), purchased post-war in Australia as RAAF surplus at £310 the pair, and VR-RBJ (84957), one of the first aircraft from limited RAF disposals in 1946 shipped out from Great Britain.

Travelling through the Malayan jungle with large consignments of cash, wages due to workers at remote mines and plantations, was hazardous and club aircraft were chartered by banks for air drops. Pilots were not paid but the flying was free. On one occasion misinterpretation of a signal caused £80,000 in cash to be thrown out of a Tiger Moth cockpit at the wrong location, never to be seen again. Leaflet drops and police charters to check on the positions of suspected terrorist hideouts were also regular requests.

Tiger Moth N522R suffered engine failure shortly after taking off from Skylark Airport, East Windsor, Connecticut on 31 August 2008 and landed straight ahead into a stand of trees. The aircraft was relatively undamaged as was pilot August Gorreck and his lady passenger but they had to remain on board for three hours whilst the Emergency Services determined the best method of rescue without disturbing the aircraft which was finely balanced in the branches. *Andy Shefrin*

None of the pilots wore parachutes and in case of emergency were taught to stall a Tiger Moth into the tops of trees where the aircraft was more likely to be found during a subsequent search. Although all three Kuala Lumpur Flying Club Tiger Moths were subsequently written off in local accidents, none was damaged during the political emergency. The only lady pilot known to have volunteered was never forced to demonstrate engine out landings, her name was Joan Glyde.

Isobel Moller learned to fly Tiger Moths with the Royal Aero Club of Western Australia from Perth's Maylands Aerodrome late in 1949. Described by the press as a '22 year old typist' she was employed as a telephonist by the Western Australian Department of Transport and embarked on a scheme to create a new height record for a woman pilot flying a Tiger Moth. The plan was to utilise Club Tiger Moth VH-ARA (DHA226), an aircraft fitted with a hinged Wackett canopy, in an effort to beat the previous record of 16,500ft set in New South Wales by a Sydney waitress, Margaret Clark, only a few weeks previously. Suitably dressed in a fur-lined flying suit and equipped with a mask and portable oxygen system supplied by Royal Perth Hospital, on 18 March 1950 Isobel Moller persuaded VH-ARA into a climb which lasted two hours and five minutes. No official barograph was carried and instead 'Belle' Moller took photographs of the altimeter but at an indicated height of 14,500ft she believed the aircraft would climb no

Members of the Kuala Lumpur Flying Club and their Tiger Moth VR-RBJ who were recruited into assisting the authorities during the Emergency of the 1950s. *deHMC Archive*

Tiger Moth VR-RBJ which was used for general duties in Malaya was one of the ex-RAF aircraft sold to the Royal Aero Club in 1946. She was operated by the Airwork Flying Club at Gatwick until 1949 when she was acquired by aircraft broker W S Shackleton and sold to Malaya. She was written off under unknown circumstances in 1957. *deHMC Archive*

On 18 March 1950 Miss Isobel Moller took Tiger Moth VH-ARA to a corrected height of 17,000ft when flying from Maylands Aerodrome, Perth, Western Australia. The aircraft was fitted with a Wackett canopy and an oxygen system was supplied by the local hospital. *Ray Johnson*

further and used the last of her film. After circling for a few minutes VH-ARA was persuaded to climb again and reached an indicated height of 16,400ft, an actual height of 17,000ft when corrected for temperature. Although unofficial the 'record' stood unchallenged for thirty years.

A bizarre incident with a happy ending occurred at Broxbourne Aerodrome in June 1951. An ATC cadet enjoying the fruits of his flying scholarship was letting down from high level in Tiger Moth G-AIDS (84546), without warming the engine, an operational necessity overlooked by the instructor. Finding himself too high for a safe touchdown the cadet opened the throttle to go around but the only response from the engine was that it gently died. With commendable speed, the instructor took control:

> "Neatly sideslipping toward the line of trees and shrubs that separated the aerodrome from a riverside bungalow estate, he pulled the machine into a stall above a handy may tree. By luck or superb airmanship or a combination of both, the Tiger Moth slipped stern first into its warm foliated embrace, suspending itself on the tree top by the undercarriage radius rods, with the elevator trailing edge two inches above ground and brushing the grass."

Joan Glyde and Tiger Moth VR-RBB of the Kuala Lumpur Flying Club. Flying the Club aircraft at no cost to themselves, members were employed as unpaid observers and messengers during the Malayan crisis of the early 1950s. *Joan Ellis*

Not every CFI could taxy his Tiger Moth straight from the airfield to the local public house at the end of the day even if he wished to. Would he be allowed to taxy back to the aerodrome after his pint? The opening of the new Tiger Moth public house at Rochester in April 1959 was celebrated in style with several pints of Courage Best. *deHMC Archive*

Daily encounters with trees was the lot of Jim Tiffen from Griffith, New South Wales, who operated his Tiger Moth VH-BIL (82473), from an 800ft strip situated in the middle of an orchard. On approach it was essential to drag the wheels through the top of an orange tree else an overshoot was a certain requirement. On take-off one day the engine stopped and with no prospect of escape the Tiger Moth landed in a peach tree, breaking everything except the propeller. That season the tree produced an outstanding crop of fruit. In later years Jim Tiffen established a new landing area on a dirt road with a right angle bend in it which he referred to as his cross wind runway. Most visitors revealed that they were worried at just having to taxy along the tree lined strip which was only 66ft wide.

Under different ownership the aircraft crashed in 1982 after which the remains were exported to the USA where, after several changes of direction and a forced landing after the propeller burst after take-off, the aircraft is airworthy in Tennessee as N80660, displaying the British letters G-ATDK, a reflection of the initial letters of the names of her owners.

This description was penned by Harry Smith, an engineer with the Herts and Essex Aero Club. On the day, Harry Smith and his colleagues were called from their lunch in the famous Monty's Cafe to supervise the retrieval of G-AIDS which was painlessly accomplished with the aid of a dragline working in a neighbouring gravel pit. Ironically, Broxbourne Aerodrome was itself closed and sold for gravel extraction the following year. Damage to G-AIDS amounted to a broken propeller, two inches neatly clipped off each tip, dented cowlings, a bent port undercarriage radius rod and a broken wing rib, all repaired within a week. G-AIDS was a survivor. She was evacuated from the Club hangar on 23 June 1947 when it was destroyed in a fire which consumed twelve aircraft, seven of which were Tiger Moths.

In June 1951 Tiger Moth G-AIDS lost power during an attempted overshoot at Broxbourne and gently subsided into a hedge of blooming may trees on the aerodrome boundary from where she was extracted with almost no damage using a dragline that had been operating in the adjacent field. *Harry Smith*

The remains of a Tiger Moth standing in the hangar at Broxbourne which was destroyed by fire on 23 June 1947. Twelve aircraft packed into the hangar for the night were lost, seven of which were Tiger Moths. *Jim Mead*

Unlike their brothers in most parts of the world aircraft registered in the USA are allowed to display any spurious markings provided the real numbers are carried externally too. G-ATDK is really N80660 and the pseudo-British registration letters were chosen to represent the initials of the joint owners. *Dale Grubbs*

On 17 May 1953, VH-BNF (DHA863), taxied out at RAAF Base Wagga following six Sea Furies which took off singly but joined together for a high speed, low level formation flight to the RAN base at Nowra. The Tiger Moth was airborne and had climbed to 150ft when the Sea Fury formation appeared overhead and at 250 knots the lead aircraft collided with VH-BNF's tail unit and starboard wings. The Tiger Moth spiralled out of the sky and hit the ground hard, wrecking every component except the rear seat and propeller. The pilot brushed off the wreckage and was unhurt, continuing his interest in aviation to the stage where he was later appointed senior pilot with a commercial airline in Australia.

Almost exactly twenty four years later, on 15 May 1977, Tiger Moth G-ANDE (85957), was letting down into Biggin Hill when a joy riding helicopter lifted off and climbed up into her, its rotor blades shearing off the whole of the undercarriage and snapping away at the pilot's heels through holes in the floor. While the helicopter fell back to earth fatally injured, G-ANDE flew the circuit and landed on her belly when further damage was inflicted although neither occupant suffered more than a few scratches.

Tiger Moth G-AHVY (83315), crashed on landing at Christchurch on the morning of Sunday 12 October 1958. The Club CFI had taken a positive stand against unauthorised dual instruction and he always insisted that the front control column be removed when friends of club members were taken aloft. This attitude led to at least one adaptable control column being manufactured which could be hidden as two pieces in the leg pockets of a flying suit.

During G-AHVY's fateful approach to land, the 'pilot' was seen standing up in the rear cockpit holding a cine camera. It is believed he had one foot on the control box which slipped, stabbing the base of the rear control column and jarring the counterfeit front stick out of its unsecured housing. A witness to the accident said he believed it was the same pilot who had once become lost due to compass deviation caused by interference from the close proximity of the rogue control column which was made of steel.

Tiger Moth PH-UDC was landed in the main street of Middelbeers, the Netherlands, in 1948 after the pilot was overcome by air sickness. via *Herman Dekker*

This is what happens to a Tiger Moth when the control column comes out of its socket during a go-around. Jan White and her passenger escaped injury when ZK-BEW subsided into the ground at Bridge Pa Aerodrome in July 2000. *via Jan White*

On 30 July 2000, a perfect day in New Zealand's mid winter, Jan White applied full power to go around for another circuit in her Tiger Moth ZK-BEW (84771), at Bridge Pa Aerodrome. When retrimming and applying forward pressure on the control column Jan White realised it had come out of its socket and at 30ft she effectively had no control. The aircraft subsided to the ground, the two starboard wings gradually absorbing the impact, allowing the pilot and her passenger to make as dignified an exit as was possible under the circumstances. Examination of the aircraft revealed that two bolts, whose purpose was to secure the control column, were missing.

A private sale effected from 5 MU Kemble in May 1947 led DE943 (85814), to Thomas Cameron in Perthshire but within the year the aeroplane had been re-sold to McDonald Aircraft Ltd. at Balado and registered G-AJVE. In 1951 she joined the Edinburgh Flying Club at Macmerry but it was at Turnhouse on 24 January 1960 that John Galt, a club pilot on his first solo, sideslipped in for a landing but misjudged his descent and was arrested between two parallel trusses on the roof of a hangar. The entire engine bay penetrated the roof structure and fuel slopped down onto the floor below but, apart from a cut lip, the pilot was uninjured. In the same hangar undergoing repairs was a BEA Viscount which had overshot the runway on landing the previous month.

Nine Tiger Moths in a diamond formation were scheduled to pass over St Albans Abbey on the occasion of the Memorial Service for Sir Geoffrey de Havilland on 21 July 1965. Gathered at Redhill that morning the weather turned sour with low cloud and poor visibility but, led by Dennis Hartas, all nine aircraft struggled through to reach their rendezvous point at Hatfield Aerodrome safely only for the hapless G-ASKP (3889), to run into the ILS aerial on touchdown. And then there were eight.

Although a replacement Tiger Moth was hastily summoned from nearby Panshanger Aerodrome it could not be made ready in time and the ninth aeroplane was the willingly volunteered and entirely appropriate DH.60 Cirrus Moth G-EBLV (188), flown in the formation by de Havilland test pilot Desmond Penrose. The diamond arrived overhead the Abbey on schedule and made two passes over the congregation as it gathered outside after the service. On the second run the sun broke weakly through the cloud for the first and only time that day.

The weather on 30 July 1997 was bright and clear but the air was in unsettled mood as Moths again made an appearance over Hatfield in salute to Sir Geoffrey de Havilland. Denied the use of facilities at the desecrated company aerodrome a stone's throw from the Hatfield campus of the University of Hertfordshire, (there was no ILS to hit any more: it had been repositioned to Chester), a fleet of thirty seven aircraft, mostly Moths, flew overhead in support of the ceremony at which HRH Prince Philip, Duke of Edinburgh, unveiled a bronze statue of the founder of the Enterprise. Led by three DH.60 Moths, the fifth group was a formation of nine Tiger Moths, but on this occasion G-EBLV was not with them; she was positioned in pole position alongside Sir Geoffrey's statue, sharing the limelight.

Above: With the assistance of Desmond Penrose flying the Hatfield based DH.60 Moth G-EBLV, a nine aeroplane formation was mustered to fly over St Albans Abbey after the Memorial Service for Sir Geoffrey de Havilland which was held on 21 July 1965. *Hawker Siddeley Aviation*

Left: It may look serene, but keeping nine low powered Tiger Moths in close formation, even on a calm day, takes considerable skill, effort and practice. The de Havilland Moth Club's Diamond Nine Team in action at Woburn Abbey. *Darryl Cott*

Tiger Moth NL985 (86417), had been in continuous RAF service from delivery to 14 EFTS Elmdon in August 1944 until withdrawn from flying duties with No 9 Advanced Flying Training School (AFTS) Wellesbourne Mountford, eight years later. Recategorised as an Instructional Airframe, 7015M, and loaned to an ATC Squadron in Birmingham, the aircraft was later withdrawn to Colerne and there restored to operational configuration with a late wartime camouflage finish, to become part of the Royal Air Force Exhibition Unit. As such, NL985 was displayed at the Royal Tournament, at the annual Battle of Britain displays on Horse Guard's Parade, and most publicly at the Royal Golden Jubilee Review of the Royal Air Force at Abingdon in June 1968.

During planning for the RAF Museum at Hendon, NL985/7015M was earmarked as the permanent representative of the type and together with a small number of other exhibits was moved onto the site in 1970 whilst final building work continued around them. Enter the brain-dead guttersnipes who evaded poor security and thought it awfully good sport to set fire to the Tiger Moth which was burned out. Other aircraft were attacked and damaged, but none fatally. The remains of NL985 were disposed of and subsequently hawked through many bazaars before the caravan temporarily came to rest at Gransden. The aircraft was issued with civil registration G-BWIK in 1995 and relocated to Old Sarum in 1999 from where notification was received in 2011 that as a restoration project she had been acquired by a new owner in Finland.

The RAF now had no Tiger Moth at all and turned to the Royal Navy for assistance. T6296 (84711), had served with the RAF until December 1946 when she was transferred to the Admiralty and was operational at a number of shore establishments until retired from flying activity at Yeovilton in September 1973. Painted in RAF brown and green camouflage, (slime and sewage), T6296 was presented to the RAF Museum to fill the vacant space and in April 1990 was transferred to the Battle of Britain Hall, although her paint scheme and spin strakes are not appropriate to the period. What price a set of bomb racks?

When Tiger Moth G-ALAD was registered to the Wiltshire School of Flying at Thruxton in June 1951, the previous identity was quoted as T6296, clearly not true, and on sale to New Zealand in 1952 the spurious RAF serial and history went with her. Not until 1997, and long since registered ZK-CDU, did official paperwork come to light confirming that the Tiger Moth in the RAF Museum was the genuine example and that ZK-CDU was probably L6926 (3581), one of the thirty civil specification Tiger Moths bought 'off the shelf' by the Air Ministry in 1937.

The RAF's travelling Exhibition Flight mounted a display on Horse Guards Parade in Central London during Battle of Britain Week for many years and Tiger Moth NL985 was a regular attendee. With others the aircraft was moved into the RAF Museum at Hendon before the site was open to the public but poor security allowed a deranged guttersnipe to break in and set fire to several exhibits of which NL985 was one. *deHMC Archive*

The pilot of a group-owned Tiger Moth operational in Norfolk was once seen standing on the rear seat of a Tiger Moth in low level flight over the Oulton Broad Regatta, by arrangement, playing a trumpet, but the occupant of the front seat was firmly in control. Perhaps spurred on by this apparent demonstration of the ease with which a Tiger Moth could be flown a seventeen year old youth removed Tiger Moth G-AMEY (85545), from her hangar at Little Snoring on 16 May 1968, somehow got her started, and attempted to take-off at which point all his ideas ran out. The aircraft was wrecked but later achieved immortality on the silver screen in a short career masquerading as a Rumpler.

Not making headlines at the time for reasons of pride as well as wartime security, was the case of a pupil from Marlborough School who helped himself to one of His Majesty's Tiger Moths dispersed with 29 EFTS at Clyffe Pypard. The aeroplane was wrecked, and apart from six of the best, details of further punishment are unrecorded.

de Havilland DH.82A Tiger Moth, G-AMNN 'Spirit of Pashley', Southern Flying Centre, Shoreham. Silver overall with blue/yellow trim to fuselage. Blue undercarriage, spinner and interplane struts. Yellow wing leading edges with blue trim. Black lettering, Southern Flying Centre badge on rudder. G-AMNN is currently owned and operated by Perry Air at Shoreham where she is available for flying instruction from *ab initio* to licence standard. Artwork ©Richard Caruana, 1:72 scale

Sydney Pickles made an agreement with the publishers of London's *Evening News* newspaper in May 1919 that he would distribute copies to the Thanet towns in Kent. The major difference from any other distributor was that Sydney Pickles had acquired a Fairey III seaplane which he landed on the river Thames near Blackfriars, collected his newspapers and flew with them around the Medway estuary. The advantage over conventional delivery was a saving in time of about two hours but although it was a short lived enterprise, hardly cost effective, the daily service was recorded as a first. To celebrate the sixtieth anniversary of the endeavour all the necessary bureaucracy was cleared to permit the Sea Tiger G-AIVW (83135), to be flown by Keith Sissons with Sue Thompson as passenger, to alight on the Thames at Blackfriars on 31 May 1979 and to collect that day's edition of the newspaper. After take-off they flew at 500ft all the way to alight on the Medway at Rochester, taxiing up to the old Short Bros' works slipway where the newspaper's Editor and Rochester's Mayor and MP were on hand to receive copies with its banner headline commemorating the event.

An unhappy ending to a good day in June 1979 awaited G-ACDA (3175), acknowledged as the prototype of the 'A' model Tiger Moth. The aircraft had been impressed into military service as BB724 but, during the war and with production continuing at Cowley, was acquired by Bertie Arden in September 1943 when, he said, the RAF was selling off some of its older aircraft, and placed in secure storage on his farm near Exeter. The Tiger Moth and several other rare aircraft stored at Haldon Moor were viewed by few privileged visitors until 1977 when G-ACDA was accepted in lieu of fees for professional services by a local solicitor. Whether the aircraft was 'sold' or 'loaned permanently' was to be the subject of legal argument at a later date.

G-ACDA was overhauled at Kemble and entered for the 1979 Famous Grouse Rally but during a routine test flight on 27 June, two days before she was due at Hatfield, the newly overhauled and 'tight' engine stopped during a casual aerobatic routine and despite all efforts, failed to re-start. During the attempt at a forced landing within sight of Kemble Aerodrome, the Tiger Moth slipped round a tree but collided with an electricity pylon which had been hidden from view and, impaled on its arms, burst into flames. Both occupants escaped by using the starboard lower wing as a stepladder to reach the ground but the intensely original and historically significant aircraft was lost although her mortal remains were later subject to a prolonged programme of reconstruction under several different hands which eventually resulted in her return to airworthiness in June 2008.

Amy Johnson's 1930 flight from London's Croydon Airport to Australia in her DH.60G Moth G-AAAH (804), has been compared to the achievement of man landing on the moon only thirty nine years later. On 5 May 1980, fifty years to the day since Amy Johnson's departure, Lewis Benjamin organised a select band of appropriate aircraft and a Tiger Moth dominated air display on what remained of the usable grass at the closed Croydon Airport. A restored green and silver DH.60G Gipsy Moth G-ABEV (1823), flown by Ron Souch, offered a privileged few the chance of a circuit. It was the last opportunity ever to fly from such historic acres as the local council refused all subsequent requests to land aeroplanes on the site against the pretext that they would cause nuisance to the local residents.

The 50th anniversary of Amy Johnson's arrival in Darwin was commemorated on 24 May 1980 when Senja Robey, a past president of the Australian Women Pilot's Association, flew Tiger Moth VH-AWA (DHA824), back into her birthplace at Mascot, now Kingsford Smith Airport, Sydney.

Tiger Moth T7941 (84305), was shipped to Southern Rhodesia in March 1941 and was later transferred to the South African Air Force as 4695. With over 2,000 hours logged the aircraft was withdrawn and stored for ten years before sale to a scrap metal company in 1955, but

Prototype DH.82A Tiger Moth G-ACDA was impressed into military service in 1940 but was sold into civilian hands in 1943 at a time when production continued at Morris Motors. The aircraft was severely damaged by fire when she collided with an electricity pylon during a test flight in 1979 and led a peripatetic life until finally restored in 2008. *David McIntosh*

was overhauled for the civil market and qualified for a C of A in 1957. Six years later the aircraft was grounded for what was described as 'poor general condition', but was made airworthy only to suffer a heavy landing at Theona in November 1965 and to turn over, after which it was discovered that the pilot had no licence. Sold to a new owner in June 1966, he noted that: "The aircraft was painted kitchen table green with a red lightning stripe along the fuselage. Everything was oil soaked, and on testing the fabric, the engineer poked his finger clean through to reveal cracked main spars in both bottom wings, bandaged and varnished over. The wings were also infested with insect life although for two years prior to sale, the previous owner had developed a relish for aerobatics."

Rebuilt to pristine condition and operated successfully for more than twelve years, the aircraft was leaving Jan Smuts Airport after a celebration of South African Airways' Golden Jubilee on 9 October 1980, when all three rocker pedestal bolts for No 4 cylinder head sheared off at 800ft over a populated area. The pilot found a clump of thatching grass amongst an estate of new houses near Edenvale High School and stalled in from a tailskid touchdown, running across a barbed wire fence which had been squashed flat by cement lorries. A traffic patrol helicopter followed the Tiger Moth's descending flightpath and was able to report by radio that no damage was evident. Replacement bolts were discovered locally in an old Gipsy Major engine which had been standing in the open for twenty years. The day following the incident, the aircraft was towed onto Milford Road and flown off.

Due to a ruptured oil pipe Ed Katzen force landed his Tiger Moth N83EK on the beach at Smith's Point in the National Park at Fire Island, New York on 27 April 2009. Having effected repairs the Park Rangers refused permission for the aircraft to take off again but the local police arranged an escort for the rigged aircraft when she was carried ten miles to Brookhaven Airfield. *Bob Mott*

In March 1990 during the Tiger Moth Club of New Zealand's North Cape to Bluff Rally, the engine of ZK-AKC failed when crossing a river at Balclutha, but a hard shingle bank orientated into wind provided the perfect 'carrier' deck on which to put down and from which, after repairs, to take off. *John King*

The Golden Jubilee of the DH.82 Tiger Moth was observed in England with two events organised by the de Havilland Moth Club in 1981. In July, six military marked Tiger Moths flew from Henlow, substituting for Stag Lane (Hatfield was suffering industrial strife), to the old airfield at Grantham (RAF Spittalgate) to commemorate the anniversary of the first RAF delivery and there landed on what had become the manicured sports field of The Prince William of Gloucester Army Barracks. Group Captain Peter Heath, one of the pilots of that first Tiger Moth formation in 1931 was taken ill just before the event and prevented from assuming his rightful place in the lead aircraft, appropriately G-ANEF (83226), of the Royal Air Force College Flying Club, Cranwell. Thirty more Tiger Moths passed overhead Grantham on their way from Henlow directly to Cranwell and a celebration banquet in College Hall.

A quarter of a century later the exercise was repeated on a much larger scale when on 17 September 2006, after a foggy start, the old Grantham/Spittalgate Aerodrome once again echoed to the sound of arriving Gipsy Major engines. By now a training ground for the Royal Corps of Logistics, runways had to be cut in the long grass of the long-abandoned sports fields and all essential facilities established on the site. The centrepiece of the celebration and Act of Remembrance on that Battle of Britain Sunday was the arrival of Paul Szluha in Tiger Moth G-MOTH (85340), re-constructed to the DH.82 configuration and painted in the colours of the RAF's first Tiger Moth, K2567.

To celebrate the 75th anniversary of the delivery of the first Tiger Moth to No 3 FTS at RAF Grantham in 1931, the de Havilland Moth Club was permitted to re-establish an aerodrome on part of the original site on Battle of Britain Sunday, 17 September 2006. Star attraction of the celebration was Paul Szluha's DH.82 lookalike G-MOTH, painted in the colours of K2567. *Terry Dann*

At a 50th birthday lunch held in the old squash courts of the London Aeroplane Club at Hatfield on 21 October 1981, the crews of seven Tiger Moths which had arrived in formation from Old Warden greeted guest of honour Alan Butler who, as a young sportsman, had funded the de Havilland Company in 1922 and later gifted these same facilities. In Australia only hours before, the Antique Aeroplane Association had organised a dinner limited to fifty guests, and a birthday cake complete with fifty candles. According to reports received at Hatfield, the candles generated so much heat that the squadron of model Tiger Moths which were dispersed around the perimeter of the culinary creation suffered bent propellers, melted struts and damaged landing gear.

In London on 16 December 1931, Squadron Leader Bert Hinkler was presented with the Royal Aero Club Gold Medal in recognition of his famous flight across the South Atlantic in a DH.80 Puss Moth. The flight had its origins in Canada and the Puss Moth was the first Canadian registered aircraft to make a landing in Great Britain. On the same day as the presentation, the first Australia-Great Britain air mails to be carried by an Australian registered aircraft also arrived in London. The pilot, Sir Charles Kingsford Smith, was immediately

Alan Butler, financial saviour of the de Havilland Aircraft Company in 1922, in the de Havilland Museum at Hatfield on the occasion of the Tiger Moth 50th birthday celebrations, 21 October 1981. *British Aerospace*

invited to the ceremony to meet fellow Australian Bert Hinkler for the first time. To commemorate the famous meeting, in 1981 special postal covers were prepared in Australia and flown to London. Keith Palmer eyed the snow banks remaining after the first falls of the winter, put on several more layers of protection, took a deep breath and agreed to fly the covers and their courier over London in his Tiger Moth G-APMX (85645):

> "After a patch of foul weather, 16 December 1981 dawned bright and clear but very cold. G-APMX really did not want to go and took forty five minutes to be stirred into action. Southern Television filmed every swing of the propeller but luckily showed only one attempt on the broadcast.

> We took off at 11.20am and flew straight to Thamesmead in order to join the helicopter river route to Battersea. The visibility was excellent until we reached London and it became quite eerie flying above the cranes and chimneys. Instructions from the CAA were to ditch in the river in case of any nasties, so we wore lifejackets, just in case.

> Tower Bridge appeared through the wires and I resisted the temptation to fly under, leaving that opportunity until later. We flew on past Westminster and turned round over the heliport where we received a wave from ATC who had been most helpful, then back along the reciprocal route to Headcorn. The flight time was only one hour but it was the coldest Tiger Moth trip I have ever made, despite thermal underwear."

During a heavy snowstorm in Kent on 14 January 1987, the blister hangar in which G-APMX was housed collapsed. The roof came to rest on the Tiger Moth's centre section which bore the whole weight of the snow-covered structure and effectively prevented the crushing of many other aircraft. Extreme pressure burst a mainwheel tyre and caused severe distortion of the airframe. The insurance assessment following an independent survey declared G-APMX to be beyond economical repair and the aircraft was sold to a third party bidder. Sold again in an incomplete condition, final restoration to airworthiness was achieved by the Newbury Aeroplane Company in November 1992.

The Museum of Army Flying at Middle Wallop was custodian of an airworthy Tiger Moth exhibit, N6985 (G-AHMN/82223), on long term loan from Alan Curtis since July 1984 when the aircraft was handed over by Admiral Sir Raymond Lygo. Sir Raymond, a former Royal Navy Tiger Moth flying instructor, then acting in his capacity as Chief Executive of British Aerospace was, as he explained, making the presentation on behalf of 'the original makers'. The aircraft was extensively damaged as the result of a heavy landing at Middle Wallop in May 2000, damage that under the terms of the agreement with Alan Curtis had to be repaired before return to his charge. With limited resource the museum volunteers agreed that the job was too

For some years the Museum of Army Flying at Middle Wallop maintained G-AHMN, a civil Tiger Moth loaned by Alan Curtis, in airworthy condition and on suitable occasions demonstrated towing techniques with Second World War training gliders. *Richard Riding*

big for them and with permission G-AHMN was offered for sale and shipped to a workshop in Antwerp in November 2000.

Charlie Shea-Simonds frequently parachuted from his own Tiger Moth, G-AGZZ (DHA926), when being piloted by a friend and had been known to drop into summer garden parties in James Bond style, immaculately dressed in DJ and black tie. Having gathered around him a number of like minded and experienced Tiger Moth owner/pilots, Charlie Shea-Simonds founded the de Havilland Moth Club Diamond Nine Formation Display Team in 1985, and after a period of consolidation and practice the team's first nine aircraft diamond was displayed on 26 April 1986 at Badminton. The Diamond Nine became a popular and regular attraction at many British air displays and on two occasions in France, varying their routines annually within the limitations of their aircraft following intensive training at the beginning of each season.

Almost inevitably, the Diamond Nine fostered excellent relations with the RAF's official Aerobatic Team, The Red Arrows, having modelled themselves on a similar nine-aircraft presentation, and in July 1995 nine Tiger Moths and nine BAe Hawks shared the same box of sky over the Reds' base at Scampton. It was the team's second visit to the Red Arrows, and on this occasion managed to fly a Diamond Nine with a Red Arrow pilot tucked into each front seat. The experience prompted one Hawk pilot to observe that the Tiger Moth must surely have been one of the world's first 'fly-by-wire' aircraft.

In their first ten years, the Diamond Nine Team flew 149 individual shows, a heavy commitment for a group of 'amateur' pilots who flew together mostly only at weekends. In 1995 the team was asked to lead the Victory Parade at the International Air Tattoo at Fairford, and put up an expansive vic of twelve Tiger Moths on consecutive public days, all aircraft carrying a worthy 'veteran' nominated by the organisers on each occasion.

The Diamond Nine team disbanded in 2000 following their appearance at the Middle Wallop Air Display on 17 September and left a void which was filled for two seasons by a four aircraft formation composed of aircraft based near Cambridge. The idea of forming a new nine aircraft team gained momentum as the 25th International Moth Rally at Woburn Abbey loomed in 2005 when ex RAF Jaguar pilot Jeff Milsom volunteered to act as co-ordinator for a new group known from their formal establishment as the 'Tiger 9'. Regular practice sessions began immediately from a field on the edge of the Salisbury Plain ranges and every season since their formation the team has introduced innovations to their routine just as any of the professionals on the show circuit do too.

Cambridge Flying Group's two Tiger Moths, G-AHIZ and G-AOEI pictured during a formation training flight in the summer sunshine in 2011. *Howard Cook*

Wing Commander Rupert Clark flew his Tiger Moth G-AOGR from her base at Cranwell to visit the Red Arrows at Scampton on 11 August 2010 having heard the 'Reds' were considering re-equipping with biplanes. *Rupert Clark*

Flying downwind and forming up after a staggered take off, the de Havilland Moth Club's Tiger 9 formation team coincided with the sunshine at Woburn Abbey in August 2013. *John Stiles*

The de Havilland Moth Club's Tiger 9 formation team flying past the White Horse in Wiltshire during one of their training sessions in June 2007. *Geoff Collins*

The de Havilland Moth Club's Tiger 9 team in their familiar diamond formation during a display at White Waltham in 2012. Had all the aircraft been painted in camouflage the essence of this shot would have been completely lost. *Steve Bohill-Smith*

A perfect Diamond formation flown by the de Havilland Moth Club's Tiger 9 team during their display at Kemble on 18 September 2011. *via Jeff Milsom*

Tiger Moth C-FFDZ (DHC1179), suffered a mishap in 2001 and on 13 August 2003 was flying her first circuits at St. Lazare, PQ, following restoration. After her third touch and go the engine lost power and the aircraft descended into standing corn which, although causing her to flip over, absorbed all the energy and inflicted very little damage. Fortunately, having been converted into the 'A' configuration, the pilot was able to wriggle free with relative ease. It was decided that for a number of reasons the easiest, quickest and most economical way to recover the Tiger Moth was by lifting her from the field by helicopter. Slung from the lower wing rear attachment points and the engine mountings C-FFDZ was gently lifted and carried inverted the few hundred yards back to base where she was delivered with equal grace thanks to the outstanding professionalism of the helicopter pilot.

John Bergh, a man with 20,000 hour cropspraying experience and chief pilot of the Sport and Vintage Aviation Society of Masterton in New Zealand, was practicing low level aerobatics in Tiger Moth ZK-BLK (82812), on 6 January 2013, about three miles from Hood Aerodrome when the newly overhauled engine stopped during a slow roll. A friend's helicopter was called in to assist recovery once the load had been reduced to a maximum of 500kg, a figure reached by draining the oil and removal

Following the formation of the de Havilland Moth Club's Diamond Nine Team in 1987, it was decided to put together a formation of all participating members during the Woburn Abbey Moth Rally two years later. The team flew a unique Diamond Sixteen for a single north-south pass across the airfield. *Ian Oliver*

Tiger Moth N838KC experienced engine failure on take-off from Schellville-Senoma Valley Airport in California in May 2001 and was arrested when she slipped down a bank and into a river. Although intact and there were no injuries, the airframe and engine suffered considerably from water damage which took several years to rectify. *Kenneth Copp*

of the fuel tank, engine cowlings and some controls. The high ambient temperatures produced thermals which required caution in handling the load and it took twenty minutes to cover the three miles back to Hood where ZK-BLK touched down to an immaculate three point landing in front of her hangar.

What is believed to have been the first de Havilland aircraft airborne in the new century, Tiger Moth ZK-BAH (83589), was taken off by John Baynes from Mandeville in New Zealand at 0520 NZDT on 1 January 2000. John also claims to have been the last de Havilland aeroplane airborne in the previous century after he viewed the sunset from 2,500ft over Mandeville and spiralled down to land although that distinction may have gone to a Moth in California.

Left: The newly overhauled 'stiff' engine installed in Tiger Moth ZK-BLK stopped during an aerobatic manoeuvre on 6 January 2013 and the aircraft was safely landed about three miles from Hood Aerodrome. The most expeditious form of recovery was by helicopter and after the load was lightened the Tiger Moth was lifted by Tim Williams flying a Hughes 500e helicopter and, exercising great care, was safely carried to Hood Aerodrome. *Tom Williams*

Below: To stay within the lifting limitations of a Hughes 500e helicopter Tiger Moth ZK-BLK was lightened by the removal of some easily accessible component parts and, due to local thermal activity, ferried with extreme care to Hood Aerodrome. *Tom Williams*

CHAPTER TWENTY THREE

Out and About

A Tiger Moth is an incredibly difficult aeroplane to draw or paint due to her many different lines and angles and if one is wrong it usually throws all else out of balance. There are certain aspects within which the aeroplane photographs well, and others not, sometimes dependent on the need for the occupant of either cockpit, or both, to be fully faced or merely tolerated.

Before the Second World War Tiger Moths were regarded strictly as pilot trainers by civil and military operators alike save for the brief interlude when the instructors of the Central Flying School, Royal Air Force, were allowed to demonstrate their abilities surrounded by eye-catching chequers, carefully chosen. The role continued during the war when around the world only two basic colour schemes prevailed: camouflage of limited differences or Trainer Yellow, 'Sunshine' yellow to be correct. Apart from the odd excursion into territory created by boredom or devilment or stupidity the utilisation of the aeroplane was welded to her sole purpose: the indoctrination into the art of flying of a whole generation of enthusiastic young men.

But at the end of hostilities it was possible to acquire one of these reliable and practical little aeroplanes for not much money, a fraction of their true cost, and for individuals or groups of friends to operate them not only in their design role but simply for the joy and fun of doing so. The shackles were broken and the use of the aeroplanes broadened to new horizons quite apart from the innovative range of commercial activities to which they were introduced.

For a short post-war period, Tiger Moths might have been regarded as nondescript toys and the number of airworthy aircraft declined along with their asset values until the situation bottomed out in the mid 1970s when aeroplanes were sought out, well kept aeroplanes with healthy engines in particular, and a number of cottage industries encompassing the right level of skills and interest developed to tend to them. It was the perfect fit: a pre-war biplane with history and charisma available at modest prices and still affordable to operate in a private capacity. Did not Grandpa learn to fly a Tiger Moth in the winter wastelands of Canada before he aspired to captaining his Lancaster or Halifax or Spitfire? Or was it Uncle Fred who suffered the heat of Southern Africa or Australia and progressed via a Tiger Moth to a Catalina or a Sunderland to protect the seaways during patrols of massive endurance. Modern owners are much more aware of the history of the type and some go to extraordinary lengths to establish details of the working lives of their own cherished aeroplanes.

Perhaps a Tiger Moth is more photogenic than many others when in the company of other aeroplanes or when flying over land and seascapes of infinite variety or is posed against a moody background or in some unusual situation. There are few aeroplane types with such evident qualities and even fewer with four wings.

Tiger Moths lined up in the shadow of Belvoir Castle during the de Havilland Moth Club's International Rally in August 2011. *Mick Bajcar*

Slow flying race in progress. Tiger Moth and Harrier, both two seat trainers, in competition at Boscombe Down. *deHMC Archive*

Below: Langley Park Airfield is situated in the heart of the city of Perth, Western Australia, and is brought into commission on a regular basis for special anniversary events. *Paul Falconer-West*

Tiger Moth G-BPHR was part of a de Havilland Moth Club tour to Germany in May 2013 to commemorate the 70th anniversary of 617 Squadron's raid on the Ruhr dams. She is seen here approaching the Eder dam, in daylight and at considerably more than sixty feet above the water. *Klaus Stewering*

Tiger Moth G-AYIT seen flying overhead Biggin Hill during one of the very popular 'Air Fair' series, lived alongside Belfast Lough in Northern Ireland until she was sold to Brazil and is now based in Sao Paulo. *deHMC Archive*

Below: A sextet of Tiger Moths in line at Luskintyre on 22 October 2011 as part of the world wide celebration of the 80th anniversary of the first flight of the prototype DH.82. *Wayne Brown*

Left: When playing to the crowd extreme concentration and good judgement is essential for a well rehearsed manoeuvre to look casual but gripping. Members of the Tiger 9 in action at Halton in June 2011. *Victoria Wood*

Bottom: To maintain a close formation of Tiger Moths with a limited power range even on a calm day means that each pilot must work hard. The end result is utmost satisfaction of everybody on the ground or in the air. The Tiger 9 was shot during a practise session in 2007. *Geoff Collins*

Below: The Tiger 9 soloton's break is as dramatic in real life as it is in print especially if viewed from immediately in front as the two Tiger Moths approach the crowd. They were caught on film at the Best of British Airshow at Kemble on 26 August 2012. *Glen R L Johnson*

Above: What better way to end a stable display of sedate close formation flying than to burst all over the sky to the roar of Gipsy Major engines? The Tiger 9 team displayed at the Marshall Aerospace Anniversary Day at Cambridge in September 2009. *Terry Burke*

Right: At the Gothenburg Air Show held on 28 August 2010 a trio of Swedish Tiger Moths was joined by a guest from Norway to create this tidy finger four. *Jens Mardh*

Below right: After the original US-based 'Woody' was rebuilt and sold to Israel, an exact copy was produced by Tom Dietrich in Canada when DH.82C C-GMTH was converted to assume the role which transformation included the provision of wooden interplane struts. She visited Brodhead in Wisconsin in September 2005. *David Welch*

Above: Tiger Moth N838KC merges with the bulk of a camouflaged B.17 during Veteran's Day at Petaluma, California in 1998. *Kenneth Copp*

Right: Perhaps one of the most convincing of all conversions of a DH.82C into the `A' configuration is ex-RCAF Tiger Moth 5806. Completed at Guelph, registered C-GMTH and painted in the Woody Woodpecker scheme carried for many years by Linley Wright's N10LW before she took up residence in Israel in 2001, the wooden interplane struts are a major factor but the other clues are raked undercarriage, mass balanced elevators, tailwheel and ply covered leading edges to the lower mainplanes. *Gilles Auliard*

Left: One time F-104 instructor Bert Davis parked his DH.82C Tiger Moth C-FSAI alongside the replica of the Avro Arrow which is part of an outdoor exhibition at the Reynolds Museum at Wetaskiwin, Alberta. The CF-105 Arrow replica was built by local resident Allan Jackson between 1989 and 1996 and featured in a mini-series made by the Canadian Broadcasting Corporation telling the story of the project and its controversial cancellation. *Bert Davis*

Below: Tiger Moth I-GATO was caught in perfect harmony with Fokker Triplane replica I-LYNC during the Eliexpo 2006 organised by the Aero Club Francesco Baracca at Lugo di Romagna. *James Lawrence*

Above: Tiger Moth N85882 in pre-war Swedish Air Force markings was a visitor to the Chino Airshow in May 1988 where she witnessed the arrival of a B.29. *Jim Meads*

Above: When not flying his Tiger Moth VH-DDA from RAAF Base Elizabeth, Rod Lovell was captaining an RAAF Orion. In this shot the Tiger Moth appears to be full-out downhill whilst the Orion glides past without a hint of flap. *via Rod Lovell*

Left: The Italian formation team the Rusty Angels developed a most efficient and patriotic smoke generation system for use on their Tiger Moths. This photograph was used on their 2009 Christmas card. *via Carlo Bucciarelli*

Carsten Ølholm and his Tiger Moth OY-ECH were never likely to be able to outrun a Danish Air Force F-16, even when displaying a high angle of attack. *via Carsten Ølholm*

Even at the extraordinary angle of attack achieved by this English Electric Lightning, David Cyster's Tiger Moth G-BAFG was always going to come in a poor second. *via David Cyster*

Left: Blue Mediterranean sky is the perfect backdrop to the New Year greeting posted by the Italian Rusty Angels formation team. *via Carlo Bucciarelli*

Below left: Some wartime pilots who trained on the Tiger Moth would progress via Oxfords and Wellingtons to the Lancaster. John Baxter took the opportunity to allow G-BPHR to fraternise with the Battle of Britain Memorial Flight's Lancaster at Kemble in July 2007. *John Baxter*

Below: Jacek Mainka flying his Polish based Tiger Moth G-AFVE over Goraszka Airfield on 8 June 2008 accompanied by a Spitfire from the RAF's Battle of Britain Memorial Flight. In 2014 Jacek achieved a life's ambition by himself flying a Spitfire in Poland, and later over the White Cliffs of Dover, occasions recognised within Polish aviation as being of great historical significance. *via Jacek Mainka*

Left: In the summer of 2000 Serge and Marie France Maigrot were invited to visit a French Air Force Mirage IV squadron at Reims with their Tiger Moth F-BGCS, one of the few that survived the mass exodus of the type in the early 1970s. *Marie France Maigrot*

Below: A DH.82C in open cockpit configuration flying in company with an F-117, or by herself, depending on the quality of the radar. *Ted Leonard*

When frozen to a clearly defined specification, the Schwarzsee in Switzerland situated at 3,000ft, provides an operational area of 1,000 metres by 500 metres for an almost unique gathering of invited aeroplanes. Flown by Bruno Vonlanthen, Tiger Moth HB-UBC based at Ecuvillens, was one of twenty visiting types in February 1998. *Bruno Vonlanthen*

Below: Built at Hatfield early in 1939 and exported to Los Angeles on board a 747 Freighter in 1988, N555XB was painted in this unusual red and blue scheme by her new owner, but retained British civil registration G-ASXB on the fuselage. *Tim Jacobson*

On the declaration of war in 1939, RAF Reserve School aircraft adopted the camouflage scheme of the day whilst retaining civil registration letters. By 1991, when she was caught slipping in to land over the lakes at Woburn Abbey, this adopted scheme had already been worn by G-ARAZ for several years. *Don Conway*

Above: Sea and coastline will always provide some of the best possible background for air-to-air photography. Tiger Moth G-BFHH was captured flying against the exposed chalk of the South Downs near Beachy Head in Sussex before January 1999 when a chunk of it fell into the sea. *Gordon Bain*

Above: Kurt Hofschneider and his Tiger Moth N39DH were welcomed into the team when they met the USAF 'Thunderbirds' at the Atlantic City Trans-Fair in 1978. *Kurt Hofschneider*

Left: Bless 'em all. de Havilland Aircraft of Canada DH.82C Tiger Moth N18840 operating in open cockpit configuration meets Lockheed C.5 Galaxy at Bozeman, Montana in October 1988. *Bud Hall*

Rebuilt in Great Britain in 1986 from the wreck of an aircraft imported from the USA, G-AHAN took up vacant markings and was photographed with new owner Lloyd Owens over Gransden. The rear door is not disturbed by airflow when opened in flight and the configuration is often considered 'more comfortable' by broad shouldered pilots operating solo from the rear cockpit. *via Lloyd Owens*

To celebrate the 60th anniversary of RAAF Base Pearce in July 1998, previous equipment (DH.82A Tiger Moth VH-NMD/A17-640 cruising speed 72 knots), was flown in formation with a current RAAF trainer (Pilatus PC-9 A23-058 stalling speed 70 knots). *Kirsty Chambers, RAAF*

Commander Philip Shaw RN, Squadron Commander of 360 Squadron RAF, Wyton, flying his hobby interest Tiger Moth G-AFVE, shadowed by his working day aeroplane, English Electric Canberra T.17A WD955 flown by Squadron Leader Terry Cairns. At the time this shot was taken from a Casa 131 Jungmann in August 1994, WD955 was the oldest operational aircraft in the RAF. *Gordon Bain*

Below: In 1982, as part of the DH100 celebrations honouring the centenary of the birth of Sir Geoffrey de Havilland, multifarious Moths transited through Farnborough Aerodrome and were briefly at rest adjacent to the famous black hangar, close to where Geoffrey de Havilland took his first paid employment in aviation. *British Aerospace*

CHAPTER TWENTY FOUR

The DH.82 Queen Bee

In the sunshine at Hatfield Queen Bee L5902 takes on fuel alongside the running Gipsy King engines of DH.91 Albatross 'E.2'. Well illustrated is the cover over the rear compartment housing the radio control apparatus and sight of some of the host of essential external fittings. *de Havilland Aircraft Company*

During the First World War investigations were conducted into the possibilities of using radio to control unmanned aircraft which could be used for reconnaissance, as targets or as flying bombs, although the latter prospect was regarded as secret and not openly discussed. The requisite technology existed but practical difficulties were severe including a lack of range. Between the wars limited development continued at the Royal Aircraft Establishment, Farnborough, (RAE) and the RAF tested a pilotless aircraft called the Larynx which was launched from a transportable catapult in a remote area in Iraq. In 1932 the Pilotless Aircraft Co-ordinating Committee met at Farnborough when arrangements were made for three Fairey IIIF aircraft to be fitted with floats and radio control apparatus at a cost of £5,000 each. The converted aircraft was to be known as the Fairey Queen. Farnborough scientists with experience of the previous experiments were gathered into a team which produced the necessary equipment in two years. Led by G J R Joyce, he was able later to report that:

> "The trials witnessed two spectacular crashes, one after take-off and one after a left hand turn, but with the aid of ciné records each trouble was shrewdly estimated, countered and finally eliminated. The culmination of these experiments was a full scale flight over the English Channel followed by two Fleet exercises at Gibraltar and Malta for catapult and gunnery trials off HMS *Valiant*. Our pleasure in recovering the aircraft after each shoot was considerable but we shared the Navy's satisfaction after a direct hit off Malta. During the last few months of her working life Service interest was great and in embryo began the idea of a target aircraft, less expensive and more easily handled."

Wireless control apparatus for the new project was designed at the RAE. The airborne R1088A receiver was a simple four-valve set but the ground base station, a mobile M11 unit, stood four feet tall and eighteen inches wide and weighed 1,500lb. Transmission frequency range was 160-180 Kcs (LW) requiring an aerial array 250ft high. At sea, base control was effected through the mother ship's wireless room and the masts acted as supports for the aerials.

The M11 was fitted with nine push-button functions each initiating a single command: lights on, lights off, right turn, straight, left turn, climb, level, glide and dive. The autopilot was geared to provide standard settings for each manoeuvre: rate one turns, climb at 400fpm, descend, and throttle settings were included as part of the command with no separate engine control. The 'lights off' command (a dash and two dots and known as a 'D' signal) was used as an automatic signal to reset a contacting clock at a given time interval. If no signal was received, after about fifty three seconds the controls were activated by the clock to put the aircraft into an emergency left glide if above a certain height, converting to a straight glide at that height. The 'D' signal at forty seconds after the last transmission prevented the emergency action.

DH.82 Tiger Moth Seaplane S1675 mounted on Short floats on the slipway at Rochester in March 1932. It is possible that the type was being considered for duties other than as a conventional seaplane even at this early date in her career. *Ulster Folk and Transport Museum*

When the DH.60 Moth and DH.82A Tiger Moth were suggested as likely candidates for the scheme Farnborough requested details of the DH.60GIII Moth and DH.82 Tiger Moth configured as seaplanes. A formal proposal was then made to the de Havilland Company on 21 December 1932 to modify a Tiger Moth for launching from a catapult at 65mph but, following a visit to Hatfield next day to inspect a DH.60M, DH.60GIII and DH.82 with Gipsy III engines, it was decided that the best option was to use the DH.60GIII Moth wooden fuselage on the grounds that it would be stronger, lighter and cheaper, more easily repaired and simple to modify in the light of operational experience, plus the stronger Tiger Moth wings, suitably adapted. The non-conducting wooden fuselage of the DH.60GIII Moth would be heavily bonded as maximum protection against interference with the wireless control. Although initial discussion suggested that motive power would be supplied by a proposed Gipsy Major Series 3 engine with fully screened ignition driving a moderately fine pitch de Havilland wooden propeller, DH5220/MX, a standard Gipsy Major 1 was chosen which would incorporate a number of necessary modifications appropriate to the task.

A large number of detail and more fundamental changes were necessary in order to create a practical target aircraft from the pure DH.60/DH.82 lineage. The engine mounting feet and wing attachments were strengthened to accept the high forces of acceleration experienced during catapult launch and the rear fuselage was reinforced to protect the integrity of the tail unit. An Eclipse starter was provided on the engine's starboard side and the carburettor redesigned to ensure a full fuel flow during the high 'G' take off segment.

To cope with water based operations control cables were designed in stainless steel although rudder and elevator were operated by pistons actuated by gyroscopically controlled air valves whose 30psi working pressure was supplied from a wind driven compressor attached by an arm to the port side of the fuselage, taking fullest advantage of the propeller slipstream. Cable operated ailerons would be locked into neutral for catapult launches. Electrical power was generated by a pair of accumulators.

A pilot's instrumented cockpit was to be provided to allow for 'manual' test flying and occasional positioning when the aileron control would be fully functional. Fitted with an ASI, an altimeter and engine gauges and controls, the front cockpit location was the chosen option fitted with standard flying controls except that the stick was riveted in position. An RAF 'Tiger Moth harness' was specified with 'special lugs' on account of picking up on the wooden fuselage. A stiffened seat and a pilot's headrest were supplied later as the result of experience. The front cockpit was scheduled to be faired over when not occupied although in practice most operations appear to have been conducted with it left open and the windscreen still in place.

Substituted for the rear cockpit was a compartment redesigned to accommodate the R1088A wireless receiving apparatus and Mk.1A Automatic Pilot. The fuel tank was increased in capacity from the Tiger Moth's nineteen gallons to twenty five gallons with an unfulfilled proposal for a further increase to thirty one gallons. Numerous additional external fittings were necessary to assist with ground handling, lifting by ship's derrick or site crane, for tethering and catapult attachment. The aircraft was to be equipped with an easily detachable wheeled undercarriage for convenience in ground handling which could be quickly changed for a Short Bros float chassis for operation from water.

The RAE referred to the contracted prototype aircraft as a DH.60 Moth which was to be delivered to Farnborough by mid January 1933, fully bonded and screened and fitted with Short floats, there to receive a Mk 1A automatic two-axis control system manufactured by R B Pullin and Company with the Automatic Telephone Manufacturing Company and Plessey supplying remote control gear and wireless receiver. The contract letter which was not issued to de Havilland until February 1933 recommended that stainless steel fittings be supplied for two 'Tiger Moth' aircraft but this was rejected in favour of the same corrosion-prevention measures recently applied to a DH.83 Fox Moth Seaplane sold to a Spanish company for exploration in the Amazon basin.

An Instruction to Proceed was issued on 23 March 1933 for a 'Special Moth', K3584 (5027), which was built against Air Ministry contract 232902/33. She was ready on 26 April, fitted with Gipsy Major engine No 5140, but issues with screening and the fitting of extended water rudders resulting in both aircraft and floats shuffling between Farnborough and Hatfield before K3584 was returned to the RAE on a wheeled undercarriage. Flight trials resulted in a recommendation for stiffening of the fuselage structure.

In support of the target aircraft contract the de Havilland Company raised their first modification to the Tiger Moth Type Record (based on the DH.60X Type Record) on 26 April 1933, the day K3584 was declared 'ready'. Addendum 83A, for which preparatory work had begun at the beginning of March, called for "Tiger Moth (wooden fuselage)" No 5027 to be modified by the "incorporation of wooden fuselage in RAF Tiger Moth." The Addendum required certification of the aircraft at the standard weights for normal and aerobatic flight (1,825lb/1,750lb Landplane and Seaplane), on the grounds that these had been agreed previously. The new fuselage was now submitted for close scrutiny and approval:

> "... this component is of 60G.III type, but has been modified by increasing the size of the centre section fuselage vertical side struts and by modifying the fuselage float chassis fittings and centre section strut fittings to accommodate increased weight. As the fuselage is ply covered, detailed stressing is not possible. Comparison, however, has been made between loads in 'Tiger' Moth metal fuselage (in Seaplane and Landplane cases) with the size of members in this centre section fuselage. The comparison indicates a fair reserve factor on all members."

On 5 May 1933 Addendum 83B was issued which confirmed suitability of the Short Bros floats and chassis. The date of her first flight from Farnborough is unknown but subsequently she was positioned to Rochester and flown from the river Medway on 11 May 1933:

> "The aircraft flew for 55 minutes. It handled well on the water and took off in nineteen seconds in a 5mph wind smoothly and in a straight line. It was laterally stable and made turns with rudder and elevator only. It was stable fore and aft and climbed to 1,000ft at 65mph in one minute and forty six seconds. Maximum speed was 108mph at sea level."

The flight is not recorded in Hubert Broad's logbook although as Chief Test Pilot he was almost certainly in command. He had been responsible for trials of the Spanish Fox Moth in January and would also fly two Tiger Moth Seaplanes, E.2 (3203), and E.3 (3204), from the river Medway in October. Meanwhile, radio control trials were delayed due to the failure of the Pullin company to deliver their equipment after misunderstanding the sequence of actions required by government paperwork.

On 21 June 1933 the Air Ministry issued invitations to tender for the supply of two 'target aircraft' to be built against specification 18/33, one to be a landplane and the other a seaplane, both to be fitted for launch by catapult. It was accepted that the de Havilland Company was likely to be the sole respondent and an Invitation to Proceed (ITP) was issued to them on 4 August calling for two aircraft to be supplied, the landplane at £1,038 with an additional £320 to cover floats and other marine equipment. While Flt Lt Vincent caught up on radio trials with K3584, which was never intended to be launched by catapult, the two new aircraft, K3597 (5038), and K3598 (5039), were delivered to Farnborough in October 1933.

The weighing report for K3597 dated 17 October 1933 refers to the aircraft as 'Special Machine for Catapult and Automatic Pilot Research' whilst both it and K3584 and K3598 are all reported to be a 'Wooden Tiger Moth'.

When compared to the first aircraft there were many essential differences designed to enable catapult launching. The bottom longerons of the wooden fuselage had an additional spruce member attached to them which extended over nearly the whole of the fuselage length and the thickness of the ply covering in the two centre bays was doubled. Catapult spools were built into the fuselage with additional side members to cope with local loads and the joint which accepted attachment of the flying wires was strengthened. As a result the authorised catapult weight was increased from 1,650lb to 1,860lb.

A modified form of slinging gear was arranged to fold compactly against the centre section fuel tank which was protected against damage and now was accommodated between solid ribs, designed to deal with the increased loads from the sling. The tank itself was fitted with diagonal tubes through which sling cables were routed and it was noted that the difference to capacity was 'negligible'. The lower mainplanes were provided with a ply covering to part of the leading edges and all control surfaces were fitted with locking bolts; the instrument board in the front cockpit carried a placard warning the pilot of this fact.

K3597 was trialled aboard an E.IIH catapult not only to confirm her compatibility but the effects of acceleration on her radio apparatus. The aircraft was launched without a pilot and with the engine stopped and was landed straight ahead at speeds no greater than 25mph.

After the Admiralty stated in October 1933 that it required four aircraft to be stationed in Malta, and four others at home, a further order for twelve aircraft was placed with Hatfield at an estimated cost of £25,000 and on 22 November it was confirmed that all were to be fitted with non-adjustable Handley Page slots. In January 1934 K3597 was damaged during catapult launching trials at Plymouth and was broken down for parts, some of which, by agreement, were incorporated into the construction of K4293 (5089), delivered in August 1934.

The name 'Queen Bee' was not officially confirmed until 22 March 1934 and within the de Havilland organisation the hybrid aircraft type was known as the DH.82 Queen Bee and not as the DH.82B Queen Bee. In early references it may have been natural for de Havilland staff to assume that following the progression of DH.82 Tiger Moth to DH.82A Tiger Moth, the next DH.82 would be designated 'B' and some documentation does reflect their assumption. However, this aeroplane was not a Tiger Moth and the DH.82 matriculation was adopted as a matter of convenience for the process of the Type Approval for which it also fed on those already established for the DH.60X Moth. The DH.82B Tiger Moth was an entirely different experimental aircraft flown in 1939 which was some years after Canada assumed title to the DH.82C Tiger Moth in which 'C' stood for Canada as did the 'C' when applied to the Gipsy Major 1 engine.

A new contract for the supply of nineteen Queen Bees was placed with Hatfield in 1934 when production was integrated with that of the Moth Major. One of the first of these aircraft, K5055 (5116), was despatched to the Royal Indian Air Force but served in isolation; targets for 'silent' gunnery practice were provided under contract by the civilian flying clubs whose Moth Majors and Tiger Moths operated without fear of collision with practice rounds.

Topping-up contracts against Specification 20/35 followed for the next several years: 1935 (42), 1936 (24), 1937 (30), 1938 (192) and 1939 (28). The average price of a Queen Bee ex-works was quoted in September 1937 at a few pence less than £1,023 each but there was no estimate for business in the following years as the company believed the type was 'unlikely to continue'. When prices were

Queen Bee production in full swing at Hatfield in 1939. Although the wing and structure of the empennage was similar to a Tiger Moth the fuselage was completely different and adorned with special fittings. It was arguably wrong even to refer to the type as a wooden Tiger Moth. *via BAE Systems*

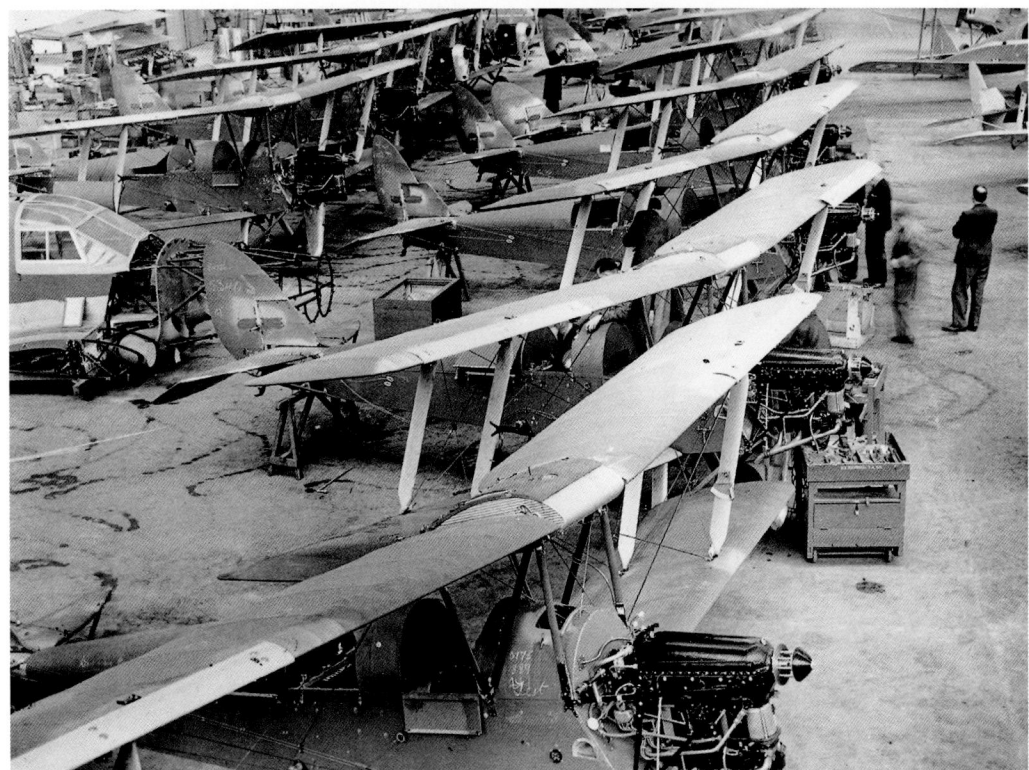

DH.82 Queen Bees in the Hatfield erecting shop in April 1939. The aircraft nearest the camera, No 5175, RAF serial K8642, has a gauge let into the fuselage side adjacent to the footstep. Note the engineless DH.93 Don fuselage on a pallet on the left. *via British Aerospace*

analysed after the aircraft became fully operational it was estimated that the cost of the ammunition used during a single training shoot far exceeded the value of the target.

An early concept was that the Queen Bee should be launched from alongside a Royal Navy warship at sea and flown for the benefit of naval gunnery practice but they were usually despatched from catapults built onto the decks of cruisers or battleships. A fleet involved in a firing exercise would sail with as many as six Queen Bees to ensure as far as was possible that a target would be available for the duration of the exercise. The aircraft would be flown at high level to simulate a bombing attack else at 500ft or less than 100ft to cover fighter or torpedo tactics and would be fired upon by different types of guns considered most appropriate to the situation. Within a fleet only one ship was allowed to fire at a time to ensure that the accuracy of the shooting by individual vessels could be identified.

The target aircraft were to be considered expendable with losses anticipated due to accurate, lucky or even poor shooting. The usual brief was for the gunners deliberately to angle off and for the position of shell bursts to be recorded but it was later considered more realistic in training to be encouraged to aim to hit the target which actually revealed the level of expertise.

The owner of a DH.82A Tiger Moth based in the USA and sold to Denmark painted his aeroplane in the yellow and black stripes more correctly applied to target tugs in an effort to dissuade gunners rather than attract their attention. Queen Bees were painted more traditionally. *via Johan Wiklund*

The special fittings on a Queen Bee which allowed the rudder to be locked during a catapult launch. The locking bar was connected to a static cable and was withdrawn as the launched aircraft became airborne. *Ian Grace*

The launch sequence from a catapult was very much a team effort whether at sea or later on land. Prior to a take-off the controlling gyroscopes were spun up using an external supply of compressed air, sufficient to sustain erection until the on-board compressor could provide a sufficient flow. Propeller and compressor speeds were checked by a stroboscope before jacks and trestles were removed. With the 'launch' valve set, controls centralised and the Gipsy Major running at full throttle, the armourer would load the magazine and hold the firing cable. If all was considered to be in order the aircraft was released under the command of an officer armed with green and red flags.

Ailerons were physically locked in the neutral position when under automatic control and control locks fitted to hard points on rudder and elevator were disconnected by static lines as the aircraft moved down the ramp. The leading edge slats fitted to both upper mainplanes were fixed in the open position and required no pre-launch adjustment. Once airborne a winch box ran out a trailing aerial and contact was established with the M11 operator; if the aerial failed to deploy the aircraft would crash.

Normal operating height was limited to 9,000ft amsl which was considered realistic for simulated bombing attacks and at which height the aircraft could still be seen against a cloudless sky. Observers worked in pairs using high powered binoculars. It was necessary for the controller to keep the Queen Bee in line of sight; he had no other indication of the aircraft's flight attitude or geographical location.

Signals were similar to those produced by a 1930's state of the art telephone dialling system (dash tone followed by dots). To guard against push-button failure a telephone hand dial was incorporated on the M11 console to duplicate signals if necessary. A similar device was included in the Queen Bee's front cockpit with which a human

An airman in a perilous position near the leading edge of Queen Bee N1846, mounted on the catapult and with the engine running. Control was exercised from the wooden hut alongside the Bessonneau acting on instructions from the launching officer at the aircraft side. *The Aeroplane*

The front cockpit of a Queen Bee displaying a number of standard flying instruments but also connections to the one time top secret wireless control apparatus in the rear compartment. *Ian Grace*

test pilot could over-ride ground signals if he believed there was a problem with the auto controls. Part of the human disconnect procedure was to cut off the pneumatic system after which the aircraft could only be flown manually. When test flown the pilot of the aircraft maintained a log of every control input which on landing was compared with that recorded by the aircraft's radio controller.

The automatic landing sequence was set up by the controller using a visual sight mounted on a tripod. Applying a corrective allowance for wind the aircraft could be accurately positioned on approach at the right speed. On the command 'glide', the throttle closed and the Queen Bee descended until at about 20ft the proximeter, the weight attached to the end of the aerial, made contact with the surface. Sensing resistance the ignition shut off automatically, the gyro was caged and 'up elevator' was set in two distinct movements. To prevent the proximeter from bouncing back towards the aircraft spikes were added which were of little assistance on land when it was dragged through a hedge or contacted a tree or a building during the latter stages of approach and caused a premature shutting off of the engine. To overcome such tendencies when monitored by a pilot in the front cockpit he was provided with a guillotine control which cut the cable. When landing on the surface of the sea the proximeter might contact the top of a swell which would cause a premature shutdown and undignified arrival.

Should the controller lose sight of his charge or a close shell-burst disrupt wireless contact a safety feature was automatically triggered. Having received no new command for a set time the remote control would close the throttle and initiate a left hand descending turn and the 'glide' sequence, hopeful that the touchdown would be onto an acceptable sea state and moderately into wind.

On one occasion a near miss by an exploding shell caused the guillotine to sever the trailing aerial in mid-action and the aircraft entered a series of uncontrolled circles overhead Aberporth until it crashed in open country.

The Royal Navy continued with its trials off the British coast and from Malta throughout 1934 when the Queen Bees were encouraged to fly in anything but straight and level patterns, simulating various forms of attack. The strike rate by the naval gunners proved disappointing and apart from some splinter damage the most serious injuries were caused by heavy landings on the open sea when struts, floats and wings were frequently carried away. Analysis of the behaviour of the 'proximeter' indicated that instead of breaking off on contact as designed it sometimes bounced. As an experiment the mass was doubled to 4lb but it bounced even more violently and on one occasion the aerial whipped forward and the weight hit the petrol tank.

To counter splinter damage to floats it was suggested that each be filled with 15,000 ping-pong balls but the cheaper and alternative remedy was to install extra bulkheads. The manufacturer was asked to consider what strengthening would be required if a pilot were to occupy the front seat during a catapult launch and the prospects of increasing the fuel supply to thirty one gallons. The question of folding wings was raised but was dismissed as being difficult to achieve and not essential and a shock-absorbing undercarriage was proposed for K4229 (5051).

Three Queen Bees were despatched to St Lucia in the West Indies in January 1935, including K3598 and where, prior to flying a trial, poor co-ordination between the pilot on board who had taxied the aircraft alongside HMS *Guardian*, and the winch operator who was to lift the aircraft onto the catapult, resulted in her capsizing. The aircraft was salvaged, returned to Hatfield for repair but having previously led a charmed life in Malta was despatched to Gibraltar in March 1936 where she was shot down in April. The two surviving aircraft based at St Lucia, K4226 (5048), and K4294 (5090), had been fitted with night flying lights which was considered to be a satisfactory development but did not prevent either from crashing into the Caribbean in February and May respectively.

In March 1935 it was first proposed to form an RAF Development Flight to exploit Queen Bee potential as the Army was taking more of an interest. Under conditions of great secrecy a party of five RAF wireless experts were gathered at RAE Farnborough in May 1935 to learn the Queen Bee radio control techniques from the system designer, G J R Joyce, an RAE Experimental Officer. The party was joined during the year by more personnel specialising in instruments, radio and hydraulics and collectively they were called the Queen Bee Base and Training Unit. Later in the year the Unit was posted to Lee on Solent to enable a naval shoot in the English Channel. In November 1936 the Base Flight was transferred to Henlow where their task was to establish a production line to equip newly delivered Queen Bees and to test them and train personnel, a task previously undertaken by the RAE at Farnborough. It was at Henlow in January 1937 that the Flight became The Pilotless Aircraft Section (PAS) and developed there the technique for taking off and landing back on a wheeled undercarriage under radio control. Following a number of automatic landings the first complete circuit was flown on 19 November 1937 but carrying a safety pilot. This was a significant development as it allowed flexibility in the siting of bases independent of catapults and also saved the expense of providing floats and the associated services necessary for a marine operation. The development also allowed further research into the prospects of aircraft being used as flying bombs directed by radio control.

Since 1933 the whole Queen Bee programme, and especially the wireless control systems, had been classified as secret but were demonstrated to the press at Farnborough on 26 June 1935 when, with an aircraft in reserve, the seventh production Queen Bee, K4227 (5049), painted silver with yellow wings and blood-red outer wing panels denoting that a pilot was not carried, and operating on a wheeled undercarriage, was taken off and landed again. On this occasion, due to Air Ministry rules concerning 'remotely controlled flight over built-up areas within a radius of five miles', Flt Lt C McC Vincent DFC, was on board for the whole exercise. Three days later the aircraft was publicly displayed for the first time during the RAF Pageant at Hendon when all items of a sensitive nature were thoroughly concealed.

On 17 July 1935 as part of the celebrations of the Silver Jubilee of their Majesties King George V and Queen Mary, the Admiralty

arranged a Queen Bee demonstration in the Solent for members of the Royal Family and invited VIP guests and agreed to selective coverage by the newsreels. The combined might of naval fire-power failed to score a hit as Queen Bee K4227, one of the aircraft demonstrated at Farnborough the previous month, continued defiantly to cruise along its prescribed flight-line. The story may be apocryphal but has endured: to save further embarrassment the controller was advised by a senior officer to press the button which might bring the demonstration to a timely and satisfactory conclusion.

Queen Bees K5113, K5114 and K5118, (5162-5164), were all delivered to Farnborough in August 1935 and in the spring of 1937 had been taken on charge in Malta. Their specification had been changed slightly and in exchange for increases in the diameter and gauge of the launching spools, a larger section top longeron in two areas, and a slight reduction in maximum catapult weight from 1,860lb to 1,800lb, increased acceleration factors of up to 5.5G at the start of the launch and 3.5G at the end were acceptable assuming a maximum airspeed of 70mph and a crosswind not exceeding 10mph. The aircraft were engaged in naval exercises until all three were lost in August 1937.

Below: DH.82 Queen Bee K4227 at Farnborough in June 1935 where she was demonstrated to the press. Note the wind driven compressor above the oil tank and how the front cockpit is faired over leaving the head bumper 'crash pad' exposed. *The Aeroplane*

Above: The first public acknowledgement of the Queen Bee programme and associated press demonstration was in June 1935 when K4227 was flown under wireless control at Farnborough although Air Ministry rules dictated that a pilot be carried on board. *deHMC Archive*

Below: Members of the press were introduced to the Queen Bee at Farnborough in June 1935 although some of the control apparatus was still classified as secret and remained hidden under cover. *deHMC Archive*

The float equipped Queen Bee N1835 following recovery from the sea after a shoot in Malta. Under most circumstances more damage was caused by a bad landing on the sea than anti-aircraft rounds, excepting a direct hit. *deHMC Archive*

As Royal Artillery anti-aircraft ranges mostly were situated along the coast, Queen Bee launch sites were established as close as practicable to the batteries and until more experience was gained operating with conventional wheeled undercarriages, all aircraft were fitted with floats and launched from catapults of various designs recovered from warships. The catapult rails could be rotated on a concrete base through 180° to seaward to give the best advantage of wind and the launch was effected by compressed air and glycerine fired by a cordite charge.

A major survey of potential Queen Bee sites around the British coastline had been undertaken in August 1936 as the result of which launch facilities were set up at Aberffraw (later renamed Bodorgan to prevent confusion over names), Aberporth, Cleave, Gosport, Kidsdale, serving the Army camp at Burrow Head, Manorbier, Morfa Towyn and Weybourne.

Due to delays in the installation of the catapult on shore at Watchet in Somerset HMS *Neptune* had been the seaborne launch vehicle at the end of July 1935 when two Queen Bees were deployed for exercises of more than three hours each. On the last day of the month K5100 (5134), failed to respond to commands and glided inland over Blue Anchor Bay where she collided with a tree and was reduced to a collection of spare parts which were salvaged and reused.

Farnborough was the controlling centre for No 1 Anti Aircraft Co-operation Unit (AACU), and a Flight based at Watchet was joined for a summer camp deployment by a detachment from Henlow's PAS in July 1937 where they launched their first pilotless aircraft on 3 August using the Larynx catapult previously installed at Farnborough. Additional launches were from the light cruiser HMS *Neptune* off the coast and three Queen Bees, K8641 (5174), K8642 (5175), and K8661 (5194), were all reported to have crashed into the sea on the same date, 20 August.

The Watchet site was inspected in August 1938 by the Secretary of State for War, Rt Hon Leslie Hore-Belisha MP, accompanied by fifty other MPs and the mayors of sixteen London Boroughs. Whilst most of the twelve Queen Bees lost from Watchet were as the result of take-off or landing accidents, K8664 (5197), was reported to have been shot down on 25 August 1938, possibly during the Parliamentary visit and L7728 (5239), on 3 August 1939, a month before war was declared.

A camouflaged Queen Bee being lowered onto a rotatable catapult on a cliff-top launch site somewhere in Great Britain, November 1939. The catapult was operated by a mixture of compressed air and glycerine fired by a cordite charge. *The Aeroplane*

K8669 on the catapult at Watchet prior to launching for the benefit of a group of visiting officials. The catapult could be rotated to take advantage of the wind. The aircraft was held securely by an elaborate cradle which picked up on special fittings on the fuselage. *via BAE Systems*

K8669 being launched from the catapult at Watchet, Somerset, on 16 August 1938. The occasion was a demonstration, during a Territorial Army camp, to invited military officers and Members of Parliament. The aircraft's lifting strops can be seen attached to the centre section. *deHMC Archive*

K8632 launching from the catapult of a Royal Navy cruiser in July 1937. Flying operations were commanded by RAF officers carried on board. *Keystone*

Queen Bee K8669 being launched from the catapult at Watchet, 16 August 1938. *deHMC Archive*

Watchet based aircraft were flown as targets for the neighbouring Army camp at Doniford and, when put down in the Bristol Channel with planned intent or not, were secured by military launches and tenders. A pilot was put aboard who shut down all the systems and attached salvage cables. In early operations the salvaged aircraft were recovered onto the SS *Adastral* but she proved to have too deep a draught for the tidal conditions in Watchet harbour and was transferred to Appledore or Padstow on behalf of RAF Cleave. Requisitioned in 1938 and converted for the exclusive rescue of Queen Bees, the SS *Radstock* was a ship originally used to carry railway lines for the construction of the Somerset and Dorset Joint Railway and later for the transport of coal from Cardiff for the Wansborough Paper Mill. When carried back to Watchet harbour the salvaged aircraft were landed on the quayside for which the War Office was charged a fee by the local council. Recovery at the Manorbier site was contracted to Crockfords who landed aircraft at Tenby.

The Queen Bees were quickly de-salted and dismantled on the dockside and returned by lorry to their launch site where they were repaired if necessary, reassembled and tested prior to re-allocation.

The SS *Radstock* in a West Country harbour with a K-serialled Queen Bee (possibly K8659) coded '69' on the deck and looking in prime condition. The ship's captain had two daughters both of whom married locally based airmen. *deHMC Archive*

The engine had already been removed from the camouflaged N1833 before the broken airframe had been landed. Note the hook and cable from the derrick attached to the lifting strops on the centre section. The treatment of engines which had been immersed in salt water was given top priority. *via Richard Riding*

In its basic form the automatic control system was required to obey 1,000 signals in succession before it was considered satisfactory for pilotless flight. If the engine had suffered immersion it was immediately stripped down and all parts were boiled in caustic soda before despatch to a base servicing unit.

Having established the project on a secure and practical footing there was time to investigate refinements. When taking off from a runway the aircraft would fly off in what would normally be considered a dangerous tail down attitude and climb away at full power under the command of the controller. Had the aircraft been flown in the conventional manner the pilot would have pushed the control column forward to lift the tail after which the remainder of the short take-off run would have been achieved by balancing on the main wheels. When landing, a pilot would have played the aircraft down to a three point touchdown with use of the elevators. In an automatic landing the proximeter caused the ignition to be cut and the elevators raised leaving the undercarriage to absorb the inevitable impact. Two schemes were investigated which aimed to improve the pilotless take-off and landing technique by lifting the tail permanently to the level flight position on the ground. The first was to consider mounting what was in effect a lengthened tailwheel strut positioned much further forward underneath the fuselage. A system designed and manufactured by British Landing Gears Ltd. (BLG) had been fitted to an Avro Sports Avian by Rollason Aircraft Services at Croydon in April 1936 and flown at Hanworth. A similar arrangement was trialled on Fairey Gordon K2748, possibly during a deployment with No 1 AACU during the summer of 1938. In response to a request dated 26 May 1938 Hatfield had drawn up a scheme by October to cover a BLG proposal which added a pair of struts for attachment at the Queen Bee's main undercarriage central knuckle joint, and a wheel with pneumatic tyre fitted to an oleo and strut tripod assembled underneath the fuselage, just behind the front cockpit.

Queen Bee K8654 (5187), delivered to Cardington in October 1936, was returned to Hatfield in November the following year where she was subject to developments with the BLG arrangement. These included the attachment of an extra panel of 2mm ply on the fuselage sides adjacent to the rear tripod. K8654 was delivered to Farnborough in January 1939 and flown by an RAE test pilot who recommended a stiffer and improved design of fuselage attachment for the front legs of the tripod and a reduction in the length of the tailwheel compression leg in order to increase wing incidence at take off. The BLG system was not universally employed and after detachment to Manorbier K8654 was scrapped in July 1945.

Meanwhile the RAE championed an alternative system. BLG was contracted to design and fit a nosewheel to a Fairey Seal and Farnborough converted a GAL Monospar to the same configuration. In November 1937 the de Havilland Company was encouraged to participate in the investigations and the following year a demonstrator DH.87B Hornet Moth visited a number of southern airfields with a crude nosewheel arrangement although there was never any suggestion that it was for advancement of the type. At the same time, during a period of remarkable innovation by the small Hatfield group responsible for the DH.94 Moth Minor, they unveiled an aircraft with a nosewheel attached to the front fuselage bulkhead by a long steel tube employing a rubber block suspension. The Air Ministry had started their search for a possible successor to the Queen Bee as early as April 1935 and the Moth Minor, apart from participating in the nose wheel trials, even if they were not in support of the target aircraft programme, fitted exactly into the category of aircraft they were analysing. The net result of the combined efforts was that the working Queen Bee remained in her original configuration.

To increase the operational range of the Queen Bee and allow her safely to fly out of sight of her controller, especially where this could result in a safe touch down in calmer waters, for example, trials were undertaken with an airborne shepherd and the RAE reported that with control fitted in a Hawker Demon flying at a distance of about 1,500 yards, these had been completely successful. Although thought never to have been used operationally in a Queen Bee the developing technology was carried forward.

'V' Flight of No 1 AACU was based at Cleave in Somerset from May 1939 where the 'anti-aircraft co-operation camp' came under the command of Sqn Ldr E R Pearce, previously with the trials unit at Henlow. The catapult was operational from June but the team believed it could launch just as easily from the grass using a wheeled undercarriage and conventional take-off techniques. The first completely automatic take-off and landing in Great Britain was claimed by the unit at Cleave with Pearce monitoring in the cockpit of P5743 (5413), in July 1939, although the honours had already been awarded to Farnborough some four years previously.

On the overcast morning of 13 November 1941, Sqn Ldr Bill Young, Officer Commanding 'G' Flight, No 1 AACU Cleave, with eight hours logged on Hawker Henleys that month and a one hour 'silent gun' sortie in Tiger Moth T8180 (84472), was invited to sample an automatic take-off in Queen Bee V4758 (5445). He recorded his impressions:

"On the cliffs of Cornwall I found myself sitting in a Queen Bee cockpit ready for take-off, only this time things would be very different. My arms were folded across my chest; my feet away from the rudder bar and the inside of my helmet felt a little moist in spite of the cold air outside, more I think from apprehension than fear. I had flown a Tiger Moth many times before, usually on engine tests, or occasionally on ferry duties. But this time it was going to fly me!

I adjusted my straps over my parachute harness and wondered whether I should put a bit of air into my Mae West, because at the end of the grass strip, due west, was a 600ft sheer drop from the edge of the cliff to the rolling Atlantic swell below. At least, I thought, it would give me extra height in an emergency. Would my climbing speed cope with the downdraught at the edge of the cliff fairly quickly followed by an up-current coming off the face? We would rock for a bit, that was for sure! I had already run up the engine against the chocks to test the magnetos and tried to give a brave wave to the wireless operator standing a few yards away. He held the black box ready to give the necessary signals that would get me airborne. The wind-speed had been checked half an hour ago. If it increased considerably the angle of climb would be wrong, perhaps we would just hang there with the ASI needle going off the clock. I am very much against stalling on the approach or undershooting!

Without further warning the throttle half-opened and we were off. What was it the other pilot had said? If we veered left or right or dipped a wing or looked like going into buildings, I was to take over manually. I did not really need telling; my hands and feet were inches from the controls.

Full throttle, the tail was off the ground and we were bumping over the rough grass gaining speed. The stick came back and we were airborne and climbing. I checked the ASI. All correct. We passed over the Army's 3in guns in a gentle climbing turn to the left and levelled out at about 1,000ft. I remember thinking, should I log this flight under 'pilot times' or 'passenger' until I reminded myself that I was in charge, or was I? The three little dots on the edge of the aerodrome obviously thought they were! The angle of glide was checked and the aircraft was now on the approach. Had the wind remained constant in speed and direction? Would the operator judge the drift correctly? This time I did the landing because the 30ft of trailing aerial with a weight on the end had a habit of snaking up and hitting the pilot on the head. Previous test pilots had been forced to wear tin hats. I pulled the stick gently back, closed the throttle, straightened up and landed."

Some of those on the ground may have breathed just as big a sigh of relief as Bill Young. The Queen Bee could become unstable below 20ft on automatic approach and the controller caused a warning hooter to be sounded when this happened. Little more serious than a need to replace the undercarriage was often the result.

At Bodorgan in 1940 after a delayed start 'Z' Flight of No 1 AACU, transferred from Watchet, provided Queen Bee targets for the range at Ty-Crose. Their first pilotless launch on a wheeled undercarriage from the grass airfield occurred on 2 December, the aircraft held during pre-take off checks by a special quick release unit designed and manufactured on site and fitted to the tailskid by Mick Smith. After P4804 (5382), had flown for a two and a half hour sortie she was guided down by a jubilant Commanding Officer only for the trailing aerial to snag causing her to crash on landing. In some official channels her loss was reported as due to having been shot down.

Losses in the sea were accepted as part of the routine; Queen Bees were not expected to disappear inland. One from Bodorgan that did so crashed on Snowdon and a mountain rescue team which had been alerted searched fruitlessly all night for the pilot, embarrassing the Queen Bee units into revising their emergency communications procedures. On an early test flight a radio had managed to engage a frequency used by the BBC for domestic broadcasting after which there was only one outcome.

To demonstrate how the system was working to the Flight's satisfaction the aircraft controller at Cleave set up a spectacular stunt for a party of visiting 'brasshats' in 1941. His idea was to guide his charge through a Bessonneau hangar before making a circuit and landing. All went well except he chose the wrong hangar; the Queen Bee flew in at one end but not out of the other.

By June 1940 the headquarters of the Pilotless Aircraft Section had become established within 70 Group at St. Athan and was renamed the Pilotless Aircraft Unit (PAU) at the end of the year, their establishment of eighteen Queen Bees, rising to thirty five by September 1941, having lost their bright yellow colours to the camouflage scheme of the day on declaration of war. The Unit moved to Manorbier in May 1942, operating in support of the guns at Tenby.

Hatfield-built V4760 (5447), was flown at St Athan in 1941 by one of the PAU's resident test pilots, Sqn Ldr Michael Adderley and, following repairs to damage caused by anti-aircraft fire, was packed for despatch to the USA where she arrived in December. Delivered to Wright Field she was flown in March, April and May 1942 by Sqn Ldr Peter Bathurst, Commanding Officer of the PAU, in a series of demonstrations totalling just over twenty three hours after which Peter Bathurst turned his attention to evaluation of the AT6A. The Queen Bee trials were conducted at a time of blossoming interest in automatic controls and aids and signified close co-operation between British and American researchers. Plans for a batch of Queen Bees to be built in the USA under a reverse lend-lease agreement were not pursued.

V4760 was stored until she was acquired in 1955 by Hayward Leland Productions of California and, civil registered N2726A, was used to gather aerial footage for the film *The Spirit of St Louis,* the aircraft providing an ideally configured camera platform. With the pilot operating from the front seat, a 180° arc of almost uninterrupted view towards the tail was available to the camera operator working from his own uncluttered compartment. The Queen Bee even made a brief appearance in the film herself as set dressing, re-painted as NC726A and wearing Pathé News titles for the occasion. By 1977, N2726A had moved to museum storage in St Paul, Minnesota from where for almost twenty years she was frequently advertised for sale as her condition gradually deteriorated. In 2002 the aircraft was registered to the Townsend Aero Museum at Chimacum, Washington State where, in an effort to start a restoration to flying condition, students from the associated aircraft engineering school removed all the original Queen Bee parts and replaced the wooden fuselage with a battered Tiger Moth frame donated for the purpose. A local enthusiast, realising that history was about to be destroyed, provided an airworthy metal frame in exchange for the wooden fuselage and other parts and spirited them away for future attention.

Production of an anticipated replacement type, the Airspeed Queen Wasp, had been sanctioned in 1939 but the order was curtailed in 1940 due to a change of priorities and the realisation that for the time being there were enough live targets available. At least seven DH.82A Tiger Moths were 'converted' to the status of Queen Bees at Manorbier and several others were scheduled but subsequently reprieved. Those engineers involved in the conversion work reported that it was a most difficult task more easily achieved by production of a new aeroplane.

For a type which in 1937 the manufacturer considered had limited future potential there was constant development and dozens of minor and more substantial modifications were incorporated: the propeller type DH5220/MX was changed to a coarser pitch DH5220/H, all night flying equipment was deleted, a new oil pressure gauge and tachometer with a shorter drive were fitted and a Mk VIIA pressure head. The launching valve was repositioned and the compressed air system revised and, not surprisingly, there were improvements to the mounting systems for the radio equipment.

In October 1941 the de Havilland Company issued details of what they described as a 'land based' version of the Queen Bee which

Queen Bee No 5447 (N2726A) in the USA, painted with representative registration NC726A, which featured with DH.60M 'NC1510V' just visible at right, in the film *The Spirit of St Louis*. The Queen Bee served both as a camera platform and set dressing. *via Barry Dowsett*

deleted all the modifications required for catapult launching and operation on floats in a marine environment whilst retaining the enhanced structure of the fuselage. DH.82A Tiger Moth II type mainplanes and ailerons were substituted incorporating multi-laminated spars which had long been the subject of research at Hatfield. There were alterations to the automatic control system and the trailing aerial was deleted in favour of fixed aerials strung between a bracket on the fin and short aerial masts on the top mainplanes.

A review of the situation in 1942 predicted an increase in attrition during the continuing training programmes and an additional 150 Queen Bee aircraft were ordered at a price of £2,000 each in a contract dated 18 August 1942, later amended to include the manufacture and delivery of spare parts. Hatfield sub-contracted the job to their associated business, Scottish Aviation Ltd., (SAL) who, according to some accounts, established a production facility in a Glasgow bus garage at 39 West Campbell Street, premises

The fuselage of N2726A still wearing the titling applied for her appearance in the film *'The Spirit of St Louis'* was delivered to the Townsend Aero Museum at Chimacum, Port Lawrence, Washington in 2002 after almost twenty five years in store in Minnesota.
Gareth le Sueur

requisitioned from a former customer for DH.83 Fox Moths, the Scottish Motor Traction Company. Subsequent research by Scottish aviation historians believe this not to be correct.

In January 1941 Scottish Aviation had been awarded a contract to incorporate modifications into the wings of up to 680 RAF Tiger Moths, a figure later reduced by 400, and the work was undertaken by the Glasgow based furniture manufacturer H Morris and Company. The new production order for Queen Bees together with sets of floats was placed by SAL with Morris who began work in February 1943. To help speed the initial process Hatfield supplied SAL with a 'pattern aircraft' in October 1942, V4772 (5459), which remained in Glasgow until September 1944 when she was delivered into storage with 19 MU at St Athan. Completed aircraft were transported to Prestwick where they were test flown prior to delivery. Another change of policy by the Ministry of Aircraft Production in December 1943 reduced the SAL order to sixty aircraft and also slowed the rate of acceptance.

The PAU was disbanded in March 1946 after sixty one Queen Bees had been sold from St Athan the previous year. In January 1946, thirty nine Queen Bees in 'as new' condition were notified still to be in long term storage. Declared obsolete in May 1947 all were removed from store and scrapped. Only three Queen Bees are known to have survived. The vast majority of the aircraft sold into the civil market in 1945 were broken up for extraction of their engines and Tiger Moth content and the remains heaped onto bonfires.

By a process of elimination a task group at the then named Mosquito Aircraft Museum at Salisbury Hall identified the shell they inherited in 1986 as probably the Scottish-built LF789 (SAL110), sold in 1945 after storage at Manorbier where it is believed she flew on just three occasions on behalf of the gunners at nearby Lydstep Camp. In view of no positive confirmation of her identity the aircraft acquired a new one, BAPC 186, issued by the British Aircraft Preservation Council. Over a nine year period only the wooden fuselage was restored for exhibition purposes and was fitted with a full set of wireless equipment and an autopilot capable of activating the tail surfaces, accompanied by a replica of the M11 control unit complete with authentic relays sourced from a redundant telephone exchange. As a result of their endeavours in the year 2000 the project, steered by Paul Doyle and Chris Rowe, was awarded the Transport Trust's Ron Wilsdon Trophy.

LF858 (SAL150), was delivered to 19 MU St Athan in April 1944 and sold as surplus stock to Wales Airways at Bridgend in December 1946. The hulk was acquired by the Shuttleworth Collection at Old Warden and sold to Barrie Bayes after a periodic clear out in the 1970s. Following a restoration programme riddled with trauma during which she was fitted with two standard cockpits and a wheeled undercarriage and painted in camouflage colours, the aircraft was registered G-BLUZ in 1985 prior to her first flight from Meppershall Airfield in October the following year, the world's only airworthy Queen Bee.

The world's only airworthy Queen Bee G-BLUZ, operating in a two seat configuration, and the fuselage of LF858 restored by volunteers at Salisbury Hall, together at the International Moth Rally at Woburn Abbey in 1997. *Darryl Cott*

DH.82 Queen Bee G-BLUZ which is operated in a two-seat configuration by the Bee Keepers was subject to a major refurbishment at RAF Henlow in the spring of 2014 when the opportunity was taken to check on many of the original external fittings peculiar to the Queen Bee and to repaint the airframe in the appropriate matt finish. *Peter Finch*

Apparently sold to a South African bidder as the result of a London auction in July 1995, the purchaser requested that all official documentation should refer to the aircraft as a 'Tiger Moth' to avoid foreseen difficulties with import and registration. After normal business deadlines had expired with no receipt of payment, the sale was declared void and the aircraft subsequently was syndicated in England to be based, very appropriately, at RAF Henlow.

The first two Jackaroo aircraft flying together over the green fields of England. Although the concept of cheaply converting an old airframe into something modern and the flow of optimism that accompanied it was not original the Jackaroo team must have been disappointed that the orders did not flow as anticipated. Although performance and economics were good, over the years most of their creations were converted back into Tiger Moths. *Flight*

CHAPTER TWENTY FIVE
The DH.82A(Mod) Thruxton Jackaroo

A shortage of dollar exchange contributed to a British Government decision to ban the post-war import of light aircraft from the USA. The vacuum thus created gave rise to a number of home grown projects, most of which failed due to a serious lack of development capital and a general inability to support the optimism and promotional claims made to an expectant market.

During the early 1950s Sqn Ldr J E Doran-Webb, a former RAF Bristol Bulldog pilot and now Managing Director of the Wiltshire School of Flying (WSF), a company founded in 1931 at High Post but now relocated to Thruxton in Hampshire, considered building a high-wing four/five seat touring aircraft using only Tiger Moth components by which he appeared to be surrounded.

Contacts at the Royal Aero Club (RAeC) assured Doran-Webb that his proposals would be well received and he was introduced to Ronald Prizeman, well known at the RAeC after his submission for a 1953 design competition earned him second place only to a syndicate entry from Boscombe Down.

Ron Prizeman soon proved that a high wing configuration incorporating the lower mainplanes and ailerons of a Tiger Moth was not a practical proposition. Instead, he schemed a four seater using the same biplane layout as a Tiger Moth but with a revised fuselage. A meeting held at the Air Registration Board (ARB) on 10 October 1956 proposed an aircraft with a target all-up-weight of 2,180lb based essentially on the argument that for the Tiger Moth wing truss, a semi aerobatic loading of 4.5g at 2,180lb would be less than the DH.82A's full aerobatic loading at 1,770 lb. After a great deal of time, effort and money had been wasted in chasing tails this view was eventually accepted by the ARB and formed the basis for certification. At the time the project was developing Ron Prizeman was Chief Engineer of Baynes Aircraft Interiors, working in the old Hawker Aircraft drawing office at Langley Aerodrome, busy with contracts covering Vickers Viscount and Bristol Britannia airliners. Of necessity plans for the four seater were drawn at weekends and during the evenings. Much had to be achieved by the end of 1956 when Ron Prizeman was scheduled to take up a Fellowship at a leading American business school.

The name 'Jackaroo' was coined by Captain Joe Taylor who had recently spent time in Australia and returned home to England with the definition of a slang farming term: 'Jackaroo', meaning a 'new chum' or 'an apprentice jack of all trades'. The name seemed apposite and was adopted without reservation.

To create sufficient elbow room with reasonable comfort for four people, the side frames of a Tiger Moth front fuselage were moved apart by 12.5in within which enlarged space four seats were installed, port and starboard pairs in tandem, the starboard pair staggered slightly forward. The fundamental change called for re-design of the critically important space frames at the front and rear of the parallel sided fuselage box, picking up on existing Tiger Moth joints. The

Tiger Moth fuselages under conversion to DH.82A (Mod) Jackaroos by engineers of the Wiltshire School of Flying in an ex-RAF workshop at Thruxton Aerodrome. *deHMC Archive*

basic control box was retained, sited on the port side of the cockpit floor. Centre section strut geometry was maintained, more widely spaced with longer carry-through spars, the consequent gap between wing root and the normal nineteen gallon fuel tank simply faired in.

New seats of tubular construction were designed by Ron Prizeman and upholstered by the wife of the WSF chief engineer, Australian J A Golbert, who was responsible for the canopy and new cockpit appointments. In addition to his normal school duties he also supervised manufacture of test rigs, the erection of an engineering mock-up and two flying prototypes complete with all necessary trial instrumentation.

The basic structure and rigging of wings, tail and rear fuselage were not altered from basic Tiger Moth practice but it was necessary to increase the undercarriage track by designing a new 'W' shaped centre strut, effectively doubling the Tiger Moth's 'V' system, picking up on an otherwise unchanged layout. An 8in welded tubular bay was added between the front fuselage box and rear pylon to facilitate joining them due to their dissimilar width.

Slots were retained and the locking lever was moved outside the cabin to a position on the centre section port rear strut, within easy reach of the captain through the sliding window; the ignition switches were re-positioned inside and mounted on the panel. No provision was made for engine self-starting due to extra weight and expense.

An increase in mass aft of the certificated centre of gravity (CG) of the Tiger Moth resulted in the addition of a 6in welded tubular bay at the forward end of the front fuselage to which standard engine bearers were attached. At first the gap between the bulkhead and rear case of the engine was merely faired over but at a much later stage longer cowlings were built to regularise the appearance of the extended nose.

The Jackaroo was intended to be flown solo from the left front seat although it was difficult to slip into that position from standing on the wing-walk until a pair of grab handles was strategically placed. In a reversal of the Tiger Moth role, during instructional flying the tutor sat in the back having to share the only instrument panel by peering over the pupil's shoulder.

With CG restored, a refined centre section, increased wingspan and the tail volume provided with a longer moment arm, spinning characteristics were expected to be better than a Tiger Moth, degraded only by the increased gyroscopic forces generated by repositioning the engine and propeller forward. Working under the close scrutiny of the ARB who only ever recognised the aircraft type in official documentation as a 'DH.82A (Mod)', the carriage of spin strakes became a mandatory but probably unnecessary requirement.

Two prototypes were built at Thruxton in 1956. G-AOEX (86483), was finished as a standard four seater with enclosed cabin and known as a Series 1. She was test flown from Thruxton by Lt Cmdr 'Pat' Shea-Simonds on 2 March 1957. G-AOEY (85899), a Series 2, was conceived as a cargo carrier or crop duster as an emergency business measure while waiting for the ARB's deliberations on the use of the Jackaroo for the carriage of passengers.

After removing the whole of the canopy structure in one easy operation, the cabin could be converted to carry a load of 550lb. An alternative, quick-fit, low profile superstructure neatly converted the Jackaroo Series 2 into a single seater with an open cockpit at the port side rear position from where the pilot was expected to read instruments on the front (and only) panel, sighting below the level of the decking. For insurance and convenience an independent Air Speed Indicator (ASI) was mounted in a teardrop housing on top of the forward decking, adjacent to the rear centre section strut.

The team responsible for the Thruxton Jackaroo. Left to right: Ron Prizeman, designer; J A Golbert, chief engineer, Wiltshire School of Flying; Squadron Leader J E Doran-Webb with a broken leg, managing director; Lieutenant Commander Pat Shea-Simonds, test pilot. *The Aeroplane*

The sparsely instrumented panel of the prototype Jackaroo G-AOEX and a view of the control box and remodelled front seat on the port side of the cabin. *The Aeroplane*

Removal of the standard canopy and three seats, installation of a hopper or container and a low profile decking, and the Series 2 Jackaroo offered opportunities for light freighting or cropspraying. *The Aeroplane*

The manufacturers claimed on launch to have received orders from agricultural contractors in New Zealand, Rhodesia and Argentina and 'earnest interest' from Germany. By July 1957 they were quoting an order book for 150 aircraft, fifty of which were for South Africa, and were anticipating production would reach at least six aircraft per month almost immediately. In spite of the optimistic publicity the single seat version of the Jackaroo never found favour but, although both it and three other aircraft were used successfully as crop sprayers, all operated in the configuration of the Series 1 with the cabin structure in place.

Test flying duties devolved to Cmdr W 'Doc' Stewart after Pat Shea-Simonds left the programme. On one occasion Doc Stewart, a Boscombe Down test pilot, conducted a series of full throttle climbs with Ron Prizeman as observer. During the final descent he expressed his pleasure at the way the aircraft could be trimmed to land. Ron Prizeman remembered the occasion well:

> "Doc set the throttle and trim and looped his hands with fingers touching two or three inches in front of the joystick. As far as I was concerned he had proved his point when the wheels first contacted the ground. As four or five gentle, arcing bounces consumed the airfield and his hands showed no sign of moving, my anxiety and pulse rate rose in a manner I can still recall."

Having seen the first two prototypes and first two production Jackaroos safely into the air, Ron Prizeman took up his academic appointment in the USA in 1957. Design responsibilities were ceded to Eric H Smith who had worked as Number Two to him at Baynes Aircraft Interiors and had been responsible for checking all the design calculations. Eric Smith became a freelance consultant and later joined the staff of the ARB.

Prototype Series 2 Jackaroo G-AOEY was developed as an emergency business measure to counter alleged procrastination by the ARB in the certification process. In spite of many public demonstrations and a short racing career, the Series 2 was not a commercial success. *The Aeroplane*

There were great hopes for the Jackaroo manufactured at Thruxton by the Wiltshire School of Flying and later an associated company, Jackaroo Aircraft. The initial price was expected to be about £900 but by July 1957 was quoted at £1,095 complete ex-works, with a nil-houred engine. An agricultural conversion kit was available at £150. Overseas owners were encouraged to convert their own Tiger Moths by purchasing a packaged kit at £600. Tiger Moths flown into Thruxton could be taken off again after ten days, fully converted, at £700. Special deals were also available for overnight engine changes or a complete engine overhaul to zero time for £150.

To a private owner with a new licence like Kenneth Irvine, the Jackaroo was a delight. He bought G-APAO (82845), in 1976, the sole Series 3, fitted with mainwheel brakes and a metal framed cabin:

> "The view from the Jackaroo is much better than from a Tiger Moth: one sits so high in the front seat that the nose is well below the horizon in level flight, she is steadier in the air (and on the ground too due to the wider undercarriage), much slower at 60 kts (1,900 rpm) and much more suited to a nervous and heavy handed beginner. I do not mind her lack of aerobatic qualities as I find that the most satisfying and demanding aerobatic manoeuvre is the execution of a good landing."

During her agricultural career, Jackaroo G-APHZ (82168), was operated by Airspray from Boxted where she was joined in 1959 by sister Jackaroo G-APAP (83018). The pair had been flown to Khartoum, contracted to spray the cotton crop, when the Sudanese Government fell to a military coup. Airspray sent a manager with a bag of cash but both disappeared shortly after arrival. Airspray's owner, retired RAF pilot Percy Hatfield, flew out to investigate and discovered the two Jackaroos picketed in the desert and for which he was presented with a bill for 'hangared parking' which he simply tore up and took both aircraft back to England. G-APHZ found her way to Canada in 1970 having long since returned to passenger configuration, where she was upgraded by the substitution of a modified DH.82C Tiger Moth style undercarriage, mainwheel brakes and a tailwheel and has been a welcomed visitor to

PRODUCTION OF THRUXTON JACKAROO
List in order of aircraft laid down for conversion.

Wiltshire School of Flying

(Mockup)	G-AMTX	83850 Completed as aircraft 13 and re-registered G-APJV.

Series 1

1	G-AOEX	86483 Under restoration in Hampshire.

Series 2

2	G-AOEY	85899 Assumed abandoned in Ghana.
3	G-ANZT	84176 Rollason 'improved'. Airworthy at RAF Henlow.
4	G-AOIR	82882 Current. Airworthy at Baxterley.
5	G-APAI	85838 Damaged 1964. Cancelled 1969.
6	G-ANFY	86349 Broken up for spares.
7	G-AOIX	83472 Broken up for spares at Thruxton. Parts to G-BPAJ at Sywell.
8	G-APAJ	83314 Commercial joyrider in Australia as VH-KRK from 1979 to 2002. Returned to GB for restoration in 2004.
9	G-APHZ	82168 Airworthy at Guelph, Canada as C-FPHZ.
10	G-AOIO	82151 Current. Dismantled and stored in Australia.
11	G-AOIV	85146 Reported derelict in Argentina 1966.
12	G-AOIT	83190 Broken up for spares in Canada.
13	G-APJV	83850 Overturned 1960. Cancelled 1962.

Series 3

14	G-APAO	82845 Airworthy. Re-converted to Tiger Moth.
15	G-AOIW	85147 Broken up for spares in the Netherlands.
16	G-APAL	82102 Airworthy. Re-converted to Tiger Moth.
17	G-APAP	83018 Current. Re-converted to Tiger Moth.
18	G-APAM	3874 Airworthy. Re-converted to Tiger Moth.

Rollason Aircraft and Engines Ltd.

19	G-APOV	83012 Crashed 1961. To school playground 1964.

Jackaroo Aircraft Ltd.

–	G-APAK	84286 To India as VT-DOF 1962. Cancelled 1969.
–	G-APRB	3971 Not completed. Parts to G-AOIR and Rollason Aircraft Ltd.
–	G-APRC	84489 Not completed. Broken up for spares.
–	G-APSU	3879 Not completed. Broken up for spares.
–	G-APSV	85358 Not completed. Broken up for spares.
–	G-ALIV	84673 Not completed. Broken up for spares.

In 1959 Jackaroos G-APAL and G-APAO were competitors in the National Air Races at Baginton. Certificated as DH.82A (Mod) Jackaroos they were entitled to participate in the Tiger Moth class races in which they fared well but were heavily handicapped. *David Welch*

G-APHZ was operated as a cropsprayer fom Boxted for two years from 1958. She reverted to standard configuration in 1960 for operations in Belfast and was sold in 1970. Her new owner took her to Canada where initially she took up registration CF-QOT and almost became an American citizen but remained in Canada with new letters, C-FPHZ. *deHMC Archive*

A sheared undercarriage bolt caused the starboard compression leg to come loose when C-FPHZ took off from her home base at Guelph on 30 June 2002 and she was damaged in the inevitable ground loop when returning to earth. *via Tom Dietrich*

Oshkosh from her base at Guelph almost every year since. G-APAP took up glider tugging and continued in that business after re-conversion to a standard Tiger Moth in 1986. In 2011 she was acquired by a new joyriding business based in Sheffield from where her speciality was, at regulation height, touring the local lakes and other landmarks used by 617 Squadron when working up towards their famous raid on the German dams in May 1943.

Of the other two sprayers, G-AOIV (85146), was sold to Argentina in 1959. Her subsequent career in South America is obscure and she was last reported with a group of derelict Peruvian registered Stearman at Don Torcuato Airport in Buenos Aires in 1966. G-AOEY (85899), the sole Series 2 Jackaroo, was eventually converted into a Series 1 sprayer and sold to Italy but she was re-sold to Nigeria and registered VR-NCY before redeployment to Ghana where she was abandoned.

The prospective orders never reached maturity and even the chance of exporting Jackaroo kits to India in 1962 was denied after G-APAK (84286), perhaps an inappropriate choice of registration, was sent as a production example. Import permits for five other Jackaroos already on the line at Thruxton were refused and each was broken up for spare parts.

These photographs of Jackaroos G-ANFY and G-ANZT, painted in the black fuselage and silver flying surface scheme adopted by the Wiltshire School of Flying, allow direct comparison of the different design of rear deckings. G-ANZT carries the high back decking favoured by Rollason Aircraft. *Hugh Evans and Peter Clifton*

A Rollason Aircraft version of the Jackaroo was G-APOV, operated by the Tiger Club for a little over a year from April 1960 when she was written off as the result of a forced landing in a Kentish hop field. The remains were donated to Staplefield House School near Haywards Heath in 1964. *David Hammond*

Ever anxious to be involved with innovation, Rollason Aircraft acquired a Thruxton-built Jackaroo, G-ANZT (84176), in 1957, ostensibly for use by their employee flying group. The company incorporated a number of what they considered to be 'improvements', the most obvious of which was the 'high back', eliminating part of the tadpole-like appearance of the original rear fuselage shape. The slat locking control was also moved back inside the cabin. In April 1960 Rollason Aircraft completed a Jackaroo of their own, G-APOV (83012), in which the decking was further modified, in plan the rear fuselage tapering smoothly from the wide cabin to the tail. Ron Prizeman was to comment wryly: "I know of no speed, handling or weight advantage being demonstrated by change."

The aeroplane enjoyed a short career. She was repaired after hitting parked cars when landing at Little Snoring in October 1960 and in July 1961 suffered engine failure with four-up and crashed into a hop field near Staplehurst in Kent. Her remains were returned to Croydon and were still evident in 1964 when she was loaned to a film company for which a fictitious German then a New Zealand registration was applied. After her appearance on the silver screen the airframe was donated to Staplefield House School in Sussex where the children made an art form of her eradication.

Although never certificated as aerobatic the aircraft was spun and on at least one occasion with all four seats occupied, an experience none of those on board said they ever wished to repeat. During early test flying, 'Doc' Stewart managed to persuade G-AOEX into a right hand spin but only with considerable difficulty. Months later he still had not succeeded in creating a developed spin to the left. A world class aerobatic pilot positioning a Jackaroo with three passengers was dismayed to see his companions beginning to doze. In his hands the immaculate slow roll was effortless but not encouraged. Many solo pilots in later years admitted to looping and rolling Jackaroos without apparent harm.

The prototype Jackaroo GAOEX suffered in a number of accidents when operating from Thruxton but recovered from each except the financial dive which put an end to the company. The aircraft subsequently led a mostly non-airworthy peripatetic life until the fuselage was acquired by Arthur Christian in the early 1980s and removed to his farm near Basingstoke where, thirty years later, the restoration programme continued.

Jackaroo G-APAM was named *'Myth'* when owned and raced between 1959 and 1964 by Sheila Scott. The aircraft was replaced by a Piper Comanche which allowed her owner to circumnavigate the world. In spite of her fame G-APAM was converted back into a standard Tiger Moth in 1988. *David Welch*

The fuselages of Jackaroo prototype G-AOEX and of G-ANZT came to rest in a barn north of Reading in 1974. Dennis and Trish Neville restored G-ANZT to flying condition in 1996. Arthur Christian took on the prototype in 1986 and on which work continues near Basingstoke. *Joe Iliffe*

As a racing, record breaking and touring aeroplane, the Jackaroo was most famously promoted by Sheila Scott who learned to fly at Thruxton and bought G-APAM (3874), in 1959. Sheila Scott named her Jackaroo *Myth* and flew her until 1964 when she was replaced by a long ranging Piper Comanche, *Myth II*. With the doors removed from both sides of the cabin the Jackaroo could be easily converted into a parachute platform, a feature recognised by British Skydiving Ltd. who purchased G-APAM and operated her from Thruxton under their own name for over a year. A pilot could concentrate on flying the aeroplane whilst a parachute instructor briefed two students in the cabin in relative comfort. When Ken Broomfield requested in June 2000 that the C of A for his Jackaroo G-AOIR (82882), be amended to permit the dropping of parachutists, the CAA insisted that the aircraft had never been cleared for such activities and demanded a fee of £250 in order to raise a Major Modification. The CAA was reminded of the commercial activities of 1964 and that the only structural difference was the addition of a grab handle.

Jackaroo G-APAJ (83314) was sold to Australia in 1979 and, registered VH-KRK, operated as a joyrider in Queensland until sold to Tiger Moth World at Torquay, Victoria in 2002. Due to weight and performance limitations it was impossible to fly the aircraft with all four seats filled and one solution to lighten the weight appeared to be to remove the superstructure and fly with only a fixed front windscreen. Although the climate may have been ideal for such an adventure there were many second thoughts and the aircraft was eventually withdrawn in 2004 and sold back to an owner in England. In 2007 John Fisher acquired the second Jackaroo sold to Australia in 1978, G-AOIO, (82151), although she was never re-registered or airworthy in the country. John Fisher had started to accumulate spares in order to rebuild the aircraft at his museum at Maryborough when he was killed in an accident in his Tiger Moth.

Even with such famous connections and log books full of triumph, no buyer was found when *Myth* was offered for sale in 1984 by her then owner, Tim Williams. Having a vintage touring aeroplane already in the form of DH.80A Puss Moth G-AAZP, Tim Williams decided he would only keep G-APAM only if she was converted back to a standard Tiger Moth, which she was the following year.

Including the airframes whose conversion was started but not completed a total of twenty five Jackaroos can be identified amongst which is the engineering mock-up G-AMTX (83850), which was re-registered G-APJV when she was fully converted as the twelfth Series 2 aircraft. The Wiltshire School of Flying operated the biggest fleet of Jackaroos from their base at Thruxton in the early 1960s, usually a minimum of ten on line each day. Residential accommodation and a good summer assisted some pupils to qualify for a private pilot's licence within a fortnight and then continue immediately through with any commercial aspirations. When the operation finally stopped and the school was sold, the aircraft were dispersed, their training days apparently done. Not so! In 1990, husband and wife team Dennis and Tricia Neville acquired and rebuilt the Rollason 'improved' example G-ANZT which flew again in

G-AOIR changed her red and silver traditional Jackaroo colour scheme to blue and silver before taking up residence at Baxterley from where owner Ken Broomfield often flew her in aid of local events and charities, dropping parachutists and poppies. *Barry Dowsett*

Jackaroo G-APAJ was sold to Australia in 1978 and operated as a joyrider under the name 'Tiger Jack' by Tiger Moth World at Torquay, Victoria. In order to maximise load in the generally hot conditions some consideration was given to removing the canopy and flying as an open cockpit four-seater but the idea was dismissed and VH-KRK was sold back to England in 2004. Restoration was continuing ten years later when she was sold to become a joyrider at Shoreham Airport. *David Reader*

Once a Tiger Moth then a Jackaroo and now a joyriding Tiger Moth, G-APAP operates in military colours in Yorkshire where flights are conducted around some of the training routes once used by 617 Squadron in preparation for their Dams raid in May 1943. *Mick Bajcar*

High-back Jackaroo G-ANZT was restored to pristine condition by Dennis and Tricia Neville between 1990 and 1996 and soloed by Mrs Neville during her PPL course in 1998, possibly the first pupil to achieve such an ambition on this type of aircraft for more than thirty years. *Norman Pratlett*

Below: Having logged several hundred hours since qualifying for her licence, Tricia Neville became one of the star turns of Captain Neville's Flying Circus with regular performances in Jackaroo G-ANZT at shows in Great Britain throughout the summer season. *Philip Stevens*

1996. In September 1998 Tricia Neville soloed and qualified for her licence on the family aeroplane, almost certainly the first pupil to do so on type for over thirty years, and probably the last.

Born into a situation created by government import restrictions, the Thruxton Jackaroo programme was fatally wounded when foreign light aircraft finally were allowed to flood into the country. Designer Ron Prizeman viewed it all quite dispassionately. He had achieved all that he had been asked and was professionally satisfied. His total fee, an agreed royalty payment of £2 per aircraft sold, he never received.

CHAPTER TWENTY SIX

The Circus Comes to Town

The 'New Ideas' department at the Tiger Club was tasked with developing an additional 'act' after their 1959 season and, on 4 March 1962, inventor Lewis Benjamin with Dennis Hartas flew the first live trials of what became known as 'Stand on Wing' (SOW). In truth, the participant was standing on a near horizontal platform secured above the centre section fuel tank with the aid of a stressed tubular frame made from parts of a Tiger Moth fuselage, which picked up on the top wing root end fittings, and provided a backrest and anchorage for a midriff security strap. Although considered somewhat tame in comparison with the freestyle gambollings of true definition wing walkers who participated in pre-war air displays, particularly in the USA, the 1960s revival in Great Britain was faced not only with the use of a Tiger Moth, barely adequate due to modest power even when combining a Gipsy Major IC with a Fairey Reed metal propeller, but also the jungle of rules and regulations which had sprung up since the war in an effort to keep civil aviation in its proper place.

Once proven in Great Britain the same configuration for the 'Stand on Wing' rig was officially approved in Sweden, Australia and New Zealand. In Australia Dr Susannah Sherlock was photographed on the rig attached to VH-GVA flown by Ray Vuillermin. *deHMC Archive*

The first live trials of the SOW rig were conducted at Redhill in March 1962 during which Lewis Benjamin was heavily protected against the elements. As experience was accumulated and a diversity of passengers carried aloft, weatherproof clothing became less of a concern.
deHMC Archive

Having constructed the rig the airworthiness authorities insisted on flight trials with a 'dummy passenger' at representative weight. Adrian Deverall and his fellow engineers at Redhill assembled 'Brother Ben', a 150lb mass complete with a painted face, flying helmet and a pair of the chief engineer's cast off shoes. Following a series of taxy tests the first circuit was flown by Lewis Benjamin followed by David Phillips and Dennis Hartas when lessons were learned not only with respect to the behaviour of the aeroplane with a tall load above the fuel tank, but also the best speeds and attitudes necessary for optimum performance.

The live trials on 4 March were conducted by Lewis Benjamin on the rig with Dennis Hartas piloting Tiger Moth G-ARAZ (82867). The flight was around a Redhill Aerodrome liberally sprinkled with snow and 'Benjy' was sensibly protected by multifarious layers of flying clothing, boots, a leather helmet, goggles and an oxygen mask connected to atmosphere. Having proved that the system was safe and practical two lady club members were enrolled, alternating with each other to stand on the wing at the club's regular displays, but it was Benjy and pilot David Phillips, performing at Rearsby in May 1962, who discovered a dark secret and how badly a Tiger Moth in the SOW configuration performed if the aircraft was allowed to unstick at too low a speed. Their circuit at 15ft, dodging trees, hedges and washing lines, completed in style by hooking the tailskid on to the airfield boundary fence at the moment of tension-relieving touchdown, promoted a close examination of the situation and resulted in a maximum permitted 'passenger' height of 5ft 8in and weight of 140lb, minimum fuel and flight with a suitably fine pitch propeller. The right take-off speed was absolutely critical.

The configuration was approved for operation in Australia, New Zealand and Sweden where Pierre Hollander carried aloft an energetic fairy-tale character, Pippi Longstocking, who was permitted to perform handstands on Tiger Moth SE-CHG (85867), as the aircraft flew around the centre of Stockholm and under some of the city's bridges. Dennis Hartas flew G-ARAZ from Lympne across the English Channel to Berck on 11 August 1963 while Allanah Campbell took in the view from her position on the top deck. In New Zealand, ZK-CDU (3581), flown by Tony Renouf with Cheryl Butterworth occupying the rig, stayed airborne for three hours and eight minutes on 4 March 1990 to create a feat of endurance recognised by the Guinness Book of Records but not the FAI. The thin divide between success and failure was sadly demonstrated at Luskintyre on 1 May 1994 when Bob Copas took-off in Tiger Moth VH-UNA (DHA1045), with Lace Maxwell on the rig to

Susan Scott who had recently qualified for her PPL flew with Graeme Wood at the Tiger Moth Club of New Zealand's fortieth birthday party at Taumarunui in October 2009 following a tradition set by her grandmother, Hilda Alexander.
John King

Ann Jackson atop Tiger Moth G-AHAN flown by Adrian Read at the International Moth Rally at Woburn Abbey in August 1999. Take off performance was so critical that the combination took off from the longer runway at Old Warden but landed at Woburn after their display.
deHMC Archive

Pierre Hollander taking an interest in the antics of his SoW passenger, the Swedish fairy tale character Pippi Longstocking. On one occasion the combination was allowed to fly under the river bridges in Stockholm, an activity which brought the city centre to a halt. *via Pierre Hollander*

demonstrate to a party of visiting schoolchildren. The engine coughed during the initial climb at low airspeed and during the attempted turnback VH-UNA stalled and spun into the ground.

Until the British Civil Aviation Authority prohibited its use for such occasions the SOW routine was used frequently as a tool for charity fund raising and had the power to attract a large television audience when a celebrity 'wing-walker' was featured, carried aloft in pursuit of a good cause, usually to the accompaniment of much well intended guffawing. Members of the general public were carried to celebrate special birthdays or anniversaries, or just for self satisfaction or to neutralise a bet or a dare. 'Colonel Crackshot' and 'Lolita' have ridden the rig, firing off blanks from a pistol or rifle yet mysteriously smashing galleries of bottles ranged in public view. The heavy protective clothing of the initial trials quickly gave way to more glamorous but practical attire when the show arena became the near exclusive domain of the ladies, but to the disappointment of many the blonde stripper who was engaged during a convivial evening in the clubhouse at Rochester failed to keep her appointment with the Tiger Moth in the cold light of the following morning.

Tiger Moth G-AVPJ (86322), operating in the SOW configuration with the Barnstormer Circus at the Nottingham Festival on 17 June 1979, hit a wire suspended above the river Trent causing aeroplane and crew to be pitched into 10ft of water, 45ft from the river bank at West Bridgford. All were rescued unhurt and both they and G-AVPJ were dried out to fly again, the Tiger Moth taking a little longer.

Standing on top of a Tiger Moth in level flight is guaranteed to keep the adrenaline pumping although other aircraft with greater reserves of power are capable of flying complete aerobatic sequences while one or more slinky figures lithely cavort through their choreographed programme of airborne aerobics. While a Tiger Moth would never be persuaded into a rolling manoeuvre with a passenger on the rig, moving the passenger to the walkway on a lower wing was a practical proposition. In a stunt to demonstrate the stickability of his line of Pattex adhesives, Marketing Manager Uwe Drews arranged to be 'stuck' to the upper surface of the port lower mainplane of Tiger Moth ZS-DND (DHA737). A detachable

As SOW operations were perfected it was inevitable that some variation on the theme should be introduced. The Barnstormers enrolled 'Colonel Crackshot' who miraculously destroyed rows of bottles set up on the flightline by shooting at them during a number of low passes. *Air Portraits*

Colin Goodman and Tiger Moth G-AHRC with the Barnstormers Flying Circus in a variation on the theme of balloon bursting. The crowd marvelled at the skill of the pilot and the bravery of the supporting cast. *via Paul Goodman*

Barry Tempest and the Super Tiger G-ANZZ *'The Archbishop'*. Note the metal Fairey Reed propeller and the relaxed attitude of the pilot. *deHMC Archive*

Barry Tempest was flying G-AVPJ in a SoW configuration in June 1979 when the aircraft hit a suspended wire and aircraft, pilot and passenger were propelled into the river Trent. All were rescued without serious hurt, dried out and made serviceable to fly again. *David Welch*

As a publicity stunt, the flying suit of Uwe Drews, marketing manager of an adhesive manufacturer in South Africa, was glued to a special panel wrapped around the port lower mainplane of Tiger Moth ZS-DND at Stellenbosch in 1985. Flown by aerobatic champion Scully Levine, at least four slow rolls were completed, all filmed from a chasing helicopter and later used in a series of television commercials. Not seen was a loose harness and a parachute concealed under Mr Drews' flying suit at the insistence of the local airworthiness authorities. The session was curtailed when it was discovered that the parachute had started to unfurl. *Henkel*

panel was wrapped around the wing to which Drews' flying suit was bonded with a Pattex product. On 4 June 1984 the aircraft was flown through a series of slow rolls, piloted by South African aerobatic champion Scully Levine, while the whole exercise was filmed from a helicopter. Faith in his company's products or not Uwe Drews was equipped with a parachute hidden inside his overalls, just in case.

An advertisement for the Durban Wings Club's 'Winter Air Pageant' scheduled for July 1982 was headed by a photograph of an anonymous Tiger Moth, tail high, wheels off the runway, with a man clad in open necked shirt and shorts sitting on the hard leading edge of the starboard lower wing, midway between the fuselage and the interplane strut, and with no visible means of restraint. In the publicity photograph the passenger door is folded down, confirming perhaps the advertised attraction of 'wing walking' at its most literal. The stunt is believed to have occurred again later, this time involving a full circuit of Johannesburg.

Circulated stories did implicate some wartime instructors in the business of terrorising their students by standing on their seats and cocking a leg over the side of the fuselage in the pretence of checking the security of the rigging prior to aerobatic practice. In England in 1969 the stunt was put on a formal level by Ron Prizeman, designer of the Jackaroo: "The young Brian Lecomber stepped out of the cockpit of a Tiger Moth operated from Denham by the Biplane Club. I drafted the display application to the Ministry of Civil Aviation which included calculations to show that the CG remained within limits, plus a scheme for a safety lanyard!"

From the earliest days of the movies, film makers have enjoyed the wide range of opportunities offered by photogenic biplanes. The aviation film industry was spawned in the days immediately after the First World War when thousands of surplus aircraft could be bought for almost nothing. There was a seemingly infinite supply of 'props' for the Barnstormers and film makers, especially in the United States, to fly, stunt and crash with a spectacularly choreographed intent. But having generated just so much firewood and torn linen, the craze wore off, especially when the Second World War brought awful realism and then new inspirations for the peacetime entertainment industry.

The British comedy actor Jack Hulbert starred in a film entitled *'Jack Ahoy'* in 1933 when a Tiger Moth "dressed up to look like the Ruritanian or some other Air Force," flew over Weymouth for the benefit of the cameras. That film appears to have sunk unlike one of the great classics of the silver screen, *King Kong*, also released in 1933. To mark Kong's Jubilee on 14 April 1983, an eight storey, 3,000lb inflatable monster was launched from the base of the Empire State Building, to whose summit he was to be tethered for ten days. Unfortunately, the monster impaled himself on the structure just below the roof which slightly spoiled the publicity opportunities. Kurt Hofschneider flying his camouflaged Tiger Moth N39DH (85674), in company with John Bussard in a Waco UPF-7, were hired to simulate the aerial attacks which featured in the original film. Authorised to circle the Empire State Building four times, neither the Tiger Moth nor Waco was permitted to dive bomb the monster. "It was very difficult to get FAA approval for the flight at all, let alone

After learning to fly in Canada Ray Morgan was posted home to his native Australia where he was attached to 11 EFTS at Benalla where he was given these photographs. Photographed from another Tiger Moth, the front seat passenger of A17-187 is clearly seen enjoying the view from the interplane strut position of the port lower. *Ray Morgan Collection*

Kurt Hofschneider ensured a place in history for his Tiger Moth N39DH when he was granted clearance by the FAA to fly over the Empire State Building in New York City, as part of the fiftieth anniversary celebrations of the legendary King Kong. *via Kurt Hofschneider*

permission to do anything fancy. Having fifty year old biplanes flying around over New York City is not part of their procedures," said an otherwise highly satisfied Moth pilot.

Having decided to give up flying, Kurt Hofschneider was approached by the Smithsonian with a view to acquiring his monster-baiting Tiger Moth but instead he decided to present her to the USAF Museum at Wright-Patterson Field, Dayton, Ohio, who were pleased to accept in view of the aircraft's structural integrity, originality and camouflage paint scheme. However, they insisted that in the quest for total authenticity the Gipsy Major 1C be replaced by a basic Gipsy Major 1. N39DH was delivered by truck in September 1998 to become part of a 'Battle of Britain' section also featuring a Spitfire and a Hurricane.

The flying sequences for David Lean's 1952 film '*The Sound Barrier*' were shot at Hatfield Aerodrome and apart from background shots of Comet, Vampire and Swift and a brief appearance by John Cunningham, Tiger Moth G-AHRM (3861), was a brief star. Through cinema magic actor Richard Attenborough manages to crash her on his first solo although the real flying was in the hands of Wing Commander Cyril Arthur, CFI at Fairoaks where G-AHRM was based. The aircraft was damaged in real accidents in 1954 and 1957 before she was completely demolished at Fairoaks in August 1958 when she hit first a flagpole and then the unyielding control tower during an attempt at landing.

The unconverted Tiger Moth T7438 (83817), was, after lengthy and careful negotiation, released from store at Croydon in April 1960 and delivered on temporary loan to the Headquarters of the 16th

Kurt Hofschneider was approached by the Smithsonian when he decided to stop flying his Tiger Moth N39DH but decided instead to donate her to the USAF Museum at Wright-Patterson Field, Dayton, Ohio. To ensure total originality the new owners insisted the engine be changed but the civil markings and much else were not. *Kurt Hofschneider*

Hounslow (London Airport) Air Scout Group situated in the grounds of the historic Meadowbank House at Cranford, then in use as a BOAC Sports and Social Centre. Although believed to be a secure site the image of an erect biplane standing in the open was too much of an attraction to local guttersnipes who broke in, slashed the wing fabric and stole all the instruments. Not surprisingly the wounded aircraft was soon collected and returned from whence she had come. For filming of the epic *Lawrence of Arabia* in 1961 the director, the same David Lean, required a Fokker D.VII and a pair of Rumpler C.Vs for action in the Jordanian Desert, and the contract to produce all three replicas was awarded to John Crewdson's Film Aviation Services at Croydon. The airfield's briefly absent Tiger Moth T7438 was converted into a Turkish Air Force D.VII and the two Rumplers were created around G-ANNF (83028), and G-ANLC (85154), each a spin-off from the mass military redundancy of 1953. Although the Rumplers featured prominently in the film, giving Alec Guinness' horse a fright, and in all the orchestrated pre-release hype, the pair succumbed to the accountants' whimsy and were abandoned on location. Delays during film production resulted in the Fokker D.VII never getting closer to the desert than her hangar at Croydon and in which she was destroyed by fire late in 1963.

In April 1960 a composite Tiger Moth was delivered to the headquarters of the 16th Hounslow Air Scout Group at Cranford, near Heathrow, where it was erected on a small island open to the weather and vandalism. On return to Croydon she was converted into a film replica but was destroyed by fire prior to delivery. *David Welch*

The direction of hand swinging the propeller betrays the presence of a Gipsy Major engine under the cowlings of this replica Fokker D.VII based on Tiger Moth T7438. The aircraft was allowed to fast taxy across the closed Croydon Airport but never flew and was destroyed by fire in her hangar. *Laurie Harris*

Paint an iron cross or two on a Tiger Moth and she instantly became sinister and an 'enemy' aircraft when a raft of films was made during the 1960s, mostly in Ireland where this fuselage was discovered in a shed. *Geoff Green*

The film industry relied on water-wash paint for cheap and instant conversion of aircraft into new roles. One problem encountered was that some paints contained lime which played havoc with metal fittings. Bayard Dupont was caught midway during the removal of an RAF roundel from a Tiger Moth fuselage. *Gerry Schwam*

An aura identified only by art directors has almost always caused Tiger Moths to be cast to act with menace 'not on the Allied side'. Given a coat of dappled waterwash paint, a gas-powered machine gun mounted over a faired front cockpit, liberal application of Maltese crosses and a pilot wearing a black helmet and heavy framed goggles, and the gang of Tiger Moths featured in *The Blue Max* in 1965 looked every inch as sinister as intended. Cheap and expendable to the film makers perhaps, all three aircraft, G-AIRI (3761), G-AIRK (82336), and G-AMTK (3985), survived their ordeals over the Western Front re-created in Ireland and after further cinematic excursions were eventually returned unharmed to private ownership.

To star in *The Blue Max* the production company commissioned two full-size replicas of the 1917 Pfalz D.III. For purity of line Vivian Bellamy's Hampshire Aeroplane Club built a Ray Hilborne-designed model starting from scratch. In the quest for reduced workshop time Doug Bianchi at White Waltham and later Booker elected to build his contracted Pfalz G-ATIF around the core of an anonymous Tiger Moth airframe. Filming was largely completed in Ireland: the Hampshire Pfalz flew behind an inverted Gipsy Major engine with an elaborate vertically mounted exhaust but the aircraft required 50lb of lead hidden behind the line of the spinner to achieve a satisfactory balance.

One of a pair of Albatros C.II replicas built by Jean Salis at La Ferte Alais in France, based on cheap and discarded Tiger Moth components. *Starliner*

When *The Blue Max* was premiered in Southern Rhodesia in 1967 a Tiger Moth fitted with a much-modified tailplane and rudder, an upright engine complete with vertical exhaust stack, squared cowlings, a machine gun mounted alongside a faired-over front cockpit and painted in a lozenge-style camouflage scheme, was hauled up onto the canopy overhead the entrance to the Rhodes Cinema in Union Avenue, Salisbury. The work had been undertaken by the SRAF at New Sarum during the early years of the terrorist war and after Ian Smith's declaration of Independence.

The simple structure and basic configuration of the Tiger Moth lead to easy conversion and First World War fighter aircraft were obvious profiles to copy. The resultant 'replicas' could be flown less reverentially in display and film work. *Aeroplane Monthly*

Replica Pfalz D.III commissioned for *The Blue Max* and based on a Tiger Moth frame was built by Doug Bianchi at White Waltham and later at Booker before delivery to the film set in Ireland. To ensure some degree of legality during ferry flights the British registration G-ATIF was applied in masking tape on the fuselage sides. *Stuart McKay*

What the art director wants, the art director gets. Tiger Moth ZS-BCN carried her civil registration on the fuselage side under the shadow of the tailplane when she was repainted at Rand Airport, Johannesburg, for her role in the film *King Solomon's Mines* shot in 1986. *Dave Becker*

Two years earlier during the premier of *Those Magnificent Men in their Flying Machines*, September 1965, a Tiger Moth in basic SRAF markings had been displayed in the same location. On that occasion her only modification had been the removal of the two starboard mainplanes to allow the airframe to nestle closer to the facade.

In 1975, the film *Aces High* mixed repainted Tiger Moths with Stampe SV-4s when the Western Front was created yet again, this time at Booker, but it was the thinly disguised Tiger Moths that bolstered the squadron bearing Iron Crosses to do spectacular aerial battle with Stampe-like S.E.5s.

For the premiere of *The Blue Max* in Southern Rhodesia in 1967 a reconfigured Tiger Moth was prepared at New Sarum which was displayed at the Rhodes Cinema in Salisbury. *via Bill Teague*

A squadron of enemy fighters descends against a backdrop of cumulus cloud ready to attack the Allied patrol. It is more likely that in modern films such scenes are achieved not with real aircraft but with more controllable computer generated graphics. *deHMC Archive*

Two Tiger Moths were prepared against an identical formula, the second as insurance against mishap, for flying sequences in the 1968 film *Villa Rides* which was shot in Spain. A third was used for the crash sequence. Most Tiger Moth film conversions involved new squared cowlings, the addition of fake interplane struts and external horns and reprofiling of the cockpits. *via Matthew Boddington*

A Tiger Moth was cast in a pivotal role in the 1968 Spanish-made Western V*illa Rides*. As an insurance two aircraft were flown to Cuatro Vientos in Spain, G-AHRC (84555), and G-AHVV (86123), which, under the direction of Charles Boddington who was to be the film pilot, were cleverly modified on site to simulate what was supposed to be a stylised version of a Curtiss Jenny with padded edges to the rounded cockpit, squared engine cowlings, dummy exhaust pipes, additional interplane struts and an array of horns and fixtures bolted to the top surfaces of the upper mainplanes in pursuit of nothing but visual effect.

In the plot, the aircraft is running guns to the army of Pancho Villa and is requisitioned by Villa's forces, together with pilot Robert Mitchum, to drop an apparently inexhaustible supply of bombs held at readiness in the cockpit on to the opposition. All is in vain until the aircraft is hit in the engine by one of cinema's magic bullets which, as expected, causes wild gyrations in the vivid blue sky to the orchestrated tones of inebriated vacuum cleaners. Inevitably, the aircraft crashes fatally onto a section of heavy fortification, creating a breach through which Villa's army surges to victory, whilst protecting every unruffled hair on her gallant pilot's head.

For film purposes the task was simple: crash the Tiger Moth into a barbed wire entanglement on a river bank at a precise spot where the barricade was secured by balsa wood posts; do not undershoot to land in the river or overshoot to hit a cliff face which was too close to avoid by turning either left or right in case of a fumble, and remember it is a real aircraft, in flight, and the crash contrived for the multi camera positions could be achieved once, or, using the second aircraft, perhaps twice.

Charles Boddington thought the director was asking too much and declined the scene. Instead, Derek Piggott, a professional gliding instructor and ex-RAF pilot, who twenty years previously had watched a salvage party cut up and throw down an Indian well the Tiger Moth he had only hours before forced landed into a paddy field, was contracted to perform the crash. He had been recommended to the producers on account of considerable experience in piloting for films including flying between narrow uprights of a bridge in *The Blue Max* and work on *Darling Lili* and *Those Magnificent Men*, for which twenty take-offs were made in a 'sabotaged' Bristol Boxkite and twenty landings successfully accomplished on the one remaining set of wheels.

Drawing on his experience with the Indian Tiger Moth incident in 1946 Derek Piggott devised a scheme to weaken the main undercarriage to ensure certainty of total collapse on touch down provided position and speed were absolutely correct. The centre pin in the undercarriage V strut was radically reduced in diameter to create a very loose fit and was to be extracted in flight with the aid of a drawstring leaving the axle tubes attached only by a twist of soft iron wire. The instrument panel was padded with polystyrene sheeting with holes cut to display vital dials, and all equipment in the vicinity of the rudder bars was cleared away. An additional safety harness was installed, and only four gallons of petrol put on board.

Although a Tiger Moth was crashed into the barricades by Derek Piggott during filming of *Villa Rides*, film actor Robert Mitchum escaped from the arranged wreckage of a DH.60 Moth Major. Two camera crews can be seen in the background under the tailplane. *via Matthew Boddington*

On the occasion of the shoot, Derek Piggott flew a cautious reconnaissance then set up the aeroplane for a controlled touchdown at an intended 55mph:

"I consciously take a grip on myself and remind myself just to concentrate on the touchdown point and not to see the cliff ahead. To my surprise it all comes easily. I watch the barricade ahead and gradually reduce speed skimming over the river a few feet above the water. Then at the exact moment I close the throttle and put the aircraft down just ahead of the barrier. A spray of muddy water covers the cockpit and windscreen and I feel the jolt as we plough into the ground, slithering to a stop. The noise stops abruptly. I look round wondering if I have touched down in the right place, or if I have stopped short of the barrier. But all is well, I see the barrier behind me, although to my amazement I realise the aircraft has stopped short of the sandbag gun emplacement. I hear the director shouting 'cut' and begin to unstrap and climb out to survey the damage."

Everybody appeared to be happy. For a screen time of about four seconds the pilot had earned a fee equivalent to a year's salary at his gliding club, but later he learned that the shot could have been completed at a different location without the glowering menace of a cliff face. That made him less happy. When analysed, subsequent action filmed in the near vicinity of the wrecked aeroplane clearly show that the Tiger Moth has been replaced by the wooden fuselage of a DH.60G Moth, several of which were reported to be lying in various states of dereliction in Spain at the time. The Tiger Moth which was crashed was neither G-AHRC nor G-AHVV but a third aircraft specially

The Reading Flying Group's Tiger Moth G-ANFM appeared in a number of British films but most spectacularly in a big screen production of the famous *Thunderbirds* television series, when Joan Hughes flew the aircraft from Booker accompanied by a cast of life-size dummies. *Ted Lay*

prepared for the scene and was remarkably undamaged considering the ordeal. The airframe was returned to Northamptonshire by Charles Boddington in the back of The Barnstormers' old coach to live again.

A 1968 production with an aerial team operating from Booker was *Thunderbird 6,* a feature-length film based on the famous *Thunderbirds* television puppet series. Painted in multi-coloured swirls, Tiger Moth G-ANFM (83604), was required to fly with a number of dummy figures clinging to the interplane struts and the undercarriage. Piloted by the petite Joan Hughes, a former ATA pilot who, with the sole assistance of a flight engineer, had delivered Lancaster bombers to wartime RAF bases, G-ANFM could be safely operated only on full throttle. Approval was given to fly low along the new but still unopened M40 Motorway which skirted the edge of Booker Airfield but because of unfavourable sidewinds in the cutting Joan Hughes was forced to fly under a bridge. Although permission had been sought for an identical scene as part of the script the police raised a prosecution and the film crew was taken to court, where they won their case. G-ANFM appeared in a number of other films taking on a French disguise to play in the life story of the writer and aviator, Antoine de Saint-Exupéry, *The Little Prince* (1974*)*, *The Awakening of Emily* (1976*)* and *Agatha* (1979*).* When the DH.60 Gipsy Moth scheduled to appear in *The King's Speech* (2010*)* went unserviceable almost immediately before her grand arrival on a frosty morning in the grounds of Hatfield House, it was her stablemate, Tiger Moth G-ANFM, that was hastily wheeled out at White Waltham Aerodrome. There was no time to disguise her registration letters this time and in spite of the film crew's meticulous attention to detail in capturing the essence of the 1930s, these letters allocated in 1953 where clearly in focus.

Perhaps the classic starring role was taken by Tiger Moth G-AMIU (83228), in the summer of 1969 when she was featured in Richard Wade's *Two in a Tiger*, a bittersweet study of teaching and learning the art of flying in a Tiger Moth. 'The Instructor', Roger Neaves, indoctrinates 'The Pupil', television actor Dudley Foster, with sufficient lore, practical expertise and self confidence to fly solo, and the entire process, although filmed against a script, is wholly believable. 'The Pupil' never flew again following his solo efforts and after the film was completed, but not thought to be in any way connected with it, Dudley Foster committed suicide. A year later, during an attempted overshoot from an apparently bad approach when being assessed by two prospective purchasers on board, G-AMIU slipped into the ground and cartwheeled, each pilot believing the other had control.

Operated as a tug aircraft by the British European Airways Silver Wing Gliding Club at Booker between 1962 and 1969, Tiger Moth G-AMIU was featured in the film *Two in a Tiger* in which actor Dudley Foster was taken to solo standard. *John Ellis*

Tiger Moth N523R (82960), was one of three acquired by American film actor Cliff Robertson whilst in England in 1965 during production of the Mosquito wrecking *633 Squadron*. In the 1972 production *Ace Elli and Rodger of the Skies*, a film starring the owner of the Tiger Moth, Frank Tallman was briefed to crash the aircraft disguised as a First World War scout onto a wooden shack in such a manner that he dropped through the roof whilst gyrating. To achieve the necessary turning effect he decided he first had to hit a tree with the wingtip of the port lower mainplane, which he did to remarkable effect. Pilot protection was provided by ice hockey equipment and a football helmet.

In an early sequence in the film *The Great Waldo Pepper*, made in 1975, Frank Tallman crash-lands N523R in a lake, the Tiger Moth standing-in for a Curtiss Jenny and amply decorated with the obligatory excess of interplane struts and external bracing. For post crash shots of the aircraft in the water a pair of dummy top wings of increased span were fitted so she could be more easily compared to a genuine JN-4 as it flies low overhead. She was rebuilt again but committed to a more devastatingly destructive landing, visually abetted by intercut shots of models, in the opening sequence of the 1985 film *The Aviator*, an action drama starring real life Tiger Moth pilot Christopher Reeve. The aircraft supposedly dives into a building where her stand-in model explodes and is consumed by fire.

The component parts of an airframe which had never flown together in ordered formation were carried to the second floor of a factory building in Newtown, Sydney in 1983 to make a name in the film *Spirit of Australia*, then the pieces were carted down the stairs again and off to Maitland, to be joined together in the interests of a first flight almost two years later. An abandoned Tiger Moth, supposedly the result of an accident when playing aerial farmers, stars in *Spirit of the Tiger*, when a couple discover the remarkably well preserved and complete wreckage in the bush, and fantasise about its past history and bright future. In real life and to create the set the airframe had been persuaded out of storage in Queensland, assembled in a pseudo damaged state which was enhanced for filming, then sold on by the production company as a viable restoration project.

Frank Talman dunked one of Cliff Robertson's three Tiger Moths, N523R, in the 1975 classic *The Great Waldo Pepper*. The aircraft was heavily disguised as a Curtiss Jenny which was obviously considered more valuable. *deHMC Archive*

In a perfect tied-together formation, Shaun Davis, John Dawson and Ray Vuillermin under blue skies at the Bundaberg Airshow in July 2009. *Craig Justo*

Water skiing with a difference was the choice of David Phillips flying his Tiger Moth ZK-BEN on Remembrance Day 2013 when he skimmed Lake Karapiro, a hydro lake on the Waikato river near Hamilton, New Zealand. *Grant Finlay*

In September 1996, Tiger Moth G-ASKP (3889), was contracted to play the villain's get-away vehicle in a television episode of Enid Blyton's *The Famous Five*, to be shot on a narrow strip, formerly part of a railway line, at Westbury-sub-Mendip in Somerset. An arrival in a gusting crosswind resulted in G-ASKP being blown off the strip and down an embankment, suffering grievously. The pilot later explained that he had expected the aircraft to adopt a natural weathercock attitude once settled on the ground but the presumption was sabotaged by the possibility of a puncture coinciding with touchdown. On the same day a friend crashed the pilot's car which was being driven to the site and the owner of the replacement aircraft, G-ADPC (3393), refused to land at Westbury, resulting in the baddies appearing on the small screen committing mayhem at Bristol's expansive Lulsgate Airport instead.

The 1997 film *The English Patient* almost swept the board at Hollywood's Oscars ceremony. Some of the opening sequences featuring a Tiger Moth were filmed in a studio in Rome in September 1995 using with an odd-job airframe stitched together for the purpose, largely based on the remains of never civilianised ex-RAF airframe N6665 (3969), supplied from England. The live action was filmed in the Tunisian desert with G-AJHU (83900), an aircraft bought for the exclusive purpose and which survived the sand and cinematic experience of being shot down in flames to continue an airworthy post-production career in Italy. She had led a chequered life as a calibration and communications aeroplane from the start of her commission as T7471 in 1941 until release in 1947. Her first 'incident' occurred in January 1943 when the curtain fastenings of her archetypal RAF blister hangar at the evocatively named Colby Grange Airfield in Lincolnshire, worked loose in high winds and the heavy cover smote her on the nose. From such beginnings, it was her destiny to star in this passionate five star drama, the creative masterpiece of an internationally assembled crew working under the commercial banner of 'Tiger Moth Productions'.

Her previous starring qualities had been witnessed in a 1985 television commercial for Windmill Bread. The two-second shot of the propeller being swung, an image fusing into the rotation of the rustic sails of a giant windmill, had taken a day and a half to shoot but the fee paid for what was probably the most exhaustive professional overhaul ever enjoyed in the aeroplane's civil life. Just over a year later G-AJHU was almost completely smashed when she failed to clear trees during take-off, against advice, under difficult wind conditions although she was eventually rebuilt at Membury to Public Transport standard.

Apart from dressing the sets, Tiger Moths have been stars in their own right particularly in feature films made in Australia and New Zealand, and promotional material shot in Canada. They have appeared too in numerous advertisements and commercials, almost inevitably with a corny and overblown 'Biggles' angle, a view countered by highlighting a product of enduring quality or contrast, as illustrated in major promotions run on behalf of Mercedes cars and Agfa film in 1997.

The 1998 television film *Jilting Joe* is another in which there seems to have been no technical oversight unless the director was only considering the human drama to the exclusion of all else. Following an unconvincing lover's tiff the lady in the story is preparing to depart in Tiger Moth G-AKXS (83512). She slams the engine cowlings without attending to the latches and by the time of the next shot has managed to seat herself in the cockpit and the engine has started by itself with the switches off.

In 2005 Dame Judi Dench was the star of *Mrs Henderson Presents*, a story surrounding the wartime activities at London's Windmill Theatre. During filming at a private strip near White Waltham in September 2004 Judi Dench flew in Tiger Moth G-ACDJ (3183), with Bob Gibson before which experience she had declared: "I will fly once, and only once, and we must come straight down again!" Bob Gibson flew the sequence but was not satisfied and asked his 'passenger' if

Tiger Moth D-EDES was rebuilt in Germany over several years which culminated in her first post-restoration flight from Alle-Ems Airfield near Papenburg on Friday 13 March 2009. The colour scheme is the owner's choice. In an earlier life as a glider tug during the 1960s the aircraft was fitted with mainwheel spats and a single cockpit and painted in a manner which gave her a rounded and dumpy appearance. *Daniel Dirkes*

Joe Pape's DH.82C Tiger Moth of uncertain origin has been fitted with sculpted open cockpits and a five piece engine cowling in addition to colour embellishments. She has the ability to taxy on vast areas of concrete apron such as that provided at Madison Municipal Airport. *Michael Montgomery*

Australian built Tiger Moth DHA428 is unusual in that it is one of three aircraft of the same type to have carried the registration VH-ASC. Acquired in 1976 by Neil Cottee, the charismatic owner of a mail-order film processing company, VH-ASC was painted very cleverly to represent the stripy camouflage of a four legged beast.
via Bill Hitchcock

Following sale in 1979, Tiger Moth VH-ASC replaced her tiger stripes for representation of a First World War scout, complete with sculpted cockpit and dummy machine gun. In conventional configuration but wearing the same colours, VH-ASC later operated aerial tours of Sydney Harbour under the title of Red Baron Scenic Flights.
via David Voight

they could go again. They did, and on return the cast and crew surrounded the aircraft for a glimpse of the star's contorted face. They were rather surprised when she stood up in the cockpit with a huge grin and announced in a loud voice: "I do not want to be an actor any more, I want to be a Tiger Moth pilot!" That quick conversion made up for the 'flying' shots which clearly showed the ignition switches to be turned off and the pilot in the rear seat holding a normal conversation with the front seat passenger without the need for any form of intercom. Perhaps that was why the switches were in the off position!

The Flying Lesson was the title of a short and moody video which appeared on the internet in 2013 featuring Tiger Moth G-AHUF (86221). It was a film the viewer enjoyed or hated: the story line was fairly preposterous but some of the flying shots were worthy. What a pity that to add artistic effect some of the close up views of the aeroplane and cockpit had been reversed putting the throttle on the right hand side and of course that aeroplane too flew well with the switches mostly in the off position.

The most salutary lesson ever to appear on film was a product of the RAF's own safety, training and education services. Tiger Moth DE685 (85626), is seen taxiing towards some seemingly deserted airfield buildings and a close up of the pilot's puckered visage reveals annoyance at being accorded no welcoming party. Leaving the engine ticking over, our hero unstraps and levers himself out of the cockpit but he slips on the walkway, knocks the throttle lever far forward and is distressed to watch his late mount waddling off into the distance. The moral of course: never leave an aircraft unattended with a live engine.

No matter how much energy he commits to his hot pursuit, the film makers of RAF Reserve Command ensure that the Tiger Moth 'RCVG' of 24 Reserve Flying School (RFS) Rochester, well and truly collides with the corner of a hut, neatly demolishing both port wings. How did they do it? When did they do it? According to official records, DE685 was written off after striking trees during a forced landing in Kent on 8 August 1950. Was that how the film makers disguised their dastardly deed, or was the 'RCVG' of the instructional safety presentation a ghost of the original, cobbled together for effect?

The viewers are left with an image of the grimacing face of the pilot whose agonies are blotted out in time honoured fashion with the enduring caption: 'The End'. But for a lady with pedigree such as the de Havilland DH.82 Tiger Moth, it was merely the closing of another chapter in a story that just keeps on running. With little doubt many more achievements and some surprises are yet in store.

Pre-war, Tiger Moths trained pilots who were to fly in combat. For almost ten years post war Tiger Moths were engaged in the pilot selection process and in satisfying the needs of the Reserve and Auxiliary Air Force. Her new and expanded civilian career was just over the horizon. *British Aerospace*

Appendix 1

Variant Specifications

On the threshold of what appeared to be an in inevitable war with Germany, and during an accelerating programme of re-armament, the de Havilland Aircraft Company decided in May 1939 to issue a clarification of the differences in specification between the various civil, civil with military connections, and pure military Tiger Moths which had been manufactured until that date. Apart from relatively minor or locally inspired production modifications yet to be conceived, the list was to prove definitive:

DH.82 Tiger Moth. Civil

Gipsy III with carburettor mounted aft.

Fuselage: The fuselage had a drop rail top longeron enabling deep front cockpit doors to be fitted. The rear fuselage cowling was of the stringer type, fabric covered. The compasses were mounted on the fuselage inner sides, adjacent to the doors.

> Chassis: This was the standard split type 'Air Wheel' chassis with exception that the compression legs were of the rubber block pattern.
>
> Empennage: The rudder had a peg type of fitting which located the tail skid to make this steerable on the ground.
>
> Oil tank capacity 2.1 gallons; petrol tank capacity 19 gallons; short stub exhaust; fixed parachute type seats.

DH.82 Tiger Moth. RAF Mk I

The Mk I denotes that this is the type supplied to the Royal Air Force and the main differences between that and the civil type machine are: ailerons mass balanced; rudder mass balanced; instruments to Air Ministry pattern; 4:1 reduction gear on the engine tachometer; fire extinguisher to Air Ministry pattern; auto slots with cockpit operated type of locking gear fitted.

DH.82A Tiger Moth. Civil

Engine: Gipsy III and Gipsy Major Series I. Aircraft with early Gipsy III engines had the carburettor mounted aft; later models were fitted with the down draught type carburettor which entails modifications to the engine controls, fireproof bulkheads, heater pipes and engine cowling. The Gipsy Major Series I superseded the Gipsy III and is now fitted as standard. It should be noted that early models were not fitted with a flame trap carburettor.

> Fuselage: fitted with parallel type top longerons. Early models had the stringer type rear fuselage cowling fabric covered, as fitted to the DH.82. This was superseded by the ply decking extended to the stern.
>
> Mainplanes: spars strengthened to take a greater all up weight than on the DH.82 and DH.82 Mk I.
>
> Chassis: Standard split type with Dowty spring legs.
>
> Empennage: rudder fitted with plates on the bottom for ground steering in lieu of the peg type as fitted to the DH.82 and DH.82 Mk I.
>
> Instruments: compasses are mounted on the centre of the instrument panel. Instrument boards of the latest type are slung on shock absorbers which allow the panels to float.
>
> Oil tank capacity 2.1 gallons increased to 2.25 gallons on later models; petrol tank capacity 19 gallons; exhaust system, long extension type; ignition switching dual with master switch.

DH.82A Tiger Moth. RAF Mk II

The Mk II denotes that this is a type supplied to the Royal Air Force, and the main differences between that and the civil type machine are: propeller, drawing number 5220MX, finer pitch than standard; mainplanes equipped for night flying with navigation lamps on top planes and flares on bottom planes; ailerons mass balanced; rudder mass balanced; instruments to Air Ministry pattern with transmitting type oil gauges; fixed type instrument boards, 4:1 reduction drive fitted to engine tachometer; first aid stowage; battery type electrical equipment; auto slots with a locking device in the rear cockpit; dual ignition switching less a master switch; special fireproof bulkhead; oil tank capacity 2.1 gallons; short exhaust; special map case to accommodate stowage for course and height indicator, riveted to the back of the front pilot's seat; special floor incorporating a large inspection door and protective accumulator mounting.

DH.82A Tiger Moth Trainer

Thirty of these aircraft (L6920-L6949) were supplied to the Royal Air Force in full service markings. These are standard civil specification training aircraft.

The following two contracts are brought to notice as it is thought that difficulties may be experienced when dealing with items concerning the servicing, owing to their rather unorthodox construction:

DH.82A Tiger Moth machine Nos 82555-82574 inc. Gipsy Major Series II

These machines were supplied less engines to the Australian Company on behalf of the Australian Government. The Australian Company installed Gipsy Major Series II engines with fixed pitch propellers, doing all the modifications that were necessary themselves. These included the following items: modified cross stay in the engine compartment; modified oil system; modified engine cowling; new oil tank; new carburettor heater pipe; new exhaust manifold; new fireproof bulkhead.

These items are covered on Instruction drawings Nos M.6455, sheets 1 and 2, and M.6500. With the exception of the items mentioned above plus the instruments and instrument boards, the remainder of these machines were built to DH.82A Mk II RAF drawings and specifications. The electrical system was Air Ministry pattern throughout with the exception of the accumulator which was the Rotax type.

DH.82A Tiger Moth machine Nos 82677- 82683 inc. Gipsy Major Series I

These machines for the Indian Government were built to the DH.82A Mk II RAF drawings and specification with the undermentioned exceptions:

> Instruments and boards to the civil type; electrical system, wing tip, tail lamp and signal lamp to Air Ministry pattern, Rotax dash lamp, accumulator and P.T.18 switchbox. Harley landing lamp, see drawing 982044; ailerons, civil type; provision for a camera gun; provision for bomb gear and racks; oil tanks 2.1 gallons capacity, civil type; 10 gallon auxiliary petrol tank; auto slots and locking gear removed from RAF type top planes; flare brackets and fittings removed from RAF type bottom planes; civil type fire extinguisher.

Bibliography

Magazines and Periodicals

Aeroguide Classic No 6, Ray Rimell
Aeroplane, The
Aeroplane Monthly
Air Extra
Air Pictorial
Canadian Warplane Heritage, R D Page
Care and Maintenance Manuals, de Havilland Aircraft Company
de Havilland Gazette, de Havilland Aircraft Company
de Havilland The Golden Years, Richard Riding
Enterprise, de Havilland Aircraft Company
Enterprise Newsletters, de Havilland Moth Club
Flight
Flugsagan No 3, Baldur Sveinsson
Gilze-Rijen Historical Flight, Stichting Vliegsport
Historie Letectvi, Hurt Kvcera and Chalas
Manx Aviation, Gordon Kniveton
Pilot's Assessment, Tony Morris
Pilot's Notes, de Havilland Moth Club
Popular Flying
Profile No 132, A J Jackson
RAF Flying Review
Recollections, Richard M Clarkson
Sales Brochures and Price Lists, de Havilland Aircraft Company
Schedule of Spare Parts, de Havilland Aircraft Company
Super Profile, Michael F Jerram
The Moth, de Havilland Moth Club
Tiger Country, Noel Oxlade and Les Bushell
Tiger Moth, Aviation Historical Society of Australia
Tiger Moth Construction Manual, Kurt Sagasser and Werner Ulmer
Yellow Wings, Dave Becker

Books

Aeroplane Affair, John O Isaacs
Behind the Cockpit Door, Arthur Whitlock
Britain's Military Training Aircraft, Ray Sturtivant
British Civil Aircraft Since 1919, A J Jackson
British Racing and Record Breaking Aircraft, Peter Lewis
By The Seat of Your Pants, Hugh Morgan
de Havilland Canada Story, The, Fred Hotson
de Havilland Aircraft Since 1909, A J Jackson
de Havilland DH.60 Moth, Stuart McKay
Delta Papa a Life of Flying, Derek Piggott
DH.82A Tiger Moth in Australia, Julian Forsyth
DH, A History of de Havilland, C Martin Sharp
Dicci Giorninei Cieli d'Europa, Frezza
Eight Wings To The North, Jonathan Elwes and *Freddy Rikken*
Fighting Grasshoppers, The, Ken Wakefield,
Forgotten Pilots, The, Lettice Curtis
From Gipsy to Gem, Peter Stokes
Glasmoth, Jonathan Elwes
Halfway to Heaven, Fred Hoinville
Mach One, Mike Lithgow
Marshall Story, The, Sir Arthur Marshall
Matilda Mission, The, Brian Edwards
New Zealand Tiger Moths 1938 to 2000, Cliff Jenks and David Phillips
New Zealand Warbirds, John King
Pigs and Wings and Other Things, W H Llewellyn
RAF Squadrons, C G Jefford
Sir Ernest Lemon, Terry Jenkins
Six Feet Over, Peter Charles
Sky Fever, Sir Geoffrey de Havilland
Solo to England, Barry Markham
Sywell Aerodrome 1928-1978, Christopher Paul
Test Pilot, Neville Duke
Tiger Moth A Tribute, The, Stuart McKay,
Tiger Moth in Australian Service, Stewart Wilson
Tiger Moth Story, The, Alan Bramson and Neville Birch
Toolbox on the Wing, Geoffrey Ellis
Topdressers, The, Janic Geelen
Vintage Aeroplanes in New Zealand, John King
Wings over Woodley, Julian Temple

Index

INDEX OF NAMES

Abbott, Clive 20, 30, 200
Adachi, Lt Gen Hatazo 139
Adderley, Sqn Ldr Michael 369
Akersveen, Arne 162
Alden, Geoffrey 92
Alexander, Hilda 381
Alfaro, Lt Luis 39
Alington, Geoffrey 208
Arbeltier, Dr René 53
Arden, Bertie 342
Arfa, Major 23
Armstrong, Art 265
Arnold, Doug 245
Arnold, Jack 278
Arthur, Wing Cmdr Cyril 384
Ashton, Sqn Ldr George 128
Assis, Darci 37, 287
Attenborough, Richard 384
Auliard, Gilles 351
Austin, A B 144
Austin, Chuck 170
Austin, Jack 170

Bader, Douglas 72
Bailey, Roger 137
Bain, Gordon 254, 255, 301, 304, 356, 357
Bajcar, Mick 267, 348, 378
Baker, David 300
Ballantyne, W T W 38, 39, 50
Ball, Frank 178
Balls, Jack 193
Barnato Walker, Diana 74
Barnes, Steve 76, 166
Barnet, Cliff 276
Barratt, Malcolm 246
Bartlett, Geoffrey 14
Barton, Paul 156
Bathurst, Sqn Ldr Peter 369
Baxter, John 299, 354
Bayes, Barrie 371
Baynes, John 347
Beaverbrook, Lord 66, 79
Beck, Tom 279
Becker, Bill 322
Becker, Captain Dave 239, 386
Beja, Major 167
Bellamy, Vivian 385
Bellin, Paget 296
Benest, Peter 37
Ben-Gurion, David 33
Benjamin, Lewis 283, 317, 318, 323, 328, 342, 380, 381
Bentley, Frank 19
Bentley, Jack 85
Berg, Victor 64
Berger, Even 159
Bergh, John 346
Betts, Fred 193

Bevis, F/O 128
Bianchi, Doug 272, 385, 386
Biddle, Richard 27
Billing, Peter 165, 166
Birchall, Roger 143
Birtles, Philip 289, 319
Bishop, R E 60
Bisshopp, Garry 272
Blake, J 305
Bleck, Carlos 12, 22, 50, 167
Blériot, Louis 280, 317
Blick, W T 237
Blomberg, Sven 163, 167
Blount, AVM Charles 129
Blyton, Enid 390
Boddington, Charles 282, 387, 388
Boddington, Matthew 387
Bohill-Smith, Steve 37, 277, 301, 345
Bohnemeier, Friedrich 239
Bonar, Eric 325
Bonner, Reg 130
Borsberry, Ben 298, 299
Boubeta, George 38, 39, 154
Bouval, Candice 277
Bower, Charles 85
Bower, Michael 122
Bowker, Bill 312
Boyes, P/O 134
Bracey, Len 113
Brackley, Ian 190
Bradbrooke, Francis 15, 20
Bragg, Lady Alice, ...213
Brant, Albert 14, 84, 92, 93
Brazier, Bill 195
Brazier, John 305
Bremridge, Flt Lt Godfrey 115
Bremridge, Wing Cmdr Philip 100, 123
Bridgman, Leonard 166
Britten, John 306
Broad, Hubert 10, 11, 12, 13, 14, 15, 20, 27, 42, 163, 164, 360
Broadie, Russell 296
Brookhouse, Roger 282
Broomfield, Ken 228, 378
Broomhead, Ken 107
Bromwich, Lt Cmdr Herbert 217
Brorup, Eric 228
Broughton, Richard 268
Brown, Jack 280
Brown, Wayne 268, 349
Brunsby, Sten Arne 159
Bryan, Percy 96
Bucciarelli, Carlo 352, 354
Buckingham, Hugh 17, 48, 50, 51, 58, 59, 87, 91, 165, 193, 194, 195, 196, 197, 198, 199, 200, 201
Buckingham, Pamela 104, 193, 196
Burges, Sue 327, 328
Burgess, P/O 134
Burke, Aubrey 201

Burke, Damien 136
Burke, Terry 229, 267, 351
Burns, J A 304
Burson, Dr John 178, 274
Bush, Ron 308
Bussard, John 383
Butler, Alan 53, 67, 192, 343, 344
Butterworth, Cheryl 381

Cairns, Terry 357
Caliendi, Charles 80
Cameron, Thomas 340
Camm, Sydney 33
Campbell, Allanah 381
Capreol, Leigh 170
Carbert, Lloyd 260
Carey, Gordon 92
Carlaw, Harold 287
Carlin, Basil 288
Carlisle, Malcolm 144
Carnarvon, Lady Fiona 37
Carnarvon, Lord 37
Carns, General Mike 188
Carter, Flt Sgt 128, 129, 132
Cecil, W/O M L 140
Cederqvist, Par 166
Chalking, Charles 246
Chambers, Kirsty 357
Chambers, Wing Cmdr 78
Charles, Peter 309, 311
Chichester, Francis 304
Child, P/O 133, 134
Christian, Arthur 377
Christie, F/O D D 19
Churchill, Winston 91
Clark, Ed 278, 288, 310
Clark, Lionel (Wilf) 49, 61, 64
Clark, Margaret 336
Clark, Nobby 150
Clark, Wing Cmdr Rupert 294, 345
Clarkson, Christopher 21, 22, 46, 47, 167
Clarkson, Richard 8, 64, 95, 96
Clason, Capt Richard 157
Clayton, Grp Capt G A V 242
Clayton, William 204
Cleyndert, Bill 227
Clifford, Peter 228
Clifton, Peter 376
Coates, Ed 270
Cobham, Alan 14, 24, 34, 228, 296
Coetzee, Dr H J (Manie) 101
Cole, Bob 102, 103, 284
Cole, P/O 134
Coles, Mr (Cowley) 75
Collins, Geoff 118, 135, 324, 345, 350
Collins, Flt Lt Jack 112
Colman, Pete 327
Conway, Don 355
Cook, Howard 345

Cooper, Ben and Jan 155	Doyle, Paul 371	Fulton, Ken 281
Copas, Bob 381	Dressler, Dr Michael 321	Galpin, John 139, 192
Copp, Kenneth 347, 351	Drews, Uwe 382, 383	Galt, John 340
Cordy, David 284	Duke, Neville 85, 115, 329	Galt, Sgt 134
Cornish, Charles 124, 269	Dumigan, Eric 261	Gandet, Eric 274
Costex, Louis 40	Duncan, Colonel USAAF 151	Garratt, Phillip 39, 59, 60, 96, 102, 172, 173,
Cott, Darryl 18, 99, 130, 267	Dunn, Jerry 208	174, 175, 176, 178
Cottee, Neil 391	Dunsworth, Terry 74	Gaskin, Len 83
Coutroubie, Mr (Greek Agent) 59	Dupont, Bayard 385	Gaughan, Shane 226
Cox, George 82, 85, 142		Gautier, F/O 129
Cramb, Adam 310	Eckhoff, Captain 158	Gay, Leo 286
Crewdson, Captain John 384	Edwards, Brian 294, 295, 298	Geelan, Janic 313
Cross, 'Baron' 80	Elgood, Terry 235	Geiselhard, P 90
Crumplin, Kevin 125, 229	Elliot, Liz 238	Geoghegan, Dr V P 128, 129
Cubitt, Wally 286	Ellis, Joan 337	George, Bill 126
Cunningham, Grp Capt John 315, 317, 384	Ellis, John 322, 388	Geraty, Nick 296
Curley, Aidan 244	Ellwood, Dr Ken 150	Gerdes, Willie 278, 280, 298
Curtin, Bob 303	Elmgren, Gunnar 167	Gestido, Major 40
Curtis, Alan 344	Elsnorth, Sgt 123	Gibbs, Michael 299
Cyster, Cherry 317	Elwes, Jonathan 272, 292, 293, 294	Gibson, Bob 390
Cyster, David 288, 289, 290, 294, 302, 317, 353	Elwes, Tatiana 294	Gilbert, Bill 193
	Engebretsen, Dan 159	Gleeson, Gerome 310
Dalton, Mike 129	Eschner, Joseph 325	Gliddon, Dick 146, 217
Dann, Terry 98, 343	Essendon, Lord 21	Glubb Pasha 217
Daunt, Michael 92	Ethiopia, Emperor of 182, 205, 206	Glyde, Joan 336, 337
Davidson, Neil 291	Evans, Hugh 49, 376	Godber, Sqn Ldr Frank 242
Davies, Sgt J K 140	Evans, Pat 306	Goddard, Paul 235
Davies, Mike 153	Evans, Sgt 86	Goddard, Air Comm R V 87
Davies, Richard 147	Everal, Walter 177	Golbert, J A 373
Davis, Bert 177, 178, 352	Everard, Sir Lindsay 48	Golding, Frank 26
Davis, Shaun 389	Everett, Cdr Robert 333	Gooch, Peter 172
Daw, N K 252	Ewing, R L 306	Goodman, Colin 382
Dawson, John 389		Goodman, Paul 382
Day, Roy 257, 258	Falconer-West, Sqn Ldr Paul 298, 329, 349	Gorbatov, Anatoly 293, 294
de Beauregard, Costa 53, 59	Farquhar, John 133	Gordon Marshall, Philip 109
de Bunsen, Mary 146, 147	Field, Herbert 151	Gorton, John 186
de Havilland, Captain Geoffrey 10, 15, 22, 37,	Fiennes, Roger 293, 294	Gordon, Philip 140
43, 49, 54, 63, 80, 194, 266,	Fieseler Gerhard 22, 47	Gorreck, August 336
269, 302, 340, 357	Fillingham, Pat 40, 64, 72, 74, 84, 85, 95,	Gosling, Leslie 257
de Havilland, Geoffrey Jnr 72, 80, 93, 118, 201	218, 316, 317	Gower, Pauline 59
de Havilland, Major Hereward 80, 83, 84, 179	Finley, Grant 389	Gowrie, Lady Zara 180
de Havilland, John 72, 201	Finn, Mr (RAE) 96	Grace, Ian 362, 363
de Havilland, Mrs Louie 269	Firth, Cmdr Charles RN 133	Grayson, Air Marshal Barry 231
de Havilland, Peter 40, 50, 194, 195	Fisher, John 297, 298, 299, 302, 378	Greeff, Richard 236
Deisher, Walter 170	Fitch, Ray 85, 86	Green, Captain Geoff 385
de Jounge, Lars 166, 295	Flagg, Richard 131	Greenberg, M L 239
Dekker, Herman 104, 106, 323, 339	Fonseca, Jose 287	Gretton, J D 77
Dench, Dame Judi 390	Forster, Lyn 189	Grey, C G 193
Dent, Richard 181, 272, 274	Forsyth, Julian 141, 247	Grierson, John 72
Denyer, Jimmy 275, 317	Forsythe, Mr and Mrs J H 206	Griffith, Idris 86
de Saint-Exupéry, Antoine 388	Foster, Dudley 388	Griffiths, Murray 294
Détroyet, Michel 47	Foster, Rodger 297	Grubbs, Dale 339
Deverall, Adrian 312, 381	Fotheringham, Jerry 175	Guinness, Alec 384
Dick, Iain 98, 126	Fourie, H E 239	Gundry, T H 54
Dickson, Captain Robert RN 331	Frame, Pete 334	Gunn, Dr Bernie 109
Dietrich, Otto 259	Fricker, John 20, 108	Gurl, Les 75
Dietrich, Tom 351, 376	Francis, R H 96	Gustavsson, Lars 167
Dirkes, Daniel 390	Franklin, Jack 142	Guttu, Mr (Norway) 160
Doran-Webb, Sqn Ldr J E 372, 373	Franklin, Peter 290	
Douglas and Clydeside, Marquess of 33, 48	Freeman, David 249	Hagby, K 225
Douglas, Bruce 176, 177	French, Ben 56, 82, 83, 92, 143, 149	Hagg, Arthur 8, 10, 15, 38
Douglas, Colonel Rod 206	Fulford, Eddy 92	Hagger, Phil 18, 91
Dowsett, Barry 119, 137, 212, 370, 378	Fuller, Edward 134	

INDEX OF NAMES continued…

Håkensen, Anders....159, 268
Håkensen, Marius....163
Halford, Frank....8, 20, 176
Hall, Bud....356
Halliday, Bernie....112
Hambrook, Peter....324
Hammond, David....377
Hanks, Julie....326
Hanna, Ray....300
Hansen, Lt Michael....44, 45, 158
Hardy, Professor Bill....249
Harris, Alan....72, 73
Harris, ATC cadet....122
Harris, Laurie....385
Harris, Mike....320
Harris, Steve....232
Hartas, Dennis....317, 340, 380, 381
Harvie, Flt Lt E F....192
Hassall, LAC....120
Hastings-Winch, Charles....125, 218
Hatfield, Percy....375
Hawes, Ted....223
Hawkesworth Sgt....87
Hearle, Frank....10, 33, 47, 54, 55, 57, 58, 62, 68
Heath, Grp Capt Peter....8, 16, 343
Hempel, Barry....296
Hendriks, Ton....230
Henley, Clay....320
Hennenson, Isaac....33
Henshaw, Alex....72
Herbert, Sqn Ldr P H....217
Herne, Garry....315
Herron, Mr (Jordan)....217
Higgs, Nicholas....201
Hilborne, Ray....385
Hildred, Sir William....204
Hills, Barry....251
Hindmarsh, John....263
Hingston, Ben....249
Hinkler, Sqn Ldr Bert....170, 288, 290, 343, 344
Hitchcock, Bill....317, 318, 391
Hitchcock P/O Ron....123
Hitchman, Nigel....274
Hoddinott, Stanley....112
Hodgkinson, P/O....134
Hodgson, Harry....287
Hoekstra, Captain J K....105
Hofschneider, Kurt....356, 383, 384
Hoggkvist, Bo....268
Hoinville, Fred....321, 322, 328, 329
Holland, Charles....14, 222, 246
Hollander, Pierre....381, 382
Hollins, Ray....292
Hooks, M J....147, 204, 212, 277
Hore-Belisha, Leslie....365
Houdini, Harry....140
Houlberg, A F....68
Howe, Stuart....167, 324
Howes, Flt Lt H A....48
Hoyle, P/O....133, 134
HM King George V....363
HM King George VI....82
HM Queen Mary....363
Hotson, Fred....171, 173, 175, 177
HRH Prince Andrew....325
HRH Prince Bernhard....10, 74
HRH Prince George....82
HRH Prince Philip....340
HRH Shah of Iran....51
Hubbard, Ralph....294
Hughes, Bryn....135
Hughes, Joan....388
Hulbert, Jack....383
Hunter, Douglas....10, 178
Hutchings, Jim....218
Hutton, Bruce....334
Hyland-Smith, Sqn Ldr....207
Hyslop, Graham....324

Iliffe, Joe....377
Inskip, Michael....98
Irvine, Kenneth....375
Isaacs, John....219
Issa Khan, Colonel....23
Izmailov, Andrei....293

Jackson, A J....271
Jackson, Allan....352
Jackson, Mrs Ann....381
Jackson, David....284
Jackson, Peter....284, 327
Jacobsen, Lt....44
Jacobson, Tim....355
Jakimiuk, Wsiewolod....218
James, Anthony....320
Jenkins, P/O....86
Jenks, Alfred....321
Jenks, Cliff....141, 196, 252
Jerram, Mike....19
Johannsen, Kurt....309
Johns, W H....191
Johnson, Amy....342
Johnson, Brett....51
Johnson, Glen....350
Johnson, Patrick....21, 22
Johnson, Ray....337
Johnston, Dr Jeremy....290
Johnston, John....193
Johnston, Johnnie....120
Jones, Norman....141, 275, 280, 327
Jones, George....126
Jones, Gordon....263
Jones, Michael....340
Jones, Major Alan Murray....179, 180, 181
Jones, Flt Lt Richard....72, 75, 109, 118
Jose, Keith....250
Joyce, G J R....358, 363
Justo, Craig....389

Katzen, Ed....343
Keating, Peter....270
Kelly, Maurice....234
Kennedy, Stewart....33
Keogh, Grp Capt Michael....87
Kessler, Walt....303
King, Bill....20, 21, 160
King, F/O George (Whizzy)....82, 83, 92
King, John....223, 227, 291, 331, 343, 381
Kingsford-Smith, Sir Charles....88, 343
Kingsford-Smith, Flt Lt John....88, 89
Kinne, Colonel Knut....160, 167
Kirby, Paul....34, 136, 231
Kirk, Fred....315
Kjellgren, Åke....167
Klingenberg, Colonel Trygve....158
Knebel, Dr Martin....137
Knight, Mrs Hope....302
Kolbjørnsen, Birgir....159
Krayerhofff, Jonkheer....62
Krosby, Arild....161, 225
Kvil, Åge....159
Kydd, Sergeant....87

Labouchere, Henry....166, 196, 266, 292, 301, 302
Lachal, Air Comm....88
Langeveld, Chris....236
Langridge, Reg....219
Langstone, Peter....281
Lankester-Parker, John....275
Lapidus, Alan....290
Larkin, Johnny....88
Larsen, Captain C C....43, 44
Lawrence, Don....14
Lawrence, James....352
Lawrence, Ted....36
Lay, Ted....388
Lean, David....384
Lecomber, Brian....383
Ledingham, W E....172
Lee, Martin....263
Le Gallais, Viscount Yves....226
Lemon, Sir Ernest....64, 66, 88
Lennon, Norm....70
Leonard, Ted....354
Le Sueur, Gareth....370
Le-Vien, Steve....266, 268
Levine, Scully....383
Levy, Howard....119, 262
Levy, Roger....53
Lewis, Hon. Brian....21
Liddell, Charlie....291
Linkous, Danny....133
Lipson, David....301
Lithgow, Mike....329
Livett, Robin....269
Loader, Bob....169, 170
Lodge, Marcus....286
Long, Don....60, 171, 172, 174, 176
Longden, Mike....229, 296
Longmore, D D....54
Longstocking, Pippi....381, 382
Lovell, Rod Flt Lt....352
Lowdell, George....48, 85
Lowe, Graeme....320
Lundin, Lars....164
Lusk, Bill....295, 301
Lygo, Sir Raymond....344
Lyons, D J....97

MacDonald, John 291
MacGillivray, Fr John 264
MacMillan, A R O 74
Madigan, Thomas 259
Mackie, George 122
Maigrot, Serge 354
Maigrot, Mrs Marie France 354
Mainka, Captain Jacek 147, 325, 354
Maniatis, Mike 285
Mano, A (Bucharest) 53
Mansell, Sgt S J 19
March, Peter 61
Mardh, Jens 351
Markham, Barry 298, 299
Markham, John 189, 285
Marsh, Bill 258
Marsh, Maurice 218
Marshall, Sir Arthur 120, 122, 213
Martin, Temple 308
Martin, Watt 173, 178, 244, 262, 278, 279
Masters, David 134, 135
Masterton, Geoff 272
Maxwell, Miss Lace 381
Maxwell, Captain Roy 169
Maynell, Bill 320
Mazny, Sergei 287
McAully, Elwyn 280
McGarvie, Bruce 324
McIntosh, David 342
McIntyre, David 33
McMahon, Jim 306, 314
McNulty, Jack 279
McPhee, Harry 320
Mead, Jim 339
Meads, Jim 352
Meincke, E B 44
Menasco, Al 176
Menaul, Wg Cmdr 122
Menzies, Robert 186
Meredith, AVM Sir Charles 111, 205
Micklethwaite, Flt Lt 113
Miers, Murray 314
Mikkelsen, Paul 296
Miles, Bob 250
Mill, Douglas 191
Millar, Ted 301
Miller, Charlie 318
Miller, 'Dusty' (RAF Instructor) 126
Miller, Dr Mark 100
Milne, Mr and Mrs G R 112
Milsom, Jeff 345, 346
Mitchell, Eric 8
Mitchum, Robert 387
Mohr, Lt 158
Mohr, Bill 162
Moller, Isobel 337
Molloy, Bud 290, 291
Monro, Hamish 77
Montgomery, Michael 390
Moon, F/O V R 14, 19, 82, 83, 92
Morgan, Lt Cmdr 92
Morgan, Roy 383
Morgan, W/O 76
Morris, Flt Lt Antony 107, 67, 267
Morris, Sir William (later Lord Nuffield) 66
Morse, Arthur 68
Morton, Jack 282
Morton, Cmdr Eric 330
Mott, Bob 343
Mounce, John 201
Moxham, Flt Lt F W 92
Moxon, Ginger 140
Mozambique, Governor General, ...206
Muller, Bob 321
Munro, Boyd 291
Murray, Lee 53, 54, 60, 62, 64, 67, 97, 170, 171, 172
Murray Jones, Alan 131, 132, 135, 139, 142, 179, 186, 193, 198
Myhr, Morten 159

Naish, F 24
Nathan, S/O J A 75
Neave, John 201, 202, 209, 271
Neaves, Roger 388
Nell, Dick 269
Nepean Bishop, Flt Lt Charles 36, 112, 113, 114, 282
Nesbit-Dufort, Flt Lt John (Whippy) 92
Neville, Dennis 311, 377, 378, 379
Neville, Hap 306
Neville, Tricia 377, 378, 379
Newhall, Domingo 263
Newman, David 48
Nichi, Grrr 109
Nicholson, R 238
Niestadt, Jaap 320
Nilsson, Birger 167
Nixen, Wilfred 9, 201
Nojaroff, Ivan 53
Noors, Ton 105
Nordgren, Loran 264
Nordquist, Colonel Alis 23
Norman, Desmond 306
Normann, Captain 158
Norris, Family 247
Nuffield, Lord (see also Sir William Morris) 67

Ohrn, Kenneth 165, 166
Ølholm, Carsten 353
Oliver, Bill, ...92
Oliver, Ian 77, 166, 346
Osborne, John 272
Ostby, K 158
Outram, Col Harold, ...62
Owens, Lloyd, ...356
Oxley, David 298

Page, F 24
Pallett, Dick 263
Palmer, Bob 150
Palmer, Keith 344
Paltridge, Shane 314
Pape, Joe 390
Parker, Chris 26
Parker, Richard 272
Parker, W R 170
Parkes, John 62
Parkhouse, Nicholas 293
Parnell, Neville 138, 314, 318
Parry, Norman 298, 299, 300, 302
Parssinen, Pekka 323
Paul, Air Comm Christopher 130, 275, 276, 277
Payne, Tom 122, 259
Pearce, Air Comm E R 248, 368
Pearson, John 259, 260
Peck, Dennis 186
Peden, Murray 152, 177, 258
Pederson, Captain Victor 248, 249
Penn, Archie 75
Penna, Les 284
Pennant-Rea, Flg Off 114
Penrose, Desmond 266, 268, 340
Perkins, Sgt 132
Perrin, Cmdr Harold 209, 214, 228
Perrior, Geoffrey 165, 298
Pesch, Dr 46
Peterson, Hans 164
Pheasant, John 227
Phelps, Anthony 74
Phelps, Ted 258
Phillips, David 281, 381, 389
Phillips, David (NZ) 141, 196, 252
Pickles, Sydney 342
Piggott, Derek 115, 243, 387
Pike, Clem 46, 53, 65, 92
Pike, Geoffrey 64
Plank, Steve 327
Plumb, Fred 10, 178
Popplewell, Ian 236, 238
Pothecary, John 18, 118, 266, 270
Poulter, Gordon 246
Povey, Harry 23, 68, 71
Power, Charles 16
Powis, Charles 176
Pratlett, Norman 379
Prince, Jimmy 309
Prizeman, Ron 372, 373, 374, 377, 379, 383
Pugh, Cyril 155
Pullen, Roger 301, 302
Pye, Ken 272

Rasmussen, Ritchie 320
Rayner, Raymond 223, 317
Read, Adrian 381
Reader, David 378
Reber, Alan 134, 139
Reeve, Bob 82
Reeve, Christopher 389
Reid, Blake 175, 176, 261
Reid, George 85
Remonte, Bob 290
Renouf, Tony 381
Rhodes, Sir Heaton 306
Reynolds, Cliff 232
Richardson, 4 EFTS Instructor 122
Riding, Eddie 35
Riding, Richard 25, 26, 33, 49, 93, 110, 112, 214, 222, 283, 306, 316, 344, 368

INDEX OF NAMES continued…

Riihela, Hannu....169, 277, 323
Roberts, Chris....272, 273
Roberts, Captain Claire....272, 273
Roberts, Stan....210, 228
Robertson, Cliff....161, 288, 389
Robertson, Doug....265
Robey, Senja....342
Robins, Arthur....169
Robinson, Paul....295
Robson, Jim....135
Rogers, Mike....126
Rogers, Nigel....251
Rolfsen, Jens....225
Rollason, William....280
Roskilly, Don....121
Roth, Mats....164, 166
Rowe, Chris....371
Rusconi, Captain Stefano....278
Russell, Captain Mike....17
Russell, Robin....267
Rushton, Mr (Luton Aerodrome)....78
Rust, Mathias....293

Sagi, Captain Aharon....136, 303
Salis, Jean....385
Sanchez, Colonel Oscar....246
Sanders, Captain....217
Sandford, W T....43
Sansome, Reginald....241
Sarjantson, Bill....115, 116
Saunders, Percy....75
Saunders, Dr Stuart....190
Savage, Michael....194
Sayer, Johnny....129
Sayward, Cyril....115
Sayward, Richard....115
Scanlan, Hugh....307
Schenk, Aard....106
Schermer-Voest, Miklos....107
Schoning, Harry....178, 273, 274
Schulte, Fr Paul....228
Schwam, Gerry....177, 290, 325, 385
Scott, Charles W A....29, 34
Scott, Miss Sheila....377, 378
Scott, Susan....381
Segerqvist, Lennart....167
Sem-Jacobsen, Einar....159
Setterfield, Barbara....328
Sharp, Martin....63, 193
Shaw, Cdr Philip RN....325, 357
Shea-Simonds, Charles....326, 345
Shea-Simonds, Lt Cdr Pat....373, 374
Shefrin, Andy....336
Shelmerdine, Lt Col Francis....82
Sheppard, Lt Cdr RN....266
Sherlock, Dr Susannah....380
Sherron, Captain Roger....225
Shipper, Mr (Pratt and Whitney)....183
Sidhu, Brig Amardeep....245
Sinclair, Sir Archibald....203
Singfield, Tom....228
Singh, Captain Dalzit....304
Sissons, Captain Keith....342
Skov Nielsen, Jorgen....312
Smeitink, Henri....106
Smith, Alex....153
Smith, Donald....150
Smith, Eric....374
Smith, Harry....338
Smith, Sqn Ldr Mick....369
Smith, Stanford....26
Smith, S V....68, 71
Smuszkowicz, Adam....244
Souch, Ron....342
Spencer, E H....206
Spencer Bower, Simon....196
Spong, Mansfield....18
Stacy, Mike....184
Stampe, Jean....43
Stansgate, Viscount....243
Starck, G H....233
St Barbe, Francis....9, 16, 17, 23, 38, 43, 49, 50, 52, 53, 54, 62, 67, 169, 170, 179, 186, 191, 192, 206, 209, 220, 224
Stedman, AVM E W....97
Stevens, Mr (Air Ministry)....96
Stevens, Neil....318, 320
Stevens, Philip....284, 379
Stewering, Klaus....349
Stewart, Cmdr 'Doc'....374, 377
Stiles, John....345
Stirling, Mitch....238
Stokes, Flt Lt L K....19
Stoneham, Don....83, 217
Strauss, George....221
Strecker, Bok....236, 239
Strong, Desmond....201
Sullivan, W....189
Sumner, Tom....144
Sund, Thorbjorn Brunander....312
Sundgren, Jarl....167
Sutherland, Miles....236
Svedfelt, Bjørn....136
Svenningsen, Elvind....162
Swinton, Lord....66

Tack, Rusty....6
Taghvaee, Babak....52
Tallman, Frank....389
Tansley, Hugh....318
Tavares, Luis....168
Taylor, Grp Capt Bill....120
Taylor, Captain Joe....372
Taylor, John W R....310
Teague, Bill....139, 235, 386
Tempest, Barry....269, 382
Terra, President Gabriel....38
Terry, Captain Fred....217
Thielst, Christian....43, 44
Thomas, Sir Miles....76
Thompson, Richard....9, 11, 12, 13
Thompson, Sue....342
Thorn, Bill....126
Thorn, Pete....126
Thorval, Maurice....40
Thretheway, Frank....169
Tiffany, John....280
Tiffin, Jim....338
Tillett, P/O....132
Tomkins, Bill....282
Tomlinson, David....116
Tomlinson, Doug....263
Towers, Graham....246
Trelles, Gualberto....38
Trenchard, Lord Hugh....82
Tripp, Robin....264
Tucker, Guy....72, 80, 100
Tucker, Col Sid (USAF)....151
Tymms, Sir Frederick....243
Tyler, Jack....11
Tyson, Geoffrey....34, 280
Tzoorberger, Instructor (Israel)....33

Ullings, Ben....230

Vaisey, Michael....227, 295
van Dam, Pim....231
van Dam, Sjors....216
van den Heuvel, Jan....162
Van der Maas, H J....17, 104
Vanneck, Hon Peter....227
van Oosterom, T....105
van Overvest, Captain H J....104
van Swijndregt, J Montauban....104
Vause, Alan....193
Veitch, Robert....181, 183, 188
Vernon, Captain David....186, 205, 227
Viera, Juan Benito....263
Villa, Sqn Ldr J W....153
Villa, Pancho....387
Vincent Flt Lt C Mc C....360, 363
Viroli, E....37
Voeten, Jan....107
Voight, David....391
von Eltz, Nikolaus....33, 49, 163
Vonlanthen, Bruno....355
Vuillermin, Ray....297, 380, 389

Wade, Richard....388
Wall, Bob....245
Wallace, Harry....250
Walpole, Peter....303
Walters, Dr Barry....251
Wardell, Sqn Ldr....125
Warren, Brett....292
Warren, Stan....292
Waterfall, Charles....219, 224
Watson, Courtney....235, 288, 292
Watson, Roy....292
Watt, Flt Lt P M....18
Webber, Matthew....186, 314
Weedon, Sid....142
Weighill, George....92
Welch, David....137, 148, 168, 191, 192, 224, 272, 274, 276, 285, 287, 303, 351, 376, 377, 382, 384
Wells, Oliver....121, 122
Wesson, Alan....101

Wheeler, Air Comm Allen 85, 93, 97, 98, 101, 102, 104, 266, 288
White, Jan 340
Whitehouse, Ted 193
Whitlock, Captain Arthur 290, 291
Whittaker, Tim 191
Wignall, Michael 297
Wiklund, Johan 362
Wilcox, Mary 309
Williams, Gar 264
Williams, R G 253
Williams, R P (Tim) 302, 378
Williams, Tim 347
Williams, Tom 347
Willies, Bob 302
Wilson, Bill 92
Wilson, Neil 125
Windingstad, Ivar 161
Windred, Ray 180, 298, 314
Winley, Bruce 182
Wood, Graeme 381
Wood, Sir Kingsley 65, 66, 67
Wood, Victoria 350
Woods, Jimmy 298
Woodward, Sqn Ldr W L 234
Worsdell, Sqn Ldr Leslie 213
Wright, Lawrence 116
Wright, Linley 351

Young, Sqn Ldr Bill 368, 369
Young, Frank 309

Zaitzev, Sasha 293
Zalesky, Ed 263
Zeederberg, Brian 180, 238, 269
Zipfell, Mark 76, 77
Zotos, Sqn Ldr Stephan 59

LOCATIONS

Where place and country names (e.g. Hatfield, Stag Lane, Australia, New Zealand, South Africa and Canada) occur profusely throughout the text, they have not been listed in this index.

Aachen 293
Abadan 33, 51
Abberffraw 365
Abbeville 129, 130
Abbotsford 244
Abbotsinch 132, 133, 135
Aberdeen 34, 85, 132, 133, 134
Aberporth 363, 365
Abingdon 341
Abu Sueir 16
Abyssinia 232
Accrington 75
Acklington 131
Addis Ababa 206, 295
Adelaide 182, 186, 251
Aden 7, 29, 227
Afghanistan 216, 243, 244
Africa 227, 288
Agra 243
Ahvaz 51
Aitape 139

Akershus Castle 162
Akureyrar 262
Akureyri 262
Alaska 262
Albany 263
Alberta 309
Alconbury 149
Aldergrove 132, 133
Alexandria (Australia) 186
Alexandria (Egypt) 299
Alice Springs 138, 139, 297, 309
Algeria 209
Alleberg 164, 165, 166
Alle-Ems 390
Altoona 309
Alton Barnes 124
Alverca 167, 168
Amager 44
Amana 280
Amiens 129
Amman 216, 217
Ancienne Lorette 264
Andover 7, 129, 131
Andrewsfield 150
Anglesey 282
Ankara 59
Ansty 94
Antarctica 193
Antwerp 345
Apethorpe 282
Appledore 367
Appledram 153
Arabian Sea 137
Arakan Yoma 140
Arborg 172
Arbroath 334
Archerfield 185, 189, 251, 296
Arctic Circle 292
Ardmucknish Bay 240
Argentina 39, 374, 376
Arkonam 241
Arnhem 116
Arras 129
Asanol 242
Ascot Vale 182
Aston Down 137, 209, 212
Athens 59
Atkinson Strip 139
Atlantic City 356
Auckland 191, 196, 253, 291, 331, 333
Aurland 158
Austria 31, 33, 90
Avebury 33
Aveiro 167
Ayr Racecourse 109
Azraq 217

Badminton 345
Baginton 77, 219, 271, 281, 317, 376
Bagumpet 139
Bahrain 289
Bairnsdale 250
Balaclava 294

Balclutha 343
Bald Faced Stag 10, 12
Balkans, The 46, 59
Bandoeng 62
Bangalore 207, 230, 237, 242, 244, 245
Bankstown 185, 189, 297, 321, 333
Baragwanath 232, 237
Barkarby 12, 13, 163, 165
Barnstaple 149, 150
Barrackpore 245
Barton 56, 62, 125, 146, 288, 290
Barton le Clay 74
Bassano 309
Bass Strait 250
Batavia 186
Battersea 344
Baxterley 228, 378
Beachy Head 356
Bedford 135, 294
Beja 168
Belfast 78, 132, 227, 349, 376
Belgium 34, 75, 106, 212, 232, 272, 293
Belgrade 58, 212
Bell Block 253
Bellingham 320
Belvedere 111
Belvoir Castle 348
Benalla 188
Benoni 207, 234, 235, 237, 239
Benson 86, 228
Berkshire 123
Berlin 24, 30
Berwick 274
Bexwell 310
Biarritz 21
Bibury 153
Biggin Hill 150, 226, 228, 339, 349
Billacombe 75
Binbrook 295
Birkenhead 132, 215
Birkenheide 136
Birmingham 66, 298, 341
Blackfriars 342
Blackpool 131, 133
Blarney Garage, Witney 75
Bloemfontein 232
Blue Anchor Bay 365
Bluff 300, 343
Bodorgan 365, 369
Bois de Boulogne 21
Boiso Lanza 246, 307
Bologne 129
Bombay 140, 240
Bonga 139
Bonn Hangelar 228
Booker 96, 116, 153, 385, 386, 387, 388
Boscombe Down 84, 85, 93, 94, 97, 100, 123, 124, 202, 266, 288, 324, 349, 374
Botswana 292
Bottisham 48, 212, 214
Boxted 375, 376
Bozeman 356
Bramcote 333

LOCATIONS continued…

Brantford 278
Bratislava 282
Braunstone 85
Brazil 31, 38, 39, 307, 308, 349
Breddan 138, 139
Brest 151
Briansk 293
Bridgend 371
Bridge Pa 191, 340
Brie 53
Brighton Technical College 43
Brindisi 210, 211, 299
Brisbane 189, 198, 296, 333
Bristol 29, 50, 74, 115
Bristol Channel 135, 367
British Columbia 235, 264, 291, 309
British Guiana 257
Brize Norton 132
Brodhead 351
Broken Hill 180
Brooklands 31, 35, 36, 74, 112
Brough 9, 16, 29
Broxbourne 337, 338, 339
Brussels 58, 59
Buc 209
Bucharest 53
Buckinghamshire 148, 149
Budapest 58
Buenos Aires 38, 376
Bulawayo 54, 111, 112, 187, 233
Bundaberg 389
Burgos 21
Burlington 263
Burma 125, 140, 185
Burnaston 219, 224
Burrow Head 365
Burtonwood 76
Buttergask 75
Buttonville 278
Bydalen 163

Cabo Frio 287
Cairns 141, 296
Cairo 51, 311
Calais 215, 280
Calcutta 123, 125, 138, 242, 245
Calgary 172, 177, 178, 309
California 176, 241, 273, 275, 279, 305, 347, 351
Calshot 42
Camber 277
Cambooya 322
Cambridge 16, 118, 120, 122, 130, 148, 156,
                213, 214, 219, 298, 299, 345, 351
Cambridge Gulf 248
Camden 251, 287, 322
Campbellford 287
Camp Borden 170, 171
Campo dos Afonsus 37, 287
Canberra 89, 189, 314
Cannanore 137
Cape Town 111, 112, 207, 233, 237, 244, 296, 304
Cape Wom 139

Captain Boiso Lanza Aerodrome 38, 39
Cardiff 76, 223
Cardington 368
Carew Cheriton 132, 135
Caribbean 61, 363
Carlisle 134
Caron 258, 259
Carrollton 178
Casablanca 209
Castle Bromwich 35, 50, 56, 57, 61, 66, 72
Castle Water 296
Catterick 131
Cawnpore 139
Caxton Gibbett 120, 121, 150, 214
Centennial Exhibition Buildings 195, 200, 201
Cerro Largo 39
Ceylon 50, 153, 212, 216, 331
Chakeri 244
Challock 283
Chalmington Manor 304
Champs Elysées 53
Chandigarth 304
Charlbury 75
Charmy Down 348
Châteauroux 209, 210
Cheltenham 64, 127
Cheshire 76
Chessington 272
Chester 16, 218, 340
Chichester 153
Chile 38, 39, 206, 216
Chiltern Hills 148
Chimacum 369, 370
China 8, 11, 31
Chindwin river 241
Chino 295, 352
Chittagong 139
Christchurch (Hampshire) 228, 339
Christchurch (NZ) 253, 291
Church Fenton 82, 86, 100, 290
Clacton 155
Cleave 365, 367, 368, 369
Clyffe Pypard 78, 120, 214
Cochin 137, 138
Cognac 209, 210
Colby Grange 390
Colerne 209, 341
Coleshill 82
Coley's Scrapyard 282
Cologne 58
Colombo 153
Coltishall 150, 155
Colwick 75
Comilla 242
Compton Abbas 118
Connecticut 336
Cootamundra 185, 272
Copenhagen 44, 45, 47
Corfield 251
Cornwall 132
Cosford 154, 155, 209, 220
Coulomiers 53
Coventry 77, 125, 316

Cox's Bazaar 242
Cranbourne 111, 208
Cranfield 122
Cranford 384
Cranwell 7, 16, 125, 135, 136, 225, 333, 343, 345
Crecy 129
Crete 299
Crimea 272, 294
Croft 223
Croy 135
Croydon 14, 26, 62, 112, 147, 150, 155, 203,
                213, 222, 224, 225, 226, 227, 271, 275, 280,
                298, 318, 326, 328, 342, 368, 376, 384, 385
Crux Easton 302
Cuatro Vientos 387
Cuba 263
Cuers 209
Culdrose 156
Cumberland 63

Dagenham Docks 76, 216
Darlington 131
Daru 141
Darwin 248, 249, 290, 298, 342
Dartmouth (Canada) 264
Dartmouth (GB) 229
Dayton 384
Debden 125
de Lesseps Field 169
Delhi 230
Denham 116, 217, 219, 272, 320
Den Helder 216
Deniliquin 294
Denmark 31, 46, 136, 163, 167, 293, 362
Derby 125
Desford 31, 35, 48, 50, 85, 92, 119, 125, 331
Desseau 46
Devizes 124
Devonport 333
Devonshire 46
De Winton 259
Dhoapalong 241
Dieppe 294
Digby 16, 126, 153
District Park 180
Dombås 162
Donibristle 333
Doniford 367
Dorset 229, 249
Dover 129, 354
Dovrefjell 162
Downsview 11, 57, 58, 59, 60, 169, 170, 171,
                172, 173, 174, 175, 176, 177, 178, 269
Drakensburg Mountains 292
Dublin 282
Dubbo 296, 322
Dum Dum 242
Dumfries 33, 149
Dungate Farm 271
Dunkeswell 209, 302
Dunedin 253, 271
Dunnottar 237
Dunsfold 288, 289

Dunstable....................................46, 92, 322	Fort Langley..309	Halmsted..136
Durazno...246, 308	France...........46, 61, 75, 128, 129, 153, 163, 295, 298, 345	Halton...................95, 266, 268, 277, 305, 350
Durban............187, 207, 233, 292, 299, 300, 330	Frankfurt..58, 59	Hamble...16, 29, 57
Dushan Tappeh..51	Frenchman's Creek....................................277	Hamilton (Canada)..............................172, 178
Duxford..............................109, 120, 286, 317	Friston..150	Hamilton (NZ)....................................314, 389
Dyce..............................85, 132, 133, 135, 136	Frobury Farm...147	Hamsey Green.......................................14, 26
		Hanworth....................................36, 150, 368
Eagle Creek..139	Gaillac..53	Harewood...253, 255
Eagles Nest...279	Galveston...225	Hartlebury..81
Eastleigh..................................75, 219, 331	Garbutt...189	Hatfield House...388
East Sussex..288	Gardermoen...142	Hatfield Park..214
East Windsor...336	Garsington Road..72	Havana...263
Ecuvillens...355	Gatwick.......................55, 56, 75, 226, 301, 337	Hawiya...217
Eden Vale...343	Garston..59	Hawkinge..118, 129
Eder Dam...349	Gatooma..206	Haywards Heath..377
Edgware..10, 27	General Artigas Aerodrome.........................39	Headcorn...................................294, 295, 311
Edinburgh..66	Geneva...90, 91	Heany..187, 207
Edmonton..173, 263	George..296	Heathrow......................14, 153, 257, 277, 282
Eelde..322	Georgia (USA).....................................178, 275	Hedmark..160
Eiffel Tower..22	Germany........31, 55, 62, 123, 304, 323, 349, 374	Helderberg Mountains...............................236
Effingham..142	Germiston..237	Hendon...........7, 18, 19, 21, 30, 34, 43, 67, 77, 82, 86, 115, 129, 130, 156, 341, 363
Egypt....................................16, 33, 50, 310	Ghale Morghi..51, 52	Henley on Thames.....................................144
Eidsfoss..158	Ghana..376	Henlow..............16, 18, 19, 42, 43, 85, 343, 363, 365, 368, 371
Eket...164	Gibraltar.............................272, 292, 358, 363	Henstridge..125, 229
Electrolux Factory...............................199, 201	Gillham Lane Farm....................................295	Hertfordshire...227
Elgin...133	Gillingham...275	Hesketh Park...228
Elizabeth..352	Gilze-Rijen......................15, 104, 106, 230	Heston............................21, 53, 59, 134, 151, 153
Elliott Lake..172	Glasgow......53, 63, 66, 132, 210, 217, 331, 370, 371	High Ercall...77, 85
Elmdon...144, 208, 298	Glastonbury...227	High Post...372
Elvegårdsmoen..162	Glen Innes...296	High River..263
Ely...312	Gloucester...223, 296	Hilversum..322
Empengani...288	Goderich..263	Hindon...231
Empire State Building.........................383, 384	Gold Coast...305	Highclere...277
Essendon..180, 248	Goraszka..354	Hinaidi...29
Ethiopia...118, 216	Goring on Thames.....................................212	Hitchin...312
English Channel.......129, 137, 280, 358, 363, 381	Gosport...332, 365	Hobart...249
Eskisehir..59	Gothenburg...351	Hobsonville.......................................191, 192, 291
Evans Bay...199, 201	Gower Peninsula.......................................132	Hollola...323
Exeter (Devon)....................................150, 153	Goxhill...151	Holme-on-Spalding Moor.........................124
Exeter (Ontario)...178	Grand Union Canal.....................................72	Holwell Hyde..67, 82
	Grangemouth..56, 66	Hong Kong............................42, 301, 333
Fairford..345	Gransden..130, 341, 356	Honiley...227
Fairoaks..............61, 78, 136, 149, 152, 215, 271, 280, 293, 300, 327, 384	Grantham.........13, 16, 19, 20, 21, 27, 155, 343	Hood...201, 346, 347
Falkoping...164, 167	Granville..146	Hooton Park..............58, 132, 133, 134, 135, 136
Farnborough..........27, 66, 79, 85, 93, 94, 95, 96, 100, 202, 266, 272, 290, 357, 358, 359, 360, 363, 364, 365, 368	Gravesend..241	Horn Island..141
Felixstowe..34, 42	Greece...233, 296	Horrmundssjoen.......................................160
Felthorpe...246	Greenfield..258	Horse Guards' Parade...............................341
Fetsund...162	Greve Strand...136	Houston...244
Fiji..230	Greenland..45, 47, 318	Hucknall..317
Filton...............................19, 26, 31, 33, 35, 240	Greenvale..186	Hullavington...............30, 74, 85, 124, 153, 220
Finland.........................160, 163, 292, 341	Greytown...296	Huntingdon...284
Fintroy..135	Griffith..252, 338	Hurn..231
Firth of Forth..144	Grorud...158	Husbands Bosworth.................................321
Fisherman's Bend......................................185	Guaviyu...308	Hyderabad...244
Fiveways Night Club............................14, 26	Guelph..........................150, 178, 351, 376	
Fleet Street..74	Guinea Fowl..111	Iowa..258
Florennes...212	Gum Creek..178	Iceland..262, 318
Florida...166, 279, 280	Gwanda..292	Idaho...320
Ford...34, 325		Imphal...242
Fornebu..160	Habbaniyah...51	Indianapolis..134, 139
	Hague, The..206	Indian Ocean...207
	Haldon Moor...342	

401

LOCATIONS continued...

Location	Pages
Indo-China	40
Indore	245
Induna	111, 112, 114
Invercargill	300
Inverness	135
Ipswich	12
Iraq	7, 31, 61
Ireland	385
Irish Sea	227, 282
Isle of Wight	155, 306
Israel	33, 136, 262, 351
Italy	53, 59, 210, 212, 310
Ivanovo	287
Jacksonville	263
Jahore Strait	42
Jan Smuts Airport	343
Jandakot	295
Japan	31, 183, 186, 188, 233, 242, 243, 257, 275
Jaquinot Bay	139
Java	62
Jeddah	217
Johannesburg	206, 232, 291, 295, 383, 386
Jordan	33, 216, 384
Juba	299, 300
Juhu	240
Kaiapoi	196
Kai Tak	42, 333
Kaladan	140, 241
Kaluga	293
Karachi	239, 240, 244
Karljohansvaern	158
Kastrup	44
Katherine river	249
Kelso	272
Kemano	309
Kemble	27, 30, 74, 155, 208, 209, 342, 350, 354
Kenley	27, 42
Kent	77, 125, 342, 343
Kenya	212, 233, 240
Key West	263
Khoramshahr	51
Khormaksar	29
Khartoum	299, 311, 375
Kiarivu	139
Kibutz Afikim	33
Kidlington	131, 228
Kidsdale	365
Kiev	294
Kilimanjaro	239
Kingsclere	147
Kingston (Canada)	172
Kirkbride	85
Kirton in Lindsey	30, 126, 136, 150
Kitimat	309
Kjeller	157, 158, 159, 160, 161, 162, 163
Klovermarken	46
Kongsvinger	158
Koppang	160, 162
Korea	218, 273, 275
Kota Bahru	123
Kroonstad	237
Krugersdorp	238, 258, 288, 292
Kununurra	298
Kuringai	180
Labrador	318
Laddingford	125
Ladyland Moor	135
La Ferté Alais	385
Lake Borrevannet	158
Lake Lesjaskog	162
Lake Ellidavatn	262
Lake Hopkins	309
Lake Karapiro	389
Lake Ossjoen	160
Lake Parker	280
Lake Puslinch	279
Lake Winnebago	262
Lancashire	75
Lancaster (USA)	177
Langarvatn	263
Langham	166
Langley	372
Langley Park	295, 298, 349
La Ribero	53
Lasham	166
Latvia	163
Launceston	249
Laurenço Marques	114
Lavenham	137, 282
Laverton	88, 138, 139, 182
Lesja	162
Le Touquet	129, 226, 280, 295
Leamington Spa	78
Leavesden	78
Le Bourget	46
Lee on Solent	137, 276, 278, 334, 335, 363
Leicestershire	75, 224, 231
Lethbridge	275
Le Tréport	129
Leuchars	132
Lidingo	166
Lima	50
Lincolnshire	126, 150, 221, 246, 295, 305
Linkoping	164, 165, 166, 167
Linton on Ouse	335
Linz	58
Lisbon	26, 167, 217
Lista	159
Lithuania	33
Little Rissington	133, 134, 209
Little Snoring	341, 376
Liverpool	132, 167
Ljungbyhed	48, 163, 164, 165, 167
Llandow	118, 209, 212, 216
Loch Lomond	63
Locking	95, 137
London Airport	112
London Docks	41
Lord Howe Island	241
Los Alcázares	53
Los Angeles	176, 192, 355
Lossiemouth	156, 333
Louisiana	305
Ludham	77
Lugo di Romagna	352
Lulsgate	94, 390
Lundtofte	26
Luskintyre	180, 186, 268, 298, 349
Luton	78, 156, 213, 222, 273, 324
Lydstep Camp	371
Lympne	34, 58, 280, 315, 316, 317, 318, 381
Lyneham	95, 136, 220
Lynn of Lorn	240
Lyttelton	233
Madison	390
Madras	230, 239, 241, 242, 244, 291
Madrid	21, 22, 26
Magdalen College	66
Maharashtra	245
Maitland	297, 317, 389
Malaya	50, 215, 218, 330, 336, 337
Malay Cove	331
Malmö	163
Malmslatt	166
Malta	7, 358, 360, 363, 364, 365
Mandeville	77, 230, 300, 347
Mangalore	320
Mangere	145, 192, 253, 255
Manitoba	172
Manmon	242
Manorbier	135, 149, 365, 367, 368, 369, 371
Manston	153, 301
Maputu	114
Mareeba	189
Margate	153
Maringo	287
Marlborough Downs (GB)	147
Marlborough School (GB)	341
Marseille	288, 289
Martlesham Heath	11, 12, 13, 16, 21, 27, 29, 43, 95, 153
Maryborough	181, 298, 378
Maryville	291
Mascot	61, 66, 88, 89, 107, 139, 146, 179, 180, 181, 182, 183, 185, 186, 187, 188, 189, 194, 198, 202, 233, 248, 249, 251, 272, 290, 298, 342
Mashhad	51
Masterton	192, 201
Maylands	336, 337
Mazango	39, 307
McMerry	340
Mediterranean Sea	299, 310
Megiddo	136
Mehrabad	51
Meir	48, 122
Melbourne	45, 180, 182, 185, 248, 250, 302, 303
Membury	151, 390
Meppershall	371
Metfield	151
Metz	129
Middlebeers	339
Middleton St George	130, 131
Middle Wallop	77, 219, 220, 344, 345

TIGER! INDEX

Mildenhall 45, 302
Millers Field 133
Milne Bay 139
Milson....192
Milton 278, 279
Minnesota 369, 370
Moncton 318, 320
Montreal 263, 320
Mooresville....133
Mombasa 240, 299, 300
Montjoie 129
Montrose....76
Morfa Towyn 365
Montana....356
Montivideo 38, 39
Monty's Café 338
Moorabin 189, 250
Moose Jaw 172
Morocco 209
Moscow 272, 292, 293, 294, 295
Motueka....291
Motunau Island....201
Mozambique 114, 167, 168
Mt Dennis....169
Mt Hampden....114, 238
Mt Hope....278
Mud Bay 235
Mundijong 285
Munich 24, 228
Muskoka 278

Nadzab....138
Nairobi 113, 299, 300
Nanton 263
Narromine....249
Narvik....162
Natal 296
Neepawa 261
Nelson....192
Netheravon 229
Netherlands, the....17, 33, 75, 104, 106, 107, 137, 186, 206, 212, 280, 339
Netherlands East Indies....62, 186, 188, 275
Newark 263, 287
New Brighton 272
New Britain 138, 139
Newbury 249
Newcastle (GB)....75, 142, 275, 317
Newcastle (NSW)....89, 180, 297, 299
New Delhi 97
New Guinea....138, 139, 189, 272
New Jersey 262
New Plymouth....191, 195, 253
New Sarum....386
New South Wales 179, 317
Newtown 389
New York....20, 192, 265, 290, 318, 320, 343, 384
Nibley 33
Nigel....237
Nigeria....376
Nisshyttan....166
Nitelva 159
Nithsdale....33
No Man's Common 83
Nordre Osen 160
Norfolk 135, 147, 227, 246, 310
Norfolk Island 291
North Atlantic Ocean....132, 134, 176, 320
North Africa....125,, 210, 243, 269, 272, 292
Northamptonshire....25, 282
North Canterbury....201
North Cape 272, 292, 300
North Carolina....176
Northern Territories....248
Northland....313
North Luffenham 115
Northolt 16, 128, 130, 153
North Sea....107
Norway 87, 162, 167, 321, 351
Nottinghamshire....75
Nowra 339
Nympsfield....155

Oban 129
Odiham 272
Ohakea....223, 230, 270
Ohio....305, 384
Okavango Delta....292
Old Marston....72
Old Rhinebeck....20, 21, 265
Old Sarum 82, 341
Old Warden....30, 266, 269, 272, 288, 317, 343, 371, 381
Olmutz....163
Onerahi 88
Ontario....178, 279, 287
Oparau 256
Oregon 301
Orleans-Saran....210
Orsa 164
Osario 287
Oshkosh 273, 275, 376
Oslo 142, 158, 160, 161, 162, 163, 225, 321
Ostersund....160
Otago 308
Otahuhu 196
Ottawa....170, 171, 172, 174, 178, 230, 257, 264
Oulton Broad....341
Ouston 75, 153
Oxford 16, 67, 75, 76
Oxley 189
Oyeren 160

Pacific....87
Padstow 367
Pakistan 244, 298
Palam....230
Palestine 31, 33
Palm Desert 178
Palmerston North....194
Pando....39
Panshanger 33, 51, 67, 77, 82, 137, 214, 217, 220, 221, 308, 312, 340
Papenburg....390
Parafield 296
Paris....21, 22, 46, 59, 209, 210, 317
Park Royal....72, 73
Parndorf....163
Pasir Ris....42
Paso de Mendoza....38
Patillas 247
Pearce 357
Pearl Harbor 233
Pedro da Aldeia 287
Pembroke Dock....120
Pennsylvania....17, 135, 177, 309
Perranporth....151
Pershore....209
Persia 23, 31, 51, 52, 87
Perth (Scotland)....31, 56, 85, 147, 204, 217
Perth (WA)....89, 245, 285, 295, 297, 298, 329, 349
Peru....33, 50
Petaluma 351
Peterborough 100, 149
Petersfield....156
Piccadilly....62
Pietersburg....292
Plymouth 34, 75, 146, 156, 217, 229, 330, 332, 334, 360
Point Cook....107, 231, 248, 249, 250, 252, 315
Poix....129
Poland....31, 33, 147, 233, 354
Pontypool 137
Port Alfred....232
Port Elizabeth 237
Portland 301
Port Macquarie 298, 318
Port Moresby....139
Port Piper....88
Porto Alegre....287
Portsmouth 19, 223
Portugal 12, 21, 31, 46, 50, 167, 168
Potchefstroom....237
Prague....22, 293
Prestwick 31, 33, 35, 48, 67, 75, 142, 320, 371
Pretoria....114, 119
Prince William of Gloucester Barracks....343
Prippet Marshes....217
Prkos....212
Puerto Rico....247
Pyingaung....241

Queensland....89, 181, 189, 251, 296, 310, 322, 324, 389
Que Que....54

Ramree Island....140
Ranchi....242
Ratcliffe....224
Reading....31, 36, 176, 298
Rearsby....381
Redhill 112, 276, 282, 296, 328, 340, 380, 381
Red Road Airfield....125
Red Square 293
Reenens Pass 292
Reigate....271
Reims....354
Rena....160
Renfrew (Scotland) 34, 43

LOCATIONS continued…

Renfrew (USA)	16
Reykjavik	262, 263
Rhodesia	100, 114
Richmond (Australia)	88, 89, 181
Rio de Janeiro	287
Risalpur	240, 241
River Caladan	140
River Cam	123
River Clyde	132, 330, 331, 333
River Don	34
River Medway	41, 169, 275, 342, 360
River Mersey	272
River Severn	223
River Thames	153, 342
River Trent	269, 382
Rivne	294
Roborough	146, 333
Rochester	41, 131, 169, 276, 338, 342, 359, 360, 382
Rocky Mountains	259, 291
Rome	278, 298, 390
Romney Marsh	153
Romorantin	209
Rongotai	87, 189, 193, 194, 195, 196, 197, 198, 199, 201, 202, 253, 254, 269
Rose Bay	89
Rosieres	129
Roskilde	312
Rotorua	154, 192, 254
Rotterdam	106, 107, 299, 322
Royston	299
Ruhr	349
Ruislip Lido	153
Russia	129, 217
Rye	147, 276, 277
Safdarjung	97
Salem	137
Saleve	59
Salisbury (SR)	55, 205, 206, 238, 385
Salisbury Hall	371
Salisbury Plain	82, 345
Salonica	58
Saltby	155
Sandskeid	262
Sandown	155
Santa Cruz	240
Santiago	231
Sao Paulo	349
Saskatoon	263, 265
Saudi Arabia	216
Scampton	345
Schiphol	104, 106
Schleissheim	228
Schwarzsee	355
Scone	204
Scotsburgh	292
Scotland	76, 331
Sealand	16, 42, 76, 78, 216, 232, 235
Seattle	320
Seletar	42
Senoma	347
Seven Barrows	37
Shaftesbury	249
Shahbaz	52
Shaikpet	139
Shanghai	24
Shawbury	76
Shearwater	264
Sheffield	376
Shellingford	73, 125
Shempston	133
Sheremetyevo	293
Shipdham	246
Shiplake	144
Shoreham	101, 128, 129, 341, 378
Silloth	133
Silver Sands	277
Simferopol	294
Sinsheim	136
Sintra	167, 168
Skopje	58
Skå Edeby	167, 268
Smarden	295
Smith's Lawn	78
Smithonian	384
Smiths Point	343
Smorum	44
Snailwell	212
Snitterfield	212
Snowden	369
Sofia	53
Sola	158, 160, 162
Solent, The	364
Soloman Islands	333
Solway Firth	124
Somaliland	227
Somerset	311
Southampton	16, 128, 153, 219
South Bagley Park	291
South Downs	356
Southend	240
Southerland	63
Southern Rhodesia	54, 111, 112, 113, 114, 123, 187, 204, 205, 206, 216, 218, 233, 237, 241, 282
Southern Sudan	299, 300
South Marston	78
Southport Beach	228
South Wales	135
Spain	22, 31, 46, 59, 387
Speke	76
Spitalgate	16, 155
St Albans Abbey	340
St Athan	369
St Cyr	210
St Eval	135
St Hubert	178
St Johns	263
St Lazare	346
St Lucia	363
St Mary's	178
St Mawgan	209
St Paul	369
St Thomas Mount	239
Staffordshire	122
Staplefield House School	76
Stapleford Tawney	48, 77, 272, 328
Staple Hall, Witney	75
Staplehurst	376
Stavern	158
Staverton	56, 127
Steinfjorden	160, 225
Stellenbosch	236
Stenlille	44
Stepney Mens' Institute	43
Stockholm	12, 163, 381, 382
Stockton	151
Stoke	76
Strait of Otranto	210, 211
Strathallan	148, 149, 290, 317
Stukeley	284
Sudan	310, 311
Suffolk	77, 137
Sunderland	317
Surabaya	186
Surcin	212
Surfers Paradise	329
Surrey	288
Svinndal	159
Swanton Morley	271
Swartkop	239
Sweden	12, 31, 160, 162, 164, 166, 167, 225, 262, 268, 321, 380, 381
Swindon	78
Switzerland	274, 295
Syderstone	276
Sydney	66, 88, 179, 182, 187, 221, 250, 286, 290, 291, 295, 296, 298, 304, 317, 320, 329, 333, 391
Syria	58
Sywell	25, 26, 36, 50, 115, 143, 147, 282, 283, 286
Tabriz	51
Tacuarembo	308
Tadjj	139
Taieri	253, 254, 255
Taif	216, 217
Taihape	223
Tai Tapu	306
Takoradi	305
Tamu	242
Tamworth	250
Tangmere	87
Tanzania	239
Tasik Malaja	186
Tasmania	182, 247, 249
Tasman Sea	88, 291
Tel Aviv	103
Tehran	23, 51
Te Kao	291
Te Puke	192
Temora	138, 250, 302
Tempe	232
Tenby	135, 367, 369

Tennessee 338	Vienna..49, 58	Wittering..19, 115
Tengah 42	Vincennes 46	Woburn Abbey............18, 77, 143, 166, 231, 266,
Ternhill 155	Viroqua 264	267, 269, 284, 297, 298, 345, 346,
Teversham 120, 121, 122, 214	Vizagapatam..242	355, 371, 381
Texas....................................225, 244, 262, 290		Woensdrecht......................................76, 104
Thailand..304	Waalhaven..104	Wollongong...89
Thame..251	Waddington..22	Wolverhampton 33, 218
Thamesmead...344	Wadebridge..151	Wonderboom 139, 233
Thanet 342	Wagga Wagga............................89, 181, 339	Woodbourne 254, 255
Theona 343	Waikato River...389	Woodley............21, 49, 123, 125, 144, 146, 176
Thruxton 130, 136, 228, 341, 372, 373,	Wales 223	Woodstock..307
375, 377, 378	Wanaka 226	Woolsington..275
Thurmaston................................75, 85, 120	Warton 151	Worcester..149
Tibenham..131	Washington (DC)...................203, 204, 205, 263	Wrexham 137, 227
Tilbury...286	Washington (State) 320	Wright Field......................................369, 384
Timmins..278	Watchet 365, 366, 367, 369	Wroughton..216
Tocumwal 252	Watchfield...125	Wyberton..246
Todmorden 75	Waterbeach..122	Wyndham..248
Tollerton 97	Waterkloof..237	Wyton 120, 147, 357
Tong...209	Watford 78	
Toowoomba............................185, 321, 322	Wellard 285	Yarra Glenn 251
Toronto ..30, 58, 60, 169, 170, 172, 178, 192, 244	Wellington 87, 192, 193, 194, 195, 196, 198,	Yarra River..180
Torquay (Victoria).............................324, 378	201, 202, 230, 333	Yate...33
Toulon...209	West Bridgford.......................................382	Yatesbury................33, 100, 140, 141, 239, 240
Tours 21	Westbury sub Mendip.....................296, 390	Yellahanka..241
Toussous 318	Westerleigh Common...............................33	Yeovilton 34, 118, 137, 156, 228, 229, 240,
Tower Bridge..343	Western Australia 140, 189, 190, 248, 249,	266, 324, 331, 341
Tower Hill Garage, Witney 75	285, 314	Yorkshire 125, 135, 140, 246, 378
Townsville 141	Western Junction 249	Young Field...296
Trenton 173, 263	West Freugh...132	Yugoslavia 75, 210, 233
Trichinopoly..241	West Germany 136, 215, 225	
Trincomalee..331	West Indies 363	Zagreb...212
Trivandrum...137	West Malling..130	Zaire..314
Trollhättän 164	Westminster...343	Zambesi River..114
Trondheim......................................158, 225	West Raynham.......................................136	Zemunik.....................................210, 211, 212
Tunisia..310, 390	Weston-super-Mare........................30, 92, 239	Zestienhoven..322
Turkey 59	Wetaskiwin.......................................309, 352	Zimbabwe..238, 292
Turnhouse...340	Wevelgem...293	Zwartkop 114, 233, 237
Turweston...282	Weybourne.......................................135, 365	
Ty-Cross..369	Weybridge.........................21, 27, 36, 115	**ORGANISATIONS, GOVERNMENT and**
	Weymouth..383	**MILITARY DEPARTMENTS, CIVIL CLUBS**
Ugerupsfalter..164	Wheathampstead.....................................83	**AND SCHOOLS, OPERATORS AND**
Ugglarp...136	Whenuapai...........................87, 253, 331, 333	**MUSEUMS**
Ukraine 294	Whitchurch..74, 280	61 Squadron Flying Group....................384
Upavon 74	White Rock...309	Aeroplane and Armament Experimental
Upwell...312	White Waltham.......22, 35, 59, 62, 74, 76, 78, 85,	Establishment (A&AEE)
Upwood 228	115, 118, 137, 156, 166, 216, 224, 272, 278,	See Boscombe Down
Uruguay 6, 38, 246, 287, 307	283, 290, 293, 295, 297, 298, 304,	See Martlesham Heath
USA 103, 106, 137, 183, 185, 186, 188, 246,	345, 385, 386, 388, 390	Ace Flight Training 302
274, 275, 286, 320, 324, 338	Whitley..58	Aerial Advertising Ltd............................192
Usworth 320	Wigram...230	Aero Club Catalunya................................53
	Willingdon Island 137	Aero Club d'Arcachon 210
Vaernes 162	Wiltshire 33, 326, 345	Aero Club de France 46
Valkenburg..76	Winchester...301	Aero Club de Moçambique 114
Valley..282, 288	Windhoek..239	Aero Club de Porto.................................168
Vancouver.........................278, 290, 318, 320	Windsor 78	Aero Club de Suisse 59
Vannes..53	Windmill Theatre...................................390	Aero Club Francesco Baracca 352
Vaerlose 26, 44	Wing..149	Aero Club of British Columbia 173
Vasteras...164, 166	Winkfield..22	Aero Club of East Africa 113, 205
Vereeniging..237	Winnipeg..172, 178	Aeronautical Inspection Department
Victoria (Australia)...............179, 186, 220, 251,	Wisconsin 264, 302, 320, 351	(AID)..62, 68, 96
274, 290, 324	Witbank..237	Afghanistan Government 216, 243
Victoria Falls 206, 289, 292	Witney 35, 62, 67, 68, 71, 72, 75, 77, 100,	Air Askari Corps.....................................113
	109, 118, 146, 147, 206, 244	

INDEX

ORGANISATIONS, GOVERNMENT and MILITARY DEPARTMENTS, CIVIL CLUBS AND SCHOOLS, OPERATORS AND MUSEUMS continued…

Airborne Forces Establishment (Ringway) 116
Air Command South East Asia (ACSEA) 243, 244
Air Contracts Ltd..192
Air Council.............30, 57, 64, 67, 184, 185, 216
Aircraft Disposal Commission 205
Aircraft Engineering Co Ltd (NZ) 255
Aircraft Research and Development Unit (RAAF)...107
Aircraft Service (NZ) Ltd................................255
Air Defence of Great Britain 21
Air Estimates 29
Air Inventions Committee 85
Air League 275
Air Registration Board (ARB) 101, 372
Air Scouts (16th Hounslow Group) 384
Air Service Training 57
Airspray..375
Air Squadron 294
Air Survey and Transport 191, 192, 193, 194, 201
Air Training Corps (ATC) 112, 135, 155, 156
Air Training Corps Touring Flight (NZ) 253, 254, 269
Air Training Scheme 109
Air Training Wing (ATW), Southern Rhodesia....................207, 237
Air Transport and Travel 67
Air Transport Auxiliary (ATA) 74, 86, 144, 146, 147
Airwork Ltd...217, 251, 337
Airwork (NZ) Ltd....................................255, 306
Airwork Pty Ltd (Australia) 204
Akureyrar Flying School 262
Alleberg Central Gliding School............164, 166
Alleberg Gliding Museum 164
American Moth Club......................................290
Amman Flying Club.......................................216
Antique Aeroplane Association of Australia 320, 343
Arab Airways..217
Arab Airways Flying Club 216
Arab Legion..216
Arnhold and Co (DH Agent) 24
Association of British Aero Clubs (ABAC) 154, 214, 223
Auckland Aero Club................................191, 192
Australian Air Board 181, 187, 248
Australian Air Department 184, 185
Australian Associated Aero Clubs............53, 249
Australian Bureau of Air Safety Investigation (BASI)................................285
Australian Department of Aircraft Production 183
Australian Department of Supply....................181
Australian Directorate of Civil Aviation...............................119, 249, 309, 310
Australian Government 182, 183, 184, 248
Australian Ministry of Supply and Shipping...247
Australian National Airways 182
Australian Women Pilots' Association 342
Austrian Government and Air Force ...49, 50, 163
Auto Techniks Museum..................................136

Auxiliary Air Force 16, 132
Aviation Historical Society of Australia.......185, 189
Aviation Historical Society of New Zealand.......103
Aviron Company (Israel)................................103
Barnstormers Flying Circus 282, 382, 388
Bathurst Soaring Group..................................303
Behala Flying Club...245
Beira Aero Club..114
Belgian Air Force and Initial Training School 212
Belgian National Flying School 212, 272
Bengal Flying Club...245
Blackburn School of Flying 16
Black Watch..115
Blue Eye Aviation...135
Bomb Disposal Squad 120
Bomber Command Museum (Hendon) 116
Bomber Command Museum (Canada)............263
BOAC..216, 320
Brazilian Air Force and Government 8, 48 287
Brazilian Navy.......................................8, 37, 287
Brian Lewis and Co..21
Bristol School of Flying 16, 20
British Air Attaché, Berlin...............................29
British Air Attaché Paris..................................29
British Aircraft Preservation Council (BAPC) 371
British Airways.......................................257, 288
British Arab Flying Club 33
British Columbia Agricultural Museum..........309
British Commonwealth Air Training Plan 176, 178, 257, 262
British European Airways 153, 215, 340, 388
British Expeditionary Force (BEF) 128
British Parachute Association.........................326
British Skydiving Ltd.....................................378
British South American Airways....................257
Brooklands Flying Club 36, 104
Bulawayo Flying Club....................................112
Bulgarian Government 53
Burmese National Air Force...........................215
Burmese Volunteer Air Force 242
Butler Air Transport 182
Cambridge Flying Group 77, 130, 345
Canadian Government.....................60, 175, 256
Canadian Aviation and Space Museum 230
Canadian Commercial Corporation.................264
Canadian Navy School of Maintenance 264
Canterbury Aero Club....................................201
Cape York Aero Club 296
Captain Neville's Flying Circus 379
Castle Bromwich Aeroplane Factory 66
Cathay Pacific Airways 182
Centennial Exhibition Buildings 254
Central Flying School Display Team ...16, 19, 25, 28
Cercle Aéronautique de Coulommiers et de la Brie..53
Chief of the Air Staff (RNZAF)........................87
Chilean Air Force and Museum 231
Chilean National Aeronautical Collection......231
Chinese Government 53
Chipperfield's Circus......................................215
Chrisair..272, 273

Christchurch Aero Club..................118, 226, 266
Cinque Ports Flying Club........................35, 104
Civil Air Guard...59, 66, 382
Civil Repair Organisation................................66
Clube de Planadores Albatroz 387
Coastal Patrol Flights (CPF) 62, 128, 132, 137
Commonwealth Disposals Commission (Australia)..247, 250
Condor Gliding Club.......................................334
Connellan Airways..................................138, 139
Controller of Research and Development 77
Cotswold Aviation Society.............................287
Coventry Aero Group.....................................219
Coventry Aeroplane Club................................58
Crop Culture Ltd 306
Cumulus Flying School 262
C W A Scott's Flying Display 34, 35
Czech Government...282
Danish Army Air Corps and Government 26, 43, 44, 46
Danish Air Force 353
Dansk Luftfartsselskab.....................................46
Darlington and District Aero Club 148, 220
Defence Flying Club 239
Defence Research Agency..............................325
Defford Aero Club..154
de Havilland Aeronautical Technical School 12, 27, 46, 90, 123, 192, 281, 312
de Havilland Civil Repair Unit (Witney) 35, 62, 118
de Havilland Moth Club.........228, 266, 269, 277, 285, 286, 290, 295, 297, 317, 324, 343, 348
de Havilland School of Flying 14, 16, 20, 21, 28, 30, 31, 38, 95
de Havilland Support Ltd 286
Delhi Flying Club...241
Department of National Defence (Canada)...172, 173
Department of Transport and Transport Canada............. 102, 103, 172, 173
Derby Aviation 224
Diamond Nine Display Team 297, 298, 345, 346
Directorate of Aeronautical Production (DAP)..55
Directorate of Civil Research and Production (DCRP)..................................62
Director of Home Operations 79
Directorate of Technical Development............94
Director General of Civil Aviation (GB) 74, 82, 204
Director General of Civil Aviation (India) 243
Director General of Research and Development (DGRD).........................76, 93
Director General of War Supplies (SAAF) 233
Director of Coastal Air Force (SAAF) 233
Director of Operational Requirements 81
Director of Training (RCAF)...........................97
Djibouti Aero Club 227
Drammen Flyklubb 224, 225
Durban Wings Club..383
Department of Civil Aviation (RLD)..104, 105, 106
Dutch Government 206, 216
Dutch Government Aviation School (RLS) 104
Dutch National Aviation School (NLS)........43, 104

406

Dutch National Flying Laboratory (NLL)..........104
Edinburgh Flying Club....................................340
Egyptian Air Force 50
Empire Air Training Scheme 111, 182, 187, 198, 232, 248, 256
Empire Central Flying School................123, 124
Empire Test Pilots' School (ETPS) 102, 107, 325
English Club, Buenos Aires 38
Entertainments National Service Association (ENSA) 140
Experimental Aircraft Association (EAA) 264
Farm Aviation Services 312
Film Aviation Services 384
Finnish Air Force..163
Fleet Air Arm Museum....................................34
Flying Training Services 16
Forest Fire Patrol (NZ)...................................254
French Air Force......................................209, 354
French Naval Air Service..................................59
Flugsport Vereinigung Speyer.........................136
Flygstyreisen...163
Flygverkstaden Vasteras (CVV)................164, 165
German Airline Pilots' Flying School 24
German Government.......................................24
German Ministry of Aviation 46
Glasmoth 293, 294
Glider Pilot Regiment.....................115, 120, 218
Goulburn Valley Aero Club............................297
Grading System 30, 110, 120, 121, 126, 256
Greek Air Force and Government 59
Halmstad Aero Club...46
Hamilton Downs Pastoral Company 139
Hamilton Flying Club...............................173, 176
Hampshire Aeroplane Club 219, 385
Hawera Aero Club..192
Herts and Essex Aero Club......................314, 338
Huntingdon Aviation 215
Iceland Gliding Club 262
Imperial Airways 115, 296
Imperial Ethiopian Aero Club 206
Imperial Ethiopian Air Force....................31, 206
Indian Air Force 97, 230, 231, 237, 240, 241, 243, 244, 315
Indian Air Force Historic Flight and Museum 230
Indian Army Historic Flight 245
Indian Disposals Board 243
Indian Government..................72, 140, 182, 230, 239, 243, 244
Inspector General Army Air Force (Norway)..158
Interim War Training Scheme 252
International Commission of Air Navigation (ICAN)..23
Iranian and Persian Ministries.........23, 32, 41, 51
Iraq Government 215
Italian Air Force 296
Jagervingen (Fighter Flight) Norway..............160
James Aviation..314
Jewish Agency..33
Johannesburg Light Plane Club......................235
Joint Air Training Plan (JATP)......................233
Joint Air Training Scheme (JATS)................................114, 205, 236, 244

Karachi Aero Club..140
Kemsley Flying Trust......................................227
Kenya Auxiliary Air Unit (KAAU)................233
Kenya Government...................................113, 208
Kingsford-Smith Aviation Services................249
Kitchener-Waterloo Flying Club....................173
Kooy Gliding Club...216
Kuala Lumpur Flying Club 336, 337
Leisure Sport..277
Le Tigri Display Team...................................328
Lebanese Air Force...215
Legacy (Australian charity)............................295
Lietuvos Aero Club 33
Light Aeroplane Clubs 1925 8
Liverpool District Aero Club...........................58
Local Defence Volunteers (Home Guard).........76
London Aeroplane Club 10, 34, 35, 46, 58, 77, 90, 123, 195, 214, 220, 254, 257, 316, 319, 343
London Air Park Flying Club..........................36
London Fire Brigade 146
London Gliding Club................................92, 322
London Transport Flying Club......................300
Lone Star Museum (Texas) 225
Lucht Strijd Krachten (the Netherlands) 106
Luftwaffe...........................46, 153, 154, 162, 163
Luton Corporation 78
Luton Flying Club..215
Madras Flying Club.........................239, 244, 245
Madyha Pradesh Flying Club 245
Malayan Government.....................................336
Marine Aircraft Experimental Establishment (MAEE).........................41, 42
Marlborough Downs Aero Club.....................192
Maryborough Aero Club................................298
Mashonaland Flying Club......................207, 238
Mediterranean Allied Air Force (MAAF)....205, 209
Merseyside Aero and Sports Co 58
Merton Park Film Studio.................................84
Middle Districts Aero Club 192, 256
Middlesex Flying Club...................................217
Midland Aero Club....................................57, 61
Midland Bank Flying Club............................215
Ministry of Aircraft Production (MAP) 76, 79, 93, 94, 131, 145, 149, 177, 185, 203, 205, 209, 237, 243, 248, 371
Ministry of Civil Aviation 207, 214
Ministry of Home Security..............................78
Ministry of Supply 207, 248, 322
Misr Flying Institute.......................................205
Mitair Agricultural Aviation 310
Montevideo Aeronautical Museum 246
Moose Jaw Flying Club..................................173
Mosquito Aircraft Museum 371
Mozambique Government..............................205
Museum of Army Flying................................344
Museum of Flight and Transportation (Vancouver) 264
Nagpur Flying Club................................245, 246
National Agricultural Advisory Service 310
National Aviation Day Display........14, 24, 30, 34
Newark Air Museum.....................................287
New Brighton Lifeboat...................................222

Newcastle Aero Club, (later Royal) 53, 113, 180, 233, 245, 249, 250, 286, 298, 317, 318
Newcastle upon Tyne Aero Club..............50, 275
New Plymouth Aero Club 255, 270
New Zealand Air Department 333
New Zealand Government 193, 254, 255
New Zealand Permanent Air Force 191
Norsk Aero Club..167
Norsk Teknisk Hogskole Flying Club 225
Northern Alberta Aero Club 173
Northern Aviation School..............................62
North Queensland Aero Club 296
Norwegian Aero Club (NAK) 225
Norwegian Army Air Force.....157, 158, 159, 160
Norwegian Aviation Historical Society (NFF) 160, 162
Norwegian Government 157, 158, 166
Norwegian Navy 157, 158
Norwegian State Aircraft Factory (Kjeller).........157
Nottingham Flying Club..................................97
Nuffield Organisation.........................57, 66, 76
Ontario Provincial Government 169
Oxford Aeroplane Club 131
Pakistan Air Force and Government 243
Palestine Flying Club................................33, 103
P & O Shipping Line 20, 240
Parachute Regiment..115
Pathé News...369
Perry Air 341
Pilotless Aircraft Coordination Command 358
Pilotless Aircraft Section 363, 369
Pilotless Aircraft Unit (PAU) 120, 149, 369
Plan Banquet 79
Plan Banquet Civil 79
Plan Banquet Comm..79
Plan Banquet Light..79
Plan Banquet Master 79
Plan Julius Caesar..79
Polish Air Force..325
Port of Spain Aero Club 61
Portsmouth Naval Gliding Club....................334
Portuguese Air Force and Historic Flight.....167, 168
Portuguese Air Force Museum.......................168
Portuguese Government and Ministry of War......167
Portuguese Military Aeronautical School 167
Portuguese Naval Air Service 167, 168
Qantas Airways...290
Quebec Soaring Club 264
Queen Bee Base Training Unit.......................363
Quelimane Aero Club.....................................205
RAAF Directorate of Technical Services........189
RAAF Museum.......................................107, 231
RAF College Flying Club 333
RAF Development Flight 363
RAF Disposal Branch.....................................223
RAF Exhibition Unit 341
RAF Flying Club......................................33, 82
RAF Home Aircraft Depot (Henlow)..........16, 19
RAF Museum (Hendon).................................341
RAF Red Arrows..345

INDEX

ORGANISATIONS, GOVERNMENT and MILITARY DEPARTMENTS, CIVIL CLUBS AND SCHOOLS, OPERATORS AND MUSEUMS continued…

RAF Research and Development Unit (India) 139
RAF Reserve of Air Force Officers (RAFO)...16, 17
RAF Special Reserve 16
RAF Volunteer Reserve 29, 132
Reading Flying Group 388
Red Baron Scenic Flights...........................391
Reynolds Alberta Museum (Wetaskiwin).................................309, 352
Rhodesian Air Training Group (RATG)..............111, 112, 114, 205, 207, 233
Robertsbridge Aviation Society.....................147
Romanian Government 53
Roslagen Aero Club 166
Rotterdam Aero Club 17, 104
Rous and Meeuwenoord Co (DH Agent) 62
Royal Aero Club.......46, 209, 214, 215, 217, 228, 317, 337, 372
Royal Aero Club of New South Wales...............................180, 250, 298
Royal Aero Club of Western Australia 89, 336
Royal Artillery...365
Royal Canadian Air Force First mention.........256
Royal Canadian Flying Clubs Association......263
Royal Canadian Navy..................................264
Royal Dutch Shell 62
Royal Flying Corps 143
Royal Flying Doctor Service..................298, 314
Royal Hellenic Air Force........................112, 215
Royal Indian Air Force Volunteer Reserve 239, 360
Royal Naval College 229, 322, 341
Royal Navy Historic Aircraft Flight..................................137, 229, 240, 325
Royal Netherlands Air Force.............15, 76, 104, 105, 106, 216, 230
Royal Netherlands Air Force Historical Flight.....230
Royal Netherlands Navy 76
Royal New Zealand Aero Club 254, 255
Royal New Zealand Air Force First mention 191
Royal New Zealand Air Force Historic Flight 230
Royal New Zealand Air Force Museum................230
Royal Norwegian Air Force 142
Royal Queensland Aero Club 185
Royal Swedish Aero Club (KSAK)..............164
Royal Swedish Air Force................8, 48, 50, 163, 164, 165, 166
Royal Swedish Air Force Museum.................166
Royal Sydney Golf Club 89
Royal Thai Navy 122, 124
Royal Victorian Aero Club 180, 189
Rusty Angels Formation Team 352, 354
Sabena 212
Salisbury Flying Club.................................112
Salvation Army....................................248, 249
Saskatoon Technical College.......................172
Saudi Arabian Government 216
Scarecrow Patrols 95, 98, 99, 128, 132, 133, 134
Scottish Flying Club...................................217
Scottish Motor Traction Co 34, 43, 371

Seaplane Club.................................147, 275, 276
Seaplane Training Flight (Calshot) 41
Secretary of State for Air.................................74
Selfridges Aviation Department 21
Service de l'Aviation Légère et Sportive (SALS)...210
Shahbaz State Aircraft Factory........................51
Shreiner and Co (Agent) 206
Shuttleworth Collection.........................288, 371
Silver Wing Gliding Club......................153, 388
Skovde Aero Club 166
Skyway Air Services 309
Skyspray of Canada.....................................309
Société Français de Transports........................53
Society of British Aircraft Constructors (SBAC)..21, 209,
Soerabaja Flying Club....................................62
South African Air Force 114, 232, 329, 342
South African Air Force Aero Club................239
South African Air Force Defence Flying Club....239
South African Airways 343
South African Government Departments 232, 233, 236, 237, 239
Southern Flying Centre 341
Southern Rhodesia Air Service and Air Force..54, 205, 208
Southern Rhodesia Flying Training School 53, 54
Southern Rhodesia Government........54, 207, 208
Southern Rhodesia Government Disposals Office.....................................206
Southport Aero Club....................................227
Soviet Air Force Museum 287
Spanish Air Force....................................22, 46
Spencer's Airways and Garage....................206
Sport and Vintage Aviation Society of Masterton 346
Standard Telephone and Cable Co 34
Strathallan Collection..................................148
Sunderland Flying Club 320
Stockholm Aero Club 166
Svedinos Bil Och Flygmuseum....................136
Tasmanian Aero Club 250
Taylorcraft CRU Thurmaston.........................35
Thames Aerial Topdressing 227
Thunderbirds (USAF) 356
Thunderbirds 388
Tiger 9 Formation Team 345, 346, 350, 351, 380
Tiger Club.........112, 155, 271, 280, 312, 323, 327
Tiger Club (Seaplane Section) 276
Tiger Moth Club of South Africa 292, 301
Tiger Moth Club of New Zealand 302, 381
Toronto Central Technical School..............12, 170
Toronto Flying Club 169, 170, 172, 173, 177
Torpedo Training Unit.................................137
Townsend Aero Museum..............................369
Townsville Aero Club..................................189
Ukraine National Aviation Museum.............294
Ukraine Parliament......................................294
United States Army Air Force 176, 178
United States 5th Army Air Force 189
United States 8th Army Air Force 151
United States Air Force 296
United State Air Force Museum (Wright Patterson) 384

United States Foreign Liquidation Commission 243
University of Hertfordshire 340
University of Oslo (Meteorology).................158
Uruguayan Military 246, 308
VASP 38
Vasteras Aeronautical Engineering College 164
Vicy French Air Force 209
Vintage Aero Services 258
Waikata Aero Club 256
Walcha Historical Society 314
Wales Airways..371
War Assets Corporation (Canada) 262, 263
War Assets Realisation Board (NZ) 254, 255
Wellington Aero Club......................193, 194, 201
Western Federated Flying Club 192
West London Aero Club 137
Whyalla Aero Club......................................180
Wideroes Flying School 158
Wiltshire School of Flying 113, 136, 223, 341, 372, 373, 375, 378
Woolgrowers Agency Co.............................249
Wolverhampton Flying Club 155
Yellow Air Taxis...215
Yugoslav Air Force 210, 211
Yugoslav Aviation Museum.........................212

BRITISH MILITARY UNITS

RAF Commands

Bomber Command 124, 219
Coastal Command 131, 132, 135
Flying Training Command 79, 84, 92, 93, 96, 101, 120, 121, 123, 130, 137
Home Command 84
Reserve Command 55, 219, 391
Technical Training Command 137

Anti Aircraft Co-operation Units

1 AACU.....................35, 86, 135, 365, 368, 369
4 AACU..42
7 AACU..131

Coastal Patrol Flights

1 CPF Aberdeen (Dyce) 85, 132, 134, 135, 136
2 CPF Glasgow (Abbotsinch) 132, 135, 137
3 CPF Hooton Park 133, 134, 135, 136
4 CPF Belfast (Aldergrove).....133, 134, 135, 136
5 CPF Carew Cheriton 135, 136, 137
6 CPF St Eval 132, 135, 137

Pre-war Elementary and Reserve Flying Training Schools (ERFTS)

1 ERFTS Hatfield..............14, 31, 35, 56, 65, 92, 95, 118, 142
3 ERFTS Hamble 57
6 ERFTS Sywell....................................25, 26, 27, 118
7 ERFTS Desford 118
9 ERFTS Ansty..57
10 ERFTS Yatesbury 33, 110
11 ERFTS Perth......................................75, 77, 118
12 ERFTS Prestwick...........................33, 81, 109
13 ERFTS White Waltham 35, 59, 62, 118
14 ERFTS Castle Bromwich 29
16 ERFTS Shoreham......................................29
18 ERFTS Fairoaks 28, 117
20 ERFTS Gravesend..................................329
22 ERFTS Cambridge 214

29 ERFTS Luton 78
34 ERFTS Southend 149
Elementary Flying Training Schools
1 EFTS Hatfield 35, 37, 82, 83, 92, 95,
99, 115, 149
1 EFTS Panshanger 217, 222, 225
2 EFTS Staverton 93
3 EFTS Shellingford .. 72, 100, 115, 125, 137, 151
3 EFTS Watchfield 72, 82, 100, 125, 126
3 EFTS Hamble 80
4 EFTS Brough 99, 122, 135, 151, 257
6 EFTS Sywell 67, 80, 97, 100, 115
7 EFTS Desford 85, 92, 125, 331
8 EFTS Woodley 95, 137
9 EFTS Ansty 86, 93, 94, 95, 127
10 EFTS Yatesbury 93, 101, 239
10 EFTS Weston-super-Mare 92, 93, 94,
97, 137, 239
10 EFTS Stoke Orchard 95
11 EFTS Perth 77, 85, 135, 136, 151, 204
12 EFTS Prestwick 33, 72
13 EFTS White Waltham 82, 85, 86, 115
14 EFTS Elmdon 137, 144, 147, 153, 341
15 EFTS Carlisle 121, 126, 135, 147, 148
16 EFTS Burnaston 95, 118, 125, 150
17 EFTS Peterborough 86, 100, 149
17 EFTS North Luffenham 115
18 EFTS Fairoaks 20, 142, 147, 152, 154
19 EFTS Sealand 72, 137
20 EFTS Yeadon 241
21 EFTS Booker 59, 96, 100, 115, 116, 148,
149, 218, 234
22 EFTS Cambridge 82, 86, 100, 118, 120,
121, 122, 130, 148, 180, 214
24 EFTS Belfast 78
24 EFTS Luton 78
24 EFTS Sealand 72
25 EFTS Hucknall 127, 147, 152
26 EFTS Theale 95
28 EFTS Wolverhampton 125, 153, 154, 218
29 EFTS Clyffe Pypard 119, 135, 341
31 EFTS Elmdon 92
Flying Training Schools (FTS)
1 FTS Leuchars 29
3 FTS 9, 16, 19
4 SFTS Habbaniyah 112
4 SFTS Cambridge 93
6 FTS Ternhill 155
7 FTS Cottesmore 155
Pot war Reserve Flying Schools (RFS)
1 RFS Panshanger 83
2 RFS Barton 218
6 RFS Sywell 225
7 RFS Desford 218
8 RFS Woodley 218
11 RFS Perth 136
12 RFS Filton 150
22 RFS Cambridge 154, 218
24 RFS Rochester 124, 137, 391
25 RFS Wolverhampton 218
RAF Maintenance Units (MU)
4 MU Cowley 20
5 MU Kemble 35, 85, 120, 340

6 MU Brize Norton 36, 130, 132
8 MU Little Rissington 75, 95
9 MU Cosford 118, 137, 224, 228, 322
10 MU Hullavington 85, 120, 124, 132, 137, 326
12 MU Kirkbride 20, 131
15 MU Wroughton 75, 76, 97, 155
19 MU St Athan 35, 132, 137, 371
20 MU Aston Down 75, 84, 137
24 MU Stoke Heath 72
24 MU Ternhill 305
25 MU Hartlebury 80
33 MU Lyneham 95, 136
36 MU Sealand 195
38 MU Llandow 35, 75, 76, 86, 223
39 MU Colerne 75, 78, 130
45 MU Kinloss 135
47 MU Sealand 76, 305
222 MU High Ercall 77, 95, 140
RAF Squadrons
2 Sqn 85
19 Sqn 290
24 Sqn 16, 19, 21, 30, 43, 130
36 Sqn 123
56 Sqn 288
57 Sqn 129
59 Sqn 129
66 Sqn 151
72 Sqn 150
76 Sqn 124
81 Sqn 129, 130, 131
116 Sqn 86, 150
141 Sqn 155
164 Sqn 77
167 Sqn 77
181 Sqn 153
198 Sqn 153
206 Sqn 134
217 Sqn 132
219 Sqn 83
224 Sqn 132
263 Sqn 76
289 Sqn 131
306 Sqn 150
312 Sqn 152
316 Sqn 150
351 Sqn 212
360 Sqn 357
401 Sqn 111
418 Sqn 130
455 Sqn 142
502 Sqn 134
603 Sqn 85
610 Sqn 132
612 Sqn 132
617 Sqn 135, 349, 376
654 Sqn 97
University Air Squadrons
Cambridge 154
London 137, 218
Oxford 177
Fleet Air Arm Squadrons
727 Sqn 332
768 Sqn 329

785 Sqn 329
804 Sqn 331, 333
812 Sqn 331, 333
898 Sqn 330, 331
Miscellaneous
9 Advanced Flying Training School
 (AFTS) Wellesbourne 341
215 Advanced Flying School Finningley 136
2 Aircrew Grading School Digby 136
2 Air Gunners School 135
2 Aircraft Servicing Unit, Cardington 19, 43
Avro Tutor Communications Squadron 128
Britannia Flight, Royal Naval
 College 229, 332, 333
British Army EFTS (Middle Wallop) 220
1 Camouflage Unit 77, 78
Central Flying School 7, 18, 19, 21, 30, 34,
74, 92, 94, 348
3 Ferry Pilots Pool White Waltham 74
1424 Flight 85
1483 Flight 95
6 Flying Instructor School (FIS) Staverton 149
10 Flying Instructor School (FIS)
 Woodley 123, 125, 137
Glider Pilot Exercise Unit (GPEU) 120
Glider Pilot Operational & Refresher
 Training Unit (ORTU) 120
1 Glider Training School (GTS) 116
1 Grading Unit Digby 126, 136, 221
2 Grading Unit Kirton in Lindsay 136
41 Group, Andover 76
1651 Heavy Conversion Unit Waterbeach 122
13 Operational Training Unit 130
55 Operational Training Unit Annan 77
1 Photographic Reconnaissance Unit 135
15 Pilots Advanced Flying Unit (PAFU) 131
1 Radio School Cranwell 155
Royal Air Force Pageant 7, 18, 21, 82, 363
Royal Air Force Golden Jubilee Review 341
Royal Corps of Logistics 343
Schools of Army Co-operation 79
3 School of Technical Training Blackpool 43
3 TAF Communications Sqn 139
Tiger Moth Communications Squadron 128
Torpedo Training Unit Abbotsinch 137

COMMONWEALTH MILITARY UNITS
Australia
1 Air Depot Laverton 182
2 Air Depot Richmond 181, 182, 185, 189
1 Air Observer School Cootamundra 188
2 Communications Flight 89
3 Communications Flight 89
8 Communications Unit 138, 139
9 Communications Unit 139
1 EFTS Parafield 186
2 EFTS Archerfield 182, 183
3 EFTS Essendon 186
4 EFTS Mascot 88, 89
5 EFTS Narromine 182, 185, 249
6 EFTS Tamworth 249
7 EFTS Western Junction 182
8 EFTS Narrendera 89, 146
9 EFTS Cunderdin 89

COMMONWEALTH MILITARY UNITS
Australia continued…
11 EFTS Benalla 383
12 Local Air Supply Unit (LASU) 139
1 Reserve and Communications Sqn............138
1 Technical Supply Depot 189
3 Wireless/Air Gunner School.........................181
5 (Army Co-Op) Sqn 189
33 Sqn...139, 141
36 Sqn..189

Canada
10 Air Depot Calgary 259
5 EFTS High River..................................262, 263
6 EFTS Prince Albert 257, 260
10 EFTS Pendleton.................................262, 265
12 EFTS Goderich..263
19 EFTS Vinden..258
20 EFTS Oshawa.....................................258, 262
28 EFTS Oshawa...269
31 EFTS Calgary......................................256, 257, 260
31 EFTS De Winton 256, 257, 258
32 EFTS Swift Current............................256, 257
32 EFTS Bowden...256
33 EFTS Caron.........................177, 257, 259, 260
34 EFTS Assiniboia 256, 263
35 EFTS Neepawa 256, 259
36 EFTS Pearce 256
3 FIS Arnprior 258
6 Repair Depot Trenton 173
8 Repair Depot Winnipeg 260
8 Service Flying Training School Moncton 236
418 Sqn..130

India
RAF Depot Karachi...239
1 Coastal Defence Flight 239
5 Coastal Defence Flight 137
1 EFTS Begumpet 243, 244
2 EFTS Jodphur 244
221 Group Comms Flight..............................242
229 Group..240
1 Repair and Salvage Unit 242
2 Repair and Salvage Unit 241
3 Repair and Salvage Unit 241

New Zealand
1 EFTS Taieri 87, 253
2 EFTS New Plymouth 87, 253
2 EFTS Ashburton 145, 148, 152
3 EFTS Harewood.........87, 150, 194, 196, 201, 253
4 EFTS Whenuapai 87, 196, 253
4 Technical Training School Woodbourne 255
CFS Tauranga..87
FAFAI Scheme 87, 88, 150, 195
Flying Instructor School Hobsonville 192
20 Sqn...88
75 Sqn...305
486 Sqn...87
488 Sqn...130

Southern Rhodesia
4 FTS Heany 40, 113, 205, 237
5 FTS Thornhill 113, 237
25 EFTS Belvedere (Salisbury) 111, 113, 205
26 EFTS Guinea Fowl (Gwelo)....111, 112, 113, 114
27 EFTS Induna (Bulawayo) 111, 113
28 EFTS Mt Hampden (Salisbury) ..111, 112, 114

South Africa
3 Air Depot Cape Town 237
4 Air Depot Lyttelton.....................................233
15 Air Depot Zwartkop 237
1 Air School Baragwanath..............................233
2 Air School Randfontein 234
5 Air School Witbank 125, 235
7 Air School Kroonstad 234, 237
62 Air School, Bloemfontein.........................233
2 Pilot Despatch Centre, Nigel 235
3 Pilot Despatch Centre, Standerton 235
24 Group Communications Flight................233
Central Flying School......................232, 237, 239
Transvaal Air Training Squadron 232
Union Air Training Group 232
Coastal Patrol Flights 232

AIRCRAFT, ENGINES, EQUIPMENT, SUPPLIES AND SERVICES
ADC Cirrus engine 1, 7I
ADC Cirrus II engine 7
ADC Cirrus Hermes IV 24
Aerocontacts... 223, 226
Aero Material 43, 163, 167
Aeronca Sedan...148
Aircraft Components Ltd. 64
Airscrew Co..27
Airspeed Co... 58, 66, 77
Airspeed Oxford........ 63, 64, 65, 66, 67, 87, 115, 122, 150, 201, 209, 233, 254, 354
Airspeed Horsa..75
Airspeed Queen Wasp 369
Alfa Romeo 53, 287, 323
Alta OHC racing car......................................320
Armstrong Siddeley Genet...........................7, 18
Armstrong Siddeley Jaguar 26
Armstrong Siddeley Lynx 9
Armstrong Siddeley Mongoose........................8
Armstrong Whitwall AW16 46
Armstrong Whitworth Albemarle....................67
ASJA..164, 165
Auster 209, 214, 249
Austin Motors..185
Australian Aircraft Sales Ltd.........................251
Automatic Telephone Mfg Co 359
Avro Company 50
Avro 504N 8, 16
Avro 621 Tutor...................................9, 11, 16, 27
Avro 626..23
Avro 631 Cadet..167
Avro 640 Cadet..43
Avro 643 Cadet................................26, 58, 59, 180, 181
Avro Anson and XIX.............76, 81, 87, 132, 133, 135, 139, 178, 182, 188, 205, 209, 216, 233, 237
Avro Avian...43, 368
Avro Lancaster.............57, 219, 257, 295, 324, 348, 354, 388
Avro Tutor..43, 128
Avro York 257
Avro Canada CF-105 Arrow..........................352
Baynes Aircraft Interiors 372, 374
Beech Staggerwing..290

Beech Musketeer 277
Bell P-39 Airacobra 189
Bellanca Co 170
Bendix Brakes 175
Bentley Motors..74
Bendix Scintilla magnetos.............................185
Birkett Air Services 78
Bjorkvallsflyg Co 46
Blackburn Aircraft Co 21, 122
Blackburn Bluebird 21, 22
Blackburn B2...9
Boeing B.17..188, 351
Boeing B.29...352
Boeing PT-17 Stearman.........................257, 308
Boeing 707 320
Boeing 727 213
Boeing 747F 301, 355
Boudoin Aviation..210
Boulton and Paul 153
Breda...40
Bristol Aeroplane Co 24, 26, 33, 35, 77, 140, 164, 186, 201
Bristol Beaufighter 142
Bristol Beaufort...186
Bristol Blenheim 76, 83, 120, 125, 129, 242
Bristol Britannia 372
Bristol Bulldog 372
Bristol Mercury engine...................................86
British Aerospace and BAE Systems 102, 285, 286, 288, 344
BAe Concorde 277, 286, 288, 301, 325
BAe Harrier 349
BAe Hawk 345
BAe Jaguar 345
British Landing Gears Ltd............................368
Britten-Norman Co.......................................307
Brooklands Aviation 25, 36, 101, 115, 118
Brown DNF Hood 123, 124
Browning machine gun 79
BTH magnetos.......................................134, 135
Bücker Co...62
Bücker and CASA 131 Jungmann.............54, 357
Caproni Ca.100......................................21, 167
Cessna 172..293
Cessna 182..300
Chance Light 116
Cierva C.40 Autogyro 129
Clyde Engineering Co 146
Cobham Plc 34
Colt machine gun 160
Commonwealth Aircraft Corporation (CAC) 181, 183
CAC Wackett.................................272, 274, 336, 337
CAC Wirraway......................................89, 182
Consolidated Aircraft Catalina 85, 242, 250, 348
Consolidated Liberator.................................244
Croydon Aircraft Co (NZ)...................76, 77, 301
Cunliffe Owen Ltd..75
Curtiss Jenny 305
Curtiss P-40 Kittyhawk 89, 237
Curiss SNC-1...38,39
Curtiss-Wright Primary Trainer......................48
Czechoslavakian Arms Factory 32

Dalli Apparatus 159
Dassault Mirage 354
de Havilland Technical School TK.2 317
DH.9 .... 26, 80, 88
DH.18 67
DH.37 53
DH.51 72
DH.60 Cirrus Moth 146, 149, 340
DH.60 Moth 221, 234
DH.60G Moth 24, 47, 169, 315, 342
DH.60GIII Moth Major 8, 24, 47, 90, 359, 360, 387
DH.60M Metal Moth 7, 18, 21, 24, 90, 170
DH.60T Moth Trainer 8, 17, 22
DH.60T Training Moth T1 11
DH.60T Tiger Moth 7, 8, 9, 11, 12, 170
DH.60X Moth 13
DH.61 Giant Moth 38, 169
DH.80 Moth Three/Puss Moth 8, 9, 13, 14, 21, 122, 170, 175, 191, 194, 220, 343, 378
DH.81 Swallow Moth 13
DH.82 Tiger Moth (first mention) 13
DH.82A Tiger Moth (first mention) 26
DH.82A Tiger Moth Ambulance 138, 139
DH.82A Tiger Moth Fighter 31
DH.82A (Can) Tiger Moth 172
DH.82A High Technology Tiger Moth 284
DH.82A Sea Tiger 276, 277, 278
DH.82A Super Tiger 155, 281, 282, 283
DH.82A Tiger Moth Seaplane 184, 360, 359,
DH.82B Tiger Moth Mk III 63, 64, 96, 99, 176
DH.82C Tiger Moth (first mention) 176
DH.82C Tiger Moth (USAAF PT-24) 178, 263
DH.82C2 Menasco Moth 177
DH.82C3 Wireless Trainer 178
DH.82C4 Menasco Moth II 178, 179
DH.82 Queen Bee 20, 42, 63, 75, 120, 135, 149, 184, 360, 361, 362, 363, 364, 365, 367, 368, 369, 370, 371
DH.83 Fox Moth 21, 24, 34, 47, 51, 72, 140, 171, 179, 201, 221, 254, 277, 314, 360, 371
DH.84 Dragon 179, 221, 251, 272
DH.85 Leopard Moth 47, 49, 77, 90, 221, 251, 272
DH.86 .... 137, 179, 221
DH.87 Hornet Moth 47, 49, 53, 59, 77, 87, 134, 135, 180, 221, 234, 251, 317, 368
DH.88 Comet 10
DH.89 Dragon Rapide and Dominie 48, 49, 53, 62, 63, 74, 76, 77, 87, 209, 212, 306, 317
DH.90 Dragonfly 76, 195, 221
DH.91 Albatross 49, 58, 59, 62, 65, 358
DH.92 Dolphin 49
DH.93 Don 49, 65
DH.94 Moth Minor 54, 59, 62, 66, 67, 181, 193, 195, 221, 247, 271, 368
DH.95 Flamingo 59, 62, 65, 67
DH.96 project 54, 59
DH.97 62
DH.98 Mosquito 10, 64, 66, 67, 130, 147, 178, 201

DH.100 Vampire 97, 167, 208, 315, 317, 384
DH.106 Comet 311, 319, 384
DH.114 Heron 317
DHC.1 Chipmunk 10, 218, 220, 273, 275, 312
Demec navigation lights 48
Derby Aviation Ltd 224
Dornier Do 217 85
Douglas Boston 130
Douglas Dakota 73, 140, 241, 242, 244, 248
Dowty Ltd 26, 64, 165
Eclipse starter 41, 359
Edo floats 186, 275, 279
English Electric Canberra 357
English Electric Lightning 77, 288, 353
Entwistle and Kenyon 75
Everel Propellers 177
Fairchild Argus 125
Fairchild PT-19 and PT-26 Cornell 38, 112, 114, 204, 233, 243, 257, 259, 263
Fairey IIID 295
Fairey IIIF Seaplane 342, 358
Fairey Barracuda 153
Fairey Battle 182, 329
Fairey Firefly 331
Fairey Gordon 87, 368
Fairey Queen 358
Fairey Seal 368
Fairey Swordfish 264
Fairey Reed propellers 59, 278, 282, 380
Fiesler Storch 162
Fiesler Tiger II 22
Fisher R80 287
Fleet Fawn 169
Fleet Finch 176, 257, 263
Fleet Trainer 21, 22, 53, 172
Focke-Wulf 44 Stieglitz 48, 50, 164, 165
Fokker Aircraft Co 104, 157
Fokker C.V-D 157
Fokker C.V-E 157, 160
Garnham Aviation 223
General Dynamics F-16 353
General Motors (Holdens) Ltd 183, 184, 185, 187, 196
Gipsy I engine 7, 23, 173
Gipsy II engine 11, 173
Gipsy III engine 8, 9, 11, 12, 13, 21, 23, 24, 172
Gipsy IIIA engine 23
Gipsy King 49, 358
Gipsy Major 1 (first mention) 14
Gipsy Major 1C 59, 176
Gipsy Major Series II 59, 181
Gipsy Major Series IIA 63
Gipsy Major Series III 63, 359
Gipsy Minor 221
Gipsy Six 37, 38
General Aircraft (GAL) Monospar 76, 368
Gloster Gamecock 282
Gloster Gladiator 159, 160
Gloster Meteor 155, 290
Gosport tube 211
Grumman Avenger 305
Grunau Baby 321
Gyorizon 48

Haerens Flyfabrikk 157
Handley Page Aircraft Co 23
Handley Page slots 22, 90, 158, 360
Handley Page 0/400 86
Handley Page HP. 75 181
Handley Page Halifax 124, 324, 354
Hants and Sussex Aviation 223, 311
Harley landing lights 48
Hawker Audax 29
Hawker Demon 29, 88, 368
Hawker Hart 26, 79, 85, 240
Hawker Hector 116
Hawker Henley 368
Hawker Hind 87, 142, 202
Hawker Horsley 42
Hawker Hunter 114, 288, 318, 329
Hawker Hurricane 66, 72, 77, 86, 116, 123, 125, 129, 153, 186, 212, 233, 240, 241, 242
Hawker Sea Fury 331, 339
Hawker Typhoon 78, 87, 153
Hawker Tomtit 8, 11, 16, 316
Heinkel He III 240
Helliwells 322
Hendon Aeroplane Co (Australia) 286
Heston Phoenix 146
Hindustan Aircraft Co 237, 244, 245
Holt Flares 182, 242
Hooper and Co 72, 73
Howard DGA 254
Hughes Compass 22
Hughes Helicopters 347
Huntingdon Aviation 215
Jackaroo Aircraft Ltd 113
James H Sutcliffe and Son 75
Junkers Ju 88 .... 67, 375
Kilfrost paste 133
Kinner Co 50
Kirby Kite 116
Koolhoven Company 43, 104
Koolhoven FK-46 104
Laidlow Propellers 176
Lawrence Engineering 251, 287, 310
William Lawrence and Co 75
Leavens Brothers 178
Link Trainer 210
Lockheed C.5 Galaxy 356
Lockheed C.130 Hercules 231, 290
Lockheed F-104 352
Lockheed Hudson 88, 132, 138
Lockheed Jetstar 51
Lockheed Orion 352
Lockheed P-38 Lightning 150
Lotus Cars 320
Lundy and Atlantic Coast Airlines ... 75, 94, 150
Lycoming Engines 277, 323
Mack and White Trucks 75
Mae West 255
Marconi AD22 wireless 22
Marshall of Cambridge 119, 120, 213, 219, 223, 322
Maurice Farman MF.7 Longhorn 159
McDonald Aircraft Ltd 340

AIRCRAFT, ENGINES, EQUIPMENT, SUPPLIES AND SERVICES continued...

Menasco Manufacturing Co 49, 173, 176, 177, 178
Menasco Pirate engines 176, 183, 262, 263, 323
Messerschmitt Bf 109..211
Messerschmitt Me 110 121
Micronair Ltd 306
Miles Aircraft Co..176
Miles Hawk 49, 176, 232
Miles Hawk Trainer 50, 176
Miles Master.....................78, 79, 100, 176, 233
Miles Falcon 76
Miles Magister........54, 55, 57, 72, 76, 78, 79, 80, 81, 131, 135, 150, 183, 204, 209, 212, 214, 232, 243
Miles Martinet 131
Miles Whitney Straight 201, 305
Morane Saulnier 47, 225
H Morris and Co..371
Morris Motors..........64, 69, 196, 209, 225, 233, 342
Morrison and Co..38
Mosawa Co (Japan)...30
MRC (Teleflex Controls) 85
Muir and Adie Ltd...223
W Mumford CRU.............................75, 146, 217
Napier Lion engine 67
Newbury Aeroplane Co 155, 344
Norcom Stretcher 138
Norfolk Aerial Spraying 286
Norwegian State Aircraft Factory 157
Norwegian State Engine Factory (NOHAB) 164
North American AT-6 Texan................38, 51, 369
North American Harvard.............74, 87, 98, 125, 210, 211, 237, 240, 241, 254, 329
North American NA-16.......................................58
North American P-51 Mustang 85, 150, 151
OGMA Portugal 50, 167
Ottley Motors 322
Pander Co 104
Pattex Adhesives 383
Peacock Aviation 223
Percival Aircraft Co..78
Percival Proctor 209
Percival Gull..24, 49, 176, 192
Percival Vega Gull.......................................76, 194
Personal Plane Services....................................272
Peter Clifford Aviation 228
Phillips and Powis 21, 49, 50, 63, 176
PiK Sailplanes 323
Pilatus PC-9...351
Piper Comanche 377, 378
Piper Cub...177, 247
Piper Navajo 291
Pirelli webbing 258
Plessey Co 360
Potez Company 40
Power Jets..77
Pratt and Whitney Co 183
Pratt and Whitney E-4 Gun Synchroniser...32, 33, 41
Pratt and Whitney Wasp 169
RAAB Katzenstein..164

R B Pullin and Co...359, 360
Reid and Sigrist 48, 85
Reid and Sigrist Desford, ...85
Renault engines 183
Republic P-47 Thunderbolt 125, 151, 241
W A Rollason Ltd 26, 124, 203, 212, 223, 225, 227, 326
Rollason Aircraft and Engines Ltd 226, 227, 271, 277, 280, 281, 282, 283, 290, 312, 327, 328, 377, 378
Rolls-Royce Merlin 66, 151
Rootes Group..76
Rotherham pump 281
Rover Group..76
Ryan ST-A 232
SAAB 166, 167
SARO Skeeter 63
Schoning Spitmoth 275
Scottish Aviation Ltd 33, 35, 370
W S Shackleton Ltd.................53, 62, 186, 239, 243, 245, 337
Shell Oil Co 206, 290
Short Bros................41, 77, 131, 158, 169, 342
Short floats 278, 359, 360
Short Stirling 122
Short Sunderland 73, 348
Shreiner and Co 206
Sidcot suit 119, 134, 142
Sir W G Armstrong Whitworth Aircraft......271, 272
Skyway Air Services 309
Skyspray of Canada...309
Slick magnetos 278
Sopwith Camel 82
Specialised Mouldings Ltd................................59
S and S Propellers 176
Southern Aircraft CRU.................................75, 85
Stampe and Vertongen.......................................43
Stampe SV-4 ....54, 272, 293, 386
Standard Motors 184, 185
Stinson Sentinel..140, 170
Supermarine Sea Otter 331
Supermarine Spitfire 57, 66, 72, 74, 75, 76, 77, 85, 109, 111, 123, 125, 131, 150, 151, 153, 240, 241, 246, 275, 317, 324, 348, 354
Supermarine Swift....................................329, 384
Supermarine Walrus 201
Sutton harness 145, 286, 310
Tata Industries 240
Taylorcraft CRU (Thurmaston) 35, 75, 85, 120, 225
Technical and Aeronautical Exploitations Ltd 59
Thruxton Jackaroo 113, 150, 244, 372, 373, 374, 375
Tupolev Tu104..311
Union Carbide Co..305
Vauxhall Motors 78
Vickers Company 77, 78, 281
Vickers Vincent 29, 87
Vickers Viscount...............................340, 372
Vickers Vildebeeste 87
Vickers Wellington 67, 76, 122, 149, 242, 354
Victorian and Interstate Airways 248
Vintair 246

Vokes air filter 233
Vosper Co 77
Vultee Vengeance 125, 131
Waco Company 39, 47, 48
Waco UOC Custom 194
Waco UPF-7 383
Walter Engine Company 38
Walter Castor 164
Walter Minor M332...287
Walter 420hp..22
Westland Aircraft..76, 77
Westland Lynx 319
Westland Lysander 79, 81, 82, 86, 87, 129, 135, 242
Westland Sea King 325
Westland Wapiti..88, 137
Westland Whirlwind...76
A J Whittemore (International Aeradio)..........226
Wolseley Aero Engines 66
Wolseley Leo 66
Wolseley Scorpio 66
Wright engines 50
Yale and Towne locks.......................................226
Zlin Z.226 Trainer 282
Zlinn Z.526 Trener 293

MISCELLANEOUS
Events
Boer War..233
Botswana Moth Safari 288, 292
Charge of the Light Brigade............................294
Daily Mail London-Paris Air Race.................317
DH100 Rally 1982 357
Empire Air Day 7, 83
England-Australia Air Race 2001 302
Famous Grouse Rally 1979 ....137, 290, 317, 318, 319, 342
Great Tiger Moth Air Race......................317, 318
Geneva Aero Show 19, 90
Glasmoth to Moscow 293, 294
King's Cup Air Race 275, 317
Lockheed Trophy.......................266, 281, 282
MacRobertson International Air Races 1934 49
Munich Agreement..55
National Air Races 316, 317
Millennium Vintage Air Rally........................300
St Germain Aviation Meeting..........................22
Tiger Moth Challenge Trophy 317
Transatlantic Air Race 1969 318
World Aerobatic Championship 1960..........282, 293
World Vintage Air Rally 1990.........................295

Films
633 Squadron..389
Ace Ellie and Rodger of the Skies 389
Aces High 386
Agatha 388
The Aviator 389
Awakening of Emily..388
The Blue Max 137, 385, 386, 387
Darling Lily...387
The English Patient 390
Famous Five 390
The Flying Lesson..391

The Great Waldo Pepper 389
Jilting Joe...390
King Kong 383
King Solomon's Mines 386
The King's Speech 388
Lawrence of Arabia 384
The Little Prince 388
Mrs Henderson Presents 390
The Sound Barrier 384
Spirit of Australia 389
Spirit of St Louis 369, 370
Spirit of the Tiger 389
Those Magnificent Men 386, 387
Thunderbirds 388
Two in a Tiger 388
Villa Rides 387

Replica aircraft
Albatros C.11..385
Bristol Boxkite 387
Curtiss Jenny 387, 388
Fokker D.VII 384, 385
Fokker Triplane 352
Pfalz D.III 385, 386
Rumpler C.V 384, 391

Civilian ships
SS *Adastral* 367
SS *Athenia* 131
SS *Breda* 240
SS *Camilla* 137
SS *City of Lancaster* 167
SS *Empire Moonrise* 167
SS *Empire Nightingale* 167
MV *Gamma* 46
SS *King George V* 129
SS *Lycaon* 217
SS *Maraquesa* 192
SS *Margrethe* 26
SS *Opawa* 195
SS *Ponto* 76, 216
SS *Port Campbell* 191
RMS *Queen Mary* 192
SS *Radstock* 367
SS *Rangitane* 195
SS *Rangitata* 195
SS *Rangitikei* 195
SS *Somerset* 195
SS *Tjinegara* 186
SS *Wairangi* 195

Royal Navy Ships and Establishments
HMS *Bambara* 331
HMS *Colossus* 209
HMS *Eagle* 330, 332, 333, 334, 335
HMS *Gamecock* 333
HMS *Glory* 331
HMS *Guardian* 363
HMS *Hermes* 334
HMS *Jackal* 133
HMS *Nabberley* 333
HMS *Nabcatcher* 333
HMS *Neptune* 365
HMS *Phoenix* 119
HMS *Pursuer* 330
HMS *Ravager* 329
HMS *Theseus* 331, 333
HMS *Valiant* 358

Miscellaneous
Abe Bailey Aviation Coronation Gift................54
British Sugar Corporation 310
James Capel Ltd 293
Chinook wind 259
Christie's 269
Clayton Report 204
Farmhand Appeal 296
Hartemann Agreement 209
Hayward Leland Productions 369
Helm wind 135
Hurricane Hazel 237, 278
Hurricane Ike 225
Larynx aircraft catapult 365
Lord Mayor of London 227
MacBrayne Steamships 129
Netherlands Indies Aviation Fund 62
Operation Violet 128
Operation Zipper 330
Paraslasher..85
Paris Green 305
Q Site 32
Rolls-Royce Silver Phantom 240
Stand on Wing (SOW) 297, 380

For details of all our books or
to order a copy of our latest FREE catalogue contact:

Crécy Publishing Limited
(+44) 161 499 0024

www.crecy.co.uk